The Politics of the New Europe

Atlantic to Urals

Ian Budge
Kenneth Newton
R.D. McKinley
Emil Kirchner
Derek Urwin
Klaus Armingeon
Ferdinand Müller–Rommel
Michael Waller
Matthew Shugart
Michael Nentwich
Stein Kuhnle
Hans Keman
Hans–Dieter Klingemann
Bernhard Wessels
Peter Frank

Longman
London and New York

Addison Wesley Longman Limited
Edinburgh Gate
Harlow, Essex CM20 2JE, England
and Associated Companies throughout the world.

Published in the United States of America
by Longman Publishing, New York

First published 1997

ISBN 0 582 23434 4 PPR

British Library Cataloguing-in-Publication Data
A catalogue record for this book is
available from the British Library

Library of Congress Cataloging-in-Publication Data

Budge, Ian.
    The politics of the new Europe: Atlantic to Urals /
Ian Budge, Kenneth Newton.
        p.   cm.
    Includes bibliographical references and index.
    ISBN 0-582-23434-4 (pbk.)
    1. Europe—Politics and government—1989–   I. Newton, Kenneth,
1940–   .   II. Title.
JN12.B83   1997
320.94—dc21
                                                            96-47848
                                                                CIP

Set by 34 in Perpetua
Produced by Longman Asia Limited, Hong Kong.
NPCC/01

The Politics of the New Europe

Contents

List of tables

List of figures

List of briefings

List of maps

List of abbreviations

(The following list includes abbreviations and acronyms which are used more than once in the text, but not the hundreds of parties and pressure groups listed in various tables and figures.)

ARRC	Allied Rapid Reaction Corps
BBC	British Broadcasting Corporation
CAP	Common Agricultural Policy
CDU	Christian Democratic Union
CEE	Central and Eastern Europe
CFE	Conventional Armed Forces Agreement
CFSP	Common Foreign and Security Policy
CIS	Commonwealth of Independent States
CMEA (COMECON)	Council for Mutual Economic Assistance
COCOM	Co-Ordinating Committee
COREPER	Committee of Permanent Representatives
CPSU	Communist Party of the Soviet Union
CSCE	Conference on Security and Co-operation in Europe
CSFR	Czechoslovak Federal Republic
EC	European Commission
ECB	European Central Bank
ECJ	European Court of Justice
ECPR	European Consortium for Political Research
ECSC	European Coal and Steel Community
ECU	European Currency Unit
ECU	European Customs Union
EEA	European Economic Area
EEC	European Economic Community
EFTA	European Free Trade Agreement
EMS	European Monetary System
EP	European Parliament
ERM	Exchange Rate Mechanism
ETA	Basque Homeland and Liberty
EU	European Union
Euratom	European Atomic Energy Authority
FDP	Free Democratic Party
FRG	Federal Republic of Germany (West Germany)
G-7	Group of Seven
GATT	General Agreement on Tariffs and Trade
GB	Great Britain
GDP	Gross Domestic Product
GDR	German Democratic Republic (East Germany)

GLC	Greater London Council
GNP	Gross National Product
GOSPLAN	Central Planning Office (of the USSR)
IBRD	International Bank for Reconstruction and Development
IGC	Intergovernmental Conference
IMF	International Monetary Fund
IRA	Irish Republican Army
ISSP	International Social Science Programme
KGB	State Security Agency (of the USSR)
MEP	Macro-economic policy-making
MP	Member of Parliament
NACC	North Atlantic Co-operation Council
NATO	North Atlantic Treaty Organisation
NEP	New Economic Plan
OECD	Organisation for Economic Co-operation and Development
OEEC	Organisation for European Economic Co-operation
Party ID	Party Identification
PASOK	Pan-Hellenic Socialist Movement
PR	Proportional representation
Quango	Quasi-non-governmental organisation
RAI	Radio – Television Italy
SALT	Strategic Arms Limitation Talks
SCPR	Social and Community Planning Research
SEA	Single European Act
SMSP	Single member, simple plurality (voting system)
SPD	Socialist Party of Germany
START	Strategic Arms Reduction Talks
STV	Single transferable vote
TACIS	Technical Assistance to the Commonwealth of Independent States
UK	United Kingdom
UN(O)	United Nations (Organisation)
UNHCR	United Nations High Commission for Refugees
USA	United States of America
USSR	Union of Soviet Socialist Republics
WEU	Western European Union
WTO	Warsaw Treaty Organisation

Preface

Pioneering an integrated treatment of the whole of Europe is such a large undertaking that it requires the work of many hands. Textual unity has been assured because the principal authors have assimilated all chapters to the main themes and written seven, where they were expert, themselves. All the chapters have, in fact, been written by specialists: R.D. McKinley (1,18), Emil Kirchner (2,17), Derek Urwin (4), Klaus Armingeon (7), Ferdinand Müller-Rommel and Michael Waller (8), Matthew Shugart (10), Michael Nentwich (14), Stein Kuhnle (15), Hans Keman (16). In addition Hans-Dieter Klingemann and Bernhard Wessels provided advice and briefings that shaped many aspects of the discussion, particularly in Chapter 9: and Peter Frank provided material on Soviet bureaucracy in Chapter 12. Naturally, these co-authors are responsible only for their specialist parts. For overall questions of fact and interpretation, Budge and Newton take responsibility.

Our contributors come from many different countries, constituting in themselves a microcosm of the New Europe. Maintaining contact during the writing of the book would have been impossible without the framework provided by the European Consortium for Political Research. It was in fact at the ECPR Joint Research Sessions of 1993, organized by the Department of Political Science, University of Trondheim, Norway that the whole project was launched. Subsequently, an International Research Seminar on the New Europe, sponsored by the Austrian Political Science Association in Vienna (November 1993) gave an opportunity to relate the specialized topics to each other within the context of the whole book.

Budge was generously supported for ten months in 1995–96 by the Netherlands Institute for Advanced Research, during which most of the chapters were written or edited. Shugart had support from the Center for Iberian and Latin American Studies, San Diego, The Center for German and European Studies, Berkeley and the Stefan Batory Foundation, Warsaw. We warmly acknowledge this essential help. It has resulted in an account which combines authoritative, detailed treatment of each topic with a clear overview of general developments. We hope that this avoids the weaknesses, and combines the strengths, of single-author treatments on the one hand, and collections of specialized papers on the other.

If so, this is largely due to the role of the European Consortium in bringing the authors together and providing a forum for the meeting of like (and sometimes unlike) minds. We also owe much to advice from Sarah Birch, Neil Robinson, Francesi Pallarés, Carlos Flores, Natasha Gaber and Joseph Farrugia, and to the secretarial and research help of Linda Day, Chris Wilkinson, Julie Lord, Jane Toettcher, Steven Studd, Octavio Amorim-Neto, Vladimir Jevremovic and Bernd Schossadowski.

Chris Harrison, Director of Social Science Publishing at Addison Wesley Longman, first suggested the idea of such a book, and has been a staunch source of support and encouragement all along. We hope he and the others like the result. With such help we should have avoided errors altogether, but in such a detailed and wide-ranging coverage this would be too much to expect. We hope they are limited, however, as we must collectively assume responsibility for them – the specialized contributors for their parts and Budge and Newton for any general errors of fact and interpretation.

Bearing in mind the need for a free-running and uncluttered text we have deliberately omitted footnotes and references except where discussion has relied exclusively on one source, or where statistics and figures are cited. A vast amount of technical and general information is packed into free-standing briefings throughout the book which we hope will prove useful for students and teachers alike. Suggestions for further reading at the end of each chapter provide guidance to the core literature in each area. We hope this allows for a discussion which is wide-ranging without being superficial, and enjoyable as well as being informative.

Studying European politics today

Thinking of Europe as a whole has been difficult ever since communists and Nazis split the continent, ideologically and militarily, after the First World War. From the 1970s, it became increasingly possible to write about 'Western Europe' owing to the convergence of national politics round a common model of liberal democracy, capitalist economics and opposition to Soviet power. Much writing still goes on along these lines. Most books about 'European' politics turn out to be books about Western Europe, with a chapter or two on Central Europe and the East tacked on.

The change from communist to democratic regimes in 1989 subverted the whole basis on which 'Western' Europe had been distinguished from 'the East'. It also shattered the cozy world of text-book writers who based themselves on this distinction. All European countries, including Russia, now subscribe to the same model of democratic politics. While many depart from the ideal in practice, this is a situation which occurs everywhere, not just in the East. The 'winner takes all' practices of 'elective dictatorships' like Britain and Greece bear some resemblance to what is going on in Bulgaria and Lithuania. The breakdown of the established party system in Italy renders elections there just as fluid as in Poland or the Ukraine. The transition from dictatorship took place only the decade before in Spain, Portugal and Greece, so there is plenty of scope for developing comparisons across Europe as a whole. 'Western Europe' is not even geographically distinctive. Finland and Greece are further east than much of Central Europe! Though Russia is undoubtedly different, it is also a country which cannot be ignored, because of its sheer impact on the rest of the continent.

There are other reasons for developing an integrated approach to European politics at the present time. In an era of globalization Europe must become increasingly sensitive to the need for common solutions to shared problems. The European states may eventually combine in a vastly expanded European Union. At the very least they need to work out a common security policy. This implies solving not only military problems, but also economic, territorial, and political tensions. These threaten national and international security and human rights, and generate vast population movements, international crime, nuclear risks and environmental pollution. The time is past when these can be handled on anything but an all-European basis, a fact which again justifies comprehensive treatment of the continent's politics.

It also explains why Part I of this book deals with overall security and peace, before dealing with the internal functioning of European States. Internal democracy is dependent on inter-European relations as much as on the capacity of nations to shape their own destinies. For example, democratic aspirations were nurtured in Spain, Portugal and Greece by the prospect of joining the European Union, and sustained by the desire to stay inside it. Similarly, the viability of the new European democracies depends, in part, upon international developments, as it did after 1945 when the Marshall Plan was implemented by the USA in order to help democracy in

West Europe. Thus the progression of this book from a general consideration of pan-European security and integration, to the internal political arrangements of individual nation-states is logical, and helps keep the primacy of the overall European order firmly in mind.

What is Europe?

Nevertheless, our decision to look at Europe as a whole does raise certain problems which we have to confront from the start. The first of these, quite simply, is what *is* Europe and where does it end? This is a problem which did not arise with older treatments of 'Western Europe', which was politically defined as those countries east of the Atlantic and north of the Mediterranean not under communist regimes. The Eastern, landward, frontiers of Europe have always been hazier. With the disappearance of the old political criterion it is clear that geography is ambiguous. Does 'Europe' now include Russia and extend across Siberia to Vladivostock on the Pacific? Russia is such a weighty actor in the continent's affairs that we cannot leave it out; and it makes no sense to consider only that part of it west of the Urals, the mountain chain traditionally taken as marking the Eastern boundary of Europe.

Similarly, should Europe take in the trans-Caucasian, ex-Soviet, Republics of Georgia, Armenia and Azerbaijan? The first two at any rate share European traditions and culture. But if we include them should we not also take in Turkey, Cyprus, Lebanon and Israel – countries which in one way or another are strongly Europeanized and closer to the continent.

Fortunately, we have no need to legislate about such definitions in the abstract. It is clear that there is a solid bloc of countries everyone would accept as being in 'Europe'. There is ambiguity about which countries to the east of these actually belong: we may wish to cast the net wider for some purposes than for others. As our chapters deal with different topics it makes sense to vary our coverage in line with the purposes of each individual discussion. For some purposes – when considering peace and security, states and territories, and constitutions – it makes sense to have as comprehensive a coverage as possible. For others – such as the discussion of political culture and attitudes – the availability of survey and other evidence necessarily limits the range of countries considered.

Pragmatic decisions like these are inevitable at present. But perhaps a pioneering book on the New Europe will encourage the collection of data on an all-European basis and thus make possible a consistently wide geographical coverage of all topics. At the moment, however, we are often driven to select a few countries to represent a larger number (e.g. of particular kinds of bureaucratic or welfare systems in Chapters 12 and 16). Whatever the selection of countries, however, we stick to the principle of always including examples from all parts of the New Europe.

Is a comparative coverage of Europe possible?

This raises another problem. The former communist regimes of the Centre and East aimed at creating a 'new Soviet man' geared to the needs of their society and state. Can we really discuss these countries in the same context as ones with a long

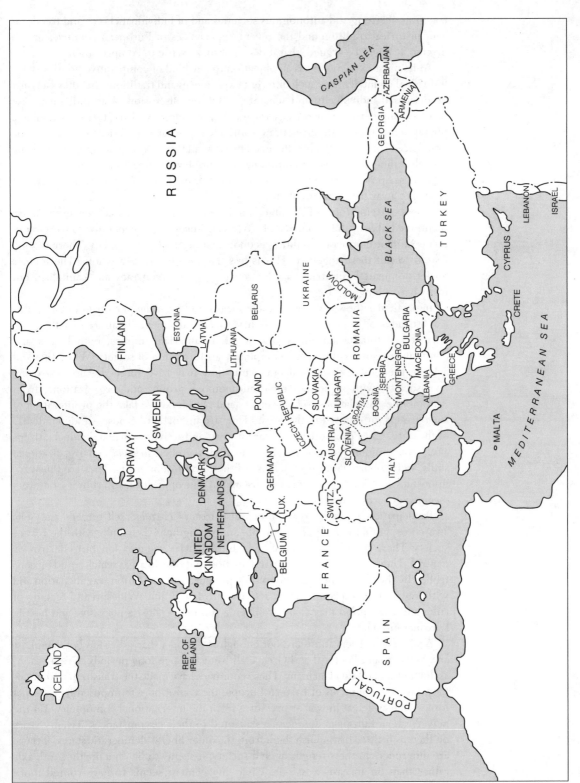

The new Europe of the 1990s

tradition of strong and autonomous societies and of individual choice and freedom? This historical tradition and the recent experiences of European countries are so diverse, it might be argued, that it does not make sense to compare them.

At its most extreme this is an objection to any kind of comparative politics at all. Individual countries have such different experiences and traditions that they can only be discussed individually and separately. But any discussion of an individual case involves implicit comparisons. We cannot, for example, characterize Britain as a liberal democracy without forming some idea of what liberal democracy is in the first place. This is inevitably influenced by what all the countries we think of as being liberal democracies have in common. Such implicit comparisons influence all the other descriptive terms we use, even in single, historical, case studies, so we cannot really get away from making them.

A less extreme form of the objection is not so easily dismissed, however. As we mentioned above, the countries of 'Western Europe' are generally converging in terms of their democratic politics, economic style and foreign policy. There is good reason to put them together. This is less true of Europe as a whole. The former Soviet-dominated countries may be converging on democracy and capitalism but many have a long way to go.

In particular the structures of their society and even the personalities and polit-ical attitudes of their citizenry may have been fundamentally altered by their ex-perience of totalitarianism. As the word 'totalitarian' implies, both Fascist and communist regimes aimed at a complete transformation of society. While they did achieve their own ideological blueprint, they may have succeeded in destroying civil society, with its innumerable autonomous groups and organizations, from Automobile Associations to bell-ringers and ramblers. We take the proliferation of such groups for granted in the West. They are important because – independently of the state – they promote particular interests and activities, give individual citizens a sense of community and belonging, train their members in social and organizational skills, and mobilize citizens in defense of their political interests. They are thus very important in fostering democratic discussion and opposition to arbitrary or over-weening government action.

Participation in such organizations also fosters citizens' self-esteem and self-awareness, gives them a purpose in life and strengthens their links with the rest of society. These are all aspects of life which totalitarian regimes sought to destroy or control. They promoted political participation, but only in areas which could be con-trolled by the state. One reaction to such pressure and regulation was alienation and withdrawal from social or public activity into family life. Widespread breaking of rules and corruption may also have been a reaction against a pervasive and hostile bureaucratic state.

Again, such observations are not enough to set up a sharp division between East and West. Spain, Portugal and Greece all went through long periods of repression, as did Italy and (West) Germany. These countries have made the transition to democ-racy. Like the countries of Eastern Europe, the transition was imposed by external forces such as defeat in war or pressures from the international community. Yet the new Western European democracies adapted to their circumstances. Twenty years on there is little to distinguish them from the older liberal-democratic states. If there are differences in the strength of civil society, it seems to lie on a north–south axis rather than on an east–west one. Civic engagement seems to have rooted more successfully in Germany than in Italy, for example, and more in the north of Italy than in the south.

Something similar seems to be occurring in Central and Eastern Europe. The overthrow of communism has encouraged vigorous activity on the part of the churches. Communist regimes never succeeded entirely in dominating these. Along with other groups and organizations, they have provided a basis for the parties and social movements of post-communist politics. All this indicates the strength and resilience of civil society in most countries, whatever their former history, and again reinforces a belief in their comparability rather than in their inherent differences.

The countries of Central and Eastern Europe passed through a terrible economic crisis immediately after their move to democracy. In some cases the economy shrunk by a third, throwing millions out of work and destroying factory-based welfare systems. Such an experience produced widespread discontent with political leadership. What is interesting, however, was that discontent was expressed democratically, at elections, and did not manifest itself as disillusionment with democracy. On the contrary, it often involved the constructive use of the central democratic mechanism, that is the opportunity to elect a new government.

Empirical support for the claim that civil society has quickly re-established itself is contained in a study carried out in 1992 by Klingemann and Hofferbert which compared political attitudes in the former West and East Germany. The latter had long experience of full-scale totalitarianism – almost sixty years of Nazi and communist attempts to control popular thinking. Yet the Klingemann and Hofferbert survey uncovers few significant differences of attitude between the two halves of the country.

As we shall see, democratic political change in Europe has often been powered by military victory and defeat, or by the demands of security, rather than by internal national movements. Once democracy and its institutions have been put in place, individuals seem to adapt their behaviour, to emerge from the family, and form new social groups and public movements. In this way Central and Eastern European states are coming to resemble their West European counterparts. Differences in the strength of civil society in the Europe of the future may not follow the East–West divide, but some other division such as that between North and South.

■ The advantages of comparison

In defending our comparative and pan-European emphasis against possible criticisms, we do not wish to lose sight of the positive benefits it bestows. We have already pointed out that no national study can be done without making implicit comparisons, which are often smuggled into the discussion and consequently less illuminating than they might be. Too often they are downright mistaken. For example, one may shake one's head over the threat to strong majority government in Britain posed by proportional representation, and fear that such reform would result in perpetually weak and unstable coalition government. But this is to forget that Ireland, Austria and Malta have had single-party majority government with various forms of proportional representation, and that German and Dutch coalitions have been stable and effective. The Italian experience of weak and unstable coalitions has been the reference implicitly used in the British debate as if it were the only one available, but this is not at all the case. This is a cogent example of the biases which come from neglect of an explicit comparative perspective.

On the other hand, the fact that Italian coalitions presided over an economic miracle in the 1950s and 1960s suggests that we should not necessarily view coalitions as a bad thing. In this case, the comparison cuts both ways. More to the point, it enables us to analyse and criticize the assertions which flow incorrectly from single nation studies.

■ Plan of the book

Because of the prime and pervasive influence of international relationships on Europe, particularly in the security dimension, Part I is dedicated to the new supranational order there. Chapter 1 considers security and peace – that is, how military and foreign alliances may develop in the future and their effects on the major countries of Europe.

One possible realignment is the extension of the European Union into Central and Eastern Europe. The widening and deepening of the Union obviously brings in the crucial matter of relations with Russia and its allied CIS (Confederation of Independent States). It also involves examining relations between the current members of the European Union, and the complex set of factors which affect its 'widening' and 'deepening'. These will determine whether the Union matures into a European Federation or whether it evolves a different kind of political structure (see Chapter 2).

Although European states may be losing both external autonomy and internal sovereignty, they are still the most important political building blocks of the continent. Chapter 3 accordingly surveys the different states within their regional European groupings. The nation-state today, however, is hardly the hard-shelled, homogeneous, and politically autonomous entity of classical theory – if indeed it ever was. Most European states have sizeable internal minorities, sometimes straddling their borders and merging with the populations of contiguous states. The most isolated of island races have been changed by the arrival of immigrants from other countries, a phenomenon which has characterized all the major European countries in recent decades. Territorial and ethnic conflicts within and between states are considered in Chapter 4.

Ethnic conflict is only one of the divisions that underlie national politics in Europe. Religion is another source of tension – classically pitting Roman Catholic against Protestant, as in the West. In the East it also involves Greek Orthodox and Muslims. Mixed in with religious and ethnic conflicts there are also, of course, the economic interests institutionalized in pressure groups such as trade unions and business associations. Part II of our discussion accordingly looks at the way in which political systems mediate internal conflicts and turn them to constructive rather than destructive use. Dictatorial regimes characteristically try to suppress conflict so as to create a façade of homogeneity and unity. European democracies often try to do this too, particularly in regard to ethnic minorities. However, democracy owes its special character to a recognition that conflict is inherent in living together. It may even be valuable in drawing attention to neglected interests and suggesting solutions to problems. In many ways, therefore, democracy is best seen as a set of institutions, from elections through interest groups to political parties and parliaments, which are designed to manage conflicts peaceably, rather than suppressing them.

Conflicts manifest themselves first of all in individual attitudes and social behaviour. Chapter 5 examines these and goes on to discuss how citizens evaluate their governments and political institutions. The mass media play an important part in shaping attitudes as well as influencing other political processes. Their influence is considered in Chapter 6.

Democratic freedoms give individuals and groups the opportunity to organize and promote their particular interests. This is a freedom employed by both national and multinational businesses and economic interests, and Chapter 7 looks at how they and trade unions organize in European countries. The following chapter then considers how a different set of social interests organize themselves politically – that is, the new social movements. These combine some of the features of interest groups and political parties, as well as claiming an exclusive mandate to represent certain moral causes such as environment and peace. They are often seen as a new political phenomenon which threatens established political parties. Social movements are discussed in Chapter 8, and political parties in Chapter 9.

Parties are a way of linking society with government through elections. The ways in which votes are aggregated into parliamentary seats, and thus into governmental authority and power, is the subject of Chapter 10. This opens Part III of our discussion – steering the state. Power is also affected by relations between parliament and president, particularly where the latter is directly elected. Other constitutional provisions may also be important. Chapter 10 reviews these over all the European countries.

Chapter 11 focuses on the actual work of parliaments and presidents, rather than on purely constitutional relationships. Governments may formulate public policies to meet voter aspirations but depend on the permanent bureaucracy to implement them. We consider their relationships in Chapter 12. Disputes among powerholders, and between them and citizens, are often settled by law. We consider judicial institutions in Chapter 14, noting, however, that the power of the courts often goes beyond the regulation of relationships and spills over into the autonomous formulation of policy.

So far, we have discussed only the central political institutions within European states. We have noted, however, that the central state often has to cope with linguistic or ethnic minorities, often territorially concentrated and with their own special demands. Such demands may put pressure on the very structure and territorial integrity of the state. One way of handling the problem is to delegate powers to regions and localities. Even in nations without deep ethnic or regional divisions, the central state has to find ways of managing its territory and implementing its legislation. This involves systems of territorial government which are considered, together with two peculiarly European forms of federalism, in Chapter 13.

Part IV deals with outputs of governments – the policies they make and implement. The two most important areas here are welfare (Chapter 15) and the economy (Chapter 16). Both have been particularly affected by political controversy and economic depression in recent years. It is, therefore, appropriate to consider current developments and how far these have been exacerbated by other problems such as migration (Chapter 17). These require important decisions to be made about

European security arrangements, as well as about the shape and content of the new European order (Chapter 18). These bring us back to the initial discussion on security and peace, which Chapter 1 takes up.

■ Further reading

David Gowland, Basil O'Neill, *et al.*, *The European Mosaic* (London, Longman, 1995).

H-D. Klingemann and R.I. Hofferbert, 'Germany: a new "wall in the mind"?, *Journal of Democracy* 5 (1994), pp. 30–44.

Richard Rose, *What is Europe?* (New York, HarperCollins, 1996).

Gordon Smith, *Politics in Western Europe* (London, Gower, 1988).

Part 1

The new European order

Chapter 1

Security and peace

■ **The post-war settlement**

Europe today has been shaped primarily by the collapse of communism in 1989 and the break-up of the Soviet bloc in Central and Eastern Europe. Previous changes of this magnitude have occurred only as the result of major wars, of which Europe has seen two this century (1914–18, 1939–45). The end of the Second World War in 1945 saw Nazi Germany defeated and partitioned between the USA, France and Britain, on the one hand, and the Soviet Union (Russia with its satellite states) on the other. Not only was Germany prostrate, but most other European states had also been decisively weakened by the conflict. Many had been occupied during the war. Even Britain, the only one successfully to defy Germany, was greatly enfeebled.

Possibly the only European power in a better military position after 1945 than before was the Soviet Union (the USSR). In spite of massive destruction, its vast natural resources, large population, and highly centralized and militarily effective dictatorship enabled it to play a major role in defeating Germany. In the process, the Soviet army occupied most of Central and Eastern Europe. In the following years the Soviet Union absorbed much territory to the west of its pre-war frontiers (notably the western Ukraine and the Baltic states). It also converted most governments of Central and Eastern Europe into satellite dictatorships dominated by communist parties subservient to Moscow.

These moves were undertaken largely for defensive reasons – to put a massive belt of territory between the Russian heartland and any possible invader. However, the United States and its West European allies interpreted them as aggressive – an impression intensified by the efforts of the large French and Italian communist parties to take over their countries electorally.

The extent to which Western communist parties, once in power, would have been puppets of Moscow is debatable. Yugoslav communists, under President Tito, defied the Soviet Union as early as 1948, and other communist parties asserted their autonomy between 1948 and 1985: Romania and Albania successfully, Poland and Czechoslovakia unsuccessfully. However, communists were seen in the West as agents of the Soviet Union. The USSR itself was credited with an unlimited appetite for expansion.

To counter this perceived threat America, Canada and practically all the non-Communist countries of Western Europe formed NATO (the North Atlantic Treaty Organization). In spite of its title, NATO also included Italy, Greece and Turkey – about as far east in the Mediterranean as one could go! The United States also consolidated the economies and the democratic stability of its wartime allies through an extensive programme of aid in the late 1940s known as the Marshall Plan. This laid the foundations for a sustained economic boom from about 1950 to 1975.

As part of the consolidation of 'Western Europe' the western parts of Germany – occupied after the war by British, US and French troops – were united in the

BRIEFING 1.1

North Atlantic Treaty Organization (NATO)

Created after the Second World War, NATO is the most important international military organization for the defense of the Western world. It provides for a unified military command in war time. For much of its history it has concentrated on the perceived threat of the Soviet bloc. In this sense, its opposite number in Eastern Europe is the Warsaw Pact (see Briefing 1.2). Membership includes the USA and Canada, and most west European nations, although after 1966 France was only a partial member, and Switzerland, Sweden, and Ireland maintained their neutral status by remaining outside. The USA contributes disproportionately to the costs of NATO and for this reason it has always been under the leadership of a US military officer.

When the Warsaw pact was dissolved in 1991, and the Soviet Union was no longer the same sort of threat, NATO redefined its role somewhat by creating a smaller, lighter and mobile strike force. It was involved in the Gulf War, and played a peacekeeping role in Bosnia. France re-established formal links in 1995.

BRIEFING 1.2

Warsaw Treaty Organization (WTO)

The Warsaw Treaty Organization was set up by the Warsaw Pact which was signed by the countries of the Soviet bloc in 1955 primarily as a military response to the creation in the West of the North Atlantic Treaty Organization. Its members were the Soviet Union and most other countries in the Soviet bloc in central Eastern Europe, except Albania which formally left the organization in 1968. Hungary tried to leave in 1956, and Czechoslovakia tried again in 1968, both provoking Russian invasion of their countries as a result. The USSR dominated the organization and provided most of its military capacity – perhaps more so than the US dominated NATO. The USSR was the only country in the WTO with nuclear weapons, and it provided by far the largest and best equipped part of the alliance. The WTO was formally dissolved in 1991 after the Soviet bloc collapsed.

Federal Republic of (West) Germany. In the eastern part of the country the USSR set up a communist regime (the German Democratic Republic). The division of the country came to symbolize the Cold War – that is, a state of constant military preparedness on both sides, the stockpiling of huge nuclear and other military armouries, and the maintenance of huge armies. As part of their commitment to NATO and the European allies the Americans maintained a large military presence in Germany to guard against the (perceived) threat posed by the Soviet empire.

In response, the Soviet Union formed the Warsaw Treaty Organization (WTO) creating a unified military command in the communist dominated states of Central and Eastern Europe. This was buttressed by the Council for Mutual Economic Assistance (CMEA) which operated on a barter basis, trading, for example, Russian oil for consumer goods from Central Europe. These arrangements contrasted with mechanisms intended to broaden and deepen the operations of the free market in the West. Countries in West Europe participated in the International Monetary Fund (IMF), established to stabilize monetary transactions between countries: the International Bank for Reconstruction and Development (IBRD), established to finance large-scale capital projects such as roads or factories: the General Agreement

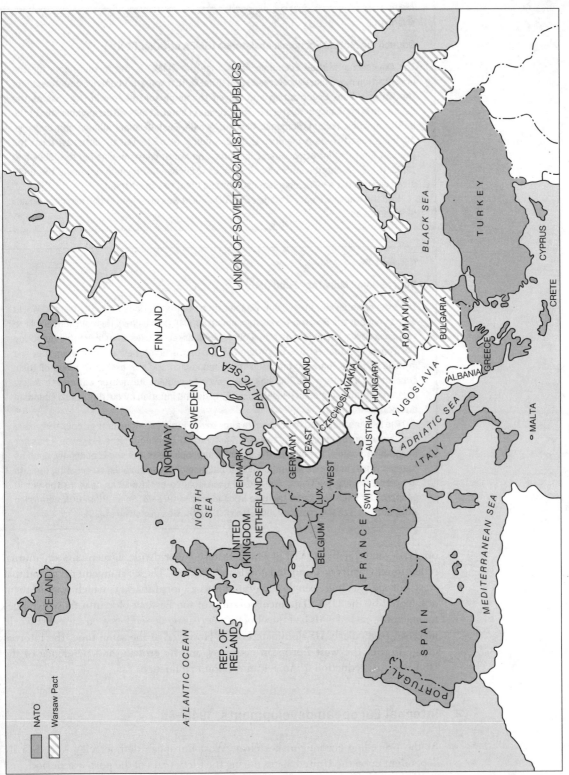

Map 1.1   The cold war: Europe divided between NATO and the Warsaw Pact (1948–89)

BRIEFING 1.3

Council for Mutual Economic Assistance (CMEA or COMECON)

The Council for Mutual Economic Assistance (or CMEA) is the formal name for the organization more usually referred to as COMECON. It was the economic counterpart of the Warsaw Pact Organization and played the same sort of role in the east as the European Community in Western Europe. It was created in 1949 with a membership of the USSR, Hungary, Poland, Romania, Czechoslovakia, East German, Albania and Bulgaria. Albania ceased to be a member in 1962, when it also started to withdraw from the Warsaw Pact Organization. Mongolia, Cuba, and North Vietnam joined in the 1960s and 1970s. It implemented economic plans for East Europe but members outside the USSR often regarded it as a mechanism used by the USSR to exploit them.

Like the Warsaw Treaty Organization, COMECON was dissolved in 1991 after the Soviet bloc collapsed.

BRIEFING 1.4

International Monetary Fund (IMF)

The International Monetary Fund was set up by United Nations after the Second World War as part of the Bretton Woods agreement of 1944 (see below). Its main concern is to secure stability in the international currency market. It tries to achieve this by acting like a bank for nation-states which allows them to overdraw their account when they are in need of extra funds to maintain their economies and the exchange value of their currencies. In return the IMF has the power to require its debtor nations to follow certain national economic policies, usually reducing inflation by cutting public spending and borrowing.

The IMF has managed to achieve its aims to a certain extent insofar as countries have used their borrowing capacity to avert financial and currency crises. However, it has not been able to deal with some of the structural problems of the world economy, such as nations which have a large and constant balance of trade surplus, so creating deficits for other trading partners. Nor has it been able to avoid shocks dealt to the world economy by such things as the rise in oil prices in 1973–74. Some COMECON countries were admitted to IMF membership after COMECON was dissolved in 1991.

on Trade and Tariffs (GATT), which fostered worldwide agreements on mutual reductions in tariffs on imported goods and services. These arrangements meant that west Europe was increasingly integrated into a global market, which was, in turn, dominated by the USA. The incorporation of the Eastern bloc into these arrangements in the early 1990s had the effect of increasing dependence on capitalist world markets, particularly US dominated ones. However, at the same time, the internal integration of the west European economy, and its growing independence of the USA, led to a reduction in American economic influence.

Internal European developments, 1945–89

As the preceding account makes clear, West European democracies were heavily dependent upon the United States during the forty years of the post-war period, just as Eastern European communist regimes were heavily dependent upon Russia. However, neither superpower was totally hegemonic within their respective sphere of influence. Autonomous developments occurred among the allied states which had consequences for the shape of the new Europe after 1989.

The loss of empires

In the nineteenth century, Britain, France, the Netherlands, Belgium and Portugal had all built up overseas empires. Britain's was the biggest, extending at its height to a quarter of the total land area of the globe. France controlled much of north and west Africa and Vietnam The Netherlands governed Indonesia, with a population ten times its own. Belgium and Portugal had conquered enormous chunks of Africa. Consequently, the governing of dependent territories absorbed much attention and offered markets and trading opportunities to both individuals and firms in Europe.

In the thirty years after the war these empires were gradually broken up under the pressure of nationalist movements in the dependent territories, often involving Europeans in protracted guerrilla warfare. The Dutch lost Indonesia in 1948–49. Belgian rule in the Congo broke down in 1960, with the colonial administration leaving in a matter of weeks – causing a financial crisis in Belgium from which the country has still not wholly recovered.

Perhaps more seriously, Portugal and France were involved in protracted wars of independence. Portugal stretched its resources beyond their limits by fighting two large-scale wars in the vast African territories of Angola and Mozambique. The eventual recognition that the wars were unwinnable brought about a withdrawal from Africa and an internal revolution in Portugal itself, leading eventually to the establishment of democracy in 1973/4.

France passed through the same experience in Vietnam (1946–54) and Algeria (1954–62). It suffered humiliating military defeat, but was able to withdraw in Vietnam. More than a million French settlers in Algeria turned a war of independence into a particularly brutal civil war, led to the downfall of the (parliamentary) Fourth Republic of 1945–58, and the inauguration of the (presidential) Fifth Republic, with General de Gaulle as president. De Gaulle quickly realized that the Algerian war was unwinnable and arranged to withdraw in 1962, sparking off a near civil war in France itself. He managed to secure the support of the political right, and of the military, by building up the armed forces and adopting a strongly nationalistic attitude abroad. France's remaining African colonies were offered independence with economic, military and cultural links with France, a situation that continues to influence French foreign and domestic policy today.

In contrast Britain, with the largest overseas empire, had least trouble. This was partly due to the precedent of granting independence within the Commonwealth to the white colonies of Canada, Australia and New Zealand, leaving a government modelled on the British, and with continuing policy and trade links. Britain had also had early experience of fighting a guerrilla war in Southern Ireland (1918–22) which had resulted in the creation of an independent breakaway state (the Republic of Ireland).

As a result, British policy concentrated on reaching an accommodation with nationalist movements in colonial countries and converting colonies into

Commonwealth members. These retained British parliamentary and administrative systems, with sympathetic governments in charge. British-educated and trained, these governments were anti-communist and maintained strong links with Britain. Limited colonial wars were fought in Malaya, Borneo, Cyprus, Kenya and Southern Arabia during the 1950s and early 1960s, but resulted mainly in the installation of sympathetic governments. The two great waves of British de-colonization were India, Burma and Palestine (1948) and Africa (1960–64).

This relatively untraumatic withdrawal from the colonies left Britain with stronger overseas links than the rest of West Europe. These were reinforced by a 'special relationship' with the United States, another former colony. Both trading and financial relations were geared, therefore, towards the Commonwealth rather than to Europe. As a consequence, Britain did not take part in the first steps towards European economic and financial integration which began in the early 1950s. When Britain did eventually join Europe it became a reluctant partner, torn between its new continental and old global links.

The parallel to West European overseas empires was the agglomeration of countries forming the Soviet Union – basically the old Russian Empire of the nineteenth century. The break-up of the Soviet Union in 1991 might therefore be seen as a belated form of decolonization similar to that enacted earlier by the West. Even the shrunken Russia of today, however, has enormous numbers of distinct racial groups and autonomous Republics within its vast territory, with consequences for European security which we will discuss later.

Mavericks within the alliances, 1948–89

Russian control over Central and Eastern Europe was far from complete, even during the period of the Cold War. It was forced to use troops to put down popular uprisings against Soviet policies in Hungary (1956) and Czechoslovakia (1968). It also had to accept deviations from the established ideological line in Poland (which had an autonomous Catholic Church and privately owned peasant farms) and Romania, where the government refused to back Soviet foreign policy. Pressures for partial autonomy became more obvious in the 1980s, when most Central and Eastern European states experimented with ways of running their economies more independently.

Moreover, two communist countries had broken openly with the Soviet Union. Yugoslavia (a federation of present-day Slovenia, Croatia, Serbia, Bosnia and Macedonia) had defied the Soviet Union in 1948 and maintained a neutral position thereafter. In the 1960s tiny Albania adopted a more extreme form of communism than the Soviet Union itself.

The Western alliance was generally more solid than the Eastern one, but nevertheless, it too had its difficulties. France blamed the United States for some of its colonial defeats, and subsequently withdrew from NATO, partly in order to develop an independent nuclear and military capability. This may have been the price paid to the military for having accepted the ignominious withdrawal from the colonies. Britain and (West) Germany, on the other hand, concentrated their foreign policy on backing NATO and maintaining an American military presence on their soil. In spite of individual acts of defiance most European countries were compliant partners of the two superpowers in their Cold War stand-off.

European Union

The most important autonomous European initiative during the Cold War was the creation and expansion of what eventually became the European Union. This was of such importance that it will have the following chapter all to itself. It is enough to note here that the Treaty of Paris (1956) which set up the European Economic Community (EEC) was inspired by economic and security interests which cut across those of the USA and the USSR. The Community was a way of integrating France and Germany so thoroughly that they would never go to war with each other again. As Franco-German rivalries had been a major factor in precipitating the two World Wars, this was an understandable preoccupation of Europeans. It also quietened worries about rearming (West) Germany and granting it political independence. It was easier for the founders of the EU to work immediately for economic and trade integration. This aroused fewer worries among nationalists in the countries concerned than straightforward political union. However, the creation first of a free trade area, then its extension, and then a common market, stimulated a need for political institutions to manage them.

Because of the overseas preoccupations mentioned earlier, Britain stood aloof from the European Community at the outset and only joined, with Denmark and Ireland, in 1973. These countries were followed by Greece (1978), Spain and Portugal (1984), and Austria, Finland and Sweden in 1995. The expansion of the Union attests to the success of the economic inducements used to attract members, leading towards a Federal Union with a single economic, political and security policy. In other words, the expansion of the Union is intimately related to the question of the deepening of the Union. In this respect, what European countries do, even with regard to purely European affairs, influences wider global security. This raises the question of what kind of security order prevails in Europe and how it is likely to develop. We discuss this in the rest of this chapter.

■ The end of the Cold War, 1983–94

Whatever initiatives European states took on their own, they were still overshadowed by the confrontation of the United States and the Soviet Union. Europe was literally caught in the middle between them. But in the 1980s the Cold War came to an end. The Soviet communist elite realized that that they could not win a full-scale war against the USA. Even attempts to match the pace of American military developments meant straining Soviet social and economic resources beyond their limits.

Under Brezhnev, effective ruler of the Soviet Union from 1964 to 1982, nothing was done, either internally or externally, to change things. The social and economic stagnation which his 'do nothing' policy fostered was exacerbated by a need to meet the new US challenge, the so-called 'Star Wars' initiative began under President Reagan (1980–88) which aimed to create an electronic shield to protect the United States from nuclear attack. Whether or not this was technically possible is a moot point. However, Soviet decision-makers recognized that they were incapable of meeting the US challenge, if it did happen to succeed, leaving them without the means of retaliating effectively to a US attack.

BRIEFING **1.5**

Commonwealth of Independent States (CIS)

This is a loose association of most of the former Republics of the Soviet Union. It was established almost concurrently with the dissolution of the old union in order to provide for military and economic co-operation between the successor states.

Only the Baltic states (Estonia, Latvia, Lithuania) and the trans-caucasian Republic of Georgia refused to sign up. However, Georgia was forced to join in 1993 as the result of a Russian-backed minority ethnic revolt in South Ossetia. This underlines the fact that the CIS has been used by Russia, its biggest and most powerful member, to dominate the other Republics and define its sphere of influence. Only the Ukraine has stood up to Russia inside the CIS, but their outstanding quarrels were patched up in 1995–96, acknowledging Russia as the most influential member.

The effort to keep up with the United States had in any case strained the hugely inefficient command economy of the Soviet Union. The combination of internal and external crisis caused Gorbachev, First Secretary and effective ruler of the USSR from 1985–91, to seek an accommodation with the Americans. In the course of this he renounced the 'Brezhnev doctrine' that the Soviet Union would intervene in Eastern European countries if they sought to change their communist regimes. This touched off a series of popular protests in these countries against unpopular and arbitrary government. In Poland and Hungary, reformist communist governments had already reached some accommodation with opposition groups.

1989 thus saw a series of peaceful but momentous revolutions – except in Romania where violence broke out – resulting in the installation of democratic governments pledged to undertake free elections. As a result of these 'velvet revolutions' the Iron Curtain separating Eastern and Western Europe disappeared almost overnight, symbolized most dramatically and effectively by the dismantling of the wall dividing Berlin into two separate cities. As a result, international relations between East and West Europe were entirely changed. The two principal international organizations, which tied the states of Eastern Europe to the Soviet Union – the Council for Mutual Economic Assistance (CMEA) and the Warsaw Treaty Organization (WTO) – were dissolved in June and March of 1991. The two Germanies were re-united and the 'satellite' Soviet states became independent. Czechoslovakia split to form the Czech Republic and Slovakia, and Yugoslavia divided into Slovenia, Croatia, Macedonia, Serbia and Bosnia. The fifteen former union republics of the Soviet Union became independent. Twelve of these joined the Russian-dominated Commonwealth of Independent States (CIS), established by the Minsk Agreement of December 1991 (though Azerbaijan did not ratify the Agreement until September 1993, and Georgia did not join the CIS until October 1993).

These are enormous and epoch-making changes but there are some important continuities. Indeed, the changes did not materialize out of the blue, nor did they create entirely new circumstances unconnected with the past. One notable continuity is the importance of what is now the Russian Federation, partly because of its population size (150 million), but also because of its economic and military capabilities. Appropriate international recognition of its central role is signalled by the fact that Russia took over the former USSR seat on the Security Council of the United

Nations. Of the other CIS countries, the Ukraine is largest with a population of 52 million, while in Central and Eastern Europe, Poland is largest with 38 million. Most other nations of the former Soviet bloc have populations of 10 million or less and are relatively poor. Although gross domestic product (GDP) estimates are unreliable and vary quite widely, the wealthiest Eastern European states are roughly on a par with Portugal or Greece. In comparison, unified Germany, with a population roughly equal to the remaining Eastern European states, has an economy which totally dwarfs them. While the independent states of Central and Eastern Europe now play a more important part in security considerations than they did during the Cold War, the Russian Federation remains the commanding player.

Apart from the importance of Russia, there is still no general consensus on what needs to be done to preserve peace and stability in the new Europe. Instead, there are two differing views which might be labelled 'liberal' and 'realist': liberals believe in the efficacy of agreements and peaceful development through international co-operation and integration. Realists maintain that the bottom line is the economic and military power that can be mustered by states and alliances. Each has its own diagnosis of the security problems facing Europe. These lead to different proposals for action. We sketch those opposing diagnoses below, and comment on them in the concluding section of the chapter.

■ European security in the 1990s: the liberal perspective

Liberals are optimistic because of economic and political changes in Eastern Europe and the CIS, particularly because command economies of the old Communist states have been reformed. The reforms began before 1989, but were, nevertheless, greatly accelerated by the new governments which took over.

The grand creator of the USSR command economy was Stalin, who significantly also founded its modern military capability. It was Stalin (leader of the Soviet Union, 1929–53, and dictator in later years) who abandoned the mixed economy of the New Economic Plan (NEP) of the 1920s, choosing instead to focus upon heavy industry, defence, and the elimination of the private agricultural sector. Though Khrushchev (1956–64) did make some attempt at decentralization, the command economy remained monolithic and largely undisturbed during his period of office. The Brezhnev period (1964–82) followed by the Andropov and Chernenko periods (1982–85) halted this process. Real change began with the *perestroika* reforms of Gorbachev. Gorbachev (1985–91), however, never really believed in a market economy. He continued to think of economic restructuring within central planning parameters. His Five Year Plan maintained central control over prices and finance, and he consistently turned down major reform programmes (including the '500-Day' plan of September 1990). Nevertheless, he provided opportunities for 'reformers' such as Yavlinsky and Gaidar. His successor, Boris Yeltsin (Russian President from 1991), initially supported the 'reformers'. Most prices were freed, and a second stage of reform was instigated which concentrated on economic privatization.

Yeltsin won 53 per cent approval for his economic policies in the referendum of April 1993. But defiance by the communist-dominated parliament and its subsequent dislodging by the army in late 1993, led to a loss of influence of the 'reformers'. Thus the Russian Federation can hardly be said to be on a major and concerted

1917–18	October Revolution – Bolshevik Party under Lenin seize central power. Peace with Germany and loss of western territories.
1918–22	Civil war won by Bolsheviks.
1922–28	New economic plan. State takes over large industry but allows small capitalists and peasants to produce and sell in private markets.
1924–30	Gradual takeover of power by Joseph Stalin after Lenin's death.
1930–34	Peasant holdings grouped into giant 'collective' farms whose crops are appropriated by the state. Resistance crushed by violence. Millions killed or deported from European territories to Siberia.
1930–41	Takeover and organization of industry to provide steel-making capacity for military purposes.
1934–38	Mass terror and purges carried through by secret police under Stalin's direction. Communist Party of Soviet Union (CPSU) becomes the major instrument of personal rule by the first secretary (Stalin).
1939–41	Nazi–Soviet pact partitions Poland between USSR and Germany. Soviet takeover of Baltic states.
1941–45	'Great Patriotic War' touched off by German invasion of USSR. Tremendous destruction and slaughter. Soviet alliance with UK and USA. USSR conquers Central and East Europe and East Germany.
1945–49	USSR reincorporates Baltic States and Eastern Poland (Western Ukraine). Organizes communist regimes on Stalinist lines in Central-East Europe.
1946–85	'Cold War' between USSR and USA and its allies in 'NATO'. Military expansion on both sides, stockpiles of nuclear weapons, intervention in third world conflicts.
1953–64	After Stalin dies relaxation of internal controls in the USSR and attempts at economic reform to produce more consumer goods with greater efficiency.
1956–64	Khruschev is First Secretary CPSU (i.e. effective ruler of USSR). Tries to reform internal processes while retaining Stalinist institutions.
1964–82	Leonid Brezhnev First Secretary CPSU stops changes and reforms.
1972–85	Arms limitations talks between USA and USSR designed to avert danger of (nuclear) war. Cold War ended after USSR essentially stops trying to keep up with American development of an anti-nuclear defence ('Star Wars').
1985–91	Gorbachev is First Secretary of CPSU. Tries to institute political and economic reforms within the old structures. Rise of dissident and minority nationalist groups which in the Baltic states secede from USSR.
1991	Coup by old line communists fails. Boris Yeltsin elected President of the Russian Soviet Socialist Republic (RFSR) and pulls out of Soviet Union, causing the collapse of the old USSR.

drive to a fully-fledged market economy. However, a real counter-revolution would be required to restore the old, Stalinist, command economy. By mid-1994, over one million small private businesses existed, some 70 per cent of industrial workers were employed by the private sector, and over 14,000 large and medium-sized firms were in private hands. The Russian economy was, in other words, readily recognizable as a mixed economy, Russia, along with the rest of the CIS, now belonged to the International Monetary Fund (IMF), the World Bank, and the General Agreement on Tariffs and Trade (GATT). The East–West economic divide – sustained by the 'Bretton Woods System' of world financial management centred on the US in the West, and the Council for Mutual Economic Assistance (CMEA) in the East – had vanished. The former Soviet Union had joined the club. (Table 1.1 outlines the development of the Soviet Union from 1917 to 1991.)

The former satellites followed suit, albeit with varying degrees of enthusiasm. Even before the fall of the Berlin Wall, both Poland and Hungary had begun to unravel the command economies imposed upon them by the creation of CMEA in January 1949. After 1989 the reforms speeded up enormously and the Central European countries (Poland, Hungary, the Czech Republic and Slovakia) operated economies with large market sectors and a free currency, albeit alongside substantial state subsidies. The most dramatic changes occurred in Poland where 'shock therapy' was introduced deliberately to change a great deal in a short period.

BRIEFING 1.6

Bretton Woods Agreement

The Bretton Woods Conference of 1944, and the agreement which emerged from it, was an attempt by Britain and the United States to establish post-war economic stability, particularly of international exchange rates. Up to the great depression of 1929, most of the main world currencies were linked to the gold standard whereby their currencies had a guaranteed value in gold. This proved impossible to maintain, and by the early 1930s most countries had abandoned the gold standard in favour of floating currencies. But these were unstable in some instances, and currency problems and hyper-inflation helped the rise of the Nazis in Germany in the 1930s. Hence the allies were concerned, immediately after the war, to establish international economic stability and predictability in the West.

Another outcome of Bretton Woods was the General Agreement on Tariffs and Trade (GATT) which attempted to work towards free trade between nations. The idea was implemented by the United Nations which set up the organization after an agreement signed in Geneva in 1947.

All these economic changes, of course, signal the integration of the economies of Central and Eastern Europe into the Western system, and therefore, arguably, into the Western democratic system as well. Liberals also have grounds for guarded optimism about the political developments themselves. Gorbachev did not have a clear design for competitive multiparty politics but he did relax controls as part of his general move towards *glasnost* or political openness. Two events proved to be turning points. First, the national elections of 1989, and local and republic elections of 1989 and 1990, exposed the increasing loss of credibility of the old style communist party. Second, the failed coup, by hard-line communists in August 1991, showed the impossibility in turning back the clock. From then on attempts to suppress the development of multiple parties was virtually unthinkable.

The failed coup also facilitated two further developments. First, it paved the way for the independence of the Union Republics, a movement which Gorbachev had tried to contain in a somewhat ineffective and confused manner. Secondly, the move to independence provided an opportunity to rewrite constitutions, and thereby formally change established political systems.

With the formation of the CIS Yeltsin found himself head of an independent state, albeit one whose constitutional arrangements were largely inherited from the command economy and one-party system of the old Soviet Union. As the political and economic crisis deepened Yeltsin moved to produce a new constitution. By July 1993, the Constitutional Convention had produced one which was not dissimilar to that of France in that it provided for a directly elected President and a bicameral legislature. Opposition from the very core of the old constitution continued, however, especially from the Congress of Peoples Deputies, and from the Supreme Soviet. Violence erupted in Moscow in October of that year which was directly responsible for over a hundred deaths. This resulted in the defeat of the Congress. On 12 December, 1993 the new constitution was put to a national plebiscite and elections for the new parliament were held on the same day.

From a liberal perspective, therefore, Russia has a political system which is beginning to take on some of the features of a liberal democracy, especially after the reasonably free elections of 1996. The constitution, both in theory and practice, looks 'Western', political parties have been created, elections have taken place, and many accepted liberal democratic rights, such as a free press and right of association, have been recognized.

Similar developments have taken place in other parts of the CIS, and in the former satellite states of Central Europe. One feature of liberal democracies, for which there is empirical support, is that they do not make war on each other. This, in a nutshell, explains why the disintegration of the old communist bloc has resulted in a fundamental reappraisal of the liberal security agenda.

This change is enormously important. But it has not been uniform. There remain great internal differences within and between countries of the old communist bloc. These leave ample room for disagreement about likely future developments. The change of political direction in Russia and in Eastern Europe is not in dispute. Rather, disagreements concern the extent to which these changes will progress, and whether they can be sustained in the long term at all. There are four main grounds for concern: political and economic reform; xenophobia and extreme nationalism; ethnic and racial conflict; and the creation of a new Russian 'empire'.

One of the principal controversies centres on how far political and economic change has been institutionalized. In the political arena for example, it is true to say that many political parties still have relatively shallow roots. The party system has fragmented to a bewildering degree. Some alliances and coalitions which led the post-1989 changes have already been broken. Constitutional practices are not safely established. Elections have often increased the representation of former communists (see Chapter 9). In the economic arena there are often deep crises; high inflation, large deficits, widespread unemployment, banking problems, financial corruption and black markets, Mafia-type activity, severe shortages, and a rapid decline of antiquated industry. Even in the states most attuned to market developments stock markets are embryonic, many prices are still controlled, and state subsidies continue.

A second major difficulty concerns the rise of xenophobic nationalist movements, underpinned by the economic difficulties and shortages just mentioned. Few wish to return to the old communist ways. But many have been acutely disadvantaged by economic change, and have every reason to express disaffection. The success of the misnamed Liberal Party (in reality a populist and nationalist right-wing party) in the December 1993 election in Russia is a case in point. The resurgence of the old Communist Party of the Soviet Union in the elections of 1995 is another.

The third source of anxiety lies in ethnic and minority problems. Eastern Europe contains several historical and cultural fault lines: Muslim and Christian, Roman Catholic and Protestant, Orthodox, and Eastern Catholic. Indeed these cleavages contributed significantly to the break-up of the former Yugoslavia. Large populations were also disturbed or divided by border changes following the First World War. Hungary for example, lost two-thirds of its population, and some 2 million ethnic Hungarians live outside Hungary. Enforced population movements under Stalin's rule, combined with the movement of Russians into satellite countries, account for the large number of Russians who now find themselves living outside the Russian Federation.

At the extreme, ethnic tensions can produce extremist, racist, and nationalist movements which incite political conflict and violence. At worst they have produced the brutal 'ethnic cleansing', or in simple language, genocide, of the Bosnian war

(1992–95). There have also been several violent, though less brutal conflicts, in the former Soviet Union; in Nagorny Karabakh, an Armenian enclave in Azerbaijan; in Moldova between the eastern part, dominated by ethnic Russians, and the western sections, dominated by Romanians; in South Ossetia in Georgia; and in Tajikistan where civil war has claimed over 20,000 lives. In Russia itself there has been a vicious repression of an uprising in Chechenia. Similar ethnic tensions, though without serious violence yet, can be found in the Baltic states, the Ukraine, the Crimea. They also contributed to the Czechoslovakian split (1992). Moreover, there are deep-rooted anti-Semitic traditions in many parts of Central and Eastern Europe. Concern among Western liberals centres on violations of human rights, racism, extreme nationalism and the rise of quasi and neo-fascist movements. These problems are known to exist. The question is how acute they are, or how acute they may become.

The fourth controversy centres on the re-creation of the old Soviet sphere of influence. From the outset the CIS was a confusing mixture of confederal and federal elements. As it has developed thus far the federal elements are gaining, along with Russian predominance. Although the currency situation is unclear, a rouble zone seems to be developing, and Russian exports and imports dwarf those of other CIS states. Under the Agreement on Armed Forces and Border Troops of December 1991, all CIS states have their own armed forces, but the Russian military by far outweighs any other. Decisions on the use of nuclear weapons are taken, according to the Agreement on Strategic Forces, by the President of the Russian Federation, albeit in consultation with the other CIS states. Six states have now signed defence treaties with Russia. While the Soviet sphere of influence in Eastern Europe now seems to have disappeared, there is little doubt that Russia can easily dominate the CIS states should she choose to do so.

Externally, the collapse of the WTO (Warsaw Treaty Organization) and the dissolution of the former Soviet Union into the CIS, have not had a serious impact on the relative military capabilities of the Russian Federation, at least not in the short term. In the long term, loss of 'empire' may force Russia to reduce its military capacity. One sign of this may be President Yeltsin's abolition of conscription in 1996. Meanwhile, Russia's present military capabilities vastly outweigh those of any other European state. Consequently, a military strike still remains a possibility in theory, if not in practice. The Baltic states of Estonia, Latvia, and Lithuania could prove to be a flashpoint. Strong connections with Scandinavia give them a symbolic importance for Western Europe. At the same time, their large Russian minorities are of continuing concern to Moscow.

There are two liberal responses to possible security threats from Russia: one revolves around questions of economics and trade; the other concerns political strategies. These involve particularly strengthening the Conference on Security and Co-operation in Europe (CSCE). There is, however, disagreement on the relative importance of each area, and on the component parts of a possible response.

Those who favour economic links do so on the grounds that increasing economic ties will help consolidate reforms, thereby removing the most fundamental security threat. In practice, two related sets of measures are possible: to expand and intensify economic relations; and to extend membership of international economic organizations.

The economic strategy covers financial aid, investment and trade. In practice all have increased, but Liberals disagree about their form, magnitude, and likely effects.

BRIEFING 1.7

The Marshall Plan

Set up in 1947 by George Marshall, Secretary of State in the Truman Administration, the plan provided millions of dollars for the post-war reconstruction of Western Europe, both economic and political. The idea was to eliminate, as far as possible, the economic conditions which provoked political instability and extremism within nations, and bitter economic competition between them. Although the countries of Eastern Europe might have been included in the plan, the Soviet Union opposed it on the grounds that it would result in US domination. In Western Europe the Marshall Plan provided for post-war reconstruction and laid the foundations for the long economic boom of the 1950s and 1960s.

   The money was first administered by a special organization set up for the purpose, the Organization for European Economic Co-operation (OEEC), which became the Organization for Economic Co-operation and Development (OECD). Some people advocated a 'new Marshall plan' for Central and Eastern Europe in the early 1990s, but money on the same scale was not provided.

For example, aid can be given either as grants or loans, it can be for longer-term development or for standby loans (such as International Monetary Fund – IMF – credits), it can be conditional or unconditional, it can be disbursed bilaterally (by separate states) or through multilateral bodies (such as the International Bank for Reconstruction and Development – BRD – or IMF), and it can be substantial or piecemeal. Political liberals in the west tend to favour the Marshall Plan model because it would be both substantial and unconditional, and help to consolidate liberal democracy and human rights. In actual fact Western aid to central and Eastern Europe has not been like this, in that it has been conditional and piecemeal. Free market liberals in the west have broadly approved this aid strategy.

   The second set of economic options involves extending membership of various international or supranational bodies to central and east European countries. The IMF, World Bank and GATT are seen by liberals as extremely important in this respect. Less important, so far, has been the establishment of the European Bank for Reconstruction and Development (EBRD), even though this funds the east. Most liberals approve of this body in principle, but those on the left are disappointed with the small scale of its activities to date.

   Probably the most serious and complicated debate has centred on the extension of the European Union (EU). For liberals, extension of membership of the EU is a high priority, and strong pressure for membership has indeed come from central Europe. In 1991, the EU signed 'Europe Agreements' providing associate status for Poland, Hungary, and (the then) Czechoslovakia, to prepare the ground for full membership. The 1992 Edinburgh Summit further committed the EU to their eventual membership. As yet, however, nothing approximating a timetable has been agreed. Furthermore, the 'Europe Agreements' have been used to restrict rather than expand trade.

   These are enormous and complex issues which raise questions about the very future of the EU – as we will see in the next chapter. Free market liberals are for 'widening' as opposed to 'deepening'. They would expand the EU as extensively and rapidly as possible, eliminating the Common Agricultural Policy and restricting regional and social funds. Social democrats, however, want a substantial expansion of

BRIEFING 1.8

General Agreement on Tariffs and Trade (GATT)

Set up by the United Nations and operating under it, the General Agreement on Tariffs and Trade was signed in 1947. Its main goal is to reduce barriers to international trade, such as import duties and controls, and international tariffs and duties, in order to achieve free trade between nations. By and large this has been successful so far as manufactured goods are concerned. By the seventh round of negotiations signed in Tokyo in 1979, international tariffs on manufactured goods were around 5 per cent, although many non-tariff restrictions were imposed in different parts of the world. The main difficulty, however, was agricultural trade between the USA, the EU, and many third world countries, all of which tried to protect their own agricultural interests against foreign competition. Years of negotiation after the Uruguayan round of 1986 produced an agricultural agreement only at the last minute.

the budget, much of which would be used to promote economic growth in the less-developed regions and to redress inequalities. In other words, the issue of expanding the EU into central Europe is intimately tied up with the debate about deepening its operations, and both are based upon a fundamental conception of what the EU is and should be about.

The second Western liberal response to Eastern Europe involves a more political strategy, notably the development of the Conference on Security and Co-operation in Europe (CSCE). The CSCE originated in 1972 from discussions which led to the Helsinki Final Act of 1975. Upon its inception the CSCE met broadly with both 'liberal' and 'realist' approval. Liberals were encouraged by its broad approach to reducing tension, including provisions for cultural, scientific and environmental co-operation. Realists were impressed by its military measures. It also formalized a commitment to human rights. A feature of the 1975 Act was provision for follow-up conferences which were held, prior to 1989, at Belgrade, Madrid and Vienna. In the pre-1989 period, the CSCE was one of the rare European initiatives which spanned the East–West divide. Since 1989 the extension of the CSCE, has become of substantial importance to liberals.

Two major developments have taken place in the CSCE since 1989. First, by the Charter of Paris for a New Europe in 1990 it was transformed from an *ad hoc* forum (as its name states the CSCE was a conference) into a permanent organization. Second, it has become substantially more active. Principal developments include: the creation of a High Commissioner for National Minorities; the establishment of the Office for Democratic Institutions and Human Rights; the establishment of a Pan-European Assembly; the extension of confidence-building measures; the negotiation of the Open Skies Agreement; the initiation of discussions on CSCE 'peacekeeping forces'; the establishment of the Forum for Security Co-operation; and the negotiation of the Conventional Armed Forces Agreement (CFE). These extensions are of enormous significance because the CSCE, though it has a substantial distance to travel, could provide a basis for collective security across the whole of Europe. It could even replace NATO and the Western European Union (WEU) (see below, p.29–30). Nevertheless, we must emphasize, once again, that there is considerable disagreement about what the CSCE is able to do. From the perspective of 1996 it seems to have less potential than it did in 1992. Only time will tell.

BRIEFING **1.9**

Conference on Security and Co-operation In Europe (CSCE)

The Conference on Security and Co-operation in Europe started off as a series of conferences but by the early 1990s had become an organization. The first conference agreement was signed in 1975 by all European states (except Albania) and by the USA and
Canada. It was intended to reduce Cold War tension by means of agreements on such
things as international economic co-operation, human rights, and most important, arms
agreements and control. After its first meeting in Helsinki (1973–75) it convened again in
1977–78 (Belgrade), 1980–83 (Madrid), and 1986–89 (Vienna) by which time it had taken a
major role in arms control and agreement.

   After the disappearance of the iron curtain, the CSCE converted itself from a conference into an organization with a permanent office and secretariat in Prague, and over
fifty nation-state members. It is now mainly concerned with peace and security in
Europe, but it has no separate military power of its own, and its relations to the
West European Union, the European Union, the Council of Europe, and NATO remain
problematic.

■ European security agendas after 1989: the realist perspective

Opposed to the 'liberal' view of European security are the 'realists' within Western
governments who believe in the fundamental importance of power and military force
in determining international relations. In general, realists are less optimistic, mainly
because they see more continuity than change since 1989. The dissolution of the
Soviet bloc has not created as many nation-states with independent power as it might
have done. In population and economic terms, the Russian Federation outweighs all
the other states. Most importantly, Russia continues to be a military superpower.

   It is important to remember that realists are not concerned with the internal
political and economic structure of nation-states. So the conversion of Central and
Eastern European states to liberal democracy and market economics, so crucial to
liberals, is for them simply not relevant. What preoccupies realists is the stability of
these states which may allow them to reach and keep international agreements. This
leads on to a second source of realist concern – namely, that the *modus vivendi* and the
balance of power developed in the international system before 1989 might be lost.

   Two concerns are particularly acute here. The first is the proliferation of nuclear
weapons. With the establishment of the CIS, four states, as opposed to the previous
one, had nuclear weapons. Although the reassertion of nuclear control by Russia over
weapons held in Belarus and Kazakhstan proceeded smoothly, this was not true of
the Ukraine. Discussions with the Ukraine have, to put it mildly, been confusing.
Parts of the Ukrainian government – it is clearly not united – have been reluctant to
relinquish their nuclear weapons. However, a deal was signed in Moscow in 1994
between Russia, the Ukraine, and, significantly, the United States. The agreement
showed a willingness on the part of the Ukraine to remove nuclear weapons if compensated by Russia and the United States. This indicates the enormous importance
the US government attaches to the Ukraine, not least because of the ramifications for
the nuclear arms reduction treaties SALT, START I and START II.

   A second cause for concern was the prospect of armed conflict, following the

BRIEFING 1.10

Negotiations and treatles between USA and USSR to limit their holdings of arms (Salt, Start, Inf)

Strategic Arms Limitation Talks (SALT)

In the early 1960s both Russia and the United States came under military and economic pressure which led them to look for ways of limiting the arms race; the USA was heavily engaged in the Vietnam War and the USSR was struggling to keep up with the military development of the USA. It suited both to sign the SALT I Treaty in 1972 which tried to establish an upper limit for missiles in each country. This was only a provisional agreement and given the absence of inspection, it did not go far. However, it proved an important start and a later round of talks (SALT II) followed. These were implemented in the early 1980s and took the further step of regulating not just the number of missiles but the number and destructive capacity of each nuclear warhead. Though it was never actually signed by either the USA or the USSR, SALT II was implemented by both sides. SALT talks gave way to START in the early 1980s.

Strategic Arms Reduction Talks (START)

Strategic Arms Reduction Talks between the USA and the USSR started in 1982 in Geneva and after some difficulties were resumed in 1985 after Gorbachev had come to power in the USSR. An agreement reducing long and intermediate-range missiles was signed in 1991 only months before the dissolution of the USSR, and paved the way for a more far-reaching reduction in nuclear forces and the destruction of warheads and missiles.

Intermediate Nuclear Forces Treaty (INF)

The Intermediate Nuclear Forces Treaty (INF) ran parallel to the SALT and START talks but concentrated on intermediate range missiles, rather than intercontinental missiles or the short-range battlefield missiles. After initial difficulties – the Russians walked out of talks in 1983 – agreement was reached by Reagan and Gorbachev and a treaty signed in Washington in 1987. This provided for the destruction of all medium-range missiles (with a range of 500 to 5,500 kilometres), including Russian SS–20s and the US Cruise missiles.

demise of the old Soviet Union and its satellites. Conflict in the former Yugoslavia is precisely the type which concerns realists. They do not oppose secessionist movements, necessarily, but are concerned with those which fail to establish viable and internationally recognized states, and which, therefore, cause local instability, with international ramifications. As has already been indicated the scope for secession in Central and Eastern Europe is substantial. More than liberals, realists express concern about the development of Islamic regimes along the southern rim of the former Soviet Union.

A further source of concern involves the former 'satellite' states of Eastern Europe, and in particular their relationship to Western Europe and the CIS, especially Russia. From a realist point of view, Russia is overwhelmingly the most important European state. Consequently, the maintenance of a *modus vivendi* between the West and Russia is vital. One of the reasons for the increasing optimism of realists over the course of the Cold War was the development of a balance of power between the East and West, based partly on the recognition of a Soviet sphere of influence in Eastern Europe. The failure of the West to react to the Soviet invasions of Hungary and Czechoslovakia in 1956 and 1968 is a classic illustration of realist thinking.

Eastern European states have moved out of a CIS sphere of influence, following the rejection of the Brezhnev Doctrine by Russia, the abolition of the WTO, and the decision to withdraw Russian troops. For realists, evolving relationships between the West and the former satellite states should not be such as to antagonize Russia. The allegiance of the former satellite states to the West needs to be secured, so that a new Russian sphere of influence cannot be reimposed, but this has to be achieved without constituting an intolerable threat to Russia.

A final source of concern has emerged for realists in their guise of neo-mercantilists – that is, as supporters of a protected market which increases national prosperity and hence military potential. Prior to 1989, economic ties between the East and the West were not strong and were monitored in the West by the Co-ordinating Committee (COCOM) which was charged with the job of restricting exports to the Soviet Union which might prove of military assistance. The office of COCOM was closed in 1994. In contrast, the CIS and central European countries have been allowed into the IMF–World Bank–GATT club, and trade has expanded substantially. Of particular concern to some western neo-mercantilists is the damage that might be done to the economies of Western Europe – especially in agriculture, coal, and manufacturing – by extending EU membership.

Realists are not agreed on these issues. For those emphasizing the continued nuclear status of Russia, the main danger is the potentially catastrophic loss of life through nuclear war. For those emphasizing changes in the international power system, the main threat is conflict and destablization caused by the emergence of new states. For those emphasizing the power of Russia, the danger is one of provoking a new 'iron curtain' and a new cold war. For those emphasizing economic changes, the main threat comes from cheap Eastern European imports and the export of investment capital to the east.

Concomitantly, there is disagreement about the appropriate response to these threats. The first concerns the necessity of continuing arms control. Many realists are encouraged by the tradition of arms control which has moved through Start I, Start II, and the INF, to acceptance of the principle of military balance as the single most important basis on which stability can be engineered. Realists also approve of some CSCE activity, particularly in the confidence building area, though they dislike any increase in its capabilities which might distract attention from the 'real' task of mutual arms reductions.

A second realist response concerns the need to recognize and support Russia. A good illustration of this was the rapidity with which the Soviet Union's permanent seat on the Security Council of the UN was transferred. Another illustration would be the incorporation of Russia into the Group of Seven (the leading economies in the world).

More importantly, realists build arguments upon the distinction which the Russians themselves term their 'near abroad' and their 'far abroad'. The near abroad is roughly the CIS territory, while the far abroad is Central Europe and beyond. Realists accept that a Russian sphere of influence within the near abroad should be tolerated, even encouraged. According to this argument the CIS can only be managed by Russia, and Western intervention in its affairs would be intolerable to Moscow. Besides, Russian co-ordination of the CIS could in fact prevent instability. In this context control by Russia of nuclear weapons is vital and ought to be supported. The development of defence treaties between Russia and other CIS states should also be supported, as should the stationing of Russian troops and development of military bases in the 'near abroad'. The partial reappearance of a Russian sphere of influence, generally deplored by liberals, is greeted by realists as a positive development.

The 'far abroad' is, however, another matter. The onus here falls on Russia to recognize that the former satellite states now fall outside its sphere of influence. Generally speaking, realists are encouraged by the willingness on the part of Russia to accept the termination of the Warsaw Pact and withdraw its troops. An incorporation of the former satellite states into a Western military alliance could be seen by Russia as threatening. In practice this means that NATO should proceed slowly and cautiously in extending to Central and Eastern Europe. Before elaborating this point, it is useful to consider a third response which centres directly on the role and position of NATO.

The idea that the end of the Cold War has made NATO redundant is anathema to realists. Russia continues to be a nuclear superpower, and so it follows automatically – so the argument goes – that nuclear deterrence under the NATO umbrella is essential for the West. Besides, there is no evidence that NATO *is* withering away in the wake of the end of the cold war. On the contrary, a major review of its role was initiated in 1990 and led to a summit meeting and the Rome Declaration of 1991. While recognizing the need for continued dialogue and further reductions in military forces, the declaration provided for the creation of an Allied Rapid Reaction Force (ARRC) operational in 1995. Given NATO's continued strength, attention shifted mainly to its relations with the CSCE and to the WEU. For realists, the CSCE has developed as far, if not further, than it should. The issue of the WEU is more complicated.

The WEU was a product of the collapse in 1954 of the idea of a European Defence Community and of the belief that West Germany should be incorporated into NATO. Although the agreement establishing the WEU was ratified in 1955, little was actually done until the mid-1980s. In 1987 it adopted the 'Platform on European Security Interests' which called for more cohesion on defence by Western European states, but also reiterated the centrality of NATO. It was used as a framework for mine-clearing following the end of the Iran–Iraq War in 1988, and for a military presence in the Kuwait conflict in 1990. It was, however, the Maastricht Treaty which pushed the issue of the WEU to the fore.

The French and German governments were keen on the WEU being integrated into the European Union (EU), while the UK and Netherlands wanted it to be a bridge between the EU and NATO. This debate on the relative importance of the WEU, *vis à vis* NATO, is important and complex. The more ambitious plan is that the WEU would progressively supplant NATO and provide the EU with its own integrated nuclear force. This fits happily with the plan to 'deepen' the EU and turn it into a superpower. At the same time it is anathema to those who see 'deepening', especially military deepening, as the means for developing a 'fortress Europe', closed and isolated from the outside world.

How the WEU will develop is still far from clear. The Maastricht Treaty (1992) puts it very firmly on the agenda, stating that it is 'an integral part of the development of the EU' and requesting the WEU 'to elaborate and implement decisions and actions of the Union which have defence implications'. It also committed members to the 'eventual framing of a common defence policy which might in time lead to a common defence'.

This was a relatively firm and explicit declaration. But it was, of course, simply a statement of intent. Furthermore, it was promptly followed by a statement that NATO was still crucial. However, the statement of intent is being translated into practice to some degree. In 1992, the WEU was given an operational capacity to use military units for humanitarian tasks, peace-keeping, and crisis management. The same units, however, were also available for NATO use under an arrangement which has come to be known as 'double hatting'. A further illustration of the move from intent to practice involves the decision by the French and German governments to establish a 'Eurocorps' as a joint defence force under the aegis of the WEU. Concern, voiced particularly by the governments of the United Kingdom and United States, that this would undermine NATO, led in 1993 to a decision that this corps could also serve under NATO command.

This brings us back to the realist appraisal of the present role of NATO in the Western alliance. Thus far NATO, as urged by realists, has proceeded relatively cautiously. Despite pressure, particularly from the countries of central Europe, NATO has not rushed to embrace the Eastern European states. Rather, in October 1993, full membership was rejected in favour of a more gradual extension. At a NATO Summit in January 1994 the Partnership for Peace Programme was launched which extended a degree of military co-operation to individual states of the former Soviet bloc – a rather confusing way of not saying 'no' to NATO membership, while not saying 'yes' either. Russia agreed to sign up for the programme in May 1994.

The North Atlantic Co-operation Council (NACC) is another NATO initiative designed to cross the East–West divide. Established in 1991 as proposed in the Rome Declaration, the Council is a forum for consultation on security and military matters which covers all sixteen members of NATO and the states of the former Soviet bloc.

The response to the alleged economic dislocations caused by extending EU membership is quite simple. It is argued that extension should not harm what realist neo-mercantilists take to be the economic interests of the EU. In its most extreme form this position has been lost in the sense that EU extension to central Europe is already on the public agenda and associate membership has been granted to the Central European countries. However, the EU has proved much more enthusiastic about giving full membership to Austria, Finland and Sweden than it has to any of the former Soviet bloc. Furthermore, associate membership includes numerous protective measures. The membership of Bulgaria, Romania and the Baltic states has been delayed until the 'medium term'.

Realists and liberals are very much at loggerheads over the issue of EU extension. Liberals see it as a major way to consolidate the situation in Eastern Europe. Quite how this important argument will be resolved remains to be seen. All we can say is that a clear resolution appears unlikely in the near future. Instead, Western Europe, with or without the USA, will no doubt muddle through with a variety of strategies, some complementary and some contradictory.

■ A new (but confused) European order?

This chapter has avoided bold statements about security problems and solutions for Europe. There are already many of these. Rather than add to their number and increase the confusion, the chapter has presented the main outlines of the problem and the main proposals debated by policy-makers. These boil down to two broad alternatives. Liberals encourage democratic transformation of the new states of Central and Eastern Europe and their integration into the Western economy. This includes the eventual integration of central Europe, and possibly Romania, Bulgaria and the Baltic states into the EU. Transition to democracy in the CIS is also to be encouraged together with trade agreements with the EU, and possibly also the USA and Japan. The other alternative is the realist one which centres on the balance of military power between alliances. It is concerned with keeping both NATO and Russia strong – partly from fear of the wars and instability which would ensue if either collapsed.

Though they stress different priorities – economic and political on the one hand, military on the other – these two alternatives can be reconciled within a general European security policy. Both liberals and realists agree on the need to maintain the stability of the Eastern states and Russia, both economically and militarily, and both approaches can be found in the various initiatives undertaken by NATO and the United States in recent years.

The events of 1989 changed relationships between the two halves of Europe, but did not totally transform the situation. European security, and the prospects both for democracy and international co-operation, still depend heavily on factors beyond the control of European states themselves, notably on US–Russian relationships. To this extent the Eurocentric world of pre-1914 will not reappear. Nevertheless, Europeans currently have an opportunity to construct and control their own security agenda, perhaps more than at any time since 1945. While many Europeans recognize the opportunities clearly enough, and have devised initiatives to capitalize on them, chances have been lost simply because there is so much disagreement within Europe. European security continues to be riddled not only with dilemmas, as it always will be, but also with competing views on what these dilemmas are.

One of the most important dilemmas is the choice between widening or deepening the European Union, and whether, in widening, it should embrace central Europe. Is deepening incompatible with widening, and how far should widening go? The resolution of these questions will affect developments in the New Europe profoundly, within individual countries and between them. For this reason we consider the EU and prospects for its extension in the next chapter, before going on to consider the separate European states in Chapter 3.

▪ Further reading

Ken Booth and Nicholas Wheeler, *Security and Strategy in the New Europe* (London, Routledge, Verso, 1991).

Adrian Hyde Price, *European Security Beyond the Cold War: Four Scenarios for 2010* (London, Sage, 1991).

Geoffrey Pridham and Tatu Vanhanen, *Democratization in Eastern Europe* (London, Routledge, 1994).

Gwyn Rees, *International Politics in Europe: The New Agenda* (London, Routledge 1993).

Chapter 2

European union and *the* European Union

■ The problems of growth

The European Union's (EU) internal influence and its role in international relations have grown enormously over the past thirty years. The domestic powers of member states are increasingly being taken over. Yet more states seek to join in the hope of gaining economic benefits and avoiding political isolation. On an international level, the EU is an important global actor in terms of trade, aid, foreign and security policy. As a supranational arm of European government it has been a hugely significant and, in many ways, successful enterprise.

Yet there are still many questionmarks over its future. How far can its influence grow without provoking opposition, backlash, or even threats of withdrawal from individual nation states? There are strong socio-economic and political pressures to enlarge the EU eastwards. But can such a complex organization continue to extend without, at the same time, undermining its own policies, institutions and authority? Does the inability of the EU, to deal effectively with international conflicts such as the Bosnian problem (Chapter 3) show up its limitations as an actor on the world stage? Or will Bosnia prove a catalyst in establishing a common foreign and security policy? Many of these questions can be answered by examining the relationship between EU development and member state interests. This will also open up questions about European security and about relations with both the USA and Russia.

Where exactly is the EU heading? As with the projects for European security discussed in the last chapter, there is no clear and simple answer to this, only various dilemmas, paradoxes and possibilities. These emerge particularly in regard to the states of Central and Eastern Europe (CEE) and the related issue of whether widening will weaken the Union. Can some of these states actually conform to EU criteria in order to secure membership? This raises the possibility of co-operation without membership, and of the wider role the EU can play in the establishment of more stable economic and political conditions within Europe as a whole.

The impact of the EU on European states takes a variety of forms, depending on whether states are full, associate or potential members, or partners in co-operation. As far as the core members are concerned (fifteen countries in 1996) membership means the acceptance of a wide range of common policies, of a defined set of EU rules, and of the authority of the various Union institutions we will describe below. Countries outside the EU may have a variety of relationships with it. For example, Turkey is an Associate Member – a status which confers certain trading privileges. But her application for full membership has been indefinitely postponed, even though she is an important strategic and military partner. Iceland is a member of the European Economic Area (EEA) and thus bound by many EU directives without having much influence over their content. Norway is also a member of the EEA but has a closer relationship with the EU, for example through joint management of the

BRIEFING **2.1**

The European Economic Area (EEA)

This is an intergovernmental organization set up to administer the single market formed by the member states of the EU with Norway and Iceland. The single market is based on freedom of movement of goods, persons, capital and services but excludes agriculture. Research, cultural, environmental and other forms of co-operation are envisaged. Given the imbalance between members, the EEA is run mainly on EU terms, but it is important for Norway and Iceland to secure their access to Union markets.

North Sea fisheries and co-ordination of immigration requirements with the other Scandinavian countries who are EU members. On the other hand, Norway rejected Union membership by a referendum in 1994. Countries which have applications pending for membership, such as Cyprus, Malta and the central European countries, tend to harmonize their policies and procedures with those of the EU in order to make eventual membership easier.

In these ways outside countries' relationships with the Union vary considerably. What one can say in general is that EU decisions have considerable importance for non-members – perhaps even more so in some cases than for full members.

Central institutions

Before dealing with the 'wider' versus 'deeper' argument – that is to say geographical enlargement versus the greater integration of the existing membership – it is appropriate to examine the role, policies, decision-making processes and jurisdiction of the EU itself, to see what might be 'deepened'.

The original six countries which set up the European Economic Community (EEC) by signing the Treaty of Rome in 1958 (France, West Germany, Italy, Belgium, the Netherlands and Luxembourg) were later joined by Britain, Ireland and Denmark in 1973, Greece (1978), Spain and Portugal (1984) and Finland, Sweden and Austria in 1995. With these graduated accessions, charted in Table 2.1, the Union now covers a vast geopolitical area stretching from the Arctic to the Mediterranean and from Ireland to the Balkans. Harmonizing public policy in such a diverse range of countries is an enormous, complex and delicate task. Therefore, it is little wonder that disputes arise about the wisdom of enlargement and whether the fragile internal cohesion of the EU will be threatened by the integration of new members from central Europe.

Compounding the difficulties in forging a single policy for a wide variety of states each with their own national interest, is the fact that the EU itself is not governed by an integrated set of institutions. In fact there are two executive structures rather than one (the Commission and the Council of Ministers), alongside a vigorous European Court of Justice which often makes policy through judicial decisions, plus an elected legislature. Perhaps the best known central institution of the Union is the European Commission, made up of nineteen technocrats based in Brussels, two nominated by each of the big countries in the Community (Britain, France, Italy, Spain and Germany) and one by each of the other countries. The

Map 2.1   The European Union in the mid-1990s

purpose of the Commission is to initiate community legislation, and send policy
directives to the Council of Ministers for consideration and decision. It also medi-
ates Council decisions. In the process of forwarding proposals, the Commission
also consults the various national governments, interest groups, the European
Parliament and advisory bodies. Additionally, the Commission implements the
numerous regulations laid down in the Treaty of Rome and subsequent EU agreements, and judgments of the European Court. The Commission ensures that the
obligations of member states under EU legislation are observed and reports any
infringements of those obligations to the European Court of Justice, which sits
in Luxembourg.

The Commission is often seen as the EU institution most likely to interfere in the

Table 2.1 The development of the European Union

1951	Treaty of Paris. Belgium, the Netherlands, Luxembourg, France, Italy and West Germany (The Six) set up the European Coal and Steel Community (ECSC).
1957	Treaty of Rome. The Six set up the European Economic Community (EEC) and the European Atomic Energy Authority (Euratom).
1962	Common Agricultural Policy (CAP) created. The EEC regulates farm prices and decides on agricultural priorities right across the community.
1966	President De Gaulle establishes the right of national veto (the 'Luxembourg Compromise').
1967	Creation of the European Communities (EC) by the merger of EEC, ECSC and Euratom under a Commission and Council of Ministers.
1968	Creation of European Customs Union.
1973	Denmark, Ireland, and the UK join the EC.
1974	Heads of Government meet as European Council. The Regional Fund created to help poor or declining regions inside member states.
1979	First direct elections to the European Parliament. The European Monetary System (EMS) with its Exchange Rate Mechanism (ERM) and European Currency Unit (ECU) created.
1981	Greece joins EC.
1985	The Milan Summit and the Single European Act (SEA) amend the Treaty of Rome to introduce the principle of qualified majority voting in areas related to setting up a single market, and take the first steps towards a common foreign policy.
1986	Spain and Portugal join the EC.
1989	Strasbourg Meeting. Germany insists that political union is necessary for monetary union.
1992	Treaty on European Union (Maastricht Treaty) amends the Single European Act and presents a plan for economic and political union. The Treaty covers co-operation on political, economic, defense, social, environmental, cultural, and legal matters. Britain and Denmark opt out of the Social Chapter on welfare and regulation of working conditions.
1992/3	Maastricht Treaty narrowly approved in a French referendum and, at the second go, in Denmark.
1992	UK is forced by a currency crisis to withdraw from ERM and EMS, to be followed in the next few months by many other EU currencies.
1993	Single internal market inaugurated.
1995	Austria, Finland and Sweden join EU.

BRIEFING 2.2

The European Commission

The European Commission is the highest administrative institution of the EU – that is, its senior civil service – but shares executive functions with the Council of Ministers. It can initiate policy and propose legislation to the Council. It is also the 'international' branch of EU government which is supposed to represent the interests of Europe as a whole, rather than individual member states. It oversees the internal work of the EU, especially financial and budgetary management, and ensures that member states implement EU policies satisfactorily, reporting those who fail to do so to the European Court of Justice. The Commission also represents the EU as a trading bloc in international organizations such as GATT.

Members of the Commission are nominated by their respective national governments and are appointed by the Council of Ministers. It is the Council of Ministers who also appoint the President of the Commission, which can be a powerful office. The Commission is able to take decisions by majority vote, but naturally prefers to reach decisions through unanimity. Each Commissioner is directly responsible for a given policy area. The Maastricht Treaty (1992) provides for European Parliament approval of new Commissioners. Their period of office was also changed to coincide with the Parliament's.

The Commission has a permanent staff of over 16,000 people in Brussels. Most work in one of the directorates general which are roughly the equivalent of national ministries.

BRIEFING 2.3

The Council of Ministers and COREPER

The Council is made up of ministers from member states. It is the main policy-making body of the EU. It meets in different forms depending upon the subject for discussion. The General Council is made up of the foreign ministers from member states, and is charged with the task of supervising and co-ordinating other council meetings. The specialist Councils bring together ministers of agriculture, finance, transport, and so on, according to the business to be transacted.

Decisions can be taken by unanimous voting, majority or weighted majority. That is, the vote of each member state is weighted roughly in proportion to the size of population, where a certain proportion of the votes cast is enough for a measure to pass. Thus there is no country veto if weighted voting is adopted.

Preparatory work for the Council is undertaken in Brussels by the Committee of Permanent Representatives (COREPER) of national and EU civil servants and officials. The Council is not able to initiate or draft legislation but must depend upon the Commission. The President of the Council tries to integrate proposals on different matters for presentation to the Council. The presidency rotates every six months between member states. The Council has a permanent secretariat of some 2,000 people.

BRIEFING 2.4

The European Court of Justice (ECJ)

The European Court of Justice (ECJ) interprets EU law, ensures that it is applied uniformly across member states and ensures that acts of the Council and Commission are indeed lawful. The Court considers cases brought before it by either member states, or the Commission, and by individuals or organizations from within member states. The justices sit in Luxembourg.

It is a supreme court; there is no power of appeal against its judgements. This, plus the fact that its decisions take precedence over national law, gives it great importance. Additionally, the nature of EU law and its application across countries means that in interpreting the law the ECJ at the same time often also makes it. Although it has no direct sanctions it is rare for its decisions to be ignored. The Court has, therefore, a powerful place within the EU, often extending EU powers as against those of member states. (For further detail, see Chapter 14.)

domestic affairs of member states. It is certainly the case that the Commission is vested with an authority which is independent of national jurisdiction. The Commission must also abide by decisions made by the Council of Ministers, who are appointed in turn by the national governments to whom they are accountable.

Perhaps a more significant development within the European Union is the growth of the authority vested in the European Court of Justice, which can override domestic courts and national parliaments. In the past, courts in many European states have merely interpreted acts of parliament. The explicit task of the European Court, however, is to ensure that national legislation and law does not conflict with EU legislation and law, a function which gives it broad ranging powers of interpretation and judgement. Additionally, the European Court has often taken a broad view of

> BRIEFING 2.5
>
> **The European Parliament (EP)**
>
> Until 1979 members of the European Parliament (EP) were appointed by national govern-
> ments from the membership of their own elected assemblies. After 1979 the EP was
> directly elected, as agreed by the Treaty of Rome, every five years. Seats in the EP are
> allocated among member states in rough proportion to their population.
>
> Although the EP is charged with the duty of supervising the Commission and the
> Council of Ministers it lacks power and has mainly a secondary and advisory role. The
> jurisdiction of the Parliament has expanded, but it is still primarily a delaying or amend-
> ing body, with limited powers of veto. It is logistically and bureaucratically hampered by
> having to meet in Brussels, for committees, and in Luxembourg and Strasbourg, for
> plenary sessions. Moreover, the main secretariat is located in Luxembourg. Business is
> conducted in all the official languages of the EU, which necessitates a huge burden
> of translation.
>
> Members of the European Parliament (MEPs) sit in international party groupings.
> There are eleven of these, with the Socialists and the Christian Democrats being the
> largest. Compared with national legislatures party organization is relatively weak. Much
> work is carried out by various Committees.

those powers invested in it. It has been particularly active in extending citizens'
social and political rights in employment and in matters directly affecting national
government legislation. It has argued, for example, that economic provisions
for free movement of labour must respect the individual's right to both security
and dignity.

The third major Community body is the Council of Ministers which, like the
Commission, is also located in Brussels. The Council consists of the General Council
and various technical sub-councils. The foreign ministers of member states meet in
the General Council, while ministers for particular policy areas such as agriculture
meet in the technical councils. Associated with each of the Ministerial Councils are
Councils of Permanent Representatives (COREPER in Community jargon), which
in turn are divided between COREPER I, which 'shadows' the Foreign Ministers and
is made up of national ambassadors to the Community, and COREPER II, which is
made up of deputy ambassadors to the Community. There are, as one might expect,
numerous committees and working parties staffed by appropriately qualified national
civil servants which undertake the necessary preparatory work for regularly held
meetings of ministers.

The single-chamber European Parliament is the fourth of the major EU institu-
tions. It was first directly elected in June 1979 and divides its time between
Strasbourg and Luxembourg, while often holding committee hearings in Brussels.
The European Parliament carries out a great deal of work in specialized committees.
Although its members belong to five major party groupings (Socialist, Liberal,
Christian Democrat, Gaullist and Conservative) and some small ones, party loyalties
do not predominate. This is partly because the powers and competences of the
Parliament are limited, so as yet there is little to divide over. Its two major powers –
to dismiss the Commission and to reject the budget – require a two-thirds majority,
which is a particularly difficult threshold to overcome. Therefore, the main influence
of the Parliament is via publicity and investigation where it has extensive and increas-

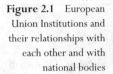

Figure 2.1 European Union Institutions and their relationships with each other and with national bodies

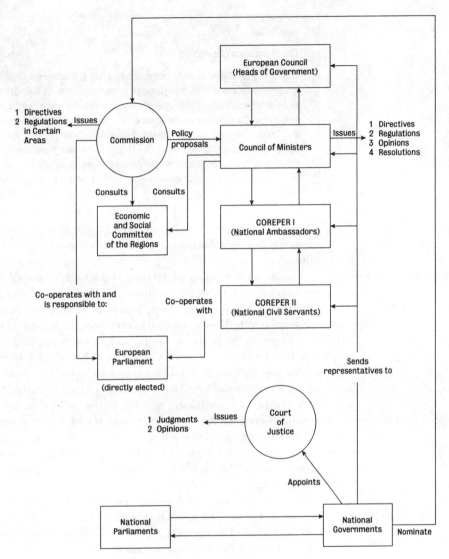

ing scope, particularly in regard to the Commission. Apart from the Parliament the other main representative bodies are the Economic and Social Committee and Committee of the Regions. However, these are merely consultative and enjoy no formal power.

As shown in Figure 2.1, Community deliberations are expressed in the form of directives, regulations, opinions and resolutions from the Council of Ministers, and in some areas the Commission, and in judgments and opinions laid down by the European Court. We shall consider later how these impinge on member governments and how in turn member governments are influenced by them.

One of the institutions shown in Figure 2.1 has not yet been discussed and needs to be commented on. Its role goes some way towards illustrating relationships between the Union and its member states. This is the European Council, a gathering of heads of government of constituent States, which meets two or three times a year

---

BRIEFING 2.6

The European Council

The European Council has become an important, if informal, forum for heads of state and government (along with their foreign ministers) to meet in order to discuss any matters of interest and concern. Its role still awaits precise definition, but since its first meeting in 1975 the Council has made some of the most significant policy decisions, affecting the EU. These include the European Monetary System, the Single European Act, the Maastricht Treaty, direct elections to the European Parliament, and admissions of new members. The Council meets about twice a year and the Presidency of the Council and of the Union rotates between member states on a six-monthly basis.

---

to discuss Union policy and to launch new initiatives. It undertakes the vital role of resolving deadlocks between states which cannot be settled by the Council of Ministers.

The limited extent to which the EU dominates national interests is reflected in the existence of these two bodies – the European Council and the Council of Ministers – which are, in effect, arenas for negotiation between national governments, rather than bodies elected to represent the interest of the EU as a whole. The only executive body which can be said to focus on the Union, independently of member state interests, is the Commission. Yet in many areas of policy-making the Commission is limited to putting proposals to the European Council and to implementing the Council's decisions and those of the Council of Ministers.

It can be said, therefore, that the EU is still primarily an intergovernmental organization rather than being truly Federal with reserved supranational powers and institutions. This is particularly true in foreign and security matters, where EU policies are merely those agreed by member states. The fact that member states often disagree rather than agree helps explain the incoherence of much of the Union's foreign policy.

Nevertheless, the Commission's powers of independent action have gradually increased over the past thirty-five years. Whereas it is the European Council which agrees on a line of policy, the Commission is independently authorized to implement it. The Council has been quite consensual in agreeing on the creation of a single market. This has meant that the Commission has been entrusted with powers of implementation which have transcended national sovereignty. For example, a common market necessarily involves the free movement of citizens across national borders. This was a matter traditionally controlled by individual sovereign states, but is now under EU regulation, thereby illustrating how the Commission's powers have been steadily increased over the years.

The European Council has also moved progressively towards a system of majority decision-making. This represents one more step along the road towards turning both itself, and the Council of Ministers, into truly European bodies. With majority voting it is easier to make clear decisions. Consensus voting invariably takes longer and is more likely to involve compromise and indecision. Deadlock in the absence of complete agreement can also prolong conflict between member states By using the majority principle member states are more likely to accept proposals and move on to the next issue for discussion.

Styles of decision-making within the Union

The complicated relationships between EU institutions and member States helps explain why decision-making is often slower and more complicated within the EU than it is within individual countries. First, the procedures and functions of the EU are limited and laid down in the agreements and founding treaties of the organization itself, namely the Treaties of Rome, Maastricht, and the Single European Act. Secondly, the allocation of powers among the various institutions means that they have to work co-operatively in order to get anything done at all. The provisions for unanimous or majority voting within the various EU institutions directly affect the speed and decisiveness of the policy-making process.

These factors combine to produce a intergovernmental, that is consensual, as opposed to a Union, that is majority type, of decision-making. In certain fields like coal and steel, the common agricultural policy (CAP), commercial trade, competition policy, and the internal market, the EU proceeds by the Union model of majority decision-making. In these areas, treaty provisions have been agreed, and common policies can therefore be adopted, often employing majority procedures. These policies can then be either enforced or amended by judgements handed down by the European Court of Justice. In other fields, however, member states co-operate through established conventions rather than on an explicit treaty base. This makes for a slower and more *ad hoc* process requiring negotiation and unanimous decisions. The term intergovernmentalism describes this method of getting everyone's co-operation which prevails on monetary, cultural, and foreign policy. Thus it might be said that the Union style of decision-making has the effect of expanding EU jurisdiction and eroding national sovereignty. The intergovernmantal style tends to sustain national sovereignty as it is based upon unanimity and the power of the national veto. However, the intergovernmental method can also regularize policies in a way which can then provide a springboard for the adoption of the Union method. That is to say, intergovernmentalism can introduce policies and practices which are then amenable to being formalised and legitimatized by Union procedures.

The Single European Act (SEA, 1986) and the Treaty on European Union (Maastricht, 1992) utilized both methods of EU decision-making. By expanding the Treaty of Rome through the establishment of the internal market, the SEA advanced the Union method. In keeping the European Court of Justice out of foreign policy, it enhanced intergovernmental procedures. The SEA also fostered 'mutual recognition' of national standards and the principle of 'subsidiarity' (deciding policies at the lowest appropriate level of government) which helped smooth over the links between EU and national jurisdictions and promoted a 'pooling of sovereignties' among member states. The Maastricht Treaty on European Union similarly utilized both methods of decision-making by adopting a 'three pillars' method. The first, consistent with the Union method, united a number of new policy directives under EU treaty jurisdiction, economic and monetary union was the main one. The major role in bringing this about was assigned to the Commission. The second and third pillars depended on intergovernmental arrangements within the fields of foreign and security policy (CFSP), and immigration (including visa issuance, political asylum, and policing). The CFSP covers all matters relating to the security of member states, and aims at a common defence policy which might lead, in time, to the establishment of a truly European defence. All decisions taken under pillars

II and III require unanimity and as such can be subjected to the veto of a single government.

These two methods of co-operation mark a growing economic, cultural and political interdependence transcending borders and penetrating deeply into national jurisdictions. They also combine national and EU competences, through the 'pooling' and 'mixing' of national sovereignty with Union powers. However, the use of these two methods, combined with the different roles of national governments and of the Commission, European Parliament and Court, in different policy areas, make it difficult to generalize about the characteristics of EU decision-making.

Underlying all these developments is the fact that national governments increasingly engage in transnational activities to achieve national goals. As a result, they increasingly depend on the goodwill and co-operation of other countries. They also run up against the cumulative effects of common EU policies. As far as possible, national governments try to retain control in national affairs. This is most evident in the principle of subsidiarity, affirmed in both the SEA and the Treaty of Maastricht. This may, however, ultimately mean taking decisions at the regional or local government levels, rather than at the national level.

The EU is therefore increasingly characterized by a sharing of functions and powers between its central institutions and those of national governments. This may help to reduce member state fears of losing too much power to a heavily centralized and bureaucratized EU. Overall, a strong element of national control pervades EU decision-making. This allows the pooling of sovereignties in certain fields but also ensures that there is no wholesale transfer of power from the national to the Union level. Governments act as gatekeepers between domestic political considerations and wider Union considerations wherever possible. While this helps to preserve the national interest of the member states, it simultaneously impedes EU attempts to get away from internal negotiation towards collective problem-solving. Power-sharing is currently most obvious in the field of foreign and security policy and goes some way towards explaining the failure of the EU in the Balkans, the area most likely to create intra-European conflict (see Chapter 3).

■ Towards a more perfect Union?

Considerable progress has been made under the two decision-making styles of the EU. The scope of EU policy has widened considerably, institutions have been strengthened, decision-making has become more efficient with the adoption of more majority voting. The EU now has powers over agriculture, external trade, the internal market, social, environmental, monetary and foreign and security policy and is expanding its responsibilities in financial affairs.

The genesis and dynamics of the internal market deserve special mention here. In hindsight, it is remarkable how far the success of the internal market has provided a springboard for other initiatives. To begin with, many commentators were sceptical about prospects for collective EU economic decision-making in the aftermath of the recession of 1974–84. Commission proposals for a single market made in the early 1980s, culminating in the so-called White Paper of 1985 (the Cockfield Report) were couched in very general terms. The report was characteristically long on aims but short on practical solutions, a mistake the EU has often repeated. What made the

BRIEFING 2.7

The Exchange Rate Mechanism (ERM) and the European Monetary System (EMS)

Exchange rate volatility between member states of the European Union is a hindrance to international trade and economic stability. The European Monetary System of the EU attempted to stabilize exchange rates by using the Exchange Rate Mechanism (ERM) which was established in 1979. If the currencies in the EMS fluctuated too much, central banks intervened to bring the currency back into line.

The system worked well and the UK joined it in 1991. However, recession in the early 1990s, plus the fact that the UK had set the exchange rate for the pound too high, brought about a crisis in 1992. The UK and Italy were forced to leave, and Spain and Portugal devalued their currencies. However, something like the EMS is seen as an integral part of the further economic integration of the EU, and as paving the way to a single European currency.

difference was that the business community, through round-table discussions among leading industrialists, were able to forge links with governments in order to free markets and eliminate trade barriers. The coalition was supported by clever and effective Commission proposals, with the President, Jacques Delors, giving an important helping hand from 1985. This resulted in a policy dynamic which seemed like a highspeed train in comparison with previous efforts. Major obstacles were overcome and four freedoms agreed; the free flow of goods, services, capital and people. In order to achieve this, resistance on specific points was gradually met by compromises or over come. Examples are the German opposition to importing foreign beer, the restrictions placed upon the transfer of financial capital between countries, the protection of monopolies in the insurance, telecommunication and transport sectors, and internal border checks within the EU.

In spite of undoubted success, future development came under serious challenge by the mid-1990s. Enlargement decisions, and German pressure for deeper integration among members, had widened the cleavage between EU aims and domestic strategies. The ensuing controversy is so important that its background and implications demands closer examination. The period between Summer 1992 and Summer 1994 saw significant events which were to set back EU co-operation. Among the most prominent were the two Danish and French referenda which ratified the Maastricht Treaty by the narrowest of margins, the enforced withdrawal of the British and Italian currencies from the Exchange Rage Mechanism (ERM) and breakdown of its narrow bands. Member states were also deeply concerned by German unification (1990) and the Bosnian conflict (1992–95).

With the apparent waning of support for deeper integration in several countries, and with pending elections in Germany and France, Germany went onto the offensive in September 1994, proposing a significant stepping-up of moves towards closer European Union. Besides reacting to indifferance in other countries, domestic motives were also a factor. On the one hand, the German government wished to avoid the mistakes of the Maastricht Treaty, where minimal public debate over issues such as the single currency had provoked near-defeat in the national referendums. On the other, Germany wanted to send signals that holding a pivotal role between East and West had been troublesome in the past, not only for itself but for the rest of Europe also. The opening up of Europe might lead to indecision which could force

Germany to go it alone on economic and foreign policy. This could rekindle the national rivalry and hostility which provoked the Second World War. Rather than risk this, the German government opted for a federally-oriented EU as a guarantee against having to take crucial decisions alone. As *The Economist* (30 September 1994) succinctly put it, 'Germany sees integration as a means of dissipating the destructive force of German nationalism and of acting in Central and Eastern Europe not as the old imperial monster but as the leader of an unimpeachable alliance.'

In order to resolve the threat of insecurity to its east, Germany supported the membership applications of some Central and Eastern states, insisting at the same time that 'deepening' the EU was also a precondition for its widening. A drift back towards intergovernmental decision-making would lead to institutional deadlock and lethargy. In order to prevent this and maintain momentum, it was necessary to reform the institutions of the EU and promote the expansion of joint EU policies. Further integration could pave the way for additional membership.

The adoption of a single currency was already seen as sensitive. The issue caused consternation not only in Denmark, France and Britain, but also in Germany itself. To go further, by calling for an alteration in the balance of power between the Council of Ministers, the Commission and the European Parliament, was a significant departure, which could be seen as an attack on national sovereignty itself. It would transform the Commission into a European government through the introduction of a bi-cameral system. This would put the European Parliament (EP) on an equal footing with the Council of Ministers. If such a development were permitted, it would in all likelihood reinforce the prospect of a multispeed Europe – that is, one in which individual member States would stand in different relationships to the Union, some being at the core with others remaining on the periphery. The way in which other EU member states, Britain and France in particular, reacted to the proposals was crucial.

For France a European approach seemed to provide the answer. If Germany could be tied to a strengthened EU, its economic power could be diluted or at least harnessed, giving France an enhanced role in future developments. However, different views surfaced within France during the French referendum of 1992, and were to re-emerge in the subsequent presidential elections of 1995. Chirac, who was eventually elected, went as far as to advocate a French referendum on the introduction of a single European currency.

Britain, who viewed the whole Maastricht negotiations with deep scepticism had negotiated op-outs on European Monetary Union (EMU) and the Social Chapter (welfare and working conditions). The British did not see further EU integration as an appropriate vehicle to either control or harness German influence. Instead, they sought to maintain a US commitment to Europe (with NATO as the main security organization) and preserve their own status as a permanent UN Security Council member. However, US indifference to the Bosnian conflict in its earlier stages (1992–94) suggested that US attention towards Britain was dependent upon its being a part of a wider Europe. Moreover, deep-seated divisions within the Conservative Party led the British government towards yet another acrimonious internal debate about Britain's place in Europe. Once more the British seemed incapable of choosing between their overseas links and the further integration of Europe.

In common with France, the UK rejected the EU's federal ambitions and stressed that the EU should remain an organization of sovereign states. Both France and

---

BRIEFING 2.8

The idea of a multispeed Europe

Deepening and widening the European Union involves a large number of complex political and technical problems. Some member states, such as Germany and France, have been keen to press on as fast as possible. But others like the UK and Denmark want to slow the process down, or even halt it. One solution might be a multispeed or 'variable geometry' Europe, in which there are two classes of members. Core members would press ahead with greater political and economic integration, others would be like associate members with more limited involvement. Such a multispeed European Union would be like the asymmetric or 'differentiated' federalism discussed in Chapter 13 which exists for regions within Spain and Italy.

Britain had found the separation of powers between the Council of Ministers and the EP satisfactory and were opposed to any fusion of power as proposed by the Germans. They were also sceptical about further powers for the EP. For the same reasons, changes in the selection or election of Commissioners, through either the EP or by direct popular vote, were dismissed as giving too much power to the EP, or investing too much control in a directly elected president. Both France and the UK preferred the Council of Ministers to dominate both the Commission and the EP and the UK also tried to abolish the Commission's sole right to propose European legislation.

Beyond these points of agreement there were also differences. The British were highly sceptical of monetary union, and saw the 1996/97 Intergovernmental Conference simply as a 'tidying up' exercise after Maastricht. France was much more committed to further EU reform. France believed that the British wanted a large free trade area without political solidarity or direction, in thwarting rather than integrating EU efforts towards deepening.

The current challenge is to reconcile these conflicting positions in order to reach an amicable agreement. Whether compromise is possible depends on developments. One relevant point, raised by Germany, refers to popular desires for the preservation of national identity and resistance to European centralization. The principle of subsidiarity, already mentioned in the SEA (Single European Act) and the Maastricht Treaty, was a reaction to concerns about excessive regulation and interference from the Union bureaucracy in Brussels. Increased subsidiarity might go some way to lessen fears of supranational encroachment. It is questionable, however, whether it would be enough to entice Britain into conceding institutional and policy reforms.

The prospects for deeper integration seem to rest therefore on whether France is willing to move closer to the German proposals for a 'multispeed' Europe. The Maastricht Treaty already provides for this. In effect, it already exists on fiscal policy, immigration and justice, and the CFSP. In these areas some member states have already opted for closer co-operation and integration than others.

Serious institutional and logistical problems would emerge from a multispeed Europe. Various questions would need to be answered such as: should the president of the Commission and the Commissioners responsible for EMU, CFSP and immigration and justice be appointed from inner-circle members only? As we have already seen, these are the most federalized of the policy areas. Would the Parliament need to change its composition when debating these issues, while broadening its membership to include core and peripheral countries when discussing intergovern-mental policy areas? Would there, indeed, be separate sets of Union institutions to reflect this two-speed membership?

As the momentum towards a federal Europe has slowed, counter-proposals have emerged which combine elements of subsidiarity with less radical institutional reforms. One proposal is to avoid extending EU jurisdiction into new policy fields (such as education), and to give the Parliament greater powers in existing fields. This would retain the Council of Ministers and the European Council as the locus of deci-sion-making and allow majority voting to continue. A lower threshold for the so-called 'qualified majority' could be set, and member states could have their votes weighted according to their size. Thus national governments would continue to play a major role in shaping the EU, while moderately enhancing the role of the Commission, the EP and the Court of Justice. Whether these reforms would be suf-ficient to maintain a coherent strategy after admittal of Central European members remains to be seen. The whole matter is closely tied to the issue of widening or deep-ening, which we will consider in the next section.

EU enlargement – wider versus deeper?

Although the Treaty of Rome states that membership is open to any country that is both European and democratic, decisions about enlargement are often contested in practice. Different member states have different interests which consistently impede the smooth process of accession. The present debate on the entry of Cyprus, Malta and Turkey and of the Central European states (the Czech Republic, Bulgaria, Hungary, Slovenia, Poland, Romania and Slovakia) is no exception. The number of countries, their geographical location, and their economic and political development, all present difficulties. Three different but interrelated factors are involved: (a) European leader-ship, (b) economic concerns, and (c) security interests. We will consider each in turn.

European leadership

The question of which countries would play a leading role within Europe and the likely subsequent policy consequences of this was a major concern of President De Gaulle's in the 1960s, particularly with regard to the entry of the UK. De Gaulle feared that Britain would undermine French leadership. Britain would serve merely as a Trojan horse for the spread of American influence throughout Europe. Leadership is again at issue with regard to central European membership. With the dismantling of the iron curtain, Germany has become the main market of the central European countries, for both imports and exports. Bringing them into the EU might create a powerful pro-Germanic voting bloc which would be seen as detrimental to the national interests of other member states, particularly France and Britain.

Economic concerns

Each enlargement of the EU has brought to the fore particular issues of concern to the countries involved. In the past these have mainly involved agriculture and fisher-ies. The admission of Austria, Finland and Sweden issues brought in other, in particular internal market policy, economies of scale, and budgetary matters. Most of these proposed changes were seen as benefiting the EU. Some southern members expressed concern about the growing influence of industrially advanced countries, especially those favouring free-trade policies. Enlargement into Central Europe will probably add a new layer of problems, particularly in agriculture and regional aid. Estimates of the likely cost of central European membership indicate that the agricultural budget will rise from ECU30 billion to about ECU45 billion, while regional aid will increase from ECU25 billion to ECU60 billion. This would probably have a strong negative effect on the four poorer members of the current Union – Ireland, Greece, Spain and Portugal – for the following reasons.

1. The Common Agricultural Policy would have to be reformed in order to keep costs within tolerable limits, and this might well mean reducing agricultural subsidies to the four.
2. A larger proportion of the Social and Regional Funds would probably be paid to central European members thus, by implication, cutting funds to the poorer countries of Western Europe.
3. A flow of cheap imports from central Europe may have a bigger impact on the economies of poorer than of richer countries in Western Europe. In 1989 the EU imposed restrictions on iron, steel, textile, and meat imports from Central and Eastern Europe. These were later relaxed and in 1994 the Commission approved modest proposals to increase trade and investment. As a result, France and Portugal complained of losing some 100,000 jobs in their textiles industries alone. EU enlargement into central Europe would have a far larger impact on Western European economies.

Competing trade interests create dilemmas and hard choices. Central and Eastern Europe need direct access to EU markets if they are to attract more foreign investment. But at the same time they need to protect themselves, particularly since their export potential is concentrated in 'sensitive sectors', such as agriculture and manufacturing. The EU could possibly afford to be generous here, since it enjoyed a favourable balance of trade of ECU8.5 billion in 1992. On the other hand, the opening-up of Eastern markets since 1989 may have undermined some Western European economies. Before 1989 annual average growth in Italy, Spain, Portugal and Greece was 3.5 per cent, 0.3 percentage points above the EU average. Between 1990 and 1994, it fell to 1.2 per cent, 0.4 points below the EU average. This puts a strain on EU cohesion. If Southern economies continue to suffer (or seem to suffer) from expansion into the East, plans to extend membership may be strongly opposed.

Economic performance in the EU, a key variable in EU development, was improving by 1995. Growth rates were up, but unemployment remained stubbbornly high. While in the final analysis reforms and the success of enlargement depend on economic growth, the EU is also concerned with these countries for reasons of general peace and stability. With this in mind the EU has recommended increased co-operation among the Associates (Bulgaria, the Czech Republic, Hungary, Poland, Romania and Slovakia), to ensure political and economic stability along the EU's eastern flank, and has promised to involve the Associates more closely in internal discussions on foreign and security matters. Indeed the six leading Associate countries attended the closing session of the EU Essen summit in December 1994. There were even proposals to invite the six to send deputies to the EP in a non-voting, consultative role.

BRIEFING 2.9

The Council of Europe

The Council of Europe was established in 1949 to promote European co-operation across all policy areas except defence. The Council is not concerned with European integration which is the job of the European Union. Nor are its conventions and agreements legally binding on member states unless they explicitly endorse them. It is a forum for discussion and it has few substantive powers. However, it was Europe's first political organization and is now its largest. Membership covers all the non-communist states of the European continent, and since 1989 has been extended to include some of the democratic states of central Europe. Eventually, all democratic states in Europe may be members.

The conventions and agreements of the Council are wide-ranging and some, such as the 1950 European Convention on Human Rights, are important. In 1960 it took on the social and cultural responsibilities of the Western European Union (WEU). The expanding membership and powers of the European Union threaten to by-pass the Council. It is useful at the moment, however, as a way of bringing together Western and Eastern countries and putting pressure on members to strengthen democratic practices. For its influence on legal convergence in Europe see Chapter 14.

Security interests

Security is a constant concern in debates about enlargement. Historically, France and Germany were at odds over British membership. Germany believed it would strengthen NATO and the US commitment to Europe. France believed it would undermine EU unity and threaten French leadership within it. However, the membership of Greece, Portugal and Spain was generally seen as contributing to the political stability of these three countries and of the Mediterranean region in general. Security is a key feature of the current debate about Turkey and Central Europe. On the one hand, German worries about instability on its eastern borders push for early expansion, possibly around the turn of the century. France is less enthusiastic, and, backed by southern members, fears that rapid enlargement would weaken the political unity of the EU and push it towards the more limited role of free-trade area. The UK shares German concerns about stability in central Europe, but fears that enlargement may trigger faster political integration. There are also worries about the situation in the Middle East and Algeria, linked to the spread of terrorism and Islamic fundamentalism. To counter-balance this, France and Spain have called for the development of a Mediterranean economic area, aimed at promoting peace and stability in that region.

■ The EU and European stability

Events are pushing the EU towards assuming a greater role in world affairs, commensurate with its economic might. It is the biggest trading bloc in the world, accounting for 15 per cent of global exports. However, it has been unable to translate economic power into political influence, or to convert economic strength into a common foreign and security policy. The issue is highly sensitive and goes to the core of national sovereignty.

BRIEFING 2.10

EU involvement in the Bosnian crisis, 1992–95

Bosnia was a constituent Republic of the former Federation of Yugoslavia (1945–91). Its population was just about 45 per cent Moslem, 32 per cent (Orthodox) Serb and 18 per cent (Catholic) Croat. After the other Yugoslav Republics of Slovenia and Croatia declared their independence in 1991 Bosnia did so too. The Serbs population then tried to seize control of as much Bosnian territory as they could, covertly abetted by neighbouring Serbia. The Muslims slowly organized themselves to resist and fight back, sometimes helped and sometimes opposed by the Croats. United Nations peacekeeping forces, contributed in part by Britain and France, were built up in 1992–93. However, the EU itself confined its role to mediation and attempts at reconciliation. It did impose a trade embargo on Serbia which helped in the withdrawal of support from the Bosnian Serbs. However, it was hampered in its efforts to do anything more by internal differences between Germany, which consistently supported Croatia, and Britain and France, more favourable to the Muslims. Fighting was only resolved by forceful US intervention in 1995. The inability of the EU to do anything effective to stop fighting on its doorstep illustrates its basic weakness, and failure to reconcile the national interests and divergent views of member states.

Because of the difficulty of integrating the diplomatic and strategic activities of its members the EU itself has relied too much on its economic leverage. It has not developed a military capacity to mount effective peacekeeping efforts. The Bosnian case is a prime example. The causes of failure include: (a) the idea that the EU is essentially a 'civilian power' with economics, human rights, democracy and diplomacy as primary concerns; (b) divergent interests in foreign and security matters among member states; (c) distrust between member countries, especially with regard to Germany; and (d) an inability to raise defence expenditures against the backdrop of 'peace dividends' and economic recession.

Among the factors helping to explain this failure, different state interests are of crucial importance. For example, Denmark has anti-federal and pro-pacifist leanings. Germany and Greece are geographically close to Bosnia, whereas Spain and Portugal are distant. Austria, Finland, Ireland and Sweden have histories of political neutrality, while Germany had constitutional limits on military intervention abroad. The UK still seems to be torn between its Commonwealth role, its special relationship with the USA, and Europe. France seems to have a nostalgia for past greatness and for going it alone. To add to all this, there is the uncertainty caused by the break up of the Soviet bloc. Western Europe has lost the unifying force of an external, common enemy. East and West are nervous about Russian political stability and ethnic conflicts.

In addition, the US has reduced its defence commitments to Europe and sent signals to the effect that Europe should take greater responsibility for its own security. In response new forms of security co-operation have emerged. But they are not shared all by EU members. France and Germany have taken the initiative by establishing an integrated military force – the Eurocorps. Other countries favour strengthening the Western European Union (WEU) (see Chapter 1). Some wish to retain close links with NATO.

Nowhere is the failure to agree illustrated more clearly than in the Bosnian conflict. The EU took many initiatives – it dispatched monitors, and distributed humanitarian aid. Member states participated in different ways in UN and NATO forces. But these had little success. This failure to resolve the conflict was worrying in two ways. First, the inability to act in concert caused deep psychological damage within the EU. Secondly, disagreements over lifting the earlier weapons embargo on Bosnian Muslims caused a deep rift in relations between the Americans and the Europeans, and introduced a split between Britain and France, on the one hand, and Germany, supporting Croatia, on the other. This may have repercussions for NATO's effectiveness and future role, and for European public opinion. In addition, the disagreement raised the spectre of unilateral national action. In the future, Germany, France and the UK may go it alone in the Balkans and clash over their perceived interests there – an uncanny repeat of the disturbing events which led up to the First World War.

In the absence of an effective foreign and security policy, the EU has put much emphasis on co-operative relations with the Central and Eastern European states. In line with the liberal point of view outlined in Chapter 1, the assumption is that democratic and economic reconstruction will ensure long-term stability. By stressing the economic dimension in European security, the EU also hopes to standardize, if not control, the flow of migration from east to west (see Chapter 17). Last but not least, these measures go some way to meeting German demands for a collective EU response to the situation. Thus they can soothe German worries about its pivotal role between East and West.

Besides discussing membership with the Central European states, the EU has encouraged general co-operation with the East. This co-operation has taken a variety of forms – trade agreements with Albania, the Baltic states and Slovenia and partnership and co-operation agreements with Kazakhstan, Russia, and the Ukraine. Under the Phare programme (organized by the EU to provide technical and economic assistance to Eastern Europe), starting in 1992, the EU gave support for education, training, research and development, general technical assistance and privatization. In 1992, the EU and its member states contributed 61 per cent of total assistance to Central and Eastern countries. The EU is also the majority shareholder in the European Bank for Reconstruction and Development (ERBD) which specializes in projects in Eastern Europe.

A programme known as TACIS has aided the transition to market reform and democracy in the CIS. TACIS provides technical support in a number of key areas. These include the development of human resources, food production and distribution, support for business, energy, transport and telecommunications, and nuclear safety. Through TACIS, the Union provides more than 70 per cent of the outside technical assistance received by Russia and the other former Soviet republics.

The EU has promoted a European Stability Pact with the expressed aim of resolving regional and ethnic conflicts and aiding democracy and economic reconstruction. It is hoped to extend this towards the Mediterranean region and to include North Africa. This is because of concern about the growth of Islamic fundamentalism, missile proliferation, and the upsurge in terrorism. The EU strategy is thus to tackle instability through closer political ties, exchange of information, and aid for economic development. In early 1995, the EU was considering a large, specifically Mediterranean, aid package. Turkey has been singled out for the development of a strategic partnership, and serious consideration has been given to EU membership for both Cyprus and Malta.

■ Conclusions: the role of the EU in the New Europe

The EU has become an influential actor in the New Europe. Its impact is growing not only within member states and aspirants for enlargement, but also within the successor states of the former Soviet Union and in regard to its southern European neighbours. However, it has yet to assume the structure, powers and functions of a federation. Both the constituent states and the EU have increased their functions in tandem over the last decade or so. This tendency seems likely to continue in the foreseeable future. Consequently, the EU's power remains potential rather than actual. It has problems in translating aims and economic strength into collective action in either the internal or external arenas. With some notable exceptions (agriculture, the internal market, external trade), the EU still reaches decisions by adopting the lowest common denominator among the competing policies of member states – rather than by designing policies of its own, representing the highest common denominator for the EU as a whole.

Solutions are enormously difficult and complex. They require a satisfactory response to all sorts of pressures. At the same time, they point to reforming the internal machinery in such a way that decision-making effectiveness is enhanced alongside democratic control. The 1996/7 Intergovernmental Conference (IGC) is again confronting that fundamental concern – how to strike a balance between the expansion of EU functions and powers, while at the same time maintaining the national control in areas marked out by the principle of subsidiarity.

What makes the exercise that much harder is the question of eastward expansion. Enlarged membership would enforce the streamlining of decision-making and demand significant institutional changes. This might well involve: reducing the number of Commissioners; altering the system of six-monthly presidencies; amending the weighted voting system giving smaller states a disproportionate influence over decision-making; and relying more on majority voting. A German discussion paper of September 1994, also called for increased powers for the European Parliament.

If it is to reap the full benefits from its new internal market, the EU will need to establish common policies in economics, finance, and social and environmental policy. No later than December 1998, Heads of State and Governments have to decide by qualified majority which countries meet the criteria for the third stage of Economic and Monetary Union (EMU). This is intended to set up a single currency and establish a European Central Bank (ECB).

While EMU is an important step in itself, questions have also been raised about the link between EMU and political union. Can EMU exist without political union, or is political union a precondition for successful EMU? Cases of monetary union without political union have existed in the past (Ireland and the United Kingdom, Luxembourg and Belgium). But some believe that successful political union is a prerequisite for monetary union. The German Bundesbank argues for a political framework, in particular a strengthened European Parliament, which would guarantee the complete independence of the new Central Bank.

EU members will also come under pressure to develop a common foreign and security capability which meets both US demands for greater self-reliance and the need to adopt a common approach in international affairs. By 1996, signs were emerging that EU members, for different reasons, were preparing for closer security co-operation, including the establishment of a cross-border European police intelligence agency. There were also acts of co-operation between member states. The UK and the Netherlands agreed to a joint amphibious force, while Britain and France combined to form a joint European Air Group, based at High Wycombe, near London, to help run joint peacekeeping and humanitarian operations. France, Spain and Italy took steps towards a common air and naval force. However, it was also significant that these attempts were, in the words of Malcolm Rifkind, the British Defence Secretary, based on the 'fundamental and unshakable' conviction that defence and security should be based on co-operation between autonomous nation-states.

The Intergovernmental Conference has to start from the uneven development of the EU so far. But it may also have the effect of enforcing more common policies. If so, certain members may be tempted to opt out of some aspects of EU activity. This, in turn, may hasten moves towards a multi-speed Europe. The IGC may also widen the gap between countries like France and Germany, which see EU development as an end in itself, and Britain, which seems more interested in using it as a framework for its own foreign and economic policies. For Germany, the EU can help avoid the mistakes of the past and create a framework for future peace and stability, in the East as well as the West. This is a view shared in varying degrees by most countries in Europe, whether inside or outside the EU itself.

■ Further reading

S. Garcia (ed.), *European Identity and the Search for Legitimacy* (London, Pinter, 1993).

Emil J. Kirchner, *Decision-Making in the European Community* (Manchester, Manchester University Press, 1992).

N. Nugent (ed.), *The European Union* (Oxford, Blackwell, 1994).

W. Wessels and C. Engel (eds), *The European Union in the 1990s – Ever Closer and Larger?* (Bonn, Europa Union Verlag, 1993).

Chapter 3

The European states

States and nations

Prospects for peace and stability, and of European Union, depend immediately upon the relationships between States – or at any rate, between the most powerful of them: Russia, Germany, France, Britain and the extra-European United States. This is not coincidental, as Europe gave rise both to the ideal and reality of the modern state. Between the two there is often a disjunction, as actual states often do not match up to the 'ideal type' of a central government in full control of a surrounding territory, able to enforce clear boundaries and to defend these against all comers. Indeed, the basic reality of the twentieth century is that the European states were unable to defend themselves first against Germany and then against Russia, and had to form alliances to counteract their power. As we have seen, these alliances pivoted on the United States. This was a clear admission that single states were not strong enough even to defend their own independence. It was only when Russia gave clear evidence of having abandoned any desire to threaten Western and Eastern Europe that the American-dominated NATO became less relevant and attempts at framing a European Federal Union could proceed.

The boundaries of the modern European states are shown in Map 3.1. They developed from the ruins of extensive Empires which survived up to the outbreak of the First World War.

The Austro-Hungarian Empire was divided in 1918 between Austria, Hungary, the Czech Republic, Slovakia, Poland, Romania, Slovenia, Croatia and Bosnia. Its boundaries are still relevant seventy years later because it succeeded in converting most of its populations to Catholicism. The religious divides of Protestantism to the west of it and Greek Orthodoxy to the east and south still exist.

The second multinational empire was the Turkish (or Ottoman) Empire, which extended at its height across most of the Balkans, covering what is today known as Bosnia, Albania, Greece, Bulgaria, Romania, Macedonia, Serbia and Croatia. While it contained pockets of Muslims, notably in Bosnia and Albania, and Catholics in Croatia, most of its populations were Orthodox Christians.

The third empire, the Russian, lasted the longest. In the seventeenth and eighteenth centuries Russians swept across the Eastern European and Siberian plains, conquering many territories on their borders such as Georgia, Armenia and Azerbaijan, Belarus, the Ukraine, most of Poland and the Baltic States of Estonia, Latvia, Lithuania and Finland. As the successor to the old Russian empire the Soviet Union (USSR) took over many of these territories again after the Second World War. In this sense, the Russian empire lasted until the dissolution of the Soviet Union, and continues today in a much diminished form as the Confederation of Independent States (CIS) (see Chapter 1).

The lines of division between these old multinational empires are still important

Map 3.1 European Empires in 1914

because they broadly coincide with the religious division between Catholic (Central and Southern Europe) and Orthodox (the Balkans and the old Russian lands), with an admixture of Muslims in a central belt across the Balkans. The empires also encouraged patterns of multi-ethnic settlement which produced substantial minorities in many countries, especially in the east and south of Europe. Ethnic and religious conflict in these areas have become a major threat to peace and democracy in Europe today.

Western Europe is also a mosaic of minorities embedded inside its current states. Although these groups are often assimilated into the dominant culture they are important in the internal politics of most European countries (see Chapter 13 and 17). Ethnicity, religion and class, have been major influences on the development of

BRIEFING 3.1

The European state

States in Europe generally developed out of the feudal holdings held by kings. In the six-teenth and seventeenth centuries they expanded and consolidated their territories often by military conquest. The territories were controlled by an army, and an administration which collected taxes to pay for the army. These differed from feudal organizations in that they were not held together by personal loyalty to the current ruler but institutionalized through rules and procedures which gave them a permanent existence.

States thus consist of an administrative apparatus operating over a defined terri-tory, which to maintain control monopolizes the use of force. In the nineteenth century, two further ideas came to be associated with the state. One was the concept of the nation. Each 'people' defined by a particular language and culture should have its own state. In practice, this often meant that the dominant majority in each state imposed its own language and culture on the minorities, using compulsory education as a tool. The second idea was democracy. The directing body of the state, the government, should be elected regularly so that state policy reflected popular wishes.

Neither democracy nor nationalism are essential elements in the definition of the state, however. Many states have made no pretence of being democratic, and true nation-states are the exception rather than the rule.

European political parties (Chapter 9). In other cases the geographical concentration of religious, linguistic, or ethnic minorities within a state has presented political problems which have been solved by regionalism or federalism, which gives minor-ities a degree of autonomy within their own areas (Chapter 13). But in some coun-tries this solution has been resisted because the central state has wished to maintain total control over all its territory. Indeed, one of the guiding ideas of nationalism is that each nation should have its own state and its own central political institutions which safeguard its identity.

The cultural and linguistic diversity of Europe, however, makes this simple idea problematic. Are Italians one people, or divided between Sicilians, Sardinians, Venetians, Ligurians, and others? As Italians they all inhabit the same peninsula and their regional languages have strong affinities (as they do with Spanish). But they also differ culturally and linguistically, and hence there are tensions between north and south, and even nascent separatist movements.

In practice, the dominant groups of the nation-states which emerged in earlier centuries have usually tried to assimilate all the groups within their state boundaries and define them as one people – for example, German, Spanish, British. This suc-ceeded in France, where a new reality, the French were created. But in places like Ireland and Yugoslavia it provoked violent secession. In other cases – such as in Scotland, or the Basque region of Spain – nationalists still demand political inde-pendence to preserve their distinctiveness (see Chapter 4).

This underlines the point that national boundaries and identities are problematic. Political boundaries are lines on maps which are often created by military power and enforced or changed by political will. They are not natural or inevitable or timeless divisions which can be taken for granted. On the contrary, they are fought over in war and often the subject of controversy during peace.

BRIEFING 3.2

Scandinavia and the Nordic countries

Scandinavia consists of Denmark, Norway and Sweden. All have close historical and linguistic ties.

The *Nordic countries*, or the Nordic area, consist of Denmark, Norway, Sweden, Finland, Iceland, the Danish dependencies of the Faroe Islands, and Greenland. Greenland is geographically part of North America.

The *Nordic Council* was set up in 1971 to formalise the strong links and co-operation between the five Nordic countries of Denmark, Norway, Sweden, Finland, and Iceland. The Council aims to integrate the Nordic area and to extend co-operation over a wide range of matters including social, economic, cultural, and legal affairs, but not (formally) defence or foreign policy. The Council is not a supranational organisation in the sense that it does not have final authority over the parliaments of individual countries.

Nevertheless, states are likely to remain the basic building blocks of European politics well into the twenty-first century. Notwithstanding the development of powerful supranational and international units of government such as the EU or NATO, nation-states are proliferating in Europe, as in other parts of the globe. Any account which left states out of the picture would therefore ignore a major reality of contemporary European politics. Accordingly, this chapter reviews the different states of Europe. It describes their recent development and current characteristics. In doing so, it fleshes out the account of their interrelationships provided in the two previous chapters. To aid comparison and contrast, we discuss states within their main geographical and cultural groupings with other states. In Chapter 4, we go on to look in more detail at the ethnic problems which threaten internal state homogeneity and integrity, and which may provoke external tensions between them.

Scandinavia and the Baltic

The Scandinavian countries, generally have small populations scattered thinly over vast, inhospitable terrains. They are strongly Protestant but their Lutheran tradition of subservience of church to state means that religion has usually been a stronger cultural than directly political influence. Their traditions of egalitarianism and individualism are associated with strong social democratic governments which have pioneered the distinctively Scandinavian model of the welfare state.

This tries to provide comprehensive public services and support for everyone, from education and housing to security against sickness, old age, and unemployment (see Chapter 15). The political dominance of the social democrats in the face of a fragmented middle-class opposition has enabled them to implement these reforms, but they have also taken care to get the maximum possible political support for them. The dependence of their economies on world markets has given businessmen considerable leverage, as governments depend on a high level of general prosperity to support the costs of the welfare state. Thus, neither governments nor the powerful social democratic trade unions have been obstructive to economic reorganization or innovation. For their part, governments have not

Map 3.2   Scandinavia and the Baltic

generally engaged in large scale planning or direction of business. They have nationalized some economic sectors because of market failure or the threat of unemployment, but they have not tried to replace a mixed economy with a state controlled,
command economy.

Sweden

With a population of more than 8 million, Sweden is the largest of the Scandinavian
nations and has traditionally played a dominant role in the region. In the past, Norway
(1814–1905), Finland (900–1814) and the Baltic states (1550–1710), were politically subordinate to it. Its population is now very homogeneous with the exception
of small pockets of third world immigrants in some cities. Its characteristic political
features are:

BRIEFING 3.3

The welfare state and the mixed economy

The welfare state

The provision by the state of collective goods and services to its citizens, especially in the areas of health, education, housing, and personal social services for the children, the old, the sick, and the unemployed. The state uses public funds to provide a minimum standard of living, or safety net, for its citizens. There are many different forms of welfare state: some work primarily through cash benefits, others by providing services directly; some provide universal benefits, others selective benefits; some try to redistribute incomes and resources; others are more concerned with raising sufficient funds for basic services; some are highly developed, some are more minimal. But in modern west European states the proportion of national wealth spent on the welfare state rose during the post-war period. The welfare state has traditionally been a crucial part of socialist or social democratic thinking in west European politics.

Mixed economy

A state which mixes both market and public sector economies, as against a state which leaves everything to the market, on the one hand, or controls every aspect of the economy, on the other. The public sector often intervenes in cases of market failure (natural monopolies or where there is no incentive for the market to produce a good or service), or those which are not thought proper to leave to the market (for example, prisons, or the regulation and/or production of medical drugs).

1. The Social Democratic Party which is the strongest party of the left in west Europe, and which usually gets almost half the popular vote. This has usually been enough to form a government for much of the twentieth century, with the exception of a period in the 1980s. The social democrats benefit from the consistent support of a small Communist Party (3–5 per cent of the vote), and from the fragmentation of the 'bourgeois' parties – the Centre (former Agrarian Party, 10–15 per cent) and the Conservatives (20–30 per cent). The latter grew in the 1980s, but this was mainly at the expense of their potential coalition partners, the Liberals, and thus there was no shift in voting power between the left and the right. The emergence of the Greens has not changed the balance either, for the Greens are generally supportive of the sort of state intervention associated with social democracy in order to protect the environment and ensure sustainable development. (For more on political parties and their ideologies see Chapter 9.)

2. The social democrats created widespread support for their welfare state plans with a system of parliamentary committees and Royal Commissions with extensive powers of inquiry and recommendation, on which all parties and interest groups were represented. Because governments are willing to accept their recommendations, their advice often has a direct impact on policy and legislation, thus creating broad support for it. In their attempts to create this broad consensus, governments also benefit from the lack of deep social divisions within society.

3. In foreign affairs Sweden has traditionally been neutral – even during the two world wars. It remained outside NATO. When Sweden joined the EU in 1995,

at the same time as Finland and Austria, its interest was primarily in economic integration rather than defence.

Norway

Norway broke its union with Sweden in 1905. The nationalism of this period also expressed itself with a new Norwegian language. But, at the same time, a combination of economic, religious and linguistic differences created internal divisions within the country. Agrarians and Christians were strong in the west, Labour in the north. Labour also gained support from a strong and unified working-class movement, which, like the social democrats in Sweden, was in power for a long time and able to consolidate a comprehensive welfare state. It had thirty years of almost unbroken power from 1935 to 1965 (except for the war and a few months in 1963), and then again in the 1970s, and from 1990 onwards. In the intervening years, a centre-right coalition was in power.

Politics in Norway are less consensual than in Sweden, mainly because religious, territorial, and urban–rural cleavages result in a more fragmented party system. Nevertheless, the population of four million is remarkably homogeneous, though scattered over an enormous area, including an Arctic region which would be depopulated without heavy subsidies. As a result there has been controversy over the question of whether to join the EU. This was favoured by the central region around Oslo, but strongly opposed in the North, which feared a loss of subsidies and resources. A bitterly fought referendum was defeated in 1972, and a less controversial one was narrowly lost in 1994. Nevertheless, Norway has various agreements with the EU, and is a member of NATO.

Denmark

Denmark is physically smaller but more fertile than its Scandinavian neighbours, and its population of 5 million is almost entirely homogeneous. Its party system resembles that of Sweden and Norway, although with about 40 per cent of the poll its Social Democratic party is electorally somewhat weaker. Nevertheless, the party is almost twice the size of its nearest rival, the right-wing Conservatives, and has been able to form governments for most of the post-war period. These have often alternated with 'bourgeois' coalitions of conservatives and right-wing liberals (Venstre) – most recently the 'four-leaf clover' coalitions of the bourgeois parties in the 1980s.

Denmark is unlike Norway and Sweden in that both single-party and coalition governments have generally depended upon parliamentary minorities. Average government duration has been two years or less, compared to three and four in the other countries.

In order to get measures through parliament, Danish governments have often formed coalitions around particular policies. For example, on welfare policies, a socialist minority government would rely on left socialist support, but on commitment to NATO it would rely on the bourgeois parties. A further consequence of minority government is that executive authority has been left to parliament and its committees on some matters. This is particularly the case with issues relating to the European Union, where policy is directed by an all-party committee.

The relative weakness of parties and governments renders the Danish

Parliament perhaps the most powerful in Europe. It also has the effect of requiring broad support for all policies, somewhat like the Swedish committee system. The fragmentation of the Danish party system is due, in large part, to the way popular votes are translated into parliamentary seats. Like Norway and Sweden, Denmark has a voting system which distributes seats in proportion to votes. The other two require a minimum of 4 per cent of the poll, for a party to get a seat, but Denmark requires 2 per cent. This gives very small parties parliamentary representation. A major example was in 1973 when three new parties gained seats, changing the parliament in the process. However, the traditional pattern re-emerged in the 1970s and 1980s, demonstrating the resilience of the established parties.

Iceland

Iceland has a population of 264,000, mostly dependent on fishing. It departs from usual Scandinavian patterns by having a multi-party system dominated by the 'bourgeois' Independence party, which gets 35–40 per cent of the vote, and by the centrist rural-based Progressive Party, with 20–25 per cent. Coalition governments of these parties have alternated with alliances of Progressives, Social Democrats and People's Alliance (communists).

The two major issues in Icelandic politics concern NATO and the economy. NATO's use of the island as a base has been controversial, but this is fading in the post-Cold War era, to be replaced by the threat to the national economy (and its welfare state) from the decline of fish stocks.

Finland

Though united with Sweden for most of its recorded history (900–1814), Finland is in many ways the odd country out in Scandinavia. Its language is totally different, and between 1809–1917 it was an autonomous grand dutchy of Russia. It fought against the Soviet Union during the Second World War, losing a massive amount of territory as a result of defeat.

The influence of the USSR on its borders had two major effects on Finnish politics. One was strict neutrality in foreign affairs (something known as 'finlandization') so that joining the European Union became possible only in the 1990s. The other effect is a strong presidency. The Russians preferred to deal directly with the president on foreign policy, thus buttressing his powers.

The president also has a decisive role in deciding which combination of parties will serve in government, which is important because there is no dominant party. The Social Democrat party gains about a quarter of the vote, the Conservatives about a fifth, and Agrarians and Communists around 10–18 per cent each. The president usually comes from the Agrarian party, which, as a result, has been at the centre of most post-war coalitions. Russian disapproval of Conservative nationalism kept them out of most post-war governments which, as a result, were cobbled together, leading to internal divisions and stalemate. Consequently, Finland has had unstable governments with an average duration of only about ten months. Political continuity has been provided by the presidency, the Agrarians, and the presence of the small (5 per cent) Swedish People's Party in almost all coalitions.

> BRIEFING 3.4
>
> ## The Baltic states
>
> *The Baltic states* consist of Latvia, Lithuania, and Estonia, three nations which are geographically grouped on the eastern shores of the Baltic sea. The three countries have a similar twentieth-century history, becoming independent states in 1918, then being part of the Soviet bloc in 1940, and then independent states again in 1991/2. They are dissimilar in other respects, especially in language and religion. Estonia and Latvia have Protestant traditions but Lithuania (see p.83) is strongly Catholic.
>
> *The Baltic Council* was set up in 1990 by Latvia, Estonia and Lithuania with the aim of co-operating on foreign policy, economic development, and domestic government and politics. The Council has signed a free-trade agreement which ended virtually all trade restrictions.

The Baltic states: Estonia and Latvia

Latvia and Estonia became independent republics in 1991. Before that they were parts of Russia and the Soviet Union for three hundred years, with a brief period of independence from 1920 to 1939. However, they have had close links with Sweden and Finland (itself a Russian province from 1814–1918). The fact that they now look to these countries for political inspiration and aid means that they should be considered here along with Scandinavia.

Estonia

Estonia is the most northerly Baltic state and has a very large Russian minority (30 per cent of the population of a million and a half) which causes acute political tensions. It gives Russia grounds for threatening action to protect its minority but in fact aimed at forcing Estonia to follow a Russian line, particularly on foreign policy and trade. In reaction, Estonia has sought to preserve its new independence from the Soviet Union by strengthening its western links, particularly with Scandinavia. A liberal democracy with a prime minister, council of ministers and parliament has been set up on the Scandinavian model.

Latvia

Latvia, south of Estonia, shares many of the same characteristics, but its Russian minority forms 34 per cent of the population of 2.6 million. As a result Russia did not complete the withdrawal of troops until 1994 and relations between the countries are difficult. Nevertheless, Latvia is a developed and relatively prosperous country (literacy is almost universal). The centre-right party, Latvian Way (LC) has formed coalition or minority governments since 1993.

Voting tendencies in all the Scandinavian countries are recorded for the elections of the mid-1990s in Table 3.1. Though minor parties have been gaining more votes, established parties have held their own. In particular, social democratic predominance continues in Norway and Sweden, though elsewhere moderate Conservative parties are making the running.

Table 3.1 Scandinavian general elections, 1993–95

	Percent valid votes	Number of seats
SWEDEN, 18 September 1994		
Social Democrats (SAP)	42.25	161
Left Party (Vp)	6.17	22
Ecology Party (MpG)	5.02	18
Moderates (M)	22.37	80
Liberal Party (Fp)	7.19	26
Centre Party (C)	7.65	27
Christian Democratic Community Party (KdS)	4.06	15
Others	2.29	0
NORWAY, 12–13 September 1993		
Norwegian Labour Party (DNA)	37.0	67
Centre Party (SP)	16.8	32
Conservative Party (Hoeyre)	16.9	28
Christian People's Party (KrF)	7.9	13
Socialist Left Party (SV)	7.9	13
Progressive Party (Frp)	6.3	10
Liberal Party (Venstre)	3.6	1
Red Electoral Alliance (RV)	1.1	1
Others	2.5	–
LATVIA, 30 September–10 October 1995		
Latvian Way (LC)	14.6	17
National Conservative Party of Latvia (NNK)	6.3	8
National Harmony Party (TSP)	5.6	6
People's Movement	7.1	16
Unity Party	14.9	8
For the Fatherland and Freedom (TUB)	11.9	14
Union of Christian Democrats (LKDS)	6.3	8
Democratic Party (DP)	15.1	18
Others	18.2	5
FINLAND, 19 March 1995		
Finnish Social Democratic Party (SDP)	28.3	63
Centre Party (KESK)	19.9	44
National Coalition Party (Kokoomus-Kok)	17.9	39
Left-wing Alliance (VL)	11.2	22
Swedish People's Party (SFP)	5.1	12
Greens (Vihrät)	6.5	9
Finnish Christian League (SKL)	3.0	7
Young Finns (NS)	2.8	2
Finnish Rural Party (SMP)	1.3	1
Ecological Party (EP)	0.3	1
Others	3.7	0
DENMARK, 21 September 1994		
Social Democrats (SD)	34.6	62
Liberals (Venstre, V)	23.3	42
Conservative People's Party (KF)	15.0	27
Socialist People's Party (SF)	7.3	13
Progress Party (FP)	6.4	11
Social Liberals	4.6	8
Unity List	3.1	6
Centre Democrats	2.8	5
Others	2.8	1
ICELAND, 8 April 1995		
Independence Party	37.1	25
Progressive Party	23.3	15
Social Democratic Party	11.4	7
People's Alliance	14.3	9
Awakening of the Nation	7.2	4
Women's Alliance	4.9	3
Others	1.8	0

Table 3.1 *(cont.)* ESTONIA, 5 March 1995

Coalition Party and Rural Union Bloc	32.2	41
Estonian Reform	16.2	19
Centre Party	14.2	16
Union of the Fatherland + ERSP Bloc Republican Conservative People's Party	7.8	8
Moderates Bloc	6.0	6
Our Home Is Estonia Bloc	5.9	6
Right wingers	5.0	5
Others	12.7	0

BRIEFING 3.5

Britain, Great Britain, the United Kingdom and the British Isles

There is often confusion among England, Britain, Great Britain, and the British Isles. This is partly because geographical entities get mixed up with political ones. The largest geographical entity, *the British Isles*, consists of two main islands and many smaller ones. The larger contains England, Wales and Scotland, and the second Northern Ireland and the Republic of Ireland. The largest political entity is the *United Kingdom of Great Britain and Northern Ireland* which consists of England, Scotland, Wales and Northern Ireland. This is often shortened to the *UK*, or *Great Britain (GB)*. The largest part of the UK is England, often confused with Britain or even the UK.

Geographically, *Ireland* (its Irish name is Eire) is the smaller of the two main islands of the British Isles. Politically, it consists of the *Republic of Ireland*, and *Northern Ireland*, which is part of the United Kingdom. The Republic of Ireland was part of the UK until 1922 when it broke away after an armed insurrection.

The British Isles

While the British Isles are on the periphery of the continent, the proximity of the south and east coast, and of London, to France and the low countries have brought them into the mainstream of European developments. At the same time, they have a world trading history and links with North America and the Commonwealth. Even when Britain eventually joined the European Community (1973) it was more interested in economic than political union.

Britain is the only European state outside the Balkans to have experienced violent territorial secession this century. Armed struggle occurred between 1918 and 1922 in Ireland, as a result of which the Republic of Ireland (Eire) was created. Northern Ireland, which remained in the United Kingdom was involved in what is, in effect, a civil war between Irish nationalists and British loyalists from 1969 onwards, and it is still not clear if or how this will be resolved. At the base of these struggles lie cultural, and, above all, religious differences: there are one and a half million Protestants in Northern Ireland but hardly any in the South.

The United Kingdom

Differences between Protestant denominations, sometimes combined with language, also underlie variations in other parts of the United Kingdom. Scotland and Wales have produced their own independence movements which have been resisted

Map 3.3 The British Isles

by central government so far, but which may yet obtain regional assemblies with powers over local affairs.

Within the United Kingdom, England is dominant. It has a population of 47 million out of a total of 56 million, and the greater London area alone has a population of about 10 million. English is overwhelmingly the dominant language, even in Ireland, and politics is all but monopolized by nationwide parties, even in Scotland and Wales. The Conservatives, on the right, have formed single-party governments for most of the post-war period, alternating with Labour. The centrist Liberals and Social Democrats, after a brief period of electoral success in the 1980s, returned to being a minor party in the 1990s and fused as the Liberal Democrats.

Territorial divisions in British politics are sharpened by the single member, simple majority voting system. The country is divided into 651 constituencies, each of which elects a single Member of Parliament. Most of these are members of the two major, national parties. The candidate with a simple majority of votes wins the seat: in the extreme case, one with 34 per cent of the vote wins over two others with 33 per cent each. Consequently, the system produces disproportionate results. In 1983, for example, the Conservatives under Thatcher won 61 per cent of the seats with 42 per cent of the votes.

Moreover, constitutional conventions place all power in the hands of the government: the party with majority support in the House of Commons controls all government offices and has full power over policy. This 'elective dictatorship' has been used by Conservative governments since 1979 to put the country on a radically free-market basis.

■ The Republic of Ireland

British parliamentary and other institutions were already implanted in Ireland at the time of the Republic's secession and have been retained. However, there are two significant differences from British politics:

1. With a homogeneous population of 3.5 million, there are few of the cleavages of other European countries. There is a small, class-based Labour Party, and a larger Fine Gael (Gaelic) Party which is increasingly radical and liberal. The largest party is Fianna Fail (Heroes of Destiny), which is populist and nationalist.
2. The electoral system is a form of proportional representation (PR) which uses the single transferable vote (STV). However, because this system ideally requires large constituencies returning six or more members, and because in Ireland they are smaller, the results are not very proportionate. Increasingly, parliamentary seats are distributed across all parties, which makes coalitions (usually with Labour) necessary. The ideological looseness of Irish politics simplifies this task.

Heavily dependent on farming and hence a large net gainer from the Common Agricultural Policy (CAP) within the EU, the Republic is an enthusiastic supporter of the Union. Being traditionally neutral, it is not a member of NATO.

Table 3.2 underlines the pivotal role of Labour in Ireland and the general predominance of the Conservatives under the UK system, with voting figures and seat distributions for the last general election.

■ The Low Countries

The geographical position of the Low Countries (also known as the Benelux nations – Belgium, the Netherlands and Luxembourg) means that they have close links with their large neighbours, France and Germany, and in the case of the Netherlands, with

Table 3.2 Irish and British general elections, 1992		% valid votes	No. of seats
	IRELAND, 12 November 1992		
	Fianna Fail (FF)	39.11	68
	Fine Gael (FG)	24.47	45
	Labour Party	19.31	33
	Progressive Democrats (PDs)	4.68	10
	Democratic Left (DLP)	2.78	4
	Green Party	1.40	1
	Others	8.24	5
	UNITED KINGDOM, 9 April 1992		
	Conservative Party	41.93	336
	Labour Party	34.39	271
	Liberal Democrats	17.85	20
	Scottish Nationalists	1.87	3
	Plaid Cymru	0.47	4
	Official Ulster Unionists	0.81	9
	Democratic Unionists	0.31	3
	Ulster Popular Unionists	0.06	1
	Social Democratic and Labour Party	0.55	4
	Sein Féin	0.23	0
	Others	1.43	0

BRIEFING 3.6

The Benelux countries or Low Countries

The Benelux countries consist of Belgium, Luxembourg and the Netherlands. The Benelux Economic Union was set up as a customs union in 1948 and gradually expanded into an economic union by 1960. It was an important example for, and component part of, the European Economic Community set up in 1958. As the role and importance of the EU grew, so that of the Benelux Union declined. The Low Countries is another collective term for these countries, due to their location on the flat coastal plain of the Rhine Delta.

Britain. This helps to explain why the group is of a strongly internationalist disposition and confirmed supporters of both NATO and the EU. (See Table 3.3 for general election results for 1994–95.)

The Netherlands

The population of the Netherlands is 15.3 million. It was originally formed as a federation of provinces united against the Catholic powers, first Spain, then France. However, its Calvinistic form of Protestantism was soon diluted by the conquest and incorporation of neighbouring Catholic provinces. Since these were also Dutch-speaking, the main internal divisions were religious, but in pre-democratic times this diversity was accommodated by a long-standing tradition of religious toleration.

With the centralization of the modern state and the introduction of popular elections, religious cleavages emerged again in nineteenth-century politics. Catholics and Calvinists formed their own parties and set up their own trade union movements. In opposition to them, the secular and modernizing liberals also organized themselves, particularly over the issue of who was to control and pay for education. Working-

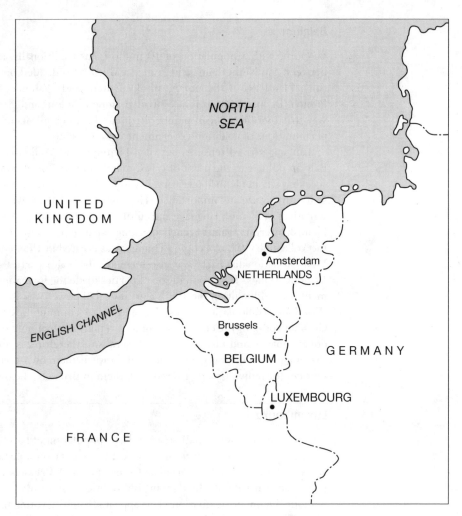

NORTH
SEA

UNITED
KINGDOM

●Amsterdam
NETHERLANDS

ENGLISH CHANNEL

Brussels
●

GERMANY

BELGIUM

LUXEMBOURG
●

FRANCE

Map 3.4   The Low Countries

class interests were also organized by the secular Labour Party, and each movement sought to provide for its members by creating its own occupational, social and cultural associations. Thus each movement or 'pillar' was a microcosm of wider society with its own leadership, communities and institutions. The leaders of the pillars negotiated and compromised with each other over the distribution of public resources for health, welfare, education, and so on.

This system, termed 'consociationalism', began to break down after the Second World War. It was particularly associated with the religious parties. With the gradual secularisation of society after the 1950s, they had to amalgamate to form the Christian Democratic Appeal (CDA) in 1980. In 1994, The Labour Party (PvdA) and the right-wing Peoples' Party for Freedom and Democracy Liberals (VVD) formed a coalition which excluded religious parties for the first time. With the rise of the progressive liberals (called the D'66) this marked the ending of the old system of religious pillarization, and greater freedom for secular parties to remodel the old, segregated institutions of Dutch society.

Belgium

Belgium, with a population of 10 million, has traditionally acted as a buffer state between the Netherlands and France and it is also divided between them linguistically; Flanders, in the north, speaks Dutch, and Wallonia, in the south, speaks French. Belgian politics is also divided along religious and class lines, but in such a way that there have been points of contact between all major parties so that many permutations of coalition government were possible.

Language-based tensions between Flemings and Walloons in the 1960s brought Belgian politics to the point of crisis, mainly over the position of Brussels, a French-speaking city in Flemish territory. Brussels was the capital of the European Union and so it grew in size and importance. The Christian socialists, who were the main representatives of Flemish language and culture, were increasingly seen as unable to defend Flemish interests against French-speaking expansion. A new Flemish nationalist party, the Volksunie (VU, or People's Union), was created in 1954 and in reaction to this a Walloon nationalist party was also formed. The major parties split into Flemish and Walloon Wings. The proliferation of parties made the formation of coalition governments very difficult. In the 1990s a great deal of power was devolved to three regions (Flanders, Wallonia and Brussels), and three communities (Flemish, French and German speaking). Central government retains control only of defence and foreign policy, finance and justice. Belgian federalism, therefore, is interesting because the two linguistic-cultural groups not only govern their own territories, but organize services for individuals registered with them in Brussels, the disputed capital.

Luxembourg

Luxembourg is a very small area and has a population of barely a third of a million. Its main significance is as a commercial centre with favourable tax and company laws, and as the location of the European Court and (with Brussels and Strasbourg) of the European Parliament. Luxemburgish politics are similar to those of Belgium, without the linguistic division. This appears from the voting figures for recent elections. Throughout the Low Countries the vote of the religious parties is in decline so that they are no longer able to dominate government coalitions as they used to.

France

France is the prototypical unitary European state, expanding from its centre in Paris to take over its periphery and, from the seventeenth to nineteenth centuries, to conquer territories from its immediate neighbours. With Britain it was the dominant military power in Europe from 1670–1870, but its role was then taken over by Germany, giving rise to the hostility and rivalry which helped start two world wars, and then inspired the European Union, as the antidote to war in Europe.

France has exercised its influence on the world not only through military power, but also through the ideas of the Enlightenment and of the French Revolution whose rallying cry of Liberty, Equality, and Fraternity have since echoed throughout Europe and North America. French culture and language also assimilated minorities within the nation in the nineteenth century to make the French Republic one and indivis-

Table 3.3 General elections in the Low Countries, 1994–95

	% valid votes	No. of seats
NETHERLANDS, 3 May 1994		
Labour Party (PvdA)	24.0	37
Christian Democratic Appeal (CDA)	22.2	34
People's Party for Freedom and Democracy (VVD)	19.9	31
Democrats 66 (D'66)	15.5	24
SGP/RPF/GPV*	4.8	7
General League of the Elderly (AOV)	3.6	6
Green Left	3.5	5
Centre Democrats (CD)	2.5	3
Socialist Party (SP)	1.3	2
55+ Union (Unie 55+)	0.9	1
Others	1.8	0
BELGIUM, 21 May 1995		
Christian People's Party (CVP)	17.2	29
Social Christian Party (PSC)	7.7	12
Flemish Liberals and Democrats (VLD)	13.1	21
Liberal Reform Party (PRL-FDF)	10.3	18
Socialist Party (SP)	12.6	20
Socialist Party (PS)	11.9	21
Vlaams Bloc	7.8	11
Volksunie	4.7	5
National Front (FN)	2.3	2
AGALEV	4.4	5
ECOLO	4.0	6
LUXEMBOURG, 12 June 1994		
Christian Social People's Party (CSV/PCS)	30.3	21
Luxembourg Socialist Workers' Party (LSAP/POSL)	25.4	17
Liberal Democratic Party (DP/PD)	19.3	12
Green Alternative	9.9	5
The Action Committee for Democracy and Justice	9.0	5

Note: *Political Reformed Party/Reformational Political Federation/Reformed Political Association (Right–wing Protestant Parties)

ible – a political and social fact. Cultural uniformity has succeeded to the point where support for minority nationalist parties, except in the outlying island of Corsica, is among the weakest in Europe.

Nevertheless, ethnic divisions remain, although they are not territorially organized. There are 1.5 million second generation, Arabic speaking people. In reaction to their presence an extreme-right Fascist party, the PNF, has gained 10–15 per cent of the popular vote. The main political division, however, is between reformed communism and socialism on the one hand, and centre-right Conservatism and Gaullist nationalism on the other.

The constitution of the Fifth Republic was created in the wake of colonial conflict and the threat of military intervention in 1958 (see Chapter 1). It provides for direct election of the president, who shares political power with a nominated prime minister, and a government the prime minister selects. Both are subject to votes of confidence by the National Assembly (the lower house of parliament). The Senate (the upper house) enjoys nearly equal status in most legislative matters.

The president has other prerogatives which make him the most powerful individual office holder in Europe: he has a seven-year term; he may call referendums to obtain approval for his proposals, thus bypassing the Assembly; and he has special responsibility for foreign affairs. If the president's party is the largest in the Assembly, he can invoke party loyalty to get his legislation passed, but if it is not he

Map 3.5   France

may use his prerogative to call an election in the hope of changing parliament's composition.

Elections in France involve two ballots on successive Sundays: the first eliminates weaker candidates; the second is a run-off between the stronger – in the case of the presidential election, between the two strongest. The system encourages alliances between parties of the same ideological tendency because defeated parties endorse candidates in the second election. The socialist Mitterrand was President from 1981 to 1994, and was succeeded by the Gaullist Chirac in 1995. However, it is the legislative elections which show the balance of strength between individual parties. The results for the last one, in which the left also did badly, are shown in Table 3.4.

■ The Western Mediterranean

The countries in this group are dissimilar in size but similar in other ways. Spain (40 million) and Italy (60 million) are two of the big countries of Europe and of the EU. By comparison Portugal (actually on the Atlantic not the Mediterranean) has 10

Table 3.4 Voting in the French legislative elections, first and second rounds, 21 and 28 March 1993

	% valid vote		
	1st Round	2nd Round	No. of seats
Communist Party (PCF)	9.2	4.6	23
Socialist Party (PS)	17.6	28.3	54
Left Radical Movement (MRG)	0.9	1.2	6
Presidential Majority	1.8	2.2	10
Rally for the Republic (RPR)	20.4	28.3	247
Union for French Democracy (UDF)	19.1	25.8	213
Various Right	4.7	3.6	24
Front National (FN)	12.4	5.7	0
Others	13.9	0.3	0

million. The small but strategic islands of Malta (population 360,000) can be included with the group. The main characteristic which these countries have in common is their strong Catholicism, which has created equally intense secular-socialist movements. Apart from Malta, all have recent experience of Fascist dictatorship, overturned in Italy by the Second World War, but continuing in Spain and Portugal into the 1970s. Their subsequent transition to liberal democracy has interesting parallels with east European countries in the 1990s.

The countries share an agricultural basis and similar social problems, particularly in their poor, southern regions. They are heavily subsidized and protected by the Common Agricultural Policy (CAP) of the EU. But in spite of this, the farming population is leaving the land, which is being taken over by large factory farms (*latifundia*) worked by a landless proletariat, often illegal Arab immigrants from North Africa.

State administrative structures have not been much modernized since the Fascist period, and consequently are over-manned, under-financed and subject to corruption and political pressures. Bureaucrats find it easier to do their minimal formal duties; more zealous performance may draw attention and invite trouble. National legislation is often loosely enforced and European Union directives lax in application. An added problem is organized crime and involvement in the world drug and arms trade, particularly in Italy. However, the judiciary and police have proved surprisingly effective in the face of both terrorism and crime, without infringing democratic guarantees. In Italy they have uncovered corruption at such high levels that there have been changes in government and in the party system itself.

A positive achievement in Spain and Italy has been an ability to accommodate strong minority nationalist movements by giving them considerable regional autonomy. Piecemeal arrangements have been made depending upon local circumstances, which give regional authorities different powers and functions, and different relations with the political centre. This is logical when some regions make strong separatist demands and others none. The success has important and interesting lessons for other European states with separatist movements, as for the idea of a two-track Europe at the supranational level. Though 'differentiated' federalism of this sort is found also in Belgium and to a lesser extent in Britain, it contrasts with the federalism of other countries where states or provinces have the same relationship with the centre. (See Chapter 13 for more detailed consideration of this point.)

Spain

By European standards Spain devolves much power to its regions, largely because the new democracy had to accommodate militant Basque and Catalan demands. Lesser

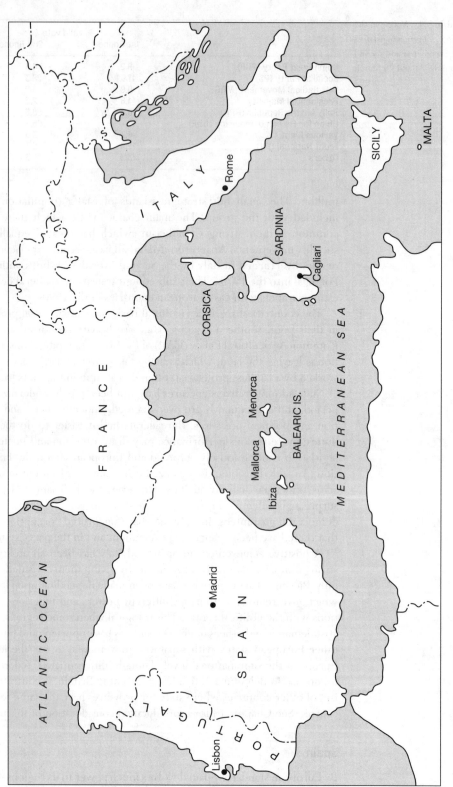

Map 3.6 The Western Mediterranean

but extensive powers have been delegated to Galicia, Andalusia, Valencia and the Balearic Islands, while the rest of Spain is divided into 'ordinary' regions.

Spain's transition to democracy has been guided and safeguarded by the King (Juan Carlos), who was installed in 1975 after the death of the former dictator, Franco. Many of the countries discussed so far in this chapter are monarchies, though constitutional ones. In Spain, Juan Carlos's role as Commander-in-Chief of the military has been important in keeping it loyal to democracy, in backing a series of settlements which produced the new and democratic constitution in 1978, and in defeating an attempted right-wing coup in 1981. Since 1976 a series of moderate right-wing and socialist governments have consolidated democracy, and carried out largely successful reforms, particularly in welfare, and in modernizing the economy.

Portugal

Portugal was as isolated as Spain by its conservative authoritarian regime up to 1974. The regime had been dedicated to maintaining its African empire in the face of decolonization elsewhere. The army's realization that it could not win the struggle led to a coup in 1974 organized by young left-wing officers. A new and democratic constitution was implemented in 1976 and the first government was a coalition led by the socialists. A relic of the dictatorship is to be found in the directly elected president who has powers equivalent to those of France and Finland. The president appoints a government, although this is dependent on parliamentary support.

The main political parties are the (centre-right) social democrats (PSD) who lost the last election, the socialists (PS), and an electoral alliance led by the communists. The PSD has led most coalition governments since 1980. The communist vote is higher than in most other west European countries, but it has declined with socialist and social democratic success. Governments have promoted social and economic reform. But the poverty of much of the country, heavily dependent upon agriculture, remains a major obstacle. On the positive side, Portugal is a homogeneous country and has no threats of regional secession, or minority protest against what seems to be an increasingly stable democratic system.

Malta

This is a characteristic it shares with the tiny island state of Malta, south of Italy. Because of its strategic location between the east and west Mediterranean, Malta was a British base for 160 years from 1800, but became independent in 1964. The language is basically Arabic, but both language and culture have been influenced by Italy (particularly with regard to its fervent Catholicism) and Britain (particularly with regard to its political institutions). Intense competition between the Church-backed Nationalist Party and the secular Labour Party, which have alternated in government since the war, has created a two-party system in spite of a proportional electoral system (STV). The Labour Governments of 1972–86 re-oriented the economy and created a full welfare state after independence. Nationalist governments from 1986 concentrated on de-nationalizing and diversifying the economy particularly into electronics. In spite of its barren terrain and small size, Malta is prosperous and has no unemployment. Few problems would be created by entry to the European Union, which is expected in the next few years.

Italy

Italy is one of Europe's heavyweights, a founder member of the EU, and one of the world's Group of Seven leading industrial countries of the world. It owes this to its spectacular industrialization of the 1950s and 1960s, when a quarter of the population migrated from the agricultural south and east to the north and west. Regional dispar-ities remain acute: the south, still with a third of the population, is chronically under-developed and dependent on agriculture in contrast to the bustling north, centred on Milan and Turin, which has integrated itself with the European industrial heartlands.

This has created a desire in parts of the north to free itself from the tax burden of supporting the south. A northern Nationalist party (the Northern League) have advocated a loose federation in place of the centralized Italian state. It had consider-able success in elections from 1992 onwards, gaining about 9 per cent of the vote.

The problem is also political. Italian governments since the war were dominated by the Christian democrats, backed by the United States and the Church in order to counter the largest communist party in Western Europe (20–30 per cent of the vote), which would have taken Italy out of the NATO alliance. To maintain their posi-tion, the Christian democrats allied with smaller parties, above all the socialists, tempting them to abandon their own policies in return for government spoils – a process known by a peculiarly Italian term 'trasformismo'. The Christian democrats consolidated their vote, particularly in the south by heavy transfers of money there and by protecting the Mafia and other criminal organizations in return for political support. In turn, they demanded and received money from all the large businesses and on all government contracts.

Among other things this meant that the bureaucracy was used as a source of patronage and thus rendered corrupt and inefficient. The whole system was exposed by courageous judges and police in the early 1990s and in effect brought down the old parties, as government ministers up to the level of premiers and presidents were charged with corruption and malpractice.

Much progress was, however, made under Christian democratic dominance. We have noted the 'economic miracle'. Regional autonomy was given to minority areas such as Sardinia and to French and German speakers in the Alps. The Italian welfare state was founded in the 1970s through popular initiatives and votes which by-passed the blocked parliament. Popular votes finally changed the electoral system in the 1990s from PR, which favoured the Christian democrats to a mixed system of con-stituency representation (75 per cent)and PR (25 per cent). It was hoped this would replace weak and short-lived coalitions with two-party competition and strong, accountable, single-party government.

These hopes were not realized in the first elections under the new system. The communists split between the Democratic Party of the Left (PDS) and the old com-munists (Rifondazione Communista). Even though they formed an electoral alliance of the left, this was defeated by a right-wing alliance consisting of ex-Fascists (the National Alliance), Forza Italia (Come on Italy!) led by the television owner Silvio Berlusconi, whose TV channels pumped out propaganda on his behalf; and the Northern League, whose support was essential to form a coalition government. These quarrelled internally over Berlusconi's plans to cut back welfare and stop judi-cial investigations into corruption. It broke up in confusion in early 1995. This led eventually to another election in early 1996 which did have the effect of creating

Table 3.5 General elections in the Western Mediterranean, 1992–96

	% valid votes	No. of seats
PORTUGAL, 1 October 1995		
Socialist Party (PS)	43.9	112
Social Democratic Party (PSD)	34.0	88
People's Party (PP)	9.1	15
United Democratic Coalition (CDU)	8.6	15
SPAIN, 3 March 1996		
Popular Party (PP)	38.85	156
Spanish Socialist Workers' Party (PSOE)	37.48	141
United Left (IU)	10.58	21
Convergence and Union (CiU)	4.61	16
Basque Nationalist Party (PNV)	1.28	5
Canary Islands Coalition (CC)	0.89	4
National Galician Bloc (BNG)	0.88	2
United People (HB)	0.73	2
Catalan Republican Left (ERC)	0.67	1
Basque Solidarity (EA)	0.46	1
Valencian Union (UV)	0.37	1
MALTA, 26 October 1996		
Nationalist Party (PN)	47.8	34
Malta Labour Party (MLP)	50.7	35
ITALY, 21 April 1996		
Olive Tree Electoral Alliance		
Democratic Party of the Left (PDS)	21.1	
Italian People's Party (PP1)/PROD1 List	6.8	
Italian Renewal (DINI LIST) (RI)	4.3	284
Greens	2.5	
Other Olive Tree	0.1	
Freedom Alliance		
Forza Italia	20.6	
National Alliance (AN)	15.7	246
Christian Democratic Centre	1.9	
United Christian – Democrats (COU/CCD)	1.9	
Northern League (LN)	10.1	59
Communist Refoundation (PRC)	8.6	35
Others	3.5	6

competing alliances on left and right. The elections were won by the centre-left 'olive tree' coalition which formed a government pledged to reform. If it succeeds it is likely to usher in a new era of political stability.

Elections have thus been very important in all these countries in producing a peaceful changes of regime and important policy changes. The most recent results are shown in Table 3.5, illustrating the important transfers of power which took place in 1996 from socialists to the conservatives of the Popular Party in Spain; in contrast to the leftish takeover in Portugal and Italy.

■ German federations

The German-speaking lands consist of Germany, Switzerland and Austria. They have the same federal form, with the Länder in Germany and the Cantons of Switzerland having real power and functioning as autonomous parts of national administration (Länder in Austria are much less autonomous). In this respect, they are good examples of second type of European federalism in which each region has the same

Map 3.7   Germany, Switzerland and Austria

politico-juridical standing with central government. At the same time, the system is not like classic US federalism, where the functions and powers of the states are clearly separated from the federal government. In the Germanic model, the federal government has limited administrative capacity to implement its legislation and relies upon the Länder and Cantons to do so.

This arrangement gives the lower levels of government a major share of public spending and an effective veto over government policy. National governments must gain the consent of the Länder even if most are in the hands of opposition parties, which is often the case. Länder also send delegations, elected by their governments, to the upper House of the Federal Parliament, whose consent is necessary to all decisions. Hence, most policies have to be negotiated and widely agreed, especially in Switzerland with its complex religious, linguistic and territorial divisions.

Switzerland

Switzerland is often regarded as the best example of a European multi-ethnic state. German-speakers form almost two-thirds of the population, French-speakers just under 20 per cent, and Italian about 5 per cent. Foreign nationals form almost one in five, the highest in Western Europe, with Italians, Yugoslavs, Spanish, Portuguese,

BRIEFING 3.7

Federal and unitary states

In *federal* constitutions the power of government is divided between a central government (the federal government) and a set of territorial entities known as states, provinces, or regions. Each level usually has distinct competences which are derived from a written constitution. Other functions and powers may be shared between federal and state governments more informally. In Federal systems, the federal or central government often consists of two chambers, one of which (the upper house or senate) contains representatives of the states. The division of powers and functions between federal and state governments varies in different systems, but in most states have considerable powers to tax and spend. Local government, a third level of government, usually falls under the direction of state rather than federal government. Constitutional courts are important in federal systems because they adjudicate in case of conflict between state and federal government. The main political significance of federal government is the autonomous power it gives to territorial units of government within nation-states, and its ability to defuse national conflict by decentralizing it to lower levels of government. In Western Europe, Germany, Switzerland, Austria and Belgium are federal states where the Länder have equal status. In Italy and Spain different regional governments have different powers in relation to the centre. The EU increasingly resembles this other model ('multi-speed Europe').

In *unitary states* constitutional power is not divided between central and territorial units of government, but is concentrated in national government. In unitary states, therefore, the powers and functions of lower levels of government within the nation are derived not from a written constitution but from central government. Consequently, central government can change these powers, duties, and functions. In Western Europe the main unitary states are Denmark, Finland, France, Greece, Ireland, the Netherlands, Norway, Portugal, Sweden and the UK. Most Central and Eastern European States are unitary, apart from Russia.

Germans and Turks among the larger groups. Switzerland is also divided almost evenly between Catholics and Protestants. In the federal system it is the distribution of groups among the twenty-six cantons which is important in the sense that a majority formed by a religious or linguistic group in any canton is likely to control it politically, and the consent of a majority of cantons is necessary for most legislation. Some cantons have even split: a new Canton of the Jura was formed in 1979 to accommodate French speakers wanting independence from the predominantly German Canton of Bern.

The cantons have a good deal of administration and legislation delegated to them, to the extent that they often have a greater influence over citizens' lives than central government itself. Switzerland was originally formed as an alliance of independent cantons for defence against common enemies. Only limited powers have been transferred to Federal level. In a successful attempt to accommodate complex societal cleavages, the principal of delegation to the lowest level is followed to its limits. Indeed, within the cantons, the local government communes deal with a wide range of public services. (This is the principle of 'subsidiarity' which we encountered in the context of the European Union in Chapter 2.) Much is also left to the individual – health insurance, for example. Switzerland has the smallest public expenditure of any west European country.

The individual also has great scope for direct participation. Many decisions are made by referendum, and citizens can demand a vote on any matter if they get enough signatures and the wording of the proposal is approved by the courts. Votes can be called at the national, cantonal or communal level, and outcomes can be important. For example, one canton restricted the size and number of container lorries passing through it, and since there were no alternative routes between Northern and Southern Europe this resulted in a major switch of EU transport to rail. Small wonder the Swiss did not want to join the EU when they could unilaterally impose such conditions!

Swiss political parties have adapted themselves to the federal system by decentralizing policy-making powers to cantonal and communal branches. Parties contest national elections but the executive Federal Council is relatively unimportant, and is run by a permanent centre-right coalition of the four largest parties – Social Democrats (who gained 19 per cent of the poll in 1991) , Radical Democrats (right-wing liberals, 21 per cent), Christian Democrats (Catholic, 18 per cent), and the People's Party (agrarian, 12 per cent).

Germany

With 7 million people, Switzerland is dwarfed by the Federal Republic of Germany. Its population of over 80 million, its prosperous economy and efficient industrial base make it the strongest country in Europe. But defeat in two world wars, occupation and partition, make it extremely wary of bold foreign initiatives without general European agreement. Hence its strong support for the European Union. Since it borders with Poland and the Czech Republic, Germany is greatly concerned with central and eastern Europe. This interest was heightened by the re-unification of Germany in 1990 – that is of West Germany, the Federal Republic of Germany (FRG), with East Germany, the former communist German Democratic Republic (GDR).

Unification produced considerable social, political and economic strains. It was accompanied by the immigration of almost 2 million people from east Europe who joined the 2 million guest workers already in west Germany, mainly Turks. Unification also meant that much inefficient industry in the former GDR collapsed, causing high unemployment and east German ('Ossie') resentment of 'Wessies' (West Germans). Some of these strains are expressed in racial attacks and support for neo-Nazi movements.

Overall, however, unification has been managed notably well. The east has been organized into six new Länder. The leading western parties have amalgamated with their eastern equivalents – the Christian Democrats (CDU, with CSU 41.5 per cent of the vote in 1994), the Social Democrats (SPD, 36.4 per cent), the Free Democrats (FDP, or Liberals, 7 per cent), the Green alliance (7 per cent) and the former communists (PDS, 4.4 per cent). The electoral system is a major influence on parties and governments. The system is a mixed proportional one, in which half the members of the lower house of parliament are elected by plurality (as in Britain) and half by proportional representation. There is a voting threshold of 5 per cent, below which there is no representation. However, parties like the PDS with three or more seats are represented.

Since 1961 the FPD has formed coalition governments with either the SPD (1969–82) or the CDU/CSU (1961–69, 1982 onwards). Underlying national politics, however, there is a general consensus about the need for a mixed economy and welfare state, for a conciliatory attitude towards Russia and Eastern Europe, and for a widening and deepening of the EU. The homogeneity of Germany has rendered local nationalism unimportant, even in Bavaria, the most distinctive area.

Table 3.6 Germanic general elections, 1991–94

	% valid votes	No. of seats
SWITZERLAND, 20 October 1991		
Radical Democratic Party (FDP/PRD)	20.9	44
Christian Democratic People's Party (CPV/PDL)	17.8	37
Social Democratic Party of Switzerland (SP/PS)	19.0	41
Swiss People's Party (SVP/UDC)	11.8	25
CPS/PES	6.4	14
Liberal Party (LPS/PLS)	3.0	10
Car Party (APS/PSA)	5.1	8
LdU Adi	2.7	6
Swiss Democrats (SDS/DS)	2.8	5
Evangelical People's (EVP/PEV)	1.9	3
Others	8.6	7
AUSTRIA, 9 October 1994		
Social Democratic Party (SPÖ)	35.23	65
People's Party (ÖVP)	27.74	52
Freedom Party (FPÖ)	22.64	42
Greens	7.01	13
Liberal Forum	5.74	11
Others	1.64	0
GERMANY, 16 October 1994		
Christian Democratic Union (CDU)	34.2	244
Christian Social Union (CSU)	7.3	50
Free Democratic Party (FDP)	6.9	47
Social Democratic Party of Germany (SPD)	36.4	252
Greens (Grünen, including Alliance 90, B'90)	7.3	49
Democratic Socialist Party (PDS)	4.4	30
Others	3.5	0

Austria

Austria (7.5 million population) is probably better included with the German federal states than with the central European countries with which it has historic ties. On the one hand, the Austrian Empire, which lasted until 1918, included Hungary, the Czech lands, Slovenia, and Serbia in Eastern Europe. On the other, Austria is German-speaking, has a federal system of government on the German/Swiss model, has been firmly in the west European camp for most of the post-war period, has a functioning and stable democracy, a high standard of living, and has been a member of the EU since 1995.

After the war Austria was occupied by the Americans, British, French and Soviets until 1955 when it gained independence and pursued a neutral, non-aligned policy. For the first twenty years after the war the government was a grand coalition formed by the Austrian People's Party, and the Socialist Party (SPO). It consolidated the welfare state, and created a system of government by 'social partnership' (corporatism) in which government, business, and trade unions collaborated closely in order to minimize social and political conflict, and maximize social stability and economic growth. The result is one of the most developed countries in Western Europe.

As in Germany, the Austrian party system is dominated by a Christian democratic party (the OVP) and a social democratic party (SPO), with a smaller party (the Freedom Party, FPO) with a strong nationalist not to say xenophobic policy, and a Green party. Since 1966, when the post-war grand coalition came to an end, the SPO has been in power almost continuously, either on its own (1970–83), in coalition with the FPO, (1983–87), or with the OVP (since 1987). In 1994 the SPO got 35 per cent of the vote, the OVP 28 per cent, while the FPD increased to almost 23 per cent. These figures can be compared with those for Germany and Switzerland in Table 3.6.

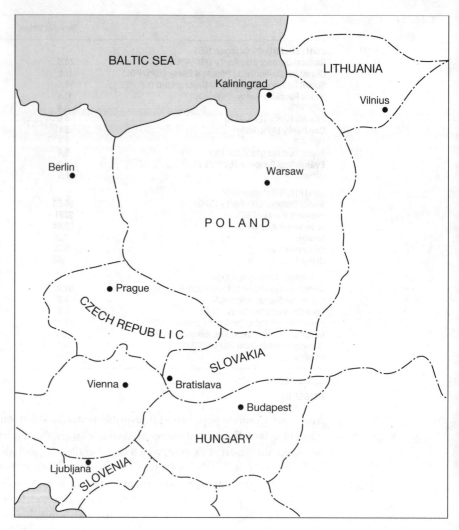

Map 3.8 Central Europe

Central Europe

Central Europe consists mainly of the western Slav nations of the Czech Republic, Slovakia, Poland, Lithuania and Slovenia, but also includes Hungary which speaks a language related to Finnish. The Hungarians, Czechs, Slovenes and Slovaks have historical ties as parts of the Austrian Empire, and as a result have Catholicism in common as well. After the war they were parts of the Soviet Empire, but they all now aspire to membership of the EU. The Czech Republic, Slovakia, Hungary and Poland formed an international alliance in 1991 known as the Visegrad group.

The collapse of communism and the opening up of national economies to the West has had a disastrous effect, at least in the short run. In spite of severe economic problems, however, the central countries have sustained free and competitive elections, due in part to the willingness of the old communist parties to remodel themselves as social democrats and play the democratic game.

> BRIEFING 3.8
>
> **Liberalization and the command economy**
>
> In the *command economies* of the Soviet bloc, the state owned and controlled all sectors of the economy, leaving little room for private ownership or market forces. All means of production and distribution were controlled by the state. This applied both to industry and agriculture, and entailed the collectivization of the farms in the earlier periods of Soviet power after the revolution of 1917.
>
> *Liberalization* here means that the dual processes of political and economic change undertaken in central and eastern Europe after the fall of the Soviet system. In the political sphere democratic constitutions were adopted, freedom of speech, association, and assembly recognized, and free elections held. In the economic sphere economies were, to varying degrees, geared to the market, much state property was privatized, and trading relations with Western countries were opened up. The short-run economic effects of liberalization for many Central and Eastern European countries were disastrous. Because of old and inefficient factories and equipment, and backward business, management, and marketing practices, the ex-Soviet countries could not compete effectively with the West. As a result industrial production fell rapidly, unemployment climbed quickly, and the standard of living collapsed. The question is whether democracy in these countries can survive such shocks, even though the economies recovered to some extent in the mid-1990s (see Chapter 16).

The Czech Republic

The unitary state of Czechoslovakia was created as a communist republic after the war, but was then reorganized to create the Federation of Czech and Slovak republics in 1969. Czechoslovakia had a hard line communist government which resisted change and was ejected by popular demonstrations in 1989. Russian troops withdrew in 1990 when anti-communist and centre-right reformers won the first election, and in 1992/3 the Federation broke up into the Czech Republic and Slovakia. The Czech lands (population 10.4 million) are fortunate in having a good industrial base and some inter-war experience of democracy.

The current government is a coalition led by the centre-left Social Democrats who replaced a free-market, centre-right coalition in 1996. The main opposition is provided by the left bloc (14 per cent) and the Social Democrats (7 per cent), survivors of the old communists. Party consolidation has been helped by a high voting threshold, on the German model, although this has not prevented party splits and fragmented voting in Parliament.

Slovakia

Slovakia (5.3 million population) was part of the Federation of Czechoslovakia until 1993, when it parted from the Czechs in the 'velvet divorce'. With Spain and Belgium, discussed earlier, and with Yugoslavia discussed below, this demonstrates the power of nationalism in the modern era, especially since the new constitution defines the State as 'of the Slovak people', thereby ignoring the substantial Hungarian minority in the south. The paradox of nationalism, long illustrated by events in south and east Europe, is that secession does not always solve minority problems, but sometimes creates new ones by drawing new borders.

The nationalist Movement for Democratic Slovakia (HZDS) was the largest party at the time of independence negotiations. It was close to an absolute parliamentary majority after the 1992 elections and dominated a coalition it formed with the Slovak National Party. Since then, however, there have been difficulties with state control of the media and an attempt to close down the new University of Trinava for political reasons. However the HZDs re-emerged as the strongest party after the election of 1994 (see Table 3.7). Splits in the fragmented party system are common. Nationalism is strong and political leaders faced with economic problems at home are always tempted to play a strong nationalist card.

Hungary

Hungary has a population of 10.3 million, but there are substantial Hungarian minorities in most neighbouring countries, except Austria. In spite of the dominance of a nationalistic, Christian, and conservative party, the Hungarian Democratic Forum (MDF) from 1990–94, Hungarian foreign policy has been moderate and aimed at maintaining cultural links with Magyar-speakers abroad. The only substantial minority within Hungary itself are the Roma (Gypsies) (6 per cent), a semi-nomadic group living on the margins of several Eastern European and Balkan societies. With the depopulation of the Hungarian countryside, the Roma are taking over whole villages which are bereft of all services and facilities.

In the 1980s Hungary was governed by a group of reform communists led by Janos Kadar who managed to introduce liberal reforms into government and the economy. This changed the old communist command economy into so-called 'goulash communism'. Even so the full transition to a market system in the early 1990s depressed output and caused extreme hardship (see Chapter 16). This brought the former communists (the Hungarian Socialist Party, MSzP) back into power in the election of 1994 with only a third of the vote but more than half the seats. This was due to an extremely complicated voting system which favours the leading parties which are the MSzP (33 per cent of the poll in 1994), and Alliance of Free Democrats ((SzDSz, 20 per cent). The party system is extremely fragmented with two agrarian, a social democratic, a Christian democratic, and a liberal party. Hungarians and Poles refer to their small parties as 'sofa parties' – they have just enough members and supporters to fill a sofa.

Poland

With an estimated population of 39 million, Poland is the largest partner in the Visegrad group of nations. It has never played the leading role in eastern Europe that its size might justify, because it is situated between two even larger neighbours, Germany and Russia. They partitioned the country in 1939. Polish identity has been sustained by a fervent nationalism closely connected with Catholicism.

This was a feature which distinguished Poland from other countries under Russian hegemony after 1945. It also fuelled effective peasant resistance to collectivization, and, as a result, Poland did not have to cope with the problems of large inefficient factory farms and a malfunctioning food distribution system. The corollary of this was the survival of a large subsistence peasantry which supported its own Polish Peasant Party (PSL) – a satellite party of the communists before the 1980s but more independent thereafter.

After the war the communist regime industrialized the country, but it also compromised with the peasants and the Catholic church. Unofficial workers' movements, backed by the church, evolved into the Solidarity movement led by Lech Walesa. Solidarity was officially recognized and won a sweeping election victory in 1989. When the USSR collapsed the new Polish government pressed ahead with rapid economic reforms which aimed to move to a competitive, market economy as rapidly as possible – a process known as 'controlled shock' or 'big bang' – starting in 1990. The resulting economic hardship caused Solidarity to split. Problems also arose because Walesa, elected president of the republic in 1990, tried to extend his executive powers, particularly over national security and defence. In addition, a highly proportional electoral system without a voting threshold helped the fragmentation of parties (twenty-nine parties and electoral groups gained representation in the 1991 election), which made it difficult to form stable and effective government coalitions. Nevertheless, economic reform continued, and in 1992/93 Poland was unusual in central Europe in showing signs of economic recovery. An electoral threshold was imposed of 5 per cent for parties and 7 per cent for electoral coalitions for the parliamentary elections of 1993.

The leading parties of 1993, therefore, had an advantage and the outcome was a coalition government consisting of the Democratic Left Alliance (DLA, former communists) and the Peasant Party which wanted to soften the impact of economic reform. In 1996 the reformist of the DLA also defeated Walesa in the presidential elections.

Lithuania

Commonly grouped with the Baltic states Lithuania was absorbed into the USSR after the Second World War along with Latvia and Estonia, and like them gained independence in 1991. However, its population of 3.8 million is largely Catholic, and some 7 per cent are Polish so it has more in common with Poland than with the other Baltic states. Ten per cent of the population is Russian although Russian troops left the country in 1993. Like Poland, Lithuania also has a strong, directly elected president.

Protest in the last years of the Soviet period consolidated around the Reform Movement which won the first election of 1990. In the following election of 1992 the ex-Communist Democratic Labour Party (LDDP) got 45 per cent of the vote and 51 per cent of the seats and formed the government. The LDDP lost the 1996 election to the Reform Movement (now called the Homeland Union). Lithuania is a well-developed nation which has stabilized itself quickly with a viable constitution, and a cohesive, unfragmented party system.

Slovenia

Although Slovenia (population 2 million) was part of Yugoslavia, it was an Austrian province for hundreds of years up to 1918, and shares its Catholic background. The Communist regime of Yugoslavia was relatively liberal, so Slovenia was already progressing towards social, economic and political reform and international integration in the 1980s. After a ten-day war, Yugoslavian federal forces withdrew from the area in 1991, and Slovenia was internationally recognized as an independent state in 1992. After an election in the same year, a broad coalition government was formed consisting of liberal, social and Christian democrats. Slovenia was the most economically developed region within Yugoslavia and thus has been reasonably prosperous during the 1990s.

The second elections in all these countries has been fairly crucial in stabilizing the

Table 3.7 General
elections in Central
Europe, 1992–96

	% of valid votes	No. of seats
CZECH REPUBLIC, 31 May 1996		
Civic Democratic Party (ODS)	29.6	68
Social Democratic Party (CSSD)	26.4	61
Communist Party (KSCM)	10.3	22
People's Party (CSL)	8.1	18
Republican Party (SPR–RSC)	8.0	18
Civic Democratic Alliance (ODA)	6.4	13
Others	11.2	0
SLOVAKIA, 30 September 1994		
Movement for a Democratic Slovakia (HZDS)	34.96	61
Common Choice Bloc	10.41	18
Hungarian Coalition	10.18	17
Christian Democratic Movement (KDH)	10.08	17
Democratic Union of Slovakia (DUS)	8.57	15
Association of Workers of Slovakia (ZRS)	7.34	13
Slovak National Party (SNS)	5.4	9
Others	13.06	0
HUNGARY, 8, 29 May 1994*		
Hungarian Socialist party (MSzP)	32.9	209
Alliance of Free Democrats (Sz DSz)	19.8	70
Hungarian Democratic Forum (MDF)	11.7	37
Independent Smallholders (FKGP)	8.9	26
Christian Democratic People's Party (KDNP)	7.1	22
Federation of Young Democrats (FIDESz)	7.0	20
Agrarian Association	2.1	1
Liberal Civic Alliance (Entrepreneur's Party)	0.6	1
Others	10.0	0
POLAND, 19 September 1993		
Democratic Left Alliance (SLD)	20.4	171
Polish Peasant Party (PSL)	15.4	132
Democratic Union (UD)	10.6	74
Labour Union (UP)	7.3	41
Confederation for an Independent Poland (KPN)	5.8	22
Non-Party Bloc in Support of Reforms (BBWR)	5.4	16
German Minority Organisations	na	4
Others	35.1	0
LITHUANIA, 20 October 1996		
Homeland Union	29.8	70
Christian Democratic Party	12.2	16
Centre Movement	8.2	13
Democratic Labour Party	9.5	12
Social Democratic Party	6.6	12
National Party	3.8	1
Women's Party	3.7	1
Others	26.1	16
SLOVENIA, 10 November 1996		
Liberal Democratic Party (LDS)	27.0	25
Christian Democratic Party (SKD)	9.6	10
Associated List (ZLSD)	9.6	9
Slovene Nationalist Party (SNS)	3.2	4
Slovene People's Party (SLS)	19.4	19
Pensioners' Party	4.3	5
Social Democratic Party of Slovenia (SDSS)	16.0	16
Others	11.4	2

Note: *Vote percentages are for the regional party lists including single-member constituencies.

party system, as we shall see in Chapter 9. In Poland, Lithuania and Hungary the ex-communists have returned peacefully to power and governed democratically. In others, the centre-right have held their own. These tendencies are documented in Table 3.7.

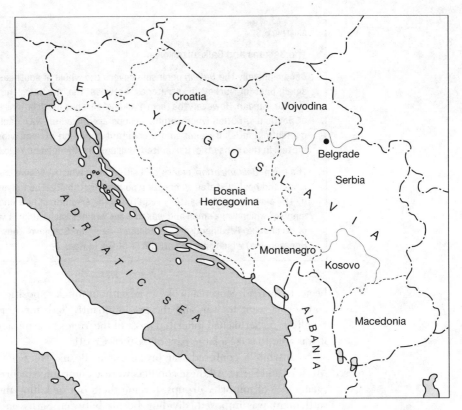

Map 3.9   Balkans (ex-Yugoslavia and Albania)

◼ The Balkans (ex-Yugoslavia and Albania)

This area is inhabited by a Slav group speaking the same language (Serbo-Croat) but split three ways by religion and culture. The original Serb kingdom was Greek Orthodox, Hungarian domination in the north combined with Italian influence along the coast converted these areas to Catholicism. Catholic Serbs became known as Croats. Turkish rule over five centuries converted many to Islam, particularly in Bosnia. Intermingled with the Serbs in the south there were Albanians who spoke a different language and were mainly Muslim. Part of the Albanian-speaking block constitutes an independent State (Albania) but also carries over into southern Serbia and western Macedonia.

In the nineteenth century, the Orthodox Serbs won their independence from the Turks and set up the kingdom of Serbia. After the First World War this became the dominant element in the newly created state of Yugoslavia, which united Serbia with Bosnia and the Catholic areas in the north and along the coast (Croatia), and Slovenia. During the Second World War, the Germans set up a Nazi state dominated by the Croatians, who, in their turn, fought a brutal guerrilla war with a communist resistance, composed heavily of Serbs.

After the war, communists took over the government, but this very soon defied Russia and followed an independent, national line. The external threat of the USSR, together with a communist monopoly of government positions, held Yugoslavia together as a Federal Republic till 1990. The groups dominant in each Republic then

---

BRIEFING 3.9

The Balkans and Balkanization

Geographically the *Balkan* peninsula covers the whole of southeast Europe, including a small part of Turkey. It stretches between the Adriatic, the Black Sea and the Mediterranean. However, the term 'Balkans' also has associations with a particular type of political situation where ethnic groups are mixed up with each other and generate conflicting national claims and a constant condition of semi-violent tension between states. In this sense the 'Balkanized' Balkans are the former Yugoslavia and Albania.

The term '*Balkanization*' refers to a situation in which a region is split into a number of small and hostile states so creating political instability. The fall of the Ottoman Empire by the early twentieth century resulted in the creation of new and autonomous states, many of which were small and waged wars against each other. It was the assassination of Archduke Ferdinand by a Bosnian Serb in Sarajevo (now capital of Bosnia-Herzegovina) which sparked off the First World War.

---

began to quarrel. Slovenia broke away without much opposition in 1991, but Croatia and Serbia went to war, and the predominantly Serb territory inside Croatia also revolted. As Serbia had inherited most of the Yugoslav army and munitions factories it was able to seize a large part of eastern Croatia.

Meanwhile a confused war broke out in Bosnia-Herzegovina between Croats, Muslims and Serbs. All these conflicts were accompanied by brutal 'ethnic cleansing' (genocide) of minority groups, forcing them out or killing them. In 1995, a peace settlement was imposed, dividing Bosnia between Serbs on the one hand, and a Muslim-Croat Federation on the other. Mutual exhaustion and foreign guarantees will probably ensure peace for a while, but violent tension will remain.

Bosnia–Herzegovina

Since Bosnia-Herzegovina is at the centre of the current conflict, little can be said except that the mainly Muslim government has been confined to half the area by the much better equipped Serbs. Internal tensions remain with the Croats, so elections – probably corrupt anyway – serve more to validate each group's national leadership rather than to reconcile one with another.

Croatia

Croatia has managed to stabilize itself with a mainly Croat population estimated at between 4 and 5 million. The war has consolidated political support for the nationalist Croatian Democratic Union which holds both the executive Presidency and majorities in the legislature. The main political opposition is from the Centre Right Liberals (HSLP) and smaller, extreme, nationalist parties.

Serbia

Serbia (population 10 million) and Montenegro (700,000 – also Serb) are united in a rump Yugoslav federation which may hold together if not too many demands are put on the Montenegrins. Both have substantial Muslim and Albanian minorities, and Serbia also has Hungarians in the north, where most Croats have been cleared out. The mainly agricultural economy is supplemented by some heavy industry and armaments.

The former communists used the wars in Croatia and Bosnia to win elections and remain in power. Thus government remains pretty much as it was under the old regime though regular elections have been held. In 1996, government controlled media gave the opposition little coverage. The communists now call themselves the Socialist Party of Serbia. The main opposition, the Serbian Movement for Renewal, has only a limited popular base and heads a left-coalition government.

Macedonia

In the far south, on the Greek border, Macedonia has remained outside Yugoslav conflicts so far. The old province of Macedonia did not gain independence from the Turks until 1912, and even now Greece disputes its name and flag, while Bulgaria claims that Slav Macedonians are Bulgars, and the Serbs that they are Serbs! In addition, the large Albanian minority in the east look to Albania. In short, the new Republic of Macedonia has potential disputes with all its neighbours. It has a population of 2 million: two-thirds are (Slav) Macedonians; a fifth are Albanian; and there are other Muslims, Roma, Serbs and Turks.

Most parties are based on ethnic groups. The Internal Macedonian Revolutionary Organization (IMRO) is the main Slav nationalist party, but it did poorly in the elections of 1995. The ex-communist Social Democratic Alliance also supported by Slavs, has formed coalition governments since independence with the (Albanian) Party of Democratic Prosperity. The governments have been held together by external threats but weakened by ethnic clashes in the north-west of the country. There is a strong presidency under the former communist leader Gligorov, which acts as a steadying force.

Albania

Although Albania was never part of Yugoslavia the two are linked because the latter has an Albanian minority. Albania also has a Greek minority in the south. It is perhaps the poorest country in Europe. Its population of 3.2 million lives in a small mountainous territory, and it suffered from a repressive and backward looking communist regime until 1990. The ex-communists, organized as the Socialist Party (PSS) managed the transition and won the first parliamentary elections in 1991. The liberal Democratic Party (PDA) won a majority in Parliament in 1992 and formed a coalition government with the Social Democratic Party. The PDA also won the Presidency in direct elections, and reaffirmed its mandate in 1996, although there were claims about electoral irregularities which were, in part, confirmed by international observers in 1996.

The eastern Mediterranean

Although Greeks and Turks have been protagonists in the Balkans, the focus of their rivalry is now in the Mediterranean, particularly Cyprus. The history of their

Table 3.8 General
elections in the Balkans,
1992–96

	% of valid votes	No. of seats
ALBANIA, 26 May and 2 June 1996		
Democratic Party (PDA)	55.5	122
Socialist Party (PSS)	20.4	10
Republican Party (PRS)	na	3
Human Rights' Party (PMDN): Greek	na	3
National Front (BK)	na	2
SERBIA, 19 December 1993		
Socialist Party of Serbia (SPS)	35.1	123
Democratic Movement of Serbia (Demos)		
Serbian Renewal Movement (SPO)	17.4	45
Serbian Radical Party (SRS)	13.7	39
Democratic Party (DS)	12.1	29
Democratic Party of Serbia (DSS)	2.8	7
Union of Vojvodina Hungarians (VMDK)	2.0	5
CROATIA, 29 October 1995		
Croatian Democratic Union (HDZ)	45.2	75
Joint List Bloc (Alliance of Right-Wing and		
Centre-Right Parties)	18.3	18
Croatian Peasant Party (HSS)		
Istrian Democratic Assembly (IDS)		
Croatian National Party (HNS)		
Croatian Christian Democratic Union (HKDU)		
Croatian Party of Slavonia and Baranja (SBHS)		
Croatian Social Liberal Party (HSLS)	11.6	12
Social Democratic Party (SDP)	8.9	10
Croatian Party of Rights (HSP)	5.0	4
MACEDONIA, 16 and 30 October and 13 November 1994		
Alliance of Macedonia (SM)	na	58
Social Democratic Alliance of Macedonia (SDSM)	na	29
Liberal Party (LP)	na	8
Socialist Party of Macedonia (SPM)	na	10
Albanian Party of Democratic Prosperity (PDP)	na	4
National Democratic Party	na	1
Democratic Party of Macedonia (DPM)	na	3
Others	na	7
Independents	na	0
IMRO-DPFME	na	0

disputes replicates many of the features of the Yugoslav conflict, and may well anticipate the way this conflict will be settled.

The Turkish Empire, established in the fifteenth and sixteenth centuries, extended over most of the Muslim Arab lands as well as over the Christian Orthodox Balkans. While the Turks provided military force, Greeks provided many of its administrative personnel. This symbiotic relationship broke down when the core Greek lands established their independence in the late 1820s with foreign help. A continuing goal of Greek foreign policy and diplomacy was then to unite all Greek-speaking lands. Steady progress in this direction was ended with defeat by the Turks on the east coast of Asia Minor in 1922–23. The ensuing massacre and flight of Greeks led to an exchange of population with Turkey. This left Greece with an almost totally Greek-speaking and Orthodox population of approximately 10 million, and only 100,000 Muslims on the border in Greek Thrace.

The modern Turkish state was founded in the core Turkish lands by a modernizing, secular officer class after the collapse of the old empire in the First World War. Based on a repudiation of the old multi-lingual empire it emphasized Turkish nation-

Map 3.10 Eastern Mediterranean (Greece, Turkey, Cyprus)

alism and homogeneity. This was secured by the expulsion and massacre of Greeks and Armenians, and an attempt to assimilate the Kurds on the eastern border of Asia Minor, where they are a majority. The state of near civil war in this area has stained Turkey's human rights record and created difficulties in joining the EU – a move also implacably opposed by the Greeks. But the forced assimilation of Kurds really stands in the tradition of Balkans nationalism and 'ethnic cleansing' of the type seen in the Yugoslav conflict.

Greece

With an homogeneous population secured by previous 'ethnic cleansing' of Turks and Slavs, Greece now has little internal ethnic conflict. Its post-war politics have been dominated by a violent civil war between communists and their opponents. This led to witch-hunts and Army influence over politics even before the establishment of a military dictatorship from 1967–74. Full democracy was restored only after the Army provoked a Turkish invasion of Cyprus. Since then government has alternated between New Democracy (ND), a moderate conservative party, and PASOK, a left-wing socialist party. Between them these parties have modernized the

Greek state and taken the country into the EU, from which it benefits substantially. However, large government deficits cause recurrent financial crises in the economy.

Cyprus

The 700,000-strong population of the large island of Cyprus is 80 per cent Greek and 20 per cent Turkish. As the last Greek-speaking land outside Greece, it has been a focus of Greek efforts to incorporate it even when it was a British colony (1878–1960). A Greek blockade of the island Turks provoked a Turkish invasion in 1974, which forced partition, the northern third of the island being secured for the Turks. The Greek-speaking two-thirds is now the Republic of Cyprus. It has a uni-cameral parliament and a directly elected executive president. After the 1991 election a centre-right government was formed consisting of the Democratic Rally (DISI) and the Liberal Party (DIKO) – which also did well in the 1996 elections.

Turkey

Turkey has a large population of almost 60 million and a strong military force of almost half a million. As the founder of the modern secular state the army occupies a special position as guarantor of the constitution. It took over the government in the early 1960s, again in 1971–74 and in the early 1980s, when it believed that the modern constitution was threatened.

A major problem is that the middle class and the west of the country have been secularized, while the bulk of the population, particularly in the rural areas and the east, remain attached to Islamic traditions. They support an Islamic party, the Justice Party and its successors, which is opposed to the modernizing right-wing Motherland Party and the secularizing republicans. Other left-wing, nationalist, and Kurdish parties complicate the picture and render coalitions necessary. In spite of a strong military-backed president and occasional military pressure for party co-operation, coalition governments have been racked by internal quarrels. The army sees integration into Europe as the way to consolidate Turkish modernization, but extreme nationalism and military intervention in politics impede entry to the EU which will only accept liberal democracies as members.

The elections of late 1995 promised a continuation of the internal and external stalemate (see Table 3.9). The Islamic Welfare Party gained ground while the two right-wing parties were rent by quarrels, which brought down the first coalition government. The second coalition between the true path and welfare parties will probably also be unstable. This contrasts with the increasing predominance of PASOK in strong single-party governments in Greece.

The Trans-Caucasus

The Trans-Caucasus region, located between the Black and Caspian Seas, contains some of the most rugged mountains in the world, and is even more of an ethnic mosaic than the Balkans. Part of the Soviet Union until 1991, the three Trans-Caucasus nations of Armenia (5.5 million), Azerbaijan (7 million), and Georgia (3.5 million) are all members of the CIS, the Russian-dominated grouping of former Soviet Republics. All three are an ethnic mix and have been involved in conflict; Georgia over its Ossetian

	% valid votes	No. of seats
GREECE, 10 October 1993		
Pan–Hellenic Socialist Movement (PASOK)	46.9	170
New Democracy (ND)	39.3	111
Political Spring (POLA)	4.9	10
Communist Party of Greece (KKE)	4.5	9
Others	4.4	0
CYPRUS, 26 May 1996		
AKEL (Communist)	33.0	19
DISI (Conservative Liberal)	34.5	20
DIKO (Conservative Liberal)	16.4	10
EDEX–SK (Socialist)	8.1	5
KED (Free Democrats)	3.7	2
TURKEY, 24 December 1995		
Welfare Party (RP)	21.38	158
True Path Party (DYP)	19.18	135
Motherland Party (ANAP)	19.65	132
Democratic Left Party (DSP)	14.64	75
Republican People's Party (CHP)	10.71	50

minority, and Armenia and Azerbaijan over the Armenian enclave (Nagorny-Karabak) within Azerbaijan. Ethnic hostilities are compounded by religion. Georgia has its own Orthodox Christian church but its minorities are Muslim. Armenia is mostly homogeneous, with its own distinctive Christian church, but also has a small Kurdish minority. Most of the Azerbaijani population is ethnically related to the Turks, speaks a similar language and is Muslim. With large oil reserves it is potentially the richest of the three republics. However, it has suffered Armenian occupation of its western border region.

Wars in the region have interrupted the transition to democracy. In both Azerbaijan and Georgia the first presidents were overthrown in internal fighting involving the military, and conflict continues. Armenia has held elections for its Assembly and directly elected president, but the latter has used conflict to justify wide-ranging executive powers and to ban the Dashnak opposition party.

Russia has used these troubles to re-establish its influence in the region and to force countries into membership of the CIS, if they had not joined already. The situation thus remains unstable, particularly since Russia itself is fighting its own wars in Chechnya just north of the area.

Eastern Europe

Eastern Europe consists mostly of Slav countries speaking languages akin to Russian, although two countries (Romania and Moldova) speak a Romance language similar to Italian. All countries of the area have close links with Russia. They are mostly Orthodox in religion, but there are also strong Uniate churches in Romania and the Ukraine. The Uniates are a group who acknowledge the supremacy of the Pope but are Orthodox in church organization and ritual.

Politically, these countries have had governments dominated by reformed communists since the break-up of the Soviet bloc. These governments were elected, however, in reasonably free and open voting, so they are certainly on the road to democracy. Reforms and liberalization, particularly of markets and the economy, have gone forward more slowly than in Central Europe.

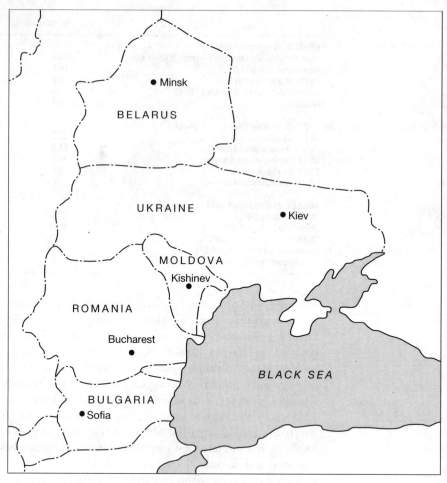

Map 3.11 Eastern Europe (Bulgaria, Romania, Moldova, Ukraine, Belarus)

Most of the countries have also chosen to have a fairly active executive Presidency, again perhaps a relic of the communist period and reflecting a current desire for strong leadership in the face of confusion caused by political and economic change.

Bulgaria

Although Bulgaria (8.5 million population) has never been under direct Russian rule, it has at various times had close relationships with it and was a loyal satellite from 1945–89. Its considerable minorities of Roma and Turks (1 million) were persecuted under the previous regime. Bulgarian communists, although not particularly reformist, saw the way the wind was blowing in the late 1980s and deposed the old-style Stalinist dictator Zhivkov in 1989. They were rewarded with an absolute majority of parliamentary seats in the first free elections of 1990, having changed their name to the Bulgarian Socialist Party (BSP). However, the main opposition alliance, the anticommunist Union of Democratic Forces, obtained the Presidency and retained it in

1996, encouraging coalition governments. The only other significant parties are an agrarian movement, the People's Union, and the Turkish Movement for Rights and Freedom. This has been pivotal in supporting coalitions (sometimes with the BSP) which have tried to tackle the serious economic problems.

Romania

Bulgaria and Romania have a similar post-war experience, except that Romania had a particularly brutal dictator, Ceausescu, who pursued an independent (of the USSR) policy abroad and a Stalinist one at home. At the end of 1989 he suddenly lost support and was captured and shot by his associates, who realized they could only stay in power by repudiating the previous regime. The army also changed sides and repressed the notorious secret police, the Securitate. The communists formed the National Salvation Front (NSF) with prominent non-party figures. This won the presidential and parliamentary elections overwhelmingly under reasonably free conditions but organized quite brutal repression of leading opposition parties, the Liberals, Peasant Party, Social Democrats, Ecologists and Hungarian Democratic Union. The NSF split on how fast to pursue market reform and a new coalition government led by the anti-NSF Democratic Convention was formed in 1996. Romania was the last European country to turn out the ex-communists.

There is a Hungarian minority in the Transylvanian region of Romania (7 per cent of the total population of about 23 million) and a large Roma (Gypsies) population estimated at about a million. Both minorities have been sharply discriminated against.

Moldova

Moldova (population 4.4 million) was a Republic of the Soviet Union which became independent in 1991. It is largely Romanian-speaking, but a large Russian-speaking minority has seceded to form the Trans-Dniestr Republic backed by elements of the Russian army stationed in the locality. The complicated struggle for survival has left power in the hands of nationalist ex-communists but there has been little chance for consolidation of internal democracy in the midst of the continuing struggle.

Ukraine

With a population of 52 million, the Ukraine is one of the largest countries in Europe. Even so it had no history of statehood until it became formally independent of the USSR in 1991. This was opposed by a substantial Russian minority in the Crimea.

Outside the Crimea the main political cleavage is between the east and the west of the country. The west was part of Poland in the inter-war period, its first language is Ukrainian, and it is mainly rural. The east is Russian-speaking, and has the large Donbas industrial complex. There is also a religious cleavage: the west is more Uniate; the east more Orthodox. Consequently, the east has closer ties with Russia, and the west is more nationalist.

The first president, the former Communist First Secretary, gained Western support for his nationalist line, but electoral defeat in 1994 brought in a rival with eastern support, and a more conciliatory policy towards Russia. Both presidents supported economic reform which may, in time, improve the awful economic situation.

Political parties are not well developed in the Ukraine, and have no real grassroots organization. This makes the media – above all TV – overwhelmingly important. The old Communist Party retains its organization, however, which gives it a great advantage and allows it to dominate parliament. Nevertheless, the president is largely independent of parliament, and in a battle with it in 1995 the president won increased powers.

The Ukraine has very rich agricultural land. It also has an international bargaining counter in the shape of nuclear weapons left by the USSR. It has agreed to return these to Russia in return for foreign aid. It has also reached agreement on a division of the armed forces and navy with Russia. At the heart of the Ukrainian problem is the fact that it existed until 1991 only within the Russian state. What and who is Ukrainian remains obscure. Anything less like the classic state, with historically defined and defensible borders, a sense of nationhood, and central control of its territory, is hard to imagine, yet Belarus may be just such a case!

Belarus

Belarus (or Byelorussia, population estimated at 10.3 million), has existed only as a province of other countries since the fourteenth century, most recently as part of the Soviet Union. It seems, in fact, to have fallen back under Russian influence as a member of the CIS. Starting with a parliament dominated by former communists, it adopted a presidential constitution in 1994 which gives the president sweeping powers. In May 1995 the ex-communist president was defeated by a pro-market, pro-Russian challenger. There are a number of parties but they lack organization and support: this is where the communists have the advantage. There is an agrarian peasants' party and a Green party, spurred on by the poisonous remains of the Chernobyl nuclear disaster whose seeping radioactivity has not been properly contained.

All the countries of Eastern Europe have had elections since independence. These have changed governments and imposed a different policy direction on the country. To this extent democracy can be seen as working remarkably well in these countries near the centre of the old communist power bloc. Table 3.10 gives the voting figures. From these it is clear that the further east one goes, the less parties have consolidated themselves.

The Russian Federation

The Russian Federation (Russia) has the same borders and population as the old Russian Soviet Federative Socialist Republic which, in turn, was the dominant Republic of the Union of Soviet Socialist Republics (USSR). Indeed, the Russian Federation is internationally recognized as the successor of the USSR. Its population of 150 million covers an area of 6.5 million square miles, which makes the Federation the largest country in the world. Moreover, as the central power of the Commonwealth of Independent States, formed by most former Soviet Republics in 1991 (see p.18), Russia maintains a wide sphere of influence. Its inheritance of most of the old Soviet military machine and nuclear arsenal makes it a world super

Table 3.10 General
elections in Eastern
Europe,1992–96

	% valid votes	No. of seats
BULGARIA, 18 December 1994		
Bulgarian Socialist Party (BSP)	43.5	125
Union of Democratic Forces (SDS)	24.2	69
People's Union/Bulgarian National Agrarian	6.5	18
Union/Democratic Party		
Movement for Rights and Freedoms (DPS)	5.4	15
Bulgarian Business Bloc (BBB)	4.7	13
Others	14.5	0
ROMANIA, 3 November 1996		
Democratic Convention of Romania	30.2	53
Social Democrats	21.5	41
Social Democratic Union	12.9	23
Hungarian Democratic Federation (UDMR)	6.6	11
Greater Romanian Party	4.5	8
Party of National Unity	4.4	7
MOLDOVA, 27 February 1994		
Agrarian Democratic Party, pro-independence		
(favouring co-operation within CIS)	43.2	56
Socialist Party and Yedinstvo/Unity Movement Bloc		
(favouring closer ties with Russia)	22.0	28
Peasants and intellectuals Bloc (pro-Romania)	9.2	11
Christian Democratic People's Front (pro-Romania)	7.5	9
UKRAINE, March–April 1994		
Left		
Communist Party (KPU)	12.72	90
Socialist Party (SPU)	3.09	15
Agrarian Party (SelPU)	2.74	19
Centre		
Party of Democratic Renewal (PDVU)	0.83	4
Social Democratic Party (SDPU)	0.36	2
Labour Party (PPU)	0.40	4
Civic Congress (HKU)		2
National Democrats		
Rukh (NRU)	5.15	20
Republican Party (URP)	2.52	11
Democratic Party (DemPU)	1.08	2
Christian Democratic Party (KhDPU)	0.35	0
Far Right		
Congress of Ukrainian Nationalists (KUN)	1.25	5
Conservative Republican Party (UKRP)	0.34	2
National Assembly (UNA-UNSO)	0.51	1
BELARUS, 14 and 28 May, 29 November and		
10 December 1995		
Party of Communists of Belarus (PCB)	na	42
Agrarian Party of Belarus (AP)	na	33
Party of Popular Accord (PPA)	na	8
United Civic Party (UCP) Liberal	na	7
Social Democratic Hramada (SDH)	na	2
Party for All Belarussian Unity and Accord (PABUA)	na	2
Belarussian Patriotic Movement (BPM)	na	1
Belarussian Party of Greens	na	1
Republican Party of Labour and Justice (RPLJ)	na	1
Belarussian Farmers' Party (BFP): Agrarian	na	1
Belarussian People's Party (BPP)	na	1
Belarussian Social Sport Party (BSSP)	na	1
Belarussian Ecological Party: Green	na	1
Belarussian Popular Front (BPF): Centrist	na	1
Independents	na	95
Vacant	na	62

Note: Independent candidates took 66.5 per cent of votes and 227 seats
Source: Calculated from the 'Vybory-1994' database constructed by the Petro Mohyla Scientific
Society of Kyiv. For the sake of consistency and comparability, figures were calculated on the basis
of vote and seat percentages for the March–April electoral rounds only.

power, though now distinctly weaker than the United States. Stretching 3,000 miles from the Baltic to the Pacific, and with immense natural resources, it is larger and potentially more powerful than any other European state. It is weakened by a defective economic base and distribution system, which wastes even the sub-optimal harvests produced by collective farms. Its outmoded heavy industry is uncompetitive without state subsidies, and is declining rapidly as the economy is privatized.

Privatization has been unplanned and disorganized, so the new business is controlled by *apparatchicks* (bureaucrats) of the old system. The collapse of the old political and administrative structures, and the dismantling of the command economy, has also produced organized crime on a vast scale, which has now spread beyond Russian borders and into Western Europe. In spite of dire effects on ordinary people, privatization of the economy proceeds and is unlikely to be reversed.

However, presidential and parliamentary elections have been held without too much political corruption. The first president of the Russian Federation, Boris Yeltsin, was elected in 1991 when the Federation was still part of the USSR. Yeltsin precipitated the break-up of the Soviet Union by refusing to recognize its authority, taking over its military, economic, and media organizations, and banning the Russian Communist Party (later re-legalized). His position was strengthened by the failure of an attempted coup in 1991.

Yeltsin then appointed himself head of the new Council of Ministers and set about radically reforming the government, the media and the economy. This brought him into direct conflict with Russian parliament. His refusal to organize an effective party to support his position meant that the parliament was dominated by two groups of opponents – old-style communists and a Liberal Democratic Party which was, in fact, right-wing and xenophobic. With ambiguous popular support in referendums and wide powers under the constitution, Yeltsin was able to maintain power, while edging parliament out of the limelight. Economic reform slowed in response to votes for protest parties, but it did not stop. Russia also took a stronger line in foreign affairs.

To a considerable extent Yeltsin's strength, in spite of sometimes erratic behaviour, is that the alternatives to himself are unappealing. The lack of any other strong party with grass-roots organization gives the old communist apparatus a great advantage electorally. However, attempts by Yeltsin supporters (before the elections of 1995 and 1996) to organize a party, 'Russia is my Home', had only modest success: It was proposed to use the state electricity company as its base because the prime minister had previously been chairman! (Though one must not forget that Berlusconi successfully organized Forza Italia in Italy round his TV companies.) The idea of a 'government party' based on state agencies is common in the localities of Russia, in the absence of any other organization (see Chapters 12 and 13). The presidents of the sixteen Autonomous Republics inside Russia have also secured office in this way. With these alliances, Yeltsin beat off a strong challenge from the communist candidate in the presidential elections of June 1996 to secure a second term of office. Results are shown in Table 3.11 for both the presidential and earlier legislative elections.

According to the census of 1989, 83 per cent of the inhabitants of Russia are Russian by descent and language, so the country is more homogeneous than many others in Europe. However, in the past the Russians conquered and assimilated many other

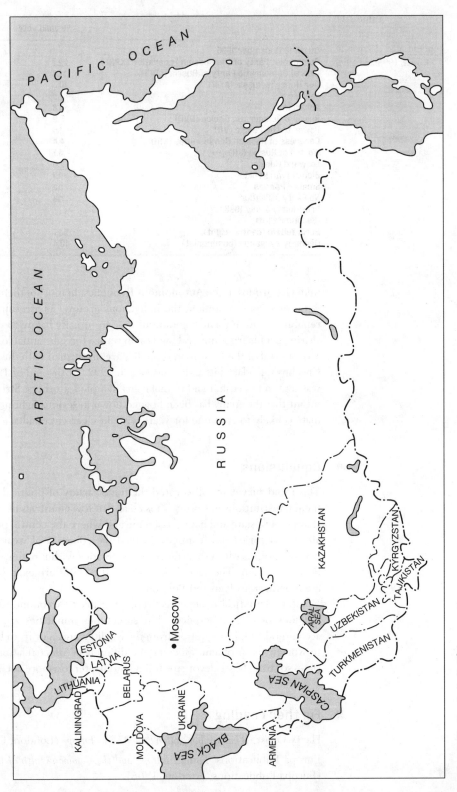

Map 3.12   Russia (to Pacific)

	% valid votes	No. of seats
DUMA 16 December 1995		
Communist Party of the Russian Federation (KPRF)	22.7	157
Liberal Democratic Party of Russia (LDPR)	11.4	51
Our House is Russia (NDR)	10.3	55
Yabloko	7.0	45
Agrarian	3.8	20
Russia's Democratic Choice (DVR)	3.9	9
Power to the People (VR)	1.6	9
Congress of Russian Communities (KRO)	4.4	5
Women of Russia (JR)	4.7	3
Forward Russia	2.0	3
Bloc of Ivan Rybkin	1.1	3
Smaller Parties	na	13
No Party Affiliation	na	77
Presidency 3 July 1996		
(Second Ballot)		
Boris Yeltsin (centre–right)	53.7	na
Gennady Zyuganov (communist)	40.4	na

minority groups in the Autonomous Republics. In most of them, Russians now mingle with, or even outnumber, the indigenous groups. As a result, the presidents of the republics – often former communists – are usually happy to do deals with Moscow, sharing profits from minerals and oil in return for substantial local autonomy (Chapter 13). Several of the Caucasian republics are dissatisfied with this arrangement and one, Chechnya, declared its independence in 1992. At the end of 1994, the Russian Army was sent in to crush it and to make an example for others. Strong Chechen resistance meant that the Army has been bogged down in serious fighting ever since. This stalemate is likely to continue for years without clear-cut results.

■ Conclusions

This rapid survey has illustrated the huge variety of political practices and governmental institutions in Europe. It is clear that few countries fit the classic model of the state, where state and nation coincide and where the central power is able to control all its territories and frontiers. Instead the cohesion of weak states with contested constitutions is often threatened by minorities within national boundaries or which flow over them. The successor states of the USSR are examples of this, but so also are Northern Ireland and Belgium.

Internal political arrangements are often able to accommodate ethnic minorities, or religious or class differences. But sometimes minorities are repressed rather than accommodated. Immigration from the Mediterranean or from Eastern Europe is likely to worsen the problem. Since ethnic differences affect relations within and between states so strongly, we devote the following chapter to a more detailed discussion of them.

■ Further reading

Harry Drost, *What's What and Who's Who in Europe* (London, Cassell, 1995).

Europa Publications, *Eastern Europe and the Commonwealth of Independent States 1994* (Europa Publications, London, 1966).

Europa Publications, *Western Europe, 1996* (London, Europa Publications, 1996).

Michael Gallagher, M.J. Laver and P. Mair, *Representative Government in Western Europe* (New York, McGraw-Hill, 1992, 1996).

International Institute for Democracy, *The Rebirth of Democracy: 12 Constitutions of Central and Eastern Europe* (Strasbourg, Council of Europe Press, 1995).

Jan-Erik Lane and Svante Ersson, *Politics and Society in Western Europe,* 3rd edn (London, Sage, 1994).

Jan-Erik Lane, David McKay and Kenneth Newton (eds), *Political Data Handbook*, 2nd edn (Oxford, Oxford University Press, 1997).

Gordon Smith, *Politics in Western Europe* (London, Gower, 1989).

Jonathan Story (ed.), *The New Europe: Politics, Government and Economy since 1945* (Blackwell, Oxford, 1993).

Stephen White, Alex Pravda and Zvi Gitelman (eds), *Developments in East European Politics* (London, Macmillan, 1993).

Chapter 4

States, territories and ethnonationalism Variations on one, or two, themes?

Nationalism west and east

There is an idea that nationalism should not exist in a fully modernized political system. Modernization should eradicate territorial and nationalist politics within and between states. Political boundaries should become geographically viable. Regimes should govern homogenized populations which, through ongoing processes of cultural socialization, increasingly identify with and endorse the legitimacy of the state in which they find themselves. The implication, in short, is that modernization should herald the coming of age of the nation-state. Such assumptions reflect long-standing historical beliefs. The interrelated concepts of state and nation have become increasingly blurred ever since the French Revolution. By the early twentieth century they had become virtually synonymous.

Western Europe was widely regarded as having attained this symbiosis. At the end of the First World War therefore the Western victors restructured the old Central and Eastern European empires in their own perceived image, as close as possible to single-nation states. They hoped by doing so to unify the continent in a mix of democracy, sovereignty and national self-determination which would provide a panacea for all of Europe's ills.

BRIEFING **4.1**

The First World War settlement in Europe

The First World War (1914–18) was fought primarily by Britain, France, Russia and the United States (which joined in 1917) against the German and Austro-Hungarian Empires. The Treaties of Versailles, and St Germain (1919–22) recreated Poland and carved Austria, Hungary, Czechoslovakia and much of Yugoslavia and Romania out of the defeated Empires. The idea was to create nation-states. However, this was watered down by considerations of economic and military viability. Hence, only the defeated successor states – Austria and Hungary – of the Austro-Hungarian Empire were internally homogeneous. Even they had ethnic links over their borders: Austria with Germany and Hungary with 2 million co-nationals scattered over the neighbouring countries. Czechs and Slovaks were put together in Czechoslovakia with the Czechs dominating the country. Slovenes, Croats, Serbs and Muslims were put together in Yugoslavia. These are the major multi-ethnic states that split up after 1990, along with the Soviet Union, which was outside the First World War settlement.

BRIEFING **4.2**

League of Nations – United Nations

The First World War (1914–18) through fighting, famine and disease, killed around 20 million people, mostly in Europe. To help avoid conflict in the future the victors hoped to create a world body which would bring nation-states together and help them resolve disputes peacefully. This was the League of Nations. The League held regular Assemblies but became increasingly ineffective as national conflicts intensified in the 1930s. It was also weakened by the fact that the US and USSR were never members. It did, however, do useful work through its specialized organizations, particularly for refugees, in the 1920s and was associated with bodies like the *International Labour Organization (ILO)*, which tried to get world agreement on working conditions.

Such bodies were inherited by the League's successor organization the *United Nations*, set up in 1946 after the Second World War (1939–45). This tried to avoid the weaknesses of the League by having, besides a General Assembly in which all States had a vote, a Security Council of major powers – USA, USSR (now Russia), China, Britain and France. Each of these can veto UN action, but if they agree they control forces which other states cannot resist. The UN has proved a useful umbrella in cases where law and order has broken down and/or where disputed borders require policing. The intervention in Bosnia was a mixture of both. It was relatively ineffective in stopping fighting, however, because UN member states often disagree on objectives and are reluctant to pay for costs.

Like the League of Nations, the UN does much useful work through specialized agencies for refugees, education, children, health and also tries to get international agreements on the environment. The Secretary-General appointed by the Assembly has become a world figure but as a result is often controversial and opposed by one or other of the superpowers. The activity of the UN marks another breakdown in the traditional view of the state as a sovereign entity controlling everything that happens within its own borders.

Ironically, but also realistically – since any impartial assessment of what Europe looked like on the ground would have demonstrated the fallacy of the simplified nation-state perspective – the planners of the new Europe admitted the existence of problems with minority nationalities. A Minorities Treaty was incorporated within the covenant of the League of Nations. However, Western states were deemed not to have a minorities problem and so were exempt from the Treaty's provisions!

Such a distinction between East and West was reflected in the views of several historians who proposed a distinctive fracture line in Europe. To the west, nationalism emerged as part of the struggle for democracy and incorporated views on the rights of individual citizens. To the east, one had a cultural nationalism manufactured out of a mythological past, which stressed the collectivity of the nation. The distinction, typified almost in terms of citizenship (the state as nation) versus *Volk* (the nation as state), has been rightly criticized for being unduly simple. Yet, as twentieth-century experiences have indicated, there is perhaps a grain of truth in it.

What is certain is that after 1918 all European regimes behaved as if they were nation-states, a practice left largely unshaken by the Second World War. Previous boundaries were, wherever possible, restored in 1945. The exceptions – for instance, the contraction of Germany or the wholesale relocation of Poland – could be explained by special, non-repeatable circumstances. They were not, after all, the consequence of *internal* conflicts between nationalities. After 1945, all regimes – liberal democratic or communist – continued to see themselves as custodians of nation-state populations fused together in a common identity and allegiance.

These assumptions were challenged in Western Europe after 1960 with the emergence in several countries of minority nationalist activity. In Eastern Europe the challenge had to wait upon the collapse of communist repression. The fragmentation of Yugoslavia and the USSR and the more civilized divorce in 1993 between Czech and Slovak merely underlined the potentially disruptive power of nationalism. An equally significant reminder has been the upsurge in the 1990s of extreme right-wing 'state nationalism' across the continent, from Russia to Belgium and from Sweden to Italy. Fears of heightened immigration flows (see Chapter 17) and confusion and concern about the effects of the European Union on state sovereignty, also suggest that nationalism, in one variety or another, could well be a major item on the political agenda as Europe moves into the twenty-first century.

Nationalism and nations

'An integrated general theory of the politics of nationalism and ethnicity must be the aim of all students of the subject' (Kellas 1991: 159). But the literature on the two associated yet conceptually distinctive terms is a definitional minefield. Kellas (1991: 2–5) defines a nation as 'a group of people who feel themselves to be a community bound together by ties of history, culture and common ancestry'. He also suggests that nations possess both 'objective' characteristics such as a territory, language, religion or common descent *and* 'subjective' characteristics – essentially a people's awareness of its community and affection for it. Ethnicity he regards as a narrower concept, restricting it to groups of people who 'share certain inborn attributes'.

The distinction is artificial unless we assume that ethnic groups lack subjective characteristics. But the definition of a nation does form a starting point. However, what is stressed here is the collectiveness of community, some kind of common awareness or identity rooted in shared cultural and psychological characteristics. In the famous phrase of Renan (1970), identity and commitment are expressed through a continuous daily plebiscite, a constant reaffirmation of belonging to the community through the totality of individual daily routines. Using a similar criterion for nation, and proposing that a nation-state exists only when all members of a particular nation are to be found as an overwhelming majority in only one state, Nielssen (1992) demonstrated the limited presence of such states anywhere in the world. Very few European countries meet the criteria for a nation-state in this sense.

We need, however, to go further than the notion of community: a nation invariably has a territorial aspect. Possession, according to the proverb, is nine points of the law. In groups which can be regarded as nations, identity with community is linked with and reinforced by identity with place. It is place in which lives are lived, interests defined, and information received and interpreted within a framework of routine social interactions.

Even so, to define nations in terms of identity with community and territory is not to assume that they will behave as political actors. 'Nation' per se is not necessarily a political concept. 'Nationalism', however, is an ideology that includes 'a cultural doctrine of nations and the national will' (Smith 1991: 72–82) which are rooted in ethnic and genealogical justifications. In turn, the ideology generates 'a social and political movement to achieve the goals of the nation and realize its national will'.

To cover all significant aspects of nationalism in the contemporary world would be beyond the scope of a single chapter. The focus here will be on peripheral or minority nationalism, an ethnoterritorial phenomenon which finds its political expression within only part of the population and territory of an existing state. Its political objectives of greater autonomy for that population and territory (up to and including secession) challenge the legitimacy of that state. They entail a change – greater or lesser – in the style and structure of the management of its territory.

Only a small number of ethnonational groups have undergone any kind of meaningful politicization. In Western Europe they are present but limited. A similar point can be made about the more complex ethnic patterns in the Centre and East. Despite the gloomy predictions of 1990, fears about the disruptive effect of nationalist conflicts have not been realized everywhere within the ex-Soviet bloc (Table 4.1). While there may be problems and tensions, political opposition to the existing state has not been an automatic consequence of these.

The significance of the immediate geopolitical context is apparent as soon as individual cases of ethnonational conflict are checked against lists of identifiable national minorities. That context, further, is heavily influenced by history. For example, commentaries upon many Eastern European disputes have observed that the present is a faithful re-run of the pre-1940 situation. This does not seem to have been expected. The point is well summed up by the laconic comment of Newhouse (*The New Yorker*, 24 August 1992): 'so thoroughly did half a century of the Cold War obscure the past that all sides were surprised to see the Balkans behaving like the Balkans'. Newhouse's comment underlines the wider point. Europe, at least in terms of state and nation, is a prisoner of its history. But eyebrows were still raised when that history reasserted itself after 1960 in the West and after 1989 in the East.

Ethnonational scenarios: east–west contrasts

It is trite but true that after the freeze imposed by communism, nationalism in one form or another manifested itself everywhere in Eastern Europe, from Czechoslovakia to the Ukraine, from Estonia to Bosnia. By contrast, in Western Europe ethnoterritorial nationalism has been more contained. Either it has been accommodated by concessions like political devolution and regionalism (see Chapter 13) or accepts the need to work through the party system (Chapter 9) or interest-groups (Chapter 7). In these ways it has become just another ingredient in the political fabric of democratic pluralism not a dangerous threat to the territorial integrity of the state. What are the reasons for this contrast? We shall discuss these here before reviewing patterns of territorial management by the European states and the lessons that can be drawn from these. Several reasons can be advanced for the East–West contrast.

There is, first, the sheer age of the state in question. Eastern Europe is a region of young states, carved originally out of the post-1918 debris of empire. Communism and the hegemony of the Soviet Union prevented states working out their own destinies in significant ways. Few states were fully sovereign entities before 1989. Inevitably, all have been concerned to mobilize facts, arguments and myths to

BRIEFING **4.3**

Democratic pluralism

This is the idea that all societies contain different and often competing political groups and ideologies, which are equally legitimate if they abstain from violence. In this context politics is seen as a struggle by groups and sections to get what they want, usually by forming their own political parties, social movements and interest groups. From this perspective it is as legitimate for ethnic groups to form parties and get concessions as it is for economic interests to do so. See Chapters 7–9 below for the ways in which these ideas get institutionalized in Europe.

demonstrate their national historical pedigree and to assert their legitimate territorial status. Indeed, two new states – Belarus and Ukraine – have almost had to invent a history for the first time. This entirely natural process of justification and consolidation, which much of Western Europe went through a long time ago but which has been imperfectly understood in many Western circles, is simply part of growing up. As Ash (1989: 242) noted, 'the lack of normal access to the national past was a form of deprivation; the recovery of it a form of emancipation'.

Nevertheless, nationalist rethinking by the new states can be a political problem because of the non-congruence between ethnonational group and territory, an imbalance which creates problems for the mutual recognition of boundaries between neighbouring states. In the Balkans there is a nexus of debatable territorial and border issues between Albania, Bulgaria, Greece, Macedonia and Serbia, let alone the quagmire of Bosnia, Croatia and Serbia. Moldova sits uneasily between Romania and Russia. The Crimea is a bone of contention between Russia and the Ukraine, while the three Baltic states look uneasily towards their giant neighbour to the east. There are also boundary questions pending between Hungary and the neighbouring states of Romania and Slovakia. Ironically, Poland, whose boundaries historically have been both permeable and mobile, is one of the few Eastern states that can look with equanimity at its boundaries.

By contrast, the borders between Western European states have been enshrined as enduring mutually accepted features and become almost irrelevant. It is inconceivable that two states would move to a military confrontation over disputed boundaries. The one outstanding instance of contention is Northern Ireland. This is, however, a case where the two states concerned, Ireland and the United Kingdom, have increasingly involved themselves in mutual discussions as the only way out of the dilemma. Equally, the involvement of Austria in the status of the German speakers in the Alto Adige (South Tyrol) after 1946 was restricted to diplomacy and persuasion.

On the other hand, the various collaborative arrangements of Western states after 1945, from the Organization for European Economic Co-operation and the Council of Europe to the European Union and the European Economic Area, have, along with mass affluence and tourism, developed communication networks and cross-national production and consumption patterns, made boundaries little more than lines on a map. Ethnonationalism in the West no longer feeds upon disputed borders. In the East it may still do so if touched off by circumstances.

Those circumstances relate in the first instance to the territorial distribution of

Table 4.1 Territorial characteristics of ethnic minorities in Europe

Country	Minority	Interface	Enclave	Mosaic	Diaspora	Violent conflict
Finland Finland	Swedes				✓	No
Norway Sweden	Sami (Lapps)			✓		No
Estonia Latvia Lithuania	Russians				✓	No
Lithuania	Poles				✓	No
Denmark	Faroese	✓				No
	Germans				✓	No
Netherlands	Frisians	✓				No
Belgium	Flemings	✓				No
	Walloons	✓		(Brussels)		No
Luxembourg	Italians				✓	No
United Kingdom	Scots	✓				No
	Welsh	✓				No
	Irish			✓		Yes
	West Indian				✓	No
	Indian–Pakistani				✓	No
France	Corsicans	✓				Yes
	Alsatians	✓				No
	Algerians				✓	No
Spain	Catalans	✓				No
	Calicians	✓				No
	Basques	✓				Yes
Italy	Tyrolese			✓		Yes
	Savoyards	✓				No
	Sards	✓				No
	Venetians	✓				No
	Lombards	✓				No
	Ligurians	✓				No
	Friulians	✓				No
	Sicilians	✓				No
Greece	Muslims	✓				No
	Slavs				✓	No
Turkey	Kurds	✓				Yes
Macedonia	Albanians				✓	No
	Turks			✓		No
	Roma				✓	No
	Serbs	✓				No
Bulgaria	Turks				✓	Yes
Serbia	Hungarians				✓	No
	Muslims			✓		No
	Albanians				✓	Yes
	Montenegrans	✓				No
Albania	Greeks	✓			✓	No
Bosnia	Serbs				✓	Yes
	Croats				✓	Yes
	Muslims			✓		Yes
Switzerland	French				✓	No
	Italian				✓	No
	Romansch			✓		No
Germany	Bavarians	✓				No
	Turks				✓	No
	Sorbs		✓			No
Slovakia	Hungarians				✓	No
Hungary	Roma (Gypsy)			✓		No
Romania	Hungarians		✓			No
	Roma				✓	No
Moldova	Russians				✓	Yes
Ukraine	Russians				✓	No
	Tatars			✓		No
Russia	Tatars			✓		No
	Caucasian	✓				Yes

Table 4.1 (continued)

Country	Minority	Interface	Enclave	Mosaic	Diaspora	Violent conflict
	minorities (Chechen and others)					
	Siberian minorities (Yakhut Bakhtian and others)	✓	1			No

ethnonational populations and the style – or absence – of consensual politics. It will be useful to begin with a crude classification of different kinds of ethnonational situations. We can talk of an *interface* situation where two distinct groups are concentrated in territories between which it is possible to construct a frontier. The ease with which a separating line can be drawn depends upon the ethnonational distribution. It is a situation which more easily lends itself to decentralization or even separation as solutions to potential conflict. The clearest example was Czechoslovakia, but Western ones might be Belgium and Switzerland.

An *enclave* situation occurs when an ethnonational group, dominant in its own territory, is surrounded by a more numerous and different population. Several localized examples of enclaves existed, for instance, in Bosnia. But the most prominent European example is the Hungarian minority in Transylvania, a region lying almost at the heart of Romania. In Western Europe enclaves have been victims of historical assimilation and survive in very diluted instances such as the Romansch-speaking population in Switzerland. Enclaves can have a great potential for disruption, as illustrated by the conflict between Armenia and Azerbaijan since the late 1980s over Nagorno-Karabakh.

A *mosaic* occurs where two or more ethnonational groups are so intermingled across a territory that it is impossible to identify either interface or enclave boundaries. The most obvious mosaics exist in the Balkans, tragically so in Bosnia. Mosaic scenarios are inherently difficult to resolve when conflicts arise.

The final type of ethnonational ecology may be called the *diaspora*, the dispersion of people who are members of one ethnonational group from a state of their own to another, usually neighbouring, independent state. Diasporas can be found throughout Europe, albeit mainly in the East where many current enclave and mosaic situations are the legacy of earlier diasporas. In the Europe of the 1990s, however, the best examples are the large Russian populations in the 'Near Abroad', notably in Estonia, Latvia and the Ukraine. Other examples are Jews and Roma, and immigrant populations in Western states, which are increasing rapidly (see Chapter 17).

Examples of the four scenarios are more readily identifiable in Eastern Europe. The enclave is generally absent from Western Europe, where in addition, only Northern Ireland, Brussels, the South Tyrol and the Basque provinces of Spain come close to the mosaic scenario. From these perspectives Western Europe *is* closer to the nation-state construct. Table 4.1 maps the distribution of the principal minority ethnic groups under these four categories across Europe, noting also the presence or absence of violence in relationships with the majority.

By itself the presence of an ethnic minority is not necessarily disruptive. What can make it so, is the interrelationship with other factors. First among these is the question of frontiers. The ethnic scenarios derive from and feed upon the maturity of the state. Just as the borders of new states, because of their relative youth, may agitate ethnonational groups within and outside any one particular state, so ethnic ecology may call into question the inviolability of existing boundaries.

In addition, there is a stronger relationship between language and religion in Eastern Europe. Theories of modernization have stressed the integral role played by secularization. In Western Europe, with the possible exception of Ireland, secularization is a long-established process. The consequence is that church and state have *de facto* been separate for some considerable time. In ethnoterritorial contexts, therefore, language and religion do not interact with each other to reinforce distinctive and hostile identities. Admittedly, the linguistic cleavage in Belgium reflects in part a distinction between a more devout Flanders and a more secular Wallonia. But this is a far cry from mutually reinforcing stigmata and/or an evangelical crusade. The Belgian context is similar to others in Western Europe such as Northern Ireland, the Basque provinces or the Alto Adige. In the West either language or religious differences may buttress ethnonational identity, but rarely both.

By contrast, ethnonational sentiment in Eastern Europe is linked not only with language but also with religious loyalty. Throughout much of Eastern Europe, communist domination, because of its denial of religion and denunciation of nationalism, reinforced the link between the two. Poland is probably the best known example of the symbiosis between nationalism and religion. But from the Baltic to the Balkans and the Black Sea there has been a tradition, reinforced under communism and re-emerging after 1989, of nationalism being sustained, nourished, protected and defended by religion. The contemporary slogan to be found in Ukraine is indicative: 'an independent Church is the foundation of an independent nation'. In a region where ethnic scenarios abound, it means that ethnonational minorities may feel themselves doubly damned in an 'alien' state.

While this kind of attachment could be found in Western Europe in the past, it is no longer prevalent or significant. Indeed, in some Western countries – Italy, for example – national state unity was forged despite, or even in opposition to, the church. Eastern Europe may eventually follow the West down the secular path but in the shorter term the mutually reinforcing role of language and religion contributes powerfully to ethnonational conflict.

Two further points must be taken into account. The first is that in Eastern Europe a country's immediate neighbours are likely to follow a different religion. It is a world where Catholic, Protestant, Muslim, Uniate and Orthodox intermingle or face each other in a variety of linguistic contexts within and between states. Second, ethnonational minorities in Eastern Europe tend to share their identity, language and religion, and hence also their desires and aspirations, with the dominant population of a neighbouring state. Serbs are to be found throughout ex-Yugoslavia, Hungarians in Vojvodina, Transylvania and Slovakia, Albanians in Kosovo and Macedonia, Turks in Bulgaria, Russians in Estonia, Latvia, Moldova and Ukraine. At the extreme, the patchwork in the Balkans is such that the area represents one single problem. It means that a neighbouring state is obliged to concern itself with the condition of its external brethren. As the Albanian government has asserted, 'it was not the Albanians who divided themselves'. In such circumstances the odds on irredentist politics and ethnonational conflict become substantially higher.

Very few ethnoterritorial minorities in the West identify with a neighbouring state even when there is, for instance, a shared language or common cultural roots.

What seems to be lacking, most strikingly so in Switzerland, is the crucial sharing of a cross-national identity. Hence while a minority may be unhappy with its lot, there is little pressure for the transference of territory to another state. This may not make the resolution of an ethnonational dispute any easier, but it does reduce the complexity of the problem. Equally, Western states do not usually espouse the cause of a minority elsewhere. Hence, throughout the slow drift towards federalism in Belgium that was finally completed in 1993, neither France nor the Netherlands played a role in the issue or identified with either of the groups across the border with which they shared their language. Similarly, Austria and Sweden, while concerned about equity for their linguistic fellows in, respectively, Italy and Finland, have refrained from overt interference and have rejected irredentism. In the most obvious possible exception to this Western picture, Northern Ireland, Irish governments since the 1985 Anglo-Irish Agreement have become partners in seeking a resolution to the province's problems, with rhetoric about reunification substantially reduced.

There is therefore no single or simple explanation of an East–West contrast. Each part of the continent has been forged in its ethnonational landscapes by their history, culture and politics. One should therefore expect different styles to emerge. In the context of national minorities, the fact that groups may be clearly linked to other states necessarily changes the nature of the game. It ensures that where inter-communal tensions arise, they have not been regarded as a matter of purely domestic politics. Where internal conflicts become international issues, resolution becomes more difficult. Because the minority believes it has or should have an external guarantor, political stances become more dogmatic and aggressive.

A major factor that has contributed to contrasts is democratic political education, socialization and experience. Few countries in Central-Eastern Europe have ever been democratic. Before the Second World War only Czechoslovakia survived as a democracy until its submission to Germany in 1938. The democratic regimes in the remainder of the region had more dubious credentials. All were in any case overthrown by internal rebellion or *coup d'état*, with Bulgaria and Lithuania leading the way in the early 1920s. Moreover, they were all, in their democratic phase, extreme multi-party systems with at least two distinctive features. There were a large number of transitory movements linked to personalities and even family dynasties. Second, ethnonationalist politics were highly visible. Throughout the Balkans, minority nationalist parties were strong. In the most extreme instance, Yugoslavia, they constituted almost the totality of the party system. Further north, as in Czechoslovakia, the party system was made up of ethnonational party systems. Many of the post-1989 democracies resurrected both these characteristics. We should not reject the professions of determination to establish democracy. But the fact remains that apart from Czechoslovakia not only was there no experience of democratic practices, but also little tradition of democracy among either leaders or masses. In terms of democratic development, much of Eastern Europe is more or less where it was in the 1920s. To expect Western standards to apply to the expression and resolution of ethnonational problems may be misguided and simplistic.

It has been argued that zero-sum conflicts and oppositions are more likely when cultural issues loom large on the agenda. Some cultural issues can be resolved by a liberal use of money, as Belgium attempted to do in the 1960s. The Eastern European economies, however, are too weak and poor for economic largesse to be a possible option. It is easier to blame the other side and take out grievances on the foreigner.

Empathy is in relatively short supply. While surveys in Western Europe have tended to confirm that national stereotypes are formed by one group about another, they have also demonstrated a reciprocal degree of acceptance among national populations, a consequence of the post-1945 socio-economic and political developments that have shrunk Western Europe.

By contrast, the degree of distrust of one's neighbours in Eastern Europe after 1989 has been high (see Eurobarometer, December 1990, A-47). The degree of distrust is a reflection of the collective memory of each ethnonational group, where the them-us dichotomy is all too often enshrined in a testament of saints and demonology. Memories of massacres, genocide, deportation and oppression have created a folklore where the villain is always a neighbour. The fact that close relatives of the neighbours tend to live on your doorstep or even in your house can intensify the problem. A spokesman for the Hungarian Democratic Forum, after the party won the 1990 election, could define the country's minorities as 'strangers'.

Given the right kind of circumstances this situation has been a fertile breeding ground for nationalist sentiment. It leads, as we have said, to a black and white view of the world and no compromise with an opponent who is defined as an enemy. Where this produces discrimination, real or perceived, against an ethnonational minority, there almost automatically follows an appeal to and a protest by the external blood brother. Russia has complained about the treatment of Russians in Estonia and Latvia, Hungary about Romania's treatment of the Hungarian minority, and so on.

Even before 1940, most Western countries were more democratic, more oriented towards constitutional practices, the notion of bargaining and compromise, and a view of politics as swings and roundabouts. Post-1945, developments have simply consolidated this. It is the lack of a democratic tradition, or more precisely of the democratic and bargaining practices that emerge from the existence and acceptance of a pluralist society, that distinguishes East from West.

All ethnonational movements tend to be broad churches. Within them can be found widely divergent views on tactics and strategies, and sometimes even on ultimate objectives. Apart from a common bond of identification with group and territory there is often little in the way of a common element across and within the several manifestations of minority nationalism. In Western Europe these internal differences became more pronounced in the 1980s. Differences between pragmatists and purists have been fostered by relative success in gaining concessions and objectives, for example, in the Basque provinces, both within the Basque Nationalist Party (PNV) and between it and other Basque organizations. Elsewhere, as in the United Kingdom, internal differences have emerged from frustration because the state has responded only marginally with offers that fell far short of ethnonational aspirations.

But most major movements in the West have also become mature in the sense that they do not see the world in black and white. All have demonstrated an awareness of policy issues other than a straightforward and simple demand for territorial structural change. They accept that the land would not flow with milk and honey just because of independence or autonomy. A broader policy portfolio outlining a general political strategy across a host of policy areas was deemed essential for demonstrating that they were serious contenders for governmental power. This exposed them to internal strains and external attack.

One consequence has been a heightened tension between those nationalists willing to settle, at least in the medium term, for something less, and a more rigid nationalism intolerant of anything short of full independence. Minority nationalist leaders, as they became more involved in the political system, increasingly tended to become more moderate and more willing to accept political compromise as they found that mainstream involvement imposed restraints upon freedom of manoeuvre. In short, they have become parts of a pluralist political system, so much so that minority ethnonationalism is usually not deemed to be an embarrassment, let alone a threat to the state.

While an inability to progress far towards the desired goals may have generated frustration, it has not led to an increased acceptance of violence and direct action as a means to an end. Only in a few instances, for example Flanders, have there been manifestations of chauvinist xenophobia. And few have matched or sought to imitate the IRA (Irish Republic Army) and ETA (Basque Homeland and Liberty), the two long-established terrorist movements. Even the Basque Provinces and Northern Ireland, with a tradition of direct action against the state, have shown popular disenchantment with violence as a political means.

The Western state has proved to be more resilient in its confrontation with minority ethnonationalism than the pessimistic prognoses of the 1960s and 1970s had predicted. That resilience is due in part to the style of ethnoterritorial politics pursued and to the nature and situation of ethnonational minorities. It is also a consequence of a relatively high degree of consensus in Western societies on what constitutes acceptable and legitimate behaviour. There is, however, another important element in the equation: the nature of the state's response. In the West there has been a high degree of state elasticity, an elasticity reflected in its style of territorial management.

Territorial management: lessons from the West

Ethnonational mobilization makes claims for adjustment in the political control and management of territory. Ethnonationalism therefore challenges the major imperative of the traditional state: the preservation of its territorial integrity. For states which claim to be nations themselves it challenges the legitimacy of existence. It is therefore natural for central regimes to accept the statement made several decades ago that 'governments have a natural tendency to integrate the societies they govern' and that 'the protection of minorities is not natural to governments' (Laponce 1960: 43).

If minority protection *is* unnatural and if regimes deem themselves to be guardians of a nation-state, then they will ignore minority wishes. Over and above this, states historically have pursued a variety of repressive measures and tactics. All such responses can be considered as part of the strategy of control advanced by Lustick (1979). His argument is that ethnic identities are 'terminal', that is unchangeable, and so rejects the notion of a 'melting pot model focusing on the processes of accumulation, socialization and assimilation'. Lustick therefore sees an ethnonationally divided society as being essentially conflictual. The state survives because it becomes a control system sustaining some kind of ethnic apartheid or enforced assimilation.

Control systems are typically associated with repressive undemocratic regimes. But coercion has also been part of the Western experience, most frequently in terms of mass education in the state language. However, contemporary Western European democracies have become too open and too pluralist for coercion to be sustained. Attempts to integrate ethnonational minorities forcibly, have been less successful than the slower, more natural process that Asp (1966: 131) calls 'democratic accumulation'. As McGarry and O'Leary (1990) demonstrate in their analysis of the 'democratic control' system in Northern Ireland between 1921 and 1972, a more likely outcome in a pluralist democratic system is some kind of minority reaction or backlash. A similar observation is made by Katzenstein (1975) on the events in the Alto Adige leading up to the adoption of the *Proporzpaket* (a compromise agreement on sharing out offices and jobs so German-speakers benefited).

Lustick's argument that control can permanently stabilize deeply divided societies finds little support in contemporary Western Europe, where coercion is more likely to provoke political action than to stifle it. By choice or intuition, Western governments since at least the 1960s have not been inclined to insist upon control. More typically they have sought to develop managerial strategies that would defuse potential conflict within existing boundaries.

Where circumstances and the health of the economy permitted it, regimes could and did pursue a specifically economic policy of concessions. This may be costly in terms of money but entails least risk to the state's territorial imperatives. There have been, however, several problems with this. It tended to be adopted by central governments as an integral part of state-wide planning and only if it could also be held to benefit the state economy as a whole. It was also almost impossible to disentangle a regional policy from the whole gamut of state economic actions, so making an evaluation of its impact upon the region and group in question difficult and even contentious. Most importantly perhaps, economic action cannot by itself address or resolve the broader political concerns of ethnoterritorial identities. For these reasons alone, an economic strategy was unsatisfactory. By the late 1970s, with increasing economic difficulties and the emergence of more cost-conscious governments, it had largely been abandoned as a panacea.

Western governments have also responded politically. The list of areas receiving or offered political concessions is extensive: the so-called Celtic fringe of the United Kingdom; Catalonia; the Basque provinces and, to a lesser degree, other Spanish regions; Flanders and Wallonia; the Swiss Jura; the Alto Adige and Val d'Aosta; Corsica; the Aaland Islands in Finland. The various policies pursued by central governments suggest that the strategies available to states fall under the rubric of one or other of two broad alternatives. Either they involve some degree of decentralized or devolved autonomy to a particular region, or they entail a kind of consociational approach, a sharing of public goods, resources and benefits among conflicting ethnonational groups irrespective of where they may be territorially located. In either instance, a government can choose to impose a standard formula across all of its territory and so applicable to all groups within the state's boundaries. Or it can treat some region or group as a special case, giving it preferential treatment and leaving existing territorial management structures intact elsewhere (the two types of federal arrangements discussed in Chapter 13).

Regimes have attempted to pursue one or the other of these broad options. In Switzerland the Bernese government eventually accepted the territorial option of a new Jura canton based upon linguistic self-determination. By contrast, the 1969 and 1972 *Proporzpaket* in the Alto Adige exemplifies the group approach. In its concern

> BRIEFING **4.4**
>
> **Consociational democracy**
>
> Consociational democracy is a concept developed by the Dutch political scientist Arend Lijphart to explain how and why some nations can maintain democratic peace and stability in spite of being deeply divided by ethnic, religious, linguistic or cultural differences. In such a democracy, the different groups are divided into communities with their own political parties, trade unions and other organizations, and they provide their own services such as health, education and welfare. Such deep social cleavages, superimposed one on top of the other, within a single state might be thought to produce severe political conflict between the communities. But in consociational democracies, the political elites representing the groups co-operate and compromise in order to maintain order and stability. They make the key decisions which enable the separate communities to maintain their own autonomy.
>
> The Netherlands is perhaps the best example of a consociational democracy but the term may also be applied to Austria and Belgium. The term 'pillarization' is also used to refer to consociational arrangements in which the different communities form separate 'pillars' within the social structure.

to satisfy regional *and* linguistic demands Belgium has come closer to a mix of the two broad strategies: a territorial approach for Flanders and Wallonia, with proportionality and sharing included for Brussels. Belgium has sought an integrated package applicable to the whole territory. The territorial changes in Spain and all tentative attempts at devolution in the United Kingdom have accepted a regional differential. In Spain the Basques and Catalans gained a more extensive autonomy than other regions. In Britain, Northern Ireland, Scotland and Wales are regarded as distinctive units, each requiring, whenever thought is given to it, different strategies or solutions.

What Western national experiences illustrate is that both territorial and group options have been considered and utilized. The territorial option would seem, superficially, to be more attractive, if only because it is easier to construct and because many ethnoterritorial minorities seem to have been content with some sort of autonomist outcome. However, the territorial option presupposes that group and territory are congruent. The most difficult and contentious cases of territorial management faced by Western governments have been in what was earlier described as mosaic or diaspora cases, where there is one territory which is populated and claimed by two or more ethnonational groups. Here, as in Northern Ireland or Brussels, a straightforward geographic decentralization of political or constitutional authority will probably not suffice. What is required is some form of group accommodation.

Territorial management: lessons of Eastern Europe

While the Western experience may serve as a role model for Eastern European problems, an automatic translation, where ethnonational disputes have become politicized, will not be easy or advisable. A democratic system is not enough: democracy is not per se a political organizing principle, merely a framework in which politics can function, for good or ill. Furthermore, democratization and the opening to the West has exposed Eastern Europe to economic as well as political change. Its sudden exposure to a global economy is a further background factor that must be taken into account.

Overall, several factors govern the choice or availability of the option of territorial management. Circumstances, both central and regional, have to be in conjunction. The costs involved have to be reasonable even though regimes – with the possible exception of the Czechs – are usually willing to pay a high price to maintain their overall rule. The options pursued probably stand a greater chance of success if they fit more easily with the historical and institutional style of centralizing politics. Without an existing tradition of decentralization, for example, a territorial solution entails a radical break in the style of government. The Western European exception is Belgium which has transformed itself from a unitary to federal state. This can perhaps be explained by its style of politics, often described as consociational. The transference of the politics of compromise and accommodation from religious to linguistic and territorial divisions was not an impossible leap in the dark.

If a Western role model has to be suggested for Eastern Europe, the most suitable candidate might well be Spain. The regime introduced a limited degree of territorial devolution all round, but with more extensive autonomy to the ethnonational regions – substantially so to the Basque provinces and Catalonia, less to the political by quiescent Galicia.

These are rather a stringent list of conditions, however. Eastern European governments will have to consider territorial and/or group accommodation. But it can be argued that the circumstances for a satisfactory resolution of ethnonational problems are not yet right. Schöpflin (1993: 258) has argued that 'democracy requires a set of values from both rulers and ruled that involve self-limitation, compromise, bargaining, reciprocity, feedback and the like, which post-communist states and societies cannot be expected to acquire overnight'. The traditional role of the Eastern state has not been that of an arbitrator or peace-maker. More often it has transformed ethnonational tensions into national rivalries and hostility. This practice not only alienates minorities but also destabilizes the state.

The notion of the nation-state still seems very attractive. Historical antipathies have been reinforced by recent experiences and interpretations. It is the nation-state ideal – one territory, one people – that lies behind attempts at forcible assimilation, exclusion of ethnonational groups from citizenship rights, and ethnic cleansing. In some ways Western attitudes have reinforced this view. For example, Western acceptance of Slovenia's right to secede from Yugoslavia was based very much upon the view that it was ethnically homogeneous. What this did was to send signals to, among others, Croats and Serbs, that congruence between territory and national group was a virtue, giving rise to 'ethnic cleansing' as a way to achieve this.

In the vast majority of cases, straightforward splintering or secession into two or more separate states that would be reasonably homogeneous is not an option. Most of Eastern Europe is simply too complex for that. The Croat-Muslim Federation in Bosnia demonstrates that even mini-states can remain ethnonationally confused. The Czechoslovak 'velvet divorce' is an exception. Other possible interfaces in Eastern Europe, for instance Moldova or Ukraine, involve an external state. In that sense the situation is more similar to diaspora, mosaic and enclave scenarios in that one or more of the populations concerned believe they have a possible external protector –

a neighbouring state – that will take up their cause and with which ideally they would wish to be linked. In turn, the external state often believes it has a duty to look after its 'own people' in other states. This has occurred even with Hungary, often regarded as one of the more 'progressive' of the new democratic regimes. For example, soon after becoming premier in 1990 Joszef Antall declared himself 'prime minister of all Hungarians'. Two years later his government reiterated that it had a duty to be responsible for Magyar populations outside the borders of Hungary. While such statements may be designed primarily as comforting rhetoric, they do little to ease existing tensions or contribute to solutions.

All new democratic regimes in Eastern Europe have been tempted by nationalistic politics, irrespective of their credentials. One problem, as Schöpflin (1993: 278–79) has pointed out, is the survival of what he calls chauvino-communism, the utilization of ethnonationalist appeals by former communists to legitimize their continuation in power. The Bulgarian Socialist Party (the reborn communists) made great play of anti-Turk propaganda in their election campaigns of the early 1990s. In 1990, in one of the first post-communist disputes in Transylvania, Romania used the ethnona-tional unrest as a reason for rebuilding its security forces.

What was typical about these responses is that little evaluation of a potential problem took place. The mere existence of an ethnonational minority tended to be accepted by leaders and electorate alike as a threat and sufficient reason for action to be taken against it. In Yugoslavia the pursuance of Serbian nationalism by Slobodan Milosevic was a key factor in the break-up of Yugoslavia, generating primeval fears from Croatia in the north to the Albanian population of Kosovo in the south. But similar attitudes have been struck by new democratic leaders, most prominently in the Balkans. In 1992, the Russian minority (30 per cent of the population) in Estonia were denied a vote because they were defined as non-citizens of the new state. In 1994 Latvia introduced even more draconian citizenship criteria directed against its substantial Russian minority.

Nationalizing politics also contributed to the break-up of Czechoslovakia. Under the communist system there was a feeling that Slovakia had retained some separate-ness while still having satisfactory access in Prague. In some ways the restoration of democracy returned the country to a past of Czech domination. Slovak discontent was first generated in 1990 by a series of decisions: the parliamentary vote in April to remove the hyphen (Czecho-Slovakia) from the country's name; the decision to scale down heavy arms production upon which Slovakia was highly dependent; the decision in October to allow ethnonational minorities in Slovakia (13 per cent of the population) the right to use their own languages in official business in those local-ities where they formed more than 10 per cent of the population. These and other actions simply fuelled Slovak fears and resentment, which could be mobilized by Vladimir Meciar and his Nationalists. The final straw, perhaps, was the request in December 1990 by President Vaclav Havel for direct powers to handle the Slovak issue.

A possible solution deriving from West European experience – economic conces-sions – is not appropriate for exactly similar reasons; it cannot by itself defuse polit-ically charged ethnonational situations. In any case, the Eastern European countries, struggling to transform a command into a market economy, will not have sufficient economic largesse for some time to come.

Nor is it easy to see how territorial accommodation would be satisfactory in more than a very few instances. Most ethnic minorities live as 'mosaics' or 'diasporas' but even 'enclaves' have more than a grain of the mosaic in them. Given ethnonational distributions, it is difficult to see how territorial resolution, where it may be possible, could avoid creating another interface. Moldava, for example, has the problem of its self-proclaimed Trans-Dniester Republic; Ukraine has the Crimea, populated by Russians and Tatars. With the exception of Belgium, there is no instance of a successful federalization of a dyadic interface. If we consider Western European states which have some degree of decentralization as a response to ethnonationalism, then the best examples – Belgium, Britain, Finland, Italy, Spain – have not granted similar autonomous powers or rights to all their regional units. While this may be an appropriate route for Eastern Europe to consider, the ethnic scenarios are usually too complex for it to be easily applicable.

Given the complexity of ethnonational scenarios, some form of group accommodation would seem to be the best way forward in most instances, something which entails some kind of consociational model. However, several authors have cast doubts on the virtues of a simple transplantation of the consociational approach to ethnic ills. Others have dismissed it as useless in ethnonational disputes where ownership of territory is in contention and sovereignty becomes an issue. Successes in Western Europe like the South Tyrol in Italy, can be offset by the tragedy of Northern Ireland, where successive British governments have advocated and attempted a variety of power-sharing policies. Their failure illustrates the basic problem. Group accommodation requires not just a willingness by the regime to make concessions, but also a willingness to compromise, and a reasonable degree of mutual trust and flexibility among the populations 'on the ground'. Where this does not apply the group approach may fail, leaving a positively inclined regime little option but to practise more or less severe control. Yet in the long term, if stability is to be secured in Eastern Europe, group accommodation would seem to be the only candidate as a viable policy.

■ Marketing futures

Western governments have been drawn to group accommodation where a straightforward territorial deconcentration of power cannot reduce ethnonational unrest. However, the interplay between state, region and ethnoterritorial nationalism underlines some basic facts about Western life; the more powerful and influential foundations of political structures and institutions; a more or less positive acceptance by elites of pluralism and difference, and tolerance towards them, as an integral part of democratic practice; and the ability of many people in culturally distinctive territories to live with some kind of dual or triple identity – for example, the same individual may feel Catalan, Spanish and European. The potential acceleration of political integration in Western Europe may, like economic developments, reinforce these characteristics. European integration has already weakened the national state. Several ethnonational minorities have welcomed the opportunity to deal directly with Brussels and participate in institutions such as the Committee of the Regions. The existence of these democratic conditions has still to be clearly demonstrated in Eastern Europe. They underlie the major differences between the West and the challenges facing, and the practices pursued, by many of the new regimes.

The legacy of history lies heavier on Eastern than on Western Europe. The communist ice age heightened the temporal dislocation between East and West. These two factors lie behind many gloomy prognoses about the ethnonational future of Eastern Europe, which also point to the negative effects of globalization. As President Clinton declared in his January 1993 inaugural address, globalization has blurred the distinction between 'what is foreign and what is domestic'. The uncertainties that globalization generates about what a state or nation is may well have been a factor strengthening ethnonational allegiances and the determination of states to act in their own interest. On the other hand, the hope of economic development and modernization held out by the events of 1989 may have limited some of the potential impact of ethnonationalism. It was when instant economic transformation was not apparent or when fears that access to affluence might be pushed further into the future that discontent began to arise. The rise of extreme right-wing neo-fascism in East Germany as a reaction to unemployment parallels developments in Slovakia and elsewhere.

Yet East-West differences in this area may not necessarily hold in the future. What we may be talking about is variations upon a single theme rather than on two. There are several pointers to the possibility of Eastern Europe following the concessionary path of the West. The disintegration of Yugoslavia and of the USSR arose from a nexus of complex factors, making them special cases in much the same way as the interface did in Czechoslovakia. Although one should be wary of over-generalization, especially when applied to the Balkans, both ethnonational minorities and states have paralleled their rhetoric with more pragmatic stances. After the bloodletting, at least Bosnian Muslims and Croats have begun to consider a federation. In Moldova, it is a moot point whether the declaration of a Trans-Dniester Republic in 1990 was an assertion of independence or the first move in a misguided attempt to force a federal political system out of the government. Equally, the rejection of union with Romania in the 1994 referendum implies that Moldava must come to terms with Trans-Dniester, given the latter's identification with Russia.

Again, external guarantors have become more circumspect in their attitudes towards neighbouring states, to the extent where collaboration, or studious non-involvement along Western lines, has become possible. Co-operation, on national minorities was part of the Visegrad agreement of February 1991, between Hungary, Poland, Slovakia and the Czech Republic. By 1992, after initial recriminations, Hungary and Slovakia declared themselves willing to consider a joint commission on the resolution of ethnonational issues. The Bosnian-Croat agreement of 1994 is a small step in a similar direction. Finally, the desire for democracy distinguishes post-1989 nationalism from its predecessors. It generates support which can moderate the destructive impacts of ethnonationalism.

The desire in Eastern Europe to be associated with the West not only economically and politically, but also institutionally – within security structures as well as through common markets – will almost certainly push states away from mechanisms of control in ethnoterritorial contexts. In turn, the fact that Eastern European stability depends upon satisfactory resolution of its numerous ethnonational scenarios may ultimately have an effect in the West. Successful territorial management in the East may be difficult, but not impossible. In turn it may provide an inspiration to Western ethnonational minorities. In time we may have a single theme, with no variations, in the treatment of ethnic minorities across Europe.

■ References and further reading

T. G. Ash, *The Uses of Adversity: Essays on the Fate of Central Europe* (Cambridge, Granta Books, 1989).

E. Asp, *The Finnicization of the Lapps* (Turku, Turun Yliopisto, 1966).

P. Katzenstein, 'Ethnic political conflict in South Tyrol,' in M.J. Esman (ed.), *Ethnic Conflict in the Western World* (Ithaca, Cornell University Press, 1975).

J. G. Kellas, *The Politics of Nationalism and Ethnicity* (London, Macmillan, 1991).

J. Laponce, *The Protection of Minorities* (Berkeley, University of California Press, 1960).

I. Lustick, 'Stability in deeply divided society: consociationalism is control', *World Politics*, 31 (1979), 325–44.

J. McGarry and B. O'Leary (eds), *The Future of Northern Ireland* (Oxford, Clarendon Press, 1990).

G. P. Nielssen, 'State and national group: A global taxonomy', in E.A. Tiryakian and R. Rogowski (eds), *New Nationalism's of the Developed West* (Boston, Allen & Unwin, 1992).

George Schöpflin, *Politics in Eastern Europe* (Oxford, Blackwell, 1993).

A. D. Smith, *National Identity* (London, Penguin, 1991).

E. Renan, *Poetry of the Celtic Races and Other Studies* (London, Kenicot Press, 1970).

Mediating internal conflicts

Chapter 5

Support for democracy

■ Introduction

Nationalism, as we have seen, can affect both external relations between States and inter-group relationships within them. The previous chapters have examined its often disruptive effects on external relationships. In Part II we look at internal relationships. Here, of course, ethnonationalism is only one of the forces at work shaping individual and group attitudes. Political relationships may also be affected by differences of economic interest, notably between workers and managers. Besides class and ethnic conflicts there may also be religious cleavages – between denominations and also between church and secular groups.

In the last chapter we argued that one solution to ethnic tensions inside a state was to accept their legitimacy. Once ethnic divisions are realistically accepted as being on a par with economic or religious divisions, or any other difference of opinion, they can enter into interest group representation (Chapter 7) or party competition (Chapter 9) as part of normal political processes. One feature of democracies is that conflict is accepted as normal and not outlawed. Any group or section can voice its opinons, and organize to advance them, without being accused of disloyalty. The only requirement is that it abides by non-violent democratic procedures, above all contesting elections and accepting their results – always, of course, with the possibility of reversing them next time.

It is the working of these democratic procedures for managing internal conflicts that we examine in Part II, for all parts of Europe. We start by looking at individual attitudes for two reasons. One is that ethnic, class and other tensions come out in the first place in the attitudes of individual citizens towards the state, its political

BRIEFING **5.1**

Democracy

We all have general ideas about what is democratic and what is not, based on some notion of a democratic government being responsive and accountable to the 'people'. One of the difficulties is that the 'people' rarely agree on the best course of action to take on any given issue, so responding to the 'people' often boils down in practice to responding to the majority. But this may mean in Europe that an ethnic majority within 'its' state may want the government to suppress the minority (or minorities). These theoretical difficulties may be avoided in practice by having regular, free, competitive elections. Holding such elections requires the extension of freedom of speech, communication and meeting to minorities. In practice the ethnic majority is often divided by class and religious differences. Political parties which base themselves on these need to ally with minority-based parties to get a parliamentary majority and form a government. The minority can then get concessions for its support. We examine party processes in Chapter 9.

institutions and towards each other. If we want to see how serious and potentially disruptive these tensions are, individual attitudes provide good evidence.

The other reason for examining political attitudes, particularly attitudes towards the working of pluralist democracy, is to see how stable European democracy really is. Our assumption is that mass attitudes towards democracy are one of the factors which determine whether democracy succeeds or fails. Certainly low levels of trust, or a sharp loss of belief in democratic principles and practice are a clear indication that something is wrong wih the political system.

■ A crisis of democracy?

The post-war politics of Western Europe and the current politics of Central and Eastern Europe are comparable in an odd and surprising way. Although Western Europe passed through a period of unprecedented peace, affluence, and political stability after the Second World War, a series of theories have predicted nothing less than democratic crisis, catastrophe and contradiction. Similarly, the concern about contemporary Central and Eastern European politics is that democracy may not survive the acute social, economic and political problems which it has to face. The endemic conflicts which democracy has to manage may always end up by involving its procedures and institutions and discrediting the system itself.

Since the 1950s, political scientists and commentators have worried about the present state and future prospects of democracy in the West, often ending up by predicting disaster. We list some of the most popular below:

- In the early 1960s, mass society theory argued that rapid social and economic change would create atomized, amorphous, alienated and anomic populations which would be easy prey for the appeals of extremists and demogogues.
- In the late 1960s and early 1970s the thesis of the legitimacy crisis argued that faith in the system of government would begin to crumble as it tried unsuccessfully to solve the contradictions of late capitalism.
- At the same time, but from a different political perspective, overload ungovernability theory argued that the growing gap between what governments promise and what they deliver would generate mass disillusionment with pluralist democracy.
- In the early 1980s it was said that the new social movements (Greens, women, minority groups, anti-nuclear groups, nationalist and religious movements) posed such a challenge to the established political order that it would be thrown into crisis.
- Most recently, some theories of postmodern politics argue that because government is unable to respond adequately to the changing demands of society, people will lose their belief in its capacity to respond to citizen demands.
- A sixth school of thought argues that because bad news helps to sell newspapers and increase audiences, the media feed the population with a diet of scandal, corruption, incompetence, and horror – ethnic cleansing, terrorism, crime, racism, greed, incompetence, and failure. By reinforcing the public mood of alienation, distrust and cynicism the media undermine faith in modern democracy.

BRIEFING 5.2

Political attitudes, political culture and the political system

Discussions of political attitudes and public opinion often use terms like 'political culture', 'community', 'regime', and so on.

- A *political culture* is the whole mass of shared attitudes, amongst a given population, towards political authorities, law, government, and so on. They give an indication of how people would behave in, say, a crisis. Thus, if most people distrust the government, think democracy is a sham and that politicians are out for themselves, they are unlikely to take to the streets if there is an army takeover.
- A *political community* is based upon a sense of mutual sympathy, loyalty, and identity. It is formed by people who are drawn and bound together by virtue of their participation in common political structures and for common political purposes.
- A *political regime* consists of the constitutional order and its structures, and the fundamental values upon which they are based.
- *Political authorities* are those people who occupy positions of importance in the political system – presidents, prime ministers, members of parliament, judges, senior bureaucrats, and so on.

The distinction between community, regime and authority is important because citizens may lose faith and confidence in a particular prime minister or president and still strongly support the regime, or system of government. In a democratic system this means that governments can change without the system of government being undermined. If citizens lose faith in their political regime, there will be pressure to change the constitutional order, but the community can still hold firm. But if support for the community fails then the political system is likely to break up altogether, perhaps through territorial secession.

In Western European democracies, authorities often lose support, but general support for regimes has remained high, and support for community (a few nationalist or separatist movements apart) is generally even stronger. This gives Western systems of government a solid and stable basis. In parts of Central and Eastern Europe, however, support for both authority and regime is often low, and in some places (Czechoslovakia, Yugoslavia, the Soviet Union) the sense of community has not been strong enough to support nationhood.

There are good reasons for being even more pessimistic about the viability of democracy in Central and Eastern Europe than in the West. It takes a long time to establish a robust and healthy democratic political culture capable of withstanding economic hardship, social change, or political crisis. It is no coincidence that most of the world's stable democracies are among the wealthiest nations of the globe, and that many of the poorest have succumbed to dictatorship or military coup. Even a perfectly designed democratic constitution will not survive without a political culture to sustain it. The development of a democratic political culture requires, among other things, a period of relative peace, economic affluence and political stability.

Economic problems are often believed to be the most serious obstacle to a peaceful transition to democracy. In this respect, Central and Eastern Europe faces not a single but a double challenge: to establish democracy and to achieve economic reform and success at the same time. Over the last fifty years some Western nations have had to face one or the other; rarely both together, and even less rarely have they had to start from scratch on both fronts. In Central and Eastern Europe the fear is that the initially high costs of economic reform may provoke a slide back into authoritarianism or totalitarianism. To be effective, economic reforms may have to be radical and quite probably painful for some. But new democratic governments may fear the electoral consequences of drastic measures, thereby prolonging the economic problems.

This predicament, severe though it is, is compounded by the initial optimism which followed the 'velvet revolutions' against communism. Quite possibly these expectations were unrealistic, and once the honeymoon effect wears off, a sense of anger and frustration may grow, provoking a political backlash. On the other hand, it is also possible that a lot of the blame will be loaded onto the old communist regime, thus reducing the strain on current democratic governments.

In addition, it must be said that there are grounds for optimism about Central–Eastern Europe. The ability of totalitarian communist regimes to establish a hegemonic anti-democratic political culture should not be taken for granted. Some Balkan states seem to have been models of totalitarian repression, but the need for Soviet force in Hungary in 1956 and Prague in 1968, and the formation of Charter 77 in Czechoslovakia and of Solidarity in Poland, is evidence that their dictatorships were unable to suppress desires for freedom and democracy. Both Hungary and Poland introduced economic and political reforms in the 1970s and 1980s and, together with the Baltic states, had partly pluralist systems operating by the 1980s.

Moreover, democracy is not entirely novel in some parts of Central-Eastern Europe. Hungary, Poland and Czechoslovakia had their pre-war parliamentary experiences. In both Russia and East Germany there is evidence that government control over the political system did not mean popular acceptance of the government's agenda and values. In neither country was regime indoctrination completely successful, and both entered the 1990s with a core of democratic attitudes and aspirations.

When examining mass attitudes towards democracy there is often an assumption that we should compare contemporary Western and Eastern Europe. Possibly this is a wrong and misleading comparison. Perhaps it would be better to compare Central and Eastern Europe now with Western Europe after 1945 when it emerged from a period of foreign occupation and anti-democratic government, and faced acute economic problems. Central and Eastern Europe in 1995 will undoubtedly come off badly if compared with Denmark or Norway in 1995, but if the comparison is with Germany or Italy in 1950, for example, the picture may be very different. A democratic ethos was not widespread in German politics in 1945, but was consolidated after a period of economic success and democratic stability. The problem is, of course, that we have no systematic data about public opinion in Italy or Germany at that time. Nevertheless, we should keep firmly in mind the fact that democracy survived in places where the ground seemed, at one time, to be infertile – Germany, Austria, Italy, Spain, Portugal, Greece.

In the pages that follow, the evidence for a decline in the Western democratic political culture will be reviewed, before turning to mass attitudes towards democracy in Central and Eastern Europe. The East and the West are examined separately because political opinion surveys are usually (fortunately not always) carried out separately so that direct comparison is rarely possible. Also, while Western data often dates back to the 1970s or before, opinion polling in the east usually starts in 1990 at the earliest. Empirical evidence about the West is full and rich in parts, less satis-

BRIEFING 5.3

Major sources for Western European public opinion

The Civic Culture: A pathbreaking study when it was published in 1963, and a classic of political science ever since, is Gabriel A. Almond and Sidney Verba's, *The Civic Culture* (Boston: Little Brown, 1963). Their survey covers many aspects of political attitudes and beliefs, and the social and economic variables associated with them, in Italy, Germany, the United Kingdom, the USA and Mexico. See also a reconsideration of the work published seventeen years later – Gabriel A. Almond and Sidney Verba (eds), *The Civic Culture Revisited* (Newbury Park, Calif., Sage, 1980).

Political Action. Based upon extensive interviews carried out in Austria, Great Britain, the Netherlands, West Germany and the USA, Samuel H. Barnes and Max Kaase (eds), *Political Action* (Beverly Hills, Calif., Sage, 1979) was an in-depth and detailed analysis of political behaviour and protest carried out in 1974. An abridged version has been published (Alan Marsh, *Political Action in Europe and the USA* (London, Macmillan, 1990) and a follow-up study of the Netherlands, West Germany and the USA (M. Kent Jennings and Jan W. van Deth, *et al.*, *Continuities in Political Action* (Berlin, de Gruyter, 1990).

Eurobarometers. The Eurobarometer surveys of the European Union are the most valuable single source of information about public opinion. Carried out twice yearly, every year since 1973, they cover all the member states of the EU, and sometimes other countries as well. Random samples of between 900 and 1,500 people are interviewed twice a year. A core set of questions is included in every survey and additional ones asked at intervals.

European Values. Based on surveys first carried out in 1981 the European Values Study covers Belgium, Denmark, Ireland (Eire and Northern Ireland), France, Great Britain, Italy, the Netherlands, Spain and West Germany. The 1981 survey was replicated in Finland and Iceland a little later. The whole survey was repeated in the countries listed in 1990, when Portugal was added. Some results are published in Stephen Harding, *et al.*, *Contrasting Values in Western Europe* (London: Macmillan, 1986) and Sheena Ashford and Noel Timms, *What Europe Thinks* (Aldershot: Dartmouth, 1992).

The International Social Science Programme (ISSP). Every year since 1985 the countries which participate in the ISSP have carried out surveys on an agreed topic. The role of government was the topic in 1985, 1990 and 1996. Western European countries in the survey are Austria, Britain, Germany, the Irish Republic, Italy, the Netherlands, Norway and Sweden. Results of the surveys are published in the reports of Social and Community Planning Research (SCPR) London in association with Dartmouth Publishing Co., Aldershot.

factory in others, but for the East it is thin and patchy. We will we see what we can learn about the West before turning to Central and Eastern Europe.

■ Political, attitudes and beliefs in Western Europe

Personal and political trust

Trust is said to be an essential ingredient of modern democratic politics. This means trust between individual citizens and between citizens and political leaders. The close link between trust and democracy is not suprising since trust is an essential part of the classic political value of fraternity – liberty, equality and fraternity are said to be the cornerstones of modern democracy. In a literal sense fraternity is that sense of trust which exists between members of the same family or kin group. In the larger political community, trust is not based upon the close ties of family, of course, but upon a looser but still powerful sense of common identity built on a common background, culture, religion, history, language and national experience. Democracy in a community or in a nation cannot be sustained without such ties which generate trust – or fraternity – between citizens, and between citizens and political leaders.

In the last decade or two, the importance of trust and fraternity has been largely neglected in both popular political debate and in political science. In the 1980s, liberty (often narrowly interpreted to mean the liberty to compete in the economic marketplace) was widely assumed to be the supreme political value in Western society. Equality was largely ignored and fraternity was barely mentioned, even in passing. But when contemporary social scientists point to the importance of trust in modern democracies they are rightly rediscovering, or reasserting, the importance of fraternity as an essential quality of a democractic order.

What is the level of trust in Western democracies? Has it declined, as some commentators claim? The evidence suggests that it has not, or at least that there has been no general decline across Western Europe. In countries such as West Germany, Luxembourg, Britain, the Netherlands and Belgium, about 90 per cent of the population say that most people in their country are 'very trustworthy' or 'fairly trustworthy'. The figures seem to have declined by 3–5 per cent, from 1976 to 1986. But in Denmark the figure rose from 88 per cent to 94 per cent in the same period, and in Italy it rose from the high forty per cents in the late 1970s, to the low 60 per cents in the late 1980s.

These figures refer to trust between citizens. Evidence about trust in government is harder to come by, partly because comparable surveys have not been carried out in a range of nations or over a long period of time. However, it is possible to compare Norway, Sweden, Denmark and the Netherlands. They have a strong enough family resemblance to bear comparison, and similarly (but not identically) worded questions have been asked at regular intervals since the early 1970s. The figures show the following: signs of a continuous decline of trust in government in Sweden from the late 1960s to the late 1980s; a decline in Norway and Denmark in the 1970s, followed by a smaller increase in the 1980s; and a rising level of confidence and trust in government in the Netherlands from a relatively low level in the early 1970s to a substantially higher level in the late 1980s.

In other words, there is no consistent or clear pattern across nations, but equally there is little evidence to confirm theories which predict a widespread decay of trust in other people or in government. Instead, there are some indications that rising or falling feelings of political trust on the part of different social groups is dependent to some extent on political factors such as the alternation of governments, which party is in power, and the performance of particular governments. Supporters of the party in power feel more trustful than supporters of opposition parties. But these, if and when their party gains power, express higher levels of trust and support. Feelings tend to change and reverse with the ebb and flow of political events. There is, accordingly, no general pattern but rather trendless fluctuation dependent upon circumstances.

Table 5.1 Confidence in major institutions, 1982, 1990: Average of fourteen West European nations

	1981 %	1990 %
Public institutions		
Police	75	74
Education	64	67
Legal system	64	57
Armed forces	58	50
Parliament	50	48
Civil service	45	44
Private institutions		
Church	54	50
Major companies	41	50
Trade unions	40	41
Press	33	35

Source: European Values Studies.

Confidence in public and private institutions

A certain degree of scepticism in public and private institutions is not unhealthy and is probably fairly widespread throughout the Western world. Probably all but the most fanatically nationalistic will express a degree of cycnism, uncertainty, or doubt about their national institutions. However, a widespread lack of confidence, or a sharp drop suggests something wrong.

Fortunately we can assess the general sense of confidence in major public and private institutions from a survey of European values carried out in 1981 in Belgium, Britain, Denmark, France, Finland, Iceland, Ireland, Italy, the Netherlands, Norway, Spain, Sweden, and West Germany – thirteen nations in all. The survey was replicated in 1990, although Finland was not included the second time round, and Portugal was added. Among other things the polls examined public confidence in ten major institutions: six of them public (the armed forces, education system, the legal system, the police, parliament and the civil service) and four private (church, press, trade unions and major companies).

By and large, confidence in public institutions is higher than in private ones (see Table 5.1). Confidence in government institutions ranges from a high in Norway (70 per cent in 1990) to a low in Italy (45 per cent). The equivalent figures for private institutions are 52 per cent (Ireland) and 33 per cent (Britain). Across Western Europe as a whole, more than half and as many as two-thirds or three-quarters of citizens express confidence in the public institutions of their country. Generally speaking, the figure is highest for the police and the education system, rather lower for parliament and civil service. It is worth remembering this when we turn to Central and Eastern Europe. Between 1981 and 1990, support for government institutions remained fairly stable or declined by a few percentage points in the countries surveyed.

Confidence in private institutions remained stable or increased during the 1980s. In particular confidence in major companies rose sharply towards the end of the decade, probably because the survey was carried out shortly after the collapse of communism signalled the triumph of capitalism in the West. In general, therefore, the polls reported in Table 5.1 find little evidence of a decline of public confidence in the major institutions of Western European society. On the contrary, confidence seems to be relatively stable.

Party identification and party membership

Parties are said to be the backbone of modern liberal democracy, yet the established mass political parties of Western Europe are also believed to be in decline (for more on this, see Chapter 9). Ordinary citizens are said to be showing lower levels of attachment to, involvement in, and identification with the mass. It has been suggested that the modern mass media, social and geographical mobility, the decline of class and community, the weakening of major socializing agencies such as the family and the church, the replacement of heavy industry and manufacturing by service industry, and spread of education have all weakened the ties of party in the postmodern world.

As a result, some predict an increase in political volatility, fragmentation and instability. Others go further and argue that these developments may signal a growing political disenchantment with conventional politics and a potential growth in radical, anti-system, and even violent political behaviour. It is difficult to put such claims to an exact empirical test. In the first place, there are disagreements about the meaning of party identification, or at least a tendency to emphasize different aspects of it. In the second, there is a lack of time-series data which is comparable across many countries and which would enable us to generalize with some confidence across space and time. Nevertheless, the Eurobarometer provide evidence about nine Western European countries going back to the 1970s, and national election studies provide further material going back to the 1950s or 1960s.

This evidence has been meticulously collected and analysed carefully by Schmitt and Holmberg (in Klingemann and Fuchs: 1995) to show a steady and steep decline in identification with parties in Sweden, Ireland, Italy and France. Britain and West Germany show a decline in the 1970s, followed by something of a revival in the late 1980s and 1990s. The pattern in the Netherlands, Denmark, Norway and Belgium is relatively stable, whereas there are signs of growing partisanship, albeit modest, in Greece, Spain and, to a lesser extent, in Portugal.

In other words, there is no Western European trend, but a mixed pattern of increase in some cases, decrease in others, and of decline followed by increase in a third group. Holmberg and Schmitt uncover possible reasons for this. On the one hand, broad social and economic changes, like rising educational levels or the spread of the mass media, cannot explain trends in party identification and partisanship. These changes have swept across the whole of Western Europe in the past decades, but patterns of party ID vary from country to country. Rather, levels of partisanship seem to respond to country-specific political circumstances. In particular, the degree to which political parties are sharply divided along policy lines and the degree to which they conflict ideologically, seems to affect the extent to which the population identifies with them. Ideologically distinct parties, whether they are large or small, show an increase in partisan support.

Party membership shows a similar pattern to party identification. Figures for ten nations (Denmark, Belgium, Britain, Finland, Ireland, Italy, the Netherlands, Norway, Sweden and West Germany) suggest two things. At between 5 and 10 per cent in most countries, party membership is quite low. It is generally highest in Denmark, Norway and Finland. Second, party membership in most west European nations has been either fairly constant since the 1960s, or else in slow and gentle

Table 5.2 Political participation in Western Europe, 1959–90

	1959 %	1974 %	1981 %	1990 %
None	85	69	55	44
Some	11	27	38	46
Active	4	4	7	10
(n)	(2,734)	(6,148)	(13,315)	(15,107)

decline. In Denmark, Finland and Norway, membership seems to have declined by 6 to 10 per cent (from around 19–14 per cent to about 13–7 per cent) In other countries where the figures were lower to start with, they have tended to remain constant since the 1960s.

In sum, party membership in Western Europe is not high, but nor is it much lower now than thirty or forty years ago. This confirms the old conclusion that politics is a minority sport in Western democracies, but fails to confirm predictions of a steep decline in involvement with the established parties.

Political apathy and interest

The democratic citizen is a politically informed and active citizen – knowledgeable enough to make intelligent judgements about politics, and vigilant and active enough to make it difficult for small and unrepresentative minorities to take control of government. The fear, however, is that levels of political apathy and ignorance are growing in the West. There is said to be a growing 'information gap' between a small well-educated minority and the great mass of people. The former make the best use of the information explosion created by the mass media; the latter feed on a junk diet of soap operas, sport, sensationalism, gossip and scandal.

Have levels of political interest and involvement declined? Part of an answer may be found in the Eurobarometer surveys which asked members of EU states whether they discuss politics, and if so how frequently. With few exceptions the level of discussion in most countries is fairly similar, and with few exceptions the level over the period from 1973 to 1992 was fairly constant: about one in six claim to discuss politics 'frequently' in most countries and in most years.

Discussion is one thing, action another. Fortunately, we can get a rough and ready impression of levels of political activity and activism from four important surveys of political behaviour in Western Europe: the Almond and Verba *Civic Culture* study (1963), the Barnes and Kaase *Political Action* study (1974), the two *European Values* surveys (1981, 1990) (see Briefing 5.3). Figures culled from these surveys and re-analysed in order to make them as comparable as possible are shown in Table 5.2. Although activists remain a small proportion of the population, the figures suggest a clear increase in political activity since the 1950s among the great mass of citizens.

It may be misleading to reduce such a complex and many sided thing as 'political activity' to a set of a dozen simple figures, especially when the figures represent averages for no less than thirteen different nations in the last two years of the series. Therefore, it is worth noting that when the figures (not presented here because they are too voluminous) are broken down by country, by year, and by type of political activity, they leave the same impression – a trend towards higher levels of overall political activity across Western Europe as a whole.

Direct action

Political theorists have always defended the democratic right of citizens to disobey laws which they believe to be unjust (especially if disobediance is non-violent). One fear in Western society, however, is that individuals and groups are increasingly turning to direct political action, including forms of civil disobedience, and perhaps even to anti-democratic, illegal behaviour including violence. Some evidence suggests that the fear is not groundless. The *Political Action* survey of 1974 (see Briefing 5.3) found that direct political action is now widely acccepted as part of the standard political repertoire of European citizens. This includes strikes, sit-ins, protests, marches, occupations, street blockades, boycotts and the use of force and violence. However, although there had been an increase in the numbers who contemplated such action, only a very small percentage actually engage in them. On average, 1 per cent of European Union citizens have been involved in two or more acts of civil disobedience in a 10-year period.

A follow-up to the *Political Action* survey in Germany, Italy, and the Netherlands confirms that *legal* forms of direct political action are now firmly established in the political repertoire. It also finds evidence of a slight long-term increase in such behaviour between 1974 and 1989. However, fluctuations in the figures suggest that changes of public mood and specific political events cause the figures to rise and also to fall.

Two points stand out. First, far from declining levels of political participation, Western Europe shows overall increases. Secondly, although the political repertoire has now broadened in the public mind to include a wide range of direct political action, such behaviour has been largely restricted to petitions, protest meetings and demonstrations, marches, boycotts and political strikes. It stops short of political force and violence. (For more detail on the 'New Politics', see Chapter 8.)

Beliefs in democracy

An overwhelming majority of Europeans believe in democracy as the legitimate way to govern. According to the Eurobarometer surveys not less than 93 per cent expressed this opinion in every member state of the European Community in 1989. In this sense democracy has established itself as the only acceptable form of government for an overwhelming majority.

The acid test, however, is not whether people believe in democracy as an abstract principle, but whether they believe their own country is run along democratic lines. Since the 1960s some theorists have claimed that large sections of the population will lose their faith in democracy because it cannot live up to its promises.

The evidence does not indicate any such crisis in popular attitudes. On the contrary, rather than a progessive decline of beliefs in democracy, a consistent 50 to 60 per cent have said ever since 1976 that they are 'very satisfied' or 'fairly satisfied' with the way democracy works in their country (see Figure 5.1). In most time series figures of this kind, it is the fluctuations and overall trends which are interesting: in Figure 5.1 it is the *absence* of trends or major fluctuations. Nothing much has happened to affect satisfaction with democracy since 1976, which is fascinating. However, as one would expect, levels vary greatly between countries. In Denmark, Norway, West Germany, Luxembourg and the Netherlands more than two out of

Figure 5.1 Trends in satisfaction with democracy in Western Europe, 1976–91

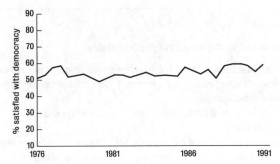

Notes: The data base is the total population. The data are pooled and weighted by population size. EC-12 consists of Belgium, Britain, Denmark, France, Germany, Greece, Ireland, Italy, Luxembourg, the Netherlands, Portugal and Spain. Northern Ireland is entered as a separate case.
Source: Eurobarometer, Nos. 6–35.

three, and as many as six out of seven, now express a high level of satisfaction. In Italy, in strong contrast, only a quarter to a third do so, and between a 30 and 40 per cent say they are 'not very satisfied' or 'not at all satisfied'.

The level of satisfaction does fluctuate a little from year to year and from country to country, but overall there is a slight (2–3 per cent) increase in satisfaction over the period from 1976 to 1991. This trend is evident in both the older democracies of North and Central Europe, and in the younger democracies of the South. Even in Italy there is a slow, though small and uneven, increase in satisfaction. Across the EU as a whole, satisfaction among the young, the better educated, and the post-materialists, has generally increased since 1976. This suggests that the slow upward trend may well continue in the future.

The fact that satisfaction with, and belief in democracy has remained at a high and consistent level over a twenty-year period and in different countries, suggests that there is a well of diffuse support for democracy. That is, support which is not dependent upon favourable political and economic conditions, but which reflects a deeper and more general commitment. Economic and political circumstances have varied across countries and across time quite considerably, but citizens in most countries express the same high levels of support for democracy in most circumstances and in most countries.

Revolution versus reform

Since 1976, twice every year, the Eurobarometer surveys have asked a sample of citizens of EU countries whether they support revolutionary action, gradual reform, or the need to defend society against subversion. The options are not really alternatives, but nevertheless, the answers tell us a good deal about how citizens feel about politics in their countries. In general, never more than 8 per cent, and more usually only 5–6 per cent, have opted for revolution since the 1970s. A solid and fairly consistent 55–70 per cent prefer reform. There is not a great deal of variation between countries, or over time.

The revolutionary minority fell from 8 per cent in 1976 to 4 per cent in 1990; the reformist majority increased from 60 per cent to 65 per cent (touching 70 per cent in 1989); those fearing subversion fluctuated between 25–30 per cent. There is

BRIEFING **5.4**

Diffuse and specific support for democracy

A useful distinction is often drawn between specific and diffuse support:

- *Specific* support of a system is based upon the particular benefits it delivers – often its economic benefits.
- *Diffuse* support is based upon fundamental beliefs and values, and upon the legitimacy of the system.

A system with strong diffuse support will easily survive periodic short-term shocks – economic depression, for example, or revelations about corruption or incompetence in high places. If diffuse support is weak, however, and the system rests upon specific support, then it will be more easily undermined by short-term failure to satisfy citizens.

Most Western European democracies have built up a reservoir of diffuse support which helps maintain stability. But many Central and Eastern European countries have not had this possibility. As a consequence they are prey to short and medium-term loss of specific support.

little here to suggest that Western Europe as a whole, or any country within it, has an untapped reservoire of revolutionary potential. Even less do they indicate that the reservoir has increased over the past fourteen years. Western Europeans appear to be as content – or discontent – with their systems of government as ever they were. There has been no noticeable increase in revolutionary feelings.

West Europe: crisis or politics as usual?

It is possible to draw out a few generalizations about mass political attitudes in Western Europe in the post-war period. First, there is little evidence to support the various theories of crisis, contradiction and catastrophe. There are few signs of a general decline in trust, confidence in public institutions, political interest, or faith in democracy; nor is there much evidence of an increase in apathy, alienation, or revolutionary feelings. Secondly, Western Europe is characterized by random fluctuation rather than general patterns of change. Indicators rise in some countries, fall in others, and rise then fall, or fall then rise in others. No single theory, or grand generalization seems to encompass all countries. Third, and perhaps most important for Central and Eastern Europe, democracy survives in spite of weak supporting mass attitudes in some cases – most notably a lack of confidence in political institutions. Italy is the classic case where democracy has managed to sustain intself in the face of widespread public dissaffection with political institutions and processes. We should bear this in mind when we consider attitudes in Central and Eastern Europe.

■ Political attitudes and beliefs in Central and Eastern Europe

Given the great diversity of their economic, social, and political circumstances, it is not suprising that mass opinions about government and politics differ considerably from one country to another in Central and Eastern Europe. Quite often they vary markedly from one year to the next within the same country! This makes it as difficult to generalize about the region as a whole as it is to generalize about any

BRIEFING 5.5

Major sources for public opinion in Central and Eastern Europe

1. *Transition to democracy*
A survey carried out in 1990/91 by the Academy of Sciences of Bulgaria, Czechoslovakia, Estonia, Hungary, Lithuania, Poland, Romania, Slovenia and the Ukraine.

2. *The new democracies barometer*
Organized by the Paul Lazarsfeld Society in Vienna this survey was started in 1991 with a survey of Bulgaria, the Czechoslovak Federation, Hungary, Poland and Romania. By 1993/94 and into its third year it had expanded to include Bulgaria, the Czech Republic, the Slovak Republic, Hungary, Poland, Romania, Slovenia, Croatia, Belarus and the Ukraine.

3. *New Soviet citizen surveys*
Conducted by the University of Iowa (USA) this survey covers Lithuania, the Ukraine, and European Russia in 1990, 1991 and 1992.

4. *Central and Eastern Eurobarometer*
This is a parallel survey to the Eurobarometer (see the discussion of Western European data). Started in late 1989, when it covered Bulgaria, the Czechoslovak Federation, and East Germany, it expanded to cover Bulgaria, the Czech and the Slovak Republics, Hungary, Poland, Lithuania, Albania, Romania, Latvia, Estonia, European Russia, Macedonia, Georgia, Slovenia, Moldova, Belarus, Armenia, the Ukraine and Kazakhstan in 1995. Like the (Western) Eurobarometer, the Eurobarometer East asks a core set of questions in its annual survey, and adds other questions at intervals.

5. *The* Times-Mirror *surveys*
Based on interviews conducted in 1991, this is a comparative East-West survey including, in the East, Bulgaria, the Czechoslavak Federation, East Germany, Hungary, Lithuania, Poland, European Russia and the Ukraine.

particular country over even a short period of time. Nevertheless, some patterns appear to emerge.

Beliefs about the old and new systems

The Central and Eastern Eurobarometer asks, 'In general do you think things in our country are going in the right or the wrong direction?' This is a deliberately general question in which the term 'things' might be interpreted in all sorts of ways. Nevertheless, responses to the question give a good general idea of how people feel, and the main impression is of a strong unease about current reforms (see Table 5.3). Although responses are highly variable from one country to another, in only three out of eight does a majority believe they are heading in the right direction. In the remaining five, most people feel that there is something wrong, and in Poland and Hungary the opinion is widespread. Clearly most people are not at all satisfied with the current state of their country.

However, dissatisfaction about the present does not mean a wish to return to the old communist days. For example, the great majority (between two-thirds and over 80 per cent) in Hungary, Poland, Bulgaria, the Czech Republic and Russia believe that the creation of a market economy is right for their country, although a majority also believe that economic reforms are going either too fast or too slow. There is a specially strong and pervasive fear of unemployment, and most people anticipate a

Table 5.3 'In general, do you think things in our country are going in the right or wrong direction?'

	Right %	Wrong %
Albania	77	17
Slovenia	62	22
Czech Republic	58	34
Slovakia	46	47
Bulgaria	42	40
Romania	42	49
Poland	27	56
Hungary	20	67

Source: Central and East European Barometer, 1993.

decline in their own household economies and their national economies in the short term.

When asked not about the immediate future, but about the likely state of affairs in five years' time, however, most are optimistic. One survey of ten nations (the 'New Democracies Barometer', which interviewed more than 11,000 people in Bulgaria, the Czech Republic, Slovakia, Hungary, Poland, Romania, Slovenia, Croatia, Belarus and the Ukraine) found that nearly two-thirds of respondents expected the economic situation to have improved in five years' time. The survey shows clearly that most people dislike their past society, are dissatisfied or fearful of the present, but optimistic about the not too distant future.

Satisfaction with democracy

The Eurobarometer surveys show a good deal of dissatisfaction with the way democracy is developing in most countries (Table 5.4). In some, the percentage of satisfied citizens is very low. At the bottom of the table, fewer than one in eight citizens in Bulgaria, Armenia, Belarus and Kazakhstan are satisfied with democratic developments. At the same time, it must also be said that some of the figures look respectable when compared with the West. Direct comparison is not possible because the questions asked in the East and the West are not identical. But satisfaction with democracy seems to be as high or higher in Romania, Lithuania, Slovenia, Estonia, Albania and the Czech Republic as in Greece, Spain or Italy. In general, satisfaction with democracy in Central and Eastern Europe is low, but this should not obscure the fact that it is comparable with Western levels in some countries (see Table 5.4).

Nor should it be assumed that reservations about the current state of democracy indicate a willingness to return to the old totalitarianism. In fact, the great majority reject a return to the old form of communist government, and even larger majorities reject a monarchy or rule by the military. Other survey evidence underlines a commitment to democracy and its operating principles. For example, most citizens understand and appeciate their personal freedoms in the new political systems. Very large majorities say the new regime is better than the old insofar as it recognizes freedom of association, freedom of religion, freedom of thought, freedom to travel and freedom from arbitrary arrest. Most citizens also recognize the rights of political parties and the press. At any rate, like citizens in the West, they are generally reluctant to express the view that any political party – even anti-democratic parties – should be outlawed. And like Western citizens, they generally disapprove of limiting the freedom of the press.

Table 5.4 Satisfaction with democracy, East (1995) and West (1994)

Western Europe (% satisfied with way democracy works)		Eastern Europe (% satisfied with way democracy is developing)	
Denmark	78	Czech Republic	44
Luxembourg	72	Albania	33
Ireland	65	Estonia	33
Netherlands	65	Slovenia	32
Portugal	55	Lithuania	31
Belgium	53	Romania	31
Germany	52	Latvia	26
UK	49	Hungary	23
France	47	Poland	23
Greece	32	Georgia	18
Spain	29	Slovakia	17
Italy	19	Ukraine	16
		European Russia (1993)	15
		Kazakhstan	12
		Belarus	11
		Armenia	9
		Bulgaria	4
Average, EU12	44		

Source: Central and East European Eurobarometer, No. 5, March 1995.

Table 5.5 Democrats and reactionaries, 1993–94

	Democrats %	Reactionaries %
Czech Republic	63	8
Poland	45	14
Romania	38	11
Slovenia	36	12
Croatia	36	13
Bulgaria	30	23
Slovakia	26	25
Hungary	24	31
Belarus	13	48
Ukraine	12	43
Average	32	23

Source: Rose and Haerpfer, 'New Democracies barometer III', 1994.

One interesting piece of research (Rose and Mischler, 1994) distinguishes between 'democrats', who favour the new regime and oppose the old, and 'reactionaries', who favour the old regime and oppose the new. In only one of the ten countries covered by the 'New democracies barometer' in 1993/4 (see Further reading list), were the democrats in an absolute majority (63 per cent in the Czech Republic), but in seven of the ten, democrats outnumber reactionaries (see Table 5.5). In the Czech Republic, Poland, Romania, Slovenia and Croatia they outnumber them heavily.

More important, while the reactionaries dislike the new regime more than the old, their liking for the old is also lukewarm. In this sense, reactionaries seem not to be hard-line Stalinists, but advocates of the semi-pluralist, semi-mixed-economy sort of 'goulash socialism' which emerged in Hungary in the 1980s. This may explain their loyalty to reformed communist trade unions (Chapter 7) and vote for new-style communist parties (Chapter 9). Reactionaries have their reservations about the new system, but this does not mean they want to return to the old. In short, democrats and reactionaries are not polar opposites; reactionaries are simply a few years behind the democrats.

Table 5.6   Trust in major institutions, 1993–94

	Bulgaria	Czech R.	Slovakia	Hungary	Poland	Romania	Slovenia	Belarus	Ukraine	Average
Public institutions										
Military	54	40	48	44	59	76	37	37	33	47
Courts	15	38	31	46	35	45	40	26	21	33
Police	17	35	30	44	43	38	37	22	15	31
Government	13	57	32	21	25	27	34	17	13	26
Civil service	16	28	28	27	23	28	37	20	17	25
Private institutions										
Churches	30	27	47	40	38	71	29	54	46	42
Media	31	45	35	32	34	22	32	32	33	33
Private enterprise	16	43	26	35	16	45	24	19	28	28
New trade unions	14	19	22	24	15	–	–	18	13	17

Source: Rose and Haerpfer, 'New Democracies Barometer III', 1994.

Supporting this conclusion, survey research in Russia, Ukraine and Lithuania finds a fairly widespread desire for strong leadership and order in 1992 (Reisinger *et al.*, 1994). More than 40 per cent in all three countries believe in strong leadership, and between 22 per cent and 40 per cent expressed a strong desire for order. At the same time, support for strong leadership is also *positively associated* with support for democratic values. While it may seem strange to combine a desire for strong leadership with a wish for democracy, it seems that the mixture does not indicate a desire for Stalinist leadership, but for good government and leadership with powers to act in the public interest.

Evidence about economic attitudes shows that Eastern Europeans are pessimistic in the short run, but more optimistic about the medium term. Political attitudes are similar in this respect. A large majority of all respondents in the ten countries surveyed in the 'New democracies barometer' in 1994/5, expected to give their regimes a higher rating five years into the future than at the time the question was asked. This optimism may help them get through what are undoubtedly hard economic and political times at present. But whether it lasts may well depend on how the economy works out in the next five years.

Trust in institutions

Table 5.6 shows that trust in the major institutions of society, both public and private, is relatively low. In the private sector neither the new trade unions nor private enterprise fare at all well. It is the churches which come off best. In the public sector, the military is most trusted, with the courts and police some way behind. Two aspects of the table as a whole give cause for concern. First, trust in institutions as such, public or private, is not well developed. Secondly, esteem for the military is relatively high. In a world in which military dictatorship is common this does not seem to be promising for civil government. More than three out of four Romanians, for example, trust the military. But only about one in four feel the same way about government, the civil service, or the media.

Compared with the West, trust in major institutions is comparatively low. The Western average across thirteen nations is higher for every public and private institution than it is for the nine countries listed in Table 5.6. In fact, the profile for Eastern countries is comparable in many ways to that of Italy, except that Italians had more confidence in their police and in private enterprise.

Table 5.7 Trust in European parliaments, 1990–91

	%		%
Ukraine	18	Italy	32
Estonia	30	Portugal	34
Poland	34	Denmark	42
Czechoslavakia	36	Belgium	43
Slovenia	36	Spain	43
Bulgaria	37	Sweden	47
Hungary	45	Britain	46
Romania	56	France	48
Lithuania	57	Ireland	50
		Germany	51
		Iceland	53
		Netherlands	54
		Norway	59

Sources: Hibbing and Patterson (1994: 577), and O. Listhaug and S. Wiberg, 'Conference in political and private institutions', in Klingemann and Fuchs (eds) (1995: 304–5).

Trust in parliament

Trust in parliament varies from a low of 18 per cent in the Ukraine to a high of well over 50 per cent in Romania and Lithuania (Table 5.7). It is more than a third but less than half in Estonia, Poland, Czechoslovakia, Slovenia, Bulgaria and Hungary. If these figures seem depressingly low, confidence in some Western European parliaments is not high either. Only one in three Italians and Portuguese express confidence in their parliaments, which makes them comparable with Poland, Czechoslovakia, Slovenia and Bulgaria. Indeed, in Romania and Lithuania, at least in 1990–1, parliaments had the support of more than half their populations. This was about the same as for Iceland, the Netherlands and Norway, which showed high esteem by Western European standards. If we allow for the possibility that the reputation of Western parliaments grew steadily during the post-war years of peace, political stability, and prosperity, then the comparison does not reflect too badly on at least some Central and Eastern European systems at this early stage .

What spoils the optimism of these observations is the fact that parliamentary trust and confidence in many parts of Central and Eastern Europe declined in the mid-1990s. There is a possibility that the gloss may be wearing off some of the new parliaments. At the same time, lack of trust in particular parliaments does not signify distrust of parliamentary democracy as a principle. People may be unhappy with their parliament, but the evidence suggests that a good proportion of them continue to believe in parliamentary democracy.

Political participation and competence

It is said that ideal democratic citizens are neither deeply involved in politics (associated with crisis and political extremism), nor withdrawn from them (suggesting apathy and alienation). Democracy requires a balance. How does Central-Eastern Europe fare in this respect? First election turnout has often been rather low by Western standards, although this may also be part of a general tendency for newly enfranchised populations to have a low voting turnout. At the same time, Eurobarometer East questions about subjective interest in politics, frequency of private political discussion, and future voting intentions suggest that the figures are not markedly out of line with the West.

Table 5.8 Internal and external efficacy, East and West, 1991

	Internal efficacy		External efficacy	
	People like me don't have a say in government (% agree)	Voting gets people like me a say in government (% agree)	Elected officials lost touch pretty quickly (% agree)	Elected officials care what people think (% agree)
UK	62	56	86	36
France	38	78	86	28
Spain	53	78	84	28
Italy	–	51	90	15
West Germany	68	61	88	33
East Germany	84	46	91	32
Bulgaria	78	86	88	24
Czechoslovakia	78	61	87	31
Hungary	86	53	86	33
Poland	90	44	91	25
Russia	–	52	92	20

Source: Kaase (1994: 259).

Nor are the figures for political efficacy very different. Efficacy is the feeling that the citizen can have an impact on political life: internal efficacy refers to a citizen's sense of being able to influence politics; external efficacy is the sense that political authorities are responsive to ordinary citizens. The figures in Table 5.8 are consistent with the general pattern that is now beginning to emerge from the survey data. First, while the Central-Eastern countries have lower levels of both internal and external efficacy than the West, the figures, on average, are not specially low. Secondly, some countries have undoubtedly low levels of efficacy. Thirdly, others have relatively high figures. Indeed, in some countries they are higher than Italy's.

■ Conclusions

History shows that stable and peaceful democracy has survived in most of Western Europe in spite of the many theories predicting that it was under threat from irresistible social and economic forces. The populations of Western European states have also maintained their faith in democracy, even strengthening it in the post-war period. Italy is something of a deviant case. But even though Italians often come out at the bottom of the Western European league tables, Italian democracy has survived, albeit in permanent crisis. On most measures, Italians are not more disillusioned with their political system than earlier generations, and in some respects they are less so.

Central and Eastern Europe presents a different picture. Apart from anything else, generalization is difficult. Countries vary so much in terms of economic development, religious and ethnic composition, nationalist divisions, political history and cultural traditions that there may well be a diversity of political patterns and outcomes. Moreover, in the present uncertain and volatile circumstances it is dangerous to make any confident statements about the likely future of any country or group of countries.

Nevertheless, some generalizations are possible. In the first place, the great majority of east Europeans seem to have firmly rejected communism and the totalitarian past. Survey research suggests that even those who are suspicious of the new order do not adhere to the old with much conviction. The fact that the transition from the old to the new was negotiated peacefully suggests that even the old guard, much privileged by the regimes they ran, knew that they had come to the end of the road. The great majority of Eastern Europeans have embraced capitalism and democracy, although some seem more favourably disposed towards the former than towards the latter. However, we cannot always be sure what is understood by either term in different parts of Central and Eastern Europe. Communism in some countries means totalitarianism and the command economy, but in others it means semi-pluralism and the 'goulash economy' of the 1980s.

Secondly, the forces of political division, fragmentation and conflict are powerful. National, ethnic, religious, geographical and ideological divisions are likely to threaten some states with division and fragmentation. Widespread anti-semitism is sometimes combined with nationalism and xenophobia (Chapter 4). A symptom and a cause of this problem is a low level of trust, both within and between countries. A 1990 Eurobarometer survey shows that the Poles and the Czechs trust Western Europeans more than they trust each other.

Thirdly, although some of the indicators of mass support for democracy are low in some Eastern European countries they are higher in others, and compare not unfavourably with some Western European nations. Italians stand out as being no more confident about democracy in their country than Poles, Hungarian, Czechs, Slovakians and Baltic nationals are about theirs. The results may be interpreted in two ways. If some Central-Eastern nations compare not unfavourably with some Western nations, despite their different stages of development, then future prospects for democracy are good. But if the comparatively solid ratings in some Eastern countries comes from the honeymoon not having worn off there are grounds for pessimism.

Fourthly, there is a good deal of optimism about both the economic and the political future. Many are not happy about the present, but most expect to evaluate both the political and the economic system more favourably in five years' time. Much seems to depend on economic conditions improving, so that this optimism may be preserved.

■ **Further reading**

The most intensive and exhaustive analysis of post-war West European public opinion about government and politics is to be found in the five 'Beliefs in Government' volumes, namely:

Olle Borre and Elinor Scarbrough (eds), *The Scope of Government* (Oxford, Oxford University Press, 1995).

Max Kaase and Kenneth Newton, *Beliefs in Government* (Oxford, Oxford University Press, 1995).

Hans-Dieter Klingemann and Dieter Fuchs (eds), *Citizens and the State* (Oxford, Oxford University Press, 1995).

Oskar Niedermayer and Richard Sinnott (eds), *Public Opinion and Internationalized Governance* (Oxford, Oxford University Press, 1995).

Jan W. van Deth and Elinor Scarbrough (eds), *The Impact of Values* (Oxford, Oxford University Press, 1995).

On Central and Eastern Europe see Max Kaase, 'Political culture and political consolidation in central and eastern Europe', *Research on Democracy and Society*, 2, 1994, 233–74; Richard Rose and Christian Haerpfer, 'New democracies between state and market', 'Adapting to transformation in Eastern Europe' and 'New democracies barometer III' all published by University of Strathclyde, Centre for the Study of Public Policy, *Studies in Public Policy*, Nos 204, 212, and 230 respectively. Other useful articles include John R. Hibbing and Samuel C. Patterson, 'Public trust in the new parliaments of Central and Eastern Europe', *Political Studies*, 42(4), December 1994, 570–92; Richard Rose and William T. E. Mischler, 'Mass reaction to regime change in Eastern Europe: polarization or leaders and laggards?', *British Journal of Political Science*, 24(2), April 1994, 159–82; William M. Reisinger, *et al.*, 'Political values in Russia, Ukraine and Lithuania: sources and implications for democracy', *British Journal of Political Science*, 24(2), April 1994, 182–223.

Chapter 6

Television, radio and press

Regulating the media in a democracy

According to modern democratic theory the mass media are of central and crucial importance. A democratic public must be informed and politically involved and it is the job of the media to supply the public with the facts of daily political life, and with a wide range of political opinion. Consequently, the mass media have been regarded as an institution almost comparable to parliament in a modern democratic state. They have a dual responsibility: to give a full and fair account of the news; and to pass critical comment and thoughtful judgement on public affairs.

Theory is one thing, however, and practice another. How should the mass media be organized? According to what sorts of principles? Should the state create a framework within which the media can perform their proper democratic role? Is there a danger that state involvement will do more harm than good, restricting the freedom of the press and making it accountable in some subtle (or not so subtle) way to the government of the day? Perhaps the least government of the media is the best government, in which case perhaps it should all be left to market forces? Experience suggests, however, that the market is an excellent servant but a poor master, especially in regard to newspapers and television. Left on its own, it creates enormous concentrations of unaccountable power, systematic political bias and poor journalistic standards. Some balance of state and market seems optimal. But what balance, and how should it be implemented and organized?

These are extremely difficult questions. They involve, as in so many other aspects of political life, complex matters of theory and practice, an attempt to reconcile incompatible interests, and a delicate balance between the competing principles of freedom and responsibility, liberty and equality, and public and private interest. Each nation has its own solution to the problems, each with a particular mix of characteristics. In post-war Europe, there have been four main ways of organizing and regulating the media. They are (1) the public service model, (2) the state control model, (3) the market model, and (4) the mixed model. This chapter will describe briefly each in turn and list the countries which adopt them. It will then turn to recent innovations in the mass media, to the transformations which these have brought about in the West, and to the extraordinarily difficult decisions which confront the new democracies of Central and Eastern Europe.

The public service model

The public service model treats political news and information as a matter of public concern. It assumes that it is the responsibility of the media to inform the population in a objective fashion, and yet to present critical opinion of all kinds. This itself

BRIEFING 6.1

Media regulation in terms of a 'public service' model

The public service model draws a distinction between electronic and print media. It regulates these sectors differently, as follows:

1. *Market regulation.* The state intervenes in the print media market only to avoid the development of monopoly or oligopoly. Spectrum scarcity means that the electronic media are natural monopolies and the state recognises this by granting broadcasting licenses to only a few companies. In the print media, there is supposed to be market competition, but in the electronic there is state regulated monopoly.

2. *Content regulation.* The print media are regulated as little as possible. They are left to regulate themselves in matters of public decency and personal privacy. The content of the electronic media are more closely regulated to produce political balance and neutrality, and to provide a wide range of programmes, including some of a cultural, minority and educational nature.

3. *Self-regulation or regulation by quango.* In order to minimize the chances of political control or interference, the media are regulated by their own bodies or by quangos which are independent of the government.

4. *Public and private funding.* The print media are usually funded by the market, while the electronic media are usually funded with public money, sometimes with general subsidies and sometimes by license fees, or a mixture of the two.

5. *Public service and profit making.* Whereas the print media are usually profit-making, the electronic media are non-profit organisations supposed to serve the public interest by maintaining political impartiality and broadcasting a mix of programmes.

6. *National broadcasting.* The public service model can only work effectively if broadcasting is limited more or less by national boundaries. Cable and satellite broadcasting from abroad render it difficult for governments to control the media.

is something of a dilemma for the media as they are expected to be neutral and balanced, yet engaged and critical. At the same time the public service model draws a clear distinction between the print media and the electronic media. In principle, anyone can set up a printing press for a newspaper or magazine and sell copies to the public. In contrast, broadcasting frequencies for radio and television are limited in number. There are only a few available frequencies and some of these must be reserved for public services such as police, fire and ambulance, or for such things as air traffic control or radio taxis. This is known as spectrum scarcity. Since the airwaves are a scarce public asset they should also be used for the public good. The public service model, therefore, regulates the electronic media quite closely, but leaves the print media to operate within looser, market constraints.

In fact the public service model involves two kinds of state regulation – *market regulation* and *content regulation*. Market regulation tries to ensure that private media monopolies or oligopolies do not emerge, for this would mean the concentration of unaccountable power in too few hands. It might also mean the media becoming narrow in their interests and politics. According to democratic theory, the media will be more likely to present a pluralistic diversity of programmes and politics if they are controlled by a wide range of people with different commercial and political interests. Therefore, it is the job of bodies such as the Federal Cartel Office in Germany and the Monopolies Commission in Britain to keep a watching eye on media mergers and acquisitions, and to ensure that oligopolies do not emerge.

Because there are only a few broadcasting frequencies, the electronic media constitute natural oligopolies or monopolies, and so they are subject to close state regulation. Only those licensed may broadcast, and programmes must observe the public interest. This brings us to the second kind of media regulation – content regulation.

According to the public service model, freedom of the press means that newspapers and magazines should operate within the loosest possible constraints, and these should be concerned mainly with privacy, decency and the laws of libel. Moreover, the press should, so far as possible, be self-regulating rather than state regulated. As with market regulation, the special situation of the electronic media means that they are subject to strict content regulation. First, they are required to provide a full and fair account of the news, and to observe strict impartiality. This means an absence of political advertising and editorializing, and a set of detailed rules about the coverage of election campaigns. Secondly, a broad range of programmes should be broadcast which appeal to different sections of the population, including quality programmes which may not be commercially viable, and minority programmes for the old or the young, or cultural, ethnic and linguistic minorities. Thirdly, public proprieties should be observed; some things should not be broadcast at all, others only after children are in bed and proper warnings given to those who might not want to watch or listen.

While the basic principles of the public service model might be acceptable in theory, they leave unanswered the difficult practical problem of how to organize and regulate broadcasting authorities. The classic solution to this problem has been the BBC – the British Broadcasting Corporation. This is a 'quango' (a quasi non-governmental organization) nominated by the government to act in the public interest with the help of public money, but not itself directly controlled by the government.

Broadly speaking, the public service model was applied in most West European democracies from the start of radio broadcasting up to about 1970, but there are variations on the theme. In France and Italy, parties and governments had considerable direct control over broadcasting. In Germany, the system was under the authority of the Länder rather than the Federal government. This was to avoid the possibility of a Goebbels-type propaganda machine being set up by the central state. In Belgium, broadcasting was divided between the Flemish and French communities. In the Netherlands, broadcasting time was apportioned to the main social and religious 'pillars'.

Even the clearest public service systems had commercial elements mixed in with them. Luxembourg has had commercial TV (CLT/RTL) from the start, and a commercial channel was licensed in Britain in 1954. After Franco, Spain was divided between a strong commercial and a strong state-run sector. Ireland, Portugal and Greece introduced commercial elements quite early. The purest public service models were to be found in Scandinavia and in Austria and Switzerland. They relied more heavily on public money than Britain, Germany or France which had somewhat larger commercial elements. Nevertheless, the whole of the democratic west had media run broadly on the same, public service lines. This contrasted strongly with the system operating the system of top-down, state control.

■ The state control model

The state control model applies to varying degree to most European dictatorships – Hitler's Germany and Stalin's Soviet Union – and to a lesser extent to the authoritarian regimes in Spain, Portugal and Greece. In this chapter, however, we will concentrate on the system operating in the Soviet empire before it collapsed.

It took some time for the state controlled model to develop in the Soviet Union and the Eastern bloc countries. After the 1917 revolution it was the job of the press to educate the population into new ways of thinking and acting – to socialize and mobilize it. All publishing was brought under the direct control of the Communist Party. The national emergency and threats of invasion during two world wars made this easier, and in the inter-war period a strong fear of invasion and of class enemies was carefully exploited by Stalin to justify tight state control of all means of communication.

At the height of Stalinism the system worked on two fronts. First, negative powers of censorship were heavily used, a responsibility of the Board for the Preservation of State Secrets in the Press (Glavlit). Secondly, on the positive side, a large number of newspapers and magazines were made available at low cost to the public, and the whole enterprise was carefully controlled by the Propaganda Department of the Central Committee of the Party. In case of a breakdown in this two-pronged approach to censorship and propaganda, the state security agency (the KGB) was used as a fast acting and powerful force to plug the gaps.

All means of communication were controlled by the state; phones were largely restricted to government and business offices, and faxes, computers, photocopying machines, even typewriters, were registered and regulated. In later years, the 'passive' media of television and film were preferred to the more 'active' print media of newspapers, magazines and books. There were four radio and four TV channels, although it was not possible to receive all of them in most parts of the USSR. Because of the enormous size of the country, the Soviet Union was advanced technically in the use of satellite broadcasting and in the use of satellite facsimile printing.

It took some time after the 1917 revolution to build up the full system of state control. After Stalin's death in 1953 it began to crumble under Khrushchev (1956–64) – a process accelerated under Gorbachev (1985–91). Nor should it be assumed that state control was total, except, perhaps, at the height of Stalin's power. After Stalin, the Soviet Union and its satellite countries produced an underground or *samizdat* ('self-published') literature which was critical of the state. In some countries, especially Poland during the years of Solidarity, there was a huge volume of *samizdat* publications, and in the 1980s this was easily available and publicly read.

The underground press was reinforced by Western radio stations which broadcast specifically to the Eastern bloc. These included BBC World Service, Voice of America, and Deutsche Welle, as well as the more propagandist Radio Free Europe and Radio Liberty. Some parts of central Europe also received Western TV. Though it was illegal to tune in, the law was difficult to enforce, and large parts of the East German population regularly watched West Berlin TV. Lastly, even in the official publications, a political debate was carried out covertly by the use of code words which could be interpreted and deciphered.

Nor should it be assumed that the Soviet state control model was completely different from the Western public service model: among many differences they had common elements. All states have secrecy laws which give governments powers of censorship. In Britain and France these powers are wide-ranging and draconian. Indeed, until the 1980s the French government largely controlled the electronic media. In the same period the British government openly criticized the performance of TV on, for example, its reporting of domestic politics, the US bombing of Libya, and the conduct of the Falklands War, as well as using direct censorship on Northern Ireland. Western governments also employ specialists in media management – a form of propaganda which tries to manipulate the media, although without the benefit of direct control. Similarly, some Western parties and governments conduct public debates in code. In the British Conservative Party open disagreement with Thatcher was strongly discouraged, so critics within the party talked about 'one-nation' politics to signal their belief in public services and the welfare state. For a time the West even had its own version of *samizdat* broadcasting in the form of pirate radio stations, although these broadcast pop music not politics.

Media in transition

Neither the public service nor the state control model survived in their pure form far into the 1970s. Technical and political developments made it increasingly difficult for national governments to exercise control. Printing has been all but revolutionized by computer-driven desk-top publishing, by fax machines, by widely available and relatively low cost photocopying and by electronic mail.

More important the electronic media have been transformed by satellite and cable TV, and by Videotext, CD-Rom and multi-media technology. Already the distinction between print and electronic media, and between private and public communication is breaking down because the introduction of the interactive information super-highway makes it possible to mix phones, computers, TV, satellites and printers to communicate in many different ways either separately or together. Above all, communication is no longer limited by national boundaries. It is no longer merely international but truly global. Suitcase-sized broadcasting dishes enable reporters to dispatch from almost anywhere on the globe, and satellites can pick up the message for broadcast to almost any other part of the globe. In this sense the global broadcasting village is now a fact.

This means, first, that national governments, whether totalitarian or democratic, can no longer control the media as they once did. Second, new technology opens up all sorts of market possibilities, and ownership and control of the media is increasingly concentrated in the hands of multinational, multi-media conglomerate corporations. This means that the old state controlled and public interest models have rapidly crumbled. We turn now to the changes which have spread so quickly across the whole of Europe.

From public service to mixed model: the West

As long as there were only a few wavelengths available for terrestrial broadcasting these were placed under public (not necessarily state) control. But the arrival of cable and satellite TV means that electronic media are no longer different in principle from print media. The availability of up to a hundred TV channels or more, and of a far greater variety of radio stations, means that they can compete in the same way as newspapers or magazines. New technology also makes it possible to pay for radio and TV in a number of different ways – by advertising revenues, subscriptions, pay-as-you view and sponsorship. The emergence of a competitive electronic media market means that there is no need for public service regulation, or so the theory says – market laws of supply and demand can take over.

In Western Europe, Italy led the way by making private radio stations legal in 1976. Once the dam was broken, there was a flood of legal and illegal commercial radio and TV stations, operating alongside the public stations controlled by RAI (Radio-Televisione Italiana – the equivalent of the BBC). A law in 1990 legalized these *de facto* developments and the result was a mainly private, but part public system. In Britain, a single commercial TV channel was introduced in 1954, though it was carefully regulated according to the public service model.

In France, direct state control of the electronic media, which reached its height under de Gaulle, was relaxed. Later an important commercial break was made in 1987 when a public channel was sold to the private sector (TF1), and new commercial channels licensed. In Germany, the public sector monopoly was ended with the inauguration of RTL-plus in 1984, and further commercial elements have been introduced since then. In Portugal, Spain, Ireland and Greece the systems were further privatized and commercialized in the late 1980s. Even in the Nordic countries, which conformed most closely to the public service model, commercial elements have been introduced in various small ways. Only Austria and Switzerland retain most, though not all, of the old state monopolies.

In some countries, changes have been forced by the existence of intense foreign commercial competition. The existence of profitable and expansionist commercial business in Luxembourg, for example, forced Belgium to follow suit. Denmark, the Netherlands, Austria, and Switzerland have been similarly affected by events across their borders. Once admitted, capitalism forces others to follow by virtue of the economic pressures it creates. By the end of the 1980s, there were more commercial TV channels than public ones in Western Europe. Such was the scale of media mergers, acquisitions, and new developments that in the financial year 1998/9 they cost a total of US$6 billion. The media have not merely become business, but very big business, on an international level. The existence of media conglomerates, often directly controlled by one person, raises all the problems of media impartiality and balance which the public service model was designed to solve. By the very nature of their operations they tend to favour free market views and centre-right parties which will give them a free hand to expand their businesses.

The extent of the movement from public service to market should not be over-estimated, however. Only one public TV channel has been sold to the private sector – TFI in France. In Germany, the courts have allowed some forms of commercialism but the Federal Constitutional Court (1986) has ruled out others. While the political right was in favour of privatization in the 1980s, it changed its mind after reunification when it realized that public service radio and TV would help in the assimilation of the new Länder in East Germany.

In Britain, the BBC's market share of radio and TV has declined but remains substantial, and the old rules governing balance and impartiality in political reporting remain in force. The introduction of commercial TV has changed the nature of BBC programmes. While there is truth in the argument that this constitutes back-door commercialization, the system as a whole is still far from a market-driven one. BBC programmes can be sponsored but commercial advertising is not allowed.

There have also been problems with the new deregulation which has sometimes

BRIEFING 6.2

The media moguls: modern multi-media, multi-nationals in Western Europe

News International – Rupert Murdoch

Murdoch owns TV stations, newspapers, magazines, book and film companies on four continents. In Britain, his daily newspapers sell 10 million copies a day, about a third of the daily total. In Australia he controls about two-thirds of newspaper circulation. In New Zealand he controls about a half. In Britain he has interests in London Weekend TV, BSkyB (claimed to be accessed by 13 million households in more than twenty countries), and cable TV, as well as books, magazines and journals (Collins, Fontana, and Granada books), films (Metromedia and Twentieth Century Fox), Reuters news agency, and in other commercial ventures concerned with trucking (TNT), gas, and oil. In Hong Kong he holds controlling interests in Star TV which has a satellite reach across Asia. Australian laws against media cross-ownership forced him to sell his TV stations in order to keep his newspapers, and in America he had to sell New York and Chicago papers in order to keep his six TV stations. He is well known for his right-wing political views, and for his involvement in the editorial policies of his newspapers.

Bertelsman – Reinhard Mohn

Though a private company this is the largest publisher in Europe and one of the half dozen largest media corporations in the world. In Germany it has reached the legal ceiling which limits its print interests. These include among other things the magazine *Stern*. It has recently bought two satellite TV channels in Germany. In the USA it owns a string of publishers and recording companies. Its world wide empire covers twenty-five countries.

Fininvest – Sylvio Berlusconi

Based in Italy, the Berlusconi empire controls TV channels in France, Germany and Spain as well as the three main commercial channels in Italy. He also controls the largest Italian publishing company (Mondadori), a film company, two national newspapers, a radio network, a chain of cinemas, and magazine publishers. Fininvest has large interests in property development, insurance, and construction, as well as owning the largest Italian supermarket chain (Standa) and a major Italian football team. Berlusconi used this media base to help in his election as Italian Prime Minister in 1994. His firms and companies provided the organizational basis for his new party *Forza Italia*, while his media pumped out propaganda on his behalf. Berlusconi represents the clearest example yet of how media control can lead on to political power. His electoral defeat in 1996 shows, however, that it is not automatic.

inhibited its progress. Serious financial problems in France, particularly with the commercial channel La Cinque and with inadequate take-up of channel capacity for TDF-1 and TDF-2, suggests the system has reached the limits of commercial funding, for the present at any rate. Some doubt that there is enough advertising revenue in Britain to support another commercial TV channel. The auctioning of TV franchises in 1991 was both controversial and embarrassing for the government, as in effect some had to be given away to the only bidder. German TV SAT 1 malfunctioned on its launch in 1987 and had to be abandoned shortly afterwards. In France, there was also political controversy over the political bias of CNCL, a controversy joined by none other than President Mitterrand.

New technology also brings political problems. For example, although the British government of the 1980s frequently stated its staunch support for market choice it was decidedly unhappy about the broadcasting of hard-core pornography from abroad (Red Hot Dutch). It was also alarmed about the possibility that some local radio stations might fall into the hands of militant ethnic groups. Across the Western world as a whole there is concern about pornography on the World Wide Web. It is not evident that the market will take care of these problems. The current wave of media de-regulation may be followed by a slower and more thoughtful process of re-regulation.

From state controlled to mixed model – the East

After the 'velvet revolution' the nations of Central and Eastern Europe knew what they did not want, which was the old state control. So they abolished it. But they did not know what they wanted, or, at least, how to get what they wanted, so they failed to replace the old system with a new one. The result is disorganization, policy-making by default, a good deal of volatility and even chaos. As a result of the inability to frame a new media structure the new system displays some of the more unpleasant characteristics of the old.

In most Central and Eastern European countries the old state media monopolies have been abolished and with them a great deal of the old apparatus of party control and censorship. In Poland for example, one of the first moves of the new Solidarity government was to abolish official state censorship and set up a Commission charged with dismantling the old state media monopoly. It put the country's leading 100 papers on the market and had sold most of them by 1994. In Czechoslovakia, censorship was officially abolished in 1990, although *de facto* this had happened some months earlier. In Hungary, the state's media monopoly actually ended in 1988 although it was not legally recognized until a law of 1989.

Dismantling the old system is one thing but setting up a framework for a new media system is another. It is not enough to leave the media to market or political forces and hope that these will produce the desired effect. The market does not answer some of the most vital questions, and does not necessarily produce solutions:

- what are the rights and duties of a free media?
- how should it be regulated, if at all, and by whom?
- what steps should be taken, if any, to prevent private media monopolies or oligopolies?
- should there be public radio and TV?
- should newspapers be subsidized by the state?
- what should be the limits, if any, of foreign ownership?
- should there be laws about pornography and violence?
- should films be classified according to their fitness for young people?
- should the old bosses of the communist media be banned from a role in the new media?

These are all very difficult questions but they have to be confronted and answered. The central difficulty of the new democracies is that they have rarely been confronted and less often answered. Quite a few draft laws have been considered but few have been adopted. Hungary has special difficulties in this respect. A two-thirds majority of parliament is necessary to pass press laws, but a draft presented in 1992 failed to get a single vote.

Partly because east European countries are in the process of fundamental transformation, and partly because few have adopted a regulatory framework for the media, the present situation is highly changeable. In 1993, Hungary had sixty-one local radio and thirty-nine local TV stations. Less than two years later this was reduced to thirty-one and twenty-six. Poland had eighty-eight newspapers in 1980, 124 in 1993; 2,500 journals and magazines in 1980, over 3,000 in 1993. The situation in Eastern countries is also volatile. In Russia the media scene involves murder, bombs, violence and intimidation, for both political and commercial gain.

Things change so quickly that it is impossible to write about them accurately. Nevertheless, across the region as a whole three general patterns are apparent: first, the penetration of the system by Western financial interests; secondly, the persistence of a strong old guard influence in the media; and thirdly, concerns about quality.

Western penetration of the eastern media market

Western financial interests have taken control of a large part of the Central and Eastern European media, and their share is increasing daily. Maxwell, Murdoch, Berlusconi, Bertelsmann, Time-Warner, Springer and many other Western media interests have moved quickly into the Eastern market. It has been estimated that Western financial interests control more than 75 per cent of Poland's national press and over a third of its regional press. Six out of ten of the best-selling weeklies are published by German companies (Bertelsmann, Springer and Bauer). In mid-1994, half of Czech national papers and two-thirds of the main regional papers were foreign owned or controlled. Most Western nations would be unhappy about such an important part of political life being in foreign hands. Not only are foreign interests expanding, but the longer the situation persists the more difficult it will be to do anything about it.

The old guard influence persists

Significant parts of the new media are under the control or influence of the old communists, and some of the new guard journalists and politicians seem to be locked into the old system. The three best-selling Polish weekly journals are in the hands of former communists. One of these, *Nie* (translating as 'No'), selling 600,000 copies a week, is a mixture of pornography, sensationalism, and anti-intellectualism, and is edited by Jerzy Urban, who was General Jaruzelski's chief spokesman during the imposition of martial law in the 1980s. In the Czech Republic the three main daily papers are all direct descendants of the communist press.

Even where new press laws have been adopted they are often sketchy and unclear, and have not prevented old-style state intervention or control of a formally free press. With a few notable exceptions (Slovenia, for example), there is widespread complaint about covert but strong government pressure on the media replacing the old overt communist censorship. One of the first acts of the government of the newly created Slovakia was to dismiss the editor of the largest 'independent' daily paper. In Poland, five changes of government have been followed immediately by the

---

BRIEFING 6.3

Western media interests in Central and Eastern European

The situation is changing so rapidly that it is impossible to give a completely accurate and up-to-date picture of Western financial involvement in the Eastern European media. But the following gives an idea of current developments.

- News International (Murdoch): shares in Hungary's private TV station, NAP TV.
- EurExpansion (a conglomerate company involving French, American and German media companies): interests in Hungarian, Polish, Czech and Russian publications.
- Fininvest (Berlusconi): advertising and foreign programming for Soviet TV (1989); financial management of Polish TV.
- Reader's Digest (a private but very large company): now sells in Hungarian, Polish, Czech and Russian.
- Ringier (a large Swiss conglomerate): owns the largest Czech daily tabloid and controls another liberal broadsheet.
- SocPresse (Robert Hersant, one of the largest publishers in France): important publishing interests in Poland; Slovakia, Hungary, the Czech Republic, and Russia. Some SocPresse stakes in Czech newspapers were taken over in 1994 by Rheinische-Bergische, a Duesseldorf company.
- Springer (one of the largest press companies in Germany): control of Hungarian newspapers.
- Astra (Luxembourg TV company): satellite services especially in Poland but also other parts of Eastern Europe.
- Time-Warner (the world's largest media conglomerate): cable TV in Poland.
- Bertelsmann (the largest west European publisher): owns half the largest Hungarian daily paper.
- Agence Havas (one of the largest western media conglomerates): interests in radio in Hungary, Latvia, Ukraine; TV in Russia, Estonia, Latvia, Hungary, Belarus, the Czech Republic, Slovakia, Lithuania and Slovenia.
- Hachette (the largest media group in France): Radio Europe 1; broadcasting interests in the Czech Republic and Russia.

---

replacement of the head of national TV. In Hungary in 1993, the directors of both national radio and TV were forced to resign after conflict with the government. In Poland, Lech Walesa (president up to 1996) has repeatedly intervened in the business of the National Radio and Television Council and changed its members – some say unconstitutionally.

The Soviet Union finalized its press laws in 1991 with sixty-two articles, one of which gives the government power to censor the publication of any specially guarded secret. The Russian Constitution guarantees the freedom of the press, but this did not prevent President Yeltsin appointing and then sacking four different directors of a TV station between 1991 and 1994. Romanian law now imposes a prison sentence on anyone who publicly defames the nation, gives false information, or presents a threat to state security. State control is often tight in the Eastern states of Ukraine, Russia, Romania, Albania and Bulgaria, and especially in Belarus under President Lukashenka.

Mass survey research in Central and Eastern Europe shows that citizens who favour a market economy are also more likely to oppose state control of the media. In terms of individual countries, Table 6.1 shows that more opposition to state

Table 6.1 Attitudes towards government control of the media in Central and Eastern Europe

	Ukraine	Russia	Belarus	Latvia	Lithuania	Estonia	Bulgaria	Czech Rep.	Poland	Romania	Slovakia
The government should control the activities of all radio, TV and print media											
% agree	63	60	56	45	27	43	45	22	30	41	29
Private/independent media will always be more objective than state media											
% agree	50	48	48	60	62	65	40	56	53	53	50
Printed material should never be banned for political reasons											
% agree	69	79	74	82	86	84	79	82	70	74	70
Censorship of films and magazines is necessary to uphold the moral standards											
% agree	77	78	71	71	58	65	64	35	54	65	49

Source: Stephen Connors, *et al.* 'Differing views on government control', *Transition*, 1 (18), October 1995, 26–9.

BRIEFING 6.4

The struggle for control of Hungarian radio and television

Illustrating the struggle for political control of the media which may affect a government's chance of re-election, is the attempt of the leading Hungarian party after the first free elections to appoint compliant directors of television and radio. The leading party of government in 1991 was the nationalist and conservative Hungarian Democratic Forum. The leading opposition party was the Alliance of Free Democrats, a liberal grouping. The president of Hungary (a position with limited powers) was Arpad Gönoz. The Forum's prime minister was Joseph Antall.

Antall first of all nominated candidates for the two directorships which were approved by the president. As they did not prove politically compliant enough, however, he asked the president to dismiss them, which he refused to do. The issue went to the Constitutional Court which ruled in favour of the president but also required parliament to pass a law on the Media clarifying the situation. Antall then appointed deputy-directors of radio and television, which he could constitutionally do without consultation. He cut financial support to television and took personal charge of their budgets.

Under constant pressure, the original directors of radio and television resigned. Their resignations were not accepted by the president but were by the prime minister. The government stalled on passing a media law while his nominees as deputies took over media administration and programming. In spite of this the (ex-communist) socialists won the election of 1994. However, they continued the tradition of forcing political appointments on the media while no regulatory law was passed by parliament. In 1996, parliament started to debate a law. The situation may soon be changed, however, through the initiation of a competing television service by some international conglomerate, possibly headed by Berlusconi or Murdoch.

---

control existed in the Czech Republic, Slovakia, Poland, Estonia and Lithuania. The more statist countries were Russia, Ukraine and Belarus. Romania, Bulgaria and Latvia fit in between the liberal and statist nations.

Media quality

In the haste to privatize the media and in the resulting scramble to buy portions of it, quality, fairness and accuracy have often taken second place to profit. A frequent complaint concerns poor journalistic standards and an old mind-set which either defends or attacks government policy, but rarely describes it accurately or analyses it objectively. In the old state system journalists were defenders of the regime. In the new system they are often defenders of one ideological line or another, not dispassionate reporters. Other commentators claim that political lies, sensationalism, partisanship, inaccuracy and bias have replaced the old 'wooden tongue' of the communist press. At the same time, many of the old communist cultural publications, some of high quality, have disappeared – although Budapest, Moscow, Prague, or Warsaw, now print their own editions of *Playboy*. Some parts of the press openly advocates xenophobia, racism and anti-semitism; other parts are simply careless, biased, or deadly dull.

The European media today

The mass media are changing rapidly in the modern world and they will continue to do so, in all probability, for the foreseeable future. When interactive information super-highways are fully integrated with satellite communications and then linked to computers, phones, faxes, TV, printers and sound systems, the possibilities are all but boundless. This may be some time in the future for the majority of people. But the current technological and political revolutions are also earth-shaking.

They have forced major changes in the old public service media systems of Western Europe. The importance and effects of these changes should not be underestimated. But it is also true that they are easily exaggerated. Most Western European countries have not ditched public service in favour of the market. Rather, change has been slow and limited, and the present arrangements are a mixture of public service and market models – a dual model, in fact.

Central and Eastern European governments have been pitched into the turbulence of technological and economic change without warning. In addition, of course, they are in the midst of basic political transformations. Hence they have had to solve the problem of how to create democratic mass media without a democratic tradition. They have been faced by a whole host of extraordinarily difficult political and technical problems which they have not been able resolve, or even face. They have been the victims of events and forces, rather than architects or pilots of them. The Baltic countries of Latvia and Estonia have probably been the most successful in establishing a free and viable media, with the help of Scandinavian investment and advice.

The mass media systems of Central and Eastern Europe have changed almost overnight. But in some important respects they have not changed enough. The old guard retains a great deal of influence, and the new guard retain many of the old ways of thinking. It will be some time before these influences wear off, although it should also be said that many transitional political systems inevitably keep some of their old elites and old ways of doing things. This was true for Italy and Germany in 1945, and for Spain, Greece and Portugal in the 1970s.

Western and Eastern Europe are both shifting rapidly towards the market as an organizing principle. Contemporary enthusiasm for the possibilities this offers makes it easy to overlook the dangers it presents for political communication. Political news is not like soap-powder, and political opinions are not like motor-cars – there are no market guarantees of their reliability, durability, or quality. There is also evidence that reliance upon profit and commercial income tends to distort the news, to threaten political neutrality, and to lower journalistic standards.

Moreover, quality news media which depend exclusively upon advertising and commercial revenues tend to be skewed towards the upper end of the market – a small and wealthy percentage of the population – and to under-provide for the rest – the great majority of low- and middle-income citizens. This may be why a market based system of political communication, such as that of the United States, is associated with low levels of political information and interest, compared with public service systems, such as those in Germany. It is not obvious that democracy is best served by exclusively commercial media, nor that they will create a well-informed and democratic public. Only time will tell whether the mixed model that currently exists in Europe is simply a transitional phase or a more permanent arrangement which encapsulates some of the virtues of both the public service and market models.

■ Further reading

On the west European media see John Keane, *The Media and Democracy* (Oxford, Polity Press, 1991); James Curran and Michael Gurevitch, *Mass Media and Society* (London, Edward Arnold, 1991); Denis McQuail, 'Western European media: the mixed model under threat', in John Downing (ed.), *Questioning the Media: A Critical Introduction* (London, Sage, 1995).

There is much less written about central and eastern Europe and the situation changes so quickly that much is slightly dated on publication. However, see Bernard J. Marguerritte, 'Post-communist eastern Europe: The difficult birth of a free press', Joan Shorenstein Center, Harvard University, John F. Kennedy School of Government, Discussion Paper D-21, August 1995; Colin Sparks, 'The press, the market, and democracy', *Journal of Communication*, Winter 1992, 36–51; John Downing, 'Media, dictatorship, and the re-emergence of "civil society"', in John Downing (ed.), *Questioning the Media: A Critical Introduction*, op. cit. The issue of media freedom is the theme of *Transition*, 1(18), 6 October 1995.

Chapter 7

Institutionalizing interests

■ Interest representation in the old and new democracies

The business conglomerates which increasingly control mass communications are in many ways typical of the special interests which seek to influence national and international politics. They may have particular political views to push, like Berlusconi in Italy, Murdoch in Britain, or Springer in Germany, or they may simply be interested in maximizing their business interests with as little state regulation as possible. In either case they need access to governments.

It could be argued that the owners of the mass media are in a special position because of the potential political power they wield. But media conglomerates are not the only powerful interests seeking to influence government. Other multinational and national firms also have favours to trade. These may be direct contributions to party funds, or even payments to individual politicians. More indirectly they may be able to invest or disinvest in depressed regions like the west of Ireland or the Spanish and Italian south – decisions which are important for local economies and party support.

Especially in the 1980s and 1990s, when governments sold off state industries on a large scale, businessmen could hope to profit directly from their dealings with politicians. In many cases, indeed, the distinction between businessmen and politicians, and civil servants is not very clear. Some of the prime beneficiaries of privatization have been ministers and civil servants, who moved into the new enterprises. This is as true of Britain as of Russia, although the major scandals arising from the nexus between business and politics have so far arisen in Spain and Italy, where they have brought down governments.

Some countries encourage close relations between civil servants and businessmen in the interests of economic development. This is perhaps most true of France, where top technocrats are produced by the specialist and elitist 'Grandes Ecoles' of Paris with a view to a double career in both public and private sectors, with free movement between them. This means that the administrators on both sides are well known to each other and have shared understandings – a system which has worked well in developing some industries. For example, armaments and associated engineering and steel enterprises need national orders to maintain their economic base, and sometimes get state help for complicated, multinational deals involving military and foreign alliances. The close involvement of armaments manufacturers with the national civil service has worked very well in making France a leading world producer. This technocratic alliance has, however, been less successful in economic sectors where more flexibility and rapid adaptation is required, as in electronics.

Whether or not they are actively encouraged as a matter of national policy, close relations between business and government are almost inevitable in the modern state. What governments do closely affects business, and business is important to governments as a wealth and job creator which provides part of the tax base. In this sense it is not even necessary for business to engage in active lobbying because governments understand its needs without being reminded. Share prices or exchange rates only need to fall for governments to become concerned and consult the bankers. Particularly for smaller or poorer countries dependent on foreign loans and capital, the approval of international money markets is crucial and will heavily influence economic policies. Bodies like the World Bank or the International Monetary Fund (IMF) may influence national policy more effectively than internal interest groups. Whatever the national benefits of business, its primary aim is to generate profits for directors and shareholders. So it is small wonder that the close relationship between businessmen and governments has been regarded with suspicion, particularly by those on the political left, quite apart from problems of bribery and corruption.

However, it is not only business which needs close relations with government. All sectors of society are affected by state policy, and must organize to make their voice heard – at the very least to convince governments that ignoring their interests will have political costs, such as a loss of votes or reduced ability to implement policies.

The need for organization is as pressing for employees as employers – more so, since the growing number of very large firms and multinationals have their own access to governments and an ability to exploit it. Individual employees, on the other hand, need to join with others to gain influence. Business apart, trade unions were often the first groups to organize this way, and both unions and business have allied themselves with, or in some cases actually created, political parties – socialists and communists on the one hand, liberals and conservatives on the other. We will discuss parties in Chapter 9. Here, however, we should note that contemporary business associations and unions often distance themselves from parties in order to remain free to negotiate with their rivals if they are in power.

This is also true of co-operative movements of producers and retailers; farmers' associations and Agrarian parties; and churches and their religious associations in regard to the Christian Democrats. These groups often have close connections with particular parties. But at the same time, they have to defend the interests of their members, whichever party is in government. Thus they maintain a certain distance from all political parties. Indeed, the classic definition of an interest group is that it tries to influence government policy without seeking to be in government – as parties do, of course.

In this sense traditional interest organizations, which defend the interests of occupational groups, differ from the more general proselytizing movements centred on a general cause such as protection of the environment, or the promotion of an alternative life style. In the case of such 'new social movements', the distinction between political and other forms of activity is blurred. Some of these movements, the 'Greens' being a notable example, have evolved a 'new politics' as well as new political parties – that is, a new political style as well as a new form of organization. We shall discuss social movements in the next chapter before looking at parties and party systems in Chapter 9.

Interest representation: theory and practice

With increasing experience of the workings of mass democracy pressure group theory has evolved from the view that the promotion of all sectional interests was

BRIEFING 7.1

Interests and groups

Pressure groups

Pressure groups are formed voluntarily by people who wish to protect or promote a common interest or cause. Unlike parties, most pressure groups have no wish to become the government of their country, and compared with parties they have a fairly narrow range of concerns, most of which are non-political. Many pressure groups are not primarily political at all. But if their interests and aspirations are affected by government they will organize themselves politically in order to influence public policy. The term 'pressure' does not necessarily imply the use of negative sanctions, such as strikes or the withdrawal of co-operation, It may simply involve passing on information to the government and the general public. Indeed, depending upon circumstances, pressure groups use a wide variety of means to exercise influence, from mass demonstrations to writing letters to representatives. There are two main types of pressure groups – sectional or interest groups, and cause or promotional groups.

Interest groups or sectional groups

Interest groups represent people in their occupational capacity and are, therefore, mainly concerned with economic interests. The three main kinds of interest groups are business, professional and trade union organizations. People often join interest groups, therefore, because of their occupation.

Cause groups

Cause groups are formed to promote or protect an idea, goal, or principle which is not directly related to the personal or material interests of their members. In other words they are voluntary organizations formed by people who have some common aspiration, apart from their jobs. The category is a broad one and covers all sorts of voluntary organizations and associations – churches, educational, cultural and leisure organizations, charities and welfare, community associations, sports clubs, social clubs, youth clubs and scientific organizations.

Peak associations

Similar types of interest groups are often brought together by a peak, or umbrella organization in order to co-ordinate activity. Peak associations are thus organizations with a membership of organizations. Most notable are the confederations which bring together business interests under one roof and try to speak for them all, and the parallel organizations of trade unions. Peak organizations do not stop with a particular country; they are often organized up to the European and world level. Nor are peak associations limited to interest groups; they cover all manner of groups.

New social movements

The term new social movements was coined in the 1970s to describe the new political organizations which were broader than pressure groups but more loosely knit than political parties. The largest and most conspicuous are concerned with the environment, with atomic energy and weapons, women and with minority groups of various kinds. They are discussed in greater detail in the following chapter.

bad and against the public interest, to the realization that there are many positive virtues in the pressure group system. At the turn of the century the main groups lobbying governments were business interests, often in pursuit of gains which had little, if any, connection with the public good. As we have seen this is often the case today, particularly when large individual firms are involved, and when government personnel benefit immediately from policies on privatization and regulation.

Yet there is another side to interest groups. Governments have a real need of two things: information and consent. They need information which is often technical and cannot be collected by public agencies and officials who, on their own, do not have the necessary expertise. Well-financed and organized interest groups have these resources, or can collect information from their own members. Hence they can help governments, even to the extent of participating in the formulation of the policy designed to regulate them.

Doing this naturally helps them influence the content of policy in their own favour. At the extreme, in fact, a group can 'capture' a ministry or public agency, which, in 'going native', may then promote narrow sectional interests rather than the public good. This is a danger, but drawing on group information and resources can also be essential for governments and generally beneficial if it produces a more sensible and workable policy. One problem of the newly emerging democracies is that neither the bureaucracy nor interest groups have a strong enough organizational base to benefit from this kind of relationship.

The other advantage the government gets from close consultation with groups is their consent and co-operation in implementing public policy. It is obviously necessary to have this, for if policy meets with resistance, implementation may be difficult or impossible. Indeed, governments often lack the ability to enforce legislation, and depend on the voluntary compliance of groups and individuals.

The opposite danger is that of strong public agencies 'capturing' private organizations which are then unable to defend their own interests against the government. Groups that develop a working relationship which is too close to government may become 'domesticated' and unable to promote the interests of their members adequately. Indeed, some organizations refuse to accept public money on these grounds. If pressure group leaders become too closely entangled with public officials, they may drift away from their members, making it difficult to implement agreements negotiated with government.

It was problems of this kind which caused the break-up of 'corporatist' and 'tripartite' arrangements in the 1980s, under the stress of economic recession. 'Neocorporatism' is a formal and informal system of negotiation and policy concertation between governments and interest groups. Each makes concessions to get agreement on general economic policy: unions might promise wage restraint; employers to retain existing employees; and government to maintain social benefits. Such corporatist settlements were credited with promoting sustained economic growth and stability, and social and political peace and co-operation during the 1960s and 1970s. The system contrasted with the rather turbulent industrial and political relations in non-corporatist countries such as Britain and France.

Since the 1980s there has been a tendency for governments dedicated to free-market economics to ignore negotiation in favour of de-regulation and competition. The Thatcher government in Britain is the best example of this, rejecting consultation with even the most established business and professional associations. Even a

BRIEFING 7.2

Corporatism, neo-corporatism and pluralism

Corporatism

Historically, the term 'corporatist' refers to the corporations or guilds of craftsmen, tradesmen and businessmen of medieval Europe. Such corporations exercised great influence on the working lives of their members. The general principle was taken up by the Fascists, Mussolini and Franco, who tried to organize all social and occupational groups into corporations or syndicates under the control and guidance of the state.

Neo-corporatism

Neo-corporatism is quite different from the corporatism of medieval guilds and the Fascist states of Italy and Spain. It refers to a system in which government and private interests work closely together within a powerful and complex set of decision-making institutions concerned with the formulation of public policy and its implementation. Each set of interests in the policy area is organized comprehensively into peak associations, or federations, which co-ordinate and monopolize their field. This means that peak associations can negotiate effectively with other peak associations and with government, and can guarantee the support of their members for the negotiated settlement. The corporatist system is usually best developed in the economic sphere where trade unions typically agree to limit wage and other demands in return for full employment, business organisations promise to maintain full employment in return for industrial peace and stability, and government agrees to maintain social benefits in return for political stability, economic co-operation, and economic growth.

Neo-corporatism developed in the 1960s and 1970s when economies were growing. It tended to break up in the 1980s under the pressures of economic stagnation or decline. Strong corporatist systems were found in Austria, Sweden, Norway, the Netherlands and Luxembourg. Less strong forms of corporatism were found in West Germany, Switzerland, Belgium, Denmark, Finland and Ireland.

Pluralism

In pluralist decision-making, groups do not co-operate so much as compete for influence over government. They are not partners with government nor bound with it in a powerful set of decision-making institutions. Groups have no formal role in decision-making or implementation, because government is the dominant force in both. Indeed, group activity may be fragmented, group membership may only be a small proportion of the possible total, and organizations in the same field of interest may be poorly co-ordinated by peak associations. However, some groups may be better organized, have more resources, and more strategic social, economic and political positions than others, and so may be relatively powerful influences on government. Business interests are often in this fortunate position in pluralist systems. France, Britain, and Italy are the best Western European examples of pluralist policy making.

strong corporatist country like the Netherlands introduced neo-liberal policies under the Christian-Liberal coalition led by Lubbers. The governments of Central and Eastern Europe had little choice about imposing free-market policies without much internal consultation as they had few national interest groups to negotiate with, other than the communist-dominated trade unions.

As the recent resurgence of Eastern trade unions and communist parties demonstrates, it can be dangerous and self-defeating not to work for widespread consent.

Even poorly organized groups which feel ignored may force the government to retreat. Such has been the case in France where government technocrats have sometimes formulated grand plans without much consultation. In the case of the high-speed rail network this has provided a coherent solution to a problem which, in countries like Britain, have tended to be defeated by local interests. However lack of consultation in France has sometimes produced violent reactions – by farmers, Catholics, or students, for example – which have resulted in sudden policy reversals, or even a threat to political stability. This is particularly true if the demonstrators occupy the streets of Paris for any length of time, as they did in 1968 and to a lesser extent in 1995.

That dangers of this type exist in some European countries today, and not all in the East, illustrates the potential uses of organized interests which offset their negative aspects. At least in the long term, organization and involvement in decision-making seem better than disorganization and alienation, so the extent of interest group organization within European countries remains an important indicator of democracy and stability.

■ Interest groups and their membership

It is difficult to obtain full information on interest groups in all European countries, but we can get an idea of their range and strength by examining a few countries. Germany is not untypical. A recent study identifies six main kinds of pressure group there (see Table 7.1) . These vary enormously in political influence and membership. For example, trade unions, with over 8 million members, are much larger than most business organizations, although the Farmers' Association is a million strong, and some other business and professional organizations are quite large.

Social organizations are also sizeable. The veterans' associations, with a million members, are a classic 'defence' group safeguarding members' pensions and other rights. The Red Cross, with 4 million, is a cause group. Amnesty International, another cause group, is concerned with civil liberties and owes some of its influence to its strong links with world organizations. There is also an elaborate array of sports associations with their own complex set of international connections.

Other Western European countries have a similar array of organizations, all with the common features of being highly varied, densely packed, and organizationally interconnected in complex ways. Many groups organised at the local and community levels are integrated into regional associations, national bodies, and then into European and international organizations. Some of their variety can be appreciated from Table 7.2, which details economic peak associations in Finland, France, Italy, Norway and Turkey.

Besides being vertically integrated, interest groups are also horizontally interconnected with other similar organizations and federations. In this way the social world of Western societies is tightly integrated by its voluntary associations which can, if necessary, be mobilized for political purposes as well. Social scientists believe that this group world is of crucial importance socially and economically, and politically it has enormous potential. Having groups which are able to organize themselves and act independently of governments and state is a major constituent of an autonomous civil society, which in turn is the principal basis for a viable democracy.

Table 7.1 Types of interest organisation, Federal Republic of Germany, 1989	Type of organization	Examples
	Economic Associations	
	Business association and associations of Self-employed	Federation of German Industry, including 34 branch associations and about 400 other organizations. Membership about 80,000. Specialized in particular for expressing demands towards the public and in the political system.
		Federation of German Employers' Associations including 58 branches and about 400 sub-organizations. Specialized in particular for conduct of collective bargaining with trade unions.
		German Farmers' Association, including about 40 associations. Membership about 1 million.
		Federation of Professions, including 65 associations for different professions (doctors, architects, etc.).
	Trade unions	German Trade Union federation, including 16 industrial trade unions. Membership about 8 million.
	Consumers' associations	Federation of consumers' associations.
	Professional associations	Association of Meteorologists. Membership 375.
	Social organizations	
	Aftermath of Second World War	Association of victims of war and military service. Membership 1 million.
	Welfare associations	Red Cross, about 4 million members.
	Other social organizations	Association of tenants (about 1 million members).
	Citizens' action committees	Environmental groups (see Chapter 8).
	Associations for leisure time activities	German Sports Federation, about 20.5 million members.
	Political associations	Amnesty International, about 28,000 members.
	Associations of territorial authorities	Association of cities and villages, about 8,000 cities/villages.

Source: Adapted from W. Rudzio, *Das Politische System der Bundesrepublik Deutschland* (Opalder, Leske und Bundrich, 1991) , pp. 61–30.

Table 7.2 Economic peak associations in selected Western European countries, 1990		
	Finland	Finnish Employers Federation (STK); Central Organization of Finnish Trade Unions (SAK), founded 1909, membership 1 million; Confederation of Salaried Employees (TVK), founded 1927, membership 350,000.
	France	National Council of French Employers (CNPF); General Workers Confederation (CGT), founded 1895, membership 1.6 million; Force Ouvriere (FO), founded 1947, membership 1.1 million; French Democratic Workers' Federation (CFDT), membership 560,000; General Confederation of Managers (CGC), founded 1944, membership 300,000; National Educational Federation (FEN), founded 1948, membership 400,000.
	Italy	General Confederation of Italian Industry (Confindustria); General Confederation of Italian Workers (CGIL – Communist/Socialist), founded 1944, membership 4.5 million; Italian Confederation of Workers (CISL – Christian Democrat), founded 1948, membership 3 million; Union of Italian Workers (UIL – Social Democrat/Liberal), founded 1950, membership 1.3 million; National Syndicate of Italian Workers (CISNAL – right), founded 1950, membership 2 million.
	Norway	Confederation of Norwegian Business and Industry; Norwegian Agricultural Workers (LO) founded 1899 membership 750,000; Confederation of Vocational Unions (YC), membership 130,000; Federation of Norwegian Professional Association (AS), membership 140,000.
	Turkey	Turkish Confederation of Employers Associations; Confederation of Progressive Trade Unions (DISK), founded 1967, suspended 1980, membership in 1980, 600,000; Confederation of Turkish Trade Unions, founded 1952, membership 2 million.

Source: Jan Erik Lane, David McKay and Kenneth Newton, *Political Data Handbook: OECD Countries*, (Oxford, Oxford University Press, 1996).

BRIEFING 7.3

Civil society, mass society and social groups

The idea of 'civil society' was very important in classical political theory of the seventeenth and eighteenth centuries. It implied that there was a society which could exist independently of the state and, if necessary, organize itself to overturn a corrupt state and reconstitute it along better lines. The term has come back into fashion, particularly to describe the social requirements necessary to sustain democracy in Central and Eastern Europe. A strong civil society would have individuals with the type of attitudes described in Chapter 5. But it would also have active and diverse voluntary groups. These need have nothing directly to do with politics. However, they provide a basis on which individuals can relate to other individuals in a spontaneous and unforced way. They give people experience in managing their own affairs, and an organizational basis for political discussion and action if they want to take it. Social groups are absent from a mass society (as contrasted to a civil society). A mass society is composed of isolated individuals who have few links with their neighbours. They have, therefore, no independent social basis on which to evaluate media or political propaganda and can thus be manipulated by leaders and the state.

We have information about group membership but unfortunately no indicators of pressure group power. Power is hard to measure. Business groups, while relatively small in terms of membership, probably gain from being better financed and organized, and from having strategic economic importance. Membership size is not the sole, or most important source of interest group influence, therefore. But it can be significant, particularly in democracies where the parties depend upon votes. In most Western societies large sections of the population belong to voluntary organizations, as Table 7.3 shows.

Outside the Mediterranean countries, more than half the population belongs to a private organization, mostly sports or athletic clubs, and churches. Although both types of organizations pursue political goals, such as increasing public expenditure on sports facilities or opposition to liberal laws on abortion, their main fields of activity are far removed from politics. Hence we will concentrate more on the other groups.

Three sets of organizations seem to be particularly influential in European politics – farmers' and employers' associations, and trade unions. Farmers' organizations usually have high membership densities; Germany is typical in that about nine out of ten farmers belong to their association. Corresponding figures for England and Wales are 80 per cent, Sweden nearly 100 per cent, and France 75 per cent. In addition these organizations historically have close links with major political parties which are (or consider themselves to be) dependent on farmers – at least on election day. Most important for farmer power may be the absence of articulate and organized antagonists, clearly present in the case of the struggle between employers and employees. There is often little organized opposition to farming interests, which can also count upon a generalized attachment to the countryside and sympathy for the rural way of life. However, since the economic importance of farming is decreasing it may be losing some of its political strength.

Employers' organizations have relatively few members but many other resources, most importantly the power to make investment decisions, and the widely shared

Table 7.3 Organizational membership in seventeen countries: Percentage of population over 16 who belonged to different types of groups, 1989–90

	Germany	Belgium	Canada	Denmark	France	UK	Iceland	Ireland
Social welfare services for elderly, handicapped or deprived people	7.2	11.6	8.4	5.5	6.6	7.1	15.5	7.4
Religious or church organizations	15.9	12.2	24.9	6.7	6.2	16.6	49.7	13.9
Education, arts, music or cultural activities	12.0	16.1	17.7	12.5	8.8	9.3	13.8	10.1
Trade unions	15.7	14.4	12.3	49.0	5.2	14.4	59.7	8.8
Political parties or groups	7.5	5.8	7.4	6.5	2.7	4.9	15.1	3.8
Local community action on issues like poverty, employment, housing, racial equality	1.7	4.3	5.2	5.0	3.3	2.7	2.0	3.3
Third World development or human rights	2.2	5.9	4.6	2.8	2.6	2.0	3.4	1.6
Conservation, the environment, ecology	4.6	6.5	7.6	12.5	2.3	5.0	4.8	2.3
Professional associations	8.9	6.7	16.4	12.1	5.0	9.8	15.0	·5.0
Youth work (e.g. scouts, guides, youth clubs, etc.)	3.6	8.2	9.8	4.7	3.2	4.6	8.3	6.3
Sports or recreation	32.3	19.5	22.9	33.5	15.7	16.9	30.3	23.7
Women's groups	5.6	9.7	6.6	1.7	1.0	4.8	6.7	4.6
Peace movement	2.0	1.9	2.0	2.1	0.5	1.1	1.4	0.6
Animal rights	4.8	7.5	2.6	4.1	2.3	1.9	2.3	1.0
Voluntary organizations concerned with health	4.4	4.2	8.7	5.8	2.8	3.5	4.7	3.2
Other groups	8.9	5.0	13.0	10.8	5.3	7.1	10.0	2.1
None	0.0	0.0	34.5	19.0	0.0	0.0	0.0	0.0
Dont know/No answer	0.2	0.5	0.0	0.0	0.4	1.3	0.0	0.2

Table 7.3 (continued)

	Italy	Netherlands	Northern Ireland	Norway	Portugal	Spain	Sweden	USA	Switzerland
Social welfare services for elderly, handicapped or deprived people	4.1	16.0	8.6	10.9	3.9	2.5	7.5	9.2	8.9
Religious or church organizations	8.0	34.9	25.0	11.2	10.5	5.2	10.3	48.7	10.7
Education, arts, music or cultural activities	4.9	34.6	10.9	13.5	6.2	4.4	13.2	19.8	18.9
Trade unions	5.9	19.1	11.8	41.7	4.5	2.7	59.1	8.9	6.4
Political parties or groups	5.0	9.4	1.6	13.9	4.0	1.6	10.0	14.5	9.0
Local community action on issues like poverty, employment, housing, racial equality	1.6	4.9	2.0	2.7	1.4	0.9	2.1	4.9	
Third World development or human rights	1.1	14.3	2.6	5.1	0.5	1.0	9.4	2.0	1.3
Conservation, the environment, ecology	3.3	23.8	2.3	4.1	0.8	1.4	10.5	8.4	10.4
Professional associations	3.9	13.1	6.6	16.3	3.5	2.7	12.0	15.2	13.4
Youth work (e.g. scouts, guides, youth clubs, etc.)	3.6	6.6	10.9	5.9	2.2	1.6	8.8	12.7	3.8
Sports or recreation	11.3	40.4	17.4	32.8	11.5	4.9	31.8	20.3	29.0
Women's groups	0.4	7.3	5.3	2.9	0.2	0.7	3.0	8.4	
Peace movement	1.2	2.9	0.7	1.5	0.4	0.7	3.2	2.0	
Animal rights	1.7	12.5	1.3	1.8	0.8	0.9	7.0	5.5	
Voluntary organizations concerned with health	2.6	19.8	3.3	12.3	2.7	1.6	2.2	7.4	
Other groups	2.1	9.9	6.6	19.1	2.1	3.4	18.0	10.7	13.3
None	0.0	0.0	0.0	0.0	0.0	0.0	14.4	18.0	34.6
Dont know/No answer	0.1	0.4	0.0	0.0	0.3	1.9	0.0	0.0	2.8

Sources: European Values Study 1990:
Question 131a: Please look carefully at the following list of voluntary organizations any, activities and say which, if an do you belong to?

assumption that business is in the public good: what is good for employers is good for the economy, and what is good for the economy is good for the polity. Employers' organizations are more numerous and fragmented than trade unions, but have higher membership densities.

Figures for the membership densities of employers in Eastern European countries are not available, but preliminary information indicates that – as in the West – they are likely to be numerous and fairly autonomous. However, due to the fact that such associations have yet to consolidate themselves, it is impossible to describe them in detail or compare them with the west. In some countries, employers' spokesmen bluntly state that they are representatives of a group which does not yet exist.

The most potent business influence in Central and Eastern Europe may be that of the groupings of ex-*apparatchiks* which have taken over privatized businesses while retaining their links with higher bureaucrats and politicians forged in communist times. This parallels developments in the West, where politicians and bureaucrats have also concentrated in the newly privatized industries. The growth of global corporations and large national conglomerates, particularly in communications and utilities, may signal a shift in the representation of economic interests from national federations of businesses to large, individual corporations. In the 1960s and 1970s, when most firms were small to medium, business interests tended to be represented through their membership of organizations designed to operate at national level (Confindustria in Italy, the Confederation of British Industry in the United Kingdom). The failure of such organizations to secure the compliance of all members to national agreements, and their subsequent lack of access to market-oriented governments of the 1980s, has put a premium on direct lobbying by larger firms. These have used professional lobbying organizations to secure immediate benefits such as franchises and favourable regulatory regimes. Such lobbying proliferated in Britain under the Thatcher governments of the 1980s. As business interests often have close relationships with national politicians and top bureaucrats, the situation in the West as far as business is concerned does not seem very different from that in the East, where individual lobbying by firms and the cultivation of personal contacts at the highest levels of government are commonplace.

Convergence, divergence and critical junctures across Europe

To what extent are Central-Eastern and Western Europe converging with regard to interest representation? We can try to answer this question in regard to trade unions, the organizations about which we have most information. There are three competing hypotheses. According to the first, national patterns of interest representation differ now, but are moving towards a common European model. The forces of convergence have been at work for decades in the West, and are now also active in Central and Eastern Europe. There, it is said, political pluralism and modernization will produce the same effects as in the West.

Some scholars argue, however, that the convergence thesis is convincing for the West, but not for the Centre or East. There, because of the communist inheritance, there is no strong civil society, that is no intermediate layer of institutions between individuals and state. A large majority of Eastern Europeans were – and still are – state-reliant and attached to egalitarian and welfarist social policies. Survey results support this point, showing that citizens are used to pursuing either individual or state-directed strategies, but not used to expressing shared interests through private organizations. Hence, even in the long run, there will be two major systems of interest intermediation in Europe: interest organizations in the West with rules about membership, organization and politics; but unstable interest groups in the East, rendered almost superfluous by a 'flattened' mass society which relies on individual action or state attachments.

A third theory suggests that systems of representation are shaped by the conditions prevailing at the time they formed. Institutional inertia and stability guarantee the continuation of the pattern once established. Western labour market structures are related to religious-cultural variables – in particular, to the role and strength of the Catholic church – and to the rules of interest representation at 'critical historical junctures' in the creation of modern capitalism. In most Western countries this was between 1871 and the 1950s. Most unions were founded in association with the political parties active at that time, which, in turn, reflected cleavages in their society. In the Low Countries, France and Italy, for example, employees were organized into separate unions by communist, socialist and Christian parties, and these countries have fragmented and competing trade union movements today.

These contrast with the unitary trade union movements of Scandinavia, Germany and Britain, although there are also important differences between the latter. In Britain, long periods of peaceful, incremental growth has produced large conglomerate unions which are not divided along ideological or religious lines, but which often compete for members within the same industry or factory, In contrast, the monolithic unions of Germany organize the whole workforce within one industry.

In Eastern and Central Europe the 'critical historical juncture' was the double transition to democracy and capitalism in the ten years between the mid-1980s and the mid-1990s. The major political conflicts were not caused by cleavages between social groups and their political organizations, but by conflicting ideas about the transition from communism to capitalism and democracy. These are to a large extent reflected in contrasts between the old communist and the new, market-oriented political elites. One would expect Central and Eastern European systems of interest representation to mirror this and to reflect, at least in part, the influence of the former communist organizations. These new Eastern institutions will change and develop – but always on a path which began in and was influenced by the crucial period of transition.

According to this theory, we can expect different systems of interest intermediation to emerge in the two parts of Europe. In the West it will be based on the historical cleavages of politics at the turn of the nineteenth and first half of the twentieth century. In the East and Centre, it will be based upon the cleavage between old and new elites in the transition to capitalism and democracy in the 1980s and 1990s.

Trade unions as a focus for comparative study

We can check theories of the convergence or divergence of interest representation in Europe by looking at the information which is available for trade unions in Western, Central and Eastern Europe. This is because, alone among European pressure groups, trade unions have been scrutinized quite systematically and comparatively. Research has focused on three main questions:

- What are the organizational features of trade union structures? This applies to external relationships (with employers and other unions) as well as internal organization (e.g. centralization of decision-making and administration).
- Who are the trade unionists? Why do they join and why do they stay?
- What do unions do? What are the similarities and differences between unions in terms of collective bargaining activities? How do they relate to the political system and to parties? Are they confined to exerting pressure from outside, or are they included in the formulation and implementation of economic policy?

In what follows we will ask these questions about trade unions in Europe as a whole, for we are interested in whether they form distinct patterns in different region of the continent. For that we have to describe their structures and recent changes.

Trade union organization

At first glance, Western trade unions seem to differ a great deal among themselves. In France they are fragmented and ideological. In Britain they are fragmented and pragmatic. In Germany they are large, concentrated and biased towards compromise. However, a closer look reveals not only similarities across the whole of Western Europe, but families of trade union systems in different countries. The differences and similarities were created during the critical junctures mentioned above.

Unions were usually born out of socialist and left-wing political movements. But in countries divided along religious lines the Christian, and particularly Catholic churches formed their own trade unions. Then, in 1917, a further division was created with the organization of communist unions. Hence, in some countries the union movement was created around the capital–labour cleavage and organized by the socialists. In others, it is complicated by church–state relations, especially those involving the Catholic church. In countries like Great Britain, with just one central (class-based, left-right) cleavage, there was no lasting political split in the labour or union movement. In contrast, countries with either a weak socialist movement, or a strong communist and / or Catholic party, produced at least two labour wings – as in France, and Italy. Third, culturally fragmented nations – the Netherlands being the best example – produced socialist, Protestant, *and* Catholic trade unions.

A second crucial question concerned who should be organized. Labour unions first emerged in small-scale businesses. Thus occupation was the obvious criterion for membership. But in the course of industrialization, the number of unskilled and white-collar workers increased and presented new opportunities for union organization. In some cases, skilled workers kept their own unions, and unskilled workers were separately organized. Later, white-collar workers also formed separate unions. Britain followed this pattern. The alternative was to have industrial unions, organizing everybody in a factory or industry in the same union, irrespective of occupation, status, or gender. Quite a number of social democratic unions still pursue this goal. However, the pattern only emerged in Germany after 1945 under the allied occupation.

Third, the emergence of the welfare state caused another critical juncture with a decisive impact on trade union systems. In the 1930s, government employment in

Western European countries ranged from around 3 per cent of the labour force in Sweden and Switzerland, to about 9 per cent in Germany and Austria. Sixty years later the figure varied between 32 per cent in Sweden to 11 per cent in Switzerland. The European average was 18 per cent. In some countries new public sector unions emerged or organizations split into a public and private branch as in Sweden. In yet others, public sector unions remained in the traditional private sector union federation.

Trade union systems in Central and Eastern Europe, however, are not shaped by these historical junctures. Rather they are determined by whether the communist trade union structures were retained into the 1990s, or dismantled to be replaced by new organizations, built from scratch. In general the decision was to maintain communist unions (Table 7.4). In some cases, the organizational infrastructure was kept, but its ideology and manifesto abandoned. This is the case in the Czech and Slovak Republics, and in Bulgaria. But in other countries trade unions changed little in terms of either structure or policies. This is true of Romania – which has retained communist personnel and structures in the trade unions as in other institutions (see Chapter 3) – and to a lesser degree of Russia. The major union federation of Poland also survives from the communist period.

In all Central and Eastern European countries however – with the exception of the Czech and Slovak Republics – traditional trade union organizations now have to compete with new labour unions. East Germany is unique, because its trade unions have been transformed by incorporation into West Germany.

The trade union question is closely linked to that of transition to a market economy. Elites favouring the continuation of the old unions are inclined towards a slow transition, if they support it at all. This is most pronounced in Russia and Romania, far less clear in Hungary, and hardly discernible in Bulgaria or in the Czech and Slovak Republics. Union leaders from new organizations more usually support fast and fundamental socio-economic change. This does not apply to some small unions like the Trade Union Association of Bohemia, Moravia and Slovakia, which was created as a Marxist opposition *against* the modernization of the formerly communist organizations.

For their part, Western trade unions have also changed. First, they have often loosened their formal ties to political parties. This was pronounced in the case of Catholic unions in France, Italy and the Netherlands. But even here, unions and political parties moved apart, rather than divorcing themselves outright. In the case of Germany, it is clear that the German Trade Union Federation continues to have a special relationship with the Social Democratic Party even though it formally declared its party political neutrality. In Britain the links between the trade unions and the Labour party have also weakened considerably.

There were, in addition, various attempts to broaden union membership. In some cases this lead to the creation of white-collar and technical unions, but in others – for instance, Great Britain – it produced union mergers. These developments changed few of the overall patterns: countries with fragmented or centralized trade union movements in the early 1950s have the same pattern forty years on. Such stability is due to institutional inertia and the failure to renew membership. Most traditional blue collar unions failed to attract the expanding numbers of white collar workers. Only in Scandinavia, and to some extent in Great Britain, did white collar union density rise substantially. In both places this may have contributed to the decline of traditional labour organizations.

Table 7.4 Trade union organizations in Central and Eastern Europe, 1992

Country	Organization	Successor organization of	Per cent share of total union membership
Bulgaria	Confederation of Independent Bulgarian Trade Unions, 1989	Bulgarian Trade Union Federation, 1947–89 Bulgarski Profesionalen Sijun–BPS	75
	Konfederacija na Nesaviznite Sindikati na Bulgarija–KNSB Independent Federation of Labour 'Podkrepa', 1989 Nesaviznata Federacija na Truda 'Podkrepa'–NFT 'Podkrepa'	None	25
Czech and Slovak Federal Republic	Czechoslovak Confederation of Trade Unions, 1990 (divided into a Czech and Slovak branch) Československá konfederácia odborových svázu–CSKOS	Revolutionary Trade Union Movement, 1945–1989 Revolucné odborové hnutie–ROH	near to 100
	Christian Trade Union Organization, 1991	None	?
	Trade Union Association of Bohemia, Moravia, and Slovakia, 1991	None (this union was founded in opposition to OSKOS, as a communist organization, headed by the president of the former communist trade union movement)	?
Hungary	Odborové zdruzenie Ciech, Moravy a Slovenska–OZCMS National Organization of Hungarian Trade Unions, 1990 Magyar Szakszervezetek Országos Szövetsége–MSZOS	National Council of Hungarian Trade unions, 1948–90 Magyar Szakszervezetek Országos Tanácsa – SZOT	66
	National Federation of Labour Councils, 1990 Munkástanácsok Országos Szövetsége – MOSZ	None	3
	Solidarity Trade Unionist Federation of Workers, 1989 Szolidaritás Szakszervezeti Munkásszövetség – SZSZM	None	4
	Democratic League of Independent Trade Unions, 1988 Független Szakszervezetek Demokratikus Ligája – FSZDL	None	6
	Forum of Co-operation Szakszervezetek Együttmüködési Foruma–SZEF (Public sector unions)	None	13
	National Co-ordination of Autonomous Trade unions, 1991 Autonom Szakszervezetek Országos Koordinácioja–ASZOK	None	8
	Intellectual Trade Union Group, 1989 Ertelmiségi Szakszervezeti Tömörülés – SZT (Union of university graduates)	None	2
Germany	(Amalgamation with trade union system of West Germany)	None	100
Poland	All–Poland Alliance of Trade Unions, 1984 Ogolnopolskie Porozmienie Zwiakow Zawodowych – OPZZ	(Sole union organization after suspension of martial law after 1983)	42
	Solidarity, Independent Autonomous Trade Unions, 1980–81, 1989 NSZZ Solidarnosc	None	21
	Solidarnosc-80	None	38
Russia	General Confederation of Trade Unions, 1990, 1992	All–Union Congress of Trade Unions, 1918–89 Vsesoyuzny Congress Profsoysov	overwhelming majority
	Free Trade Unions, 1990 – among them Miners, Air traffic controllers, Pilots, Train drivers	None	minority
	Socialist (now: Solidarity) Unions (SozProf), 1989 (Social-democratic Unions) Profsojus Rossi SozProf	None	minority
	Societal-political association 'Worker' (Marxist organizations)	None	minority
	Obscestvenno-politiceskogo objedinenija 'Rabotsii'	None	minority

Notes: Data on membership shares are highly unreliable. Quantitative indicators in this table should not be over–interpreted; they just give some idea of relative shares.

In other respects internal and external power relationships remained unchanged in the West. That is, vertical integration (between different levels of the same trade union) and horizontal integration (relations between trade unions) did not change much.

Judged by the standards of the double revolution – to both capitalism and democracy – organizational changes in Central and Eastern Europe are not profound. They do not seem to confirm either theories of convergence, or theories of the 'missing middle layer'. Labour relations are usually dominated by the same organizations, often with the same ideology, as in the 1970s and 1980s. It is also remarkable that similar economic conditions can be associated with very different trade union systems, from the highly fragmented unions of Hungary, to the concentrated ones of Bulgaria, and the Czech and Slovak Republics.

Obviously the market economy is exerting similar pressures. But the transition did not occur in a vacuum. The politics and policies of Central and Eastern Europe are strongly influenced, even determined, by elites who owe their leading positions to the old communist system. In many cases the old system and old traditions have been carried over, whether from the pluralist system of Hungary, or the centralized system of Czechoslovakian employers. A small but telling example is the Russian practice of unions running holiday resorts. As long as Russians cannot afford holidays on Western lines, the unions will continue to play their traditional role. It is too easy to overlook the capacity of trade unions to pursue individual strategies even though they operate under similar economic circumstances.

Union membership

How many employees belong to trade unions and in what respects do they differ from non-unionists? Unfortunately, data on trade union membership in Central and Eastern Europe are unreliable or frequently missing, a problem which sometimes occurs with Western unions as well. Hence our comparison will be based on the results of surveys administered by the European Union, and on comparable surveys from other sources. While subject to some error these allow us to distinguish between employed and unemployed union members – a useful distinction which helps us to avoid over-estimating union density in a given economic sector.

Trade union membership, measured as the percentage of trade unionists in total dependent employment, varies considerably across Europe (see Tables 7.5 and 7.6). In Eastern Europe, it is high where union systems are dominated by former communist organizations, probably because they continue to provide selective incentives such as holidays and welfare. Another reason might be opposition to market transition. There is a positive correlation between resistance to change and union membership in these countries. In this sense, Eastern European unions have a defensive function and are strongest where there is most opposition to market economics.

Trade unions in both the East and West share one common trait: older employees of forty years or more, are over-represented (Table 7.7). Older employees, because they are less mobile and perhaps less employable, are more dependent on the defensive functions of unions. Younger employees may be more individualistic and less convinced of the need for collective goals and worker solidarity. A third explanation is progressive socialization into union norms over the course of one's

Table 7.5 Union
density: Employed trade
union members as a
percentage of the
dependent labour force,
1992–93

Country	Trade union membership as percent of the dependent labour force
Albania	61
Armenia	34
Belgium	47
Belarus	93
Bulgaria	48
Denmark	87
East Germany	39
Estonia	44
Euro-Russia	80
France	11
Georgia	46
Greece	17
Hungary	39
Ireland	42
Italy	36
Latvia	58
Lithuania	14
Luxembourg	59
Macedonia	41
Moldova	78
Netherlands	33
Norway	61
Poland	23
Portugal	25
Romania	46
Slovenia	55
Spain	15
Ukraine	82
United Kingdom	39
West Germany	32

Sources: Eurobarometer 39, Spring 1993 (ZA 2346); Central and
Eastern Eurobarometer, Fall 1992 (ZA 2321).

working life. Even in the nineteenth century, unions had the problem of low densities among younger workers.

Are the numbers or densities of unionized workers changing in different economic sectors? The cataclysmic changes in the East have surely had a major impact? Survey evidence does point to decreasing densities, especially in the former communist unions. This is partly due to the transition to democracy, which means that workers can no longer be coerced into joining. But it may also be because unions have often scaled down their activities after having lost state subsidies. At the same time, there is also a seepage of membership across Europe as a whole. Table 7.8 shows this for four countries. In Britain, Italy and the Netherlands, densities have declined in all groups, whereas Germany has compensated for losses by recruiting white-collar and younger workers.

Reasons for the loss in European membership include (1) a failure to organize the increasing numbers of office and service workers, (2) unemployment, which has hit membership particularly among manual workers, (3) public suspicion of unions, encouraged by conservative governments which came to power during the 1980s and 1990s, (4) increasing numbers of women and part-time workers who are difficult to organize, (5) increasing heterogeneity of the workforce in terms of qualifications, type of working conditions, and so on – all conditions which make any

Table 7.6 Union density by status: Union members as a percentage of white-collar (non-manual) and blue-collar (manual) workers

Country	Union members as percentage of white-collar workers	Union members as percentage of blue-collar workers
Albania	66	47
Armenia	47	33
Belgium	31	58
Belarus	95	90
Bulgaria	54	42
Denmark	76	92
East Germany	32	40
Estonia	44	42
Euro–Russia	80	80
France	10	11
Georgia	54	44
Greece	15	10
Hungary	40	33
Ireland	28	40
Italy	28	37
Latvia	60	55
Lithuania	16	13
Luxembourg	51	69
Macedonia	56	29
Moldova	83	75
Netherlands	29	33
Norway	54	65
Poland	24	13
Portugal	19	18
Romania	39	41
Spain	10	19
Ukraine	85	80
United Kingdom	31	40
West Germany	24	34

Sources: Eurobarometer 39, Spring 1993 (ZA 2346); Central and Eastern Eurobarometer, Fall 1992 (ZA 2321).

common interests of workers less visible. Nevertheless, decline is less in some countries than others. This is partly because of variations in social and political conditions, and partly because some unions have been more adept at adjusting to changing conditions. Recruitment seems to be as high among the young as among the old. There have been no major changes in relative densities since the 1970s.

Union policies and politics

What impact do unions have on politics? We can divide the answer into two parts: their impact on bargaining (with employers and sometimes governments), and their impact on politics and public affairs generally.

Collective bargaining

Across Europe the ability of unions to negotiate good terms for their members seems to have declined in some countries but remained the same in others. It has certainly not increased. The legal basis for collective bargaining is, in any case, very restricted in Eastern and Central Europe, and to a lesser extent in Southern Europe, where it was discouraged by the authoritarian regimes. In any case, in these countries there are few

Table 7.7 Union density by age: Union members as a percentage of workers below and over 40

Country	Union members as percentages of workers aged 15–39 years	Union members as percentage of workers 40 years and older
Albania	66	61
Armenia	33	51
Belgium	51	42
Belarus	90	95
Bulgaria	41	55
Denmark	85	89
East Germany	35	44
Estonia	36	53
Euro-Russia	75	86
France	10	13
Georgia	42	57
Greece	15	20
Hungary	34	44
Ireland	41	46
Italy	33	40
Latvia	50	66
Lithuania	12	17
Luxembourg	57	62
Macedonia	39	43
Moldova	74	82
Netherlands	27	43
Norway	50	74
Poland	20	28
Portugal	20	35
Romania	46	46
Slovenia	53	60
Spain	13	21
Ukraine	78	88
United Kingdom	37	41
West Germany	30	34

Sources: Eurobarometer 39, Spring 1993 (ZA 2346); Central and Eastern Eurobarometer, Fall 1992 (ZA 2321).

Table 7.8 Percentage changes in union densities in selected countries, 1975–95

	Percent change in union density among				
	All workers	White-collar workers	Blue-collar workers	Young workers	Old workers
Great Britain	-2	+2	-17	0	-3
Germany	+2	+1	-4	+2	+1
Netherlands	-3	-2	-12	-4	-2
Italy	-5	-8	-10	-3	-11

organizations to bargain with because business associations have not really emerged. In other places, conservative governments have tried to roll back the frontiers of the state (in some respects, not others), leaving the economy to the market and to international financial movements. Also, high unemployment weakens unions, making strike action sporadic, disorganized and unofficial. These trends are not absent in the West. Although unions have well-defined legal rights, high unemployment and growing internationalization of business have weakened their bargaining power as in the East.

Governments also consult unions less – possibly because globalization seems to have weakened national trade union organizations. Again there is variation between countries Corporatist arrangements for bringing together government, unions and

Table 7.9 Average left-right self-location of union-affiliated compared to non-affiliated individuals

Country	Members of trade union households	Members of non-trade union households
Belgium	3.9	5.5
Denmark	5.5	5.7
East Germany	4.7	5.0
France	5.0	5.1
Greece	5.1	5.7
Ireland	5.5	5.7
Italy	4.2	5.0
Luxembourg	5.1	5.3
Netherlands	5.0	5.5
Norway	5.0	5.3
Portugal	4.7	5.7
Spain	3.6	4.7
United Kingdom	5.1	5.6
West Germany	5.0	5.8

Notes: Respondents were asked to locate themselves on a scale running from 1 (extreme left) to 10 (extreme right).
Sources: Eurobarometer 39, Spring 1993 (ZA 2346).

Table 7.10 Party attachments of members of trade union households compared with members of other households

Country	Members of trade union households	Members of non-trade union households
Belgium	23	19
Denmark	24	27
East Germany	17	16
France	31	20
Greece	44	21
Ireland	23	19
Italy	32	24
Luxembourg	21	11
Netherlands	32	27
Norway	25	17
Portugal	20	7
Spain	21	11
United Kingdom	36	30
West Germany	32	24

Sources: Eurobarometer 39, Spring 1993 (ZA 2346).

business are clearly out of favour in Belgium, the Netherlands and Sweden, but appear to be fairly intact elsewhere. Ireland, Britain and France never had strong arrangements for such negotiations in any case, and British unions, never strong by West European standards, are now weaker than ever.

General effects on politics

Traditionally, unions have been associated with left-wing parties. But they have distanced themselves from them in the last thirty years, as an insurance policy for negotiating with centre-right governments. In spite of this, they have not become apolitical nor have they de-politicized their membership. Table 7.9 shows that union members are more to the left than the general population of most west European countries. Table 7.10 shows that union members are more likely to support a political party than non-trade unionists. While the party was not named in the survey it was likely to be on the left.

Table 7.11 Decline in party attachment and differences in left–right placement in union and non-union households, 1973/74–1993

Party attachment	Non-union households	Union households
Great Britain	−24	−20
West Germany	−9	−5
The Netherlands	−23	−18
Italy	−28	−34

Left-right location: differences in location towards left between union and non-union households

	1973–1974	1993
Great Britain	0.8	0.5
West Germany	0.6	0.8
The Netherlands	0.5	0.5
Italy	0.4	0.8

Source: Political Action 1973/1974 (Italy 1975/1976) ZA 0765; Eurobarometer 39, Spring 1993 (ZA 2346).

Table 7.12 Trade union opposition to the market economy in Central and Eastern Europe

Country	Percent members of non-trade union households opposed	Percent members of trade union households opposed
Albania	21	19
Armenia	53	55
Belarus	61	54
Bulgaria	21	19
Estonia	28	33
Georgia	28	35
Hungary	17	19
Latvia	40	48
Lithuania	17	23
Macedonia	51	55
Moldova	63	47
Poland	24	24
Romania	26	22
Euro–Russia	41	42
Slovenia	23	24
Ukraine	44	43

Note: [a]Percentage of respective group stating that the creation of a free market economy, i.e. one largely free from state control, is wrong for our country's future. [b]Trade union households are households in which at least one member is a union member.
Source: Central and Eastern Eurobarometer, Fall 1992 (ZA 2321).

Union members are not, of course, immune from general tendencies affecting the population as a whole. In countries where party identification and support are declining, the same is true of union members, though the decline is not as sharp. Table 7.11 shows a union effect which pervades households as well as individuals. Union households are consistently more left-wing than others, even at time points twenty years apart.

It seems likely that these patterns will repeat themselves in Central and Eastern Europe, ex-communist parties will find more support among the members of the ex-communist trade unions. Unfortunately, direct evidence on the link is missing. It is interesting to note, on the other hand, that opposition to market economics is no stronger in union than non-union households (see Table 7.12). This suggests that the link between unions and politics is not strong. We can, however, look at this the other way round. In countries where opposition to the market economy is strong, union density is high. In other words, there is a connection between trade unionism and general politics, Central and Eastern Europe are similar to the West in this respect.

Interest representation: convergence or divergence?

There are some tendencies towards common trade union patterns across Europe as a whole, but these still bear the stamp of 'crucial junctures' at their time of origin. Once institutionalized within a particular social, economic, and political system, trade union characteristics are slow to change. Variations are likely to remain for the foreseeable future.

Other tendencies are common to the whole of Europe, however. The privatization and globalization of economies has increased the influence of footloose multinational corporations and international bodies, relative to national interests and national interest groups. This is also true of the modern descendants of the classic pressure groups – the new social movements – which are also directly affected by global and international developments. We will turn to these in the next chapter.

Further reading

Peter Flora, *State, Economy and Society in Western Europe 1815–1975* (London, Macmillan, 1983).

Clark Kerr, *The Future of Industrial Societies, Convergence or Continuing Diversity?* (Cambridge, Mass., Harvard University Press, 1983).

Walter Korpi, *The Democratic Class Struggle* (London, Routledge, 1983).

OECD, *The Transition to Market Economy* (Paris, OECD, 1992).

OECD, *Historical Statistics* (Paris, various dates).

Jelle Visser, *European Trade Unions in Figures* (Deventer, Kluwer, 1989).

Chapter 8

Environment and peace: a new politics of social movements?

The new politics

Economic growth and declining international tension were associated in the Europe of the 1970s and 1980s with the development of a new kind of political movement. This differed markedly from the traditional forms of interest representation discussed in the last chapter, both in terms of goals, and the means used to achieve them. The younger and better educated sections of society became concerned with citizen participation and self-determination, minority rights, women's rights, the environment, international peace, atomic energy and Third World politics. They used novel political strategies such as demonstrations, protests, boycotts, occupations, sit-ins, and passive resistance. These disconcerted both politicians and political scientists, who labelled them 'unconventional'. The label is less appropriate in the 1990s, because, as Chapter 5 shows, these forms of participation are now generally accepted in Western democratic societies.

Willingness to engage in them is still useful for distinguishing new groups from old, however. Whereas 'old politics' tended to be elite-directed, 'new politics' were aimed at mass participation and self-direction. In the first part of the post-war period, political leaders tended to set the political agenda and organize people through hierarchical organizations such as trade unions, parties and interest groups. The new politics did not respond to elites so much as try to put pressure on them. Citizens' initiatives and movements were less formal and hierarchical than orthodox parties and pressure groups. New social movements took the form of loose national networks based upon loose local networks – they were networks of networks.

These were also found in Central and Eastern Europe. Because the area was dominated by communist regimes backed by Soviet military power, dissent had different emphases from the West. But there was a common concern for individual rights and civil liberties. The Eastern movements were less concerned with the environment, while in the West the ecologically oriented Greens were probably the most powerful and best publicized of the new social movements.

Other factors meant that protests against environmental waste and destruction were – and still are – limited in Central and Eastern Europe. The major positive achievement of communist regimes had been the transformation of largely agrarian societies into urban and industrial ones. In spite of environmental costs, the transformation improved the immediate living conditions of many people, especially those of the urban working class. Thus there was only limited popular support for long-term environmental causes.

BRIEFING 8.1

The environmental movement and its political strategies in Hungary

By 1993–94, there were an estimated 30,000 interest groups and non-governmental organizations in Hungary. Two-thirds of these registered themselves in 1989 before the establishment of democracy. This in itself casts an interesting light on claims for and against the strength of 'civil society' in Central and Eastern Europe. In the midst of political turmoil and economic hardship environmental groups lacked much popular support, however. So the 'German' strategy of direct social and political action by the Greens was largely ruled out – although on the question of building gigantic dams on the Danube, where Hungarian nationalism and relations with Slovakia were involved, some popular mobilization occurred.

In order to get environmental legislation therefore, some environmental activists tried to work through the left-wing parties, particularly the Hungarian Socialist Party. This was an interesting reflection of the experience of Western ecologists twenty years before when they tried to work through the mainstream parties, and encountered the same obstacles – namely, that economic prosperity was much more important to the party as a whole than environmental considerations.

Supplementing these efforts, the ecologists tried another traditional interest group tactic. They tried to work with the environmental committee of parliament and the appropriate Ministry by submitting detailed draft legislation and documentation. The work was financed by Western sources through the Central-Eastern European Regional Centre. So far, no legislation has been passed. But a forum grouping interested groups, parliamentarians and civil servants meets regularly. So the kind of close working relationships common in the West have been established and will probably ensure better implementation of legislation if and when it is passed. The Environmental Action Plan for Central and Eastern Europe adopted by a European-wide conference in 1993 sets priorities for the Danube basin and steps up pressure for domestic legislation. A detailed description of the situation is given in Éva Najba, 'The green line in the Hungarian transition', in Attila Ágit (ed.), *The First Steps: The Emergence of East Central Parliaments* (Budapest, the Hungarian Centre for Democracy, 1994), pp. 198–207.

The first concern of the new democracies in Central and Eastern Europe was to consolidate individual rights and liberties. The second was to deal with the immediate economic crisis which threatened the survival not only of democracy but society itself. Environmental concerns were remote. Only in Bulgaria were they mixed with political and economic opposition to the old communist regime. Nevertheless, as democracy consolidates itself and the immediate economic crisis recedes, new groups concerned with ecology are beginning to emerge.

There has, therefore, been both overlap and divergence in Europe so far as the new politics are concerned. Some issues are shared, such as civil and minority rights, but environmentalism and feminism have less support in the East. These movements are also comparatively weak in the Mediterranean area – Portugal, Spain, Turkey and Greece – so this is not purely an East–West difference.

Indeed, both the East and South suffer from the legacy of authoritarian regimes which distrusted movements they could not control. The social basis for new types of organization is still lacking, and they are often dependent on support from other countries. The major forces for environmental protection in Central and Eastern Europe are still international organizations like the World Wildlife Fund, Western

BRIEFING 8.2

Materialism and postmaterialism

The terms materialism and postmaterialism were developed by the US political scientist Ronald Inglehart. He argues that basic political attitudes, ideas and values are slowly shifting from a concern with jobs, money, and material possessions to culture, quality of life, the environment, minority rights, individual autonomy and self-expression. There are two main reasons for this. First, the long period of peace, affluence and stability since 1945 freed people from the need for food, security, warmth, order, wealth and material possessions. They can now take more interest in social and political equality, job satisfaction and freedom of speech. Second, the huge expansion of education and the mass media in the Western world has made people more aware of art, culture and nature. Inglehart's statistics, based on extensive survey data from Western Europe, show that young and well-educated people are most likely to be postmaterialists. He argues that this group will become steadily more influential in Western politics as they grow older and take over elite positions. This group is also more likely to pursue its political goals through unconventional political action such as sits-ins, protests, occupations and civil disobedience.

Postmaterialism is associated with relatively high levels of political awareness and activity. Survey evidence points to a strong connection between postmaterialists and the new social movements which provide a means for expressing many of their political and other goals. The new social movements also express postmaterialist ideas about political organization in the sense that try not to be hierarchical, or bureaucratic, or centralized. Postmaterialism may also undermine to some extent the old mass parties and interest organizations which are based upon the materialist, left-right politics of class. If so, they will help transform both the ideological and organizational forms of Western politics.

For the most complete accounts of postmaterialist theory and evidence see Ronald Inglehart, *The Silent Revolution: Changing Values and Political Styles among Western Publics* (Princeton University Press, Princeton, NJ, 1977) and *Culture Shift in Advanced Industrial Societies* (Princeton University Press, Princeton, NJ, 1990).

governments, and the European Commission, which are concerned about pollution, the ozone layer, and badly maintained nuclear power stations.

However, the 'new politics' is similar in all parts of Europe in terms of attracting the young and better educated. Movements of opposition to the communists were widely supported by the young, as were new parties and social movements in the West. So a first approach to the understanding of the new European politics is to ask: why the young? This question is discussed in the next section.

■ Why the young? Why new politics?

The rise of the new movements may signal a change in citizen concerns and ideas, not just about politics but about a wide range of other matters. Theories of post-materialism maintain that a fundamental value change is taking place, particularly among the young and educated. Older preoccupations with material security and success (jobs, wages, inflation, and material possessions) have been replaced by new concerns with the environment, minority rights, social equality, participation, self-expression and alternative lifestyles. The change from 'materialist' to 'postmaterial-ist' values has come about because growing economic prosperity means that material survival, and indeed a modest affluence, can be taken for granted. Individuals are freed from worries about where the next meal is coming from and able to concentrate on other matters.

The idea that a widespread change is taking place is supported by the fact, already noted, that the new politics are practised mainly by the young and educated, and by the contrasting vigour of new social movements in the East and the West. Material survival in the East remains an acute concern. Economic hardship forces materialist concerns on citizens, as it does not in the West.

As against this, one can accept that many supporters of the new social movements *are* postmaterialists, but still argue about which is cause and which effect. One would expect a Green activist to be more concerned about the environment and less about economic security than a non-activist. But does membership of the movement foster such attitudes, or do the attitudes precede membership? Chapter 5 shows that there is as much stability as change in values among Western publics. Rather than the polit-ical agenda shifting wholesale to new values and concerns, there is, rather, a mixing of the old, materialist priorities, with some of the newer postmaterialist ones.

Other explanations of the 'new politics' emphasize secular changes in modern society, such as the growth of the middle classes and the decline of religion which incline those affected to new values. Others argue that the growing bureaucratiza-tion and anonymity of modern life has produced a humanist backlash, which then flows over into alternative social movements. In addition, modern communication techniques have made it easier to organize and mobilize outside established political parties and trade unions. They also make it easier for new leaders with new agendas to appeal directly to citizens without going through the old party organizations. However, new communications technology cannot explain why new social move-ments have the policies and values they do nor why the young and educated support them so strongly.

■ Dissenting movements in Western Europe

Widespread public awareness of environmental deterioration emerged at the end of the 1960s in all advanced industrialized countries. Air and water pollution, noise, harmful chemicals in food, scarce resources, and endangered species all joined the political agenda. The famous Club of Rome report, *Limits to Growth*, underlined the larger and longer-term problems associated with environmental destruction, often caused by government policies and driven by economic pressures.

In Western Europe, environmental issues were taken up by some social demo-cratic and socialist parties, but the larger left-wing parties either could not or would not respond, thus leaving them to independent citizen initiatives. These often emerged spontaneously on the local level, and were directed at single issues such as the provision of parks, urban renewal, new roads, or nuclear power. They used the direct and unconventional means pioneered by student movements of the 1960s – demonstrations, sit-ins, occupations, protests, direct action and civil disobedience. They also used the legal system to force public inquiries, and soon created national umbrella organizations to strengthen their political impact. The *Bundesverband*

BRIEFING 8.3

Limits to Growth

In the late 1960s and early 1970s there was a flood of reports on the consequences of economic and population growth in the world. One of the most famous and pessimistic was the Club of Rome's *The Limits to Growth*. Published in 1972, it forecast that if the world's population, industry, pollution, food production, and use of natural resources continue to grow at its current rate, the limits to growth will be reached within a hundred years. The result would be a sudden and uncontrollable decline in both population and industrial capacity – a worldwide catastrophe. Aluminium supplies will be exhausted within thirty-one years (2001), and copper will run out before that. Even if massive discoveries of copper are made, the supply cannot last long into the twenty-first century.

The report received widespread publicity and its title, *Limits to Growth*, became a rallying cry for the new ecology movement. A second Club of Rome report, *Mankind at the Turning Point*, concentrated on the Third World, arguing that the production of raw materials would suffer from acute resource shortages which would spread to the world's economy and paralyse it.

See D. H. Meadows, *et al.*, *The Limits to Growth* (New York, Universe Books, 1972) and M. Mesarovic and E. Pestel, *Mankind at the Turning Point* (New York, Dutton/Reader's Digest, 1974).

Bürgerinitiativen Umweltschutz (BBU) was founded in Germany in 1972, the *Amis de la Terre* in France in 1971, the Swedish *Miljvardsgruppemas Riförbund* (MIGRI) in 1971, and the Dutch *Vereiniging Mileudefensie* (VDM) in 1972.

In the mid-1970s the nuclear energy issue also became controversial. Frightened by the oil crisis, many West European governments decided to expand their nuclear programme, demonstrating to the anti-nuclear movement the need to organize nationally. The result was the Organization for Information on Nuclear Power (OOA) formed in Denmark in 1974, the committee for the Co-ordination of Regional Anti-Nuclear Power Initiatives (LEK) in the Netherlands (1973), the Environmental Federation (*Miljöverbund*) in Sweden (1976), the Initiative of Anti-Nuclear Power Plants (IAG) in Austria (1976), and the Action Against Nuclear Power (AMA) in Norway (1974).

Nuclear protest also focused on weapons, particularly the NATO decision to build up intermediate nuclear forces and to site Cruise and Pershing II missiles in Western Europe. This created considerable cross-national solidarity among the new social movements. Large demonstrations were organized, along with illegal occupations of missile sites. Most of these activities were initiated by national and international peace movements.

The followers of these movements tended to have a clear socio-economic profile: young, educated, postmaterialist and centre-left in politics. Research shows three main groupings involved in the new politics. In Italy and Belgium they were mainly left-wing, in Germany and Denmark mainly postmaterialist, and in the Netherlands and France left-wing and postmaterialist.

Because of their value orientations (i.e. left-postmaterialist) most new social movements leaned towards the social democrats or other large, established, left-wing parties, in the late 1970s. Efforts were made to influence the policies of these parties, but without success. There were two main reasons for this. First, many

---

BRIEFING 8.4

Michels' iron law of oligarchy

In 1911 the German sociologist Robert Michels published his *Political Parties*, in which he formulated the famous 'iron law of oligarchy'. This states that mass organizations, by their very nature, cannot be democratic, but will always be controlled by a small elite. The modern world, he said, was faced with an insoluble dilemma. On the one hand, modern life requires large scale institutions and organizations – parties, interest groups, churches, trade unions. On the other hand, large organizations will be always be in the hands of a few leaders, no matter how strongly they aspire to internal democracy. There are two sets of reasons for this. First, organizational: leaders know all the business of their organization, they control the means of internal communication, and they usually have greater political skills than ordinary members. Secondly, there are the psychological characteristics of members. Michels refers to the 'incompetence of the masses', to the fact that few know much about policy matters, or turn up to meetings, while most feel the need for 'direction and guidance' provided by leaders.

According to Michels, leaders develop their own particular interests and goals which are different from those of members. They control organization, and use it for their own purposes, not those of the members. Thus leaders of mass movements inevitably become members of the power elite. Leaders of revolutionary movements always betray their cause.

Almost fifty years after the publication of *Political Parties*, Milovan Djilas, a former second-in-command of the Yugoslavian leader Tito, wrote his book *The New Class*, in which he documents how the Communist revolution had produced not Communism and democracy but 'the most complete authority of any single new class. Everything else is sham and an illusion'.

See Robert Michels, *Political Parties* (New York, Collier Books, 1962) and Milovan Djilas, *The New Class: An Analysis of the Communist System* (New York, Praeger, 1957).

---

socialist parties were in government during this period, a time of economic slow-down and unemployment. Most left-wing governments had to work with trade union, business, and other materialist interest groups in order to manage the crisis.

Second, the hierarchical, bureaucratic, and 'broad church' character of most socialist parties made it almost impossible for new social movements to bring about any major change in their policy position over a short period of time. By and large, Michel's 'iron law of oligarchy' still applied. Though they took up some limited ecological positions the lack of a strong and immediate political response yet induced some new social movements to set up their own political parties, notably the Greens.

■ Dissenting movements in Eastern Europe

New social movements began to emerge in some strength in the East in 1975, the year of the Helsinki Accord signed by governments of both the East and the West. By endorsing human rights, governments in the East were presenting hostages to fortune in their own countries. At this time the Soviet Union was also trying to ease the Cold War and join the global economy. These events had immediate repercussions in most Eastern European countries.

Charter 77 in Czechoslovakia, for instance, used the Helsinki Accord as a weapon

BRIEFING **8.5**

The Helsinki Accords of 1975

These were the points incorporated in the Helsinki Final Act of 1975, an international agreement adopted by the States participating in the Conference on Security and Co-operation in Europe (CSCE, see Chapter 1). These included all the European countries except Albania plus the USA and Canada. The accords covered economic, scientific and technological co-operation: closer contacts between different peoples; a re-affirmation of human rights; and exchanges of military information to reduce tension. They represented an important relaxation of the Cold War. Their importance in regard to the new social movements was that they gave dissident movements in the Soviet Bloc an official reason for existence – to check up on human rights – and governmental approval, at least in principal, for contacts with Western groups. Many took the opportunity to set up 'watch committees' which monitored the applications of the accords in their own countries and publicized breaches of them by the state.

to embarrass the ruling party in the eyes of international opinion. In 1976, Polish worker disturbances re-enacted previous working-class protests in the country in 1956 and in 1970. But the workers' protest action followed the new organizational style of the Committee for the Defence of Workers (KOR). When a massive workers' protest erupted in 1980, the Solidarity movement was born, built upon continuing worker resistance to the political regime.

Dissent in Poland illustrates the new movements that mobilized discontent in most Eastern European countries, of which Charter 77 and Solidarity are the most prominent examples. Their tactics included international contacts and discussion both within the Eastern bloc and between the East and the West. Leading figures of Charter 77 and Solidarity met frequently. So did Eastern dissidents and Western peace movements on the issue of NATO missiles.

The first result of international contact was sharp disagreement, most notably over the adoption of peace as a primary objective. Members of Charter 77 argued that 'peace' had been emptied of significance by communist abuse of the term, and claimed that human rights should be the mobilizing issue. The turning-point came when the Eastern dissident movements acknowledged the strategic value of peace and other issues that Western movements were promoting.

East Germany provides another example of a broad umbrella movement of dissent. In this case the movement was orchestrated by the Protestant churches, benefiting from a concordat with the state. This, however, ruled out any overt demand for human rights. All the more prominent, therefore, was the appeal for peace and for the protection of the environment – though in neither case were these allowed to challenge the regime.

In Hungary, there was no single broad movement playing a role like Charter 77 or Solidarity, and the broadest focus of dissent was an environmental movement to fight a system of dams on the Danube. This movement was a complex one, with strong nationalist overtones, and interconnections between what are best described as 'clubs of dissent'. It was from these that the new parties and elites emerged in the post-communist period.

The first dissenting movement in Bulgaria also grew out of the environmental issue and consolidated itself around the Union of Democratic Forces (SDS), opposed

BRIEFING 8.6

New politics parties

These are political parties which emphasize individual choice, equal rights for minorities and for men and women, strong political participation by everyone, the importance of the environment and of the developing countries, and peace and disarmament. They have an unconventional political style, focused on the importance of ordinary members and electorate. In line with this they make great efforts to encourage participation within the party. For more on this see Thomas Poguntke, 'New politics and party systems: the emergence of a new type of party?' *West European Politics*, 10 (1987), pp. 76–88.

to the old Communist regime. However, the SDS did not establish itself until after the 'velvet revolution' of 1989, so it was the consequence and not the promoter of political change.

From new social movements to new political parties

In contemporary Western Europe the followers of new social movements support both Green parties and particular types of left-wing socialist parties. We refer to all of these as 'new politics' parties. Currently, there are ten small left-wing parties, which can be included under this label. Most of them were founded in the mid-1960s, and supported, initially, by the student protest movements (for instance in Denmark, Italy and the Netherlands). Now, however, they are concerned to translate their ideals into practical politics through parliamentary activity. Table 8.1 lists these parties and shows how they have performed electorally, on average, over the later post-war period.

A second type of new politics party consists of recently founded Green parties which operate in seventeen Western nations, with parliamentary representation in nine (Austria, Belgium, Finland, Germany, the Netherlands, Italy, Luxembourg, Ireland and Switzerland). While their electoral success varies considerably between countries and at different levels of the political system, the Greens are still relatively small in terms of votes and seats. Table 8.2 lists these environmentalist parties and traces their average electoral performance over the 1970s and 1980s. (This can be compared with their most recent electoral results in the tables in Chapter 3.)

The new politics parties have three main things in common. First, on policy matters, they combine a strong concern for equal rights, especially minority rights, with an uncompromising ecological and anti-nuclear stance. They also support solidarity with the Third World, unilateral disarmament, and greater social equality in the West. All advocate an alternative lifestyle with less emphasis on material goods, and more individualism, self-realization and self-determination. They strongly support wealth-sharing between rich and poor nations, and want to help poorer countries create self-sufficient economies, free of financial domination by the West. In other words, new politics parties have a programmatic and ideological way of thinking which cuts across the traditional left-right division. New politics issues challenge conventional politics on new grounds.

Second, in terms of organization, new politics parties display a strong preference

Table 8.1 Left-socialist parties and their average vote in national elections, 1965–89

Country	Party	Average % of valid votes
Denmark	Socialistisk Folkerparti/Venstresocialisterne/Faelles Kurs	12.3
Finland	Työväen ja Pienviljelijäin/Sosialdemokraattinen Litto	1.9
France	Union des Forces Démocratiques/Parti Socialiste Unifié	2.2
Ireland	The Workers' Party/Democratic Socialist Party/Democratic Left	2.0
Italy	Partito Socialista Italiano di Unità Proletaria/Manifesto/Partito di Unità Proletaria per il Comunismo	2.3
Netherlands	Pacifistich-Socialische Partij/Socialistische Partij	1.8
Norway	Sosialistisk Venstreparti	6.6
Spain	Partido del Trabajo de España	1.0
Switzerland	Partito Socialista Autonomo/Progressive Organizationen der Schweiz	1.3
Turkey	Turkish Labour Party	1.5

Table 8.2 Green and environmentalist parties and their average vote in national elections, 1975–89

Country	Party	Average % of valid votes
Austria	Vereinte Grüne Österreichs	5.0
Belgium	AGALEV/Écologistes/Regenboog	5.5
Denmark	Grøne	0.9
Finland	Greens	4.1
France	Écologistes	3.0
FRG	Die Grünen/Brüdnis 90/Grüne/Ökologisch-Demokratische Partei	6.1
Greece	Ecologists	0.4
Iceland	Women's List/Humanist Party	8.6
Ireland	Green Alliance	1.1
Italy	Partito Radicale/Lista Verde	3.3
Luxembourg	Écologistes	6.2
Netherlands	Federatieve Groenen/Grøen Links	1.9
Norway	Green party/Grone	0.3
Spain	Los Verdes	0.7
Sweden	Mijöpartiet	3.1
Slovenia	Greens	3.7
Switzerland	Grüne/Die Andere Schweiz (DACH)	6.0
UK	Ecology Party	0.3

for grass-roots participation, local autonomy and decentralization. These are seen as an essential precondition for meaningful participation at all levels of the organization, because they distribute power, make politics more transparent, and hence more intelligible (see Table 9.4 below).

Third, new politics parties have similar electorates consisting of people who are mainly young, new middle class, urban, educated, postmaterialist and left-wing. In most cases it is easy to detect links between new politics parties and new social movements. Despite some differences in structure and policies, we can refer to the followers of these parties as the 'new-left social movement activists' who consider their parties the parliamentary arm of the new social movements. Examples include the Socialist Peoples Party (SF) in Denmark, and the Radical Party (PPR) and the Pacifist Socialist Party in the Netherlands. The Green Party has been most successful in Germany.

The SF in Denmark was founded as long ago as 1959 as an alternative to the socialists and communists. Between 1976 and 1978, intensive discussions took place on the issue of nuclear energy. A discussion paper rejecting atomic power was issued, and the national parliament introduced a bill (initiated by the SF) requesting the Swedish government to close down the nuclear power station at Barseback, only twenty miles from Copenhagen. In its basic action programme of 1981 the SF repeated this rejection of nuclear power. Ever since it has had the strong support of the Danish anti-nuclear movement.

In the Netherlands, the PPR and PSP have made ecology and pacifism the central features of their programmes since the 1960s. The founders of the PSP wanted to forge a bond between anti-militarists and socialists, and give them a strong voice in parliament. The PPR was created by a loose group of Christian-radical movements and former members of the Catholic Peoples Party. Both the PSP and the PPR are committed to international disarmament and Dutch withdrawal from NATO. They argue that private dominance in the energy sector reinforces business interests in other sectors of the economy through a network of international economic links, and that nuclear energy creates another link between military and economic interests. Both parties believe world peace is threatened rather than preserved by nuclear weapons, and both supported the anti-nuclear and peace movement. After a series of debates about 'green credentials', they formed an alliance with the communists and some green movements in the 'Green Progressive Accord' which later became the 'Green-Left' alliance.

In Germany, various ecological and populist groups came together in the Green Party, founded in 1980 in opposition to the established parties. The four pillars of the Greens' national programme are their ecological, social, non-violent, and grass-roots commitments. In contrast to the smaller left-wing parties in Denmark and the Netherlands, the German Greens cannot be placed easily on a left-right continuum. Their criticism of welfare state excesses, for example, forms part of the CDU programme, but their demands for direct democracy emanate from the left. The political strategies of Green parties vary in different countries but they share common values – more democracy, more participation, more attention to minority groups, a halt to armaments and missiles, and protection of the environment by making offenders pay. These constitute the new values of the new politics.

In Central and Eastern Europe the dissident movements of the 1970s and 1980s were deeply involved in the first free elections and, in many cases, constituted the foundations upon which many diverse organizations and parties were built. Their rallying cries were civil rights and peace, but in retrospect we can see that what actually motivated them was a broader 'myth of liberation' from communism and the Russians, in which most problems would be solved by freedom and democracy. This was potent enough to keep the forces for change together during the transfer of power. But once this was achieved, hard choices had to be made, and new identities and organizations formed which would sustain a viable competitive party system.

The period from the fall of the old communist regimes in 1989 to the second series of elections in 1994 was of great significance. Developments were so dense and important that it is difficult to sum them up in a few paragraphs. They went far beyond the formation of parties and political organizations, and constituted a remoulding of groups and the political process. Although parties played a key role, the circumstances of the time discredited them in the eyes of many new social movements who were in the forefront of the challenge to old communism. The dissidents of communist times were accustomed to thinking and organizing themselves as a national and all inclusive movement of general protest. Seeing themselves as representing only one section of society and competing with other social interests was alien to them. For example, Polish Solidarity was not a political party when it took its seat at the round table discussions in Poland in the spring of 1989. Nor could it be described exactly as a trade union. It was a broad and all-inclusive movement which represented 'the people'. In the early 1990s, the boundaries between organizational forms of political action were fluid, parties themselves under suspicion, and party formation simply part of a wider process of group and social formation.

The first free elections, under new laws of association, not only enabled existing movements to convert themselves into political parties, but also exerted very strong pressure on them to do so. The anguish this caused was strong in the Czechoslovak Civic Forum and the Polish Solidarity. The very terms 'forum' and 'solidarity' suggested inclusiveness; but with free elections these movements were called upon on to follow the logic of the competitive game. That is, they had to distinguish themselves from other parties and loosen their grip on the all-inclusive call for 'liberation'. They had to set themselves apart from and against other interests and make policy choices which would define their political identity.

The shift from a 'movement' to 'party' mode of action was difficult, and it often resulted in anguish and confusion. Solidarity is the obvious case. After monopolizing opposition to the communists in the partially free elections of 1989, the movement fragmented into a plethora of parties which contested the election of October 1991, with partial success. But in the 1993 election none of the direct descendants of the Solidarity trade union movement won seats. Similarly, the Bulgarian *Podkrepa*, formed as a trade union at the height of the revolutionary period, was uncertain about its role. For a time it was enrolled in the Union of Democratic Forces. But when it left the party, its leader continued to behave like a party leader, engaging in discussions with international funding bodies and visiting the exiled monarch to discuss the political situation.

A second feature of this period also undermined the momentum of the liberation movements. Despite vast changes, the old communist institutions maintained their organizational continuity in contrast to the fluidity around them. As noted in Chapter 7, old trade unions detached themselves from their communist sponsors and succeeded in retaining the bulk of their members. A striking case was the official OPZZ unions in Poland, which greatly outnumbered Solidarity unions after 1989. Communist parties also maintained continuity. Although they changed their names and their message, they remained viable in organizational terms, achieving considerable success in the elections of the 1990s. Parties which had been forced into communist blocs under the old regime (especially Christian and agrarian parties), also contrived to make the best of their inherited organizational assets. Poland's United Peasants' Party is a good example. Its leader became prime minister after the 1993 elections, in coalition with the former communists.

Finally, international funding bodies have played an important role in the development of interest mediation in the new politics, particularly where countries were heavily indebted. Dependence on outside political actors has put governments in a good position for bargaining with social movements at home, since they could always plead irresistible external pressures which made it impossible for them to change their policy. In a different way foreign intervention has also affected the environmental agenda-setting of governments. The influence and resources of international agencies trying to ensure nuclear safety have had a greater impact than the activities of domestic environmental movements. Foreign help, however, often enabled these to build themselves up, along with the more normal types of interest organizations. Table 8.3 lists the quite impressive array of non-governmental organizations that had established themselves even in poor and isolated Macedonia by the end of 1995.

Table 8.3 Non-governmental organizations in the Republic of Macedonia, 1995

Humanitarian
First Children's Embassy – Stip
The Humanitarian and Cultural Organization 'El Hilal'
The Humanitarian and Charitable Association 'Spike of Goodness'
The Human and Charitable Association 'Mother Theresa'
The Humanitarian and Charitable Association of the Romas 'Moon'
The Humanitarian Organization 'Homos'
ADRA Macedonia
CARITAS Macedonia
Consulate of the First Children's Embassy in Macedonia
Red Cross of Skopje
Red Cross of Macedonia
Macedonia Center for International Co-operation

Human rights
Helsinki Committee for Human Rights
Helsinki Citizens Assembly
Macedonian Council for the European Movement
Forum for Human Rights
Committee for Peace and Civil Initiative
Committee for Macedonian–Greek Dialogue
League of Vlachs
Union of Romas
Association for Human Protection of Macedonians Discriminated by the Republic of Greece 'Dignity'

Ecological
Movement of Ecologists of Macedonia
Ecological Association 'Survival'
Forum of Young Ecologists
Friends of the Forest
Association for Protection of Animals 'Doe'
Humanitarian Association for Protection of Dojran Lake – for Healthy and Beautiful Children

Women's
Organization of Women of Macedonia
Women's Organization of Skopje
Albanian Women's League
Women's Club 'Spark of Life'
Women's Organization of Tetovo
Roma Women's Organization 'Daja'
Club 'Kumanovka'

Youth and Students
Youth Council
National Student Union of Macedonia
Union of Secondary School Students of Macedonia
Macedonian Medical Students Association
Scout Union of Macedonia
Holiday Union of Macedonia
Musical Youth of Macedonia
Young Writers of Macedonia
Film Youth of Macedonia
Young Explorers of Macedonia
Children's Defence Union 'Save the Children' of Macedonia
Young European Federalists

■ Social movements and social cleavages

In Western Europe the impact of new social movements and new politics parties is still controversial. On the one hand, they have mobilized supporters and enabled them to express their views by voting. They thus bring in groups of people who were previously excluded from normal electoral politics. By doing so, however, they have destabilized the system by increasing electoral volatility and party realignment, and by questioning

BRIEFING 8.7

Voluntary organizations in the Republic of Macedonia

No country is typical, but examining one in more depth illustrates the state of civil society in Eastern and Central Europe, and shows how rapidly the situation there is changing.

Macedonia (see Chapter 3) is a small landlocked country in the Balkans, bordering on Serbia, Albania, Greece and Bulgaria. It is the southernmost of the ex-Yugoslav Republics, and unlike the others has had a peaceful transition to independence and democracy. In spite of an ethnically diverse population (65 per cent Slav, 22 per cent Albanian, 4 per cent Turkish, 2.5 per cent Roma (gypsy), 2 per cent Serb and other small groups), internal peace is promoted by including the Albanian party with two Slav parties in the government coalition.

Although the Yugoslav regime was comparatively tolerant by communist standards, it still infiltrated and controlled 'voluntary' associations. Five of these had a privileged status: the League of Communists, the Socialist Union of Working People, the Union of Socialist Youth, Veterans Associations, and the Association of Trade Unions.

In the late 1980s the first real voluntary associations were formed, mostly concerned with ecology (the first, Survival, still exists). The war in nearby Bosnia created a flood of groups concerned with peace, which reached a peak in 1992–93.

After independence the trade union movement split into two. An independent trade union formed in opposition to the former Communist Association, which itself disaffiliated from the state and Communist Party, and competed quite effectively for members. Most of the other former communist associations were disbanded, but the Youth Council continued, cutting staff however from 25 in 1990 to 6 in 1994.

In 1993 a Dutch church-based organization with the backing of the World Council of Churches, sent a worker to Macedonia who, with financial backing from the Netherlands, and in co-operation with local activists, set up the Macedonian Centre for International Co-operation (MCIC). This was a support group for other voluntary movements in Macedonia, and provided them with financial aid. By 1995, the Dutch helper had withdrawn and the MCIC had become autonomous – though still with Dutch financial backing. USAID, an American government agency, has also given help and some of its personnel have worked unofficially in local groups, mainly ecological ones. Both organizations, again with international church backing, have helped stimulate water supply initiatives and co-operatives at village level.

Most of the other voluntary organizations operating in Macedonia in 1995 were small, located in the capital (Skopje), and heavily dependent on foreign or church sponsorship. However some have emerged spontaneously and have aspects in common with new social movements elsewhere, such as the ecology group, Survival. Many are like western local groups of the late 1970s, protecting features like Dojran lake. Some women's groups, especially among ethnic minorities such as the Roma, are grass roots movements with considerable impact.

Voluntary associations have difficulties resulting from the legal framework of the former repressive regime. All have to register with the Ministry of the Interior. This is relatively easy for organizations run by the Slav elite, but impedes minority organizations and those in villages far from the capital. Only the Red Cross is tax exempt, with the result that other voluntary organizations put their accounts under Red Cross control. Voluntary associations are now pressing for a new law which would grant them charitable status, and allow registration at local offices throughout the country.

An ecological party has been formed but it failed to gain seats in parliament. In spite of difficulties, international organizations have stimulated much activity, and local initiatives are now taking over.

the concerns of orthodox politics as well as its whole tone and style. For their part, the established parties will happily steal the clothes of the new parties if they can. This has happened on the environmental front to a modest extent, which, in turn, could also produce realignment within West European party systems. In sum the new social movements and parties both stabilize and destabilize the old party system.

This process is most likely to affect larger socialist parties, whose elites and members may be dividing into two groupings. The first, those with a traditional left-wing outlook, are concerned with working-class security and economic stability. They form the old left. The second, with a new politics orientation, tend to empha-size quality of life, democracy, equality, and the environment. They form the new left. The new left within the old socialist parties competes with new politics parties for the same voters, while the old left continues the class struggle by modern means. Socialists are, therefore, caught between two cultures. Whatever they might gain from one, they risk losing from the other.

At the same time, only a minority of voters identify with the new left. Consequently, the best strategy for established parties is to reconcile the old and new politics in order to retain the support of the majority of old-left voters, and to attract the small but growing numbers of new. Many socialist parties have not managed this compromise. But some have changed with apparent success, judging from their voting figures. Parties are not fools and they do try to adapt, but it is a long, slow, and difficult process in some cases. Equally, the modest success of new movements and parties demonstrates that they also have an appeal, and are here to stay as long as their issues remain on the political agenda and are not stolen by the major parties.

If the term 'new social movement' is to be applied to eastern Europe it must be with a difference. Before 1989, the communist monopoly of power ruled out free political parties and movements. But dissident movements developed in spite of this, gathering momentum after the signing of the Helsinki Accords in 1975. Nevertheless, the movements were conditioned by the system, concentrating primarily on the issue of political and civil rights. After 1989, new parties and movements also mirrored the system. Reflecting demands for liberation from authoritarian rule, they tended to equate freedom with market economics, and liberation from communism with democracy. They did not immediately appreciate that they had to go further.

Transition processes have continued to affect both the cleavage structure and the relationship between parties and movements. One surprise was the abruptness with which concerns for peace and the environment lost their prominence. This was partly because the signing of the INF Treaty in 1987 (see Chapter 1) removed immediate threats to peace. But no one event can explain why the Greens lost support (for example, the Danube Circle in Hungary).

A second feature of the transition is that a class cleavage between employers and employees did not immediately become important, in spite of a fairly strong trade union presence. This was partly because of opposition to communist ideology, and partly because of the new enthusiasm for market economics. Third, a religious cleav-age resurfaced in some countries, notably Poland, which was articulated by political parties allied with the church. Finally, the myth of liberation was not only consistent with ethnic appeals, but sometimes actively encouraged them. In the most promi-nent case this led to the break up of the Czechoslovak state, and to tragedy in Bosnia, but ethnic divisions also reappeared in other countries.

Before long, the harsh effects of market reforms were felt. This ushered in a new period in which the former communist parties recovered, all but one renamed, but all laying claim to the mantle of social democracy. While they, too, endorsed the market, they offered themselves as alternatives to the liberal or conservative governments of the transition. The bright shine on these new 'free' ideologies was tarnished somewhat by the effects of economic hardship. The transformed communist parties could, at least, lay claim to have provided a measure of economic stability and protection under the old system. Given the continuing strength of various trade union organizations, a left seems to be appearing, based on working-class support, which is not dissimilar from the old, materialist left in the West.

Thus, it is still too early to discern a full blown, post-communist, 'new politics' emerging in the East. The practice of open, pluralist politics is still so recent, the communist legacy so strong, the processes of change still so unsettled, and the economic crisis so severe that it may be a long time before anything resembling 'New Politics' emerges on any scale. There are certainly environmental movements throughout the region, in many cases well-structured as non-governmental organizations. There are other movements for improvement in fields such as housing. Some elements of alternative politics have also spread from west to east, often with the help of western organisations. The Regional Environmental Centre in Budapest is very active, and is run by one of the most prominent environmental dissidents of the late communist period. But foreign involvement with the work of the centre has so far prevented it from playing an alternative local role. The Helsinki Citizens Assembly is also interesting from this point of view. Set up by Western European peace campaigners in collaboration with Eastern counterparts, it is a vigorous 'all-European' new politics movement, which promotes democratic and alternative values in the East. However, its Western European component serves again to underline the point that purely indigenous examples of new politics in Eastern and Central Europe are few and far between.

Further reading

Russell J. Dalton and Manfred Kuchler (eds), *Challenging The Political Order* (Oxford, Oxford University Press, 1990).

Ferdinand Müller-Rommel (ed.), *New Politics in Western Europe* (Boulder, Col., Westview Press 1989).

Thomas Poguntke, *Alternative Politics* (Edinburgh, Edinburgh University Press, 1993).

Timo Pürainen (ed.), *Change and Continuity in Eastern Europe* (London, Dartmouth, 1994).

Geoffrey Pridham and Tatu Vanhanen (eds), *Democratization in Eastern Europe* (London, Routledge, 1994).

Ray Tavras, *Consolidating Democracy in Poland* (Boulder, Col., Westview, 1995).

Chapter 9

The old politics of parties

The importance of political parties

Political parties are at the centre of many of the developments reviewed in previous chapters. It is difficult to explain the configuration of interest groups and trade unions without considering the political parties which were around at the time of their foundation. In many cases parties were the creators and sponsors of a particular type of union. In other countries, trade unions themselves created a political wing – a Labour Party – to advance their interests directly in government. Or as in Poland, splits in the labour movement have produced competing political parties. New social movements have similarly supported the left socialists in some countries while directly intervening to create alternative Green parties in others.

All this goes to show the extent to which the creation and survival of political parties is integrally linked to developments in the wider society. Indeed, it is totally artificial to attempt to separate them. Political parties are simply one channel, though often the most spectacular, through which social developments take place. Parties channel these developments by articulating the needs of the sectors of society which have created and which support them.

Parties have to concern themselves with interests and needs beyond those of their immediate supporters, because they need to attract other votes in elections. They also aim to form governments – often coalitions with other parties – which will make policy for the country as a whole. They cannot therefore just pursue a narrowly sectional programme. Doing so either deprives them of votes which would make them a significant political force, or renders other parties unwilling to co-operate with them in government.

It is political parties' concern with elections and getting into government which distinguishes them from associated interest groups. As we saw, an interest group is an organization which attempts to influence government policy without wishing to formulate that policy itself. Political parties on the other hand *do* want to take responsibility for policy. In order to do so they run candidates in elections for public office – mostly, in Europe, for parliamentary positions. The balance of party deputies or MPs in the parliament then determines which party or parties will form the government. The minimum condition is that the party or parties in government can win a parliamentary investiture vote.

Parties are thus organizations which uniquely link particular social interests (represented by their members or activists) to ordinary voters, to parliamentarians (the elected candidates whom they have backed) and to members of the Government who are usually the party leaders. In government the leaders try to implement the policies in the programme with which they have attracted votes at the election. The fact that parties (again, uniquely among social and political organizations) put forward *different* short-term plans for society gives ordinary people the opportunity

BRIEFING **9.1**

Pluralism

Pluralism is both a prescriptive theory of how political life *ought* to be organized and an empirical theory of how politics actually *is* organized. The empirical theory concerns us here. It sometimes goes under the name of polyarchy, or pluralist democracy.

A pluralist system is one in which there are many, competing centres of power. Power and influence are divided between many different social groups, organizations, parties and interests. Each of these has some resources with which to fight for its political interests, and each has some influence over politics. Groups which form a loose alliance on one issue re-form different alliances on other issues. Power is therefore fluid. It ebbs and flows according to circumstances and the issues at stake.

In a pluralist system there is no permanent power structure or unified power elite. Instead competing elites represent different groups and interests and fight many political issues in many political arenas.

For an excellent analysis of pluralism/polyarchy see Robert A. Dahl, *Modern Political Analysis* (Prentice Hall, Englewood Cliffs, NJ, 1991), pp.71–80.

to choose between them and thus make some difference to what the government does. Voters would not have this opportunity if they simply voted for individual candidates, without party backing, as these could not offer a comprehensive programme nor any guarantee that it could be put into effect.

Parties therefore form the essential link between elections and governments in the European democracies. Without parties, individual voters would have much less control over government policy than they do now, and governments themselves would be less cohesive and effective. This all depends of course on parties themselves being disciplined and united round a fairly clear-cut point of view. The internal factionalism of parties in Italy, and the inability of the Russian leadership to create stable parties, have rendered governments less effective and more remote from ordinary people.

European democracies therefore are *party* democracies. Parties are often criticized for squabbling unnecessarily over policies and for bringing personalities and sectional interests into public programmes which should be pursued objectively in the interests of all. The difficulty is, as the former Fascist and communist regimes have demonstrated, that objectively 'correct' policies are hard to find. When a regime claims to have the 'correct' policy it usually means doing down minorities in favour of regime supporters, which hardly qualifies as the true general interest.

The pluralist type of democracy which exists in contemporary Europe maintains instead that the best policy is one on which all or most people can compromise once they have had the opportunity to organize support for their own views. In this process, interest groups and social movements are necessary and parties are crucial. It is indeed through their incessant squabbling and argument that the best general policy is likely to emerge.

In this chapter we shall concentrate mainly on how parties interact with the wider society, leaving the question of how they function in government to Chapter 12. The particular configuration of parties in each country is strongly affected by its history and the constitutional arrangements which we shall consider in Chapter 10. It is the diversity of European countries in terms of history, social groups and constitutions

BRIEFING 9.2

Ideology

The term 'ideology' is used in many different ways, but essentially it is a system of ideas and assumptions which help us understand and interpret the political world. It consists of a set of values and beliefs, factual assumptions and ideas which help us impose order on a complex world, and which explain what is going on, why, and our place in it. The term is often restricted to a fairly explicit, coherent and elaborate set of ideas – a theory of politics. In this sense, relatively few people are ideologues. But many more subscribe to looser and less explicit ideologies such as socialism, liberalism or conservatism. Parties are built around these conflicting political principles ('principles' are a positive term which means the same as ideology in the broader sense).

Sometimes the term ideology is used neutrally to describe any more or less worked out set of values and ideas about politics. But sometimes the term is used critically to imply dogmatism or blinkered vision. In a strict Marxist sense, ideology means a false view of the world – the false consciousness created by capitalists in order to keep the workers happy. There is a sense in which an ideology relieves us all of the need to re-think and re-analyse every single new political event; we simply fit things into the old understanding. But there is also a sense in which everybody, not just those suffering from false consciousness, depends upon an ideology to make sense of politics. In this sense Marxism itself is an ideology, but a highly developed one which is complex, subtle and general.

which accounts for the bewildering range of parties and party systems which we see today across the continent.

Are there, however, common features underlying this diversity? The fact that parties in many different countries call themselves by a similar name – Socialist, Labour, Christian, Liberal, Green and so on – gives some indication that there may be. We consider this in the next section, where we will also be raising the question of whether the new parties of Central and Eastern Europe resemble the established ones of the West and South.

Ideologies and party families

Parties are not the only groups with ideologies. Churches and trade unions have them too. Indeed, they may be necessary for any social group to function. This is because everyone needs to make sense of what is often a confusing and frightening world. We need to interpret events in order to react to them and thus exercise some control over our own destiny. This is particularly important for organized groups, who are often called upon to say and do something quickly. Ideology gives a quick answer in most situations.

Ideology provides the necessary framework for interpreting events with a view to taking action. An ideology is a theory about the world and about society, and of the place of you and your group within it. The most developed ideology is still probably that of Karl Marx, worked out in the mid-nineteenth century.

According to Marx, historical and contemporary events can only be understood in terms of class relationships. Thus two major class groups (the 'bourgeoisie', that

BRIEFING 9.3

Marxism, communism, socialism

Marxism
The creation of Karl Marx in the mid-nineteenth century, Marxism is probably still the best known political ideology in the West. Although it has many different branches, Marxism states that economic relations, particularly those between the classes created by the system of production, determine all forms of political and social life. In the late capitalist system there are only two classes: the capitalists or property owners or bourgeoisie, who are increasingly rich; and the workers, or proletariat, who are exploited and become increasingly poor. As a result, the workers develop a revolutionary class consciousness, overthrow the system, and, after a period of state socialism, eventually establish a states-less and property-less society.

According to Marx, history can only be understood in terms of class, and capitalist politics can only be understood as a constant class struggle between the bourgeoisie and the proletariat. Other ideas such as religion or nationalism might seem important, but are simply different manifestations of class interests, which are used by the ruling class to mystify politics and create the false consciousness which conceals the real class struggle. A Marxist, therefore, reacts to events by asking whose class interests are being served. Foreign wars, for example, may appear to be unconnected with the class struggle, but, according to Marxist theory, are actually a means of maintaining capitalists in power.

Communism
Although communism adopted Marxism as its official ideology it is useful to distinguish between Marxism as a theory of politics, and communism as a form of government. Communism was developed first in Russia after the revolution of 1917 and was extended by the Soviet Union to other countries of the Eastern Bloc after 1945.

Communist practice was very much shaped by the fact that its exponents took power in relatively underdeveloped societies which they had to industrialize, often by brutal repression of opposed interests. Thus, it ended up as a system where there was little or no private ownership of property, which was taken over by the state. Its other feature was the domination of a single monolithic and hierarchical party, the Communist Party, separate from the state apparatus, which it controlled through the *nomenklatura* system (see Chapter 13). Through this a closed political elite exercised control. However, communism took over from Marxism the ideal of equality and applied it in practice by trying to eliminate unemployment and provide generous social welfare for everybody in the population. The collapse of the Eastern Bloc in 1989 signalled the end of communism in Europe.

Socialism
Socialism also took over from Marxism the ideas of equality and a welfare state. It differed from communism, however, in accepting the need for democratic pluralism and thus the possibility of its own electoral defeat. This also meant in practice that it operated a *mixed economy* (see Chapter 16) rather than advocating total state planning.

is the middle class, and the workers) are the only really significant ones to be taken into account. Other groups such as Churches or minority nationalities, which might on first sight seem to be important are at bottom simply manifestations of one class interest or another. Claims that religion or nationalism are more important than class are simply bourgeois weapons to create 'false consciousness', that is to delude the workers about where their real interests lie.

These are in essence to struggle against their bourgeois employers, and eventually to overthrow the capitalist system which allows the latter to control the means of production such as factories and land. Their monopoly on these enables them to exploit workers by forcing them to sell their labour (their only resource) very cheaply and thus creates gross inequalities of wealth and social conditions in society.

A Marxist therefore can react to events by asking whose class interests are being served by them, and acting so as to advance those of the workers. Foreign wars, for example – seemingly far removed from internal class struggle – can be judged by whether they are promoting the liberation of some oppressed group of workers or are simply a selfish struggle for resources among various bourgeois cliques.

After the fall of the old communist regimes few parties in contemporary Europe would support the whole of the Marxist argument. Democratic socialists would, however, accept the point that class relationships are the most important ones and that the central issues in politics are those concerned with the distribution of resources between classes. They would argue that the working class – like all others in society – has an interest in preserving peace and stability, and that redistribution achieved through negotiation and argument is much better than imposed solutions supported by force, since these can always be reversed by greater force.

A similar acceptance of non-violence and democracy occurs among the adherents of other party ideologies in Europe. In practice, this means accepting the policies chosen by the elected governments, no matter how much one may criticize them as unfair or unjust. Indeed, if a party can persuade enough electors that they are unfair, it can hope to reverse the electoral decision next time and thus modify the policies. Because of this possibility most governments will tend to compromise with the parties out of government so that the projects they initiate will have some chance of permanency.

Within this broad acceptance of democracy, however, ideologies will differ from each other in terms of which groups are considered to be the important ones in society and how their interests should be served. Are classes so pervasive and central that the interests of the workers should always come first? Or are workers' interests only part of a more general, societal interest as 'bourgeois' parties tend to argue, and hence better served by strengthening the free market which will create more wealth for all? Or, on the contrary, is economic growth the force which is destroying the natural world in which we all have a common interest, so should it be opposed? Also perhaps, because through uncontrolled development it destroys the countryside and threatens the culture of minority groups, which needs to be defended by setting up their own state or sub-state institutions.

It can be seen that there is rich ground for controversy and argument among the adherents of different ideologies. This is particularly the case because no one can say scientifically or objectively which ideology is right. Assertions that class is the most important of social relationships, or that the world would suffer an irreparable loss if a language ceased to be spoken, are not subject to 'scientific' or 'objective' proof. They spring out of an identification with or immersion in a particular group in society. One function of an ideology indeed, is to buttress that identity, as most people in modern Europe belong actually or potentially to many different overlapping groups. Is someone from northwest Spain who works in a steel factory primarily a worker, a Basque, a Spaniard, European, Catholic or white? In a situation of multiple individual identities, parties and social movements struggle to make one predominate and thus to mobilize support for their policies and general point of view.

Ideologies are thus important not only in telling leaders what to do but in telling their supporters who they *are* and thus making them receptive to leaders' diagnoses of the political situation. Ideology is particularly important for political parties, which have to operate across different levels of society. It helps to link up often complex governmental decisions with the broadly defined interests of their supporters and voters.

Many ideologies have a general appeal across national frontiers and help define broad groups of parties – often termed 'party families'. Socialism is perhaps the best example of such an 'international' ideology, as it has an obvious message for workers everywhere. This is the reason why every European country has a socialist party. But there are also Conservatives and Liberals, Greens and Agrarians in many places. While ethnic parties differ in terms of the particular minority group they seek to defend, they make broadly the same arguments in defense of their interests and so can be identified as members of a common 'family', very pervasive in Europe, as a result of the processes of state building discussed in Chapters 3 and 4.

Even parties of the same family can disagree over strategy and tactics of course, particularly over how far one should go in opposing government policies. There can also be disagreement over which goals to emphasise out of the common set of objectives. An example of this occurs with the left socialists and established social democratic parties discussed in the last chapter. Left socialists emphasize concerns like peace and participation neglected by older parties in the same tradition, who are more concerned with the distribution of wealth and income. At the same time there is often a split between old style Marxist parties which refuse to renounce violence as a possible instrument of class struggle, and Social Democratic and Labour parties who rule out violence altogether.

The reconstituted communist parties of Central and Eastern Europe now often call themselves social democrats and have sought to establish their new democratic credentials by renouncing violence. Their behaviour since 1989 tends to support this claim.

We can summarize the points we have made about ideologies and party families, and specify some further details, by classifying them as we have done in Table 9.1.

At the side of the table are listed the main ideologies which define the 'party families' of Europe today. We have already discussed the characteristics of 'new politics' parties in Chapter 8, seeing how they evolve out of new social movements and receive the support of the young and well-educated 'postmaterialists'. We have also talked about their 'core values' of general participation and defence of the environment, as well as their support for peace. These values feed into the specific policies they promote.

A general way of judging parties, apart from their particular policies, is on the extent to which they support an extension of government activities and powers in pursuit of their aims. This is often used to distinguish 'left' from 'right' parties. The latter think that government activity should be limited as much as possible. Green and left socialist parties seek greater government intervention in defence of the environment which they see as under threat from uncoordinated capitalist activity. So they clearly belong on the left side of the general political spectrum. Indeed, it is

Table 9.1 European ideologies and party families

Ideology	Support groups	Core values	Characteristic policies	Attitudes to government intervention	Typical parties
'New politics'	Young, highly educated, post materialists, new social movements	Environment, participation, peace	Encourage sense of community, protect nature against nuclear power, help social minority groups, especially women	Supports more to achieve objectives where private initiatives insufficient	Greens, feminists left socialists
Socialism	Workers, public employees in social and service sectors, intellectuals	Equality of wealth and opportunity	Extend welfare protection (health and pensions), regulation of capitalism, peace	Necessary to a high degree to achieve objectives	Left socialists, (ex-) communists, social democrats, Labour
Christian democracy	Churches, especially Catholic churches, sectors of middle class, country and small towns	Fraternity, community, human dignity, subsidiary	Uphold traditional morality and family, extend welfare, mixed economy	Support where necessary, particularly on welfare	Christian socialists, Christian democrats and people's parties
Agrarian	Country and small towns	Agriculture, traditional rural way of life	Support farmers, preserve countryside against threats	Support where favours farmers	Farmers, smallholders peasants parties, agrarian, centre parties
Liberalism	Secular and anti-clerical sections of middle class, religious minorities, some peripheral regions	Liberty, individualism	Freedom from controls, free markets, efficient, limited government, social minimum to allow individuals to use freedom	Neo-liberal parties: role of government limited to upholding free market; progressive liberals want intervention to uphold individual liberty	Radicals, progressives, freedom parties, liberals
Conservatism	Upper and middle class, especially small towns and medium cities, country	Order, security social hierarchy	Uphold established state structures and national boundaries, oppose crime by forceful means, maintain armed forces	Wherever necessary to uphold institutions	Conservative and national parties
Minority nationalist Ethnicity regionalism	Minority groups especially with differing culture or language, peripheral groups	Cultural diversity among groups, value of all human experience	Decentralization and autonomy self-determination for cultural groups	Necessary to uphold minority cultures in the modern world	Nationalist, regional, ethnic parties and leagues

a moot point whether left socialists belong more with the new politics camp or the socialist family itself, so they are put with both in the table.

All party families can be characterized along the same lines as new politics parties, in terms of the main sectors of society where they find support, their core values, characteristic policies, attitudes to government intervention and typical member parties. All these characteristics of parties belonging to the same family are tied together by an ideology. Thus, in the case of socialists we have already seen that they put workers' interests and the need to promote them by securing a more equal society at the centre of their concerns. This leads to specific policies of extending universal welfare and limiting the full rigours of the free market through government intervention. The former communist parties of Poland and Bulgaria, as well as of

BRIEFING 9.4

Left–right differences in politics

The terms 'left' and 'right' originated from the location of supporters and opponents of political change in France at the end of the eighteenth century. Supporters of reform sat on the left of the legislative chamber while supporters of the king and established institutions sat on the right. The terms have kept their connection with those who urge change on the one hand, and those who oppose it on the other. However, the connection is more rhetorical than real, as right-wing parties often in practice introduce greater changes than left-wing ones (an example would be Thatcherite and Gaullist reforms in Britain and France).

In the twentieth century the core distinction is defined in terms of support for more government intervention, on the left, and opposition to it, on the right. Left-wing parties want more government support for the welfare state (see Chapter 15) and more regulation and planning in the economy. Right-wing parties want government to get out of society and the economy so far as possible, in order to extend individual freedom of choice. But they do support strong government measures to guarantee law and order internally, and national security, externally. Thus they support a strong, but limited, state. In contrast, left-wing parties want peace through international co-operation (this links up with the contrast between 'realists' and 'liberals' internationally, in Chapter 1). Left-wing positions have generally developed out of some variant of Marxist ideology (see Briefing 9.3).

Centre parties tend to mix these positions and support government intervention, up to a point, in most policy areas, but specifically oppose Marxist analyses of society.

The fact that parties take up these positions means that their election programmes and manifestos can be statistically analysed to see how they 'move' in left-right terms from election to election (see Figure 9.3).

For more details, see Ian Budge, David Robertson and D.J. Hearl, *Ideology, Strategy and Party Change* (Cambridge, Cambridge University Press, 1987).

Italy and France, have taken these policies on board together with a commitment to democracy. So they hardly seem to differ from established socialist parties on these points and can be grouped with them.

The other ideologies and party families in Table 9.1 have not been discussed so far except in passing. Christian Democrats have often been regarded as archetypal 'centre' parties on the left-right dimension of government intervention. They do not regard intervention as a good thing in itself, but are quite prepared to support it where necessary. This is because they regard a basic level of income and welfare as necessary to maintain human dignity and family survival — central values of the Christian social doctrine which constitutes their basic ideology. While they would prefer decentralization and 'subsidiarity' therefore (delegation of decision-making to the smallest possible unit, including that of the family and individual) they support government action where it can remedy an immediate evil. This often causes them to ally with Socialists on welfare matters while opposing them in terms of respect for property.

Agrarian parties, which in Scandinavia have often changed their name to 'centre' parties, are also opposed to government intervention in principle. The massive depopulation of the European countryside, and the integration of agriculture into a global market economy, means, however, that neither farmers nor countryside would survive without massive government support and protection. Hence in pursuit of farmers' or peasants' interests, Agrarian parties are wholeheartedly for intervention although they may oppose it elsewhere. Some agrarian parties like the Swedish centre party with its opposition to nuclear energy have taken on a greenish tinge. Intensive agriculture fostered by subsidies is however a destructive factor so far as the environment is concerned. So there is no natural convergence of interests between agrarian and Green parties.

With liberal parties we come to a family which is sharply divided between two groupings. Indeed it has sometimes been suggested that we should distinguish between them as two different families – radicals or progressive liberals (those of Scandinavia and Britain for example) and neo-liberals in most of the rest of Europe. The general split over the extent of Government intervention and preservation of the free market runs through the middle of the liberal group yet they do converge on core values of individualism and freedom.

The split comes on how one interprets freedom. Neo-liberals see freedom as non-interference by others with an individual's ability to choose – what to buy, where to work, what to do in general. Government intervention and regulation usually means prohibiting certain choices, such as buying drugs or reading pornography, or taking on risky jobs in bad conditions to earn more money, for example. Some government intervention may be necessary, particularly to stop some individuals interfering with others' choices. But it should be limited to the absolute minimum necessary.

Progressive liberals go one step further in this argument. There is no point, they say, in removing negative constraints on freedom if the end result of bad social conditions is to force certain actions on individuals willy-nilly. If the only job available is a risky and unpleasant one, so an individual has to take it or let her family starve, where is the liberty in that? To have effective freedom of choice individuals have to be assured of a certain social minimum which can only be secured by government intervention. Paradoxically, more intervention can increase freedom of choice – a proposition which neo-liberals reject.

When we review parties across Europe we shall accordingly divide the liberals into these two groups (see Table 9.2 below). Yet there is a sense in which they share the same position – one which, for example, distinguishes them from traditional conservative parties. These parties have been heavily influenced by the groups (beginning with nineteenth-century aristocrats) who were concerned with operating and upholding the traditional functions of the state. These were largely concerned with public order and external security, which have remained central values for conservatives – who often call themselves national parties (like the Italian *Alleanza Nazionale*).

Such parties have tended also to attract supporters of previous military or authoritarian regimes, like the *Partido Popular* in Spain from supporters of General Franco (the military dictator from 1940–74). In this way they provide a democratic alternative for groups who might otherwise be tempted into anti-democratic movements.

From this point of view, conservative parties have no doubts about the need for government intervention in matters of order and security. Sometimes too they see this as enhanced by making minimal social provisions, so as not to drive groups to action which might endanger public order. Parties like the French Gaullists are generally supportive of extensive welfare plans and control of sectors of industry defined as strategic, such as steel and armaments.

Recently some conservative parties have been strongly influenced by neo-liberals who are mainly interested in a strong state in order to guarantee a free market economy. This involves radical reforms which are opposed by traditional conservative groups, and have sometimes sparked strong protest – Margaret Thatcher's poll tax in the 1980s, and the proposed welfare reforms of French Gaullists in 1995, for example.

The last family listed in Table 9.1 is that of supporters of the rights of minorities (usually ethnic or religious ones) to have their own state or sub-state institutions. These might be Federal or regional ones within an existing state (as in Catalonia within Spain) or they might involve secession or union with the majority in a neighbouring state. We discussed these alternatives in Chapter 4. The imperfect coincidence between state boundaries and nations in Europe means that practically every country outside the Nordic countries, Poland and Germany has one or more ethnic minorities, which are at least potentially capable of supporting a significant party.

All such parties are dedicated to the proposition that minority culture, language or religion (sometimes all three) are intrinsically valuable and should be preserved and strengthened. Doing so in an age of universal education and television, they argue, demands a government which will act positively in support of the minority, giving them their own schools and cultural media. These need to be supplemented by measures to check the erosion of the group through emigration, and hence to strengthen the regional economy. Minority groups are often territorially concentrated on the periphery of an existing state and feel either overlooked or discriminated against by policy-makers in the capital.

Of course, minorities often have worse things to complain of than neglect: active discrimination and persecution in some parts of Europe, not to mention downright genocide, the extreme case being the former Yugoslavia. All these add to the impetus of minority parties. Yet their core appeal, exemplified in the regionalist parties of Western Europe, is that minorities have the right to exist and to safeguard their future, which can only be done by political means. Hence, if they do not actually want to secede they are pro-interventionist, certainly as regards their own and similar groups, but do not fit readily on the general left-right continuum that characterizes the other parties.

How did all these party families come into existence? We shall provide a detailed answer below. It is clear, however, that parties always base their appeals on certain groups in the population, if these were not created by them in the first place. Their ideology often appears as a rationalization of their supporters' interests. This does not render it invalid as, after all, these are important and justifiable social interests. Each group therefore, having its interests to defend against conflicting or potentially hostile ones, has tended to generate its own party when it was sufficiently organized and self-conscious enough to do so. A crucial point was often when it got the vote, during the successive extensions of the franchise in the nineteenth and twentieth centuries.

Party differences and their supporting ideologies can therefore be expected to go on so long as the social divisions or cleavages on which they base themselves continue to be important. Society, of course, is in constant change. We have already commented on the continuing depopulation of the countryside in most of Europe, with the exception of Poland and its Eastern neighbours. This has weakened agrarian parties considerably. However, parties are not simply passive upholders of social

BRIEFING **9.5**

The end of ideology?

In the 1950s and 1960s political scientists such as Daniel Bell and Seymour Martin Lipset wrote of the end of ideology and of the exhaustion of political ideas. The utopian appeals of communism, Fascism and most other 'isms', they said, had come to an end, to be replaced by a general consensus about the welfare state, the mixed economy, decentralized power and pluralist democracy. Serious intellectual conflict had ended since the main problems of the industrial revolution had been solved and the workers had gained industrial and political citizenship. The democratic struggle would continue, but without ideology.

Thirty years later, Francis Fukuyama revived the theme with his claim that history had come to an end. By this he meant that virtually the whole of the globe had reached a consensus that liberal democracy was the only acceptable form of government. As the final form of government, the triumph of liberal democracy constituted the end of history – or the end of ideology in Bell and Lipset's terms. All these theses depend on the idea that only left-wing (or extreme right-wing) beliefs add up to an ideology. We have shown that faith in liberal democracy and the free market are also ideological. In fact the struggle between conflicting political beliefs and principles has if anything intensified in the 1980s and 1990s as the left has regrouped and fought back against resurgent free market ideas, and ethnic nationalism has become stronger.

See Daniel Bell, *The End of ideology* (New York, Free Press, 1960); S.M. Lipset, *Political Man* (New York, Doubleday, 1960); F. Fukuyama, *The End of History and the Last Man* (New York, Free Press, 1992).

cleavages and will look out for related causes which will keep them going as a political force. The Swedish Agrarians' conversion into the centre party testifies to this. Still, such parties tend to suffer from the lack of a cohesive social base, as the centre party has.

Depopulation and assimilation may be expected therefore to weaken small Agrarian and Nationalist parties, while Christian ones will surely suffer from a decline in church attendance. Major divisions, however, like the extent of government intervention in society and the economy, may be expected to continue and to sustain contrasting party families and ideologies. Neither parties nor ideologies are in decline in Europe today – indeed, they have recently had an infusion of vigour from renewed party competition in Southern and Eastern Europe, as we shall see in the next section.

The political parties of Europe

Table 9.2 lists all the parties in the various European countries under their appropriate party family (as indicated above, we have divided the liberals into 'radical' and conservative liberal parties).

Parties usually make their ideological position quite clear, but there are, of course, some ambiguous cases. This is particularly so with some of the parties which have recently emerged in Eastern Europe, particularly if they have not yet had the chance to define themselves clearly through being in government.

Generally, however, it is remarkable how well parties do fit into families across

Table 9.2   The European political parties: By country, ideology and 'family'

Country	Left — New politics: Ecological	Left — New politics: Left socialist	Left — (ex-)Communist	Left — Social democratic	Left — Liberal radical	Centre — Centre, (ex-)agrarian	Centre — Religious/Christian	Right — Liberal-conservative	Right — Nationalist, conservative	Ethnic-regional	Other — Extreme right/protest
Sweden	Greens	Left Party New Democracy		Social Democrats	Peoples	Centre	Christian Democrats		Moderates		
Norway		Left Socialist	Workers	Labour		Centre	Christian People's	Liberals	Conservatives		Progress, pensioners
Denmark	Red-Green List	Socialist People's		Social Democrats	Radical Liberals, Centre Democrats	Venstre	Christian People's		Conservatives, Progress		
Iceland	Woman's Alliance	Alliance	People's Alliance	Social Democratic		Progressive			Independence, Awakening of the Nation		
Finland	Greens		Left-Wing Alliance	Social Democratic	Progressive Finns, Reform Party	Centre, rural	Christian, League		National Coalition	Swedish People's	Alliance for Free Finland
Estonia			Coalition/Rural Union	Social Democratic	Centrist Party			Moderates	National Independence, Fatherland, Democratic Union Free Estonia	Our Home is Estonia (Russian)	Right-wingers
Latvia			Latvian Way			Farmer's Union	Union of Christian Democrats (LKDS)	National Conservatives	National Harmony, Fatherland and Freedom, Democratic	Equal Rights (Russian)	
Great Britain (United Kingdom)				Labour	Liberal Democrat				Conservative	Minority Ethnic Parties (SNP, PC, Unionist SDLP)	
Ireland	Green Alliance	Workers' Party		Labour	Fine Gael			Progressive Democrats	Fianna Fail		
Netherlands	Green	Left		Labour (PvdA)	Democrats '66 (D'66)		Christian Democratic Appeal, Calvinist Parties (SGP, PRF)	Liberals (VVD)			Anti-Immigrant Union of Elderly

Belgium	Flemish Greens (AGALEV) French Greens (ECOLO)			Flemish Socialist (SP) French Socialist (PS)		Flemish Christians (CVP) French Christians (PSC)	Flemish Liberals (PVV) French Liberals (PRL)		Flemish Nationalists (Volksunie)	Flemish Block
Luxembourg	Ecologists		Action Committee for Democracy and Justice	Socialist	Action for Democracy Pensioners	Christian Social				Anti-immigrant
France	Greens	Unified Socialists	Communists (PCF)	Socialist (PS)	Left Radicals (MRG)		Union for French Democracy (UDF)	Gaullist (RPR)		National Front
Spain			United Left	Socialists (PSDE)				Popular Party	Catalan Nationalists (Convergance and Unity), Basque Nationalists, etc.	
Portugal			Democratic Union	Socialists		People's Party (Christian Democrats (CDS))	Social Democrats (PSD)			
Malta				Labour				Nationalists		
Italy	Greens		Communist Refoundation	Democratic Party of the Left (PDS)		Popular Party		Forza Italia National Alliance	Northern League, Minority Ethnic Parties (SVP, PSA, UV, etc.)	
Switzerland	Greens		Workers	Social Democrats		Christian Democrats, Evangelical People's Party	Radical Democrats, Liberals	Swiss Peoples		Auto Party, Anti-immigrant
Germany	Greens		Democratic Socialist	Social Democrats (SDP)	Free Democrats (FPD)	Christian Democrats (CDU-CSU)				
Austria	Green Alternative			Socialists	Liberal Forum		People's Party	Freedom Party		

Table 9.2 (continued)

Country	New politics — Ecological	New politics — Left socialist	(ex-)Communist	Social democratic	Liberal radical	Centre, (ex-)agrarian	Religious/Christian	Liberal-conservative	Nationalist, conservative	Ethnic-regional	Extreme right/protest
Czech Rep.			Left Block	Social Democrats	Liberal Social Union		Christian Democratic Union	Civic Democratic Party, Civic Democratic Alliance–Forum	Republican Party	Self-government Moravia/Silesia	
Slovakia			Democratic Left, Slovak Workers		Democratic Union of Slovakia		Christian Democrats	Common Choice	Movement for a Democratic Slovakia, Slovak National Party	Hungarian Coalition	
Hungary			Socialists		Young Democrats	Independent Small Holders, Agrarian Association	Christian Democrats	Liberal Civic Alliance, Free Democrats	Democratic Forum		
Poland			Democratic Left	Union of Labour		Peasants	Catholic Fatherland Coalition	Democratic Union	Independent Poland (KPN) Non-Party Block		
Lithuania			Democratic Labour Party	Social Democratic Party			Christian Democrats	National Union	Democratic Reform Party, Centre Movement	Union of Poles	
Slovenia	Greens		Associated List of Social Democrats				Christian Democrats	Democratic League, Liberal Democrats	Democrats, Nationalist Party		
Croatia				Social Democrats, Democratic Changes	Social Liberals	Peasants	Christian Democrats	People's Party	Democratic Union, Party of Rights	Joint–List Coalition of Regionalist Parties	
Serbia			Socialists			Democratic Party		Democratic Movement of Serbia	Serbian Renewal Serbian Radical Party Democratic Party of Serbia	Union of Vojvodina Hungarians Democratic League of Kosovo (Albanian)	
Macedonia			Social Democratic League	Socialists		Liberal Party	National Democratic Party		Revolutionary National Unity	Alliance of Reform Forces Democratic Prosperity	

Country	Communists / ex-communists	Social Democrats / Socialists	Socialists / Populists	Agrarians	Christian / Religious	Liberals / Republicans	Conservatives / Nationalists	Ethnic / Other
Albania	Socialists	Social Democratic Party				Republican Party	Democratic Party	(Greek) Human Rights Unity Party
Greece	Communists	Socialists (PASOK)				New Democracy, Political Spring		
Cyprus	Progressive Party of Working People (AKEL)	Social Party (EDEK)				Democratic Rally (DISI)	Democratic Party (DIKO)	
Turkey		Social Democratic	Republican People's Party; Populists		(Islamic) National Salvation Party		Motherland Party, True Path Party	
Armenia	Revolutionary Communists Freedom					National Union	Union of National Self-Determination	
Georgia		Greens		National Democratic Party		National Front Charter 21	Chavchavadze Society	
Bulgaria	Socialists			People's Union		Union of Democratic Forces, Business Block		Movement for Rights and Freedom (Turkish)
Romania	Party of Social Democracy					Democratic Convention	National Unity, Greater Romania	Hungarian Democratic Union
Moldova	Socialist-Unity			Agrarian Democracy	Christian Democratic People's			Peasants and Intellectuals (Pro-Romania)
Ukraine	Communist Party (KPU)	Socialist (SPU)	Social Democrats	Agrarian Party		Democratic Rebirth	RUKH Republicans, Democrats, Nationalists	
Belarus	Communists			Agrarians		People's Front, Democratic Belarus		
Russia	Communist (KPRF)		Yabloko			Russia's Choice	Our House is Russia	Liberal Democrats

Notes: The parties mentioned in Table 9.2 are the ones which gained legislative seats in the 1990s, i.e. which exist now.

In general the English names for parties are given, but where parties are commonly referred to in English by their native initials or name these are used.

Electoral alliances such as the Nordic 'bourgeois coalitions', the right and left in France, 'Olive Tree' and 'Pol of Liberty' in Italy, or the Yeltsin Government Coalition in Russia, are not mentioned. Only their constituent parties are listed.

national frontiers. This all goes to show how much ideology continues to distinguish parties and how important it remains. The fact that the new parties of Southern and Eastern Europe have so rapidly divided along traditional lines shows how central these are to political debate. The degree to which governments should intervene to secure the well-being of their citizens and territory, and the rights of minorities, seem the major questions which will dominate domestic politics in Europe well into the next millennium.

Of course we should always remember that the parties listed in Table 9.2 represent only a tiny fraction of those which actually exist in Europe. Most countries have literally hundreds of political parties: even tiny, recently independent Macedonia has about forty. The point about most of these mini-parties, however, is that they only compete in one or two places in some elections. In other words, they are unsuccessful and not very important for electoral or parliamentary politics. Often they exist to advertise a cause, and to promote it by getting the larger parties to think that perhaps they should ward off a potential threat to their votes by accommodating it.

Sometimes too these small parties exist because enthusiasts for a particular cause like the environment think that people *must* be concerned given the extent of destruction that is going on. Even if they have received little support in the past therefore they think they will get widespread support next time. Political parties are kept going by enthusiasts like these whose ideological beliefs incline them to excessive optimism. Since people's reactions are uncertain, particularly given the enormous social changes taking place in Central and Eastern Europe, such optimism sometimes pays off. More often it is just enough to keep a small organization staggering on from election without running many candidates or attracting many votes.

The parties in Table 9.2 are therefore the relatively significant and successful parties, which have gained enough votes to get into parliament. This does not always guarantee them large numbers of representatives there. The extent to which it does, as we shall see in Chapter 10, depends on the way in which votes get translated into seats. Systems of proportional representation, where the whole object is to get a fairly exact equivalence between votes and seats, generally guarantee parties a percent of seats in parliament which corresponds to their vote. So if a party gets 25 per cent of the vote, for example, it should get nearly 25 per cent of the parliamentary seats.

Proportional representation, by awarding them parliamentary seats, can thus make small parties significant in forming or supporting governments, usually owing to the larger parties or blocs balancing each other out. This has been the case with the Free Democrats (FDP) in Germany, in contrast to the total exclusion of the more electorally successful British Liberals from power.

On the other hand, some large parties with a considerable popular following are often excluded from government by their rivals – the Popular Party in Spain during the 1980s is a case in point. Because of their electoral support, however, such parties cannot be totally ignored in the government's calculations, for if they refused to co-operate policy could hardly be implemented. Even if never in government therefore such parties are significant in the sense of affecting State policy, directly or indirectly.

Both types of party are represented in Table 9.2, along with the large parties which normally form governments. Between them they represent all the really important political forces and cleavages in Europe, so we shall focus our discussion on them in the rest of this chapter.

Though small parties can be important the essential factor in gaining power is

BRIEFING 9.6

The concept of a party system

Basically, a party system is the overall configuration of significant parties within a state. This has two aspects, the first qualitative, the second quantitative.

The qualitative aspect is the question of what party families are represented among the significant parties (significant in the sense of having a continuing presence in parliament and affecting government policy). This shades into the question of power relationships between them. Do all types of party get relatively equal numbers of votes and share equally in government, or does one party of a particular type dominate? For example, the Nordic countries are often cited as examples of social democratic dominance. Not only are the social democratic parties substantially larger than any of the bourgeois parties, but they generally form the government and the other parties are in opposition. The Low Countries in contrast are a case where the Christian parties, through not attracting substantially more votes than other parties, can generally decide whether to form a coalition with the (right-wing) liberals or the socialists, as these parties are usually sharply opposed to each other.

The quantitative aspect of party systems is the question of how many significant parties there are. Do two major parties compete to form a majority single party government (Britain and Spain) or are there many smaller parties which have to form coalition governments (Belgium, Poland and Finland). This is obviously an important question which we consider in Chapter 10, so the question of the number of parties has been more studied than the question of what types of parties exist.

Both of these aspects of party systems can in any case be explained in the same way, by the underlying social cleavages which exist in a country. If there is only one major social cleavage, class for example, then you might expect to find a two-party system where the Socialists represent workers' interests and a Conservative or Liberal party represents the middle class. Conversely, where class, religious and ethnic/regional cleavages are all important, you could expect to find four or five parties (see 'P=C+1?' below).

However, things are not as simple as that. It is clear that the number of parties is heavily affected by the electoral system (i.e. the way votes are counted) as much as by social cleavages. There are actually three significant British parties at electoral level but only two which count in Parliament, because the system of awarding constituency seats to the party which gets most (but not a majority of) votes penalizes the Liberals. Under a PR system there would always have to be coalitions in Britain, as in Germany. We will discuss this in more detail in Chapter 10.

---

generally the parties' electoral strength among voters. The tables in Chapter 3 show the different parties' current electoral strength. In terms of the policies they can be expected to pursue and the long-term direction of the government will take, the crucial point is whether a particular party family and ideological tendency is represented in a country. This is shown in Table 9.2. A further question is how much support a particular family gets. Even if it is divided between a number of parties, these will find it easier to co-operate in government because they can all agree in similar lines of policy. Thus the overall voting strength of a tendency is important for showing which line policy will take.

Table 9.3 shows the average strength of the various ideological groupings over the last 30 years. Average figures can be a bit misleading. For example, the socialists in Greece are now stronger, and the conservatives weaker than their averages in the table

Table 9.3   Average percentage vote by country for each party family in free elections, 1965–95

Country	Ecological	Left Socialist	(Ex-) Communist	Social Democrat	Liberal	(Centre) Agrarian	Religious Christian	Nationalist Conservative	Ethnic- regional	Extreme right/protest
Sweden	4	5		45	11	15	2	19		
Norway		7		39	5	9	9	22		4
Denmark	2	10		34	10	15	2	24		
Iceland	8		16	15		23		36		
Finland	5		15	26	3	18	2	19	5	
Estonia			32		25	14		7	6	5
Latvia			33		13	11	5		6	
Great Britain				39	14			42	4	
Ireland	1	2		13	35			47		
Netherlands	2	2		29	21		39			
Belgium	6			26	20		30		13	
Luxembourg	6		7	33	20		33			2
France	5	2	17	25	19			26		
Spain			8	40				37	9	
Portugal			15	31	27		13			
Malta				49				49		
Italy	4		6	20			15	40	9	
Switzerland	6		2	22	23		21	12		4
Germany	5		3	34	8		44			1
Austria	4			44	5			34		8
Czech Republic			14	6	42		6	6	6	
Slovakia			15		19		10	40	10	
Hungary			21		28	11	7	20		
Poland			15	7	10	10		11		
Lithuania			46	6		6	12	22	2	
Slovenia	4		14		29		14	13		
Croatia				9	12	5	5	50	5	
Serbia			35		17	12		15	2	
Macedonia			50						20	
Albania			23					58		
Greece			10	34				45		
Cyprus			31	12	34			20		
Turkey				30			10	45		
Bulgaria			44		29	6			7	
Romania			59		15			8	7	
Moldova			22			43	7		9	
Ukraine			13	3	2	3		9		
Belarus			15		3	10				
Russia			18		11			5		17

Notes: The table covers the results from free elections in each country for the second half of the post-war period (1965–1995). Some countries only started to have free elections in the 1970s (Spain, Portugal, Greece, Cyprus) and others (Central and Eastern Europe) in the 1990s. Averages are only taken for these free elections, so in the latter case figures may be based only on two or even on one election. Averages also relate only to the period of time a party acatually contested free elections. So the figures for more recently formed parties are based on a more limited set of elections within the time period than is the case with longer-established parties (e.g. most Italian parties were founded after 1992 in their present form, and many Central and Eastern European parties changed between the first and second free election). The parties making up the 'family' whose average vote is shown are the ones listed it in Table 9.2. Thus, figures relate only to the parties operating now, not ones which existed at some point in the period but have now disappeared.

indicate. This is because the average still reflects Pasok's relative weakness in the 1970s. So to make a full assessment of electoral politics in each country the averages in Table 9.3 need to be compared with the latest results reported in Chapter 3.

What the averages do show is the relative strength of each ideological tendency in each country. In some, like Greece and Spain, only a limited number of tendencies are represented. In others like Ukraine and Scandinavia, there is a broad range of tendencies, with socialists predominating, however. The Czech Republic is notable in being the only country with a predominant Liberal Party.

The most widespread and generally strongest party family in Europe are the socialists, particularly if they are grouped with the ex-communists who in most cases have moved to the same policy positions. But all party families have some electoral strength across Europe as a whole. The most limited are protest parties of the extreme right, which are generally suspicious and resentful of democratic pluralism. This confirms the survey evidence in Chapter 5 that, generally, European electors strongly support democracy. Minority ethnic parties seem about as strong in Western as in Central and Eastern Europe.

Indeed a major point which comes out from both tables is the remarkable similarity of party systems in both parts of Europe. It would be hard to determine simply from the distribution of party families or from their relative strength whether a country was in East, Centre, West or South. (Exceptions are Belarus, Ukraine and Russia where all parties are weak.) On the whole, however, the emerging democracies seem to be tending rapidly to the electoral practices of the established ones – another feature which justifies looking at them all altogether in this context.

■ Party organization and membership

All parties depend upon organization. No matter how limited their electoral goals, they must perform their organizational job well if they are to survive or win elections. Forms of party organization vary considerably, however, partly depending upon their history.

Parties often began as loose groupings of aristocrats or rich merchants and businessmen joined together in opposition to the government. Their motivation might simply have been to replace the office-holders themselves, or it might have been an opposition of principle, wanting free trade and social improvements as against a protectionist and traditionalist government. Such an opposition was at the root of the Liberal–Conservative party distinction which exists today.

The government had no scruples in using all the resources at its disposal, including those of the state, in trying to keep voters on its side. This is rather like the situation in contemporary Russia where President Yeltsin and his supporters, rather than forming an ideologically distinct party, have relied on the civil service and business organizations to campaign for them.

Lacking government support, the 'country parties' of nineteenth-century Europe had to fall back on their own resources. As the leaders were persons with wealth, land, businesses and a following in their own right, they each organized their own campaign and secured their election in the regions where they were powerful. This, too, is not unlike what most of the Russian opposition does today.

Such 'parties of notables' have distinct characteristics. Each notable has his own band of supporters and secures his own election. He is thus a distinctly independent figure not bound by party discipline. The only way party action can be taken is by agreement. There may, however, be rivalries and jealousies between particular notables which lead them to abstain on particular votes, or even to secede from the party. It is very difficult, therefore, for the top leadership to give binding commitments on behalf of the party and often some members will abstain on crucial votes which the rest support. Again, such behaviour with the splitting and re-formation of parliamentary parties, is familiar from Russia, Belarus and the Ukraine.

With the coming of a mass electorate and universal suffrage, the nature of party organization changed in most European countries. Electors were now too numerous to respond to the appeals of any one personality. They were more likely to follow the lead of their own organizations like trade unions or business associations, and to respond to general ideological, rather than personal, appeals. Parties needed to operate on a more regular basis than that provided by the *ad hoc* campaign teams assembled by notables. They needed to set up permanent organizations which would raise money through membership fees, keep track of voter registration, canvass for support, mobilize voters on election day, discuss policy and report local views to the centre.

The answer was to set up some kind of central organization in the state capital, directed by the top leaders, which kept closely in touch with the party representatives in parliament. This organization serviced and co-ordinated the activities of local branches. Depending on how elections and voting were organized these branches existed in every important city and town, and usually also in the countryside.

The central organization and regional associations prepared general policy statements and recruited and organized the party lists of candidates. Branches did ground level work like listing party voters, organizing transport and publicity, raising money and so on. Members were prepared to donate money and time to party activity because they subscribed to its ideology and supported its policy. This meant, however, that their views could not be ignored. The payoff for their work was to give them a voice in party affairs, through regional and national councils and conferences whose decisions had to be considered by the leadership.

The exact extent of workers' and activists' influence varied with individual parties but also – and most significantly – with their ideology. Socialist, agrarian and Christian parties organized their mass base from the start, since they needed it – first to agitate for the franchise, then to mobilize votes to get representatives into parliament. Liberal and Conservative notables, who were already there, had to create mass organizations to safeguard their electoral base. But they did it later and more reluctantly, imitating the new mass parties previously unrepresented in parliament – a process which has been described as 'contagion from the Left'.

The notables, however, were suspicious of new ideas of intra-party democracy and generally limited the influence of the mass organization on the leadership and its policy. By contrast the Green and left-socialist parties of the post-war era have sought to extend popular participation even to the extent of not having a formal membership and allowing anybody into party meetings to discuss policy.

Figure 9.1 illustrates these points by showing the structure of the Maltese Nationalist Party. In Malta, parties first based themselves on pre-existing village social clubs and even village bands! However, the Maltese Labour Party, the great rival of the Nationalists, organized a network of explicitly political clubs and associations, and the Nationalists, to compete effectively, had to organize their own in the 1970s. The Labour Party, following the British model, has close relations with the trade unions. In response, the Nationalists have created affiliated workers', women's and youth organizations, as well as receiving consistent support from the Catholic church and its strong parochial organization. Both parties have arrangements for a strong central co-ordinating committee and bureaucracy, as well as a General Council where ordinary members can make their voices heard.

The danger with strong leadership and bureaucratic organization is that under a façade of democratic representation of members, they can actually manipulate pro-

Figure 9.1 A typical mass party organization (Partito Nazzjonalista, Malta)

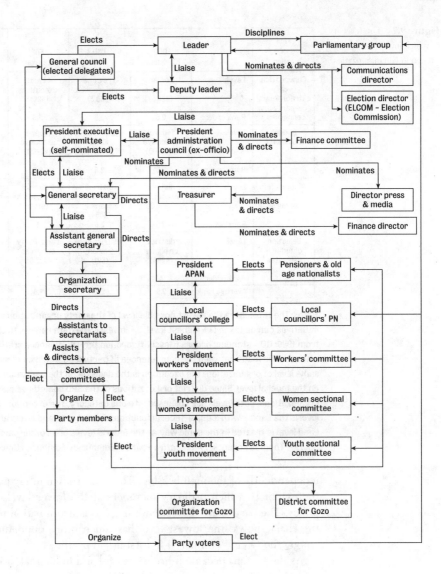

cedures so as to impose their own views on members, as Michels said (see Chapter 8). As their shared ideology makes for a convergence of views anyway it is difficult to say when this is happening. However, there have been occasions when party leaders have openly stated that they will ignore majority views inside the party, as Chancellor Schmidt did in accepting American nuclear missiles in West Germany in the late 1970s, and as the Irish Labour leaders did in going into government coalitions with Fine Gael in the early 1980s. In response, Irish Labour members secured a pledge that the members' conference would decide on party coalition participation in the future and have done so in the late 1980s and 1990s.

New politics parties, as noted in Chapter 8, distrust party organization and bureaucracy for this very reason – as stifling internal participation and ignoring or perverting popular views. In reaction the German Green Party devised extremely open internal procedures explicitly designed to prevent leaders operating too

Figure 9.2 The level at which initiatives can be taken in German parties

Kind of action		CDU (Christians)	CSU	FDP (Liberals)	SPD (Social democrats)	Greens
Convocation of extraordinary party congress	Level:	1/3 of land-organizations (§28.5)	3 regional conferences (§38.3)	4 Land-executives (§21.1)	2/5 regional executives (§21.1)	10% of district organizations (§8.4)
	Rank order:	2.5	2.5	2.5	2.5	5
Budget decisions	Level:	federal executive (§15-FO)	presidium (§24.2)	federal executive (§2-FO)	federal executive (§7-FO)	party congress (§12-FO)
	Rank order:	2.5	2.5	2.5	2.5	5
Motions for party congress	Level:	district executive (§6-GO)	district executive or assembly (§45.1)	5 district organizations (§11.1)	local organizations (§18.2)	20 members (§8.5)
	Rank order:	2.5	2.5	1	4	5
Selection of federal delegates	Level:	district or higher (§28.1)	district and region (§21)	Land-Party congress (§13.8)	region or sub-region (§15)	district (§8.1)
	Rank order:	4	3	1	2	5
	Average rank:	2.9	2.6	1.8	2.8	5

Notes: The table gives the lowest possible level of the party organization at which selected political initiatives can be taken (1 = highest level, 5 = lowest). The data referes to the relevant party statues from 1989: GO = standing orders (Geschäftsordnung); 'FO' = financial statute (Finanzordnung). No distinction is made between the competences of party leaderships and party conferences on the same level of organization. The exception is the decision on the party budget, which has to be taken on the federal level. Since district organizations of the SPD sometimes play the role of land organizations, both levels are collapsed into one category. The exception is the CSU, whose highest level is the Land – with a quasi-federal function: district and land levels are kept separate here. The Land level is treated in the same way as the federal levels of all other parties.
Source: Thomas Poguntke, *Alternative Politics* (Edinburgh, Edinburgh University Press, 1993), p. 141.

independently of the membership. These are shown in Figure 9.2, which compares the extent to which ordinary members at the lower levels of parties can initiate policy. The parties are divided into five levels, from nation to district (Level 5). As the chart shows, the lowest level has much more opportunity to take initiatives among the Greens compared to established parties.

As the Greens became more successful and influential, however, they found that leaders could, in an age of mass television, put an attractive human face on policy for the mass electorate and become major electoral assets. Secondly, leaders were necessary to make quick decisions which could not be extensively discussed through popular and often disorderly meetings.

There is an inbuilt tension between leaders and members inside all modern mass parties. Leaders cannot always consult broadly before taking decisions and the suspicion grows that they might not want to do so because general opinion might be against their own preferred course of action. Leaders also receive direct rewards from their political activities – better salaries, expenses, directorships, consultancies and gifts – so they can often be accused of having been bought off for personal gain. Party activists, on the other hand, can be written off as extremist ideologues who would prefer to stick with unworkable policies to keep their ideals pure, rather than making pragmatic compromises which give them at least something of what they want.

There will probably always be quarrels of this sort going on inside political parties, just as in the wider democracy. Conflict is not something any democracy can

Table 9.4 Party members as a percentage of all electors in eleven European countres, 1960s and 1980s	First election in 1960s	Last election in 1980s
Austria	26.2	21.8
Sweden	22.0	21.2
Denmark	21.1	6.5
Finland	18.9	12.9
Norway	15.5	13.5
Italy	12.7	9.7
Netherlands	9.4	2.8
UK	9.4	3.3
Belgium	7.8	9.2
West Germany	2.5	4.2
Ireland	na	5.3

Sources: This table is from Ware (1996: 73) and based on data in Table 1 of Richard S. Katz, Peter Mair, *et al.* 'The membership of political parties in European democracies', *European Journal of Political Research*, 22 (1992), 334.

get rid of without ceasing to be a democracy, even if it becomes wearing and distressing at times. However, there are two factors limiting disputes between leaders and members inside a political party.

The first is their shared ideology. Both want essentially the same things, no matter how much they disagree on how to get them, or what priorities should be given to their shared goals. This limits disagreement. The best leaders can persuade members to back their compromises by showing them how it advances their shared goals.

The second factor maintaining party unity is mutual dependence. Leaders and members both need each other. Without a leadership, members would be just an uncoordinated mass. Without members, leaders would lack the resources and votes to achieve their goals. So there is pressure on both of them to work together. The most successful leaders recognize and manage to achieve this.

The fact that party membership has declined in Europe over the last thirty years has been taken as a sign of decay – certainly of the established parties (see Table 9.4). It may, however, equally reflect the fact that large numbers of members are less important to parties than they were. In the past, members were more necessary to organize meetings and make direct contact with electors on behalf of the party. With television, however, leaders and parliamentarians can project their image and policies into every home, so members are less important than they were.

This argument can, however, be a double-edged one. The essential job of getting electors to the polls, and checking the validity of the votes and electoral counts themselves, still depend heavily on ordinary members. Perhaps for this reason parties which have suffered heavy losses of members are anxious to rebuild their membership base, as British Labour and Scandinavian social democrats want to do, with some success in the early 1990s. This may redress to some extent the drastic falls shown in Table 9.4.

It is clear from Table 9.4, moreover, that inter-country variation in membership is much greater than decline over time. The latter may be exaggerated by the fact that countries where membership has undoubtedly gone up, such as Spain, Portugal and Greece, are not shown. Where numbers have declined, as in Britain and Germany, parties have also acquired a new and important figure, the local politicians, active in regional parliaments, or local councils. This is a result of politics at intermediate levels now involving the parties – a development of the post-war period in its full magnitude and extent. Such activists, often managing billion-pound budgets in their own area of competence, have considerable political power in their own right. Even if numbers of activists have gone down inside some parties, therefore, their weight and influence have increased qualitatively. Germany, Britain and Italy are good examples of this process.

The continuing importance of party organization and membership are well demonstrated by the recent experience of Central and Eastern Europe. The first step towards the restoration of democracy – often taken before the collapse of the old regime – was the organization of political parties. This shows how necessary these are to democracy and effectively contradicts the idea that parties as such are in decline. Half those in Table 9.2 were formed in the last 10–15 years.

Competing parties often emerged, in Central, Eastern and Southern Europe, from the pro-democracy movement itself, as it split over the policies and choices to be made after the ousting of the old monolithic regime. Solidarity in Poland is the best known example, but this happened also in Czechoslovakia, Hungary and the Baltic states. These parties dominated the first free elections and formed the first governments in or around 1990, in most countries.

Once in office they enthusiastically set about privatizing state-owned industry, stabilizing the currency and introducing a free market, with often catastrophic effects on employment and welfare (see Chapters 15 and 16 below). The industrial working class was particularly badly hit and reacted against these policies – finding a political spokesman and defender in the reformed Communist Party which had dominated the country before the revolution.

In many countries (Germany, Poland, Hungary, the Ukraine and Russia itself) the new Communist Party won votes from people badly affected by liberalization and anxious about the state support (e.g. for welfare) which they had previously enjoyed. However, another factor helping the re-emergence of the communists in most of these countries was the fact that they had a nationwide organization with branches in regions and constituencies, records and party workers who could contact and mobilize their potential voters. In contrast, most of their rivals had only a central organization with few local affiliates. Their policies were certainly unpopular but they could have limited their defeat by organizing themselves efficiently, which they failed to do.

The point about organization is reinforced by the success of some of the communists' former allies from the old regime. From 1946–89 in many Central and Eastern European countries, various parties – Christians and Agrarians normally – had been forced into alliance with communists in a 'popular front'. They were hardly free agents but to a limited extent they could press their supporters' interests from within the government.

This inglorious collaboration did preserve their organization and assets which they were able to take with them when they withdrew from the forced coalition in 1989–90. Like the reformed communists, this gave them a much more effective political machine than their 'bourgeois' opponents, which limited their defeat in the first elections of the 1990s and enabled them to recover ground in later elections. As a result agrarians often went into coalition with the reformed communists to form a new government which limited the free market reforms. In Poland the agrarians actually provided the Prime Minister after 1993.

We can, of course, expect the other parties in Central and Eastern Europe to learn their lesson from this and form effective grass-roots organizations. 'Contagion from the left' is thus occurring later than in the West but has the same underlying logic and is recognizably the same process. In a mass democracy parties have to have a mass organization if they are to get the mass vote.

■ Party systems and social cleavages

Not only organizational logic explains the survival of parties from the old communist regimes. The cleavage lines underlying society and the various social interests that they define, have also found expression through these parties. To see how this has occurred we turn back to the processes by which parties developed in Europe in the late nineteenth and twentieth centuries. Once we have described these we can see how they are working themselves out again in Central and Eastern Europe today.

We have already made some references to the historical development of parties and party systems, particularly with regard to the original conflict between conservative and liberal parties which developed from about 1830 onwards. This derived from the social changes brought on by the Industrial Revolution. The new class of wealthy industrialists, merchants and professionals created by industrialization was mostly excluded from political power. This might not have mattered had states and governments been doing what they wanted – creating an infrastructure of roads, railways, urban services and public health which would provide a sound basis for economic expansion. The state administration tended, however, to be dominated by landed aristocrats who took a traditional view of government, concerning themselves mostly with the army, internal order, and suppressing religious and political dissent.

The new bourgeoisie was influenced by some of the ideas of the French Revolution (1789–96) and wanted liberty and equality at least for themselves. They also consisted disproportionately of religious and other minorities, such as Jews and Protestant dissenters, who had been debarred from ordinary careers under the old regime and turned to money-making. Thus, besides action on the new cities and urban areas, they wanted to take education from the hands of the church, secularize it and open it to all.

These Liberals were generally successful in extending the right to vote to the middle class, in taking over the government and in carrying through their desired reforms. In doing so, however, they stirred up opposition just as their successors in Central and Eastern Europe have done today. The church saw its very existence threatened by removal of control over the minds of the young. It might not be able to stop secular schools operating as it had in the past. But it could aim at extending church schools and having them supported by the state. To this end it turned from dependence on the conservative aristocrats who had failed to protect it, to organizing mass movements of the faithful who would have enough votes to counteract the liberals. In its turn it agitated for a wider franchise, to extend to religious adherents, including peasants and workers. These movements were the ancestors of the Christian democrats of today.

Support for the enfranchisement of the lower classes made for sometimes surprising alliances between religious, agrarian and socialist parties. As the countryside was often deeply religious, the first was not perhaps too surprising. The liberals' promotion of public works thrusting deep into the countryside, their imposition of godless secular schools, and subordination of the interests of farmers and peasants to those of city dwellers to secure cheap food – all created reactions which might lead to support of Christians or conservatives, or to the creation of autonomous agrarian parties.

The same developments were, of course, even more deeply resented where the country-dwellers were a minority ethnic group whose children were now forcibly educated in the majority language of the state. Their resistance might again be

BRIEFING 9.7

P = C + 1? The relationship between social cleavages and number and type of political parties

The formula $P=C+1$ is just a way of expressing common ideas about the relationship between the number of parties (P) and the number of politically relevant cleavages in a society (C). It says that if there is only one important cleavage in a society then there will be only two parties (one representing each side of the divide, working class (socialist) and middle class (conservative) for example. Two cleavages, class and religion, would, however, produce three parties as one might expect the higher status religious group to coincide largely with the middle class, and thus both to be represented by one party, while religion split the working class who would be represented by two parties.

Similarly, one might say $PT=TC$ where PT was party type and TC was type of cleavage: thus the existence of class and religious cleavages in a society would produce socialist, liberal and Christian parties. Generally, four types of cleavages are regarded as particularly important in explaining differences in party systems: class, religion, ethnic-regional and urban–rural (i.e. differences between cities and countryside). To this we might add age and education differences in relation to the rise of the 'New Politics' (cf. Chapter 8).

Such differences are regarded as increasingly important because the supporters of Green and left socialist parties are disproportionately young and highly educated. However, this illustrates one of the difficulties involved in using social cleavages to account for the existence of particular types of parties in a country. How do we know when a cleavage is politically important? We know because a particular party exists. Why does it exist? It exists because the related cleavage is politically important.

In other words, explaining parties by cleavages is in danger of becoming circular: we explain parties by cleavages, but we assess cleavages by parties. How do we know, for example, that Flemish nationalism is an important cleavage inside Belgium but Frisian nationalism is not an important cleavage inside the Netherlands? The answer is that there *is* a Flemish nationalist party (in fact two, the Volksunie and the Vlaamsblok) but no Frisian nationalist party in the Netherlands. We have no real explanation why this contrast should hold – not in terms of social cleavages anyway. We could say that the significant Frisian group is smaller than the Flemish and have been given concessions by Dutch governments, but this implies that politics can shape social cleavages so that these do not just have a one-way effect on party systems.

This can explain an otherwise puzzling feature of European party systems. Why should countries which mostly have rather similar social cleavages – class, regional, religious, urban–rural – not have produced rather similar party systems, rather than the bewildering diversity of systems which actually exists in Europe? One explanation is that parties are not just passive repositories of social cleavages but autonomous actors which play a large part in defining them. In Britain, for example, the Labour party has played a large part in linking class and territorial cleavages so that it represents the peripheries of the country as well as the lower classes – an alliance which the socialists in Spain were able to consolidate only partially, in Andalusia but not in Catalonia nor Euzkadi.

Another factor in the less than perfect coincidence between social cleavages and political parties is the influence of constitutional arrangements and the electoral system. The methods for translating votes into legislative seats are often designed to weaken particular parties and social interests. Even where they have not been actually designed to do so they often do anyway, as we shall see in Chapter 10.

(continued)

> *(continued)*
>
> Despite all these qualifications the explanation of party systems by social cleavage clearly has a lot of validity. In particular, it makes sense of the historical emergence of parties in Western Europe, and explains contemporary developments in the East very convincingly, as we have seen. What needs to be done is first to admit other factors (like electoral systems) into the relationship, and secondly to find a way of assessing the political significance of cleavages independently of the existence of particular parties.
>
> For the relationship between cleavages and parties, see M. Lipset and S. Rokkan (eds), *Party Systems and Voter Alignments* (New York, Free Press, 1967).

mobilized by conservative or religious parties, but might well throw up an ethnic nationalist party, dedicated to the preservation of minority language and culture.

Meanwhile in the cities the factory workers, now becoming the largest social group, were being mobilized through trade unions and parties to press their liberal employers for better conditions and wages. Sometimes Christian unions and parties played a large part in this process, sometimes it was in the hands of social democrats. As noted in Chapter 7, the shape of the union movement was very much affected by the activity of the parties at this critical juncture. Sometimes a unified movement emerged: sometimes it split between Christians and socialists; and sometimes between different types of socialist – notably social democrats and communists.

It is possible to see developments in Central and Eastern Europe as a re-run in the 1990s of these historic party conflicts, which had not been absent from the area of course in the late nineteenth and early twentieth century, before the Soviet-dictated freeze on party developments. In fact many of the parties which have now re-emerged are descendants of parties which represented these cleavages before the Second World War – the agrarian parties of peasants and smallholders, Christian parties of the church, ethnic parties of the minority groups, and ex-communist parties of the urban workers.

Tables 9.2 and 9.3 illustrate the results of this process in terms of the distribution and voting strength of these party families over most of the countries of Central and Eastern Europe. All of the types of parties represented in Western Europe also appear in the Centre-East and dominate the contests – although, as noted in Chapter 8, 'New Politics' parties are rare. The Bulgarian ecological opposition has come to be dominated by liberals. Most of the running is made by ex-communist, liberal and nationalist parties. Agrarians and ethnic regionalist parties play a significant supporting role, while liberal parties retain their strength in the Czech Republic, Slovenia and Bulgaria.

In view of these results it is not surprising that (ex)-communist dominated governments re-emerged in many countries, notably Poland, Hungary and Lithuania, in the mid-1990s. This is natural if seen as an attempt by groups in these societies to defend themselves against the hardships of the free market – an interpretation reinforced by the fact that agrarian parties were often in partnership with the (ex)-communists.

Developments in the Centre and East can thus be set in a wider framework than that of support or opposition to the move from Soviet society of the early 1990s. They mirror the wider processes which have created European party systems over the last 100 years. In this context it is significant that Portugal, Spain and Greece all witnessed the takeover of the government by socialist parties five or seven years after the collapse of the authoritarian regime, as the vulnerable groups in society sought protection against the instability brought about by the political changes.

The political developments working themselves through the new democracies of Southern, Central and Eastern Europe thus seem likely to produce party systems which closely resemble those already existing in the West. The question is how far are these party systems themselves in change? The rise of new party families – most spectacularly 'New Politics' parties but also minority ethnic and regionalist ones – since the 1960s, has called into question the assertion that established party systems were largely in place in Western Europe by the 1920s and have continued along the same lines ever since.

■ European party systems: change or stabilization?

Like many generalizations, the 'freezing' thesis that party systems have remained the same and the opposed idea that voting and parties have become totally 'volatile', both require qualification. To some extent party systems are always subject to change, as new parties try out their appeals and gain at least limited success, like the Dutch Farmers' party in the 1960s. It is hard to think of any West European system where the parties' voting support has not gone up and down at least to some extent in the post-war period. The freedom of electors to change their vote is after all a defining characteristic of democracy, so we would be disconcerned if there were not a certain fluctuation from election to election. Moreover, some of the older parties have greatly strengthened themselves at particular periods, notably the socialists and Christian democrats after the Second World War (when Germany and Italy acquired almost new party systems). Add this to the political transformations in France during the 1960s and in Spain, Portugal and Greece in the 1970s, and it can be seen that much party and voting change have occurred in Western Europe since 1945, let alone 1920.

Yet there are two senses in which an underlying stability and continuity have been maintained. Major parties have not disappeared. Even the shrunken Christian Democrats Party in Italy have re-emerged in the 1990s as a people's party keeping a shaky centre-left coalition in place. The new parties which have acquired parliamentary seats have on the whole remained on the fringes of the parliamentary game, as Chapter 8 has already pointed out with regard to Greens and left socialists.

Even the limited success of such new parties means that the established parties have lost votes. Political commentators have as a result been quick to talk about greater electoral volatility and a weakening of the social base of established parties. It is certainly true that greater shifts of votes seem to be occurring between individual parties as is almost inevitable if new parties enter into competition. Where these attract votes they must come from somewhere and inevitably this is from established parties.

When it comes to crossing the left-right divide, however, electorates seem as stable in their overall preferences as they were before the First World War and more stable than they were in the inter-war period. That is, they may transfer their aggregate support from one party of the centre right to another, or between parties of the left such as the left socialists and social democrats. But there is no sign that mass electorate are significantly shifting support between left parties as a bloc and right-wing parties as a bloc. The division over the extent and nature of government intervention in favour of underprivileged social groups, is the most widespread political cleavage across Europe. Thus the unchanging line-up of electorates on each side of this divide indicates that there is substantial continuity underlying the changes in party support that we observe from election to election.

As such changes are dramatic and exciting, they tend to catch the attention both of journalists and voting specialists and to be discussed at great length by them. Change is news, voting stability is not. Added to this there have been great social transformations in all European societies over the post-war period – industrialization in the South and East, a decline of traditional manufacturing in the West. Coupled with the fluctuating electoral fortunes of established parties, this had led some commentators and analysts to claim that traditional class cleavages – and traditional social cleavages in general – are losing their effects. Voting is becoming less rooted in the loyalties of social groups and more a matter of individual choice. Hence it shows much overall fluctuation at the level of the electorate as a whole (technically termed electoral volatility). In reaction to such individually-based voting it is claimed, parties have watered down their old ideologies and abandoned their traditional groups of supporters, seeking votes from the new individualistic electors by endorsing whatever positions seem most popular at each election and transforming themselves into 'catch-all' parties without any fixed social basis. The end of social cleavages thus implies the end of ideology and a blurring of partisan divisions, as one party becomes hard to distinguish from another. So party families are also becoming irrelevant as parties change their positions.

This analysis has been applied particularly to parties of the left, above all to the social democrats. These were the archetypal party based on a particular social cleavage, that of class, and on a particular social group, the manual, urban working class. The shrinking size of this group in Western Europe means that socialist parties have been fatally weakened at the electoral level and have been compelled to abandon their socialist ideology, each becoming just another 'catch-all' party.

The idea of a 'decline of the left' along with a general decline of ideology, becomes very attractive to journalists every time a socialist or labour party loses an election. Yet over Europe as a whole there is no consistent trend to a victory of one type of party over another. As social democrats lost control of government in Scandinavia, Germany and Britain at the beginning of the 1980s, they gained it in France and Spain. In the 1990s as they lost these two countries, they regained control in Scandinavia and Italy. The left-wing parties in the Centre and East, seemingly totally crushed in 1990, mostly staged a comeback in the mid-1990s, while Dutch labour pushed out the Christian democrats from government in 1994 for the first time in 80 years.

In other words, there is no long-term 'decline of the left' in electoral terms – nor of any other party family either. As far as ideology is concerned, Figure 9.3 plots the left-right movement of the UK, German and Dutch parties over the post-war period. Their ideological positions are estimated from the published election programmes of the parties. These are designed to appeal to electors and attract votes, so it is here if anywhere that we would expect to see parties crossing the left-right divide and coming closer together over the post-war period if they were really becoming non-ideological and 'catch-all'.

But what we actually discover is that the parties remain very distinctive in terms of their left-right positions. This is especially true of the socialist and labour parties.

Figure 9.3   Left–right positions of parties in the UK, Germany and the Netherlands

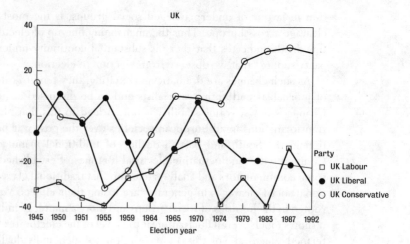

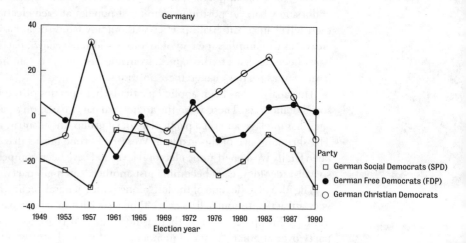

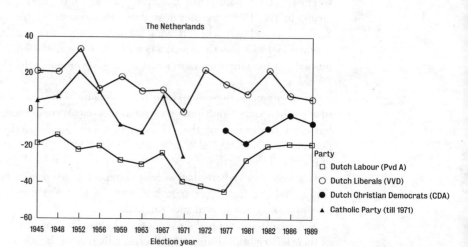

Particularly interesting is the case of the German Social Democrats. At a famous conference at Bad Godesburg in 1959, at the height of the Cold War, they explicitly said that they were no longer a Marxist party. This was taken as an indication that they had totally abandoned the left and become indistinguishable from the Christians. Indeed, it was this incident which sparked off the whole 'catch-all', 'end-of-ideology' thesis. But in terms of actual policy and their position on intervention and welfare they have always remained distinct, as Figure 9.3 shows. Indeed by the 1980s they were back in the same left-wing position they had held in the 1950s.

In terms of party reactions and policy, therefore, continuity and stability seem more characteristic of European parties than change and volatility. It is the same with underlying social cleavages and their effects on voting. Research shows little clear evidence that they are losing their effects. Of course, the numbers in various social categories change and this has an impact on the overall vote for the party which they support. Thus the numbers of unionized manual workers has gone down drastically between the late 1970s and the mid-1990s and this has had consequences for left-wing parties whose faithful supporters they are – just as declining numbers of farmers and practising believers has had an effect of agrarian and Christian parties respectively.

The remaining members of these groups continue to vote for their respective parties, however, while the latter have extended their traditional appeals to other social categories. Social changes do not cut just one way. As clerical and service jobs become more routinized and insecure, their occupants find themselves in the position of manual assembly line workers of the past, and hence more open to union and left-wing persuasion. Similarly, agrarian parties can take on a Green tinge and Christian parties emphasize their support of the family without abandoning

Figure 9.3

Notes: Party left–right movement is calculated by:

1. Categorizing the points of each election programme into 'left' and 'right'.
2. Percentaging total 'left' and 'right' points out of total number of points in document.
3. Subtracting 'left' percentage from 'right' percentage to give final party position in each election.
4. The calculation can be summarized as follows:

Right categories		*Left categories*
Sum of percentages in categories labelled:		*Sum of percentages in categories labelled:*
Freedom		Decolonization
Human Rights		Anti–Military
Constitutionalism		Peace
Effective Authority		Internationalism
Free Enterprise		Democracy
Economic Incentives		Regulate Capitalism
Anti-Protectionism	*MINUS*	Economic Planning
Economic Orthodoxy		Pro-Protectionism
Anti-Social Services		Controlled Economy
National Way of Life		Nationalization
Traditional Morality		Pro-Social Services
Law and Order		Pro-Education
Social Harmony		Pro-Labour

Source: M. J. Laver and Ian Budge, *Party Policy and Government Coalitions* (London, Macmillan, 1992).

traditional positions. While some decline in their overall vote has occurred through the erosion of their traditional support base, it has been limited.

Because of this, the broad contours of most Western party systems do not look too different from what they were in the 1950s. In taking on these features, the party systems of the Centre and East are adjusting themselves to an established model which looks likely to continue in its essentials into the third millennium. The minor modification and change it will constantly undergo (and occasional major change in particular countries like Italy) will save it from rigidity and enable it to translate new social demands into government programmes and policies. It is to the processes and institutions of government that we now turn in Part III.

■ Further reading

Stefano Bartolini and Peter Mair, *Identity, Competition and Electoral Availability: The Stabilization of European Electorates* (Cambridge, Cambridge University Press, 1990).

Ian Budge, David Robertson, D. J. Hearl (eds), *Ideology, Strategy and Party Change*, (Cambridge, Cambridge University Press, 1987).

D. J. Hearl, Ian Budge and Bernard Pearson 'Distinctiveness of regional voting: A comparative analysis, 1949–1993', *Electoral Studies*,15, 1996, 167–82.

H. D. Klingemann and D. Fuchs (eds), *Citizens and the State* (Oxford, Oxford University Press, 1995).

B. Szajkowski (ed.), *New Political parties of Eastern Europe and the Soviet Union* (London, Longman, 1991).

Alan Ware, *Political Parties and Party Systems* (Oxford, Oxford University Press, 1996).

Part III

Steering states

Building the institutional framework: electoral systems, party systems and presidents

■ The Importance of formal institutions

With the stunning collapse of European communism in 1989 and 1990, almost every European state became democratic, or is heading in the general direction of democracy. Progress is halting and bumpy in some cases, especially in the successor states to the Soviet Union and Yugoslavia. However, competitive and open elections have been held in most countries in Central and Eastern Europe, and most have drafted new democratic constitutions or reinstated older ones. This chapter will review party systems, electoral systems and presidential powers in Europe, to see whether the emerging democracies are exhibiting similar or different patterns of institutional development compared with those of the West.

Formal institutions are important because they influence the behaviour of interest groups, parties and politicians as much as social cleavages. Parties, for example, base themselves on social cleavages and emphasize them to mobilize support, but their chances of success are affected by formal constitutional considerations. In particular, the rules for translating votes into seats are crucial. An extreme case of mismatch, or electoral disproportionality, is the United Kingdom, where the Liberals attracted a quarter of the votes in 1983, but won only 2 per cent of seats.

Like many British institutions, the electoral system is a haphazard legacy from the past. Its supporters claim that it creates a simple, clear-cut choice for electors; produces two large parties, Labour and Conservative; encourages strong, united and stable government; and enforces political accountability. Other countries have borrowed the argument: Hungary, with its constituency based seats; and Greece with 'reinforced proportionality', which gives a bonus of approximately 10 per cent of seats to the winning party. The complex electoral system recently introduced in Italy is also based partly on the simple majority system of Britain. In contrast, the British system is thought unfair by many who advocate proportional representation in order to achieve a closer match between votes and seats, as do the Netherlands and Poland, for example.

Another important factor is the 'threshold' of votes which parties must exceed to get any representation at all in parliament. Poland's use of a much higher threshold after 1991 reduced the number of parties in parliament from twenty-four to six in 1993. This also helped to create disproportionality between shares of vote and shares of seats. Thus electoral rules can have major consequences for power relations within any given state. But they are not the only consideration.

On the contrary, many other constitutional rules govern the relationship between different branches of government and between different political institutions. In Scandinavia, for example, interest groups are permitted free access to Parliament and the civil service. But in Macedonia and many other East European countries they are denied even formal legal recognition. The rules regulating the media, as we have already seen in Chapter 6, are crucial in enabling it to influence the formation of governments and their policies. Some governments depend only upon parliament, others are appointed by a president with executive powers. In some countries, regional and local governments are relatively autonomous, in others they are creatures of the central state.

These are the sorts of questions considered in Part III of this book. We cannot hope to cover every constitutional variation of importance but will start with two important ones: party and electoral systems, and presidential and parliamentary powers. The countries considered here all have a population of a million or more. They include the successor states of the former Soviet Union, even though these meet only minimal democratic criteria. Countries of the Mediterranean region are also included, if they are democratic.

Some interesting patterns are revealed. Three of the emerging democracies have even more fragmented party systems than Brazil, which previously held the record. The number of 'effective' parties (see Briefing 10.1) in Georgia, Russia and the Ukraine is more than fifteen each – a staggering figure. There have also been considerable changes to electoral systems. Among those former communist nations which have held a second round of free elections, only the Czech and Slovak Republics and Hungary have used the same electoral rules in both. Reform has not been restricted to the former communist countries: France has changed from majority run-off elections to proportional representation and back again since 1986. Italy has recently adopted sweeping electoral changes.

We have seen other significant institutional innovations since 1989. The emerging democracies have given us the world's first examples of:

- an electoral system that allows voters to rank order their preferences among several party lists (Georgia in 1992);
- a directly elected head of state who is also a full member of parliament (also Georgia before 1995)
- a directly elected head of government who is subject to parliamentary votes of confidence (Israel, starting in 1996) and;
- the first system in which the directly elected president and the parliament take turns in attempting to form a government until one of them succeeds (Poland).

Clearly, we are living in a time of institutional innovation, and as we approach the twenty-first century this is as good a time as any for some stock-taking.

■ Counting parties

Our first task is to classify countries according to their party system characteristics. As a start we might simply count the number of parties. Although this simple approach may be misleading and not very informative, it can tell us a lot about a country's politics. It gives clues as to whether one party can legislate alone or must form coalitions with other parties, and it indicates how politically divided a country is.

BRIEFING 10.1

The effective number of parties

Counting the number of parties may seem straightforward, but it is not. Many countries – particularly at times of major change – tend to produce large numbers of mini-parties with one or two seats, or less, which have little impact on national politics. Therefore in counting parties we should include only those which have serious effects on governments and their policies. The most obvious way of doing this is to exclude parties that get fewer than a given percentage of votes or seats. However, a cut-off point of this kind is necessarily arbitrary and different points will yield different conclusions.

A better method is to weight the parties so the larger ones are given more weight than the smaller ones. The most straightforward method, and one that has gained wide acceptance in electoral studies, is to multiply or 'weight' each fractional share of votes or seats by itself (i.e. square it). A party with 52 per cent of the votes is given a fraction of 0.52, while a party with 2 per cent has a fraction of 0.02. When these fractions are squared, the large party contributes much more ($0.52 \times 0.52 = 0.2704$) than the small party ($0.02 \times .02 = 0.0004$).

After we have summed the squares of the fractional vote or seat shares, we divide this fraction into one (1.00) and obtain a result that is fairly easy to interpret, as we shall see. Expressed mathematically, the formula for determining the *effective number of vote-winning parties* is:

$$N_v = 1/(\Sigma v_i^2),$$

where v_i is the fractional share of votes for the ith party. If we replace v_i with s_i, we compute the effective number of *seat*-winning parties (N_s).

An attractive feature of this method of counting is that for party systems consisting of exactly equal-sized parties, N simply gives us the actual number of parties. For example, if two parties each have 50 per cent of the votes or seats, N = 2.0. ($1/0.25 + 0.25 = 1/0.5 = 2.0$). If three parties each have one-third N = 3.0. If one of the three parties then splits into two equal-sized splinter parties (33.3–33.3–16.65–16.65), then N should increase, and indeed it does: N = 3.6.

More information about this way of looking at party systems can be found in Rein Taagepera and Matthew S. Shugart, 'Predicting the number of parties: a quantitative model of Duverger's mechanical effect, *American Political Science Review,* 87, (2), June, 1993, 455–64; Markku Laakso and Rein Taagepera, 'Effective number of parties: a measure with application to West Europe', *Comparative Political Studies,* 12, (1979), 3–27, Rein Taagepera and Matthew S. Shugart, *Seats and Votes: The Effects and Determinants of Electoral Systems* (New Haven, Yale University Press, 1989), esp. pp. 77–91 and 259–60.

Table 10.1 shows how the effective number of electoral, vote-winning parties compare across Europe. The figures are based on elections in the late 1980s or early 1990s (two where they occurred in the same country). West and East European countries are shown in different columns. The figures show that post-communist party systems are clearly more fragmented than those of the West. Seven out of ten Eastern systems have more than five effective parties, compared with four out of ten Western systems. In Russia and Ukraine, such a large number of the candidates were independents that that it is not possible to calculate the effective number of parties. The figure for both countries are undoubtedly in excess of fifteen, probably far in excess. For Russia, the effective number of *seat*-winning parties is 14.1, one of the highest figures ever recorded worldwide.

West Europe/Mediterranean	Nv	East Europe/Eurasia
	2.2	Albania (1991, 1991)
Austria (1983, 1986), Greece (1990, 1993)	2.6	
Portugal (1987, 1991)	3.0	
Germany (1990), United Kingdom (1987, 1992)	3.1	
	3.5	Bulgaria (1990, 1991)
Ireland (1989, 1992)	3.6	
	3.8	Moldova
Spain (1989, 1993)	3.9	
Sweden (1988, 1991)	4.3	
Turkey (1987, 1991)	4.4	
Netherlands (1986, 1989), Norway (1989, 1993)	4.8	
Israel (1988, 1992)	5.0	
France (1988, 1993)	5.1	
	5.3	Slovakia (1992)
Denmark (1987, 1988)	5.8	
Finland (1987, 1991)	6.0	
	6.1	Czech Republic (1992), Hungary (1990, 1994)
Italy (1987, 1992, 1994)	6.2	Latvia (1993)
Switzerland (1987, 1991)	7.1	
	8.2	Slovenia (1992)
	8.9	Estonia (1992)
Belgium (1987, 1991)	9.0	
	10.9	Georgia (1992) Russia* Ukraine*

Notes: The large number of independent candidates and inadequacies of data reporting make it impossible to determine Nv in Russia and Ukraine, but the figure would be in excess of fifteen.

Vote data unavailable for Croatia (probably less than three effective parties) and for Lithuania (probably between three and five).

Only one election is used for Germany, that of 1990, because previous elections were held within different borders and are thus not directly comparable.

Sources: Generally the reports on recent elections in *Electoral Studies* or *Keesing's Contemporary Archives* and Carlos Flores, 'Electoral systems in Eastern Europe: how are they changing? Why are they changing?', Paper prepared for the XVI International Political Science Association World Congress, Berlin, August 21–25, 1994.

Of course, this table refers only to fragmentation of voting. Fragmentation of parties in parliament is a different matter. An easy way to estimate the effects of the electoral system on fragmentation of the party system is simply to compare the effective number of electoral parties (N_v) with the effective number of legislative parties (N_s). Figure 10.1 presents N_v on one axis against N_s on the other. Countries that changed their electoral system substantially have separate data points for the old and new systems.

In most countries there are minor parties which attract too few votes to get elected, so there are usually fewer parties in the legislature than in elections. Thus all countries appear on or below the diagonal in Figure 10.1. The most that can be expected is that the effective number of parties in elections matches the effect we number in the legislature – Belgium and Switzerland are the named countries that come closest to this.

The voting systems of several Eastern countries give a lower shares of seats to some parties than their votes deserve (Poland, Slovakia, Romania, the Czech Republic and Estonia, for example), and in the West the same is true of France. It is surprising to see the number of countries with proportional representation (PR) in this category, given that PR is supposed to distribute seats in proportion to votes. Included here are Poland (especially with the 1993 rules), Romania, Estonia and

Figure 10.1 Effective number of parties, votes versus seats

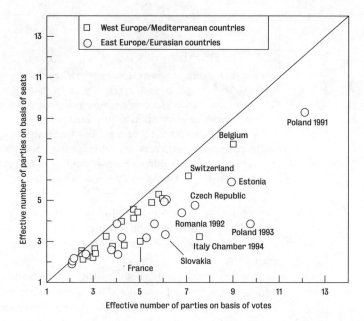

Slovakia. Each of these systems will probably see a future reduction in N_v, the effective number of electoral parties, since those which have failed to gain seats are likely to drop out of the contest, or to merge with other parties to improve their chances. The same may happen in Italy, where a new election system is designed to reduce the number of parties. Now we turn to a discussion of the electoral laws themselves.

■ Electoral systems

Numerous features of electoral systems affect the relationship shown in Table 10.1 – that is, how votes are translated into seats. Here we will focus on the four most important: district magnitude, allocation formula, supplementary seats and thresholds. The first two features are universal: every electoral system has some allocation formula and a certain magnitude. The other two features are components of some systems, but not others.

Allocation formula and district magnitude

By far the most important factor determining how closely the distribution of seats resembles the distribution of votes is the magnitude of electoral districts. Magnitude (abbreviated M) simply refers to the number of seats allocated in a district. Because allocation formulas (i.e. the precise way in which votes are matched to seats) interact with district magnitude to produce the overall effect on proportionality, it is best to talk about them together.

Many systems use single-member districts (M = 1). In single-member districts, one common formula is the plurality rule, used for example in Britain, in which the candidate with the most votes in a given district wins the one seat assigned to that district. It does not matter what the winner's vote share is. Thus in a

> **BRIEFING 10.2**
>
> **Run-off elections**
>
> This is an electoral system under which there are two rounds of elections, held within a week or fortnight of each other. Any party candidate can stand in the first election. Those who receive less than a certain percentage of the vote (sometimes all except the two leading candidates) are then eliminated. In the second or run-off election the winning candidate has to receive either a majority or a plurality of the vote. This system tends to eliminate the smaller parties in the region in which the election is held but makes it important which of the remaining candidates will receive their endorsement and get their votes. This renders party electoral alliances very important.

fragmented party system, a seat may be won with much less than a majority of the votes. The plurality formula is sometime used in multiseat districts, as in the Polish and Russian senates, where the voter gets as many votes as there are seats (usually two).

Sometime with single-member districts, instead of allowing a plurality of votes to suffice, a runoff may be required in the event that no candidate achieves a majority. The runoff may be restricted to the top two candidates, in which case one of them is assured a majority of votes cast. Or, as in France and Hungary, the run-off may be open to more than two candidates, with a simple plurality sufficing in the second round.

Because the single member, simple majority system is likely to produce distorted results, most European countries use some form of PR. In order to use PR, the district magnitude must be greater than one. In general, the higher the magnitude, the greater the proportionality, but this depends, in turn, on the allocation formula. There are many different formulas, some of which are described in Briefing 10.3. The allocation formula has a smaller impact on seat distribution than the magnitude, except when magnitudes are low.

Supplementary seats

Some electoral systems do not allocate seats by local districts, but employ some variant of nationwide allocation. Others allocate seats by groups of districts below the national level. A few countries, such as Israel and the Netherlands, use nationwide allocation in one district for the whole nation. However, most systems based on national allocation use complex districting; that is, some seats are filled by local districts, while others are allocated in an upper tier.

Supplementary seats may be divided into two categories, compensatory or additional. If seats are *compensatory*, it means that for purposes of determining seat allocation among parties, all seats – those in the basic districts as well as in the upper tier – are taken into account. This allocation procedure calculates the seat shares of the parties based on their votes nationwide (or in the regions). It then subtracts the seats already won in the basic districts and compensates the parties, as appropriate, at the upper level. In systems with compensatory upper tiers, the basic districts in the lower tier thus have little effect on the overall distribution of seats among parties.

One example of a compensatory form of PR is the much-emulated German

BRIEFING 10.3

Voting Systems – plurality and proportional representation (PR)

Free elections are the backbone of modern democracy, and although at first sight they may appear to be a simple matter – expressing a preference for one option over others – they turn out to be very complex affairs. There are two main types of electoral systems in modern democracies, simple plurality voting and proportional representation.

Simple plurality

Sometimes called the 'first-past-the-post' systems, this only requires the winning candidate to get more votes than any other candidate, no matter how many candidates there may be, and no matter how small the winning percentage of the vote may be. In a three-way contest the winner may get little more than a third of the total, and in a four-way contest, little more than a quarter. Simple plurality voting is usually linked with single-member constituencies, and the whole package is called the single member, simple plurality system (or SMSP). In Europe it is used in the UK, and outside Europe in the USA and Canada. The advantage of the system is simplicity. The disadvantage is that it is likely to produce disproportionate election results – i.e. the distribution of votes between parties does not closely match their proportion of seats in the legislature. The simple plurality system also means that minor party supporters, even large minorities, may 'waste' their vote.

Second ballot and alternative vote

The second ballot system tries to avoid the worst disadvantage of the simple plurality system, by requiring a winning candidate to get an absolute majority (50 per cent+1) of the votes cast in the first round. Failing this a second (run-off) ballot is held for the strongest of the first round candidates.

Alternative vote

Another variation on simple plurality voting is to allow voters to indicate their first and subsequent preferences among candidates, so that if no candidate receives a majority of first preferences in the first count, second (and subsequent) preferences may be brought into play in second and subsequent counts.

Proportional representation

Proportional representation (PR) is an allocation formula which tries to distribute seats in proportion to the votes. In other words, PR tries to ensure that minorities as well as majorities are represented in proportion to their voting strength. The three main ways of doing this are the party list system, the single transferable vote, and the additional member system.

Party list system

One of the simplest ways of ensuring that seats are proportional to votes is to distribute the seats on a national basis (as in the Netherlands) or in large regions (Italy). Parties draw up a list of candidates in order of preference, and they are elected in proportion to the number of votes their party receives, starting from the top of party lists. This gives a lot of power to the party leaders who decide who is going to the top of the list.

(continued)

(continued)

Single transferable vote (STV)

This voting system is widely used in Western Europe. Voters may rank order their preferences for candidates, so that their second, third, or subsequent preferences can be taken into account. If their first-choice candidate achieves the desired quota before other seats are filled, then their lower preference(s) may come into play. Or if their first-choice candidate is eliminated, then their second, or subsequent preference can be taken into account. In this way, those casting a first choice for a minor party can choose to caste a second choice for another party, thereby reducing the chances of a 'wasted' vote and making electoral alliances important. There are many different variations on STV, and many different ways of calculating the final result. In Ireland, voters can order their preferences within and across parties, so ensuring the closest possible relationship between voter preferences and candidates elected. STV must be used in conjunction with multi-member districts.

Additional and compensatory member systems

These are ways of trying to keep personal links between elected representatives and voters. Two election systems can be used: first, single-member districts elect representatives by simple plurality, second ballot, or alternative votes; second, seats are allocated on the basis of votes received in the district elections and in such a way as to achieve proportionality, in the compensatory member system, or without regard to the other results, in the additional member system. In Germany, equal numbers of seats are allotted at district and national levels, and citizens cast two votes – one for their district and another for the national party list. In Georgia, a unique electoral system is used in which eighty four members are elected from single-member districts, but the rest (146) by a PR system which allows voters to express up to three preferences, for party lists, not individual candidates. Votes are counted on the basis of 'points', with first preferences counting for five points, second for three and third for one.

system, in which half the seats are allocated in single-member districts (by plurality) and half by PR. Because the PR half is compensatory, the system is not really a mix of plurality and PR, as is often claimed. Instead it is just a PR system in which half the seats happen to be allocated in single-member districts. It differs only in degree from other compensatory PR systems, such as the Swedish, in which the basic level consists of smaller multi-member districts with PR.

The second of the supplementary systems uses additional seats. These are created in another district (or districts) above the basic districts, and seats in the two levels of districts are allocated independently of one another. No compensation for disproportionality is intended. Sometimes, as with compensatory systems, the basic districts may be single-seat. Like the German system and its imitators, these systems are often called 'mixed' systems. However, if many seats are allocated in single-member, local districts, it is unlikely that the PR allocation of additional seats will make up for disproportionality. Indeed, additional seat systems should not be confused with compensatory systems designed to achieve greater proportionality. If seats are distributed with the intention of compensating, then the resulting system is PR. If the system uses additional seats, then the system is just a 'softened' form of majoritarian allocation, as in Hungary.

Thresholds

Most systems using compensatory or additional seats employ voting thresholds, which are designed to prevent small parties from benefiting from compensatory or additional seat allocation. Table 10.2 shows the thresholds in use in European countries. In some countries (Poland and Turkey) a threshold applied to national voting may keep a party out of parliament even if it has enough votes to win at the district level. The effect is not only to reduce parliamentary fragmentation, but also to prevent regional parties from being represented. A party that is strong enough to win seats in a region may be barred from parliament if it fails to pass the national threshold. In a few countries, a threshold is applied in the basic districts themselves, as in Spain and also in the French system of 1986.

European electoral systems

Table 10.3 classifies electoral systems in Europe according to their basic characteristics. The simplest systems, in section A of the table, allocate seats in districts and there is no voting threshold at either national or district levels. In the West, Finland, Portugal and Switzerland use PR and simple district-level allocation within large districts. In the east, only a few plurality and majority run-off systems, plus Romania's small district PR system, fit the category. After 1990 Albania abandoned this voting system, leaving the Polish and Russian senates and Ukraine as the only simple district systems in the East.

Section B of Table 10.3 shows those systems in which all seats are allocated within districts, but with a threshold. In the case of Spain and the French system of 1986, the threshold was applied only to districts, but in Turkey there is a high national threshold of 10 per cent. In addition, there is a rule which is unique among European countries, which favours large parties even more. In districts with at least five seats, the first is allocated to the candidate with a plurality of individual votes, and the remaining seats are then allocated by PR from party lists.

Group C of Table 10.3 are the so-called additional-member systems of Bulgaria (1990), Croatia, Georgia, Hungary, Lithuania and Russia. These all allocate a portion of seats in single-member districts and the rest are independently distributed in multi-seat districts. Each elector casts two votes, one for a district candidate and one for a party list. The multi-seat district is usually nationwide, although in the case of Hungary there is a two-stage process. The crucial feature of additional member systems, however, is that the additional seats allocated from the lists do not compensate parties for the inevitable distortions occurring in the single-member districts. These systems therefore tend to favour large parties, despite the allocation of many seats on a nationwide basis.

The next group in section D of Table 10.3 lists systems with complex districting in which the upper tier is neither fully compensatory nor strictly additional. Poland's 1991 lower-house electoral law provided for PR voting in districts, but also for additional seats for parties above a national threshold. The threshold applied only for the national list, and there was no threshold within the basic districts, one of which was fairly large. Greece uses an extremely complex law that provides for a national tier, but one that is only partially compensatory and which favours large parties in spite of the use of PR.

Table 10.2 Legal thresholds in use in European electoral systems[a]

West Europe/Mediterranean	%	East Europe/Eurasia
	0.67	
Netherlands		
Norway		
	1	
Israel (pre-1992)		
	1.5	
Israel		
	2	
Denmark		
	3	
Greece[b]		Croatia
Spain[c]		Romania
	4	
Italy (chamber)		Albania
Sweden		Bulgaria
		Hungary
		Latvia
		Lithuania
	5	
France (1986)[b]		Czech Republic
Germany[d]		Czechoslovakia
		Estonia
		Poland[e]
		Russia
		Slovakia
	6	
		Moldova
		Poland
	10	
Turkey[d]		
	12	
Sweden[b]		

Notes: [a] Most recent election of those reported in Table 10.1 unless otherwise indicated. Thresholds based on other criteria (and percentage approximation):
Austria – one district-level seat (2.5%)
Belgium – two-thirds of a quota in at least one district (5.5%)
Slovenia – votes sufficient to elect three members (1.7%).
Thresholds pertain to nationwide share of the vote and apply only to super-district allocation unless otherwise indicated (i.e., parties that have less than the requisite threshold may be represented in parliament on account of ability to win seats at the district level). Thresholds are those in place for individual parties. Several countries (e.g. Czech Republic, Greece, Poland and Slovakia) apply higher thresholds to multiparty coalitions.
[b] In Greece, parties with over 3% of the vote are guaranteed representation, though not at full compensation.
[c] Threshold applies at district level only.
[d] Or three district-level seats. Threshold waived for national minorities.
[e] Threshold bars any party from representation even in a district unless it has also surpassed the indicated threshold.

The largest group, in section E of Table 10.3, consists of countries divided into districts at the local level. Parties exceeding the threshold are awarded compensatory seats at an upper tier of the voting system. Usually the compensatory seats are allocated from a single nationwide district, although sometimes (Austria and the former Czechoslovakia) they are based upon regional super-districts. For purposes of allocating seats to parties in the overall parliament, it makes little difference what the magnitudes of the districts are, as long as parties are compensated at the upper level. Thus the compensatory member systems, with their large number of single-member dis-

Table 10.3 Classifying the electoral systems of Europe

Simple district-level allocation, no threshold	
United Kingdom	Albania 1990
France	Ukraine
Ireland	Poland, senate
Portugal	Russia, senate
Finland	
Switzerland	
District-level allocation, with threshold	
Turkey	
France 1986	
Spain	
Additional-member systems	
	Bulgaria 1990
	Croatia
	Hungary
	Lithuania
	Russia
	Georgia
Complex PR districting, non-compensatory upper-tier	
Greece 1990	Poland
Greece	
Compensatory seats with threshold for upper-tier allocation	
Italy	Moldova
Norway	Czech Republic
Germany	Czechoslovakia
Belgium	Estonia
Italy pre-1993	Albania
Austria	Bulgaria
Denmark	Latvia
Israel	Romania
Netherlands	Slovenia
Effective nationwide allocation, no threshold	
	Romania 1990

tricts (Germany, Italy in 1994 and Albania) are included here. The rest of the systems listed in this group use multi-member districts at the local level, and thus would qualify as 'PR', even without the national compensation seats. The compensatory process simply ensures that regional variations in voting do not prevent the overall allocation from being proportional, at least among parties clearing the threshold.

Finally, in section F, we have a unique system in which full compensatory allocation is carried out within one nationwide district and there is no threshold. Only one recent election, in Romania in 1990, fits this description but it was not used a second time. It is probably the most proportional electoral law ever used anywhere in the world.

■ Electoral systems and party systems

Perhaps the two most important features of a political system discussed so far in this chapter are (1) the number of effective parties, and (2) the proportionality between party votes and seats. In general, these two characteristics of the political system are inversely related. The more devices like small electoral districts, and thresholds, are used to reduce the number of small parties, the less their voters are represented in legislatures and the less proportional the system becomes.

However, the inverse relationship between the effective number of parties and proportionality is not exact. The more the voting system discriminates against mini-parties, and the poorer their chances of winning even one seat, the more likely they are to drop out of the contest, leaving mainly the larger parties in the running. This will lower the number of effective parties and increase proportionality in future elections. Germany offers one of the best examples of this. In 1949, the discrepancy between seat and vote shares was 8.2 per cent. This was small compared to some recent East European elections. But once the parties unable to exceed the threshold had been shaken out by 1965, the discrepancy fell to less than 4 per cent. In the election of 1987, when hardly any German parties failed to cross the threshold, it was 1.4 per cent. In systems with effective nationwide compensation, deviation is only about as high as the percentage of votes cast for parties failing the threshold.

Similarly, the number of competing parties and consequent disproportionality in the new democracies is due, in part, to the experimental nature of the party system. The first Romanian election was called at such short notice that parties were poorly organized and numerous micro-parties won votes but not seats. By the second election, some opposition parties had become more established and the effective number of electoral parties surged from 2.2 to 6.8. However, given the adoption of a threshold of 3 per cent by the 1992 law, disproportionality rose even more dramatically, from 3.1 per cent to 20.9 per cent. Similarly, in Poland, fragmentation in the 1991 election was not so much caused by electoral laws, but occurred in spite of them. As Figure 10.1 shows, the number of electorally effective parties in the 1991 election was 12.1, but the effective number of parties in the Sjem (parliament) was only 9.3. The imposition of a national threshold for the 1993 election helped reduce the first figure to 9.8, and the second to 3.9, but the threshold caused disproportionality to reach 37 per cent. In the short run, a threshold may cause disproportionality. But in the long run, if the German case is anything to go by, party systems tend to adjust and disproportionality declines.

Consequently, older election systems are likely to be more proportional than younger ones. This produces the contrast which appears between the older electoral systems of the West and the new ones of Central and Eastern Europe. But the sharpness of the contrast will diminish as time moves on.

Defining constitutional systems

We now turn to another important aspect of constitutional systems – the difference between parliamentary, presidential and other forms of government. To examine the difference we must first establish clear definitions of regime types. A system will be called parliamentary if, and only if, (1) the cabinet, headed by a prime minister, is collectively responsible to the majority in parliament, and (2) there is no popularly elected president with real political powers. There may be a president elected by parliament itself who *has* some important political powers, but a president directly elected by the voters is bound to be more independent. We shall return to the theme of presidents in parliamentary systems below. But first let us consider the powers of popularly elected presidents, a theme that has proved quite contentious in several post-communist countries, notably Poland and Russia.

■ Powers of popularly elected presidents

A popularly elected president with constitutional discretion in the choice of cabinet ministers (or at least of the prime minister), and/or the right to dissolve parliament and call new elections, constitutes a form of government that is commonly called 'semi-presidential' rather than parliamentary. However, the term semi-presidential often confuses two types of government based on different principles, namely, *premier-presidentialism* and *president-parliamentarism*. In premier-presidentialism, the cabinet is responsible only to parliament, and in president-parliamentarism it is jointly responsible to the president and the parliament.

Under president-parliamentarism, the president has constitutional authority to dismiss a government even when it has the confidence of the parliamentary majority. The most prominent historical example is the Weimar Republic of Germany, 1919–33. Armenia adopted such a system in 1995. Under the more common premier-presidentialism, the cabinet is responsible to the parliamentary majority and the president cannot remain the effective head of government if he or she represents a different party or group of parties. An example of this situation occurred in France during the 'co-habitation periods' from 1986 to 1988, and 1993 to 1995 when the socialist president Mitterrand had to yield to a conservative parliamentary majority in the construction of the cabinet. In contrast, a *'pure' presidential* system entails (1) a popularly elected president who is (2) always constitutionally the head of government, regardless of the party composition of the legislature, and (3) a separation of powers such that neither the legislature nor the executive can shorten the term of office of the other.

This discussion suggests two dimensions for understanding presidential systems. The first dimension concerns the powers of the president over the cabinet. They are minimal when the choice of prime minister and cabinet ministers is left entirely to parliament, and maximal when the president appoints whoever he/she wants to the cabinet, and can dismiss them at any time. There are also intermediate positions as in Austria, for example, where the presidential nominee for prime minister must be ratified by the assembly, or in Belorus where the president appoints ministers with the consent of the assembly.

The second dimension defines the degree to which the survival in office of each branch of government is independent of the other – i.e. whether terms are fixed, or whether one branch can shorten the term of office of another. At one extreme, the assembly can dismiss the cabinet at any time on a vote of confidence, and the elected president can dissolve parliament at any time. At the other extreme, both branches have a fixed term of office which cannot be shortened by the other. There are also intermediate positions. An example is France, where the presidential power of dissolution can be exercised only once a year. Another is Russia where the power may be used only when the cabinet is censured by the assembly.

In Table 10.4 countries are scored according to degrees of presidential power on the two dimensions – presidential authority over the cabinet, and independent survival. For example, in the last column of Table 10.4 a maximum score of four is given to a country in which neither the assembly nor the president can shorten the term of office of the other. A score of zero is given to the other extreme where both have real powers over the other, and a score of one is given where such powers can only be exercised under specified circumstances.

Table 10.4 Powers of popularly-elected presidents

Scoring system: Powers over cabinet

Cabinet formation

    4 President appoints ministers without need for assembly confirmation

    3 President appoints ministers with consent of assembly

    2 President appoints ministers who need confidence of assembly

    1 President nominates prime minister who needs confidence of assembly; prime minister appoints other ministers (possibly with consent of president)

    0 President cannot name ministers except on recommendation of assembly

Cabinet dismissal

    4 President dismisses ministers at will

    3 President dismisses ministers with consent of assembly

    1 President dismisses ministers, but only under certain restrictions

    0 Ministers (or whole cabinet) may be removed only by assembly on vote of censure

Separation of survival in office (scored for both assembly and executive)

    4 No provisions compromising separation of survival (i.e., fixed terms)

    3 Survival can be attacked, but attacker must stand for re-election

    2 Survival can be attacked only in situation of mutual jeopardy

    1 Survival can be attacked, except at specified times

    0 Survival can be attacked at any time (i.e. unrestricted censure or dissolution)

(Scores of countries shown below.)

Country	Presidential powers over cabinet		Separation of survival for:	
	Cabinet formation	Cabinet dismisal	Assembly	Executive
Armenia	4	4	0	0
Austria	1	1	0	0
Bosnia-Herzegovina	2	0	0	0
Bulgaria	0	0	4	0
Belarus	3	3	4	4
Croatia	4	4	2	0
Cyprus	4	4	4	4
Finland	2	0	0	0
France	1	0	1	0
Georgia	3	4	4	4
Ireland	0	0	4	0
Israel	3	4	3	3
Lithuania	1	0	2	0
Macedonia	1	0	4	0
Moldova	1	0	2	0
Poland	1	0	2	0
Portugal	1	1	1	0
Romania	1	0	2	0
Russia	1	4	2	0
Slovenia	0	0	4	0
Ukraine	3	3	4	0
United States	3	4	4	4

Notes: The United States are included for comparison as an example of nearly pure presidentalism.

In Figure 10.2 these two dimensions of presidential power are then plotted against each other to show how they relate. Countries in the upper half of the figure have presidents with most power – that is, the president-parliamentary systems. In the upper left, a president-parliamentary regime gives the president discretion to dissolve parliament at any time, as well as the right to appoint and dismiss cabinets freely. This form of regime is probably inherently unstable because the president cannot keep his cabinet in office against the wishes of the parliamentary majority, but can always respond to a vote of no confidence by dissolving parliament and appointing a presidential cabinet in the interim. This is exactly the situation resulting in repeated parliamentary elections in the early 1930s under the Weimar Republic in Germany, until Adolph Hitler combined the offices of prime minister and chancellor.

Figure 10.2
Presidential cabinet
authority and separation
of survival: power of
popularity of elected
presidents

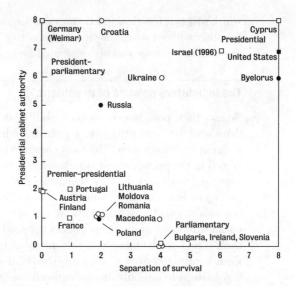

Notes:
☐ West Europe/Mediterranean countries (US and Weimar Germany shown for reference).
○ East Europe/Eurasian countries.
   Solid symbols indicate a president who has a veto that requires a two-thirds vote to override.

Presidential cabinet authority:
0   Appointment and dismissal of cabinet ministers by assembly only.
0.5   President nominates prime ministerial candidate, but assembly may propose alternate;
      assembly alone may dismiss.
1   President nominates prime minister, who then nominates other ministers; assembly alone may
      dismiss.
1.5   President appoints all ministers; assembly alone may dismiss.
2   President appoints all ministers, has restricted dismissal authority.
3   President appoints prime minister with consent of assembly, and may freely dismiss ministers.
3.5   President appoints all ministers with consent of assembly, and may freely dismiss ministers.
4   President appoints and dismisses ministers freely.

Separation of survival of cabinet and assembly:
0   President may dissolve assembly at any time; censure is unrestricted.
0.5   President's dissolution power is restricted in time; censure is unrestricted.
1   President may dissolve assembly in response to actions by assembly itself (i.e., repeated
      censures); censure is unrestricted.
1.5   Dissolution power is restricted both by time and as response to assembly actions; censure is
      unrestricted.
2   President may not dissolve assembly, or not without standing for re-election himself; censure
      unrestricted.
3   Restricted censure; no dissolution.
4   No censure; no dissolution.

Among current European systems only Armenia is in this extreme and unstable situation, but the constitutions of Croatia, Russia and Ukraine are close: cabinets are responsible to both parliament and president, and (except in Ukraine) the president has dissolution power, although only after censures (or, in Croatia, after failure to pass the budget within thirty days of its submission by the executive).

At the upper-right corner of Figure 10.2, we find Cyprus as our best example of presidentialism (albeit one with an unusual co-presidency rather than the usual single-person presidency). Belarus and Georgia have also adopted a presidential system which provides for full separation of survival and a cabinet which need maintain the confidence only of the president and not of the assembly. Israel's new system will be closer to presidentialism than to anything else. Although terms can be shortened, which makes it less than strictly presidential, neither branch can attack the survival of the other without shortening its own term too. Thus it is fundamentally different from those other regimes with non-separated survival, shown in the left half of the figure.

The legislative powers of president

Besides their powers over cabinets and the dissolution of parliaments, some presidents also have authority over legislation, while others must accept the will of the majority in the assembly. The most common presidential power in this respect is the veto (i.e. the president can stop legislation becoming law). But the rules for exercising the veto vary. In some countries the presidential veto of legislation may be overturned by a majority vote of the assembly. But in Belorus, Poland and Russia it requires a two-thirds majority. In Georgia it requires three-fifths. The Russian constitution also allows the president to issue decrees with legal force in areas where there is no law, and there have been many such areas in the period of transition from Communism to a market economy. The Polish presidency is unique in having a strong legislative veto but only limited authority in other respects – an unusual and potentially conflictual combination.

Presidents in premier-presidential systems have weaker vetoes. In Lithuania and Portugal, the Presidential veto can be overridden by a majority of the assembly. Though in Portugal, on matters relating to electoral laws and military and foreign relations, this requires a two-thirds majority. In Lithuania, a veto on constitutional law can only be overturned with a three-fifths majority. In some countries, the president is so weak that the systems are effectively parliamentary, not presidential, notably Bulgaria, Ireland and Slovenia. Finally, Switzerland stands alone. It has neither a popularly elected president, nor a cabinet responsible to parliament. Instead, the parliament elects an executive council, which sits for a fixed term.

We will now turn to the parliamentary systems, which predominate in Europe.

■ Presidents in parliamentary systems

Parliamentary systems may be divided into two main types; monarchies and republics. Our sample of European countries includes seven parliamentary monarchies, all in Western Europe – Belgium, Denmark, Netherlands, Norway, Spain, Sweden and the United Kingdom. All these countries are constitutional monarchies. With the possible exception of Spain, monarchs are ceremonial Heads of State without authority over legislation or the composition of cabinets. The re-establishment of monarchies was debated in some Eastern European countries, notably Bulgaria and Romania, but was rejected. Nevertheless, significant minorities in these and other countries, such as Greece, believe in a monarchy.

In the second set of parliamentary systems, the republics, the position of head of state is filled by a president. They are usually elected by parliament. In Germany and Italy, however, election is by colleges consisting of parliamentarians and delegates from state or regional legislatures. It often takes a large majority to elect a president, at least on the first and sometimes the second ballot. In Greece, Hungary, Italy and Turkey it requires a two-thirds majority, in Slovakia, three-fifths. Since this can be difficult to reach, many constitutions allow for run-off procedures. That is, if the initial ballot fails to produce the required majority, a second ballot can be held with new candidates, and if there is still deadlock, the necessary majority is reduced. If the parliaments of Greece and Turkey fail to reach the required majorities, parliament is dissolved and the new parliament charged with electing a president.

Presidents usually serve a longer term than their parliaments. Thus the majority electing the president will not always be the majority currently controlling parliament. Some presidents serve only a limited number of terms (e.g., two in Greece) or at least a limited number of consecutive terms (two in the Czech Republic, Estonia and Israel). The Turkish president is limited to a single term. All these measures – election by large majority, longer terms of office than parliament, and limits on re-election – are a way of giving presidents some independence from day-to-day parliamentary affairs, and the possibility of forming a check on the parliamentary majority. A president elected by parliamentarians is less independent than one elected by popular vote, but can sometimes play an important role. Of course, their ability to do so depends not only on who elects them but also, crucially, on their constitutional powers.

Some parliamentary presidents have considerable authority over the appointment of their prime minister and the formation of cabinets – more than some popularly elected presidents. For instance, Czech, Italian, Latvian, Slovak and Turkish prime ministers are all appointed by the president, although presidential freedom here is limited because prime ministers and the government they form must have the confidence of parliament. Nevertheless, the power of appointment gives the president more leverage than in other countries where the president nominates a candidate who must then be approved by parliament and then form a government, as in Estonia, Germany and Hungary. The Greek president is the only one in Europe who has no constitutional discretion in even nominating a prime minister.

Many presidents also have powers over the formation of cabinets. Most parliamentary presidents have an effective veto over the prime ministerial appointments to the cabinet (but the German, Hungarian and Israeli presidents do not). Presidents in Estonia, Slovakia and Turkey may also veto the dismissal of a minister by the prime minister. The Italian president even has discretion in dissolving parliament.

A few parliamentary presidents also have some legislative powers. Most can delay legislation by sending it back for reconsideration. In the Czech Republic and Greece, referred measures require a majority of all members (as opposed to a simple majority of those voting) before they become law.

Presidents are generally assumed either to have no power or not to exercise it in parliamentary systems. However, there are cases of presidents entering the political fray. President Vaclav Havel of the Czech Republic has certainly shown that his office need not be symbolic. On the basis of formal powers, we might also expect the presidents of Italy, Slovakia and Turkey to be politically active at opportune moments, because they have greater power over government formation than their counterparts in other countries. The one-term limit on the Turkish president means he has no worries about re-election if he does exercise full presidential powers.

For this reason, the Turkish system is sometimes classified as a hybrid, rather than a pure parliamentary system. In contrast, the Italian system is usually classified as parliamentary, even though the Italian president has considerable constitutional powers. These were used very effectively in sustaining the Dini government in 1995 against the wishes of half the parliament. By and large parliamentary presidents may have more power where a fluid and unsettled party system gives the president an opportunity to exploit political divisions. Conversely, the more established and concentrated the party system, the less opportunity the president has to exercise power. These generalizations hold for directly elected presidents too. But they apply especially to presidents who lack a direct connection to the electorate.

■ Concluding remarks

The new democracies of Eastern Europe and the former Soviet Union differ from the long-established democracies of Western Europe, particularly in their degree of party fragmentation. However, it is not clear how long this contrast will last. Countries with the greatest voting fragmentation usually have less fragmented legislatures, because many minor parties fail to win seats in the election. It is likely that many of these will soon fade away, or merge with other parties to strengthen themselves. This may also happen in Italy, where a new and controversial electoral system has recently been implemented.

Although Eastern and Western Europe display different patterns of party fragmentation at present, it is thus likely that the two will converge. In Georgia, Russia and the Ukraine, however, fragmentation may continue for a long time, since it is caused not by electoral arrangements, but by deep regional disparities and the weakness of national parties.

In countries in which party systems are highly fragmented, we may expect presidents to play an important role. This is likely in countries where the president is both popularly elected and has influence over the formation of governments, parliamentary terms, and legislation. Presidents in Croatia, Poland and Russia enjoy some or all of these powers. Even those presidents who are elected by parliament may emerge as politically important figures, especially where they have significant constitutional prerogatives, as in Italy, the Czech Republic and Slovakia. If the historical experience of the West is anything to go by, the president-parliamentary systems currently operating in Russia, the Ukraine and Croatia are likely to lead to difficult political relationships in the future.

Europe is remarkable for its wide variety of democratic arrangements. Perhaps as political scientists and the general public become more aware of the way these arrangements work, we will be in a better position to safeguard and advance the hard-won freedoms of its peoples.

■ Further reading

Juan J. Linz and Arthuo Valenzuela, *The Failure of Presidential Democracy: Comparative Perspectives* (Baltimore, Johns Hopkins University Press, 1994).

Thomas T. Mackie and Richard Rose, *The International Almanac of Electoral History* (London, Macmillan, 1991).

Matthew S. Shugart and John M. Carey, *Presidents and Assemblies: Constitutional Design and Electoral Dynamics* (Cambridge, Cambridge University Press, 1992).

Rein Taagepera and Matthew S. Shugart, *Seats and Votes: The Effects and Determinants of Electoral Systems* (New Haven, Yale University Press, 1979).

Chapter 11

Parties, parliaments and governments

■ Forming governments with parliamentary support

Our discussion of constitutional and institutional variations across European democracies should not blind us to the fact that in some essential features they are the same. The most important of these is the common dependence of governments on free elections. Indeed, this dependence is what entitles the European countries to call themselves democracies in the first place. It was the shift from self-nomination of governments to being chosen by electors that marked the change to democracy in Southern and Eastern Europe.

Elections are sometimes held to make important decisions on particular policies – ones which involve changing the constitution or the national territory. For example Finland, Sweden, Norway, Switzerland and Austria all had popular consultations in the 1990s to decide whether to join the European Union. France and other existing members voted on the Treaty of Maastricht (signed in December 1991), which extended the Union's powers. Italy and many Central and Eastern countries have had mass referendums on constitutional change.

In Europe, only Italy and Switzerland hold regular policy votes outside these areas, on matters such as divorce and abortion, transport policy and economics, a situation which is described as 'direct democracy' – decision-making directly by the people. Even in these countries most day-to-day policy is voted on by parliament rather than by the population. This is even truer of the other European countries, where popular policy voting is an exception. In general, European elections are held to decide which party or parties will get popular support and qualify to form a government. The government, with parliamentary support, then goes on to decide what policies to adopt or change. This is the political arrangement generally described as 'representative democracy', which we shall go on to examine below. (Given the importance of political parties in elections, parliaments and governments, however, a more accurate term might be 'party democracy'.)

Electors' choices between parties have of course a lot to do with what kind of programme they would pursue in office. Parties issue quite detailed 'manifestos' or 'action plans' outlining what they would do if they got into government, and a great deal of election discussion is centred around these. Still, in selecting a party, electors have to take its programme as a whole, even if they dislike bits of it and prefer some plans of the other parties. They can only, in this kind of representative election, choose the party whose policies they prefer on balance, despite disagreeing on particular items.

This is still a great deal when compared with the former Fascist and communist regimes, where electors could vote only for one party or bloc, a situation that gave them no effective choice at all. In the European democracies it is the freedom of

BRIEFING 11.1

Referendums and initiatives in Switzerland

Switzerland is a federal republic made up of twenty-three cantons. The executive is the seven-member Federal Council. Legislative power is divided between the two hundred member Federal Assembly, and the forty-six member Council of States elected within cantons. However, direct democracy plays an important part in Swiss government. Referendums (that is, popular votes which give citizens the chance to express their opinion on a matter directly, rather than through an elected representative) were introduced in Switzerland in 1874. All citizens eighteen years and over are entitled to vote in federal referendums and all constitutional amendments, emergency legislation, and major legislative change are required to pass the test of a general referendum.

In addition, a provision for popular initiatives allows citizens themselves to decide directly on an issue. A petition signed by 100,000 citizens (about 2.5 per cent of the population) requires the decision to be made by a popular vote. Usually popular initiatives involve fairly detailed legislative proposals, but for technical reasons these must be presented as constitutional amendments. Referendums also involve major issues of government and politics. In recent years Swiss popular votes have rejected membership of the United Nations (1966 and again in 1986), and of the European Economic Area (1992). Issues such as these require a double majority: that is, a national majority of all citizens voting in the referendum, and a majority within a majority of the cantons.

The cantons and municipalities have considerable autonomy and their own arrangements for initiatives and referendums, which they employ frequently. Switzerland is thus the European country which approaches most nearly to 'direct democracy' where the people as a whole rather than the parliament and government decide what to do in politics.

For more on Switzerland, see Wolf Linder, *Swiss Democracy* (London, Macmillan, 1994).

different parties to organize and to compete with each other for votes on the basis of different ideologies and programmes which gives electors a real choice (see Chapter 9).

The mechanism through which electors' preferences between parties are registered, in the European democracies, is mostly through the allocation of seats in parliament. This is true even in the semi-Presidential regimes discussed at the end of Chapter 10. Electors in these countries have an additional opportunity to influence policy by voting for a president. However, it is only in a limited number of countries – Russia, the Ukraine, Belorus, Croatia, Serbia and Cyprus (see Figure 10.2) that the president's formal powers over the government outweigh those of the parliament. Even under the powerful presidency of France, the government needs support, or at least tolerance, from the parliamentary majority.

This dependence of government on parliament in the overwhelming majority of European democracies, means that the rules for allocating legislative seats to parties on the basis of their votes are of crucial importance in ensuring that the government *does* reflect popular preferences. As we saw in Chapter 10 the rules are often imperfect, although the gross discrepancies which have occurred in some Polish and British elections are fortunately rare. In general it can be said that electors' choices between the larger parties, which are almost certain to form the government, are faithfully reflected. So in its essentials representative democracy works well, institutionally, in Europe.

The parliamentary allocation of seats between parties determines which government forms. The most common types of government formation after elections are:

One-party (near) majority

A one-party (near) majority is where one party has a majority of parliamentary seats – sometimes a near majority, as has often occurred in the Scandinavian and Baltic countries. In these cases the predominant party usually forms a single-party government which is certain of winning important parliamentary votes. Such governments tend to be the longest-lasting in Europe and are usually terminated by new elections. Britain is the classic example of such a system but a surprising number of other European countries such as Spain, Malta, Albania, Greece, Serbia and Romania also have such governments. Near-majority single-party governments are often formed by the social democrats in Sweden and Norway.

Electoral alliances

An electoral alliance falls between single-party government and the multi-party coalitions we shall consider below. Left- and right-wing parties compete as a bloc in elections on the implicit understanding that they will form a government together if they get a combined majority of parliamentary seats. Sometimes they make an explicit electoral alliance to this effect, and even issue a common programme saying what they would do together in government. This is quite a common feature of French politics where the four large parties have to form a left and right bloc to compete in the presidential elections and form a parliamentary (near) majority to support a government of the same ideological hue.

Of course parties do not need to share the same ideological position to make an electoral alliance. Parties of the centre may join with parties of the left or right (ex-communists and peasants in Central and Eastern Europe, for example; socialists and Catalan nationalists in Spain; or liberals (FDP) with both socialists and Christians in Germany, at different times). However, sharing the same ideological position helps to get agreement on policy both in elections and when it comes to forming a government, so alliances are more common within the broad ideological groups than across them.

Coalition government

The third type of government formation, the most common in Europe, is where no one party or bloc dominates and a number of parties of relatively equal size share the parliamentary seats. This is a classic situation where a first option is for parties to form a minority government, composed either of a single party or a coalition. If governments have to have a parliamentary majority to ensure they are not voted down by parties outside the government, then this must be a majority coalition, possibly of several parties directly controlling more than 50 per cent of the seats.

One country where minority governments form most of the time is Denmark (sometimes coalitions, sometimes single-party social democratic governments). Countries where majority multi-party coalitions are negotiated after elections are Ireland, Poland, Finland, the Low Countries and Italy, among others.

Just describing governments as party coalitions, however, gives little indication of how they actually function. In some countries, such as the Netherlands, the parties take a long time (up to six months in 1977) to decide who is to govern together and what they will do when in office. They make a detailed written agreement and publish it. Naturally the agreement concentrates on the areas where the partners agree. Dutch coalitions tend to cohere very well round their programme, which covers the whole period they expect to be in office. This is helped by the fact that Dutch governments tend to be two-party ones like the German, so there are fewer conflicting views to reconcile than in multi-party coalitions like the Italian and Finnish. To appreciate this point one need only contrast the multi-party coalitions in Poland from 1991–93, with their internal squabbles and frequent crises, with the relative stability of the two-party socialist-agrarian coalition which succeeded it.

Government stability may also be aided by the fact that coalitions tend to be based around one party which is almost always in office. In a multi-party situation this usually occurs because the party is centrist in ideology and so more congenial to parties of both left and right than either are to each other. It helps also if it has a sufficient number of legislative seats to make it inconvenient to form coalitions without it, thus putting it in a pivotal position in parliament.

Such pivotal parties often have ideologies which cut across mainstream left-right distinctions. Classically, they are Christian democrats as in the Low Countries and for a long time in Italy. As we noted in Chapter 9 (Table 9.1) such parties share a strong pro-welfare orientation with socialists, but also have a strong commitment to private property and traditional moral values, which render them congenial to parties of the right. Christian parties are weaker in Eastern Europe. A pivotal role can be taken by agrarian or centre parties in countries such as Hungary and Poland, since again their ideology has elements which appeal both to left and right. Minority ethnic parties are also inclined to trade their support for concessions as in Macedonia, Bulgaria and Spain.

Although some parties, notably the Christian democrats, have become almost a permanent feature of coalitions in certain countries, their indispensability can never be taken for granted. This has been illustrated graphically in the recent Dutch coalition formed after the elections of 1994 which grouped the two main parties of the left (PvdA and D'66) with the right-wing VVD, excluding the Christians from government for the first time in seventy-seven years.

Such cases can occur because government coalitions are not only based on general policy considerations, but also take into account influence over policy implementation through party control of particular ministries (see Chapter 12). Parties are also concerned about how government participation might affect future election prospects. If a country looks likely to experience an economic boom for example, parties might be anxious to take part in any kind of government so as to take credit for economic prosperity.

Such situations are temporary however. In the long run, standing policy differences, especially those related to long-term left–right divisions, are likely to reassert themselves and render centre parties more acceptable partners again. In Belgium, for example, the Christian democrats were outside the socialist-liberal coalition from 1954–8, but have been in government ever since because of their acceptability to both left and right.

BRIEFING 11.2

Changing fortunes of a pivotal party: the Dutch Christian Democratic appeal

The CDA was formed in the 1970s through the amalgamation of the Catholic party with two Calvinist parties – the Anti-Revolutionary Party (ARP) and the Christian Historical Union (CHU). The three had co-operated closely since their creation in the late nineteenth century, with the ARP and CHU closely following the Catholic lead in the post-war period. So the CDA can be regarded as essentially the continuation of the Catholic Party.

The CP and the CDA have been central to Dutch coalition-building for two reasons:

1. they had a slightly larger or equal share of seats to any other party in the Second Chamber, the popularly elected house of the Dutch parliament.
2. they held a middle position on the principal issues disputed between the other parties.

These are mostly related to the left-right dimension, on which we show party positions after the elections of 1989, together with their number of legislative seats:

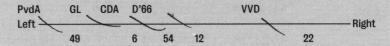

PvdA		GL	CDA	D'66		VVD	
Left							Right
	49	6	54	12		22	

The fact that the CDA had around 30 per cent of the seats made it necessary to form a three-party coalition of the other parties to get a parliamentary majority which excluded the CDA. In that case, paradoxically, the government parties would disagree more on policy among themselves than they would with the CDA. Any of them would thus get more of the policy they wanted by combining with the CDA than with parties on the other side of the left-right dimension.

These were the considerations which made the CDA (and parties similarly placed in other countries) a pivotal party, in the sense of being indispensable to any viable coalition that might form. This enabled it to claim the premiership in the government and to get more or less the policies it wanted. It also meant that its party leader was the first to be asked to form a new government, so that he could choose between a right-oriented one with the Liberals (VVD) or a left-oriented one with Labour (PvdA).

This comfortable situation came unstuck after the elections of 1994, primarily because the CDA lost votes and therefore seats. In the new parliament the CDA had only thirty-four seats compared with its previous fifty-four. In addition, the PvdA had moved substantially to the right, putting it in the pivotal position between CDA and VVD. The ideological positions and seats held by the parties in 1994 were:

	GL		D'66	CDA	PvdA		VVD	
Left							Right	
	5		24	34	37		31	

Its seat loss not only deprived the CDA of bargaining power but seemed to indicate it had been rejected by electors. The PvdA had also lost votes and seats but was still the largest party. It took the initiative in forming a coalition with the parties which had gained D'66 (a radical-liberal party) and the VVD. Its rightward shift made it easier to do this as it was now closer to the VVD than the Christians were. Thus a three-party coalition was formed without the CDA – the first time for seventy-seven years that a religious party was not in government.

Presidentially supported governments

Quite a different type of government formation occurs where there is a president with some authority independent of parliament, who is able to take the initiative in forming and sustaining governments. This may occur not only where the president has formal authority to do so, as in Russia and the Ukraine, but where party support or party divisions inside parliament give him or her the scope to do so.

An example of what powers a president can have with the backing of his own party group in parliament, is given by France. Despite his limited formal powers (Table 10.4), when his party bloc has a majority or plurality of seats the French president can, as party leader, nominate and form the government, and influence its policy. The emergence of a Polish president in 1995 from the dominant party in parliament (the ex-communists) probably means that the situation there will develop in the same way as the French. It was the failure of the first president (Walesa) to create a successful parliamentary party that limited his influence to foreign policy and defence.

Most commonly, however, presidential control over governments results from divisions and weakness among the parliamentary parties. Their inability to agree on a government in the first place, or to co-operate within one when it forms, may give the president a justification for intervention. This often takes the form of nominating a 'technical' government of 'specialists' drawn from higher civil servants.

This situation has occurred quite often in Finland, where typically the position of Minister of Finance has been taken by the Governor of the Central Bank, and Minister of Defence by the Chief of the Army General Staff and so on. Even when these governments have been succeeded by party-based governments, presidential support of the Agrarian Centre Party ensured it a leading role in governments.

Italy has been moving in this direction ever since the collapse of the Christian Democrats who dominated its governments from the end of the Second World War until 1992. Two non-partisan and largely technical governments brought together by the president then carried through the election reforms of 1993 (Chapter 10). Instead of unblocking the political situation by permitting a clear alternation of left and right, these produced a parliamentary situation in which the individual parties inside these blocs quarrelled among themselves. So in 1995, President Scalfaro produced a technical government under an economist, Dini, to avert a financial crisis. Its dependence on the centre-left parties caused it to be voted down by the right at the end of the year. But the parties could not agree on an immediate successor, leaving Dini and his colleagues in charge of the interim administration. This was quite usual, as the general practice in all countries is to leave the previous government in charge while a new coalition is being formed. Normally, such 'caretaker' governments simply carry on the routine administration, leaving new policy initiatives to the incoming government, which will have the necessary support to carry them through.

Italy, however, had just assumed the Presidency of the European Union for its period of six months (see Chapter 2) so the caretaker government had to take essential initiatives. Whatever the shape they assumed, Italy had governments formed and largely sustained by the president for most of the period from 1992–96. It was no wonder that direct election of either the president or prime minister and an enhancement of their executive powers were increasingly discussed as a means of breaking through the institutional stalemate.

BRIEFING 11.3

The European Parliament and the collective executive

We talk largely about national parliaments in this chapter but should not forget the quasi-federal European Parliament which groups representatives from the fifteen countries of the European Union. Elections for the parliament are held every four years in all member countries. As the only directly elected union body, the European Parliament claims more legitimacy than the Commission, even though interest is low in some countries and elections are dominated by national and not European issues.

One reason for this is the European Parliament's relative lack of power in relation to the other European bodies (see Figure 2.1). It can dismiss the (nationally nominated) Commission but the same Commissioners can be re-nominated by the member states. It can (and has) refused(d) to pass the budget. But in that case the European Union simply operates on the basis of last year's budget until the new one is passed.

In any case, the European Parliament and the Commission generally agree on the broad desirability of closer European integration and enhancement of their own powers in relation to the member states. The real bodies the European Parliament wants to control are the European Council and the councils of (national) ministers, over whom they have little formal power. In this respect it is rather in the position of the Russian parliament in relation to the Russian president – isolated from the real locus of power.

All the European Parliament can really hope to do is inform and mobilize public opinion, though it is hampered in this by its peripheral position. This is symbolized by its geographic isolation in Strasbourg and Luxembourg where it meets alternately. It tries to counter this by holding committee meetings in Brussels near the centres of real decision-making.

The European Parliament has one chamber, unlike most parliaments in Europe (though associated with it are the advisory Economic and Social Committee and the Committee of Regions – see Chapter 2). All the major party families have (cross-national) parliamentary groups, the two leading ones being the socialist and Christian. However, as these all consist of EU supporters and the main issue is the strengthening of the Union, party disagreement is muted. Like national parliaments the European Parliament has a strong committee structure, where most legislative work gets done (see Table 11.2).

A similar situation prevails in Russia. The constitutional powers vested in the President and the relative weakness of the Duma make it almost inevitable that the government will be nominated by, and almost wholly responsible to him. This form of strong presidentialism could be seen as a response to the relative weakness and fragmentation of the parties and parliament in Russia and in neighbouring Ukraine and Belarus. On the other hand, the situation helps to perpetuate party weakness and division, since parties have no inducement to come together in a coalition. They thus adopt negative and critical attitudes, since they do not have to assume responsibility for forming and supporting the government. The government will continue whatever they do, so parliamentarians can afford to be as obstructive as they like.

▪ Parliamentary influence versus governmental strength

In most of Europe, in fact, attention focuses more on the executive than the legislature. Parliaments simply react to what the executive does. This is clearly true of strong presidential systems such as Russia. But it also occurs where government is dependent upon parliament rather than on a president, particularly in the case of single-party majority governments. Even though such a government depends on parliamentary support, disciplined party voting enables it to act with great independence in most circumstances. Thus, the government will generally dominate parliament rather than the other way round. Using its built-in majority, the government can impose procedures and timetables, limit questioning of its activities, pass legislation, and, if necessary, win votes of confidence. Even opposition parties tolerate government domination of this kind, hoping to benefit from it when their turn in government comes. The power of the government is even greater if the Prime Minister is free to call an election. The threat of losing seats often has the effect of reinforcing party loyalty and intimidating internal party opponents.

Britain is the classic situation of a strong single-party government acting with full autonomy. This is reinforced by the fact that about a third of the majority party and a sixth of all members of parliament are members of the government. So even in terms of simple numbers there is a strong government presence in the House of Commons. The fact that there is effectively only one main opposition party reinforces the division of parliament along party lines. Under these circumstances parliament simply becomes one of the forums where opposition leaders criticize government policy without being able to defeat it.

There is more scope for parliamentary autonomy in the minority governments which sometimes occur in Ireland, Norway and Sweden. To ensure that the government wins essential votes some cross-party agreement is necessary, and legislation is often discussed at length both inside and outside parliament. In the Nordic countries cross-party parliamentary commissions often hold public hearings and consult affected interests. Great emphasis is put not just on inter-party agreement, but on a broad societal consensus. Thus in the Nordic countries parliaments have an important role independent of party conflicts and affiliations. This is most marked in Denmark where minority governments are most liable to defeat in parliament. The average life of a government in Denmark is about two years, compared with three in Norway and four in Sweden and Britain.

To survive even as long as they do, Danish governments have to get parliamentary agreement with different groups on different aspects of policy. Social democratic governments have tended to ally with the 'bourgeois' parties to support NATO and the Western military alliance against the 'peace package' of the left socialists (see Chapter 8). To sustain welfare services, however, they have allied with the left socialists against the right. In effect, they built separate coalitions on different issues.

Continual bargaining between the parties thus makes parliamentary debate very important in Denmark. In addition, minority governments have avoided trouble by leaving difficult and important policy decisions to parliamentary committees. The most important committee controls relations with the European Union. Its members are all senior statesmen. It sets national policies in regard to the EU, and Danish representatives in Brussels report back to it, rather than to the government.

In Denmark, governments depend on parliament rather than the other way round. This is unusual. But it is generally true that wherever coalitions are weak and quarrel internally, much more importance is attached to negotiations within parliament then where governments are confident of winning legislative votes. Generally,

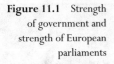

Figure 11.1 Strength of government and strength of European parliaments

coalitions are weaker the more parties they include. Having to get more agreement across party lines almost inevitably involves more bickering and squabbling.

Where governments cannot be sure of their own party support, they will try to get as wide a consensus as possible in parliament, even among parties not in the government coalition. This is the case in Italy where internal discipline is weak and factions within parties quite common. It also occurred in Poland in the first freely elected parliament (1991–93) and may account for the tendency in Hungary for even majority parties to ally themselves with smaller ones to ensure they have 65–70 per cent of parliamentary seats, instead of forming single-party governments. Figure 11.1 sums up these trade-offs between parliamentary and government powers.

The stronger the government the weaker the parliament. Either parliament is controlled by a powerful majority government – Greece, Malta, France, Spain, Britain and to some extent Hungary and Romania. Or it is ignored by governments which are dependent on presidents, not parliaments – the former Soviet countries and the European Union. These are the cases which cluster at the top left-hand side of Figure 11.1.

At the same time, a weak government does not necessarily mean a strong parliament either, for this combination often produces a weak and ineffective parliament *and* government. Again Italy is the best example. The almost continual bargaining and confusion between many parties and the weakness of coalitions, means that everyone is ineffective. Belgium also approaches this situation.

The situation most favourable for strong parliaments is found in the Nordic countries where reasonably authoritative government co-exists with cross-party debate and independent parliamentary committees. Such countries appear on the right-hand side of Figure 11.1. But there are only a few of them.

This has led some commentators to talk about a 'decline of parliaments' as though legislative powers had been whittled down compared to some time in the past. As with political parties, however, there never was a Golden Age in which parliaments had more power than they do now. British governments have always had firm control of legislative proceedings. In north-west Europe, governments appear to have been even less permissive in the past! The major example of a legislature on which governments were totally dependent was the National Assembly under the French Third and Fourth Republics (1870–1958). The continual atmosphere of crisis and the

BRIEFING 11.4

Switzerland: Parliament under a permanent coalition

Swiss politics are strongly devolved to Cantons (the regions or states), localities and affected groups. It is a working example of subsidiarity (the idea that political decisions should be taken at the level appropriate for them). The parliament thus has a powerful Upper Chamber with co-equal powers, representing the Cantons, as well as a directly elected lower Chamber. These must operate in the knowledge that some of their decisions have to be ratified by referendum, while most of the others can be challenged or reversed by popular initiatives if enough signatures can be collected to set them in motion.

All the main party families are represented in parliament and the four major ones in the Federal Council, which forms the government. The parties – radicals, (Catholic) conservatives, socialists and the People's Party – divide up council seats through the 'magic formula' of 2, 2, 2, 1. But the actual party nominee may not be chosen by the joint vote of both Houses. Another member of the same party may be elected in his place. Once elected the Council is constitutionally required to serve for four years.

As such ideologically diverse parties make up the government, and control about three-quarters of the seats in the Chamber, the concept of a cohesive government versus opposition bloc is quite absent in the Swiss case, and does not dominate parliamentary proceedings. The devolution of power of cantons and popular referendums tends to make parliament's one of checking details of what has largely been decided elsewhere. It thus meets less frequently than other parliaments in Europe and is far from being the main focus of decision-making. The most dramatic issues are voted on and decided in referendum campaigns.

monotonous fall of short-lived governments, however, simply meant that all politicians became an irrelevance, as in Italy and Belgium today.

Elsewhere in Europe, parliaments have either not existed until recently or have been rubber-stamps for the regime. Though parliamentary power and initiatives may be restricted in most European countries, they still seem greater than they were in the past. If we want to look for a Golden Age, we should search for it in the present.

How parliaments organize themselves: institutions and structures

The previous discussion has shown what a tremendous variation there is in the scope for independent debate and decision-making of parliaments across Europe. This is not simply a contrast between the old West and East but dependent on party structure and constitutional arrangements. We have not even discussed cases like Switzerland, where a quite exceptional form of politics affects the Federal Parliament's position.

Arguably, acting as a forum for relatively free discussion is parliament's most important role, whatever party or presidential limitations there are on its other powers. In this section we shall see how European parliaments organize themselves for this task, before going on in the next section to look at the most effective legislative instrument for scrutiny and enquiry, the parliamentary committee.

The parliamentary setting

First of all, we have to remember that the role of the central parliament varies very much according to what is done by the Courts, by regional parliaments (if any) and by local governments. In Switzerland, so many functions are devolved to cantons and communes that what the federal parliament does is much more limited than in most countries. The same is true of Russia in relation to the autonomous republics. We shall go into regional and local governments in Chapter 13, but the way they can affect the activities of the central parliament deserves to be noted.

The same is true of the Courts (Chapter 14). In some countries they rule on constitutional matters and take an active investigative role much more than in others. The European Union is a good example of this. The European Court has certainly done more than the parliament to enhance the powers of the Union and to enforce its authority in member states.

Again, the local governments of communes and cities may exercise extensive devolved powers in certain areas, as in Sweden over health and in Ireland over the environment. Once parliament has approved such devolution, it loses its immediate jurisdiction over it. As the jurisdiction of local government varies considerably across Europe, this affects the scope of parliamentary debate and scrutiny in the different countries to a very great extent (Chapter 13).

Bicameralism: the other chamber

Regionalism also has a direct impact on how parliament is organized through the First or Upper Chamber. Most European parliaments are bicameral, that is they have two Houses through which legislation has to pass before it becomes law. The exceptions to this, where parliament has only one directly elected chamber, are the Scandinavian countries, Bulgaria, Malta, Turkey, Greece, Slovakia, Portugal and Macedonia.

The function of the 'other house' of parliament is either to safeguard the rights of specified minorities in society (often territorially organized as regions or states) or to provide for the revision and checking of legislation, or both. Where the house represents states it may have co-equal powers, as in Switzerland, or an effective veto over legislation as in Germany. In Germany indeed the Bundesrat is made up of delegates from state governments. As a majority of these are often controlled by the opposition parties, the ruling parties at federal level often have to compromise to get legislation through parliament as a whole (for more on this see Chapter 13).

Where the other house is directly elected, this is often on a territorial basis designed to reinforce its link with regions or provinces, as in Poland. Or members may be elected by a college of local and regional councillors (France), so that the House reflects local interests in general though not those of specific regions.

Where it represents states or regions, the house is supposed to examine legislation and scrutinize state legislation from the point of view of how it affects territorial interests and/or ethnic minorities. This is because these are peculiarly important to national cohesion and unity as we saw in Chapter 4. The powers of the other house are designed to reassure minority groups that their interests will not be overridden. Unfortunately, many of the countries where minority nationalism is a problem do not have such safeguards, either in the shape of a territorially based upper house or of regional government.

Safeguarding territorial and/or ethnic interests is however just a special case, though an important one, of the role of the other chamber of parliament in protecting minorities in general. This role originated in the face of the widening of the franchise in the nineteenth century when it was felt that a popularly elected house with strong mass parties would threaten property and established interests. The other house, nominated or with a restricted electorate, was given powers to counter such threats.

In the event, they were hardly necessary, as the new parties and enfranchised electors were far from revolutionary. The other house often survived, however, as a less partisan arena where legislation could be examined on its technical merits, experts and specialists could be brought in, and scrutiny of the administration carried on in a more considered and long-term manner than where it was dominated by party debates. Even the bizarre House of Lords in Britain, where in theory all hereditary peers can vote, is effectively an arena where distinguished experts can conduct specialized debates.

The 'other' chamber is usually organized along the same lines as the popular chamber, with a president and specialized committees. Except in states with considerable regional autonomy, where it represents these units, it does not generally have great powers. Its main influence has to be through the quality of its debates and ability to pursue matters blocked elsewhere which then reach the media. In this capacity it is an enhancement to parliamentary systems but, apart from the exceptional cases we have mentioned, not a major component. Governments tend to base themselves in the popular chambers which as a result become the major focus of interest and excitement, and hence of media attention.

Structuring discussion and debate

In order to structure discussion, all legislative bodies need to have a body of rules and regulations, often quite detailed ones, specifying such matters as how time is to be allocated, who is to speak when, what matters are to be dealt with by the whole house and what by committees, how members are to be allocated to committees, how far the media are to be admitted to sessions, what kinds of contacts members are permitted to have with outside bodies, and a whole host of other matters. While details vary, these matters are handled in broadly the same way in all parliaments. Many of the rules of procedure go back to British parliamentary practice of the mid-nineteenth century. Thus they all make arrangements for legislation to be passed through a number of stages, including detailed consideration by an appropriate committee.

To administer the rules and provide for the resolution of disputes between opposing parties, most legislative chambers also have a president – sometimes a collective presidium. Even where this is chosen proportionally from party nominees, it usually consists of persons who are slightly aloof from day-to-day struggles and who do not harbour higher political ambitions. However, in the semi-presidential systems, particularly where the parliamentary majority is formed by a different party from the president, the speaker may play an important opposition role.

As the name 'legislature' applied to parliaments implies, the greater amount of their time is taken up with discussing and passing laws. It is, however, arguable whether legislation is really their most important function. Almost all laws in modern parliaments are drafted and prepared by governments. After parliamentary debate and discussion, they usually emerge much the same as when they were first proposed. This is due to party loyalty and discipline which ensures that members of each party's parliamentary group will all vote in the same way. As the government will generally be supported by a majority, this means that its legislation will not be queried.

Exceptions are the semi-presidential regimes where the government may have a very limited parliamentary base and hence cannot rely on voting support. The Russian Duma seemed almost to take pleasure in botching governmental legislation in the mid-1990s. Given the wide powers of the Russian President, however, this often gave him a reason for passing emergency decrees and regulations. In 1994, the recently elected Ukrainian president, for similar reasons, forced parliament to grant him a major package of powers so that the programme of privatization and reform would not be impeded.

Other Central and Eastern parliaments have been exceptionally busy with reform legislation. Often the whole legal and social base needs to be overhauled as privatization of enterprises raises such non-obvious questions as how pension funds need to be restructured, and whether the new firms have liability for former state employees.

In light of what has been said above it will come as no surprise that the Nordic parliaments are much freer from party control over legislation than most others. Ordinary members can introduce proposals for legislation. If these pass the scrutiny of the relevant parliamentary committee they quite often inspire the appointment of a Royal Commission to consult with interested groups. The report of the commission will then form the basis for a government-backed bill leading to important legislation. If an Environment Bill is finally passed in Hungary it will owe a lot to the activities of the relevant parliamentary committee which has taken the initiative, in conjunction with Green activists, in producing one.

One particular aspect of parliaments which closely affects their freedom to legislate and, beyond that, their whole freedom of debate and ability to form an independent collective viewpoint, is the extent to which government ministers are allowed to intervene and control discussion. In contrast to the Nordic situation, French and Hungarian ministers can pilot their own bills through parliament and committees. The French Assembly additionally has to debate the government's version of the Bill in plenary session, with changes proposed in parliament considered simply as amendments, and given less time.

Ministerial control seems relatively unaffected by whether ministers are formally members of the parliament or not. A whole variety of practices are possible. Ministers may have to be members of one of the houses of parliament and continue to be so during their term of office as in Ireland and Britain. Ministers may be drawn from parliament but then have to resign (the Netherlands). Or they may be drawn from both parliament and outside (France). Or they may be exclusively drawn from outside (Russia). In any case, what makes the difference is the extent to which they can participate in parliamentary proceedings during their period of appointment. Only in the more constitutionally separated presidential-premier regimes do they participate hardly at all, or very seldom in parliamentary discussion.

As we have said, ministerial control extends beyond participation in debates into all other parliamentary activities. From the viewpoint of attracting attention and initiating general discussion, these are probably more important than passing laws. They include questions to ministers and comments on their actions; scrutiny and criticism of the detailed work of the bureaucracy; and general debate on matters of public concern. Obviously, the freer parliament is to set up its own agenda in regard to these questions, the more it can generate a collective standpoint over and against the parties and the government, and the more individual members can get their own views over to the media. Parliamentary proceedings will become 'news', as defined by press and television, the more they are free and wide-ranging.

These are the very reasons government and parties want to control them of course! In general, the autonomy of parliaments in these areas varies with the strength of the government so it is charted to some extent in Figure 11.1 (except for the obvious fact that parliaments in semi-presidential regimes are free to organize their own proceedings but lack the power to turn words into deeds). Of the parliamentary-based regimes, Britain and the Nordic countries are almost at the opposite poles as far as autonomy of parliamentary action is concerned.

Individual legislators and their activities

In talking about the collective activities of parliaments one should not of course forget about the activities of members of parliament (MPs) or deputies as individuals, or their personal links within and outside parliament. Within parliament these are primarily with the party group, to whom they largely owe election and with whose other members they share ideological loyalties. This accounts for the pervasive influence of the parties in legislatures: identity, survival and hopes of political advancement are all bound up with the party.

Even the ties which in constituency-based systems the legislator develops with constituents are coloured by party. However desirous an individual MP may be to serve all local residents regardless of voting loyalties, the people he or she sees most locally are party activists and workers – on whom again the deputy depends for survival. Only where the electoral system puts a premium on being individually known as widely as possible may a representative make a real investment in breaking beyond party circles. Thus in Ireland where vote transfers and competition in three- or four-member constituencies means that the TD (Teachta Dála) competes against members of his own party, strong local ties are essential, particularly in country districts, to get re-elected. Of course, where parties have weak organizations on the ground, and elections are constituency-based, there is a premium on being well known, as in Turkey, Albania, Hungary and Russia, for example.

Belgium and France constitute a special case, in that national legislators often build their career on local politics, as Mayor of a Commune or city. Here the importance of their local base means that their legislative role is often but an adjunct to it, for reasons we shall go into in Chapter 13.

Most European parliaments are, however, elected through some form of proportional representation. The need to guard against distortions by having large constituencies means that candidates run on a party list where the top names are almost bound to get elected and the bottom ones equally likely to fail. This gives the leadership a potent sanction against rebels and again reinforces the pervasive influence of party. Even in constituency-based elections, party endorsement is vital to election, since local contacts at best contribute a limited number of votes.

Outside their local affiliations the main contacts legislators have is with interest groups and social movements. These may provide manpower, support and finance to individuals as well as to political parties. They may also be useful sources of information. A major way of making a legislative mark quickly is to become a specialist in some legislative or policy area. Having contacts with groups in the area provides ready access to specialized knowledge. Relationships are often formalized through the award of a consultancy to the member. Nothing is for nothing, of course: in such situations the deputy will tend to become an advocate for one point of view, unless his or her contacts have been widely spread.

Specialization forms the basis of the only other links a legislator may develop within parliament which challenge those of party – that is with his or her specialized committee. Most parliaments have permanent committees specialized according to area, often with oversight over a corresponding ministry. These often consider legislation in the area but also have more general powers of scrutiny and initiation, as with the Environmental Committee in Hungary. Members are or become specialists in the area and may, through their daily interaction with other members, develop a common loyalty across party lines. This is all the more likely if the committee is expected to be non-partisan in its approach. Generally, one might say that the more specialized the committee is the more cross-partisan its approach will be and the closer ties will be among its members.

Committees are such an important aspect of parliamentary processes that we devote the whole of the next section to them. Their effects on individual members are only one of the ways in which they contribute to the formation of 'Parliamentary', as opposed to party, opinion – as we shall see.

Parliamentary committees

Parliaments need to have committees if only because a whole house or assembly, whether it has 100 or 800 members, cannot concern itself with everything. It needs to have groups of specialists who can summarize technical details. It needs bodies with a collective memory which can track developments in particular areas or keep an eye on particular ministries. By multiplying committees, the assembly can effectively extend the time it spends on scrutiny and detailed investigation. Given the complexity of modern administration legislatures have to get down to detail if they are to be effective, so the number and activity of its committees is a prime indicator of legislative power and influence.

As we have noted, the most powerful parliament in Europe is probably the Danish one, because its committees combine oversight and scrutiny with actually laying down a mandate for national representatives. The most powerful are the all-party Committee on Foreign Affairs (Udernrigs Politiske Nævn) and the Committee on European Union Affairs (Markedsudvalg).

Despite their power the actual number of committees in the Scandinavian Parliaments is rather small, going against the point made above about the number of committees reflecting parliamentary activity and general standing (the Eduskunta, the Finnish parliament, has only eight). They are also less specialized than in other parliaments, not 'shadowing' particular ministries and with a relatively higher number dealing with legislation. This, however, reflects the relative autonomy of these parliaments in initiating and discussing legislation independently of the government. A significant point is the exclusion of ministers from committees – in Sweden for example. Clearly, this increases the committee's scope for autonomous discussion.

Contrast the French Assembly's limited number of broad functional committees, devoted largely to considering legislation, and with the relevant government minister piloting his own bill through it. These committees have specialized sub-committees more distanced from government control, but which lack the standing of the parent.

Some countries divide legislative functions from the scrutiny of policy and administration. The British House of Commons is the most obvious example of this. It has four large standing committees with about 100 members in each to discuss legislation. Quite separate from these are fifteen 'select' committees with a relatively permanent membership and a small secretariat designed to scrutinize the activities of the major ministries. The committees may be chaired by members of opposition parties and are supposed to adopt a non-partisan approach. Ministers do not participate except as witnesses.

The separation of scrutiny from legislation may be a weakness, however. The committees produce reports, tempered by the need to obtain cross-party agreement. These often attract great media attention, but once the report is produced it is often unclear what is to be done with it. The relevant ministry is expected to respond but may take two or three years to do so. There is then a fair possibility that elections will have been held, the committee will have a new membership and the report will be forgotten.

Most European parliaments combine legislation and scrutiny in one committee. Like the British select committees these 'track' the main ministries, though they may also cover other policy areas deemed important. Table 11.1 lists the main committees of the Polish Sejm, which are typical of those in most countries. It compares those with the committees of the European Parliament, which are a kind of distillation of those operating in the national parliaments of Western Europe.

The general characteristics of such committees are that they are fairly numerous – fifteen to twenty-five is the typical range. Their membership is generally limited to 15–30 members. They deal with legislation, policy review and administrative scrutiny and cover the whole range of government activities. They have convenors who are relatively independent of government, not known as extreme partisans, or who may actually be members of non-governmental parties. They can summon administrators and ministers as witnesses and may sit in private. Parties are probably represented in proportion to their numbers in the legislature as a whole, but proceedings are expected to be relatively non-partisan (not, however, in Germany where committees of the Bundestag divide along partisan lines).

To keep committees relatively non-partisan they may have to avoid the most controversial topics (except in Scandinavia where the government may be happy to unload such a topic on to them). If the overall legislative process is controlled by the party government, committees have little chance of initiating legislation on the problems they uncover (as with the Environment Committee in Hungary). Their reports may attract media attention but then be left to languish.

These are weaknesses the committees share with parliaments as a whole, and they are not weaknesses that can be transcended while governments exert the power they do, in most cases, over legislative processes. What is clear is that most of the effec-

Table 11.1   Main committees of two European parliaments

European Parliament	Polish Sjem
Political Affairs	Administrative and International Affairs
Agriculture, Fisheries, Rural Development	European Treaty
Budgets	Education, Science and Technical Progress
Economic and Monetary Affairs and Industrial Policy	Trade and Services
Energy, Research and Technology	Culture and Mass Media
External Economic Relations	Contact with Poles Abroad
Legal Affairs and Citizen's Rights	Youth, Physical Culture and Sport
Social Affairs, Employment and the Working Environment	National and Ethnic Minorities
Regional Policy and Regional Planning	National Defense
Transport and Tourism	Environment Protection, Natural Resources and Forestry
Environment, Public Health and Consumer Protection	Constitutional Accountability
Youth, Culture, Education, the Media and Sport	Economic Policy, Budget and Finance
Development and Co-operation	Urban Planning and Construction Policy
Budgetary Control	Social Welfare
Institutional Affairs	Privatization Committee
Procedure, Credentials and Immunities	Regulation and Deputies' Affairs
Women's Rights	Agriculture
Petitions	Local Government
	Justice
	Foreign Affairs
	International Economic Relations and Maritime Trade
	Economic System and Industry
	Legislative
	Health

tive work of parliaments is done in their committees. Without committees the detailed work of scrutinizing legislation and administration would be neglected, and parliament would form even more of an arena for ritual political battles and 'shadow-boxing'.

Party democracy versus representative democracy

Discussion of parliaments inevitably raises the question of whether European democracy is party democracy or representative democracy. The nineteenth-century liberals who first set up assemblies and legislatures had no doubts that they were constructing representative democracy, and in a particularly pure form. Electors would choose men of standing and distinction who would come together in parliament to apply their own judgement to questions of national policy. They would be uninfluenced by the special pleading of particular interests, as they would be sufficiently prosperous not to be beholden to them. Given these conditions, the independent judgements of legislators would be easily reconciled and the best national policy would emerge from the national assembly (at least most of the time).

Though couched in idealistic terms this is not a parody of what early reformers thought. Social interests and political parties rapidly asserted themselves, however, first of all by extending the franchise to less-educated strata, whom they organized into voting groups. Instead of electing the best men with no (obvious) social or political ties, mass parties put in their own ideologues and partisans who could be trusted to vote as the party told them to.

There has been a tension between these two roles ever since. Should representatives act according to their own consciences, as the persons individually best suited to decide what national policy should be? Or should they simply act in line with their party, whose electors put them there because of their affiliations and not because of their individual merits? The conflict is compounded in most parliaments because representation has moved away from a constituency system, where candidates had a change of being personally known, to proportional representation where he and she is simply a name on a party list.

There is little doubt from our discussion that party roles win the conflict hands down. Parties dominate parliaments and their members just as they dominate elections and governments. Indeed, they form the indispensable link between the three. If we want electors to have a choice between people and policies, which then translates into the kind of government that gets formed and into what that government does, we need political parties and their programmes. Mass democracies have to be (competitive) party democracies or they will not be democracies.

Nineteenth-century liberals saw parties as disruptive influences because they themselves were not at heart democrats and feared the consequences of having mass preferences translated into government policy without the filter of independent representatives who could interpose themselves between population and policy. With the advantage of hindsight we can realize that neither the masses nor their parties were revolutionary and in fact valued stability and order rather than upsetting it. Nevertheless, we retain some of the forms of representative democracy – the most obvious being the assemblies and parliaments of Europe. With their imposing buildings, attendant staff and mass of legislators, these must surely have some purpose beyond the mundane one of registering party strength after an election?

This chapter shows that they do, even if it is clear that their main function is that of acting as the principal arena for party debate and negotiation. For one thing, electors' wishes are often expressed in an unclear way. Where no party has a majority what kind of government will be formed? Negotiations are carried out within parliament where close party and legislative contacts ease the way to an agreement. Parliaments cannot be regarded as simple counting devices in such cases. They hold discussions which influence the formation of governments and often their termination and replacement too.

The question of whether parliament really exists in a collective sense is, of course, most sharply posed when a single-party majority government clearly emerges and distinguishes itself from the opposition. It is more difficult in this case to think of the parliament having any function or collective identity independent of the party conflict. To a considerable extent this is true. Nevertheless, it is hard to imagine any other body which could follow legislation in detail or take the initiative in scrutinizing administration. As we have seen, most parliaments have developed means of doing this.

Parliamentary discussion and scrutiny are even more valuable in presidential-premier systems. Even though the president is directly elected, one would hesitate to leave the whole cumulation of executive and legislative power in the hands of one man and his entourage. Here the checking and balancing power of parliament as a whole is more obvious (and one would say, necessary) if democracy really is to function.

In the end, there is perhaps not so much of a conflict between the ideals of representative and party democracy as is often made out. Individual representatives are after all affiliated to the party because their judgement tells them it offers the best policies for government. Besides sitting on parliamentary committees, the deputies also sit on party ones and contribute powerfully to party decisions. Put this way, one can see their activity in parliament as a seamless web, spilling over from a party to a parliamentary context and back again without much conscious distinction. Parliaments do owe their contemporary relevance to party activity, but on the other hand they provide an indispensable context for it – one which, if did not exist, would have to be reinvented, as to a considerable extent it has been in Southern and Eastern Europe.

Further reading

Attila Agh (ed.), *The Emergence of East Central European Parliament: The First Steps* (Budapest, Hungarian Centre of Democratic Studies, 1994).

Ian Budge, *The New Challenge of Direct Democracy* (Cambridge, Polity 1996).

Josep M. Colomer (ed.), *Political Institutions in Europe* (London, Routledge, 1996).

M. J. Laver and Ian Budge (eds), *Party Policy and Government Coalitions* (London, Macmillan 1992).

Gordon Smith, *Politics in Western Europe* (Aldershot, Gower 1988), ch. 7.

Chapter 12

Parties, governments and bureaucracies

■ The policy process

Government seems very remote from the ordinary person in the street. What links them together is the great social invention of modern times, the political party. As we have seen in Chapter 9, parties contest elections by offering a choice of different personnel and programmes to electors. Electors' votes are translated into party shares of parliamentary seats (or in some cases, control of the presidency) through the various constitutional rules described in Chapter 10. On the basis of their parliamentary or presidential support, parties form a government, broadly related to their electoral votes, in the various ways described in Chapter 11. In government, parties try to advance their characteristic values and policies, which form the main basis on which they have attracted electoral approval.

The whole process of election, government formation and party policy-making is summarized in Figure 12.1. Parties are not insensitive to changes in the national society and economy, or to developments in the surrounding world. They try to respond to these but always on the basis of their pre-existing ideology and values. Socialist parties for example are always likely to emphasize the need for welfare and social care more than other types of party. If an elector is particularly concerned about welfare he or she would do best voting for the socialist party because their long-standing concern is a better guarantee that they will actually do something about it in government than other parties.

The same reasoning applies in reverse to traditional moral values. Christian democrats are always more concerned about these. Other parties may also respond but your best bet as a morally concerned elector is to vote for the Christians because they can be trusted to try to do something about moral decline.

Parties thus offer electors both choices and guarantees that their choices will be effective, on the basis of their record and ideology. They are inflexibly committed to certain priorities. Their inflexibility on these offers electors a choice between different programmes and also guarantees that the policies will be put into effect by the parties in government. Electors can select a Liberal party, for example, when they are worried about inflation and under-productivity and feel free market policies are needed. If they feel by the time of the next election that these are now threatening jobs and security, they can switch their vote to a communist or socialist party to slow down change. The parties themselves offer an array of different policies from which electors can choose according to circumstances.

Figure 12.1 provides an overview of this process. The parties' programmatic priorities cover the range of societal developments and problems. Where electors are affected and worried by a problem they can select the appropriate party programme. Electors thus vote for the parties whose programme best reflects their

Figure 12.1 The democratic policy process

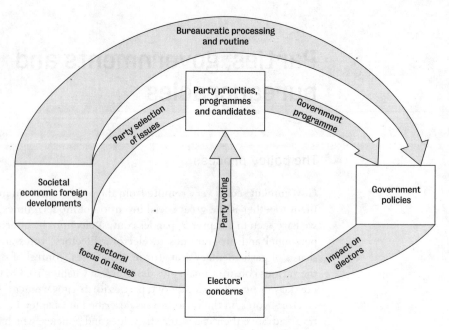

political preferences and their own estimates of social priorities. Parties go into government on the basis of their election programme. This is the only medium-term action plan they have got, and thus forms an indispensable basis for planning and co-ordinating government action, whether on their own or in collaboration with other parties.

Recent research shows that this summary of democratic policy-making has considerable validity, even though it leaves out important influences like the mass media, interest groups and social movements. Parties in the European countries as in other democracies do respond to problems and to public opinion by offering different policy priorities for action. They do carry these through reliably into government planning, in this way linking electors' preferences, as expressed through votes in elections, to what government actually does.

Of course, this is a rough and ready process operating at a broad political level, so it does not always work out perfectly in detail. Where a single party gets a majority and forms a government it has clearly gained or retained electoral approval so its programme has been broadly endorsed. The same applies to blocs and electoral alliances which form a government together. In a multi-party system, however, it may be that parties which *lost* electoral support enter the government because they are still important to coalition building. The most one can say is that some parties in the coalition will have gained votes electorally and will exert more internal influence because of it.

Another consideration in real-life politics is that winning parties often pick up items from losing party's platforms if they think they have a good point. This has happened particularly with regard to the welfare state in post-war European democracies. Socialist, communists and Christians constantly emphasize the need for welfare; other parties much less so. Whether or not these parties were in government, during the period from 1950–80 welfare and health programmes continued to expand (see Chapter 15).

This probably also reflected, at least in part, independent action by the bureau-

> BRIEFING 12.1
>
> **The party mandate, government legitimacy and authority**
>
> *Mandate* and *legitimacy* are two words you will often come across in discussions of democratic government. A party's *mandate* is its right and responsibility to carry through the policy programme which it put before electors at the previous election, and which attracted the votes which gave it the ability to form or enter government. This is, by and large, the idea lying behind the policy processes discussed in this section. *Legitimacy* is the recognition of your right to get something done and to ask for help to do it. Because its programme has been endorsed by the electorate, a government has a right, recognized by parliament and bureaucracy, to have it effected, whether by legislation or administrative action. This is because the electoral majority's verdict is final in democracies, and this gives the government *authority* – the right to be obeyed – within the area of its programme.

cracy (shown by the top arrow in Figure 12.1). As we shall see administrators are not simply neutral figures automatically carrying through government policies. They have their own views and have to plan for social needs, even if the government parties fail to pick these up. If the birth rate goes up one year, extra school accommodation will be needed five or six years on, regardless of what parties say. So the bureaucracy tackles a whole range of problems which parties often ignore, preferring to concentrate on the 'big' issues of economy, society and peace.

Party governments are thus not free agents, willing things to be done or not to be done, and having their wishes automatically fulfilled. They have to negotiate with and work through established bureaucracies. These are composed of permanent civil servants and administrative technicians who do not necessarily feel sympathy with the current government. In the rest of this chapter we examine how governments interact with the bureaucracy in Europe: how they try to get their policies implemented: and how the bureaucracy helps or hinders them. We go on to consider the ways in which bureaucrats themselves create and administer policy and how far they can be considered a unified organization separate from parties and governments as such. We begin by looking at the actual operation of party government and its interactions with bureaucracy.

Parties, cabinets and ministries

As we have seen, the predominance of political parties in European parliaments carries through into government. Governments are party governments (with the occasional exception of 'caretaker' and 'technical' administrations, appointed by the head of state, which may, however, have an implicit party bias). Even where parties are weak and fluid, as in Russia, persons appointed to government without initial party affiliations tend to group together as the 'party of government' against those outside it, and to fight the next election under a common political label.

Under parliamentary regimes, and most semi-presidential ones too, it is pre-existing parties, often with a long history, which enter office. Governments are defined by the parties which form them and by which nominee takes over the premiership and ministries.

Table 12.1   The relationship between party control of government ministries and fiscal policy for nineteen democracies, 1965–82[a]

Party family with most ministries in policy sector 2[b]	Fiscal policy aimed at avoiding unemployment (Keynesianism)	Cautious orthodox fiscal policies oriented to avoiding inflation	Cuts and withdrawal of government expenditure	Fiscal policies aimed at having a 'minimal state'	contol %	No. years in control
Conservative	33	25	0	42	100	12
Liberal	30	22	44	4	100	23
Religious	52	28	16	4	100	30
Socialist	66	24	0	10	100	38

Notes:
[a] Entries in the table are percentages of the years that a particular family type held the ministry overall democracies. The ones covered are most democracies of Western Europe plus Israel but omit Switzerland.
[b] The relevant ministries are Labour and Economy/Finance.
Source: Adapted from Budge and Keman (1993: 144–6).

The question of which party takes over which ministry is a very important one, central to the coalition negotiations described in the last chapter. Where a single party forms the government of course, whether as a majority or minority, it will take all the ministries. But in the more common case of coalition government, which ministry goes to whom is a key question, possibly more important than negotiations over the general policies the government will pursue.

This is so for several reasons. First, ministries have a place in the government's central policy-making body – the cabinet or council of ministers. The number of ministries a party holds is symbolic of its importance to the government. It could also be significant in increasing party influence within the government – provided that the cabinet does not just rubber-stamp decisions already made through party negotiations outside, or by a coalition committee; or is totally bound by a coalition agreement. If, in effect, parties negotiate as blocs, under the threat of one of them walking out and bringing down the coalition, then the actual voting strength of each within the cabinet is irrelevant.

As this is often the case, a more important reason for parties wanting to control ministries is their ability to influence policy by doing so. General policies and legislation are discussed and decided in cabinet (or in coalition negotiations). There remain, however, many points of detailed implementation which have to be decided at administrative level. In the Ministry of National Insurance for example this might involve deciding whether war widows are to be defined as those who lost husbands owing to causes connected with the war (for example, a wound which caused death twenty or thirty years after) or only as those who lost husbands during the war period itself owing to fighting. For a left-wing party seeking to extend benefits, or a right-wing one seeking to restrict them, such operational decisions are important in advancing their policy. Indeed, a strong link has been found between party control of particular ministries and expenditure in the related policy area, for many European countries.

Table 12.1 illustrates this for a very central area of government policy – management of money, credit, overall expenditure and taxation, collectively known as fiscal policy. The four main policy options governments have in this area are summarized at the top of the four columns of the table. Basically, governments can spend money in a depression so as to stimulate business activity and create jobs. This is one aspect of the economic stance known as Keynesianism, and is a natural reaction of parties of the left.

Table 12.2   Government ministries preferred by the main European party families, in order

Party families	Conservative	Liberal	Religious	Socialist	Agrarian	Ethnic-Nationalist
Government Ministries	Interior Foreign Affairs/ Defense Justice Agriculture Economy Education/Trade/ Industry/Commerce	Economy/Finance Justice Education Interior Trade/Industry/ Commerce	Religious Affairs Education Agriculture Social Affairs/ Health/Labour	Health/Social Affairs Economy Industry Education	Agriculture Fisheries	Regional Affairs Interior

As we see, socialists spent two-thirds of the time they held the appropriate ministries pursuing this type of policy and Christians less so, but still for more than half their tenure of relevant ministries. The liberals and conservatives on the right, however, spent a third or less of their tenure pursuing expansionary policies. They preferred instead to combat inflation by reining in fiscal policy or even went on to cut down state activities to 'get government out of people's lives'. Such policies were pursued by party holders of the ministry regardless of what overall government policy was. So one can see how important holding a ministry may be for a party's policy objectives.

Given their special ideologies and policy goals, specific ministries can thus become very attractive for particular types of party, as Table 12.1 shows. The party values and policies are the ones already specified for the various families in Table 9.1 above. Clearly, for a conservative party concerned above all with internal and external security, there are great attractions in having the Ministries of Internal and External Affairs, Defence and Justice. Socialists and Christians concerned with welfare and education will probably compete for these ministries if they are in coalition together, while liberals want education and finance. Where the party with similar preferences is not represented in a coalition the rival can take all the ministries it wants. If they are in coalition together the distribution will be settled by bargaining on the basis of their respective strengths.

Table 12.2 shows how the different party families value ministries differently in line with their preferred values, policies and support groups. It also shows which ministries they most want to have and which ones – at the bottom of their rankings – they would be prepared to trade to get the ones they most want. In line with their general priorities, conservative parties put order and security at the top of their lists of concerns, liberals economy and justice, and socialists the welfare-related ministries. Religious parties are naturally concerned with religious affairs but also with educating the young, the next generation of adherents. Agrarians want to serve primary producers (agriculture and fisheries) and regional and minority nationalist parties want to secure the ministries important in regional affairs. The last two types of party are more focused on one particular type of ministry than are other families, since they are also more concerned about one particular issue.

How this all works out we can see from a computer model of a European agrarian party's decisions about ministries (see Figure 12.2). As the most important thing for it is to get hold of the Ministry of Agriculture it will not join any coalition government which does not give it this ministry. However, if it is in a predominant position in the government it will take a lot of other ministries too. Even if it needs partners

Figure 12.2 How agrarian parties decide on what ministries to take in a coalition government

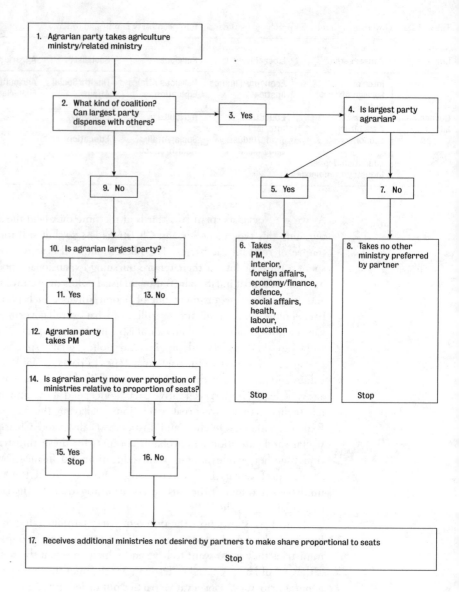

1. Agrarian party takes agriculture ministry/related ministry

2. What kind of coalition? Can largest party dispense with others?

3. Yes

4. Is largest party agrarian?

9. No

5. Yes

7. No

10. Is agrarian largest party?

6. Takes PM, interior, foreign affairs, economy/finance, defence, social affairs, health, labour, education

    Stop

8. Takes no other ministry preferred by partner

    Stop

11. Yes

13. No

12. Agrarian party takes PM

14. Is agrarian party now over proportion of ministries relative to proportion of seats?

15. Yes Stop

16. No

17. Receives additional ministries not desired by partners to make share proportional to seats

    Stop

but is still the largest party it will take the premiership as this generally goes to the largest party and gives it a general influence.

Each party familys' decision processes can be modelled in this way on the basis of their preferences in Table 12.2. Such modelling gives us a precise indication of what ministries each party will take in a particular type of government. Gaining control of the ministries it wants is a powerful inducement for a party to join a coalition, independently of the overall policies of the government. This is not necessarily (or even usually) because party leaders want the official salary, status and prestige associated with being a minister. It is because holding a ministry is another important way of getting party policies implemented. In general, parties will try to do this both at the general level, through the coalition agreement and government programme, and at a detailed administrative level within the ministry.

BRIEFING 12.2

Party bargaining about government ministries

Figure 12.1 is a 'flow diagram' which shows how one type of party (Agrarians) act on their preferences about ministries (Table 12.2) in forming a government. A flow diagram divides up their decision about participation into a large number of detailed questions. Depending on whether party decision-makers answer these positively (Yes) or negatively (No), they take different actions. Thus the absolute condition for the party to participate in the coalition is taking the Ministry of Agriculture. This gives it a central voice in the decisions that matter to it and to its core supporters (farmers and peasants). Participation without this ministry is just not worthwhile for an agrarian party.

If they are the largest party in the coalition the agrarian party will also take the premiership and whatever other ministries they can get to increase their general influence (which also, of course, strengthens their position in regard to agriculture). If the coalition partners can do without the agrarians, on the other hand, these will content themselves with agriculture alone. If they are essential to the coalition but not dominant, all parties in the coalition will generally receive a proportion of ministries equivalent to the proportion of seats they contribute. This is a fair rule of thumb everyone can agree on (though sometimes in two-party coalitions, the smaller party will insist on a 50–50 split, as its support is as essential as the larger partner's. This is noticeable in progressive-independence party coalitions in Iceland, for example). Once parties come up to their limit, however defined, the distribution stops.

The 'flow diagram' in Figure 12.2 is the basis for a computer programme which makes predictions about what parties will do about ministries under specified circumstances. It is supported by the facts. In 83 per cent of cases where an agrarian party entered coalitions in Western Europe between 1945 and 1989 it got the Ministry of Agriculture and related ministries like the Ministry of Fisheries. For more details see Budge and Keman, *Parties and Democracy* (Oxford, Oxford University Press, 1963) pp. 115–17.

Partly to keep a check on this, another party in a coalition may have the right to nominate a deputy to the ministry (in Austria and the Netherlands these are termed state secretaries, and they always come from another party than the minister's). Such a person may or may not prove an obstacle to the minister's programme. As the other party or parties interested in a ministry often have views on that policy area which are similar to those of the minister's party (for example, Christians and socialists on welfare, nationalists and conservatives on defence) they may well be able to work together quite happily.

One of the important consequences of parties having preferences for particular ministries is that if they take part in most governments they may control certain ministries almost permanently. An example of this is given in Table 12.3 for Italy, showing the extent to which the Christian democrats in their heyday 'occupied' ministries like the Ministry of the Interior and the Ministry of Education. Not only does the party generally hold the ministry but the same party nominee may stay continuously in the same office despite the rise and fall of successive governments. Thus in Italy during the 1970s and 1980s, the Christian democrat, Andreotti held the Foreign Ministry and his colleague Cossiga the Interior Ministry for periods of five to six years, despite the average life of a government being ten months!

Governmental instability may thus mask ministerial continuity – and vice versa! In British governments, which last four to five years, frequent reshuffles limit

Ministry	Number of times over 39 government ministries controlled by:					
	DC	PSI	PSDI	PRI	PLI	Independent
Premiership	37			2		
Vice-Premiership	8	5	4	2		
Foreign Affairs	32		3	2	2	
Interior	39					
Justice	28			5		
Defence	19	5	4	5		
Treasury	33		1	1		
Finance	19	6	7	3		
Budget	21	7	3	5		
Public Works	19	5	8	3		
Labour and Social Security	26	2	6			
Education	31	1		2	2	
Industry	27		4		4	
Nationalized Industries	23	5	1			
Agriculture	34					
Post	33		2			1
Health	14	6		6		
Transport	23	6	5		1	
Merchant Marine	29		4	3		
Foreign Trade	17	8	2	4		4
Tourism	17	5	3			1
South	19	5	2			
Culture	5		1	2		
Ministers Without Portfolio	74	11	14	5	4	

individual tenure of a ministry to an average of eighteen months. Stability and continuity are not always what they seem! The contrast is explained by the fact that the prime minister of a single-party majority government can move ministers around, or even dismiss them, without bringing the government down. This is impossible in a coalition where the distribution of ministries has been negotiated with the coalition partners and any attempt to move a party nominee will result in the collapse of the government. In general, however, it is ministers in presidentially nominated governments, independent of parliamentary approval, who enjoy the longest and most generally uninterrupted tenure of office.

The length of time individuals and parties hold a ministry is important from the point of view of shaping its outlook and policies. As we shall see below the civil servants in each ministry tend to develop a common set of ideas about policy and a shared outlook on the world. These are shaped by many influences: the advisers and specialists in the policy area: the research done there: interactions with colleagues: the interest groups who lobby the department (see Chapter 7 above). But an important influence is also of course the party which usually controls the ministry. Even when it is temporarily not in control, civil servants' views may continue to be shaped by the party ideology.

Another important consideration linked to length of individual tenure, is how far the minister can get new innovations accepted or pass legislative bills through parliament. It takes about six months to familiarize oneself with a ministry sufficiently well to draft good legislation or develop a programme. Then another six months are required to prepare it. It will then take yet another six months to a year to get this through parliament (given the normally crowded legislative programme). Unless a minister has at least two years in office, he or she will not be able to finalize his or her reforms and changes.

In this respect, British or Irish ministers contrast with Swiss federal councillors, who are constitutionally guaranteed a four-year tenure; or with ministers in Russia or the Ukraine, where presidential support guarantees a long term. Such ministerial stability is very important at the moment in Central and Eastern Europe, given the massive series of legislative and administrative changes needed to implement the free market, and the inertia of many bureaucracies inherited from the communist period.

In preparing his legislation or administrative measures the minister may have the help of political advisers – often organized in the form of a ministerial *cabinet* meeting regularly within the ministry. This is probably the most effective way to support his internal interventions. Or he may lack this altogether and rely on advice and help from his civil servants and permanent bureaucrats. They may be disposed to give help where the minister comes from the party which usually dominates the department, as they then tend to share the same views about policy. If he or she is a political outsider, however, the civil servants may be obstructive and even try to thwart him – possibly aided and abetted by his nominal deputy, the state secretary. Both situations occur quite frequently.

Under single-party government of course, ministers may have deputy ministers from their own party – sometimes five or six in number as in the large departments of state in Britain. While this renders the minister less isolated, the deputies will experience the same difficulties in getting to grips with a new department. Probably a *cabinet* of technical experts and consultants, brought in from outside, is the best way of empowering the politicians. But in many countries ministers lack them.

Such research as has been done on ministerial–civil servant relations indicate that it is a great advantage if the minister has a clear-cut programme for the policy area. Even unsympathetic officials find it hard to oppose this, particularly if it has figured in the party election programme and has in this sense been given a 'mandate' by voters.

Privatization programmes in Central and Eastern Europe have benefited from their initial overwhelming popular endorsement. They drew on detailed programmes made up by Western consultants and specialists and had general backing from the whole government. They thus developed a tremendous impetus which subsequent reactions against them, and even the replacement of neo-liberal parties by ex-communists, were unable to derail. The same might be said of privatizations in cases like Britain and Portugal, where the clearly specified goals of the programme and use of specialized consultants in banks, overcame whatever internal opposition there might have been from old-style bureaucrats.

In clashes with their civil servants, ministers cannot count totally upon the support of government colleagues. This is clear in the case of a coalition like the Dutch one of 1994, where the VVD oppose the socialists on many points. A minister may encounter opposition not only at cabinet level but also within the ministry, from the state secretary.

Less obviously, ministers in a single-party government may well be hampered by personal and policy rivalries. Ministers make their reputation by carrying through their programme and aggrandizing their ministries. For exactly the same reason, however, their Cabinet colleagues oppose them. Prestigious ministries are in short supply and where one minister is promoted another loses out. Compounding this, there are always two or three contenders for the leadership and premiership in a single-party government. The other ministers are grouped round them. As there is a continual struggle for dominance between such factions, a minister belonging to one may find the others opposing him simply to weaken his faction and the person he supports as the potential prime minister.

If all this makes governments seem like a seething mass of political and personal rivalries, it is quite right. Yet only to emphasize this side is to distort the picture. Members of a coalition have their agreed programme to carry through – at least to some extent, if they are to deliver what they promised. This common purpose is even more evident in the case of a single-party government. The members of any government, however, have an interest in its success. They have agreed a programme and they need to carry at least some of it through if they are to maintain a credible public profile.

The role of a prime minister is to build on this common purpose to secure at least minimal cohesiveness in a coalition and enforce unity in a single-party government. In the process of doing this he or she is likely to back the ministers whose projects are most obviously related to the party programme (or government agreement). Both internally and externally, therefore, a minister is most likely to be effective through having a clearly conceived project with the backing of his or her party. But the minister will still depend very much on the efficiency and capacity of the bureaucrats who staff the ministry. It is therefore to them that we turn in the next section.

■ Ministries and bureaucrats

We have already made a lot of references to ministries, as objects of party control and a power base for party representatives within government. Ministries are more than that, however. They are the units into which bureaucracy and administration are divided up and within which the average civil administrator will spend most of his or her working life. They are also the agencies to which the preparation and implementation of specific pieces of legislation will be delegated, so that they crucially affect the success of party and government programmes.

Ministries exist because administrative tasks have to be separated and delegated to specific bodies if they are to be made manageable. When government was essentially about preventing internal revolts and waging foreign wars, all administrative tasks could be considered by the Royal Council and discharged collectively. Even then, however, there were specialists in finance who had their own department. The eighteenth-century state had to have separate departments at least for the navy, army, and for finance. With the enormous growth of government activity, specialization has now become necessary across the board. The larger European bureaucracies are now divided into something like 20–30 major ministries, departments and agencies (the three terms are used almost interchangeably).

Table 12.4 compares important ministries and departments from countries at different ends of Europe and with very different traditions – Britain and Russia. In light of this, it is interesting to see how similar the major ministries are: Foreign and Internal Affairs (in Britain called the Home Office), Justice (the Lord Chancellor's Department), Defence, Finance (Treasury), Environment, Labour (Employment), Education and so on. Both countries also present a bit of a hodgepodge, with no clear reason why one department should be an agency or committee and another ministry.

Ministries may vary in size from quite small bodies of 50–300 civil servants to enormous administrations employing 200–300 thousand people. In the Russian

Table 12.4 Central ministries and agencies in Britain and Russia

Major departments of the British government	Major departments of the Russian government
Ministry of Agriculture, Fisheries and Food	Fuel and Energy
Crown Prosecution Service	Economy
HM Customs and Excise	Science and Technology Policy
Ministry of Defence	Agriculture and Food
Office of Electricity Regulation (OFFER)	Defense
Department of Employment and Education	Health and Medical Industry
Department of the Environment	Finance
ECGD (Export Credit Guarantee Department)	Education
Foreign and Commonwealth Office	Protection of the Environment and Natural Resources
Office of Gas Supply (OFGAS)	Justice
Department of Health	Transport
Department of National Heritage	External Economic Relations
Home Office	Culture
Central Office of Information	Internal Affairs
Board of Inland Revenue	Communications
Law Officers' Departments	Co-operation with CIS States
Lord Chancellor's Department	Social Security
Ordnance Survey	Nationalities Affairs and Regional Policy
Overseas Development Administration	Foreign Affairs
Parliamentary Counsel	Means of Communication
Paymaster General's Office	Labor
Office of Population Censuses and Surveys	Civil Defense, Emergencies and Relief of Natural Disasters
HM Procurator General and Treasury Solicitor's Department	Atomic Energy
Serious Fraud Office	State Committees (*gosudarstvennye komitety*) of the Russian Federation:
Department of Social Security	Architecture and Construction
HMSO (Her Majesty's Stationery Office)	Anti-Monopolies Policy and Support for New Economic Structure
Central Statistical Office	Higher Education
Office of Telecommunications (OFTEL)	State Security
Board of Trade	
Department of Transport	
HM Treasury	
Office of Water Services (OFWAT)	

Note: In the case of Northern Ireland, the Secretary of State for Northern Ireland is responsible for law and order and for a range of services administered through the Northern Ireland Departments. Scotland enjoys wide administrative autonomy through the Scottish Office's five major departments. Wales enjoys less administrative autonomy although certain aspects of government are administered through the Welsh Office.
Source (for Britain): Britain: An Official Handbook 1992, London, HMSO, 1992, pp. 47–51.

Federation collecting revenue, including taxes, occupied 835,000 people in 1995. Differences in size often stem from the fact that one ministry has a field administration – a network of offices and local agencies – while another relies on other agencies, or on territorial and regional governments to do local administration for them. Central civil servants administering education in Britain are small in number because schools are either autonomous or administered by local governments. This contrasts with colleagues in the Department of Social Security, where they have local branches to make benefit payments throughout the country. Because of different institutional arrangements at local level, some labour intensive ministries in Britain are not as labour intensive in Russia. Welfare in all the ex-Soviet systems for example was organized through the factory and the workplace, rather than through local offices (see Chapter 15). The collapse of many state enterprises means that welfare and other services have to be provided by other means, if at all.

This perhaps accounts for the increasing number of Federal bureaucrats in Russia – estimated at over three million at the beginning of 1995 and growing fast. The suspicion is, however, that the swelling numbers represent a migration of former

> **BRIEFING 12.3**
>
> **Russian bureaucracy**
>
> From the beginning of the modern Russian state, round about 1,700, Russian bureaucrats constituted a separate estate, apart from and above the general population. Bureaucrats were rewarded with rank and land for carrying on state administration. Mostly they were left free to exploit the local population provided they met state levies of money, goods and men for the army.
>
> The original service nobility was replaced by a more technical and professional bureaucracy in the nineteenth century, but the tradition of regarding a bureaucratic position as a secure job, or an opportunity for personal aggrandisement, remained. In this respect, Russian bureaucracy is a more extreme example of similar attitudes prevailing throughout Southern and Eastern Europe. Even honest officials saw their job as first and foremost to carry through policies decided by the central state, without regard to the wishes of the local population.
>
> This simply continued under communist rule. The difference was that the bureaucracy was infiltrated by and closely controlled by the Communist Party, which offered a parallel career to the most able bureaucrats through the party hierarchy. With the collapse of the old system the bureaucracy continues largely unsupervised, so it is generally less efficient than before. Above all, it offers secure, if badly paid, jobs to those unable to get them elsewhere.

Communist Party and Soviet bureaucrats into the Russian administration in order to secure themselves a job, rather than anything to do with efficient transfer of functions from local to national level.

Concern has been expressed in the West, above all in Britain, at the growth of bureaucracy seen as a non-productive organization hampering real enterprise. Strenuous attempts were made by British Conservatives from 1979 to 'hive off' or privatize government functions (even non-obvious ones like prisons), reduce numbers of civil servants, and cut government expenditure. In part 'reducing bureaucrats' is a question of definition. If a nationalized industry is sold, its workers cease to count as being in public employment and that cuts the nominal number of civil servants. But these were industrial workers and hardly bureaucrats anyway.

Serious and sustained attempts have been made, however, to cut numbers in the bureaucracy itself. This resulted in a reduction from 700,000 in 1979 to 590,000 in the 1990s. Attempts to cut overall government expenditure, on the other hand, have been unsuccessful. At most it has been level pegging in real terms. The paradox of neo-liberal policy is to seek efficiency by reducing numbers of employees in private as well as public concerns. But this results in them ceasing to pay taxes and drawing welfare benefits instead, thus keeping up levels of public expenditure. Unless benefits are totally withdrawn, which would cause more social disorder than the government would like to handle, this paradox of public expenditure will remain.

In a curious way, the Netherlands has for most of this century anticipated 'hiving off'. Its system of giving as much autonomy as possible to the 'social pillars' (for example, churches and trade unions) meant that welfare, health and education were administered through committees representing these – separately for each pillar. The Netherlands combines social autonomy and devolution with a French-style field

BRIEFING 12.4

Tuesday morning at the Ministry of the Interior

'On the face of it, the scene at the Ministry of the Interior the following Tuesday morning was calculated to gladden the hearts of all those who despaired of the grotesque over-manning and under achievement of the government bureaucracy, a number roughly equal to those who had failed to secure a cushy . . . post of their own. Not only were a significant minority of the staff at their desks, but the atmosphere was one of intense and animated activity. The only snag was that little or none of this activity had anything to do with the duties of the ministry.

In the ministerial suite on the top floor, where the present incumbent and his coterie of under-secretaries presided, the imminent collapse of the present government coalition had prompted a frantic round of consultations, negotiations, threats and promises as potential contenders jockeyed for position. On the lower floors . . . it was business as usual. The range of services on offer included a fax bureau, an agency for Filipino maids, two competing protection rackets, a Kawasaki motorcycle franchise, a video rental club, a travel agent and a city-wide courier service, to say nothing of Madam Beta, medium, astrologer, sorcerer, cards and palms read, the evil eye averted, talismans and amulets prepared. One of the most flourishing of these enterprises was situated in the Administration section on the ground floor, where Tania Biacis ran an agency which supplied speciality food items [using the ministry's fax and telephones to communicate with her international clients]' Michael Dibdin, *CABAL* (London, Faber and Faber, 1992), p. 41.

This is a fictional description, but not too exaggerated the further one moves south and east in Europe. From the viewpoint of the individual civil servant, bureaucratic positions are primarily secure jobs, where there is no need to go beyond mechanical routine (indeed it may be dangerous to do otherwise). From this basis second jobs and money-making enterprizes can be pursued to make up for the low pay.

administration, where the governor of a province acts as local delegate for all the central ministries. This is true for all the countries, including France itself, which have adopted the centralized prefectoral system (see Chapter 13). In Germany and Switzerland on the other hand the states do practically all the local administration, leaving federal ministries relatively small.

Whatever the division of functions, the central core of any central ministry at the civil service level is likely to consist of a limited number of high-level administrators who devise and implement policy in close contact with the political head of the department and/or his deputies and political advisers. In some countries, like Ireland, a relatively sharp distinction is drawn between permanent civil servants, who will serve under different coalitions and ministers of different parties, and the political personnel, who come and go with governments. In other countries the distinction is more blurred. In France and Belgium, both 'political' and administrative appointees are likely to have received a technocratic training and may have switched between the civil service and political and business appointments several times. Presidentially nominated governments tend to draw on technocrats and politicians impartially, and may even upgrade civil servants to be ministers. So the distinction between the two becomes very blurred. This is also true under a long-serving administration such as the Conservatives in Britain (1979–97) or the liberal-Christian coalition in Germany (1983–97). Inevitably, after working together a long time with particular politicians, top civil servants tend to think like ministers.

> **BRIEFING 12.5**
>
> **Going by the book: the case of the prison governor's secretary**
>
> Nominations to all Civil Service jobs in Italy (including universities) are made through national competitions called 'Concorsi'. The practice is borrowed from France and is meant to ensure that all Italian citizens have an equal chance wherever they come from in the country. One small Roman woman had been through several such competitions and was finally successful in being appointed provisionally as secretary to the Governor of the State Penitentiary of Arezzo, an isolated mountain town in Tuscany. It was very different from Rome, but a job was a job. She persevered and did well, and was finally nominated by her boss for the permanent position.
>
> This involved filling in a form with her personal details. Unfortunately, the Civil Servant in the Ministry of the Interior at Rome who dealt with her case, noted a rule which said everybody in the Prison Service had to be at least 1.70 meters (5 feet 6 inches) tall. No matter that the regulation dated from the Fascist dictatorship in the 1930s when the service was all male and was obviously meant to apply to those in direct contact with prisoners. A rule is a rule, so the poor Roman lady had to leave though she had given perfect satisfaction. It would be no surprise if the rule were still on the books, and still being applied by the men at the ministry.

Particularly if they can see retirement looming before the end of the government, they may become partisan in their approach.

Ministries tend to be structured hierarchically, with a formal system of appointment procedures, grades and salary separating those at the top from those at the middle. (The ones at the bottom do not count for policy-making purposes, being engaged in more routine administration.) However, the formal hierarchy is always likely to be cut across by ministers and their advisers, unless the civil service is very conscious of itself as a separate body and erects barriers against this. There are really two choices open to a career civil servant. One is to maximize the security and privileges of the position. Other countries do not go as far as to offer the special status and privileges enjoyed by German civil servants (*beamte*) or by Russian (*chinovnik*). But they are still considerable. The individual can seek to safeguard them by making it a first concern never to step out of line, to do things always by the book and never without full formal authorization. In this way he or she can avoid extra responsibility and look forward to early retirement with full pension rights.

Particularly in the Mediterranean countries, where rules and procedures are very complex, and any irregularity might be a subject of judicial enquiry, such an attitude makes for extreme bureaucratic inertia and delay. As an old Spanish saying has it: 'if death came from Madrid we would all be immortal!' Given the experiences of living under police regimes in Eastern Europe such attitudes are also pervasive there.

Bureaucratic slowness and reluctance to do anything not explicitly envisaged under the rules can place intolerable burdens on business, for example money arriving years late; licences and permits indefinitely blocked. Under such bureaucratic systems therefore there is a premium on short-cutting procedures. This might be done through direct bribery of civil servants. A commoner approach, however, is to work through politicians. They often have the influence and contacts to speed up the decision process, in return for financial and other contributions either to themselves or their party. Such contributions may be recognized as legitimate – where parties

BRIEFING 12.6

Families in Russian Bureaucracy

Under the old Soviet system, penalties for bureaucrats or factory managers who failed to fulfil the targets assigned to them in the State's Five Year Plan could be very severe. At the least they could be sacked. Under Stalin they might be put on trial and shot for economic sabotage. Within the locality everyone was encouraged to report back to the centre on everyone else: the bureaucrats on managers, the local Communist Party Secretary on the bureaucrats, the Secret Police on the Party Secretary, and so on. It was a game of dog-eat-dog, which the central authorities encouraged.

However, the local men could maximize their own security by getting together and agreeing to cover up for each other. This ensured that only favourable reports reached the centre, which had no independent means of checking their truth. Such bureaucratic 'families' could also extend to the centre. Often the local men had patrons in Moscow too, thus extending their cover up. In Russia today, the old bureaucratic 'families' are less necessary for personal security but still useful for personal advantage and promotion, as well as for benefiting from the proceeds of privatization.

are not subsidized by the state they need to get support from somewhere. They are common practice in Britain, for example. But they can easily slide over into corrupt practices as in the revelations in Italy about Tangentopoli (Bribesville) – the development of a system in the 1970s and 1980s of organized payoffs to parties on every public contract and transaction.

In this situation the individual bureaucrat can make another career choice than simply following routine, with higher rewards associated with correspondingly greater risks. He or she can cultivate contacts with politicians, helping them short-circuit the bureaucratic process in a more or less irregular way and receiving accelerated promotion, or offices within the minister's gift, as a reward. The actions that are taken may simply be necessary to get things done, but again can rapidly slide over to illegality (for example, to avoid lengthy delays, a computer contract can be awarded to one particular firm with only a pretence, if that, at competitive bidding). The action is high risk for bureaucrats since if political protection is withdrawn they may be exposed to investigative journalism and prosecution. On the other hand, if the political patrons prospers they may carry the bureaucrats in their wake.

It is important to realize that excessive legal formalism in a bureaucracy itself breeds the impulse – sometimes the necessity – to get quick even if irregular decisions. The ideal would be to strike a balance between flexibility and proper legal safeguards. Of course that is easier said than done. The way in which the countries of northwest Europe have attempted to do this is by creating a civil service with a strong professional ethos oriented to achieving collective goals, which are only secondarily associated with personal advancement.

This combines with the division of the administration into ministries to create a certain competitiveness to achieve common departmental objectives. Individual civil servants find themselves in a ministry where they will spend most if not all their working lives. The ministry will have certain priorities. These are partly given by its function – the Ministry of Education must put school building high on its agenda and defend this priority against those of the Department of Transport for more road-building or those of the Ministry of Defence for more arms.

Just like the political head of the ministry, the individual civil servant receives recognition to the extent that he or she promotes the Ministry's priorities or defends its position. In this way the desire for personal advancement is harnessed to the achievement of collective goals, buttressed by association with a group of colleagues who generally share the 'departmental view' and participate collectively in achieving it. The fact that each ministry takes a differing view on governmental priorities, and tries to promote its position, often leads to clashes within the administration. These may range from frankly adversarial and conflictual as in Britain, differences of emphasis within an overall plan as in France, or an opening to public debate and consensual resolution as in Scandinavia.

In Britain, the essential assumption, in the civil service as in the law (see Chapter 14), is that no final truth or totally satisfactory solution is to be found to any problem. However, the clash of opposing views will expose the weak and strong points of a case. Hence administrative decision-making is best organized through a series of committees in which representatives of the opposing ministries argue with each other. If they cannot make a decision this goes to a higher committee right up to the level of the cabinet, the highest committee of government. Given the obsessive secrecy of British administration, in which access to information is used as a basis of power, this battle is fought out almost entirely between civil servants and their associated interest groups until politicians get involved at the very top (but only if the civil servants cannot reach a compromise).

While differences between ministries also exist in France, they are muted by the generally shared belief that an optimal solution can be found in the context of an overarching state plan. The fact that civil servants come from a very precisely defined technological elite helps this recognition. Moreover, there is also likely to *be* an overarching plan, lacking in Britain, which relates the different ministries' priorities. Thus, extension of the rail network is likely to be considered in relation to new roads, and both used as instruments for regional development.

The generally more powerful position of parliament in the Nordic countries, which enhances its powers of administrative scrutiny and policy initiation, means that debate on policy and administration can never be confined wholly, as in Britain, to civil servants and professional politicians. Debate there is, but it is likely to be publicly conducted through a Royal Commission and/or parliamentary committees. Moreover, it does not have the adversarial tone of Britain since great care is taken to build as wide a consensus as possible.

Each of these ways of handling bureaucratic conflict has its merits and its defects. British adversarial debate is good at uncovering strengths, weaknesses and hidden assumptions of proposals. Too often, however, more weaknesses are uncovered than anything else and no proposal gets adopted. This in turn, leads to attempts like Margaret Thatcher's in the 1980s to cut through the system, promoting civil servants who are 'one of us' and allowing no debate on ill-thought-out ideas like the poll tax (which shifted local taxation from property to people).

In seeking a consensus, Scandinavian methods, like the British, may lead to stalemate, delay, or vacuous compromises. While French technological planning may avoid these, it is often not sufficiently critical of its own assumptions (the rush into nuclear power after 1970, ignoring long-term structural weaknesses of the technology, may be a case in point). The great weakness of French planning is totally ignoring popular reactions to its projects. This can provoke great explosions of popular feeling, which put the regime in crisis, notably in 1968.

BRIEFING 12.7

Max Weber's 'ideal-type' of rational-legal bureaucracy

Max Weber was perhaps the most influential social scientist of the early twentieth century. He saw society modernizing itself by becoming more bureaucratic, that is organizing its activities so that they are efficient and impersonal. This implies creating a bureaucracy with the following characteristics:

- a hierarchy of command
- salaried officials who are paid by the state
- authority coming only from position in the hierarchy
- appointments made on the basis of competence
- strict rules which determine individual decisions
- record-keeping, so that the organization can keep track of what it has done and refer to rules and precedents.

No real-life bureaucracy can function exactly like this 'ideal type'. But to the extent that it does it can be described as rational and efficient. Unfortunately, actual experience shows that bureaucracies functioning in this way may often produce bad decisions, like the Italian bureaucracy in the case of the prison governor's secretary cited above. Mechanical application of rules, and refusal to take responsibility at the lower levels, may produce decisions which are neither rational nor efficient in a broader sense.

■ Bureaucratic hierarchy or bureaucratic pluralism?

The traditional concept of a bureaucracy is of an hierarchical organization, operating according to fixed rules and regulations which it applies scrupulously to particular cases. The officials at the bottom are really no more than implementors of policies passed down to them from the top. The less they exercise their individual initiative the better, since if every local office made different kinds of decisions the results would be chaos, and people could vary their tax rates or welfare benefits at will by going from one area to another.

In order to secure uniformity over the area they are administering, bureaucracies should so far as possible have rules which state what to do in every conceivable case. Where a decision is to be made that is not covered by the rules it should be passed up the hierarchy, resolved, and promulgated as an additional rule for all to apply in similar cases which come up. There should be clear lines of command and decision so that everyone knows who they are responsible to. Information and questions about doubtful cases should be passed up and authoritative decisions and rules should come down.

This 'ideal-type' of a 'rational-legal' bureaucracy was specified by Max Weber, a turn of the century German sociologist. It has been a highly influential way of viewing bureaucracy ever since, often cited as though it were the last word on the subject. However, it is recognizably an idealized picture of what German imperial bureaucracy aimed at achieving in the last quarter of the nineteenth century. So it does have its limitations, some of which have been frequently pointed out. For example, it hardly fits with the picture of inter-ministerial competition and political penetration of the civil service which we have drawn from the European experience in the last section.

The question is however, whether this is a good or a bad thing? Does the fact that European bureaucracies do not meet Weberian standards indicate that they need extensive reform to put them on the right track? Or does this represent a realistic adaptation to developments a century later on, which require something more from bureaucracies than obsessive pursuit of routine?

Perhaps the most telling argument against the Weberian specifications for a rational efficient bureaucracy, often cited by Italian specialists, is that it fits Italian bureaucratic practices pretty well! As those are neither rational nor efficient, this indicates that Weber's prescription for a perfect bureaucracy is fundamentally flawed. At the very least we can say that actual practice which does not conform exactly to the ideal type is not automatically wrong.

Bureaucratic practice in Europe conforms to the Weberian model most closely not in the way it operates but in the way personnel are recruited on the basis of competence (with one major exception we shall note below). In most countries recruitment is through a general exam which all persons with a University or comparable training are entitled to sit. 'Competence' may be defined more or less broadly. In France, for example, it will have been necessary to go to one of the specialized *Grandes Écoles*, or associated university institutes, for relatively intense instruction before taking the civil service exam. EU structures broadly follow the French model.

In Germany by contrast all university graduates can take a state examination which qualifies them for entry to the civil service whether or not they choose to go into it. Actual recruitment to the civil service is in most countries highly centralized. In Germany and Switzerland, however, where most civil servants work for Länder and Cantons, personnel are recruited locally, though under fairly standardized national rules and procedures. Scandinavia is unusual, in that the separate agencies within central government, which enjoy a fair degree of autonomy, recruit directly from the pool of qualified people. As in Britain there is little specialized training for the job in Scandinavia, either pre- or post-entry. The ethos of the civil service is to have generalists, who can turn their hands to any administrative task, rather than specialist training for a particular function and Ministry. This is in spite of the fact that civil servants will generally spend most of their career inside one ministry.

The 'generalists' recruited to bureaucracies tend increasingly to be those that have a law degree however. This is true even in Britain, where civil service entry used to be dominated by classicists from Oxford and Cambridge. Law is increasingly regarded as a general administrative qualification. This, combined with the great expansion in graduate numbers and the limited professional openings available for lawyers, accounts for the increasing numbers of them going into the civil service (in Sweden for example around two-thirds of law graduates).

Though these social and institutional factors may act to favour some types of recruit over others, entry and promotion in most European countries are not conclusively closed against anyone with the requisite qualifications. The great exception was the Soviet system, which has been responsible for placing most of the bureaucrats currently in office in Russia and Central and Eastern Europe. The Soviets operated on the basis of a Nomenklatura system. The Nomenklatura was a) a list of bureaucratic and administrative posts; b) a secret list of nominees already vetted as loyal by the communist party. Although nominally distinct from the state bureaucracy, the communist party organization at the appropriate level actually nominated candidates for every vacant post and ensured (through its nominees in appropriate committees) that they got appointed. There was thus no pretence of 'objective' criteria being applied to bureaucratic or indeed any other type of appointment. What mattered was being acceptable to the party, which came to mean having a powerful patron in its central apparatus. This system operated throughout the Soviet sphere of influence up to 1990. It was less pervasive in its effects outside the old USSR, however, where it had to compete with the professional ethos of bureaucrats inherited from the interwar period. In the 1970s and 1980s technocratic governments wanted more competence and expertise from the civil service than one could get from party appointees.

In Russia, Ukraine and Belarus, however, not only are the communist apparatchiks still in office, but they are appointing others in their own image without any regard to regular procedures. This is indicated by the massive increase in the numbers of the Russian bureaucracy since 1991. It is now seventeen times greater than the old Soviet bureaucracy, despite there being 130 million people less to administer. From 1994–5 government expenditure as a whole grew in Russia by 74 per cent. Not only are former communist bureaucrats entrenched in state administration. They also dominate parliament, the president's circle and have migrated to business and industry, helped by bureaucratic 'family' connections.

A press release to *Izvestiya* of 7 September 1995, summarizing a speech of President Yeltsin to the Russian Civil Service Academy, is instructive about the current situation:

Outlining the ailments of the bureaucratic apparatus (its non-professionalism, its uncontrolled nature, lack of co-ordination, its corruption), the President noted the need to form a legal basis for the civil service. He announced that a decision had been taken to create a Council on Civil Service Matters, the Council to be accountable to the President.

Boris Yeltsin also considers it necessary to work out a series of normative documents, with the aim of raising the effectiveness of the work of civil servants, [and of] strengthening guarantees for their social security.

The President called upon his audience at the Academy to assist in formulating a conception of a state cadres policy.

One need not endorse the Weberian model in its entirety to agree that the Russian situation is undesirable and gives ample scope for nepotism and corruption. Some of these problems stem from the very transition to pluralism and democracy, which involved a breakdown in the old repressive structures that at least gave some cohesiveness to the bureaucracy.

One of these has already been mentioned – the Nomenklatura system that itself was simply the most obvious manifestation of the constant surveillance of the state bureaucracy by the parallel bureaucracy of the communist party. Another was the subordination of the entire state administrative structure to the requirements of the five year plans. Above the routine bureaucracy was the Central Planning Office (GOSPLAN) and its affiliates for each industrial sector. These had the responsibility for working out a five year plan for economic development in every area, detailed down to the level of each factory and farm. All normal bureaucratic activity was subordinated to this and individuals who did not meet objectives were liable to demotion if not worse.

The inefficiencies and evasions of Soviet-era planning were notorious (see Briefing

12.6 on bureaucratic 'families' above). It was, and is, particularly deficient in food distribution and agricultural management. (The classic assessment of the Soviet harvest is 'worse than last year, better than next year'.) These weaknesses, however, make it easy to overlook its very real strengths. It was after all the system that took the Soviet economy from agriculture to an advanced industrial base in thirty years (1930–60) industrializing the Central and Eastern European economies at the same time. It produced the armaments to sustain the key Soviet role in the Second World War; and nuclear and rocket technology thereafter. It even accompanied these with a modest expansion of consumer goods in the later post-war period.

Centralized planning worked when it had one overriding objective, such as 'increase steel production'; 'make tanks'; 'produce a nuclear bomb', and was backed by ruthless repression so that the inefficient were imprisoned or shot. It failed when its objectives became more diffuse and the terror slackened. It then lacked real sanctions to enforce compliance at the lower levels. The situation outlined by Yeltsin evolved over the last thirty years of the Soviet regime and in many ways has just been brought into the open by democracy. The same problem remains: the lack of effective controls and even of accurate information about what is going on at the lower levels and in the localities.

A possible response is to emphasize hierarchy and adherence to a fixed set of rules – the very Weberian stance taken by President Yeltsin in the press release cited above. Were the bureaucracy to be engaged simply in the traditional, limited activities of the early nineteenth-century state – enforcing order, applying laws, collecting taxes – this might be an adequate response. Such functions might indeed be carried on within a well-established body of rules.

The trouble is that modern bureaucracies, in both East and West, are engaged in a wide range of activities which cannot be reduced to rules or routine and which often have no precedents to guide them. In all countries the bureaucracy has been heavily engaged in industrial and economic development. In France and Italy, this has involved plans which approached traditional Soviet ones in their blanket coverage of the national economy, though they set indicative targets rather than ones rigidly worked out and enforced in detail. Elsewhere, the problem has been what to do about excessive production of steel, for example, or how to run down declining sectors like shipbuilding and textiles. There are no precedents or routines to adopt in these cases. Decisions are as much political as technocratic. If the strategic decision is taken by politicians, civil servants still have to work out the details, without precedents or binding rules.

The same applies to environmental policy or fiscal management. In health administration choices have to be made between buying high technology to prolong the lives of acute cases or improving public health in general. Such choices can hardly be routine or standardized. To pretend that they are is usually a political ploy to deflect attention from the choices that actually are made.

It is also true, with the enormous growth of administration in modern European countries, that the very distinction between administration and administered is itself getting blurred. Traditional views of bureaucracy, like Weber's, see it as a group of people set apart from the rest of civil society by their service to the state. As we pointed out in Chapter 7 however, bureaucracies often rely on bodies such as professional associations and trade unions to administer themselves, or at any rate to provide the information essential to administering the sector. The interest groups

BRIEFING 12.8

The quango

A 'quango' is a 'quasi-non-governmental organization' – so-called because set up by governments and funded by public money, but operated independently of the bureaucracy. They are an attempt to distance some important and politically sensitive public function from direct government control. Perhaps the best known quango is the British Broadcasting Corporation (BBC) which, for much of its history, has been funded by public money but (in theory) is independent of the government of the day. In other words, quangos are set up on the grounds that (a) some public body is necessary, but (b) that this body should not be controlled by government.

Quangos proliferated in all sorts of policy areas in Britain under the Conservative governments of Margaret Thatcher. They came to be collectively influential and to spend a good deal of public money. They were also widely criticized on the grounds that (a) they were not accountable to the general public, that (b) they were run by unelected officials, and that (c) the government appointed political sympathizers to them.

often ally with 'their' ministry or department to fight rival departments and their clients, both within and outside bureaucratic channels. This destroys any conception of rational bureaucracy as an ordered hierarchy operating as an autonomous force inside the national society.

Such a conception is undermined even further when interest group members are co-opted on to nominated bodies, outside the regular civil service, to run a particular service such as health delivery or mile production. The later post-war period has seen an enormous growth in such 'quasi non-governmental organizations' – the notorious 'quangos'.

Modern administration also depends on delegating many of its tasks to those it is administering – as for example with self-assessment of taxes, or filling in claims for benefits. The ordinary citizens who do this are totally outside the hierarchy. All these developments have fostered a reaction in Europe during the last twenty years against bureaucratic centralization, hierarchy and planning. The key to efficiency has been seen as the adoption of business practices. As far as possible, bureaucratic relationships should be changed and modelled on those prevailing in the free market. Several of the European countries have gone quite far along this road, while others have paid it at least lip service. Such developments are potentially very far-reaching for the whole conduct of public administration in Europe. How they have actually been conceived and implemented we shall see in the next section.

The business revolution in bureaucracy

The evident troubles of the Soviet systems from the 1970s onwards produced a sharp reaction in Western Europe in favour of capitalism and democracy. The two were seen as interlinked, and based on the freedom of the individual to make his or her own choices. These could involve voting for a particular kind of government through the processes outlined in the preceding chapter. Or they could be directed at buying what you wanted rather than having choices predetermined for you through centralized planning. The way in which goods become available in Western economics was

BRIEFING 12.9

Capitalism and the mixed economy

The term 'capitalism' refers to a particular form of economic and social organizations which contrasts with feudalism, in the past, and with both communism and socialism in contemporary times. It is a controversial term and often used in a loose and ideological way. It implies that most of the economy is in the hands of people who seek profit, that most property is owned by private individuals or interests, and that a more or less unrestricted market is the way in which the supply of goods and services is organized to meet demand.

In the nineteenth century, capitalism took a *laissez-faire* form in which governments played a minimal role. But as the twentieth century progressed most Western European states adopted a mixed form of capitalism in which state regulation, state, support for welfare and some state owned enterprises are mixed with market or capitalist or profit seeking firms. Capitalists believe in a market economy which is relatively unrestricted and uncontrolled by the state, and which has the smallest possible public sector. Sometimes this is now called the liberal or neo–liberal or free market position. Communists, in contrast, believe in state control and ownership of the economy – the 'command economy'. Most people are between these extremes and believe in a mixed economy with both state and private sectors. There is much argument, of course, about the nature of the mix, which particular economic functions should be public or private, and how public control should be exercised. This question is at the heart of party competition and left–right differences in the European democracies.

through firms and producers finding out what consumers wanted and trying to provide it for them, rather than first deciding what they should have through an integrated system of national planning. Economic freedom in this sense was seen as an essential concomitant of political freedom. If consumer choice were abolished political choice would have to be restricted too. Otherwise the populace would use it to press for economic freedom again.

Capitalist democracy seemed to have justified itself by providing the economic prosperity and political freedom which bureaucratic planning had failed to do in the East. This triggered off a reaction in the West not just against full centralized planning but even against the idea of a mixed economy, which had been generally accepted from around 1945–80. The mixed economy was a system in which certain strategic areas of the economy (energy and communications for example) were controlled by the state so as to produce the best management of these crucial resources. At the same time the government planned its economic and financial policies so as to reduce unemployment and inflation and possibly to reduce social inequalities (see Chapter 16).

The economic difficulties of the 1970s seemed to indicate that even this degree of government intervention had failed. The solution, particularly to parties of the right, seemed to lie in scaling down ambitious interventionist plans, thus freeing business to make the optimal use of resources in response to consumer preferences. The words of Ronald Reagan, President of the United States during most of the 1980s, found an echo with many Europeans: 'government is not the solution, it is the problem'.

Closer to home, Europeans found an example in the activities of Margaret Thatcher, Conservative Prime Minister of Britain during the same period. Thatcher saw in the organization and size of the British bureaucracy a major brake on the development of business. She and her governments dealt with this in four principal ways:

1. Many sectors previously owned by government were 'privatized', that is turned into private businesses or sold to business. Steel, coal, oil, water, electricity, gas, transport – all these and many other sectors were simply sold off.
2. Many government services which did not make profits were 'contracted out' in an arrangement whereby business contracted to run the service to certain standards for an agreed price. Such arrangements covered areas from accounting and catering to prisons.
3. Government agencies were carved out of the old ministries to run specific services, such as pension payments. Such agencies, like private businesses, had a contractual relationship with their sponsor specifying the money to be paid to them and what they would do in return. They were modelled on a business enterprise rather than a hierarchical bureaucracy.
4. Wherever possible agencies were encouraged to compete with each other for the supply of services. The intention was to set up an 'internal market' even where a full free market could not be created. The best example of this was in the National Health Service where doctors were organized in group practices with a specified budget provided by the government but could choose between different hospitals (also controlled by government) for the best bargains in treating their patients.

These changes were successful in reducing the core civil service from 700,000 in 1979 to 590,000 by 1990. They also succeeded in altering the bureaucratic culture to a more management and business-oriented one. By fragmenting its structure the reforms moved the civil service even further from a traditional hierarchy to a bargaining and pluralistic structure, within limits set by government ideology.

The Thatcherite reforms were emulated most enthusiastically in the Netherlands by the centre-right coalition of Christians and liberals during the 1980s (but carried on by the left-liberal coalition from 1994 onwards). Portugal pursued a vigorous privatization programme, though not one of structural bureaucratic reform. Even the Italian caretaker governments of the mid-1990s made efforts to reduce the vast state holdings but typically got bogged down in political difficulties.

The great bulk of privatizations, however, occurred in Eastern and Central Europe. Often these were organized by Western consultants who had cut their teeth on earlier privatizations in their home countries – another example of the increased international influences which now affect national policy in the various European countries.

The major structural reform of the bureaucracy in Eastern and Central Europe has occurred, however, by default – the formal, but not actual, disappearance of the Nomenklatura. The traditional departments, in many cases surviving from the interwar or even pre-First World War period, re-emerged as the foci of bureaucratic activity. These may be nominally divided between Ministries, agencies and committees as in the Russian case (Table 12.4). But as in Russia there is little rationale to the distinction, certainly not a Thatcherite hiving-off of government activities to contractually-based agencies.

Despite the lip-service paid to it, there has also been resistance or indifference to business-oriented reform of bureaucracy in most of Western Europe, for various reasons connected to the politico-administrative traditions of the countries concerned. In France, there is little pressure to reorganize the bureaucracy along business lines – quite the reverse, as traditionally French business has been organized along bureaucratic lines. We have already commented on the close relations between state and business in France and the fact that they are run by the same, interchangeable, technocratic elite. Neither the Socialist governments of Mitterrand (1981–94) nor of his Gaullist successor Chirac from 1995 onwards have seriously considered changing the strong tradition of state intervention in France. Rather they have pursued relatively orthodox financial and economic policies through the same structures, with a few privatizations of marginal enterprises on the side. No president or government in France is likely to change the structure which gives them such powers of intervention in society and the economy.

For different structural reasons this is not likely to happen in Germany either. The federal civil service is limited in numbers and heavily policy oriented. Most policy implementation is done through the states (Länder), which are often under the control of opposition parties. The costs of forcing through changes would be great and the probability of being blocked would be high. Moreover, the relative prosperity of the country and its political success in assimilating the former East Germany seem to indicate that the administrative formula works relatively well. In spite of the fact that it involves a relatively high element of corporatism and interventionism, there is no real pressure to change.

The same may be said of Scandinavia. The 'social democratic state' has achieved a high degree of social well-being. At the margins social protection is being cut down as too expensive. However, the delivery systems and overall bureaucratic structures are not under serious attack, and seem unlikely to be while social democratic dominance continues. Significantly Denmark, where social democrats are weakest, is the Nordic country which has experimented most with agency reform. But even there, change has been half hearted compared with the Thatcherite experiment in Britain.

The Mediterranean countries, Spain, Italy and Greece, have resisted Thatcherite changes for different reasons. Reform threatens established civil service careers and pension prospects. Faced with the prospect of a massive reaction from the swollen numbers in state service, parties and governments are simply too weak to contemplate large-scale reform, despite the acknowledged deficiencies of the system.

For all these reasons therefore the structural impact of bureaucratic reform has been limited to Britain and the Netherlands. The fact that it has been carried through there helps to illustrate the much greater susceptibility of Britain, compared to other European countries, to American influences. Its failure to spread more widely may also reflect doubts in Britain itself about the impact of these bureaucratic reforms on democratic accountability. For if administration is devolved to business and autonomous agencies, how far can the elected government be held accountable for a failure to deliver? Suppose, for example, there are a number of prison escapes, but the prison service blames this on the fact that it was required in its contract to improve living conditions for prisoners which in turn required reductions in strict security. Are the escapes to be blamed on the contract (approved by the government) or on the agency itself (which clearly any government would like to do to absolve itself from responsibility)? If the government is blamed directly for any escape the temptation is to take over direct day-to-day control to ensure that escapes do not happen. But this then negates the contract and the idea of 'hiving-off' functions in the first place.

The idea of cutting down on bureaucracy, introducing business methods, improving delivery, and so on, thus turns out to have too many hidden complications for the democratic system of government itself, to be immediately acceptable across Europe. This may account for the general failure to implement structural bureaucratic reforms on the continent – though as we have seen, many country-specific forces (and often selfish bureaucratic resistance and inertia) are also at work.

One way of reducing central bureaucracy is to devolve functions not to agencies but to regions. Germany and Switzerland are both cases where the federal bureaucracy is limited because most policies are implemented by Länder and cantons. Sweden has devolved most of the spending on health to local government. Such a delegation of powers may also meet criteria for greater efficiency (since delivery is carried through closer to clients and their needs) and for regional autonomy, with minorities demanding greater political power for themselves and their representatives over their own well-being. Both of these justifications are incorporated in the principle of subsidiarity being advocated by the European Union. They also have the potential to head off religious and ethnic conflicts in Europe, which as we have seen are a major threat to general peace and stability in the region (Chapters 4, 17). For all these reasons we need now to examine the territorial dimension of European politics and administration. We do this in Chapter 13.

Further reading

Ian Budge and Hans Keman, *Parties and Democracy* (Oxford, Oxford University Press 1993).

Andrew Dunsire and Christopher Hood, *Cutback Management in Public Bureaucracy* (Cambridge, Cambridge University Press, 1989).

Michael Laver and Kenneth Shepsle (eds), *Cabinet Ministers and Parliamentary Government* (New York, Cambridge University Press, 1994).

Yves Mény, *Government and Politics in Western Europe* (Oxford, Oxford University Press 1993).

Michael Moran and Tony Prosser (eds), *Privatization and Regulatory Change in Europe* (Philadelphia, Open University Press, 1994).

Edward C. Page, *Political Authority and Bureaucratic Power: A Comparative Analysis* (London, Harvester Wheatsheaf, 1992).

Chapter 13

Regions and localities: power-sharing with the periphery

■ Local government

Formulating grand national plans is one thing. Having these plans implemented by street-level bureaucrats, who find them impractical or want to ignore them, is quite another. Generally, both Southern and Eastern European countries have difficulty in ensuring national policies are applied at the local level. One of the major difficulties in Russia is the extent to which many local officials have freed themselves from central administrative control in return for political support of the presidency against parliament.

Faced with problems of local implementation, European governments have generally adopted two different solutions. The first is to impose direct central control on localities. The second is to rely on local governments performing most administrative functions for themselves under indirect guidance or inspection by the central state.

Central control in the unitary state

The first model is most evident in the traditional French system. It has spread to many of the countries influenced by France in the Mediterranean area; to the Low Countries; and it is also found in Eastern Europe. The French system rests on the prefect, a kind of local governor appointed by the Ministry of the Interior in the local Department or Province. The prefect has final responsibility for local government in his region, but he is above all a central official, charged with executing the policies of central government. Other ministries might have their own offices in the locality, but the prefect is generally responsible for co-ordinating all local administrative activities. The justification for this sort of centralized system was that it tried to guarantee citizens the same rights and duties, no matter where they lived in France.

In such a system there may be local councils and Mayors. But in a centralized administrative system the best way of getting things done locally is through central government. The traditional role of French Mayors was thus to consolidate a strong local political base which would also secure them a legislative seat and national political credit. They could then use this to get the appropriate minister to intervene locally and secure the desired result. Such a system depends, to some extent, on whether the mayor's party is in government or opposition nationally. In Italy, most local governments have been run by the communists or their successors, which soured relations with the prefects who were appointed by a minister of the centre or the right (see Table 12.3). However, even an opposition politician can contrive to make himself useful to national government, or a great nuisance to it, and hence retain some national bargaining power.

The importance of the dual mandate – central and local – obtained by so many French and Belgian politicians, accounts for the comparatively large numbers who are both mayors and deputies. They acquire power nationally in order to represent their locality effectively – a phenomenon known as the *cumul des mandats*.

After the 1960s the prefectoral system was modified in France, and in most of the other countries where it operated, with the notable exception of Greece. These modifications were encouraged by three developments. First, there was a need for economic planning and service delivery over larger areas than the traditional provinces and *départements* covered by the prefect. Secondly, local politicians became more professional and more powerful. Thirdly, there was more popular support for local control over many functions, not only from ethnic minorities and regional nationalists but also by members of the national majority living there. These were often voiced by the new social movements discussed in Chapter 8, and supported by the EU as a counterpoise to the powers of national governments.

The purely functional need for economic planning and service delivery over larger areas resulted in the grouping of traditional departments into regions. In some cases they acquired 'super-prefects' and planning councils. In France itself, regional authorities were created for administrative convenience, rather than being based upon the old provinces or historic regions. (Apart from Corsica, where nationalists succeeded in getting a local parliament with limited powers.)

For purely administrative reasons, therefore, many of the unitary states of West Europe have found it necessary to give local and regional government more power and a wider array of functions, even if, in France, this goes against the ideal of 'the Republic, one and indivisible'. As local problems of health (particularly personal social and health services), industrial and city planning, housing and the environment have become more important and more complex, national governments have found their own civil service overloaded. Thus they have increasingly delegated functions to the local level, giving local government more legal autonomy, vesting mayors with executive powers and consolidating a local tax base. Local delegation has also been spurred on by ideological commitments of socialist governments to local autonomy, as in France and Spain in the 1980s.

Localities have also changed in nature through the fusion of previously separate cities and towns in large connurbations, and the growing interdependence of urban and rural areas. This has made it necessary either to create or expand the powers of regional governments. Such governments sit between the *communes* and local authorities of the traditional local government system, and the central state. They are a way of integrating the fragmented activity of small, local units of government, of benefiting from economies of scale in the provision of public services, of planning more effectively for such things as housing, transport, and economic development, and of sharing resources such as money and space. Most countries in Western Europe have either strengthened or created this middle (or meso) level of government in the last two decades or so.

In some cases local and regional governments, particularly in large cities, have seized the political opportunity to demonstrate their capabilities over and against the national government. They have been particularly anxious to do so when they have been in the hands of an opposition political party – Paris under the Gaullists in the

BRIEFING 13.1

Policy communities

Policy communities are tight vertical networks of interested bodies, organizations, and people who have a common interest in a particular policy area and who share a common set of underlying assumptions about it and each other. They are usually made up of public officials in government (both central and sub-central) and private interests and bodies (pressure groups and cause groups) who are particularly concerned with the policy area. The main point is that these different organizations and individuals interact closely so that they develop a shared framework for thinking about the policy.

Although the distinction is not always drawn, or not always drawn clearly, a policy *network* is similar to a policy community, though more loosely knit.

1980s, or Bologna from the 1960s under a left coalition. In these cases the drive for local and regional autonomy comes from both administrative and political pressures. It would take too much political effort for the central governmental to suppress these initiatives so they have to live with them, taking as much credit from decentralizing reforms as they can.

One general phenomenon of the post-war period – throughout Europe and not confined to the countries of French administrative traditions – has been the extent to which local government at all levels has become politicized. This has had two effects. One has been to create a class of influential local politicians who act as a counterweight to national politicians, thus shifting the balance of political concerns between state and local matters to some extent. This is particularly so when regional parliaments are involved. The second effect has been to create a counter-cyclical rhythm, or mid-term election effect. Local and regional elections are usually held at different times from national elections, often when the central government is unpopular. So opposition parties tend to win locally. This creates a tension between local and national government, with the former resisting some of the latter's policies.

In Italy and Germany the ability of local opposition to block government measures has forced national governments to compromise. In other cases, such as Britain and Russia, it has led the national government to try to crush local opposition through various legal and administrative devices.

Changing local autonomy in the unitary state

The emergence of local government has brought French-inspired administrative systems closer to the other great tradition of territorial management in Europe. Instead of strong centralization and control from the centre, this has relied on local governments performing most administrative functions for themselves under indirect guidance or inspection from the relevant national ministries. A consequence of this has been that local communities have dealt with a variety of central government ministries, not simply with the Interior as in the prefectoral system. To some extent local communes have been in the position of a territorially-based interest group able to form alliances within the civil service – horizontal networks and policy communities within and between Ministries – able, to some extent, to play one off against another. With different variations this pluralist system has been prevalent in

Scandinavia, Germany/Switzerland and the British Isles. Like its French counterpart, however, it is undergoing changes which in the end may bring the two styles of field administration and local policy-making closer together.

One powerful impulse towards change derives from the political opposition between national and local government, built into the cycle of elections. Particularly in Britain, this has led to Labour and Liberal controlled local governments opposing Thatcherite policies of cutting social expenditures and reducing local budgets. In order to enforce their policies, the national governments have sought to reduce the autonomy and scope of local government through a variety of measures, paralleling those applied to the central bureaucracy which were described in the last chapter. These measures include:

1. Reduced local spending. Most European local governments have substantial autonomy over taxing and spending. But in Britain under Thatcher, central government took control both of local revenues and expenditure, determining how much each separate local authority should raise in local taxation, and how much each would spend on different services. If councils raise taxes more than central government allows, they lose a proportionate share of the central government grant ('capping'). This makes Britain unusual, in that central government now has almost complete control over local taxing and spending.
2. Functions have been removed from locally elected councils and given to appointed boards whose members are nominated by central government ('quangos, or quasi-non-governmental organizations, see Chapter 12). This has happened in many areas relating to planning, housing, and education.
3. Some services have been slowly centralized over the years. For example, the police have been brought under the *de facto* control of the Home Secretary, and the educational curriculum under the central ministry.
4. Legislation has forced local councils to sell much of their property (e.g. housing) and to privatise some of their services.
5. The abolition of the Greater London Council (GLC) and of the Metropolitan Counties which ran the largest urban areas of England.

These changes in Britain have had the effect of creating a system which is more centralized in some respects (finance, police and education, for example), but more dispersed in others (the services now provided by quangos and the private sector). Contrary to the general European trend towards decentralization, Thatcher's Britain has moved in the opposite direction. The largest units of local government have either been abolished altogether, or else reduced greatly in power; some of the most important local functions have been centralized; and other local functions have been dispersed either to the private sector or to centrally appointed quangos. This makes for a new system which is under the tight control of central government, in some respects, but locally fragmented through the intrusion of quangos and private interests, in others.

As with reforms of central administration, British developments have not been emulated much elsewhere. On the contrary, the general Western European trend is towards greater integration of services at the local level. Even where local spending has been cut, as in parts of Scandinavia, a respect for local government and democracy has resulted in co-operation and compromise between central and local government.

The same result has been achieved in Germany under somewhat different circumstances. Local government in the Federal Republic comes under the states (Länder) not the federal government. Whether or not in the hands of opposition parties, these would simply not accept wholesale local reform along Thatcherite lines. Moreover, they are in a position to resist both because of their entrenched constitutional, and their power in the Bundesrat, the second chamber of federal parliament. Federal government may sometimes apply pressure to change Land boundaries (as with Baden-Wurtemberg in the 1950s and Berlin and Brandenburg in the 1990s). But it is beyond their competence to change local communes.

This is another feature which makes Britain different from the rest of Europe. Local government boundaries have been altered frequently, usually through amalgamation to take advantage of presumed economies of scale. This has made local boundaries responsive to social and economic changes. But on occasion it has also allowed central government to manipulate the system in its own party political interests. The Greater London Council was abolished because Labour domination of the authority was a constant nuisance to Conservative central government. This was at the time when Paris set up a single administrative unit to deal with problems which demanded an integrated regional plan for the growing problems of the capital.

Federalism and regionalism in Europe

Federalism is usually identified with the constitutional relationships which exist in the United States between its fifty component states and the federal institutions. These have exerted a considerable influence over the constitutions of other English-speaking federations overseas, in Latin America, and on the Germanic federations in Europe (notably Germany and Switzerland).

In spite of Germany calling itself a Federal Republic, and the existence of autonomous units inside many of the traditional European states (Spain and Russia are notable examples) no European country really follows the US model. Whether this disqualifies them from being regarded as 'real' federations is largely a matter of terminology. What is true is that sub-state units in many European countries enjoy an autonomy that equals or exceeds that of the US states. This is not simply a matter of informal practice, as in the case of local government, but is very often constitutionally guaranteed and protected by the courts (see Chapter 14).

What distinguishes American federalism from that found elsewhere is the absolute separation of powers between constituent states and the federal union. The individual states have sovereignty, that is control over some policy areas in their territories, and the union in others. Neither has any authority or function in matters reserved to the other.

Although the constitutional doctrine is clear, the practical question of where state powers end and federal ones begin is often ambiguous and blurred. As the final arbiter is the Federal Supreme Court, Federal authority has usually been favoured at the expense of state sovereignty. Such decisions have been underpinned by the extreme mobility of the American population, a quarter of whom change residence every year. This makes it a matter of indifference to most Americans which state they are in, and renders it easier for them to relate to federal rather than to state government.

BRIEFING 13.2

Sovereignty

To be sovereign is to be the highest or the ultimate political authority in a given territory. The sovereign state is so called because there is no superior authority in the land. Sovereignty is, therefore, a crucial concept in the government of states and in the politics between states. Internationally, a sovereign state is recognized to have authority over its own territory and this authority should not be challenged by other states. Sovereignty is therefore the basis of international law. Within states the sovereign state also has power over the affairs of the nation and its citizens. In modern states this is linked with democracy: a state is recognized as sovereign within its own territory because it is deemed legitimate by its citizens. In the words of Max Weber, the state has a monopoly of the legitimate use of physical force. We talk about the sovereignty of the people to indicate that the state has sovereign power over its citizens because they believe it to be right – usually because it is democratic.

In unitary states the central government is sovereign over all other levels of government, though they may, and most usually do, delegate some of this power to sub-national units of government. However, the central state can always take back its delegated power if it wishes. In contrast, in federal systems sovereignty is shared between the federal government and the territorial units of government within the state – usually known as states, or regions, or provinces. The latter have their own constitutionally defined powers over some functions within their territory. In federal systems, therefore, power is not delegated by the central state to lower levels of government, but is exercised by these levels of government as a constitutional right.

The European Union also involves the sharing of state sovereignty, not with a lower level of government but with a higher, supranational one. It is this loss of traditional state power which concerns some nationalist opponents of the EU.

There is not such a clear separation of powers between the central government and regions in Europe. Central and regional governments are seen as working together. The centre often relies on the regions to carry through its policies because it lacks an operational field administration of its own, even in its areas of exclusive jurisdiction. Legal clashes of the US type between regions and centre are thus generally absent – which is just as well, for if they involved national minorities, they might raise political passions of a very strong kind. If a shift towards Federal power in the USA is encouraged by high rates of geographic mobility, the presence of old ethnic conflicts in some parts of Europe helps preserve the powers of the regions.

We can distinguish two broad types of European federalism: the Germanic and uniform systems, and the differentiated systems. Both are very different from US practice, but the first is closer than the second.

The Germanic model

In both the German and Swiss federations, all units (Länder and cantons) have the same standing, in theory and in practice, in relation to Federal government. Whether the unit is a single city like Hamburg, or a mixed region such as North Rhine-Westphalia, it has the same legal powers and status. The same is true of the cantons of Zurich and Schwyz in Switzerland. Size and traditions make no difference –

BRIEFING 13.3

Federalism, regionalism, devolution and subsidiarity

In a federal state power is shared between central government (usually known as a federal government) and a set of territorial authorities within the state (usually known as states, regions, or provinces). Each unit of government has its own powers within its defined territory, and each maintains its own institutions of government in order to carry out its functions. In other words, power is not concentrated in the hands of central government, as in unitary states, but is decentralized to varying degrees. Federal forms of government are particularly useful in plural societies because they allow different ethnic, religious or linguistic groups a certain autonomy over their affairs.

Regionalism is a loose term which may mean the same thing as federalism, but can also imply closer relationships between the central and sub-state governments.

Devolution is the process by which power is devolved or decentralized to lower levels of government within the state. In some cases this may be a way of defusing special religious, regional, ethnic or linguistic problems (Catalonia in Spain, or Northern Ireland in the UK). In others, it may be in the interests of local democracy and the decentralization of power. In still others it may be to promote administrative efficiency in government.

The term *subsidiarity* is usually used in the context of the division of powers within the European Union, but it applies to all systems of government. It means that government decisions should be taken at the lowest possible territorial level. Some decisions have to be taken at the highest level of government at EU level, some by traditional states, others by regional government, and some by local or community levels of government. There is, of course, controversy about what sorts of decisions should be taken at what levels, as all governments wish to extend their own competences.

though differences in population do count in terms of representation within the upper house of the federal parliament.

In respect of the legal and political equality of sub-national units of government, the Germanic federations are the same as the USA. What makes them different is the separation of federal and state competences in the USA, and the close intergovernmental relations in Europe. In Germany and Switzerland, the Länder and cantons derive their political importance from two sources.

1. They do all the field administration in their respective countries. Whether legislation is passed at Federal or Land level, it is carried out by the latter's civil service and agencies. Local agreement must be secured for Federal legislation, therefore, otherwise it will not be implemented. On the other side of the coin, the requirement of national standards of service provision means that legislation is federal, and applies uniformly throughout the country. It will vary only in terms of detailed regional application and enforcement.

2. The regions have power over Federal legislation itself. In Germany the Länder nominate the delegations which make up the Bundestag, the powerful second house of the parliament which has a veto over all matters affecting Länder. Thus the regions can directly influence federal legislation. For example, they have stipulated that further German integration into the European Union must safeguard their own position.

In Switzerland the upper house is not directly nominated by the cantons, but they exercise great power over policy by virtue of national referendums, which can be held on all important issues. They have to be passed by a majority of cantons, as well as by a national majority of those voting in the referendum. This gives the quarter of the population living in the smaller cantons a veto.

The power of Swiss cantons also rests upon the local referendums they call themselves. The canton of Gräubunden in the East of Switzerland severely restricted heavy lorry traffic. Since two of the most important Alpine passes linking the north and south of Europe go through the canton, the restriction forced a major revision of European transport policy – it shifted to trains. Gräubunden has been able to do more for itself and the environment than most national governments!

The regional administrative role, and the uniform legal status of cantons and Länder, might make them seem more of an administrative convenience to central government rather than an assertion of local autonomy. The example of Gräubunden cautions against this view. Besides, in Switzerland and Germany the Federal government cannot alter local boundaries at its own convenience. It may try to exercise political pressure for change but it has no formal powers. In Switzerland, strong linguistic and religious differences sometimes divide cantons which jealously guard their rights. The recent secession of the (French-speaking) North Jura from the (German) canton of Bern, illustrates this point. In Germany, Bavaria remains distinct, and other Länder such as Hamburg and Bremen are supported by strong local feeling. In short, the Länder of the two Germanic federations are not simply glorified local governments; they have their constitutionally guaranteed status and, in some cases, they encapsulate and protect strong local identities. This is not the case in Austria where the provinces, even those with long histories and strong traditions, are almost totally subordinated to central government.

The differentiated model

The second type of European federalism is designed to contain and defuse minority nationalism within existing states. In certain countries this is much stronger in some regions than others, and so the degree of local autonomy and decentralization may also vary. In other words, regions have neither equal powers nor similar standing at the centre. Areas which have preserved their historical distinctiveness and linguistic-religious traditions have greater powers than regions which have not. The special treatment of particular regions makes this form of federalism different from both the US and Germanic models.

This is a less neat and tidy form of territorial management, but 'differentiated' regionalism is well adapted to European needs – given the history of imperfect state building which left unassimilated minorities scattered within and across national territories in both Western and Eastern Europe (see Chapters 3 and 4). Recognizing the justice of special ethnic or cultural claims, and incorporating them into the structure of the state, may be a more effective way of coping with minorities and stabilizing the situation, than repression and forced assimilation to a uniform 'national' pattern.

Indeed, a form of federation in which the constituent units have unequal powers and differing degrees of autonomy, may also be the best way forward for the European Union. Since some countries advocate closer integration, and others resist it, the examples of differentiated federalism might well provide a model for a similar sort of 'two-speed Europe'. This would restrict the functioning of the European Union no more than the very different relationships of the Spanish government with

BRIEFING **13.4**

The autonomous republics of the upper Volga

In the sixteenth century the Russian state conquered the states on the Upper Volga river, centred on Kazan. These were inhabited by Tatar peoples, largely Muslims, survivors of the nomadic hordes from Central Asia who had invaded Europe from the fifth to the fourteenth centuries. The Russians made various attempts to convert them, creating a large Orthodox minority, which still used their own language in Church services. However, the majority remained Muslim and maintained their own culture and institutions despite Tsarist disapproval. As early as the end of the eighteenth century they became a minority in their own territory owing to Russian colonization of their cities. But they remained culturally distinctive.

Soviet rule brought some support for the language, the official position being that it was acceptable to repeat the official Party line in different languages. Minorities were also encouraged to make careers within the Party. The administrative-territorial structure of the Russian Federation, largest of the Republics of the USSR, was based on these formally autonomous national formations as well as upon the historic Russian provinces. A cluster of five autonomous Republics including the Bashkir and Tatar Republics, were created on the Upper Volga. In fact the degree of real autonomy was minimal. Each territorial unit was closely controlled from Moscow. The use of Russian was encouraged through secondary education and religious observances were discouraged.

With the break-up of the USSR at the end of 1991, the 'national' republics were encouraged by Yeltsin to 'seize as much independence as you want'. The process seemed likely to end in secession, but this crisis was averted by Moscow giving the leadership full internal autonomy in return for material supplies and political support for the President. The leaders of the republics also realized that full independence was impossible owing to their geographical position within Russia and the Russian presence within their boundaries. In all the autonomous republics there are substantial Russian populations and a great deal of inter-ethnic mixing has taken place. Moreover, both Russians and Tatars shared the Soviet experience, not all negative. At present the political compromise seems to be working well within the Russian Federation (outside Chechnya). It is too early, however, to say whether Russian regionalism constitutes a model which could really be followed in the rest of Europe.

its regions. Nobody claims that Spain has become less viable or effective as a nation-state over the last fifteen years because of differentiated regionalism. The mistake is to think that European union depends on exactly the same powers being exerted in every country.

Varied power-sharing between centre and periphery is surprisingly widespread in both Western and Eastern Europe. Two of the most prominent examples are to be found in Russia and Spain. As noted in Chapter 1, Russian expansion in earlier centuries involved the conquest and partial assimilation of many national minorities. Some of these achieved independence after the break-up of the USSR, but many remained inside Russia often because they were intermingled with the Russians or found themselves physically surrounded by Russia itself. To a surprising extent Moscow has respected their position, bargaining with minority leaders over the distribution of resources and power between the autonomous Republics and the centre.

The best-known case is one where these arrangements have broken down – Chechnya, an area on the border between Russia and the trans-Caucasian states. A

BRIEFING **13.5**

Catalonia: region or nation?

Catalonia was the most dynamic and richest part of the Kingdom of Aragon which joined with Castile at the end of the fifteenth century to form modern Spain. Centralizing governments based in Madrid tried forcibly to undermine Catalan autonomy and culture over the next three centuries.

However, Catalonia remained the most economically dynamic part of Spain. The commercial bourgeoisie supported a resurgence of the language and of fine arts at the end of the nineteenth century. Growing Catalan nationalism forced the concession of a Catalan parliament and government in the 1930s and then pushed Catalonia on to the government (anti-Fascist) side during the long and debilitating Spanish Civil War (1936–40). The victorious right-wing regime of General Franco (1940–74) attempted to assimilate the Catalans once and for all by imposing the Spanish language and encouraging massive immigration from the South.

However, reforming regimes after 1974 reconciled themselves to decentralization and restored the Catalan Generalität (government) and parliament. Dominated by a conservative nationalist party (*Convergencia i union*) this imposed Catalan as the language of education and public institutions. By supporting both socialist and conservative governments in Madrid, the party gained more autonomy for Catalonia. It is probably now the most powerful sub-state unit of government in Europe.

While the Catalans may dream of an eventual nation-state of their own, practical benefits may keep them within Spain. The most effective opposition to *Convergencia i unio* paradoxically comes from the socialist-dominated municipality of Barcelona, whose town hall is just across the main square from the parliament building in the old city.

particularly brutal war has been waged in the region to try to force the Chechens to retract their declaration of independence and accept the status of an autonomous Republic.

Russia invaded Chechnya partly to prevent other autonomous Republics from seceding. This is a danger in the Caucasus, where minorities and ethnic groups often spread over international boundaries. It is much less of a danger for Republics on the Upper Volga or in Siberia, for two reasons: first, they are territorially surrounded by Russia and cannot easily get external support for secession. Secondly, ethnic Russians are in a majority even within the boundaries of their own Republics, though the Republican governments themselves are generally dominated by leaders from the ethnic minority which gives them their names.

Under these circumstances leaders have preferred to negotiate with the Russian centre rather than defy it. Generally, they have been able to come to an arrangement which serves minority interests better than in the old days, when the Soviet leadership through the *nomenklatura* manipulated political appointments and exploited Republics' resources ruthlessly in favour of the overall Russian majority. The new arrangements also enable governments to defend minority culture and language better against informal but strong pressures for Russification and assimilation. The arrangement is surprisingly accommodating and conciliatory in most cases, and might – though it is early days – serve as a model for the way in which Eastern European countries in general could compromise with their minorities.

Spain's regional minorities also constituted one of the most pressing problems facing the new democracy at the end of the 1970s. The central government made a

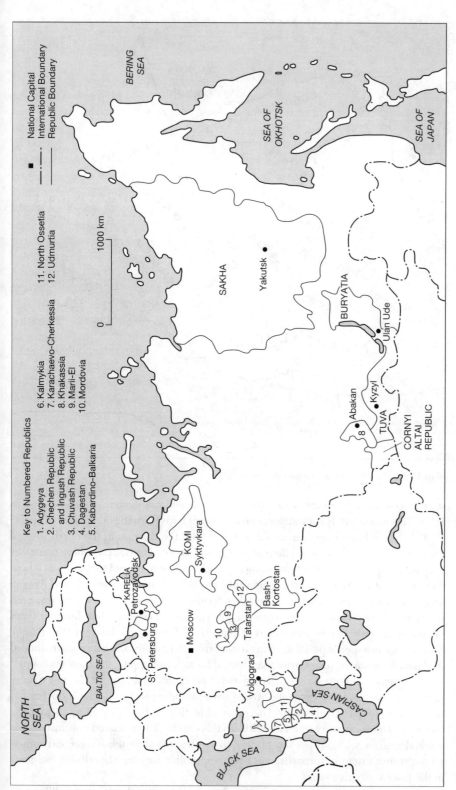

Map 13.1 The Russian autonomous republics

Key to Numbered Republics

1. Adygeya
2. Chechen Republic and Ingush Republic
3. Chuvash Republic
4. Dagestan
5. Kabardino–Balkaria

6. Kalmykia
7. Karachaevo-Cherkessia
8. Khakassia
9. Mari-El
10. Mordovia

11. North Ossetia
12. Udmurtia

■ National Capital
—·—·— International Boundary
———— Republic Boundary

0   1000 km

Map 13.2   The autonomous communities of Spain

start by concluding a treaty with the exiled Catalan administration, the *Generalität* in 1979. This immediately set Catalonia on a different basis from the other areas of Spain.

A slightly different agreement was reached with the Basques in the north-west of Spain. Some of the Catalan and Basque provisions extended to Galicia, where there was a separate linguistic group but no strong regionalist movement, and to Andalusia where there was neither. Subsequently, regions like the Balearic Islands, Valencia and Aragon have received extended powers. The other Spanish regions have less autonomy, even where they have Assemblies and regional governments. There are thus different types of region in Spain, each with different powers. Catalonia and Euzkadi (the Basque country) are in a special position owing to the strength of their local nationalism. Indeed the Spanish monarch, Juan Carlos, has defined his task as 'keeping the Catalans happy'!

These arrangements have secured general peace and stability for the last twenty years – not an outcome everyone would have predicted in 1975. The economy has functioned comparatively well. The great objective of foreign policy, to join the European Union, was achieved in 1985. To this extent differentiated regionalism has worked well in Spain. It is even undermining the appeal of the Basque extremists whose commitment to terrorism has been responsible for some horrifying incidents in the last twenty five years.

In spite of its challenge to state nationalism and territorial uniformity, differentiated regionalism crops up as a solution to minority demands in a surprising number of European countries, including ones previously committed to uniformity and centralisation across their 'national' territory. Belgium, for example, with State structures not only modelled on the French but actually operating in French (despite over half the population speaking Dutch) has recently divided itself into two largely autonomous entities, Flanders and Wallonia. The governments of these areas run practically all their own internal affairs. Brussels, the national and European capital, remains a problem as it is a French-speaking city expanding into Dutch-speaking territory. This has resulted in a different treatment of the capital and its suburbs, with the French and Flemish Councils providing personal and cultural services to those Bruxellois registered with them.

Even centralized France, strongly opposed in the name of 'the Republic, one and indivisible' to traditional identities and autonomies, has one region which it treats differently. This is Corsica, the large Mediterranean island with a strong indigenous nationalist movement. This has forced the creation of a local parliament, albeit with limited powers.

Despite the Thatcherite dislike of local autonomy it is likely that Wales and Scotland eventually will emerge as self-governing regions within the UK. Northern Ireland constituted such a region, with its own parliament and government, from 1922 to 1972. A possible compromise to end terrorism may be the reconstitution of the old province, with built-in power-sharing for the Protestant–Unionist majority and the Nationalist Catholic minority.

Italy follows Spain in having four regions with special powers (Alto Adige, Val d'Aosta, Sardinia and Sicily) as well as 'ordinary' regions. Many other countries have small regions, often islands (the Aaland Islands in Finland, the Faroes in Denmark, the Channel Islands and the Isle of Man in Britain) which are autonomous. Although neglected in most general surveys of European government, these cases show that autonomous areas are not at all uncommon. Paradoxically this often strengthens rather than weakens the unity of the State and the ties of the centre to the periphery.

The force behind differentiated regionalism is clearly minority nationalism. At this point, therefore, we ought to return to this phenomenon, to see what keeps it going and how it survives in an increasingly homogenized world. In spite of all the ink spilled on the topic of the globalization and supranationalism, local and regional identities seem to be growing in political strength. More autonomous regions, and more independent nation-states, are being created. We must ask, therefore, how far ethnic nationalism impacts on national politics, and what its demands are. We analyse these aspects of regionalism in the next section where we explicitly examine the match between minority aspirations and regional political structures, particularly assemblies and governments. The creation of such structures indicates how far governments are facing up to regional and minority problems, which remain the major threat to general European security and peace today.

■ Minorities and regions

Table 13.1 lists the major ethnic and cultural minorities of Europe and gives some information about them. A major question is how large they are. Minorities like the Sami (Lapps) in Arctic Scandinavia are too small to make a political impact and are substantially outnumbered in their own territory. One should note, however, that

Table 13.1   The ethnic minorities of Europe

Country	Minority	Approx. no. '000s	Approximate % country population	Dispersed (D) or territorially concentrated (C)	Cross-border or encapsulated by state (E)	Name of autonomous region
Finland	Swedes	250	8	D and C	C	Aaland Islands
Finland, Norway, Sweden	Sami (Lapps)	70	0.3	D	C	None
Estonia	Russians	500	30.0	D	C	None
Latvia	Russians	830	34.0	D	C	None
Denmark	Faroese	50	1.2	C	E	Faroes
	Germans	50	1.0	C	C	Faroes
Netherlands	Friesians	600	2.3	C	E	None
Belgium	Flemings	6,000	60.0	C	C	Flanders
	Walloons	4,000	40.0	C	C	Wallonie
Luxembourg	Italians and others	100	25.0	D	E	None
United Kingdom	Scots	5,000	9.0	C	E	None
	Welsh	2,200	5.0	C	E	None
	Irish	2,000	3.0	C	C	None
	Caribbean	580	1.0	D	C	None
	Indian-Pakistani	1,640	3.0	D	C	None
France	Corsicans	200	0.3	D	E	Corsica
	Alsatians	1,300	2.3	C	C	None
	Algerians	3,000	4.5	D	C	None
	Bretons	1,000	1.5	C	E	None
	Occitans-Provencals	1,500	2.7	C	E	None
Spain	Catalans	6,000	16.3	C	E	Catalonia, Balearic Islands, Valencia
	Galicians	3,000	8	C	E	Galicia
	Basques	800	2.3	C	E	Euzkadi
	Roma (Gypsies)	500	1.3	C	C	None
Italy	South Tyrolese	300	0.7	C	C	Alto Adige
	Savoyards	200	0.5	C	C	Val D'Aosta
	Sards	1,500	2.6	C	E	Sardinia
	Venetians	4,500	8.5	C	E	Veneto
	Lombards	9,500	16.5	C	E	Lombardy
	Ligurians	1,700	3.1	C	E	Liguria
	Friulians	550	1.0	C	C	Venezia Giulia-Friuli
	Sicilians	5,000	8.0	C	E	Sicily
Greece	Muslims	150	1.0	C	C	None
Turkey	Kurds	10.6	200	C	C	None
Macedonia	Albanians	400	22.0	C	C	None
	Turks	40	2.0	D	C	None
	Roma (Gypsies)	80	4.0	D	C	None
	Serbs	40	2.0	C	C	None
Bulgaria	Turks	750	8.5	D	C	None
	Roma (Gypsies)	400	4.0	D	C	None
Serbia-Yugoslavia	Hungarians	350	3.5	C	C	None
	Albanians	1,800	17.0	C	C	None
	Montenegrans	600	5.0	C	C	Montenegro
	Roma (Gypsies)	375	3.5	C	C	None
Albania	Greek	150	4.0	C	C	None
Bosnia-Herzegovina	Serbs	1,200	30.0	C	C	Serb Bosnia
	Croats	700	17.0	C	C	None
	Muslims	1,600	40.0	C	E	None
	Roma (Gypsy)	175	4.0	D	C	None
Switzerland	French	1,200	20.0	C	C	Various Cantons
	Italian	300	5.0	C	C	Canton of Ticino
	Romansch	60	1.0	C	E	None
Germany	Bavarians	12,000	14.0	C	E	Bavaria
	Turks	1,850	2.0	D	C	None
Czech Republic	Roma (Gypsies)	400	3.9	D	C	None
	Moravians	1,300	13.0	C	E	None

Table 13.1 *(continued)*

Country	Minority	Approx. no. '000s	Approximate % country population	Dispersed (D) or territorially concentrated (C)	Cross-border or encapsulated by state (E)	Name of autonomous region
Slovakia	Hungarians	600	11.0	C	C	None
	Roma (Gypsies)	400	7.5	D	C	None
Hungary	Roma (Gypsy)	600	6.0	D	C	None
Romania	Hungarian	1,500	7.0	C	C	None
	Roma	750	3.0	D	C	None
	Ukrainians	600	2.0	C	C	None
Moldova	Russian	550	30.0	C	C	Trans–Dnieper Republic
Lithuania	Poles	300	7.0	D	C	None
	Russians	400	9.0	D	C	None
Belarus	Russians	1,300	13	D	C	None
	Poles	400	4	D	C	None
	Ukrainians	300	3	D	C	None
Ukraine	Russian		22	D&C	C	Crimea
European Russia	Tatars	6,000	3.8	C	E	Upper Volga Republics
	Ukrainian	4,500	3.0	C	C	None
	Chuvash (Caucasus)	1,700	1.2	C	E	Chuvash Autonomous Republic
	Chechens (Caucasus)	400	0.2	C	E	Chechnya
Georgia	Ossetians	150	3.0		C	South Ossetia
	Armenians	350	8.0	C	C	None
	Russians	300	6.0	D	C	None

Note: Iceland, Ireland, Portugal, Malta, Croatia, Slavonia, Austria, Poland, (Greek) Cyprus, Armenia, Azerbaijan (in its effective frontiers) do not have significant minorities.

there is a Sami parliament, though there is no territorial regional parliament. Another small minority, the Roma (Gypsies), also have a significant political impact in Macedonia, though no autonomy.

Size is only one consideration, however. As we saw in Chapter 4, concentration and separation are also crucial. If a group is sharply separated from the majority (an island community like the Faroes, for example) it can be small but culturally and territorially distinctive enough to secure political autonomy. The Roma are unlikely to have a substantial impact as long as they are physically spread among the population, and do not constitute a local majority anywhere. This prevents them agitating for local autonomy as smaller, but more concentrated minorities can.

Ethnic groups are likely to be more effective if they have support from across the border from other members of their group – especially if the latter have national independence. Some minorities are not really minorities, but members of a larger linguistic or cultural group who have been cut off by national boundaries which runs through the group rather than enclosing it. Austrian support has been helpful in gaining substantial autonomy for the German-speaking Tyrolese inside Italy. Apart from direct political support, diffuse reinforcement often comes from having a friendly external state which, for example, might publish and broadcast in the minority language.

It helps, of course, if the ethnic minority is a large one, so that it can sustain itself culturally and exert some political clout. This is true of groups like the Flemings and Catalans. If a successful minority can establish an independent state or an autonomous region, it can then control education and television, which enables it to preserve its own language and culture against pressures for assimilation. The best example of this is Catalonia where the autonomous government has reintroduced the Catalan language into schools and the media, thus saving it from slow extinction. It called its programme 'linguistic normalization' though it was really a linguistic revolution.

The second last column of Table 13.1 shows whether or not minorities are encapsulated by state boundaries (cf. Table 4.1 on 'diasporas' and 'mosaics'). In Europe, minorities divide fairly evenly between those which lie within a single state, and those which spread across national borders. Significantly, there are more encapsulated minorities in Western Europe (and Russia) than in Eastern Europe – a fact which, unfortunately, encourages Eastern states to intervene in the internal affairs of their neighbours. The states most closely linked with external minorities are Albania and Hungary. Albania is smaller and weaker than its neighbours, and unlikely to intervene effectively on behalf of Albanians over the border. The Hungarian minority in Slovakia is cut off from Hungary by a frontier which runs along the Danube, rather than north of it. Hungary has always been moderate in its attitudes to its own ethnic groups in other states, even where these have not been treated particularly well. In Chapter 4 we noted Slovakia's definition of itself in its constitution as the 'Slovak national state', completely ignoring the 10 per cent of Hungarians along its southern border. Similar attitudes prevail in Romania and create constant friction with the Hungarian minority there.

Nationalist ideology argues that every national group should have its own state (see Chapters 3 and 4). The main problem is that majorities and minorities usually disagree over what constitutes a national group. The unfortunate Slavs in Macedonia, for example, were defined as South Serbs by Serbia, Bulgars by Bulgaria, and Greek Orthodox by Greece! Having constructed this categorization, all the neighbouring countries felt entitled to partition the territory and to enforce their own language on the population, expelling those who resisted.

Such action often creates 'facts on the ground' which result in the assimilation of the region into the state which has incorporated it. Greece expelled as many Slav-speakers from coastal Macedonia as it could, settled the area with dispossessed Greeks (they, in turn, came from Asia Minor as a result of Turkish 'ethnic cleansing'), and imposed the Greek language. As a result, coastal Macedonia is now Greek. The same process of expelling minorities has gone on recently in Bosnia-Herzegovina where, as a result of a brutal four years civil war, homogeneous blocs of territory have been carved out to be inhabited exclusively by Serbs, Muslims and Croats – the 'wrong sort' having been massacred or expelled.

The current distribution of minorities and majorities in Europe thus reflects patterns of war and expulsion, which have created minorities in some cases while eliminating them in others. (In Chapter 17 we shall examine other long-term factors, creating minorities, notably emigration across state boundaries.)

War, discrimination, and persecution have been employed by some European states against their minorities, while others have relied on more subtle economic and cultural pressures, such as compulsory education in the national language, and reserving state jobs for those completing such education. France, Spain, Italy and Britain have pursued this policy vigorously in the past. It ensures that the minority intelligentsia will be 'nationalized'. National TV in the state language completes the process by displacing the minority language popular level.

This type of involuntary assimilation is familiar in the Italian and Spanish regions, Wales, Ireland, Scotland and above all in France. Small wonder then that minorities, where they are strong enough, will try to preserve their distinctiveness by acquiring their own government structures to defend their identity. It is hard to resist assimilation without some degree of political autonomy.

For all the fears expressed about the threat of minority nationalism to European stability, territorial secession has not been common in modern European history if we set aside the cases where the state has collapsed as a result of defeat in war. The main cases of minority secession are Norway's peaceful split from Sweden in 1907, Finland's more or less peaceful split from Russia in 1918, and Iceland's from Denmark in 1944. More recently, there is the case of a negotiated separation in the 'velvet divorce' of Slovakia and the Czech Republic in 1992 and the peaceful dissolution of the Soviet Union in the same year. This same peaceful split may be occurring slowly in Belgium, between Flanders and Wallonia. The main case of violent secession is that of Southern Ireland from the United Kingdom from 1919–22. This left Northern Ireland as a bone of contention, and the object of repeated terrorist and guerrilla campaigns.

The Irish example illustrates another general point. Only if the break is clean, absorbs the great majority of an ethnic group, and creates a relatively homogeneous new state, can a minority problem be said to be solved. Otherwise ethnic tensions and border disputes are likely to reappear. Minorities which have recently fought successfully for independence tend to be intolerant of the struggles of other minorities within their new state. At least this is what opponents of minority nationalism argue. These include many 'realists' in international relations. If a state shows signs of fragmenting, its boundaries must be upheld, otherwise neighbours will be tempted to intervene and the area will become destabilized by conflict and violence. Whether this is really true, or is just a convenient justification for rejecting minority demands, is unclear. There have been more cases of peaceful withdrawal in twentieth-century Europe than of violent secession.

Even the break-up of multinational empires and states seems to have been followed by no more tension than if they had continued. The countries carved out of the former Austro-Hungarian empire from 1918–22 have continued largely unchanged, except for the peaceful secessions of Slovakia and Slovenia. In spite of Chechnya, the Soviet breakup has so far proved more peaceful and stable than might have been imagined in 1990. Only the dissolution of ex-Yugoslavia has provoked outright war, which, however, has been effectively contained within part of the former national territory.

'Realists' are correct to say the break-up of existing states creates a potential for international tension and violence. But to infer from this that minorities must accept the status quo, however discriminatory or punitive, is equally 'unrealistic'. The status quo may be no less threatening to peace and stability.

One solution may be international guarantees of the rights of minorities, policed by bodies such as the UN or the European Union. We consider some of these in relation to trans-European migration in Chapter 17. Another solution, however, is differentiated regionalism along the lines discussed earlier in this chapter. After all, ethnic minorities do not normally want total independence – a seat in the UN and all this implies. More usually, they want autonomy and political guarantees within the existing state. Regional decentralization can achieve this by allowing minorities to adapt state legislation to their own conditions, and by giving them a direct voice in national policy making. With powers like these, who needs an independent state?

Although differentiated regionalism is sometimes regarded as a messy compromise forced upon central states by obstreperous minorities, this discussion shows it is a promising solution to regional and ethnic problems which has been developed with notable success in Western Europe. It is a way of achieving peaceful compromises within the structure of existing States, and without upsetting either the national or international balance of power. It is capable of meeting minority aspirations without the threats of fragmentation and destabilization posed by secession. To the existing state, it offers a solution to minority problems without incurring either territorial break-up, or a blanket delegation of powers to all sub-central units of government. Concessions made to regional minorities need not be extended to regions inhabited by the majority. Since 'special regions' tend to be small and remote, the reforms are not likely to have general effects. They are thus more likely to be tolerated by established elites and the ethnic majority.

Table 13.2 shows the other side of the coin to Table 13.1, listing the historic, cultural and territorial entities of Europe which have achieved a degree of political autonomy. The table shows that some countries have strongly resisted the demands of their minorities for autonomy. This is especially the case with the United Kingdom. Others – Spain and Russia – have gone a long way towards giving minorities what they want, short of national disintegration.

Table 13.2 also shows that some regions without strong cultural or ethnic distinctiveness have extensive autonomy. It does not list most of the German Länder, Swiss Cantons, or Italian and Spanish regions. Many of these have no specially strong historical or cultural roots and seem designed more as an administrative convenience than as a response to minority pressure. They bring us back to the other main purpose behind European regional arrangements – their functional efficiency and ability to bring administration closer to the people. We must not forget that the territorial decentralization can be either a political response to local diversity (ethnic, religious, linguistic, or historical), or an organizational response to the need for better territorial administration. So far as the latter is concerned, most Western European states have increased the powers and functions of the middle levels, which fit somewhere between national and local government.

■ The survival of European minorities

Given exceptionally strong pressures for nationalization and assimilation in modern society, how have so many distinctive national minorities managed to survive? This question is not so different from asking why nation-states themselves continue to exist in Europe, and why more are being created even in the present era of globalization and international or supranational government. As we have seen, many former minorities have managed to secure nationhood for themselves – in Ireland, Iceland, Norway, Slovakia, Slovenia, Croatia, Macedonia, Ukraine, Belarus, to say nothing of the European parts of overseas empires which have gained independence since 1945, such as Cyprus and Malta. The concept of minority and nation are interchangeable up to a point – a nation being an ethnic group that has managed to create its own protective government structure. A minority, by definition, has not.

Table 13.2 Major cultural–historical regions of Europe within existing states

State	Region	Ethnically-culturally distinctive group	Autonomous?
Norway, Finland, Sweden	Lapland	Sami (Lapps)	No
Denmark	Faroes	Faroese	Yes
	Slesvig	Germans	No
Netherlands	Friesland	Friesians	No
Belgium	Flanders	Flemings	No
	Wallonie	Walloons	Yes
	Brussels	Flemings, Walloons	Yes
United Kingdom	Scotland	Scots	No
	Wales	Welsh	No
	Northern Ireland	Irish	No
	Isle of Man	Yes	Yes
	Channel Islands	Yes	Yes
France	Alsace	Alsatians	No
	Brittany	Bretons	No
	Languedoc	Occitans	No
	Provence	Provencals	No
	Savoy	Savoyards	No
	Corsica	Corsicans	Yes
Italy	Sardinia	Sards	Yes
	South Tyrol (Alto Adige)	Tyrolese	Yes
	Val D'Aosta	Savoyards	Yes
	Friuli–Venezia Giulia	Friulans, Slavs	Yes
	Veneto	Venetians	Yes
	Lombardy	Lombards	Yes
	Liguria	Ligurians	Yes
	Tuscany	Ambiguous	Yes
	Umbria	Ambiguous	Yes
	Marches	Ambiguous	Yes
	Calabria	Ambiguous	Yes
	Sicily	Sicilians	Yes
Spain	Catalonia	Catalans	Yes
	Valencia, Balearic Islands, Aragon	Catalans	Yes
	Euzkadi (Basque) Provinces	Basques	Yes
	Galicia	Galicians	Yes
Serbia-Yugoslavia	Kossovo	Albanians	No
	Banat	Hungarians	No
Germany	Bavaria	Bavarians	Yes
	Hamburg	No	Yes
	Bremen	No	Yes
Switzerland	French Cantons	French speakers	Yes
	Ticino	Italian speakers	Yes
Ukraine	Crimea	Russians, Tatars	Yes
European	Karelia	Finns	Yes
Russia	Upper Volga	Tatars	
	Caucasus	Mainly Muslim minorities	Yes
Turkey	Kurdistan	Kurds	No

It is not difficult to explain the survival of a small culture and language if they manage to create their own nation-state (the Dutch and Danish, for example). More puzzling is the survival of strong minorities which are contained within larger states. In what follows we will concentrate on minorities which persist in spite of the pressures for them to become assimilated into the state majority. In some cases, they are protected by vestigial political structures. Thus Scotland, in spite of the drastic decline of Gaelic, and the assimilation of Scots to English, still has a separate legal

> BRIEFING 13.6
>
> **Scotland: some cultural but more political distinctiveness**
>
> Scotland was a Medieval and Renaissance State absorbed by its stronger neighbour England in the course of the seventeenth century. While the Union of 1707 was hastened by commercial and political pressure, it was basically negotiated by the elites on both sides. This meant that the stronger Scottish elites such as lawyers and the (Presbyterian) church were able to safeguard their interests. Considerable elements of the old Scottish state thus survived in the new United Kingdom.
>
> The existence of separate law-courts and an autonomous church meant that, in the nineteenth-century services dependent on them, such as education and welfare, assumed a distinctively Scottish form and had to be administered from Edinburgh rather than London. Distinctive Scottish institutions did not in this case underpin cultural survival. On the contrary, the church and schools systematically imposed standard English on Scots and Gaelic speakers alike. However, they did form the focus for a semi-autonomous press and later, radio and television, based in the principal Scottish cities.
>
> Appalling social conditions inherited from the Industrial Revolution inclined most Scots to reformist and radical politics, which conflicted with the conservatism of the English heartland. This conflict was exacerbated under Thatcherite governments from 1979–97, whose cuts in public expenditure hit Scots hard. The growth of a Scottish Nationalist party aiming at total independence forced the Labour Party to promise devolution and regional government in an attempt to keep its Scottish support.

and school system, a distinct national church, and vigorous local media. These have fostered a different pattern of politics from the rest of the United Kingdom and supported a sense of distinct identity.

This has also been true of Catalonia in Spain, and is the reason why so many small minority groups survive in Russia. Providing an education in the minority language is perhaps the most important factor in its survival. This is above all a state activity in Europe – hence the importance of autonomous state or sub-state structures.

Minority survival is also facilitated, of course, the further away the minority is from the state capital. This makes implementation of centrist policies more difficult and conversely renders it easier for the minority to resist them. Difficult or isolated terrain fosters a sense of distinctiveness in the minority and again makes it harder to enforce centrist policies. More distinctive areas often have a different economic base from the rest of the state. Usually this implies that they are rural and poorer, like Corsica and Sardinia. Sometimes, however, the peripheral region is richer than the centre as Catalonia and Euzkadi are in Spain.

Where ethnic differences are reinforced or to some extent displaced by religious differences, there is an alternative basis for an ethnic consciousness. The Muslims of Bosnia-Herzegovina are a case in point. But so also are the minorities of the United Kingdom where religion has often seemed a more important basis of differentiation than pure ethnic distinctiveness.

The ability of a minority language to survive with any degree of vigour up to the present time has often depended, in the absence of state support, on the development of a minority intelligentsia who could use and develop it. Such an intelligentsia was often associated with the church. The literary basis for a language was very often the translation of the Bible into it, done at varying points between the Reformation and the twentieth century. The language of the Bible became a standard literary form which was then systematized through dictionaries and grammars – again the work of intellectuals and an essential basis if the language was to be passed on to others. The first Catalan dictionary was published at the end of the nineteenth century and the first Macedonian Slav dictionary in 1929. It can be seen just how important was official Soviet approval for minority languages, as it stimulated this kind of philological and literary activity, often with generous state subsidies.

To the extent that minority groups could emulate national majorities in stimulating literary and linguistic activity, creating an intelligentsia, propagating their work through the schools, and reserving state occupations for members of their own group, they could survive. Even so, the minority languages were often weakened in competition with the state language. Where they had no such facilities they have been weakened to the point of extinction, as has happened above all with French regional languages. In the mid-nineteenth century it was said that the majority of the French population did not speak French. By the end of the twentieth, few used a regional language as their first choice, except possibly in Alsace and Corsica.

■ Regionalism and European Union

The traditional argument used against minority nationalism in Europe is based on economic and political viability. Most regions, it is argued, are too small to form an independent state (ignoring the cases of Luxembourg, Ireland and Malta). They would break up the free market and economic union created by larger political units, and their populations would suffer a sharp fall in their standard of living as a result (ignoring the cases of Iceland and Norway, which have increased their prosperity since independence).

Although such arguments are generally specious, they have become even more outdated with the advent of the European Union. As the EU is primarily an economic union, national political boundaries are irrelevant to economic activity and flows of trade. Thus for actual or potential members, political changes carry few or no economic effects. As the EU also guarantees defence, even small regions or states are able to shelter under its umbrella.

The EU could thus make an enormous difference to the prospects for minority nationalism in Europe. Paradoxically, moves towards a wider and wider European federation at one level, and ever smaller autonomous regions and units lower down, could well support each other. Their common opponents are the existing European States (or some of them, as Federal Germany is both a keen supporter of European federation and of extensions to the power of regions). The more the powers of the existing states are reduced by being transferred upwards to Brussels, on the one hand, and downwards to regions on the other, the easier it will be to achieve full European union.

The EU has made two important gestures towards support of European regionalism:

1. In the first place it has created an (advisory) Committee of the Regions, to comment on policy proposals from a regional point of view and to aid

deliberations of the European Parliament. It seems likely that this will remain a pure 'talking-shop' like the Social and Economic Committee, which represents social interests, although it does give regions a direct voice at Brussels, by-passing central state governments. It is a 'European' recognition of their importance, if nothing else. Many regions, not to mention large cities, now maintain offices in Brussels, primarily to keep track of potential grants. These are direct channels of contact with the EU which do not depend on the mediation of central governments.

2. The doctrine of 'subsidiarity' promulgated by the EU is potentially vital for the role of regions. This doctrine commits the EU to having policies and services administered at the level most appropriate for them. Existing states, notably Britain and Denmark, have seized on this as a justification for resisting further transfers of power to Brussels, and indeed reclaiming those which have already been transferred. What these governments choose to ignore is that most of the powers they currently exercise could (and should, under this doctrine) be transferred to regions and local governments. Were subsidiarity ever to be taken seriously it could undermine their position totally, leaving little more than defence in their hands (and even that might go up to the EU).

There is thus a political alliance waiting to be formed between the EU and the regions. This has implications for Central and Eastern Europe too. One of the conditions the Union might impose if it took regionalism seriously, is that minorities in potential member states must have substantial autonomy.

The Union's own support of regionalism is, however, itself currently limited by two factors:

1. Its own bureaucracy, based in Brussels, functions primarily on the French model. This is centralized and technological in style, typically committed to grand, bureaucratically planned projects which negotiation with interests and political representatives would simply weaken. From this perspective, regions look like another obstacle to efficient administration rather than potential allies against state governments.

2. The German influence on Brussels, reinforced by the Länder's resolutions on the safeguarding of their own powers in a future European federation. This conceives of a Germany type of federalism, with all units having equal standing, rather than differentiated regionalism of the kind we have discussed. The latter is also disadvantaged by the French bureaucracy's preference for administrative symmetry and order, which rules out creating different types of regional units with different powers.

As this might well be the most promising line along which European Union could proceed, the whole project of European Federation could be held up by a preference for neatness and order which envisages exactly the same relationship holding between Brussels and every constituent part of Europe. This is mistaken, as it seeks to impose only one kind of regional arrangement on Europe, whereas differentiated regionalism is probably the best basis on which to secure compromise.

Potential allies, the European Union and European regions still have a long way to go before they consolidate their relationship. As regards regionalism itself, however, it is clearly in Europe to stay, whether as a response to minority nationalism or as a necessary complement to an increasingly overloaded central administrative machine; or, indeed, both. The fact that it can serve a variety of purposes renders it one of the most interesting European political innovations of the post-war era.

Further reading

Douglas Ashford, *British Dogmatism and French Pragmatism: Local Policy-Making in the Welfare State* (London, Allen and Unwin, 1982).

Ian Bremmer and Ray Taras (eds), *Nations and Politics in the Soviet Successor States* (Cambridge, Cambridge University Press, 1993).

Stein Rokkan and Derek Urwin (eds), *The Politics of Territorial Identity* (London, Sage, 1982).

Gordon Smith, *Politics in Western Europe* (London, Gower, 1988), ch. 9.

Further reading

Chapter 14

Judges and courts: interpreting law or making policy?

■ Introduction

Power-sharing with regions or local authorities often involves the central government in political disputes. As we have seen, some local or regional governments are bound to be controlled by political parties different from those in power at the centre. These may be able to co-operate or compromise much of the time, especially if each have the ability to block each other, as in Germany. On issues central to their core ideologies, however, neither side may feel able to give way. They thus get locked into confrontations which they cannot resolve on their own.

In such a situation one or both parties may appeal to the courts to say who should prevail. Judges are especially likely to be involved when there is a Constitutional Court whose responsibility it is to say what the relationship between political bodies should be. Political questions may go to ordinary courts too, however, as disputes often embroil individuals and groups with governments. Either these feel that governments are exceeding their powers or are not using them enough. Or else a government is appealing to the court for judgment against them.

Legal appeals are necessary because the law is often not clear on what ought to be done under a particular set of circumstances. These may never have occurred before or may never have been envisaged when legislation was written. Particularly with the pace of change in the last third of the twentieth century, existing law has to be extended to cover new contingencies. From time to time, parliaments and governments may update a particular body of law (on consumer protection for example). But the vast bulk of decisions on how the law affects a particular case are made by judges in the courts.

As the existing law is unclear, judges may be said to be legislating whenever they extend it. One question which arises from this is whether they use purely technical, objective legal criteria in coming to these decisions or whether they are swayed by political considerations. As we saw in Chapter 2, the European Court of Justice has pursued a consistent line in favour of extending European Union powers, including its own jurisdiction. This often leads individuals or groups in dispute with their national governments to appeal to the court in order to reverse a decision. Inevitably, therefore, the Court becomes involved in highly controversial issues which lead to accusations that it is playing politics.

It may be, however, that judges have little choice but to use political criteria in decision-making, since no others are available. Deciding whether a public authority enjoined in its Charter to run transport economically is within its rights in reducing fares, and thus doubling passenger traffic, is not something legal rules cover. In whatever way they resolve such a case, judges are bound to be accused of political bias.

Nevertheless, this may be truer of some areas than of others. One of the questions we shall be asking in this chapter is how far judges are pursuing a definite political line and how far they are functioning as relatively neutral arbiters in adjusting old law to new circumstances. In order to decide this we have first of all to look at the nature of law as it is made and applied in the different areas of Europe. How is it changing, particularly under the influence of international bodies like the European Court itself and the Council of Europe, which has been particularly active in the field of human rights? These points are considered in the next section.

■ The law

In democracies, law is seen as reflecting the judgement of citizens about what are right and proper actions. Often law is 'negative' in that it prohibits certain kinds of action, like murder or discrimination on racial or gender grounds, because these are considered to be wrong. Usually citizens do not vote directly on laws themselves, outside Switzerland and Italy (see Chapter 9). In representative democracies, which almost all European countries are, laws are discussed and voted on by legislators in parliament. The very words 'legislator' and 'legislature' suggest the principal function of parliament, which is to pass laws.

Similarly the term 'executive' (government and bureaucracy) implies that its main task is to 'execute' or 'implement' the laws made in parliament. The judiciary in turn is not supposed to become directly involved in legislation or administration. Rather, it checks that the law is being properly interpreted and administered. If there are disputes about how it should be applied or what it means, the courts supply the correct interpretation, after hearing arguments on both sides. Of course, they decide after hearing evidence whether someone has broken the law and what the penalties for this should be.

Our previous discussion shows that actual practice is more confused and ambiguous than this idealized description implies. Most legislation is neither planned nor drafted by parliaments but by governments or bureaucracies. Through their party majority governments make proposals which they can pass in their entirety regardless of what is said in parliament. Not only this, but governments have acquired considerable powers in the field of 'secondary' legislation – directives and orders which fill in the 'general' or 'framework' legislation passed by parliament. Under presidential regimes, the executive may also be empowered to legislate directly where parliament has failed to do so – a practice common in Russia and the Ukraine.

Globalization and increasing European integration also means that much legislation has been agreed by intergovernment negotiation or even passed directly by higher-level bodies such as the Nordic Council or European Union. In these cases the national parliament simply rubber-stamps law already made elsewhere, if it sees them at all!

Last, but not least, describing the courts as concerned simply with the implementation and interpretation of law and settling disputes ignores their important political functions. These vary, however, from one European country to another, owing to the different position of judges. No single system predominates in Europe. So the law sets different boundaries for intervention within each state. Moreover, the Courts are orga-

BRIEFING **14.1**

The three branches of government and the separation of powers

Eighteenth-century thinkers, notably the Frenchman Montesquieu, believed that a major safeguard against tyrannical rule was to have three branches of some government each operating in their own sphere and not trespassing into the sphere of the others. Parliament (the legislature) should pass laws and agree taxation. Government (the executive) should administer laws and take administrative decisions which could not be covered by law (such as declaring war). Courts (the judiciary) should decide who was right in disputes between the other two branches, and interpret existing law, and try cases where it had been broken.

Montesquieu thought this was how British constitutional arrangements, which he admired, ideally worked. His reasoning was influential among the leaders of breakaway British colonies in America who put his ideas into practice in the form of Constitution of the United States. In fact, the actual political arrangements in eighteenth-century Britain depended very much upon the executive maintaining and influencing a parliamentary majority, just as parliamentary governments throughout Europe do today, through political parties (Chapter 11).

Judges and courts, on the other hand, are not dependent on elections and generally nominated for life. Thus in practice they have a great deal of independence from the executive and legislature and enjoy a genuine separation of powers. Attempts to put them under the executive, or for it to influence their decisions are generally interpreted as a move away from democracy and a first step towards dictatorship. To that extent the doctrine of the separation of powers holds in Europe today.

nized differently and institutions matter! So we must describe judicial structures and career patterns before coming to any conclusions about the judges' political impact.

Having reviewed these points, we shall answer the main question of this chapter: do judges *make* law and policy? We proceed in three steps. First, we look at the daily work of judges and take up some of the points which emerge from the common law/civil law cleavage in Europe. Secondly, we consider the various forms of judicial review, that is the ways judges control the legality of the laws they apply. Thirdly, we look at the role special courts have in many European countries in reviewing the constitutionality of laws. We shall conclude the discussion with some hypotheses about the judiciary's influence in steering and directing European societies.

The legal families of Europe

In Europe, systems of civil law are distinguished from systems of common law. The civil law systems are quite diverse among themselves. We shall distinguish between five legal families in Europe: the common law, the Romance, the Germanic, the Nordic and the socialist. The differences among them mainly relate to private and commercial law, not constitutional, administrative or criminal law.

The common law family

Common law underlies the legal systems of most of the British Isles. The distinctive features of this family of laws are its technique and philosophy, evolved over nine

BRIEFING **14.2**

Law and different kinds of law

In essence, a law is a general rule backed by sanctions against those who break it. Who decides and applies such sanctions (international bodies, state or sub-state governments) may vary. There is debate about whether law could take the form of customs and conventions backed by public opinion in societies without government. However, in the modern world law is generally defined by having the backing of some authority which issues the rule in written form.

The *general* nature of law consists in the fact that it specifies appropriate behaviour for everyone under a particular set of circumstances. These circumstances are likely to arise, however, only for particular groups or types of people. Thus laws will have more relevance for some groups and individual than others, which is why these are more involved in lobbying the executive and legislature and in court actions designed to change existing rules.

The body of law is divided up according to the area of life it regulates. Thus there is a body of criminal law, commercial law, private law, family law, public, constitutional and administrative law, and so on. The borders between these are fluid and often depend on rather arbitrary definitions, for example whether sharp practice in business comes under commercial law or criminal law depends on whether it can be classed as a fraud (illicit deception). Legal cases are often defended on the grounds that an inappropriate charge has been brought.

Some practices like making contracts cut across a number of fields, so that the law of contract has a general applicability. So does the law of evidence. Law about procedures (such as how valid laws must be made) thus have a more general impact than most substantive law, since they affect the whole process of law-making. This is why constitutional courts generally have a higher status than ordinary courts. Very often the outcome of a particular case depends on whether the relevant laws under which it is brought are valid or not. Ultimately, therefore, decisions about political and legal procedures will affect us all.

centuries. 'The technique of this evolution has not been through the enunciation of principle, but through a continuing flow of cases and statutes. But, of the two, it is the cases that have determined its life. [Parliamentary] statutes have been and, in the field of lawyer's law, still are an exception' (Chloros, 1978: 12). Then as now common law is built upon the resolution of concrete disputes. An important feature in this process is the binding force of precedent (*stare decisis*). In the absence of legislation, every English and Irish court is bound by all decisions handed down by courts superior to it in the hierarchy. Common law is associated with the principle of equity, which prevails in cases of conflict. This principle guarantees that even where no common law rule exists, a decision can be made on the grounds of fairness. 'The philosophy of the Common law, the scale of values which it attempts to express, is one in favour of rights rather than of duties, of emancipation rather than of control, of responsibility rather than paternalism' (Chloros, 1978: 14).

Civil law is much older, with roots in ancient Roman law. It was influenced by the jurisprudence of the medieval church and the emergence of natural law in the seventeenth century. The abstract principles derived from this development were collected and put together in a systematic way in so-called codes. Although the various national codes differed, there was an underlying unity of method and of concepts.

'The method was deductive, that is, the process of reasoning was from general principles to specific cases, and the concepts were intellectual constructions, some, such
as possession, of considerable complexity' (Chloros, 1978: 16). Civil law is paternalistic, interferes more with individuals, expects a higher standard of behaviour
from them, and insists upon the need for discipline and control.

As mentioned above, there are four sub-families in the civil law traditions.

The Romance family

The core country in the Romance family of law is France. Until the French
Revolution a Roman law oriented system was in force in southern France, whereas
in the northern part many different systems of customary laws with less Roman
influence existed. From these three central codes in the field of private law emerged
the civil code, a commercial code, and a code of civil procedure. These French codes
have been very influential in the Benelux and the Iberian countries, as well as in Italy.

The Germanic family

Austria, Switzerland and Germany are the nucleus of the Germanic family of law, but
the tradition is also of great importance in Central and Eastern Europe. The recep-
tion and the updating of Roman law, in particular by the so-called Pandectist school,
is the most important factor in its development. The codes of the German group
are much more systematic than the codification within other groups. Moreover,
'general principles play a considerably more important role' (Bollen and de Groot,
1994: 104).

The Nordic family

Despite considerable differences this is usually classified under civil law families, but
it forms a special grouping by reason of close interrelationships between the various
national legal systems and common stylistic hallmarks. The similarities are due to
two factors. First, Roman law has played a smaller role than in continental Europe.
Secondly, the Scandinavian countries were frequently united with each other and
there has been close co-operation on legislation, particularly from 1962 (Bollen and
de Groot, 1994: 108). Old Germanic law forms the basis of Nordic law. The Nordic
countries maintained their local characteristics, but political and intellectual relations with Central and Eastern Europe allowed civil law thinking to make its way into
Scandinavia. However, the idea of codifying the whole of private law in a comprehensive manner has not worked out in any of the Nordic countries. Significant differences between the Nordic laws and those of continental Europe exist, for example
in the law of purchase.

The socialist (ex-communist) family

Socialist law, although of diminishing scope, still has some influence. Obviously this
is the case in those countries which still have a communist regime (e.g. Serbia), but
it also influences Soviet bloc countries which are in a process of transformation. As
far as its technique is concerned, socialist law belongs to the civil law systems because

Table 14.1 The legal
families of Europe

Legal family	Main countries	Strong influence in
Common Law	England and Wales, Ireland	Scotland,* Cyprus, Malta
Romance	France, Belgium, Luxembourg, Netherlands, Italy, Spain and Portugal	Scotland,* Greece, Turkey, EU, Poland, Romania, Malta
Germanic	Germany, Austria, Switzerland, Liechtenstein, Greece	Poland, Portugal, Turkey, Bulgaria, Croatia, Cyprus, Czech Republic, Slovakia, Hungary, Slovenia
Nordic	Denmark, Sweden, Norway, Finland, Iceland	Baltic states
Socialist	Serbia, Montenegro, Russia	Albania, Ukraine, Belarus, Baltic states

Note: * Mixed legal system.

there are codes. However, much law was created outside traditional structures, the machinery of justice differs fundamentally, and the legal concepts are completely subordinated to economic categories in the Marxian tradition (Chloros, 1978). The law is seen

> **as a tool of the state, to be used to work toward a socialist society. The state can (and should) use law to further its ends. This results in a kind of twisted logical circle; law exists to further the interests of citizens. The state knows better than any individual what the interest of the citizens are. Anything the state does, therefore, must be legal, since it is the state that writes the laws defining what, exactly, legal behaviour is. Thus law becomes simply another instrument of state policy**   *(Mahler, 1992: 155).*

Table 14.1 shows how national legal systems divide between these legal families. Except for the core countries in each family, this can only be an approximate characterization since the influences vary not only in time but from one legal field to the other (e.g. constitutional, private, commercial law). In particular, the legal systems of Central and Eastern Europe are in constant evolution away from the socialist legal tradition towards Western traditions. Thus, any exact characterization seems impossible at the moment, and may be superfluous altogether.

■ The harmonization of law in Europe

In his article on the 'Europeanization of the Law', Tomuschat states: 'The convergence of the legal orders in Europe is a fact that does not call for empirical evidence any more' (Tomuschat 1995: 21; our translation). Such convergence calls into who questions the usefulness of dividing European legal systems into the traditional 'legal families'. This seems even true to be for the common/civil law dichotomy: 'As the world becomes smaller by greater speed and through enormous but peaceful movements of population, a tendency may be detected to amalgamate the two [i.e. the common and the civil law] in a new form of European law in which those features of the two systems are retained which have proved to be of enduring value' (Chloros, 1978: 18). Thus, despite all differences there is a strong tendency in Europe to harmonize, even to unify, the law. At least three factors are of importance here: a) the activities of the Council of Europe (human rights in particular); b) the growth of EU law; c) the political as well as economic integration of the Eastern parts of Europe. We will discuss these factors in order.

Council of Europe: human rights and other unifying conventions

The Europeans, already signatories of the 1948 Universal Declaration of Human Rights by the United Nations, established an advanced human rights regime in 1950. The European Convention for the Protection of the Human Rights and Fundamental Freedoms has had a strong influence 'because of the binding nature of the decisions handed down by the European Court of Human Rights (ECHR) on the twenty states which have accepted compulsory jurisdiction. Further, the jurisprudential practice of the Court has gradually made it easier for individuals to pursue claims via the European Commission on Human Rights' (Stack 1992: 141). The Court and the Commission have thus actively shaped legislative, judicial and administrative practices in the European states. The Convention itself has in most countries legal, often even constitutional status, and is thus directly applicable in most legal systems. Consequently, it has a unifying and harmonizing power which should not be overlooked. To cite but one example, the development of advanced administrative courts in Austria is due almost solely to its influence. Kühnhardt comments that the Council of Europe and its human rights documents 'will be instrumental in bridging the present gap between the countries of Central, Eastern and Western Europe and facilitate the full-fledged integration of a new Europe, of a real European Community (Kühnhardt, 1993: 137).

The concern for human rights was intended mainly to protect individuals, but the Council of Europe has also promoted further international agreements aimed specifically at unifying the laws of European states. There are conventions on social law, data protection/privacy, criminal law, administrative law, product liability and many other matters. The explicit goal is the replacement of differing national laws and statutes by *unified legal provisions*. This has to be distinguished from the activities of the European Union (EU), which aims rather than at *harmonizing* the laws, at unifying the effects of the different national laws.

European Union law

The founding treaties of the three original European Communities (Coal and Steel, Economy, Atomic Energy) explicitly conferred powers to harmonize the law of the member states for the achievement of the Common Market. European legislators have been very active indeed. From 1986 to 1992, in particular, member states had to implement enormous numbers of directives to establish the single market. Consequently, economic law is harmonized to a very high degree, and the law in some other areas (such as social, consumer and environmental policy) is heavily influenced by European legislation. What is more, there are some areas where (previously differing) national legislation no longer exists, for example in international competition, foreign trade relations and agricultural policies. Here the European Union is now the relevant law-maker. The jurisprudence of the European Court of Justice (ECJ), in particular the preliminary ruling procedure (see below), has also had an important harmonizing effect on national legal systems.

Further proposals have been made for a unified Law of Contract. In 1989 the European Parliament passed a 'resolution on action to bring into line the private law of the Members State'. However, there is no specific provision in the EC Treaty for harmonizing private law. Doing so might touch off negative political reactions since private law covers such sensitive and cultural areas as family law, the law of inheritance, and land ownership. Nevertheless, there is much debate on drafting a European civil code outside the EU framework.

Influence of EU in Central and Eastern Europe

The law of the EU is also a strong influence on neighbouring countries. For instance, the member states of the European Free Trade Area (EFTA) began in the late 1980s to check the compatibility of any new legislation with European Community law before enactment. This was an attempt by countries like Sweden and Finland to avoid the discrepancies which would have prevented or rendered more difficult later attempts to form closer ties between the two economic entities. This strategy culminated in the 1994 European Economic Area (EEA) agreement which rendered harmonization obligatory. Most of the EEA members are now members of the EU and therefore had to accept the whole of the so-called *acquis communautaire* (existing laws and powers of the union). This will have a general impact on the Nordic legal family, since Norway and Iceland as EEA members and Sweden and Finland as new EU members are all committed to harmonization.

A similar development is taking place with respect to Central and Eastern European states, in particular Poland, Hungary, Slovenia and the Czech Republic. These countries were an integral part of the West up to the Second World War. Their socialist legal structure built on these old foundations. After 1989, the socialist superstructure was abolished, and the old laws adapted to a freer economy and society. A strong legal orientation towards the Western example was a logical consequence. The so-called Europe Agreements between some of the Eastern European states and the EU fulfil a similar role for these countries as did the EEA agreement for the EFTA countries. They give free access to each others' markets in exchange for serious efforts to harmonize the law on the part of the non-EU countries. Some of these states have already officially applied for EU membership, and some will do so in the foreseeable future. This puts implementation of EC law and practices in Eastern Europe high on the agenda. The EU has tried to facilitate this process by financing the exchange of lawyers and practitioners between East and West, under its TEMPUS initiative.

■ The diminishing common/civil law cleavage

The differences between common and civil law are becoming less important given the development towards harmonization mentioned above. In addition, two other factors are attenuating the classical dichotomy between English and continental legal traditions.

First, the growth of administrative law is a central phenomenon of twentieth-century English legal development. There are now two thousand or more administrative tribunals that handle the bulk of the disputes that arise between the administrative agencies and private citizens. Thus, the description of the common law system as one with no administrative law and no separate administrative courts is no longer valid. The specific peculiarities of the English judicial system such as the separation between barristers (who can appear in court) and solicitors (who cannot) are also being abandoned.

Secondly,

---

because a rough contrast is often drawn between common law as case law and civil law as code law, the similarity of common and civil law jurisdictions is often overlooked. It is true that the style of legal argumentation is somewhat different on the Continent than in Great Britain ... in reality [the continental judge] is acknowledging the body of legal doctrines built up around the bare words of the code by previous cases. While he does not necessarily cite the cases, other judges and lawyers know that he is not inventing new doctrines from scratch with just the bare words of the code to aid him. From the way he announces and applies the doctrines, they will be able to tell just which leading cases from the past he is following ... Continental judges are careful to phrase their commentary as if previous decisions are simply more or less persuasive discussions of what the code provisions really mean rather than independent acts of law-making. English judges, however, are usually careful to do something very similar. Typically, they treat a precedent as evidence or example of an underlying common law rule, not as a single piece of judicial legislation

(Shapiro, 1981: 136).

However, this tendency to convergence will not lead to complete unification in the short run. There are, for example, many technical difficulties in including the common law countries in the drafting of a pan-European civil code.

The courts

Common law and civil law systems

The differences in the legal systems of the European states also extend to differences in the structure of judicial systems. The first important distinction has to be drawn between civil and common law. The latter 'has a unified court system that might be represented as a pyramid with a single supreme court at the apex. Regardless of the number of different kinds of courts and of the way jurisdiction is divided among them in lower parts of the pyramid, every case is at least potentially subject to final scrutiny by a supreme court' (Merryman, 1969: 92). Although there is only a single supreme court there are two types of court at the bottom: County Courts which deal with the majority of civil litigation, and Crown Courts for criminal cases. At the very bottom, the lay magistrates' courts sit in minor criminal, family and youth cases. At the intermediate levels, we find the High Court and the Court of Appeal which, however, are unified only in name, as they have different divisions with respect to civil and criminal cases. The High Court may be the court of first instance if the amount of money at issue exceeds the County Court limit or if there is a serious criminal offence. Thus, the characterization of the English system as a 'unified court system' applies to the fact that there is no distinction between criminal/civil law on the one hand, and administrative law on the other.

The English judicial tradition is characterized by the passive role of the judge. The conduct of the judicial proceedings is in general the responsibility of the parties themselves, that is their lawyers (described as the 'adversarial principle' in civil, and

Figure 14.1 The 'common law' judicial system in England and Wales
Source: Peele (1995: 428).

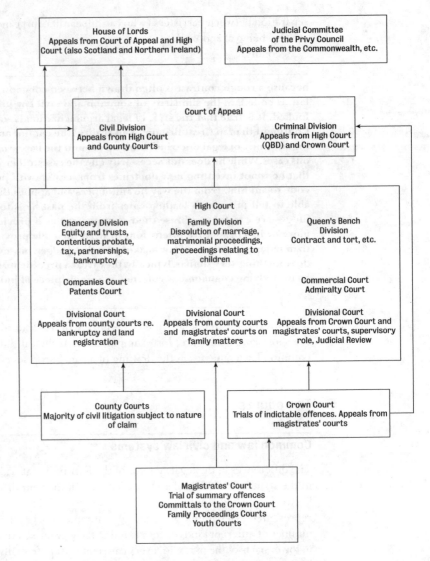

House of Lords
Appeals from Court of Appeal and High Court (also Scotland and Northern Ireland)

Judicial Committee of the Privy Council
Appeals from the Commonwealth, etc.

Court of Appeal

Civil Division
Appeals from High Court and County Courts

Criminal Division
Appeals from High Court (QBD) and Crown Court

High Court

Chancery Division
Equity and trusts, contentious probate, tax, partnerships, bankruptcy

Family Division
Dissolution of marriage, matrimonial proceedings, proceedings relating to children

Queen's Bench Division
Contract and tort, etc.

Companies Court
Patents Court

Commercial Court
Admiralty Court

Divisional Court
Appeals from county courts re. bankruptcy and land registration

Divisional Court
Appeals from county courts and magistrates' courts on family matters

Divisional Court
Appeals from Crown Court and magistrates' courts, supervisory role, Judicial Review

County Courts
Majority of civil litigation subject to nature of claim

Crown Court
Trials of indictable offences. Appeals from magistrates' courts

Magistrates' Court
Trial of summary offences
Committals to the Crown Court
Family Proceedings Courts
Youth Courts

This diagram is, of necessity, much simplified and should not be taken as a comprehensive statement on the jurisdiction of any specfic court

'accusatory principle' in criminal cases). 'The primary role of the judge during the trial is to make sure that the procedural rules are followed, although it may occasionally occur that the judge takes a more active role, depending very much on the personality and disposition of the particular judge' (Bogdan, 1994: 126). A typical common law judicial structure (that for England and Wales) is summarized in Figure 14.1.

The civil law countries have a dual system, consisting of two quite separate sets of courts, each with its own jurisdiction, its own judiciary, and its own procedures. The first set are the so-called 'ordinary' courts which hear and decide the great range of civil and criminal litigation. On the top of these, there is a Supreme Court of Cassation, a body that provides authoritative answers to questions on the interpretation of statutes referred to it by ordinary judges. Arguments about the facts of the case are excluded. The only permissible questions are questions of law. The Supreme Court thus does not decide the case, but may quash the decision of the lower court and order another court of that level to reconsider the case according to its own authoritative interpretation (Merryman, 1969: 94).

On the lower levels, we find specialized courts or courts of limited jurisdiction, for example in commercial or labour relations law. There is a division between civil and criminal courts (Weston, 1993: 69).

A typical civil law nation, however, will also have a set of administrative courts, entirely separate and exercising an independent jurisdiction.

The basic reason is, again, the revolutionary doctrine of the separation of powers ... One of the objectives of the revolutionary reforms was to deprive ordinary judges of any power to determine the legality of administrative action or to control the conduct of government officials. Just as the separation of the legislative and judicial powers denied judges any opportunity to interfere in the legislative process, so the separation of the administrative and judicial powers denied them that opportunity in the administrative process *(Merryman, 1969: 94).*

In the Romance legal family there is a so-called state council at the apex of the administrative courts. In the Germanic system, administrative courts, as such, have been created.

In general, the continental judge plays an active role in the trial. For instance, witnesses, although rare in civil cases, are questioned by the court, not by the parties or their advocates (who may, however, ask the court to put a certain question to the witness) (Bogdan, 1994: 177). This is the 'inquisitorial model'. In contrast to common law countries, juries are not very common on the continent. In the Dutch system, for instance, juries are unknown. In other countries, they play a role only in the most serious criminal cases.

Figure 14.2 summarizes the main features of a judicial system in the civil law tradition (the example is France).

Supreme courts and constitutional courts

When considering the policy-making role of the judiciary, the highest courts are of particular interest. We shall, therefore, deal with them separately.

All states have supreme courts. As we have already mentioned, the common law countries have only a single supreme court. The civil law countries have at least two, one in the 'ordinary', the other in the administrative branch. Some states have other, specialized, supreme courts; thus, for example Germany, has six supreme courts in total: one for constitutional law, one for administrative law, one for civil and criminal matters, one for tax, one for social, and one for labour law cases. All have exclusive competence to deal with cases falling exclusively into those areas. A common chamber of the courts solves possible conflicts of jurisdiction.

In some countries, the supreme court is a tribunal which differs from the other courts only inasmuch as it is the court of last (i.e. third) instance. The typical case here is England and Wales, where the (single) supreme court is the House of Lords

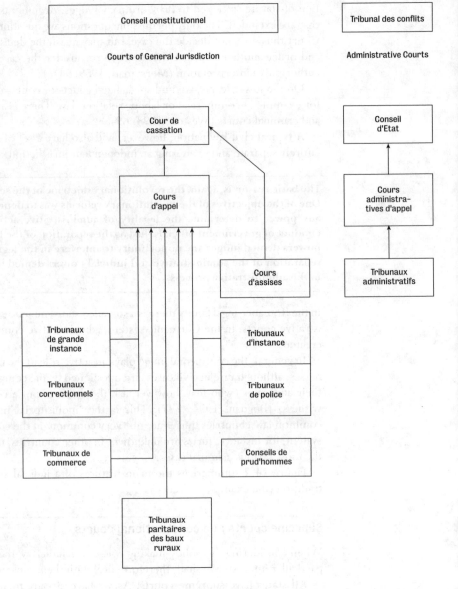

Figure 14.2 The 'civil law' judicial system in France
Source: Bogdan (1994: 174).

(and not, despite its name, the Supreme Court of Judicature which consists of the High Court, Crown Court and Court of Appeal). When the House of Lords, which is also the upper legislative chamber in the United Kingdom, functions as a court, participation is reserved to the so-called Law Lords, that is the well-respected jurists who have been elevated to a peerage just for that purpose, plus the previous holders of the office of Lord Chancellor. The House of Lords normally functions as a court of cassation, though a leave to appeal is required which can be granted not only by the House itself but also by the Court of Appeal. Leave to appeal is granted only in cases where a question of law of general interest has arisen. Some other countries follow the British model of having a Supreme Court deciding the full merits of a case, for instance Sweden and Poland.

Table 14.2		
Constitutional courts in European countries		

Country	Constitutional court	Remarks (year in (parentheses) = date of start of activities)
Albania	Yes	(1992)
Austria	Yes	(1920/1945)
Belgium	Yes	(1985): 'quasi–constitutional court'
Bulgaria	Yes	(1991)
Croatia	Yes	(1990)
Czech Republic	Yes	(1993)
Denmark	No	
Estonia	Yes	
EU	Yes	(1952); the European Court of Justice decides 'constitutional' issues, though it is not formally called a constitutional court
Finland	No	
France	Yes	(1959); but the Constitutional Council is not considered a court
Germany	Yes	(1949/1951); there are constitutional courts both at the federal and the Länder level
Greece	Yes	
Hungary	Yes	(1990) 'most active and powerful in the world'
Iceland	No	
Ireland	No	no specific constitutional court, but the High Court and the Supreme Court are granted original jurisdiction in disputes about the constitutionality of a statute
Italy	Yes	(1948)
Latvia	No	(by 1993)
Lithuania	Yes	(1993)
Luxembourg	No	
Macedonia	Yes	(1991)
Malta	Yes	(1975)
Netherlands	No	
Norway	No	
Poland	Yes	(1985)
Portugal	Yes	(1976)
Romania	Yes	(1992)
Serbia	Yes	(1964)
Slovakia	Yes	(1993)
Slovenia	Yes	(1991)
Spain	Yes	(1978)
Sweden	No	
Switzerland	No	
Turkey	Yes	(1961)
UK	No	

In contrast, the French Court of Cassation has no total jurisdiction. It cannot decide the case, but has only the power to control the correct application of the law, to quash the decision, and to refer the case for further consideration back to the lower courts. The same is true for the Belgian and Italian Supreme Courts. The Federal Court of Justice of Germany, as well as the Supreme Courts of the Netherlands, Austria, and also Switzerland to some degree, seem to be placed somewhere in the middle. For example, the High Council of the Netherlands has the last say with respect to points of law and, therefore, decides the whole case if a new appraisal of the facts of the case does not seem necessary.

Constitutional courts or review bodies play an important role in policy-making. They do not exist everywhere, however, as Table 14.2 shows. There seems to be a strong tendency to have them in the newly democratized Eastern and Central European countries. In mid-1993, twenty out of the twenty-nine former communist states in this area had established a constitutional court. We shall analyse the functioning of these courts in more detail when we consider constitutional review.

Supranational courts in Europe

European integration has brought about a new and very special type of international court: the so-called supranational court. There are two such court systems in Europe.

The first is part of the Convention on Human Rights of the Council of Europe (CoE) and consists of the European Commission on Human Rights and the European Court of Human Rights, both sitting in Strasbourg. The Commission investigates complaints of human rights abuses. Central to its function is the preliminary determination of whether or not a complaint meets the criteria for admissibility under the European Convention. If the Commission (whose decision is final and without appeal) determines that a complaint is admissible, and no amicable settlement of the dispute can be reached, it prepares a report on the facts and its opinion whether the state has breached the Convention. The report is forwarded to the Committee of Ministers of the CoE and may be brought before the Court. The Court comprises judges equal to the number of states in the CoE. The Court's decision is binding for those nations that have accepted its jurisdiction (that is to say, the overwhelming majority in Europe) and overrides any decision made by the national courts.

Within the European Union, two other very influential supranational courts exist: the Court of First Instance (CFI) and the European Court of Justice (ECJ). Both courts have as many members as there are states in the Union (fifteen at the moment). The CFI is competent to deal with a great variety of cases, such as competition law, staff cases, and foreign trade relations. Appeal to the ECJ is possible. The ECJ can be labelled the 'constitutional court' of the EC since it has the power to invalidate secondary EC legislation on the grounds of incompatibility with the EC treaties (i.e. the EC 'constitution'). It also settles disputes among the member states and between them and the institutions of the EU. Finally, its most important task is to check the compatibility of the member states' legislation with EC law, either by way of referrals of preliminary questions by national courts, or by way of a complaint of the EU Commission or of another member state.

The judges

Who are the judges? As Volcansek and Lafon note, 'the recruitment of jurists is the point where law and political culture intersect in a tangible fashion' (1988, p. 4). It seems that judicial recruitment evolves 'in some tandem arrangement with changes in a nation's political orientations' (ibid.).

'We in the common law world know what a judge is. He is a culture hero, even something of a father figure . . . If he sits on the highest court of a state or is high in the federal judiciary, his name may be a household word. His opinions will be discussed in the newspapers and dissected and criticized in the legal periodicals. He is a very important person' (Merryman, 1969:35). Most of the judges in common law countries are appointed or elected to the bench as a kind of crowning achievement relatively late in life, after having practised as a lawyer, in particular as a barrister for quite some time. In England, all appointments to judicial office are made by the Crown. In practice, they are made by, or on the advice of, the Lord Chancellor or Lord Advocate, the senior legal member of the government. Although some would voice doubts, most commentators agree that the system of appointing judges is done 'with little direct surrender to politics' (Abraham, 1993:31).

In the civil law world, a judge is not a hero, 'he is a civil servant, a functionary' (Merryman, 1969:36). There is a common pattern of judicial recruitment and personnel management across continental Europe although there are substantial variations in judicial independence and status from country to country. Unlike judges in England, judges on the continent are not recruited from among experienced practitioners. Instead, in some countries, such as France and Spain, there are special schools for training judges. In others such as Austria, Germany and the Nordic countries, judicial training is acquired in a post-law-school practical internship. Subsequently, young lawyers enter the judicial service directly at the lowest rank. Then they work their way up to higher and higher judgeships until retirement. The great majority of judicial offices, even at the highest level, are filled from within the ranks of the professional judiciary. Lateral entry into the judiciary is rare (Merryman, 1969:36). Judges are perceived both by others and themselves as government officials and share their relative prestige.

In discussing the notion of judicial independence, Shapiro (1981:151) points out the following differences with the common law judiciary. First, there is no tie between the judiciary and a politically powerful legal profession. Secondly, while English judges do not usually seek promotion from court to court, almost every European judge seeks to rise higher in his service. Thirdly, continental judges are a bureaucratic corps of government servants. 'The result is that European judicial services are likely to be closely attuned to the viewpoints of the civil servants who run the country. In short, behind the façade of judicial independence may lie an assimilation and subordination of judges to the higher civil service' (ibid.). However, the reality varies from country to country: while the Italian judiciary is 'an almost completely self-contained and self-controlled career service' (ibid.), the French judicial service remains essentially a branch of the civil service (Volcansek and Lafon, 1988:99). The German service lies somewhere in between the two. In France, as in many other countries on the continent, political patronage seems to play only a small role in the selection process. It is more the overall performance of a judge (mainly in terms of the number of his/her decisions quashed by a higher court) and the principle of seniority that influences promotion. However, the appointment for the constitutional councils/courts involves a parliamentary committee and/or the government (see below). There is only one European country – Switzerland – where judges are elected not directly by the citizenry, but by the two federal chambers sitting jointly as the National Assembly to ensure that there is a linguistic balance on the bench.

Lühmann (1975:116) noted the 'civil-service mentality' of German judges: 'The candidates for judicial careers . . . show a lesser degree of professional ambition. They tend to attribute events rather to circumstances than to themselves, they are less prepared to take risks and less capable of tolerating ambiguities. Their professional values are concentrated on security and on independence of their salaries from success or failure; they are directed more towards order than towards enterprise.' Procedures reflect this mentality. Even appellate and higher courts, where three or more judges sit on the bench and decide with a simple majority, present themselves in public as a unanimous body. Decisions are announced as decisions of the (collegiate) court, without enumeration of votes pro and con. In most jurisdictions, separate concurring opinions and dissenting opinions are not written or published, nor are dissenting votes noted.

	The judge is perceived as a:
Common law	'cultural hero', 'a father figure', 'an important person
Continental law	'an operator of a machine designed and built by legislators', a 'civil servant', a 'career judge', a 'functionary', an 'expert clerk'

Table 14.3 summarizes these contrasting judicial roles.

Another distinctive feature of the English judiciary is the tradition of having unpaid non-legally trained magistrates or justices of peace (JPs) sitting in minor criminal cases in smaller cities and towns. They are selected by local advisory committees. The approximately 30,000 JPs are generally white, middle class and in the upper age bracket (Peele 1995, p.437). In most European countries, laymen sit only in the specialized commercial courts or tribunals, and then always with a professional judge on the bench.

We must also take into consideration the recruitment of the judges to the constitutional courts. There, the picture is quite different since constitutional courts are rightly considered political players. The first difference consists in the mode of appointment. This is dominated by politicians (see Table 14.4). The second refers to the qualifications of the constitutional judges. Having served as a judge in the 'ordinary' judiciary is not always a precondition for being appointed. Law professors, for example, may become constitutional judges. At the one extreme (in France), there exist no formal prerequisites for membership beyond being aged eighteen or over and citizenship. 'In practice, the single most important criterion for selection is partisan affiliation. Since the Council's creation in 1958, former government ministers and parliamentarians have always constituted a majority of its members' (Stone 1992:31). At the other extreme, we find the Belgian rules carefully trying to establish a linguistic and political legal balance. One half of the Belgian Arbitration court, a semi-political, semi-juridical entity, consists of former members of parliament, and the other half are appointed from among the legal profession (highest courts, law teachers). In Germany, Italy and Spain law professors make up the largest group of appointees, followed by judges and lawyers. In Italy, the number of judges who had at one time been parliamentarians approaches that of France (Stone 1992a:294). To take but one of the newer Central and Eastern European examples, the Croatian court is composed of professional legal scholars and judges. Although not formally required, all members of the court are qualified to be a judge.

Judicial policy-making

'That courts make policies through even the simple act of choosing among competing interpretations is now widely accepted. That they often do far more is also not in doubt' (Volcansek 1992a: 1). This statement clearly applies to the common law systems where case law, and thus judge-made law, is an accepted and well-established feature. But it also applies to the civil law systems. Common lawyers say that the continental codes offer many (general) principles and few (concrete) rules. Continental lawyers see the code as providing rules, but very general ones that must be explicated by legal learning. 'Thus, the [continental] lawyer may insist that [continental] judges do apply pre-existing legal rules enacted by the code while the [common] lawyer might say that [continental] judges create legal rules in accordance with the principles stated in the code. Both would agree, however, that the code was not and could not be the whole of legal rules' (Shapiro, 1981:134). It seems to be rather a matter of definition whether one considers that task of the continental judge as being creative, and thus producing (new) legal rules, or as being only 'la bouche de la loi' (Montesquieu).

As a general rule, at least in civil law countries, a decision in a case between two individuals or between the state and an individual applies only among the parties involved in that trial. However, as has been pointed out, the application of the law, whether it is the common law or a statute or code, involves interpretation, and thus in some sense amendment of the law. These new rules, although only applicable between the parties in the first place, also become influential outside. In the common law system this is because of the principle of *stare decisis* (i.e. that decisions of higher courts are binding for lower courts). In the civil law tradition this happens because the judgement is part of a body of other decisions which build up to the jurisprudence and doctrine interpreting the written law. In this respect, we can speak of law-making by judges.

A brief round-up of judicial activities in European states presents a multifaceted picture of this type of judicial policy-making. For instance, Verougstraete, in a report on Belgium, writes: 'There have been numerous cases in which courts have, in effect, corrected the words of a statute, because they were convinced that the text was defective and ran counter to the intent of the legislator' (Verougstraete, 1992:98). Every observer familiar with the jurisprudence of a national legal system will agree to this as a statement of fact for his/her national system. The many blanket clauses to be found in the codes (e.g. the public order clause) give some leeway for political assessments by the judges. A report on the Netherlands by van Koppen points out that Dutch courts have been called 'deputy legislators'. This is due to the need to compromise fragmented political interests in the coalition structure. This prevents parliament from producing clear legislation on many controversial issues. 'In fact, legislators often refrain from regulating certain issues and choose to leave them to the judiciary' (van Koppen, 1992:84). Stone argues that 'French judges (not unlike their counterparts elsewhere) make law all the time . . . The ordinary and administrative courts, in sum, are national policy-makers to the extent that the aggregate effect of their decisions is to clarify, reinforce, or reshape general norms enshrined in code law' (Stone, 1992:29). Drewry reports of the British system that UK legislation is drafted in considerable detail, seeking to anticipate all contingencies. This restricts the latitude for judicial creativity. 'Judicial policy-making in Britain – exercised through creative . . . statutory interpretation and the operation of the doctrine of *stare decisis* in 'nudging' forwards (or backwards or sideways) the common law in areas where the legislature has elected to remain silent – is generally cautious, incremental and interstitial' (Drewry, 1992:14). The ECJ is another good example of a policy-making body where 'judicial activism' is the most moderate description of its activities. As Volcansek (1992b: 113) observes: 'The actions of the [ECJ] undoubtedly violated the line between interpretation (in even the loosest sense) and legislation.' The most prominent examples of the ECJ's 'legislative' activities are the doctrine of supremacy of EC law over national, even constitutional law; the doctrine of the direct effect of ECP law; and the Court's treatment of fundamental rights protected from EU encroachment.

However, there is an even more important aspect of policy-making by the judiciary. This is its role *vis-à-vis* the constitutionality of laws and statutes. There are two forms of this involvement: judicial review by the judiciary in general and constitutional review by a specialized constitutional (quasi-) court.

Judicial review

'Judicial review' in the US sense is the power of any judge of any court, in any case, at any time, at the behest of any litigant party, to declare a law unconstitutional (Stone, 1995: 287). In most European countries the courts do not have the power to invalidate laws. But in most countries, the administrative courts do have the power to review administrative acts. Furthermore, there are many ways in which the judiciary exercises considerable influence over legislation.

As Stone observes with respect to France, 'during the Fourth Republic, courts and particularly the Council of State began to discover and catalogue an array of constitutional principles that could be invoked by parties to litigation' (Stone, 1992b: 29). In Britain, the judicial process is limited by a doctrine of parliamentary sovereignty and by the fact that there is no codified constitution. Consequently, judicial review in the US sense is impossible. But, Drewry notes, 'in Britain, judicial review has been called an instrument of administrative law, encompassing a cluster of remedies available in the courts for challenging the legality or fairness of acts or omissions by public authorities' (Drewry, 1992: 19). There was a very activist phase through the 1960s and 1970s which continued during the post-1979 Thatcher years. In a series of public law cases, judicial remedies were granted not just against local authorities and civil servants, but also against ministers in their exercise of wide discretionary powers conferred on them by statute (Drewry, 1992: 20).

Ireland presents a special case since the constitution explicitly establishes judicial review. The Irish model comes close to the continental model of constitutional review since it is only the High Court which enjoys the power to invalidate acts of parliament.

The influence of European law is of considerable importance here. Within the EU, both the ECJ and the courts of the member states are required to ensure that EU law prevails over national law. 'This has placed national courts in a stronger position *vis-à-vis* parliament than they were accustomed to in the national context' (Scheltema, 1995: 207). If a court believes that a national statute is in clear breach of EC law, it is bound not to apply this statute. If in doubt, it is obliged to ask the ECJ for a decision which, in turn, has binding force. Consequently, judicial (or constitutional) review at the European level has consequences for the national level, too.

Constitutional review

'Constitutional review' is the authority to invalidate laws, administrative decisions, and judicial rulings on the grounds that they violate constitutional norms (Stone, 1995:287). If such authority is vested in a single constitutional review body – most frequently called a court – then we speak of constitutional review. This is the 'European Model' (Stone) in contrast to the US model of judicial review by the judiciary.

With respect to constitutional review, we can speak of abstract or of concrete review. Abstract review processes do not have a connection to a specific case, but are usually initiated by politicians: governments and legislators, federated member states (Länder) or regional governments (see Table 14.4). Abstract review processes have therefore been described as 'constitutional dialogues between elected politicians and constitutional judges in the making of legislation' (Stone, 1995:291). Although this is an accurate description in most states, there are nevertheless some important exceptions and new developments. In Spain, Poland and Croatia, an ombudsperson ('Defensor del Pueblo') has the power to initiate abstract review. This is a guarantee against possible abuses of power in the case of governments which hold absolute majorities in parliament. In Hungary, even individuals have the right to initiate abstract review. This has played a helpful role in the constitutional screening of the whole Hungarian legal order. In some Eastern states such as Poland and Serbia, associations and large interest groups, in others also courts and even local communes, enjoy the same rights as the politicians. In some countries (e.g. Austria, Albania, Poland and Serbia) the constitutional court itself may become active without any application. This reinforces its role as a political actor in its own right. The European Court of Justice represents another special case. Abstract 'constitutional' review can be initiated by every member state and by the main institutions of the EC, that is the Commission, the Council and the European Parliament.

All European constitutional courts practise some form of abstract review, but not all practise concrete constitutional review (France is a particular exception). Concrete review is 'a constitutional dialogue . . . established between the judiciary and constitutional courts in the defense of the supremacy of the constitution in the administration of justice' (Stone, 1995:292). Concrete review processes are initiated by either the judiciary, by individuals, or by an ombudsperson in the course of, or following, litigation in the courts. On the one hand, the judiciary is not allowed to engage in judicial review. On the other hand, the constitution is considered to be a higher law binding the judiciary as well. Therefore, ordinary judges have to refer constitutional questions to the constitutional court if there is doubt about the constitutionality of an act, or if the settlement of a case depends on the answer to this question. This system is reduplicated in the relationship between national courts and the ECJ through the so-called preliminary ruling procedure; where the constitutionality (i.e. the compatibility with EC law) of national law is at stake.

Individuals are also able to apply for constitutional review in about half the European cases (see Table 14.4). In general, the conditions are quite restrictive. In Germany, for instance, a 'constitutional complaint' may be filed by any person who claims that public officials, including judges, have deprived him or her of civil rights guaranteed by the Basic Law, but only after judicial remedies are exhausted. In Austria, an 'individual application' for invalidating a law or a decree is only possible if the applicant is deprived of his or her 'subjective rights' directly by the unconstitutionality of the law, without any other decision (of a court or an administrative body) being involved. Similar formulas also apply to other constitutional courts as well as to the ECJ. However, among all decisions handed down by, for example the German Federal Constitutional Court, some 95 per cent are initiated by individuals.

The second distinction to be made (and which applies only to abstract review) is the one between prospective or *a priori*, and retrospective or *a posteriori* review. The Constitutional Court of France, for instance, can only be involved in review of the constitutionality of a law before it has been enacted. The Irish Supreme Court can

Table 14.4   Characteristics of European constitutional courts

Country	Members named by	Abstract review	Authority to initiate abstract review	Concrete review	Authority to initiate concrete review
Albania	president and parliament	Yes	president, parliament, government, court itself	Yes	judiciary
Austria	government and parliament	Yes	fed. and Länder gov., 1/3 of National rat, 1/3 of any legis. chamber of a Land	Yes	judiciary, individuals
Belgium	senate	Yes		Yes	judiciary, individuals
Bulgaria	president, parliament, assembly of supr. courts	Yes	president, parliament, government	Yes	judiciary
Croatia	parliament	Yes	president, parliament, government	Yes	judiciary, individuals
Czech Rep.	president and parliament	Yes	president, parliament, government	Yes	judiciary, individuals
EU	member states	Yes	member states, EU institutions	Yes	judiciary, individuals
France	president of the republic, president of the two chambers	Yes	Presidents of Republic, and of the two chambers, 60 members of the two chambers	No	
Germany	the two chambers (Bundestag, Bundesrat)	Yes	Federal and Länder government, one-third of Bundestag, parties	Yes	judiciary, individuals
Hungary	parliament	Yes	also individuals!	Yes	judiciary, individuals
Italy	government, parliament and president of supreme court	Yes	national and regional government	Yes	judiciary
Lithuania	president and parliament of supreme court	Yes	president, parliament, government	Yes	judiciary
Macedonia	president and parliament and assembly of supreme courts	Yes	president, parliament, government	No	
Poland	parliament	Yes	president, parliament, government, judiciary, communes, associations, court itself	Yes	
Romania	president and parliament	No		Yes	judiciary
Serbia and Montenegro	president	Yes	president, parliament, government, court itself, associations	Yes	judiciary
Slovakia	president and parliament	Yes	president, parliament, government	Yes	judiciary, individuals
Slovenia	president	Yes	president, parliament, government	Yes	judiciary, individuals
Spain	government, judiciary, parliament	Yes	prime minister, president of parliament, 50 MPs or senators, executives of autonomous regions, ombudsperson	Yes	judiciary, ombudsperson, individuals
Turkey	president (on a proposal of the other supreme courts and high-level officers and attorneys)	Yes	president, one-fifth of parliament	Yes	Judiciary

Note: This table is illustrative not exhaustive, and may not be exactly comparable in all parts, since the sources used are mostly unsystematic. A full comparative analysis of constitutional review is still awaited.
Sources: G. Brunner, 'Die Neue Verfassungsgerichtbarkeit in Osteuropa', *Zeitschrift für Auslandisches Öffentliches Recht und Volkerrecht*, 53, pp. 819–70; N. Pesut, 'Verfassungsgerichtbarkeit Kroatien Osteuropa-Recht', 42, 1, pp. 18–47: Y Guchet (ed.), *Les Systemes Politiques des Pays de L'Union Européene* (Paris, Colin, 1994); A. Stone, *Governing with Judges* in J. Hayward and A. J. Page (eds), *Governing the New Europe* (Cambridge, Polity, 1995).

give an advisory opinion on constitutionality when asked by the president before a law is enacted. Although this court cannot be seen as a constitutional court in the narrow sense, the advisory opinion procedure is nevertheless a sort of abstract and prospective review, similar to that of France. The Hungarian Constitutional Court is also entitled to review laws before promulgation. With respect to international treaties, there is a prospective review procedure in some countries (e.g. in Germany, see the famous ruling on the Maastricht Treaty which cleared the path for its entering into force in 1993) and at the European level (see, e.g. the well-known 'opinions' of the ECJ in cases like the European Economic Area Agreement). However, most constitutional review processes start only when legislation is already enacted. Table 14.4 simplifies and summarizes the constitutional mechanisms employed by European constitutional courts.

Although constitutional review is the most relevant political task of constitutional courts, most also resolve controversies between units of government over their constitutional rights and duties, for example, the Austrian and German Constitutional Courts decide financial disputes between the communes, the Länder, and the Bund. They also decide on the validity of elections; and can hear impeachments involving the highest federal or Länder organs, e.g. members of the government. In most Central and Eastern European countries, the constitutional courts have also the power to prohibit unconstitutional political parties. However, in some countries such as France, there are separate High Courts of Justice dealing with impeachment cases.

The impact of constitutional review

Although judicial review in the US sense is formally prohibited in Europe, it does take place in disguised form. In countries which have a constitutional court, judicial review is an overt and powerful – and sometimes criticized – political reality. Unfortunately, the literature varies, so the following comparison can only give an impressionistic picture of how it currently operates in Europe.

The Federal Constitutional Court of Germany 'has been among the most energetic of constitutional courts, evoking criticisms both of "judicializing" politics and "politicizing" justice' (Murphy and Tanenhaus, 1977: 32). Decisions have involved politically sensitive issues such as freedom of speech, political parties, abortion, and federal-state relations. The main political parties were able 'to shift the battle into the judicial arena'. Up to 1992, the Court had invalidated 4.6 per cent of all federal laws, the greatest number in social policy, followed by financial and then legal policy (Landfried, 1992:51). A most powerful tool developed by the Court reduces the policy-making power of parliament. This is the 'interpretation in conformity with the constitution' which is a declaration that one particular interpretation of a law is the only constitutionally permissible one and often entails precise prescriptions for the implementation of a law. There are also cases where the Court has exceeded its competence and been heavily critized, for example, on the question of abortion. This has led members of parliament to adjust their bills to (previous) decisions of the Court and anticipate possible future judicial review, a practice has been nicknamed 'Karlsruhe astrology' after the town where the Court sits.

Similar experience in France with respect to the Constitutional Court led Stone (1992:30) to describe the Council as a 'specialised, third chamber of parliament'. He argues that the composition of the Council, its weak 'judicial' status, detachment from the judicial system, and in particular, its frequent use by members of the parliamentary opposition, have developed a political climate which has 'juridicized' policy-making in the 'other' chambers of parliament. 'Each decision was a complex annulment of the government's preferred text' . . . and each led to a second legislative process, the purpose of which was to implement the Council's policies as a means of securing promulgation' (Stone, 1992b:36). The Council is particularly concerned with codifying a bill of rights. By contrast, Bell comes to the conclusion that 'the scope and procedure of the constitutional review now operated by the

Conseil constitutionnel is very much like that of a constitutional court, but with substantial differences from the kinds of courts that exist in the United States and Germany' (Bell, 1992:55).

The Austrian Constitutional Court resembles the German. However, there is one important difference which changes the interplay between the Court and parliament. While the German Basic Law is hardly amendable at all, amendments to the Austrian Federal Constitution occur quite frequently. If they do not touch the 'core' of the constitution, these 'constitutional laws' only require a two-thirds majority in parliament. Consequently, if the Court invalidates a federal law, the legislature may overturn the ruling of the Court by simply enacting the criticized provision again, but this time with a higher quorum, as a constitutional law which then is immune from scrutiny by the Court. In times of a coalition government consisting of the two major parties, the hurdle of the two-thirds majority requirement is not a difficult one to surpass and, thus, is a frequent practice. A similar phenomenon has been described with respect to the Hungarian Court.

The Italian Constitutional Court seems to keep a low profile, due to several factors. First, there is no power of abstract review initiated by parliamentarians. Secondly, Italian constitutional judges have been conscientiously passive in their relations with sitting legislators (Stone, 1992:297). Thirdly, many cases are not heard by the Court, since a large margin of discretionary interpretation is left to the lower court judge who can prevent a case reaching the Court by issuing an interlocutory judgement, that is, noting that the claim of the case is unfounded. 'The Court has developed a relatively restrained view of its power, partially because of indifference from the executive branch and the public at large, but more so because of outright hostility from many in the ordinary judiciary' (de Franciscis and Zannini, 1992:71). Despite these difficulties, it has assumed a major role, both in protecting civil liberties and more clearly defining the relationships and powers between the national and regional governments. It has also been active on church-state relations and the validation of referendum proposals.

In Spain, abstract review is more important than concrete review. As in Germany, the Court is heavily involved not only in partisan disputes over national legislation but also in the ongoing construction of regionalism (Stone, 1992:297).

The Belgian Arbitration Court can exercise only very limited powers of constitutional review. However, its 'decisions were crucial for the cohesion of the country and do perhaps not fit completely with the prevailing view of the political parties of the majority. In other cases the court has been far more cautious and saved the government from some rather tricky impasses in which it had put itself' (Verougstraete, 1992:101).

The Croatian, like most other Eastern and Central European constitutional courts, has played an important role in the transformation of the old socialist legal order, the building of a democratic party system, and the protection of basic rights. It has sometimes been criticized for its opportunism and delays in some cases.

In Hungary, most decisions of the Constitutional Court concern the constitutionality of norms, rather than basic rights of the citizens. The conflicts between the legislature and the Court seem to be mainly 'teething troubles'.

To sum up, constitutional courts all over Europe have vetoed hundreds of legal provisions, lawfully enacted by the respective legislature, while laying down rules for how they must or must not be revised in the future.

The impact of constitutional courts on policy-making processes results from a combination of two main factors. The first of these is the existence of a leading decision (or line of decisions) relevant to the legislation currently being debated in the government or parliament . . . A leading decision has the effect of at least partly codifying these constraints . . . In this way, constitutional uncertainty is gradually replaced by constitutional obligation . . . The second factor is the extent to which parliamentary oppositions and subnational governments exploit review processes for their own political ends, facilitating or reinforcing the control of constitutional courts over policy outcomes . . . oppositions exploit abstract review procedures – which are virtually costless – in order to win from constitutional courts what they can never win in parliament . . . Indirect effects are anticipatory reactions structured by constitutional politics *(Stone 1995:300).*

Some of the most controversial social issues have been shuttled to the courts in their role as problem solvers.

Thus, constitutional courts are ambivalent, hybrid entities: they can neither be limited to functions of a purely judicial nature nor reduced to mere political bodies (Mény and Knapp, 1993:369).

◼ Conclusions

We can summarize our main conclusions about the relationship between law, judges, courts and policy-making processes in Europe, as follows:

- The law is an important means of policy-making. In an ever more complex environment the amount of legislation is growing, and therefore the role of those whose language is the law, the lawyers in general, and the judges in particular, is increasing.
- European integration plays a major role both in harmonizing laws in all European states and in enhancing the impact of courts in the policy-making arena.
- The policy process is increasingly 'juridicized', i.e. influenced by extra-political considerations such as the probable outcome of a constitutional review process. Judicial review in general ('test case' strategies), and constitutional review in particular is being used by parliamentary opposition and minority groups in order to by-pass the 'normal' processes of policy-making through government and parliament.
- The Central and Eastern European states have instituted constitutional review procedures on the Western European model. These have helped their transition to democracy and strengthened their civil society.

◼ Further reading

Much information on legal processes in Europe, particularly in the Centre and East, is available only in specialized sources. A very useful compilation, however, is to be found in the 1992 issue of *West European Politics*, Vol.15, Part 3, which contains the articles by Volcansek, Verougstraete, van Koppen, Stone, Stack, Landfried, de Franciscis and Zannini and Drewry, cited above. Another good comparative collection is edited by

Hesse and Johnson, *Constitutional Policy and Change in Europe* (Oxford, Oxford University Press, 1995). The article by Attila Àgh, on Hungary titled 'The permanent "constitutional crisis" in the democratic transition', is in this collection and also Scheltema.

A succinct comparison of the different legal systems is A. G. Chloros, 'Common law, civil law and socialist law', *The Cambrian Law Review*, 10, 1978, pp. 11–26.

Other useful comparative and specialized works are:

H. J. Abraham, *The Judicial Process – An Introduction Analysis of the Courts of the United States, England and France*, 6th edn (Oxford/New York, Oxford University Press, 1993).

J. Bell *French Constitutional Law* (Oxford/New York, Oxford University Press, 1992).

M. Bogdan, *Comparative Law* (Deventer, Cambridge, Kluwer, 1994).

C. Bollen, G. R. d. Groot, 'The sources and backgrounds of European legal systems,' in Hartkamp, Hesselink, Hondius, de Perron and Vranken (eds), *Towards a European Civil Code* (Dordrecht/Boston/London, Martinus Nijhoff, 1994).

R. M. Jackson, *The Machinery of Justice in England*, 7th edn (Cambridge, Cambridge University Press, 1977).

L. Kühnhardt, 'European courts and human rights', in Greenberg, Katz, Oliviero and Whetley (eds), *Constitutionalism and Democracy – Transitions in the Contemporary World* (New York/Oxford, Oxford University Press, 1993).

N. Luhmann, 'The legal profession: comments on the situation in the Federal Republic of Germany', *Juridical Review* 20 (1975).

G. S. Mahler, *Comparative Politics: An Institutional and Cross-National Approach* (Englewood Cliffs, Prentice-Hall, 1992).

Y. Mény, and A. Knapp, *Government and Politics in Western Europe – Britain, France, Italy, Germany*, 2nd edn (Oxford/New York, Oxford University Press 1993).

J. H. Merryman, *The Civil Law Tradition – An Introduction to the Legal Systems of Western Europe and Latin America* (Stanford, Stanford University Press, 1969).

W. F. Murphy, and J. Tanenhaus, *Comparative Constitutional Law – Cases and Commentaries* (New York, St Martin's Press, 1977).

Gillian Peele, 'Governing the UK', in *Modern Government*, 3rd edn (Oxford, Blackwell, 1995).

M. Scheltema, Constitutional Developments in the Netherlands: Towards a Weaker Parliament and Stronger Courts?, in Hesse and Johnson (eds), *Constitutional Policy and Change in Europe* (New York/Oxford, Oxford University Press, 1995).

M. M. Shapiro, *Courts, A Comparative and Political Analysis* (Chicago, University of Chicago Press, 1981).

A. Stone, 'Governing with judges: The new constitutionalism', in J. Hayward and A. J. Page (eds), *Governing the New Europe* (Cambridge, Polity Press, 1995).

C. Tomuschat, 'Europäisiering des Rechts', *Europäische Integration und Nationale Rechtskulturen* (Köln/Berlin/Bonn/München, Carl Heymanns Verlag, 1995).

M. L. Volcansek, and J. L. Lafon, *Judicial Selection – The Cross-Evaluation of French and American Practices, Contributions in Legal Studies* (40) (New York/Westport/London, Greenwood Press, 1988).

M. Weston, *An English Reader's Guide to the French Legal System*, 2nd edn (Providence/Oxford, Berg Publishers).

Political economy

Chapter 15

Reshaping the welfare state

■ Introduction

State structures have a life of their own. Although different constitutional arrangements and legal systems have effects on government policy, these are not always direct or obvious. Sometimes, very different political systems may pursue substantially the same policies, like expenditure cuts in Britain and the Netherlands in the 1980s. At other times similar governments may pursue different policies, like the socialists in France (orthodox finance) and Greece (free spending) during the same period.

However, one thing is clear: governments and states have to make policy choices, and these have to cope adequately with the problems facing society, both externally and internally. Democracies have an inbuilt safety-value, in that governments can be voted out if their policies are seen not to have succeeded (see Chapter 11). If new governments fail to make the necessary policy adjustments, however, the whole future of the state and its political structures may be endangered. Institutional arrangements may be autonomous, but their long-term survival depends on the success of the policies which emerge from them.

This is particularly true for the new democracies of Southern and Central Europe. Their authoritarian predecessors broke down because they could not cope with the problems they faced. Democratization was carried through under the shadow of a massive social and economic crisis, which we shall document in this and the following chapter. Appreciation of the political benefits of democratization carried these countries through the early 1990s, and the changes of government it permitted produced necessary modifications of policy.

However, in the long run there have to be discernible benefits for the population if democracy is to continue. Against all expectations, there was a minor turnaround in Central Europe in the mid-1990s. This gives hope that concrete economic and social benefits may emerge more quickly than expected. One should never forget, however, the close tie between the stability of institutions and the outputs they produce – a link which is easy to forget if we concentrate only on the functioning of democratic processes. That is why, in this part of our book, we concentrate on the two most basic internal policy sectors: welfare and economics. Both are intimately linked with the well-being of the population and indeed with each other. If the economy malfunctions, income goes down and unemployment rises. This throws the burden on welfare provisions – not just for those out of work, but for the vulnerable and economically inactive sections of the population, that is the children, sick and elderly.

In this century, as we shall see, all European countries have developed a network of social policies and institutions to administer them which go collectively under the name of the welfare state. Basically these are designed to prevent any citizen from

BRIEFING 15.1

The welfare state

This refers to a state that accepts the principle that it should intervene to ensure that all its inhabitants enjoy minimal standards of living, health and protection against major contingencies (unemployment, sickness, death). Whether all should enjoy state protection, or whether this should be confined only to those who cannot help themselves is a question that is widely debated, particularly between 'left' and 'right' (see Chapter 9). The term 'welfare state' also refers very often to the array of institutions – hospitals, health trusts, insurance and employment agencies – set up by the state to care for those in need.

dying of cold, hunger or lack of medical attention. How they do this depends on the institutional arrangements which have been made. As we shall see, there are strong national differences between these arrangements in Europe. These will probably tie most welfare provision to the country level rather than the European one for the foreseeable future. However, common pressures like the growth of structural unemployment, ageing populations and competition in a global market may produce limited convergence between European systems, if only in a common 'crisis of the welfare state'.

For the reasons mentioned above, this is a serious challenge to European democracies. Welfare states are above all *national*, that is they are an important legitimizing characteristic of the nation-state itself. A redistributive welfare state (i.e. one that tries to reduce the grossest disparities in life chances between rich and poor) is possible only to the extent that a common identity – a sense of community and belonging together – exists. Without some fellow-feeling for the beneficiaries, citizens will not see why their taxes and contributions should pay for the others.

This is how our present discussion ties in with previous ones of national and regional identities in Europe, and of the state structures they support. Indeed some of the developments we have discussed such as devolution of power to localities and regions, are due to the immense administrative burdens of dispensing healthcare and delivering social services. These demand a more personal and indeed individualized approach to administration than when the state was simply the guarantor of external defence, and of internal order and communication.

This chapter thus forms a crucial link between the institutional analyses of Part III and the increasingly policy oriented discussions of Chapters 16–18. The welfare state is at once a set of institutions and of associated policies. The fact that both are under pressure at the moment is a particular problem in Europe. For it is here that the welfare state originated and where it has always been strongest.

■ Initial questions and some historical lessons

'The welfare state is at a breaking point' (*The European*, 28/1/94) and 'a few bold souls are even wondering if Europe should not rebuild its welfare state, creating a more modest and affordable structure before the old edifice falls into total disrepair' (*Newsweek*, 20/12/93). These are typical of media comments on European welfare

BRIEFING 15.2

The (recurring) crisis of the welfare state

As the quotes show, the idea that the welfare state has entered into a crisis is common in academic and political debate. The question is whether this is a political crisis, brought on by right-wing groups and parties which simply want the better-off to keep what they have got; or whether welfare spending has actually come up against some kind of objective limit to what can be spent on it? Political rhetoric often rests on the second idea, that there is a fixed limit to what can be spent on welfare. When the argument is examined, however, it usually comes down to the proposition that reducing taxes is a more urgent priority than spending on welfare. Tax reductions can of course be defended on many grounds but they do not constitute an 'objective necessity' which 'inevitably' limits welfare spending.

Similar arguments about a 'crisis' have often been used in the past. Ever since the end of the nineteenth century, the welfare state has been accused of exceeding its reasonable limits and of producing undesirable side-effects. In Germany for example, a heated debate over the excessive economic burdens imposed by Bismarck's social legislation was already in full swing just after 1900. At that time the social insurance schemes spent 1.4 per cent of the gross domestic product! In 1952, *The Times* in Britain inaugurated the first of many debates on the 'crisis'. In that year, 15.6 per cent of the British gross domestic product (GDP) was spent on social security and services. In 1991, average social protection expenditure as a percentage of GDP in the twelve countries of the then European Community was 26.0 per cent (Eurostat, 1994, *Social Protection in Europe 1993*).

states. Among the questions they raise are: What is the status of European welfare states? In what direction(s) are they moving? What economic, political and cultural challenges do they face?

As background, it is useful to give a brief presentation and interpretation of the history of welfare development. Most of the post-war period has been characterized by overall welfare growth, solid cross-party commitment to such growth, and – for historical reasons – by institutional differentiation among European states. We shall draw a general picture of these developments. Within this framework we will then outline recent developments in four selected countries: the United Kingdom, Germany, Sweden and Poland. Each of these represents one of the four types of welfare states which can be distinguished in post-war Europe.

This is not the first time that the welfare state has been perceived to be at a 'breaking point'. For a perspective on its current position we begin by looking at some essential elements in the development of European welfare states.

The modern welfare state is a European invention which can trace its institutional roots, if not its concept or conception, to the last two decades of the nineteenth century. Comprehensive national social insurance, originating in Bismarck's Germany in 1883, spread all over Europe before 1920. In the inter-war period, the European ideal of social security spread all over the world. Today, about 140 countries have some type of state-backed social security system. Most commonly this covers work-related injury, and old age and survivors' pension schemes; least commonly an unemployment insurance scheme.

Social insurance represented a radical break with poor law legislation. In one way, the innovative role of Germany in providing social security was unexpected, in another way perhaps not. State social security can be seen as one response to the break-down of the traditional modes of social protection during the process of industrialization. These had been provided by the family and local community. Population movements, increased social mobility and the growth of new family patterns destroyed these, however, provoking a response by the state.

Social security can also be seen as a concomitant of democratization, as a response to political demands for greater social security, justice and equality. These could be met by extending public responsibility for social needs to propertyless workers dependent upon wages from industrial labour.

But Germany was not the most industrialized European country in the 1880s, and certainly not the most democratic. On the other hand, the economic doctrines which prohibited state interference in the free market, which were strong in the English-speaking countries, had a comparatively moderate influence. Paternalistic intervention by the state had a longer tradition and a stronger presence in Germany. An active role for the state in the social field was thus more conceivable in this historical-political context than in the more democratic and more capitalist European countries, such as Britain and Denmark. But the democratic states soon caught up.

The origin of social security as a state response to disruptive economic change teaches us a lesson which is still relevant in the modern world. Social security can be an answer both to leaders' needs for social and political stability and to popular demands for social protection and security. It can also in some cases develop as a conscious reform by humanitarian and socially minded politicians of all parties.

Identical solutions do not imply identical causes or motivations, and identical problems do not imply identical solutions. Social insurance can be interpreted broadly as an answer to problems created by capitalist industrialization. But we need only look to East Asia today to observe attempts at another interpretation of welfare problems and needs, which entails different political solutions from the European. (For example, Singapore passed a law in 1994 which gave families rather than the state the responsibility of looking after aged parents.) On the other hand, some of the factors which gave rise to the European welfare states may still become manifest elsewhere in the world. Pressures from demographic change, labour mobility and social instability, together with a push from growing national wealth and political democratization, may facilitate the diffusion of ideas about state social action.

In the first phase of European social security development, debate centred on what the fundamental and constituent principles of the state's social role should be. The idea that the state should play some kind of role quickly gained acceptance across regimes and countries at different levels of industrialization, democratization and capitalist development. But should insurance be compulsory or voluntary? Should insurance cover only certain kinds of needs or 'all' social insurance needs? Should it extend only to some groups of the population, perhaps only to the most needy, or to everybody? Should a moral demarcation be drawn between the 'deserving' and 'undeserving' poor? Should insurance schemes be financed by general taxation, employers and/or premiums from the insured? Should there be means-testing or universal benefits? Should they be organized by the state or privately – for example through trade unions and mutual benefit societies?

The period from 1870 to 1920 has been called the period of 'experimentation' (Heclo, 1981). The period was characterized by innovation and volatility in programming, and by 'constitutional' arguments on boundary problems. In the 1990s, the old debate on boundaries resumed: what should (and *can*) be the responsibility of the state? What are the limits of individual and family responsibilities?

Historically, the target groups were generally the deserving poor and the (industrial) working class, although in Scandinavia the concept of a comprehensive 'people's insurance' was invented around the turn of the century. The first social insurance policies reflected attempts to reconcile the values of liberty, equality and security – and countries differed in their specific responses to the needs and problems of social security. European welfare states developed into different institutional shapes which have persisted to this day. This warns us that the title of this chapter 'Reshaping the welfare state' could more correctly read 'reshaping the welfare states'. Institutional legacies are not easily thrown overboard and will still shape national responses even to the same set of pressures.

Institutional differentiation in post-war developments

A significant institutional difference exists between countries where claims for social transfers and services gradually came to be based on citizen rights, and countries where claims are related to employment and contribution records. A parallel distinction holds between countries where social security schemes and health and social services are uniform and universal, and countries where schemes are differentiated by occupational group and social class.

Most of the fundamental decisions on these institutional characteristics were taken relatively early. A major distinction can still be drawn between the Scandinavian-British system, with relatively strong elements of social citizenship and relatively uniform and integrated institutions: and the continental systems with much more fragmented institutions and with a smaller citizenship component. The two major dimensions of institutional variation can generally be summarized as the degree of 'stateness' (i.e. the degree to which the state or central government controls the various welfare institutions) and the degree of 'universalism' (i.e. the degree to which welfare institutions cover the whole population or specific groups only). Both dimensions are closely related to the specific national histories of state and class formation, of nation-building and cultural heterogeneity. The more homogeneous the industrial working class, the more influential big industry, and the more centralized the trade union movement, the more likely was the development of a uniform system of income maintenance. The two basic historical principles of social security in Europe are associated with the names Bismarck and Beveridge, the great British social reformer of the 1930s and 1940s. They can be summarized as in Table 15.1.

The period after the Second World War, saw a vigorous and persistent growth in social expenditure in European countries – both in real terms and, until recent years, as a proportion of gross domestic product (GDP). At least four different types of institutional arrangements for welfare developed. Most European countries would fit in one such type. Bear in mind, however, that schematic models do not provide a complete perspective on the welfare system of any given country, and they are rather static. Changes take place in all systems.

In Figure 15.1, we distinguish between four European welfare models, one of which – the communist – collapsed after 1989. The exact way it will now develop

Table 15.1 Historical European social security principles

Principles	Germany (Bismarck)	Great Britain (Beveridge)
Guiding principle	Social security as an autonomous principle	Priority on secured jobs and the right to work
Special goal	Maintenance of status and income	Guaranteeing a social level of subsistence
Coverage	Employed persons (and family members)	All citizens
Kind of transfer	Earnings-related benefits	Flat-rate benefits
Financial base	Through contributions of employers and employees	Through (progressive) taxation
Administration and execution	In the hands of the social partners; employers and employees	In the hands of employees or the State

Source: Roebroeck (1991).

Figure 15.1 Major European welfare state models since 1945

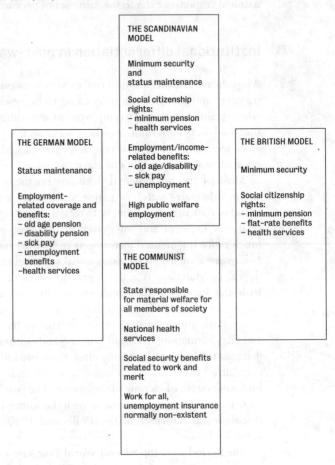

THE SCANDINAVIAN MODEL

Minimum security and status maintenance

Social citizenship rights:
– minimum pension
– health services

Employment/income-related benefits:
– old age/disability
– sick pay
– unemployment

High public welfare employment

THE GERMAN MODEL

Status maintenance

Employment-related coverage and benefits:
– old age pension
– disability pension
– sick pay
– unemployment benefits
– health services

THE BRITISH MODEL

Minimum security

Social citizenship rights:
– minimum pension
– flat-rate benefits
– health services

THE COMMUNIST MODEL

State responsible for material welfare for all members of society

National health services

Social security benefits related to work and merit

Work for all, unemployment insurance normally non-existent

is unclear but any changes are likely to build on institutional features of the old regime (e.g. the welfare functions of unions described in Chapter 7). The typology in Figure 15.1 helps specify the differentiation between European welfare states which took place after 1945. With the exception of the communist model, it is unlikely that this will rapidly disappear.

We shall take a closer look later at what has happened after 1989 in countries which represent each of the four models: the United Kingdom, Germany, Sweden

Figure 15.2 Real social
expenditure and real
GDP, 1965–85
Note: Unweighted average
of twenty-one OECD
countries.
Source: Cochrane (1993:
241), based on OECD,
1988, data from *National
Accounts and Social Data
Bank.*

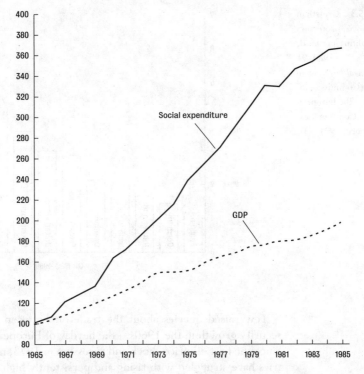

and Poland. This is one way to search for commonalities, and to look for trends to convergence or divergence in welfare state development. But first let us examine some general trends in social expenditure until the early 1990s, and the 'ideological status' of the welfare state at the beginning of the 1990s.

Social expenditure growth and ideological rhetoric in the 1980s

From 1945 to 1980 social expenditure in all countries increased as an effect of; a) the expansion of established social security schemes; b) the development of some new schemes such as family allowances and maternity benefits; c) the introduction of earnings-related elements in many pension schemes; d) demographic change; and e) higher welfare payments in general. Levels of benefit were increasingly safe-guarded through linkage to price indexes and/or to the average level of earnings, or to the level of earnings at retirement. Steadily higher proportions of the population were covered, as well as wider risks. There was a general trend towards equal rights for men and women in the labour market and in relation to social security legisla-tion. Social insurance was also extended to self-employed persons usually through the establishment of more universal systems of coverage.

The period 1950–80 thus saw an unprecedented increase in social security and welfare in Europe. Expansion was made possible by sustained economic growth, which was conducive to a political consensus on welfare expansion. As a general illustration of welfare state growth in European and other capitalist democracies in the period 1965–85, Figure 15.2 shows the growth curves of social expenditure and GDP for twenty-one OECD countries (i.e. including some non-European states).

Figure 15.3 Growth in social protection expenditure per head, 1980–91

Source: Social Protection in Europe (Commission of the European Communities, Luxembourg, 1994: 43).

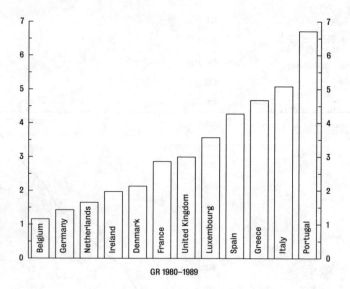

GR 1980–1989

Few raised queries about the trade-off between economic growth and social security growth in the 1960s – the heyday of European welfare state development. Since the first oil price shock and recession in 1973, most Western European countries have struggled with rising and persistently high levels of unemployment, and rising public deficits. In the Central and Eastern European countries, similar problems developed. But there they were kept off the public political agenda by the undemocratic character of the political systems, and their different ways of defining and interpreting social and political problems.

Since 1989 the change in these countries from centralized communist systems to decentralized, market-oriented capitalist democracies has also implied that a new kind of welfare system must be established. Common constraints have induced governments both in Eastern and Western Europe to cut social expenditure or increase social revenue. Demographic change will impose an increasing burden on future public budgets unless some schemes and benefits are modified. This is shown by the way in which total social expenditures have grown quite dramatically in real terms during the last decade over most of Europe, as exemplified by figures for the member states of the European Union (Figure 15.3).

In 1991, the average share of social expenditure as a percentage of gross domestic product in the European Community was 26 per cent. The Netherlands was top with 32.4 per cent and Portugal at the bottom with 19.4 per cent (Eurostat, 1994, with Greece not included). The average is the same as in 1985, while the level in 1980 was 24 per cent. Data for Central and Eastern European countries for this period are not comparable, but social security expenditure as a percentage of GDP increased substantially in Bulgaria, Czechoslovakia, Hungary and Poland between 1985 and 1991.

Thus in spite of many examples of retrenchment, total social expenditure continued to increase both in real terms, and also as a percentage of GDP. Partly because of rising unemployment, and partly because of a growing proportion of old people in most populations, the number of eligible beneficiaries of social security schemes has steadily increased. Cuts in benefit levels for sickness, old age, unemployment and social assistance in many countries have not prevented the total social budget from increasing. Gross public debt as percentage of GDP increased in all but one member state of the European Community from 1989–95 (*The European*, 28/1/94–3/2/94). All Eastern European countries are characterized by a deep fiscal crisis, which is more profound than in Western Europe, at the same time as their welfare systems face more fundamental institutional challenges than in the West.

In the governing circles of Western European countries, the beginning of the 1980s marked a change in the dominant thinking about the welfare state. Margaret Thatcher's first government stated in 1979 that 'higher public expenditure cannot any longer be allowed to precede, and thus prevent, growth in the private sector' (Walker, 1986). Similar statements were made even by the social democratic Scandinavian governments of the 1980s. During the 1980s parties, movements, and governments across the political spectrum advocated more market, less state intervention, more decentralization, and expansion of individual rights and responsibilities. The recipe for this ideological change can probably be traced back to a book published by the OECD in 1981. The Secretary-General, van Lennep, formulated the general programme for the 1980s as:

> **new relationships between action by the State and private action; new agents for welfare and well-being; the responsibilities of individuals for themselves and others reinforced. It is in this sense that the emergence of the Welfare Society is both inevitable and desirable**
>
> *(van Lennep, 'Opening Address', in OECD, **The Welfare State in Crisis**, Paris, OECD, 1981).*

The image of an expensive and inefficient welfare state was spread, and with it the idea that the public sector could not grow any more. Concern for the economic burden on the gainfully employed became widespread, and more emphasis was put on voluntary organizations and the so-called 'third sector'. Belief in the voluntary sector was on the rise across the entire OECD in the 1980s, independently of large national variations in the scope of state welfare schemes and of variations in the scope of the voluntary welfare sector. Little systematic cross-national knowledge about the voluntary sector in fact exists. In spite of this, the notion of 'welfare pluralism' (Johnson, 1987) diffused from politicians, government bureaucrats and economists to the general public.

In spite of all the rhetoric against the welfare state or its further growth, state social expenditures continued to rise through the 1980s. No major cuts in central social programmes were made anywhere, not even by neo-conservative regimes in countries such as the UK and the USA. Certainly the level of benefits and the criteria for receiving them tightened, but with little effect on overall social expenditure.

At the same time, the importance of fiscal welfare – stimulating private health and pension insurance – and occupational welfare, seems to have increased in many countries. In fact, all types of welfare provision seem to have increased simultaneously! The 1980s was not a decade of 'more market, less state', but rather one of 'more market, more state'. This development was possible because an ageing population and high levels of unemployment in countries with well established social entitlements, automatically entails higher public social expenditure. At the same time fiscal policies giving tax incentives for private insurance and occupational pensions were effective. Many people, trade unions and firms gave priority to health and welfare security needs, and could to a greater extent that in earlier decades afford personal investment in non-public welfare arrangements.

■ Common challenges

European welfare states exist in different shapes and sizes, and thus face a number of specific challenges. We shall look at some of these below. But some developments appear to affect all national welfare structures. These include: the internationalization of markets; the changing composition of the population; persistent levels of high unemployment; changes in family structure; and high popular expectations about welfare provision.

The European Union represents no direct challenge to national welfare states – within or outside the EU. Its 'social dimension' has gained in importance and visibility over the last ten years, but the guiding principle for most of its social and welfare policies has been, and most likely will be, the principle of subsidiarity. Social security systems can be harmonized only through the agreement of member states. Thus harmonization through EU institutions must be considered unlikely for technical, economic and political reasons. Stronger economic integration, harmonization of indirect taxes, and moves towards monetary union may, however, indirectly induce national governments to converge somewhat. Nevertheless, taxation for social and health security, as well as direct personal taxation, will remain a national responsibility.

Calls for minimum standards of welfare within the EU may gain political strength, and thus promote welfare in member states where such standards are poor or non-existent. The more developed welfare states, on the other hand, may come under pressure to reduce social expenditure to an average European level. At least governments may use the EU as a handy political excuse for cutting expenditures. There is a possibility that developed welfare states may also be called upon to contribute to a redistribution of welfare in Europe. But this is an extremely difficult political manoeuvre in a situation where national electorates are divided over the role of the EU.

Both the EU as such, and national governments, may develop a shared opinion on the recommended scope and role of social policy to make Europe competitive with North America and South-East Asia. This, however, is unlikely to emerge as a result of formal requirements to do so. The new GATT agreement may be one pretext for developing less expensive European welfare states. But even if governments and parliaments have ambitions to limit welfare state growth or reduce the scope of the welfare state, other factors may render this difficult. Analyses of welfare state change in Europe, North America and Japan for 1975–85 showed that welfare expenditures continued to grow faster than the economic product and public revenues – despite curtailments of welfare programmes.

European welfare states, particularly Western ones, are from a global perspective relatively well developed. People have social rights, and are entitled to benefits and services under specified circumstances. Rights and entitlements cannot easily be discarded. With the increase in the elderly and in the very old in European populations, social expenditure – especially pension expenditure – is bound to increase unless political steps are taken to limit the size of future benefits. In 1990, the proportion of voters over fifty-five in the twelve EC countries was 33 per cent, and the projection for 2020 is 42 per cent (Wilson, 1993: 96) Germany is top with 45 per cent and Ireland at the bottom with 31 per cent. Central and Eastern European countries will also be within this range.

All this carries a number of implications for welfare: pension expenditures will rise, the demand for health, nursing and social services will increase, and older voters – who for the most part only have experience of developed welfare states – will make up a stronger block voters with higher welfare demands than the present generation. Changes in the demographic composition of European populations means that the balance between workers and non-workers is affected. This may produce an increasing tax-burden on the economically active in welfare systems which basically use the pay-as-you-go principle.

On the other hand, we should not rule out the possibility of gradual behavioural, institutional and political adaptations to the changing demographic structure. Old people – exposed to less hard physical work than in earlier periods – may in the future have more part-time jobs and contribute both to the labour-free and to tax revenues. Future pensioners will on average be much better off economically than today's pensioners, and thus be able to pay directly for a lot more services which currently are covered by taxes. Although demographic ageing from 2010 onwards will certainly prove a challenge for pension, health and social service systems, one should not necessarily accept a mechanistic approach to the effects on social spending.

On the other hand, the changing age structure will develop in a period with growing competition in international product markets, and rapid internationalization of monetary markets. These offer new chances of profit to the owners of capital and thus strengthen their bargaining power vis-à-vis labour and the state. Although by 1994–95 most of Europe seemed to be recovering from recession, unemployment levels are on average high (around 11 per cent in the EU, higher in Central and Eastern Europe), and long-term unemployment is increasing. A challenge within the EU will be the potentially greater inequality between member countries – unless the economic concentration effects of the single market is met by territorial redistribution at the EU level.

In the wider Europe greater inequality may emerge between countries inside and outside the EU, unless Central and Eastern Europe are integrated in the EU/EEA economic system. Such territorial inequalities carry new challenges for national welfare systems – especially in the less developed market economies. An EU-report (Eurostat, 1994) points to the growing instability of all labour markets – with more frequent interruptions to working careers; persistently high levels of unemployment; the emergence of new forms of poverty and social exclusion. These are accompanied by changes in family structure (for example, increasing numbers of single mothers and one-parent families).

Besides these financial, demographic, socio-structural, and international problems, European welfare states face socio-cultural challenges. A number of studies have shown that welfare state programmes enjoy a high level of mass support. Cutbacks have not led to a legitimation crisis nor a welfare backlash. Citizens have on the whole tolerated curtailments of some social programmes. But popular expectations about welfare still run high. A Eurobarometer study from spring 1992 shows overwhelming support for a strong state role among all twelve-member countries of the EU. Southern Europeans seem in general to want and expect more from the state than northern Europeans. In all countries, more people prefer a 'maximalist' rather than a 'minimalist' approach to state social protection, even if it may mean increasing taxes and contributions.

A comparison of attitudes in 1986 towards the welfare state in the USA, United Kingdom, (West) Germany, the Netherlands, Italy, and Hungary indicated significant differences between the USA, on the one hand, and all the European countries, on the other. On average 60 per cent of Europeans think the state ought to be responsible for basic income, and 68 per cent that it should be responsible for reducing income inequalities. Corresponding figures among Americans were 20 per cent and 27 per cent respectively (Flora, 1993). Data on the state's role in securing work for all show a similar profile. Europeans from north, south, west and east, are consistently more supportive of a strong welfare state than are Americans (and probably also than other non-Europeans in industrialized countries).

The high legitimacy that European welfare states enjoy militates against any reduction in their responsibilities, which many governments and (economic) experts consider necessary. Welfare expectations are too high for governmental comfort. The data may reflect the historical uniqueness of European welfare state development, making state welfare a persistent and distinctive element of European political culture.

If this is so, is it necessarily a drawback in the era of international money markets and global competition – or is it a European advantage? Are not developed, consolidated welfare states conducive to democratic and social stability, which again is conducive to future investments and productivity? Can more weakly developed welfare states provide the same degree of democratic legitimacy and social stability? Is the welfare challenge more critical in the newly industrialized countries of Asia, and in capitalist America, than in European countries? There are no simple answers to these questions. They do indicate, however, that Europe is not necessarily a loser or a laggard in the global competition, and that any assessment of the welfare state is to some extent normative and value-based.

■ Reshaping welfare provision in different institutional contexts

As we have pointed out, there is not one European welfare state but many different kinds. Below we consider four main variants and the kind of changes that they are experiencing in the 1990s.

The United Kingdom: minimum security with targeted tampering at the margins

The British welfare model is universalist, but also characterized by low, flat-rate benefits. The system thus stimulates well-off groups to take out supplementary occupational and/or private insurance. A great number of studies and evaluations of welfare state development in Britain have appeared since Margaret Thatcher formed her first government in 1979. Overall expenditure continued to rise in spite of conservative rhetoric against the welfare state in the 1980s. Barr and Coulter (1991: 33) concluded in their study of developments in the 1970s and 1980s that 'although social security was regarded more as a solution in the 1970s and more as a problem in the

1980s, the changes in reality, though genuinely meeting some of the stated objectives of policy, did not come close to matching the rhetoric'. Jonathan Bradshaw (1993: 97–8) reached a similar conclusion: 'Social security is deeply impervious to change (at least from the radical right). It is ingrained in our culture, economy and system of exchange to such an extent that government can succeed only in tampering at the margins.'

However some reforms have been made during the 1990s in the direction of what the government calls targeted benefits based on means-testing. The percentage of social spending absorbed by means-tested benefits has doubled between 1978/79 and 1993/94 from 17 per cent to 34 per cent (Sinfield, 1994). Several reforms aimed at curtailing expenditure have been introduced. There have been cuts in benefits for children and single parents; in disability allowances and incapacity benefits; in sick pay and unemployment benefits – which were replaced by a much less generous 'Jobseeker's Allowance' in April 1996.

The long-term effect of the 1982 decision to change the basis for indexing retirement pensions to prices only, has been that the basic National Insurance pension fell from 30 per cent to 19 per cent of net average weekly earnings for men between 1980 and 1993 (Sinfield, 1994). According to one study, poverty is widespread and poverty rates have risen substantially in the past decade to over one-fifth of the population (Millar, 1993). Inequality has also become markedly greater in recent years, increasing faster than in most Western economies. A group particularly vulnerable to poverty have been young, especially the homeless people. Recent policy trends are likely to continue under the Conservatives. A change of direction may occur if Labour comes to power after the 1997 election and follows up on its criticisms of Tory social policy.

Germany: status maintenance with minor curtailments and consolidated expansion

The German model is based on employment-related coverage and benefits and the principle of status maintenance. As in all other European welfare states, German social security and welfare is financed through contributions from employers and employees, and from general taxes. The relative importance of taxes has increased over the last thirty years. Benefits for sickness, unemployment and old age pensions are among the most generous in Europe, but a universal (citizenship-based) pension right does not exist as in the United Kingdom, the Netherlands and the Nordic countries. However, means-tested assistance is available for persons without entitlement to a pension and with no income.

During the last twenty years, given high unemployment and rising numbers of pensioners, reforms to reduce the cost of the income transfer system have been introduced. The unification of East and West Germany in 1990 put the welfare system under tremendous pressure. Nearly all components of the income transfer system were changed in the early 1990s. This was justified in the light of demographic developments, the economic situation and German unification. Due to these reforms, West Germans relying on social security and assistance are now worse off, although slight improvements have occurred as a consequence of decisions by the Constitutional Court.

Important reforms to curb expenditure growth have been made in the field of statutory health insurance and in the law governing unemployment and labour market policy. From 1992, the social security system of West Germany was extended to cover the whole of unified Germany, although levels of contributions and benefits are different in old and new *Bundesländer*. The objective is to bring East German standards gradually up to West German. All current pensions were changed under the new pension law in 1992. As a result, East German pensioners receive an earnings-related pension, which will be adjusted in line with net wage increases in the 'New Länder'. The financial situation of families with children, especially with a single parent, has been improved through recent reforms. Changes in the indexing of social assistance benefits will produce a fall in real income for recipients if the inflation rate increases by more than standard rates (geared to the average monthly net income of workers with low income).

A major new reform was passed in 1994 to cover the need for nursing in old age. Care in old age had not been covered by social insurance, and the elderly sick had had to rely on private support from the family or from the means-tested social assistance scheme. The need for a reform was acknowledged by all parties given the present number of persons in need of care – approximately 1.65 million people (2 per cent of the German population). It was made all the more necessary through the increase in life expectancy, reduction in birth rate, and the growing number of old people. The reform covers all members of public and private sickness insurance schemes and implies a significant new tax (or contribution) from employees. The nursing insurance will be financed on a pay-as-you-go basis with compulsory contributions from employees. Payment of benefits began in April 1995 for nursing care at home and in July 1996 for people who need constant attendance in some kind of institution.

The German welfare state enjoys strong political support both at the mass and elite levels (there was general support for nursing insurance). Without sustained economic growth, more efforts to reduce expenditure in some programmes are likely, given the cost of the new reform. This is exacerbated by the ageing of the population, by unemployment, and by German unification with its new social obligations on the state.

Sweden: general universal welfare model under pressure

Sweden has the most comprehensive welfare state among capitalist democracies, and (together with the Netherlands) the most expensive one. It is still comprehensive and expensive, but a number of initiatives have been taken in recent years to curtail the growth of expenditure. This was partly an effect of too generous and costly social legislation in previous decades, partly because the recession began to affect the overall activity of the economy, partly because of the rapid increase in unemployment levels in the 1990s, partly because of the 'explosion' of public debt and budget deficits, and partly because of demographic trends, as in other countries.

The bourgeois government, with a conservative prime minister, of 1991–94 had also an ideological commitment to reducing welfare. Individual choice and family responsibilities were emphasized, as well as the view that a high level of taxation impedes economic growth. The social democrats, as main architects of the 'Swedish model', have reluctantly recognized the need for cuts in expenditure and benefits. They won the 1994 election in spite of their pledge to do so. This says something for crisis consciousness among Swedish voters and parties. The economic recession promoted a broad consensus on the need for change.

The first real cut to social expenditure came under the social democrats (but with the support of the non-socialist parties) in March 1991, against the background of increasing absence through sickness during the latter part of the 1980s. This made sickness benefits a convenient target for cutbacks. The statutory replacement rate was reduced from 90 per cent to 65 per cent for the first three days of absence, and to 80 per cent from day four to day ninety. Another reform – with the same political support – was instituted in 1992. It was decided that employers should pay benefits for the first two-week sick-pay period according to maximum levels defined in the 1991-reform, which meant 75 per cent wage compensation for the first three days, 90 per cent for the rest of the two-week period, 80 per cent from day fourteen, and 90 per cent from day ninety.

A further cutback came in 1993, with the same broad political agreement, when a waiting day for sick pay was introduced, Employees' contributions (tax deductible) to sickness benefit were raised to 0.95 per cent of gross earnings and coupled with a reduction of benefit to 80 per cent in cases exceeding ninety days.

All types of pensions were adjusted downwards during these years. The base amount was to be linked to the consumer price index in order to control expenditure growth. The most radical changes concerned industrial injury insurance, which is now completely co-ordinated with the sickness benefit scheme. Unemployment benefits were cut in 1993 to 80 per cent of previous earnings (which is still high by any international standard) and a five-day waiting period was (re-)introduced. Changes in industrial injury and in unemployment insurance were opposed by the social democrats. The reforms have reduced expenditure on several programmes, and further reforms – especially the one on the old-age pension – will significantly affect the level of social expenditure. The reform of the pension system is supported by the social democrats and the non-socialist parties.

The Swedish welfare system underwent profound reform in the 1990s. Most changes have had broad political support in parliament. The present social democratic government is prepared to cut social programmes even further. How far the generous welfare state will be rolled back is dependent upon the performance of the economy. But cutbacks in social programmes have begun from a very generous level. The general characteristics of the Swedish welfare model are still in place, and are likely to be retained in the foreseeable future.

Poland: in search of a new concept for social protection

After 1990 all the Central and Eastern European countries experienced a restructuring of industry, financial problems, inflation, and high unemployment (with the exception of the Czech Republic). Where they diverged was on the specific direction of the internal reforms they undertook. It is still too early to characterize the kind of welfare model which will emerge after the period of transition, but the Polish case offers some interesting possibilities.

Under the system prevailing from 1945 until 1989, social objectives were pursued through a policy of low prices for basic products such as food, items for children and youth, and for housing. There was also employment-based social insurance and service provision. The change to a democratic, market-type economy since 1989 meant that a major transformation of the welfare model has had to be undertaken. This had to cope with industrial privatizations, a rapid increase in unemployment

(15–16 per cent in 1994), a high rate of inflation (over 600 per cent in 1990), a large public debt, and a rise in the number of old-age pensioners.

Unemployment benefits were introduced in 1989, to be paid for a maximum period of one year. Social assistance, which played an insignificant role under the previous system, has increased in importance. The health care system had problems before the change, but its finances have deteriorated, leading to a spontaneous privatization of health services. These, however, are now out of reach for wide sectors of the population.

Fundamental changes in the regulatory regime for pensions were adopted by law in October 1991, which secured the insurance-related right to old-age and disability pension benefits. This law introduced criteria for the length of time for which social security contributions have been paid and the amount of earlier earnings. The formula for calculating old-age pension benefits also takes into account a social component which is equal for everybody.

Benefits were constrained through parliamentary and presidential decisions in 1992 and 1993. Work on pensions is being continued with the objective of adding an additional system to the existing one. The rapidly growing private sector (comprising about 40 per cent of the working population) cannot compensate for the decline in contributions from the state sector. Thus the potential for financing social insurance is weak. Public social expenditures from 1989 to 1992 diminished in real terms, but their share in the national income increased from 15.3 per cent to 22 per cent. This implies that the decline in real value of budgetary social expenditures was lower than the decline in national income. Thus one may say that social objectives were protected by state policy. However, the general reduction of social well-being explains the success of the ex-communists in the 1993 and 1995 elections.

The establishment of new types of institutions, which would implement social policies and relieve the state budget of the need to fund them directly, proved difficult owing to the myriad of political groupings present in parliament during the early 1990s. The economic situation in Poland has improved since then with an increase in real GDP in every year from 1992 to 1994. Industrial output increased by 5 per cent from March 1994 to March 1995. However, unemployment has risen continuously, and there is a widening gap in the distribution of wealth. A survey of family budgets indicates that some 34 per cent of people in Poland lived below the officially defined subsistence level in 1992.

No clear concept seems to exist in Poland at the present time of how the welfare system should be (re-)designed. The social policies pursued during recent years have been dominated by short-term considerations as a result of deep-rooted economic recession and the crisis in state finances accompanying it. Developments so far seem to point in the direction of the German model, but possibly with less organizational fragmentation of the social insurance system.

■ The future European welfare state: (again) a model for the world?

Governments across Europe are concerned about the current and future development of their national welfare states. Globalization of economic competition and money markets, ageing of the population and rising entitlements, persistent high levels of unemployment, and financial constraints – all represent common challenges. Expenditure cuts are attempted everywhere, but there are also improvements in some social programmes and the creation of new ones in some countries. Developments are thus not entirely uniform, partly because expenditure reductions and programme development occur in very different institutional contexts. Tampering with Swedish or German programmes has less dramatic consequences for dependent populations than tampering with British and Polish.

European welfare states enjoy high political legitimacy, perhaps creating voter expectations which are higher than governments can cope with. Support for state welfare is strong all over Europe. National welfare states have not been dismantled, and are not likely to be. Monetary and political integration may encourage similar expenditures and levels of provision, but institutional convergence is a much more complicated and long-term prospect – if it occurs at all.

Will 'globalization' represent a threat to European welfare states, or can Europe (again) become a model for the developing regions of the world, of the social role and responsibility of the state in society? Are market-oriented, democratic, and mature welfare states not better guarantees of social, and political stability, and thus of a productive work force and attractive investment context, than capitalist authoritarian, and less developed welfare states? The evolution of the European systems seems to support this point. It will be interesting to see if the rest of the world adopts the European model at the outset of the next millennium.

■ Further reading

J. Alber, 'Is there a crisis of the welfare state? Cross-national evidence from Europe, North America and Japan', *European Sociological Review*, Vol. 4, No. 3, 1988.

A. B. Atkinson, 'What is happening to the distribution of income?' (London, LSE, Sticero Welfare State Programme, No. 87, 1993).

N. Barr, and F. A. Coulter, 'Social Security', in J. Hills (ed.) *The State of Welfare in Britain* (Oxford, Clarendon Press, 1991).

J. Bradshaw, 'Social Security', in D. Marsh and R. Rhodes (eds), *Implementing Thatcherite Policies: Audit of an Era* (Milton Keynes, Open University Press, 1993).

J. Campbell, 'The fiscal crisis of the post-Socialist countries', in K. Nielsen, B. Jessop and J. Hausner (eds), *Strategic Choice and path Dependency in Post-Socialism* (Aldershot, Edward Elgar, 1994).

Allan Cochrane, 'Looking for a European Welfare State', in A. Cochrane and J. Clarke (eds), *Comparing Welfare States, Britain in International Context* (London, Sage, 1993).

Bob Deacon (1992) 'East European welfare: past, present and future in comparative context', in Bob Deacon *et al.* (eds), *The New Eastern Europe. Social Policy Past, Present and the Future* (London, Sage, 1992).

Gösta Esping-Andersen, *The Three Worlds of Welfare Capitalism* (Cambridge, Polity Press, 1990).

Eurostat, *Social Protection in Europe 1993* (Luxembourg, Commission of the European Communities, 1994).

Maurizio Ferrera, *EC Citizens and Social Protection. Main Results From a Eurobarometer Study* (EC Commission, Division V/E/2, Brussels, 1993).

Peter Flora, *Growth to Limits. The Western European Welfare States Since World War II*, 2 vols (Berlin, Walter de Gruyter, 1987), Vol.1, p.4.

Peter Flora, 'The national welfare states and European integration', in Luis Moreno (ed.), *Social Exchange and Welfare Development* (Consejo Superior de Investigaciones Cientificas, Madrid, 1993).

Ludwik Florek, 'Evolution of social security in Poland', in B. von Maydell and E. M. Hohnerlein (eds), *The Transformations of Social Security Systems in Central and Eastern Europe* (Leuven, Peters Press, 1994).

Hugh Heclo, 'Towards a new welfare state?', in P. Flora, and A. J. Heidenheimer (eds), *The Development of Welfare States in Europe and America* (New Brunswick and London, Transaction Books, 1981).

Norman Johnson, *The Welfare State in Transition: The Theory and Practice of Welfare Pluralism* (Brighton, Wheatsheaf Books, 1987).

Catherine Jones, *Patterns of Social Policy: An Introduction of Comparative Analysis* (London, Tavistock, 1985).

Stephan Leibfried, 'Towards a European welfare state?', in Catherine Jones (ed.), *New Perspectives on the Welfare State in Europe* (London, Routledge, 1993).

J. Millar, 'The continuing trend of rising poverty', in A. Sinfield (ed.), *Poverty, Inequality and Justice* (Edinburgh, New Waverley Papers No. 6, 1993).

Joop M. Roebroek, 'Social policy diversities in Europe', in *Social Security in Europe* (Brussels/Bruyland, Antwerpen/Maklu Uitgevers, 1991).

Adrian Sinfield, 'The latest trends in social security in the United Kingdom', in H. Ploug and L. Kvist (eds), *Recent Trends in Cash Benefits in Europe*, Vol.4 (The Danish National Institute of Social Research, Copenhagen, Social Security in Europe, 1994).

Richard H. Titmuss, *Social Policy, An Introduction* (London, Allen & Unwin, 1974).

Alan Walker, 'The future of the British welfare state: privatization or socialization?', in Adalbert Evers *et al.* (eds) *The Changing Face of Welfare* (Aldershot, Gower, 1986).

Gail Wilson, 'The challenge of an aging electorate: changes in the formation of social policy in Europe', *Journal of European Social Policy,* 3, 91–105, (1993).

Chapter 16

Managing the economy

State intervention and the 'welfare mix'

Welfare and the economy are intimately related because the welfare system deals with the casualties of the economy – the injured, sick, the old and the unemployed. In recent years their numbers have been growing in most countries. This is because modern economies and welfare systems are facing new challenges caused by the globalization of markets, competition, technological change, privatization, growing government deficits and greater demands for public spending. It is no wonder, therefore, that European governments are concerned with both the economy and welfare, or that debates about economic management have immediate consequences for welfare, and vice versa. A reduction in unemployment is likely to relieve welfare services. Conversely, an increase in economic efficiency, regardless of other considerations, may lead to increased unemployment and greater demand for welfare. This has happened on a large scale in many parts of Central and Eastern Europe where privatization in the early 1990s had a huge impact on public services (documented in Chapter 15 in the case of Poland).

Political parties across the whole of Europe are divided on the issues of state intervention in the economy and the scope of the welfare state. This is the essence of left-right distinctions (cf. Chapter 9) and holds no matter what ethnic, religious or other cleavages may separate parties. Indeed, since the earliest days of party politics, there has been a continuous and vigorous debate not only about the *extent* of state intervention, but also about the *type* of macro-economic policy best suited to good economic performance. Far from being settled after all this time, fierce discussion continues unabated about the three-cornered relationship between democracy, welfare and the economy.

The politics of economic management in the new Europe

Before 1989 the debate was largely restricted to western countries characterized either as 'capitalist democracies' or 'mixed economies'. In this chapter, however, we extend our analysis of economic performance and macro-economic policy to countries in Central and Eastern Europe which have recently adopted parliamentary democracy and simultaneously developed market economies. In this respect, both East and West face common problems, and it makes sense to see how they compare and contrast in their handling of these.

Nevertheless, comparing economic development and welfare across the East–West divide may appear hazardous for several reasons. First, the former communist countries are in transition from one-party states with command economies, to market economies and pluralist democracies. It may be some time yet before they

BRIEFING **16.1**

The market economy

A market economy is one in which the supply of goods and services is left as far as possible to individuals and firms to provide in response to spontaneous consumer demand. This contrasts with a command economy where the state tries to plan all production and distribution in accordance with its priorities. Because of the failure of the Soviet-inspired economies, the market is now often seen as the panacea for all economic ills. Central and Eastern European countries are busily engaged in deregulating markets, abolishing controls on individuals and firms, and selling off state property.

Most ordinary goods and services are probably produced and distributed more efficiently by private business. However, there are major limits on the extent to which a market economy can provide all the goods and services which people require:

a) Most obviously, functions like defense, enforcing order, providing adequate communications, and collecting taxes to pay for them are probably best performed by the state. These are only specific examples of 'collective public goods', where a service has to be provided for everyone or not at all, and individuals cannot be prevented from taking advantage of it nor can they be directly charged for services received. The environment probably falls into this category, too.

b) Businesses cannot be left to compete by any means. Paradoxically, a free market needs state regulation to keep it free. Most obviously this involves outlawing violence and intimidation, enforcing contracts and punishing fraud. However, it extends to preventing the development of monopolies and conspiracies between firms to collude in raising prices and limiting production (cartels). The easiest way of making profits is usually not free competition, so if this is desired government has to enforce it:

c) Providing what people want is all very well, but massive advertising may persuade consumers that they need things they would never have wanted otherwise.

d) The free market responds to the demands of those with money but not to those without money – unemployed, old, sick, children. Unless these groups are to be left to their fate, the (welfare) state has to provide for them outside the free market.

Thus there are complexities in the move from planned to free markets that simple political slogans do not catch.

---

settle into clear and stable patterns. Secondly, the structure of the Eastern economies is very different from Western mixed economies, not only in terms of state intervention and control, but also because economic activity is more heavily concentrated on agriculture, mining and heavy industry. Thirdly, whereas Western European countries have long been integrated into the world economy, the former communist economies were strongly tied into the structure of trade and exchange associated with the Council for Mutual Economic Assistance (see p. 14) and are still set apart from the rest of the world to some extent.

Yet both parts of the new Europe also shows similarities in economic performance and policy-making. First, there have recently been important changes of public policy in both the East and the West, apparently in response to common economic pressures. Many governments are reducing the scope of their intervention in the economy and their financial support for the welfare state. This leads to a second similarity: government attitudes towards economic management and planning have undergone something of a sea change, so far at least as political rhetoric, if not political practice, is concerned.

BRIEFING 16.2

Keynesianism

This is the common term applied to the ideas of John Maynard Keynes, a British economist active in the inter-war and immediate post-war period. Its importance is that it
justified in economic terms the success of those governments in the 1930s which reduced
unemployment by spending money and creating a public financial deficit. The traditional
idea was that in a recession government should reduce taxes and expenditure and
balance their budget. This would strengthen financial confidence and free resources for
businessmen to invest, thus gradually stimulating economic activity and mopping up the
unemployed. Keynes pointed out that without expanding markets businessmen would
not invest but simply save money. Accordingly, governments should spend at this time
and create demand, which would stimulate investment and employment.

The same reasoning indicated that in a boom when production could not keep up with
demand, governments should reduce demand by increasing taxes and cutting expenditure – a 'counter-cyclical' policy. These ideas provided a means of managing a capitalist
or 'mixed' economy without socialist planning or nationalization of industry and thus
appealed to parties of the centre in the post-war period.

To understand why, we have to go back to the history of public management and
economic policy-making in west Europe after 1945. In the early post-war years most
Western European states adopted Keynesian policies of economic management. That
is, the public sector took responsibility for managing economic activity by fiscal
means, primarily by manipulating interest rates, public debt and private credit. In
times of economic recession governments increased their own borrowing and eased
private credit in order to stimulate demand and reduce unemployment. If inflation
rose too fast, they would increase interest rates and reduce their own spending in
order to prevent the economic boom spiralling out of control.

There was assumed to be a trade-off between inflation and unemployment, in the
sense that mild inflation stimulates economic activity, whereas steep inflation
destroys confidence in saving and investment, and may lead to sharp falls in economic
activity and employment. By means of Keynesian economic management governments hoped to steer a course between the two extremes of too much inflation and
economic growth, on the one hand, and too little to mop up unemployment, on the
other.

Keynesian policies seemed to work well during the long economic boom between
1950 and 1975. But then the first oil shock of 1971/2 caused a serious economic
downturn in which both inflation and unemployment rose together in what was
called 'stagflation'.

This combination undermined the fundamental premise of Keynesian policy that
unemployment and inflation are inversely related. As a result this style of economic
management began to be questioned. Governments pursued more conservative
financial policies, trying to balance their books by cutting spending, and letting the
market sort itself out with as little state regulation as possible. The best way of
helping the economy, it was said, was to free it from restrictions and release as much
capital as possible by lowering taxes. The new approach was most enthusiastically
adopted by the Thatcherite Conservative governments of Britain.

These policies were not the only alternatives to Keynesianism, but they were

> BRIEFING 16.3
>
> **Gross national product (GNP) and gross domestic product (GDP)**
>
> The gross national product, or GNP, of a nation is the total income of all residents before providing for depreciation or capital consumption. It is broadly made up of the total value of goods and services produced by the nation plus income from economic activity abroad. GNP is usually measured over a twelve-month period and therefore serves as a measure of national wealth.
>
> Gross domestic product, or GDP, is smaller than GNP and does not allow for earnings from abroad. It is the total value of goods and services produced by the residents of a nation before allowing for depreciation or capital consumption.

congenial to many parties of the right. They were also strongly advocated by many leading economists, and eventually influenced political movements of the left, though with varying degrees of enthusiasm. They were certainly not accepted over night nor in all countries. It took the recessions of the 1980s, for example, to convince parties like that of the French socialists that things had to change. The general world recession of 1989–92 was a turning point for many governments and provided a real test of their commitment to even a weakened form of Keynesian economic management.

This was also the period in which the countries of Central and Eastern Europe initiated the vast changes necessary to transform themselves from command to mixed economies. They were under pressure from Western institutions like the International Monetary Fund (IMF) and World Bank to cut government spending and controls and to open their economies up to domestic and international competition.

For both Eastern and Western Europe, the late 1980s and early 1990s were thus an economically testing time – a 'critical juncture', which seems likely to shape developments for some time to come. Though a modest economic revival in the mid-1990s has eased the situation, we focus particularly on the decisions made from 1989 to 1992 since this period shows how fundamental approaches to economic policy have changed, and how decision-makers reacted to new economic circumstances.

This was also a period of world economic transformation. National economies were becoming more international, and the trend towards 'globalization' can be seen in the rising volume of imports and exports the world over. Imports and exports formed an ever increasing part of national economies. In all countries, not least in the new Europe, international trade and the national balance of payments are increasingly important factors in economic development. Globalization also means that national policies are more dependent on international economic developments. No country in reality ever had exclusive control over its economic affairs. But the consequences of globalization appear to be particularly great for smaller economies and for the Central and Eastern European countries, especially as they try to integrate themselves into the world system.

■ Patterns of political and economic performance

One important indicator of the economic performance of a country is its gross national product. In particular, it is necessary to take account of how economic activities result in increased domestic production and/or employment. For example, windfall profits, or 'fast money' may lead to inflation and a rise in imports, not to increased domestic production, with inevitable consequences for the national economy. In Table 16.1 the main economic indicators of economic performance are listed for nine selected European countries for the 1989–95 period.

With minor exceptions, the indicators reveal a worsening picture between 1990 and 1992. Economic growth is slow or stagnant, and unemployment rises faster than inflation. The table shows considerable variation in the West in the early 1990s, and some in Central and Eastern Europe. The important point, however, is that trends across the *whole* of Europe are broadly comparable. There were no systematic East–West differences in unemployment. Ireland and Spain, for example, experienced comparable levels of unemployment to those in Hungary and Poland.

The main difference between East and West relates to imports and exports. By importing much more than they exported the Central and Eastern European economies became increasingly indebted. This not only imposed a domestic burden, but also constrained the processes of economic transformation, since a major part of the economic surplus had to go to pay interest abroad.

There is considerable national variation from 1989 to 1992 in the economic 'misery index', measured by adding together rates of unemployment and inflation and dividing by two. Three groups of countries can be detected in Table 16.1: Austria, the Netherlands, Sweden and Switzerland score on the low side, with between 3 to 5 points; Ireland and Spain have between 10 and 11; Czechoslovakia and Hungary have 18 to 21 points. Poland has the highest misery index score at 33.5, though inflation improved dramatically after 1993, in line with the general economic upturn, and the gap with other European countries closed.

Although the misery index is a simple measure of the economic situation, it is a valid one, since inflation and unemployment are sensitive indicators relating directly to everyday life. Although economic stagnation and weak exports can threaten economic stability, they are less visible and have less effect on electoral changes and the fortunes of governments. In other words, the misery index is centrally important for understanding how and why parties and governments react to the economic situation.

As Table 16.1 also shows the economic situation in most countries improved from 1992 to 1995, in line with general world recovery. The change was particularly marked in the Czech Republic and in Poland, as attested by the dramatic fall in the misery index of around 15 per cent. No Western country achieved such a figure, but then they were less severely affected in the first place.

Table 16.2 presents a dynamic picture of how economic performance is changing. The index of domestic performance in the table (putting together growth, inflation and unemployment) summarizes the separate trends shown in Table 16.1, so a higher score represents a better economic performance. But the indices also show *relative* scores for each country compared with the others. Thus a country with a high score has a relatively good performance on growth, inflation and unemployment. Low or negative scores point to a relatively poor economic performance overall. For instance, Ireland and Spain did relatively well in 1990. Sweden and the Central and Eastern European countries did not. Conversely some economies appeared to benefit from their international trade, for example Ireland in 1990, whereas other economies are undermined by their international economic relations (like Poland

Table 16.1 Main economic indicators for selected European countries, 1989–95

| Country and year | Indicators (all in % of GDP) | | | | |
	Economic growth	Rate of inflation	Rate of unemployment	Balance of payments	Misery
1. Austria 1989	3.1%	2.9%	3.5%	-0.5%	3.20
1990	4.6	3.2	3.3	-0.7	3.25
1992	2.1	4.0	4.0	-0.2	4.00
(1995)	(2.5)	(2.1)	(6.4)	(-2.0)	(4.25)
Change 1990/1992	-2.5	+0.8	+0.7	+0.5	+0.75
(92–95)	(+0.4)	(-1.0)	(2.4)	(-1.8)	(+0.25)
2. Ireland 1989	3.9%	4.7%	13.5%	-0I9	9.10
1990	8.3	2.5	13.7	0.2	8.10
1992	2.4	3.6	16.9	3.4	10.25
(1995)	(4.0)	(2.8)	(14.6)	(5.2)	(8.70)
Change 1990/1992	-5.9	+1.1	+3.2	+3.2	+2.15
(92–95)	(+1.6)	(-0.8)	(-2.3)	(+1.8)	(-1.55)
3. Netherlands 1989	2.6%	1.3%	9.2%	5.1%	5.25
1990	3.9	2.3	6.4	3.5	4.35
1992	1.2	3.1	6.5 (7.6)	2.1	4.80
(1995)	(2.3)	(1.6)	+0.1 (+1.1)	(3.7)	(4.80)
Change 1990/1992	-2.7	+0.8		-1.4	+0.45
(92–95)	(+1.1)	(-1.5)		(+1.6)	(0.0)
4. Spain 1989	3.2%	6.9%	16.9%	0.1%	11.90
1990	3.7	16.3	16.3	-0.3	11.30
1992	2.6	15.9	16.1	-0.2	11.00
(1995)	(2.9)	(4.4)	(24.3)	(0.0)	(14.35)
Change 1990/1992	-1.1	-0.4	-0.2	+0.1	-0.30
(92–95)	(+0.3)	(-1.5)	(+7.8)	(+0.2)	(+3.35)
5. Sweden 1989	1.6%	6.9%	4.2%	-0.6%	5.55
1990	0.5	9.7	1.5	-2.6	5.60
1992	-0.3	3.2	4.5	-2.1	3.35
(1995)	(3.8)	(2.7)	(7.2)	(2.3)	(5.00)
Change 1990/1992	-0.8	-6.5	+3.0	+0.5	-2.25
(92–95)	(+4.1)	(-0.5)	(+2.7)	(+4.4)	(+1.65)
6. Switzerland 1989	2.0%	6.6%	1.5%	-0.4%	4.05
1990	2.2	5.4	0.6	3.8	3.00
1992	0.9	4.3	2.5	6.2	3.40
(1995)	(0.0)	(4.9)	(4.5)	(6.2)	(3.20)
Change 1990/1992	-1.3	-1.1	+1.9	+2.5	+0.40
(92–95)	(-0.9)	(+0.6)	(+2.0)	(0.0)	(-0.20)
7. Czech & 1989	1.5%	1.0%	NA	NA	–
Slovak 1990	-1.1	18.0	1.0%	-15.0%	9.5
Republic 1992	-8.5	32.5	9.5	-8.1	21.00
(1995)	(6.3)	(8.0)	(3.6)	(-3.5)	(5.80)
Change 1990/1992	-7.4	+14.5	+8.5	+6.9	+11.5
(92–95)	(+14.8)	(-24.5)	(-5.9)	(+4.6)	(-15.2)
8. Hungary 1989	1.5%	17.0%	1.7%	3.6%	9.35
1990	-2.4	28.9	7.5	9.2	18.20
1992	-8.5	22.8	13.3	-4.5	18.05
(1995)	(2.9)	(28.7)	(9.3)	(-2.9)	(19.0)
Change 1990/1992	-6.1	-6.1	+5.8	-13.7	-0.15
(92–95)	(+11.4)	(+5.9)	(-4.0)	(+1.6)	(+0.95)
9. Poland 1989	1.0%	60.0%	0.3%	NA	30.15
1990	-11.6	76.0	6.1	-17.4%	41.05
1992	-7.6	43.0	14.0	-9.7	33.50
(1995)	(5.2)	(22.0)	(16.2)	(-2.3)	(19.10)
Change 1990/1992	+4.0	-33.0	+7.9	+7.7	-7.65
(92–95)	(+12.8)	(-21.0)	(+2.2)	(+7.4)	(14.40)

Note: Czech Republic after only 1992.
 Economic Growth (Annual Change in GDP); Rate of Inflation (Annual Change Consumer Price Index); Rate of Unemployment (proportion of unemployed inTotal Labour Force); Balance of Payments (+ = Positive; – = Negative). Misery = Sum of Rate of Inflation and Rate of Unemployment divided by 2.
Source: OECD, *Economic Outlook* (various volumes); OECD, *Economic Systems* of Czech and Slovak Republic 1991, Hungary (1991, 1993) Poland (1992), *The Economist* (Jan. 1996: 1996–99).

Table 16.2 Comparing economic performance across the New Europe, 1990–95

Country	Domestic performance			International performance		
	1990	1992	1995	1990	1992	1995
Austria	0.488	0.849	0.820	0.465	0.654	0.150
Ireland	0.755	0.497	0.011	0.955	0.683	0.518
Netherlands	0.545	0.713	0.790	0.641	0.716	0.861
Spain	0.757	0.486	-0.708	0.604	0.427	-.107
Sweden	-0.064	0.625	0.566	-0.029	0.378	0.354
Switzerland	0.147	0.767	1.270	0.375	1.004	1.671
CSFR	-0.212	-1.182	0.168	-0.629	-1.260	-0.978
Hungary	-0.536	-1.056	-1.289	-0.023	-0.919	-1.099
Poland	-1.280	-1.078	-1.605	-2.358	-1.682	-1.370

Notes: Based on a Principal Component Analysis with a Varimax Solution. Communality for domestic performance: h^2 = 66.7% (1990) 65.5% (1992) 57.4 (1995) and for international performance: h^2 = 70.2% (1990) 61.7% (1992) 51.3% (1995).

A principal components analysis is a way of combining indicators of economic performance, in this case those reported in Table 16.1. The indicator of domestic performance shows how countries are performing in relation to each other on economic growth, inflation and unemployment (combined). The indicator of international performance shows how they are performing relative to each other on these three indicators plus balance of payments.

and Sweden in 1990). By 1995 the Czech Republic had substantially improved its economic performance, though still pulled down by its balance of payments figures.

Table 16.2 demonstrates, once again, that there is considerable variation in economic performance in Europe, both across countries and over time. The Central and Eastern European economies are generally worse off than their Western counterparts, but nevertheless, differences are considerable within the West as well. Most economies there were in comparatively poor shape at the end of the 1980s, but they recovered somewhat after 1990. Ireland and Spain did not follow this pattern and performed relatively poorly in 1992 and 1995 – a trend also revealed in Table 16.1. One can observe the emergence of two groups of countries: recovering economies (Austria, the Netherlands, Sweden and Switzerland and possibly the Czech Republic) and worsening ones. Access to, and dependence upon, the world market helps account for these differences.

International economic relations are one of the many problems of the Eastern European economies. Economic reform combined with weak currencies and comparatively poor industrial products, have grave effects on their competitiveness and economic performance. The relatively strong economy of the Czech Republic was less affected initially and after a hiccup in 1992 is now adjusting better. Poland appears to have been continuously vulnerable, whereas Hungary has declined from 1989.

These conclusions are reinforced if we graph performance in 1990 against performance in 1995, for all the countries involved. In terms of purely domestic economic performance (Figure 16.1), the Czech Republic belongs with the predominantly 'Western' cluster, while Poland, Hungary, Spain and Ireland perform less well. When the balance of payments is brought in as a consideration (Figure 16.2), all the Western countries perform better than the Eastern ones.

Regional European differences exist, therefore, but country variation is perhaps greater. Two factors stand out as affecting performance: international trade and the composite structure of the economy. These also impact on the degree of misery. Vulnerability to international developments is shown more dramatically in Figure 16.2, where Ireland and Spain are pulled up, and the Czech Republic depressed, by the performance of their balance of payments.

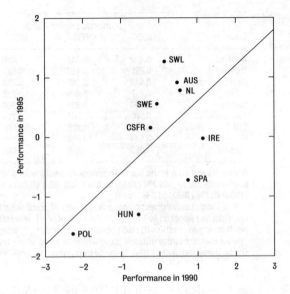

Figure 16.1 Change in domestic economic performance for selected European countries, 1990–95

The fact that inter-country variation in performance is generally greater than East–West regional differences underlines the role of national governments in managing the economy. The impact of public management strategies in these mixed economies must be considered in explaining their varying success in adapting to change. The next section is dedicated to this question of how democratic governments cope with economic changes under different circumstances.

■ The politics of economic management: the role of parties and governments

Let us, therefore, look more closely at contemporary policies of economic management. In what way and to what extent have these strategies affected economic performance? To answer this question we have developed a composite policy scale of macro-economic policy-making (MEP). This combines three measures:

1. government expenditure as a per cent of GDP
2. the public deficit as a per cent of GDP
3. tax revenue as per cent of GDP.

The more governments spend and borrow, the more Keynesian the policy. Since high tax levels limit the room for manoeuvre, the MEP index combines the first two percentages positively, and tax pressure negatively. Positive scores in Table 16.3 point to Keynesian policies of an expansive public economy, while negative scores indicate a restrictive fiscal policy.

The results once again show considerable national variation. Since governments in Europe in the early 1990s operate in rather similar economic climates, the variations suggest some independence on the part of governments to determine their own economic policies. Four countries had Keynesian policies of demand management in 1990: Hungary, the Netherlands, Sweden and the CSFR. Other countries were more restrictive, although the figures suggest that Austria and the CSFR (in 1992) were

Figure 16.2 Change in international economic performance for selected countries 1990–95

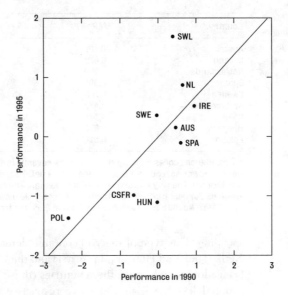

Table 16.3 Comparing macro-economic policies across Europe, 1990–92

Country	MEP 1990	MEP 1992
Austria	-0.154	0.038
Ireland	-0.772	-0.539
Netherlands	0.351	0.669
Spain	-0.975	-0.498
Sweden	1.483	2.009
Switzerland	-1.341	-1.580
CSFR	1.411	-0.023
Hungary	0.397	0.414
Poland	-0.400	-0.520

Notes: Communality h^2 = 65.1% (1990) 70.1% (1992) MEP is a composite measure, based on principal components analysis of Government expenditure as a percent of GDP, the public deficit as a percent of GDP and tax revenue as a percent of GDP. Higher scores represent a more Keynesian policy relative to the other countries. Figures for Central Europe are not available after 1992.

moving towards a broadly neutral position, somewhere between Keynsianism and the new financial orthodoxy.

Countries are generally consistent in their policy approaches. Only Sweden and the Netherlands show a shift to more Keynsian policies, Spain moves from highly restrictive to somewhat less restrictive policies. The CSFR alone switches from a Keynesian to a neutral position. The overall stability of the other countries is not surprising. It reinforces the view that policy-making in liberal democracies is not a simple matter of abstract theory or technical capacity. The state is like a supertanker, unable to change course immediately. Policy change is dependent on policy consensus, on the one hand, and constrained by inertia and incrementalism (e.g. legal entitlements and time-consuming, trickle-down effects), on the other.

Looking at the cross-national variation in macro-economic policy as a whole, it appears that Sweden has consistently taken a policy stand favouring Keynsianism. The public economy is not only large, but has been sustained by means of deficit

Table 16.4 Tax-supported spending on welfare in selected European countries, 1990–92

Country	MEP 1990	MEP 1992
Austria	−0.489	−0.281
Ireland	−0.672	−0.959
Netherlands	0.200	0.581
Spain	−0.901	−0.662
Sweden	0.700	0.917
Switzerland	−1.468	−1.566
CSFR	1.764	1.526
Hungary	0.874	0.725
Poland	0.011	−0.280

Notes: Higher scores indicate that more tax revenue is spent on welfare: lower scores that less is spent. For a detailed description of the data and the way it is scored see Hans Keman, *The Development Towards Surplus Welfare* (Amsterdam CT Press, 1988) pp. 105–30 esp. 114–17. No data are available for Central Europe after 1992.

spending. This type of macro-economic demand-management is also found in the Netherlands and Hungary. In Austria and the CSFR a 'middle of the road' policy has been adopted, whereas other countries (those with a minus sign in Table 16.3) have adopted less Keynsian and more restrictive policies. Switzerland is the clearest example. Ireland and Spain have become somewhat less restrictive.

What does all this mean? First, in most countries the capacity of fiscal policy instruments to revitalize domestic economic activity is limited because of various constraints. Secondly, economic policies are strongly influenced by political factors. These are particularly important in regard to macro-economic policy. Notwithstanding increased electoral volatility of late, ideological divisions in West European politics have remained quite stable. This means that the old divisions between the political left and right remain important, with the expected consequences for economic policy. In Sweden and the Netherlands, for example, left- and right-wing parties distance themselves, and their economic policies, in the competition for power. By comparison, the parties of Switzerland and Austria take a more centrist position. In other words, the nature of the party system appears to affect the choice of macro-economic policies.

It should be added immediately that this is not a general 'law', but a particular product of the post-war development of the West European party systems. In the three Eastern and Central European countries under review the party systems are not yet firmly formed, and competing political interests have not yet adopted firm ideological positions to guide their programmes for action. On the one hand, most parties have had to adopt policies favourable to 'market economics'. On the other hand, governments have to combat steep rises in unemployment and inflation, and compensate citizens for the radical shift from socialist to mixed economies. The result is a tension between the new orthodoxy and old Keynsian policies of macro-economic management.

An important feature of any macro-economic policy is its influence on other economic and welfare policies. Economic management is intimately related to other state policies in a mixed economy, particularly to social welfare, because a declining economy will generate a wide range of social problems. This is reflected in the so-called 'extraction-distribution cycle' of the public economy, which measures the proportion of the state's tax income used for social services and social security benefits. In Table 16.4 a negative score indicates low expenditure of taxes in these areas while positive scores represent high expenditure.

Figure 16.3
Relationship between
macro-economic policy
and tax-supported
spending on welfare in
selected countries, 1990
and 1992
Note: Scores are base.

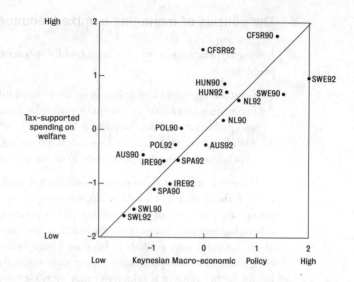

Figure 16.3
Relationship between macro-economic policy and tax-supported spending on welfare in selected countries, 1990 and 1992
Note: Scores are base.

In countries like Ireland, Spain, Switzerland and Poland relatively small proportions of tax income are spent on social services, whereas in the CSFR, the Netherlands, Sweden and Hungary it is extensively redistributed in this way. Again, one can observe a high degree of cross-national variation across the European countries. As with macro-economic policy, changes in national patterns over time are much less dramatic than is suggested by sweeping generalizations about the 'rolling back of the state', and 'the dismantling of the welfare state'.

In view of our earlier conclusions about incrementalism and inertia this is not surprising. Yet it should also be noted that there are clear national differences which are related to the commitments of parties and governments to welfare – in other words, to the left-right party cleavages mentioned earlier. This reinforces the view that different welfare policies reflect political choices as much as economic necessities. That is, countries with comparable levels of economic performance (e.g. the Central and Eastern European countries, and Ireland and Spain) score quite differently on the extraction-distribution cycle, just as they pursue different strategies in macro-economic policy.

The two are indeed closely related, as Figure 16.3 shows. Two clusters of countries stand out:

1. Countries which combine an active policy stance on economic matters with a relatively high level of redistribution of welfare-related public goods (Sweden, the Netherlands, Czechoslovakia and Hungary).
2. Countries which combine a lower level of public economic activity with a lower level of welfare distribution.

The strong relationship between macro-economic policies and redistributive welfare policies implies that the ideological choices of parties and governments cover the whole policy spectrum, from economics to welfare. Where the state is actively involved in Keynsian policies of economic management and planning, it is involved also in redistributive welfare policies. Where the state favours market economics, it also favours limiting public measures to deal with the unemployment and social problems that markets often create.

▪ The politics of managing a 'mixed' economy

Economic stagnation or decline usually present decision-makers with three problems:

1. Controlling wages and prices in order to limit inflation and unemployment.
2. Promoting international competitiveness by means of stable exchange rates and acceptable rates of productivity.
3. Avoiding budget deficits and so-called 'crowding-out' effects caused by public expenditure siphoning off money from the private sector.

However, some of these policy goals are not easily reconciled, and attempting to achieve them simultaneously is like squaring the circle. Besides, governments and parties are prisoners of their previous policy positions, to a certain extent at least. It is hard for them to change course when they find themselves in the middle of a storm at sea. Each measure is likely to become a bone of contention among different interest groups. For example, public sector wage controls can easily lead to strikes, striving for higher rates of productivity may increase rates of unemployment, and cuts in public expenditures often provoke public protest.

Recent electoral results throughout Europe demonstrate the political difficulties of attempting to deal with economic problems. Between 1989 and 1994, elections took place in all the countries considered in this chapter (cf. Chapter 3). In both East and the West established governments were turned out. In Hungary and Poland the electorate removed their first democratic (and anti-communist) governments in favour of the social democrats, that is the ex-communists. Czechoslovakia was faced with the (mainly) non-economic issue of whether the federal republic should remain intact or be split. In the end, the popular vote went to the separatist parties.

Thus in both parts of Europe the elections held between 1989 and 1994 resulted in substantial political change. Much of this was related to socio-economic circumstances as well as to the policies of austerity which had been implemented at that time. In all the countries we are examining here, there was public dissatisfaction with government policies and the established parties, regardless of their ideological complexion.

This chapter shows that it is not possible to separate out economic policies from politics. Political factors shape economic policies, but economic circumstances also strongly influence public policies. In the end the policies will come home to roost electorally. In this sense we cannot isolate economic from public policy by seeking refuge in the technicalities of 'economic science'. Rather we have to think in terms of a unified 'political economy'.

▪ Further reading

For detailed statistics the various OECD series, including *Historical Statistics*, published in Paris at various dates, are essential. Since the situation, particularly in Central and Eastern Europe, changes so fast, periodicals like *The Economist* (London) and *Keesing's Contemporary Archives* are particularly useful.

More general reviews are:

C. Clague and G. C. Rausser (eds), *The Emergence of Market Economies in Eastern Europe* (Oxford, Blackwell, 1992).

Hans Keman , H. Paloheimo and P. F. Whitely (eds), *Coping with the Crisis: Alternative Responses to Economic Recession* (London, Sage, 1987).

A. Koves, *Central and East European Economies in Transition* (San Francisco, Westview Press, 1992).

L. C. B. Periera, J. M. Maravall and Adam Przeworski, *Economic Reforms in New Democracies* (Cambridge, Cambridge University Press, 1993).

Loukas Tsoukalis, *The New European Economy: The Politics and Economics of Integration* (Oxford, Oxford University Press, 1993).

J. Winiecki, *Post Soviet Type Economies in Transition* (Avebury, Aldershot, 1993).

The future of the new Europe

Chapter 17

Minorities and migrants:
European dilemmas

■ Introduction

It is no accident that we return in our concluding chapters to the cross-border, supra-national concerns with which we began in Part I. For if anything is clear about the new Europe it is that peace and security cannot be guaranteed by any state acting on its own. Even the most powerful countries, Germany and Russia, are immediately affected by other countries' actions – above all, by the policies of superpowers outside Europe, primarily the United States, China, and Japan. Europe's destiny is largely dependent on non-Europeans. This will remain the case even if the European Union itself becomes a superpower, since a united Europe would only be one player among the four or five on the world stage.

However, without European integration in one form or another, individual countries will be even more at the mercy of international forces. This is true even for economics. National economies may remain distinctive, because of different national policies and priorities. But they have to compete and sell at a world level. Individually they respond to, rather than shape, developments like globalization.

It is indeed remarkable that Europe, with its immense political and cultural diversity, its variety of languages, its comparatively small population and even smaller geographical area, and its predominance of small to medium economies, has been so successful. Social and political development and economic prosperity have long been characteristics of Western Europe, and this seems likely to spread, perhaps slowly and unevenly, to Central and Eastern Europe as well.

European diversity, however, comprising more than forty separate states, and well established sub-state structures, creates its own problems. As if having to cope with external superpowers were not enough, Europe has its own internal hostilities and tensions. These deserve detailed consideration since both World Wars were touched off by hostilities between European countries.

The most pervasive source of national and international tension derives from the messy nature of state-building itself. As we have seen, few European states are really what they claim to be: nation-states. Either they incorporate two or more ethnic groups within their own border, or one (or more) of these ethnic groups spills over their borders into other states, creating minorities abroad and tensions at home. The violent break-up of Yugoslavia demonstrates the forces unleashed when one ethnic group seeks to dominate others. A vicious circle of retaliation follows. This draws in other countries, some of which may be fishing in troubled waters, some trying to sell arms, some trying to resolve matters peacefully. Either way, the result is instability.

Established territorial minorities within States *need* not present a great problem,

BRIEFING 17.1

The changing nature of migration in modern Europe

The immigration of the 1950s and 1960s, from the Caribbean, India, Southern Europe and Turkey, into the host countries of the North-West, left large immigrant communities inside the large cities. Immigrants came to settle. They were generally too poor to afford a return journey to their native country and communication networks were not well developed.

The situation today has changed in a way which both eases and exacerbates ethnic problems. Communications are quick and cheap. New immigrants from Central and Eastern Europe and North Africa have in many cases not far to travel home. In extreme cases, such as Berlin, Poles can work in the city and return 90 kilometres to their home country in the evening. In other cases, immigrants can work three or six months away, and return home, as do British and Irish labourers in Germany.

From one point of view seasonal labour of this kind creates fewer problems for the host country, which does not have to cope with family problems or provide social support or housing. On the other hand, immigrants have no incentive to assimilate, or to accommodate the majority culture and remain an alien underclass completing for jobs – an obvious target for xenophobic and racialist attacks.

however. Central and Eastern Europe could well defuse tensions with territorial minorities by devolving powers and granting a degree of regional autonomy, as some other European countries have done. This has a fair chance of reconciling minorities with their host state, especially since some traditional state powers may increasingly be shifted upwards to agencies of supranational or international government, such as the European Union.

More alarming and potentially destabilizing is the prospect of large-scale population movements across state boundaries. This has the effect of introducing radically different ethnic and language groups into established societies. The *modus vivendi* evolving between majorities and long-standing minorities is not easily extended to new ones, especially if they carry with them non-European cultures, languages, and in the case of Muslims, religions.

Such immigration has already caused tensions. The economic boom of 1950–75 sucked immigrants into some European countries from all over the world – mainly because they were needed to supplement the native work force when labour was scarce. Caribbean and Indians flowed into Britain, Algerians into France, Turks and Italians into Germany, and Surinamese and Moluccans to the Netherlands. As recession succeeded boom, the situation of these immigrants worsened. Most had settled permanently, but found themselves in the worst housing areas of big cities, often in abysmal social conditions, with overcrowded schools, and poor public services. High unemployment and competition for jobs sparked resentment among the indigenous population. Sometimes rioting occurred, and political tensions escalated. Host governments were often accused of discrimination, indigenous residents of racial prejudice.

A major problem for Western Europe would be huge population movements from the Central and Eastern European states if their economies collapsed. There would be no way of keeping immigrants out, short of creating a new Iron Curtain, or the kind of fence, patrolled by border guards, which exists between the

USA and Mexico. A heavy influx of new immigrants might give enormous impetus to the racialist parties already active in Western politics. Fortunately these are small and marginal at the moment, but small parties can always grow (see Chapter 9).

Economic collapse in the East is unlikely thanks to the modest world boom which has stimulated their economies. However Russia, the country doing least well economically, also has the largest population. The fragile social and political situation there is capable of generating large population flows into Western Europe. Immigrants might come not only from Europe, but also from the Middle East, Asia, and North Africa.

The possibility of mass immigration creates problems not only for peace and stability but also for civil rights inside European countries. In liberal democratic theory, two principles run side by side. One calls for minorities to abide by majoritarian decision-making rules. The other defends the rights of individuals, and argues that we should judge civilization by the protection it gives minorities. Their human rights are clearly stated by such organizations as the United Nations (UN), Council of Europe, and the Organization on Security and Co-operation in Europe (OSCE). However, the charters of such bodies make provision for individuals, whether majorities or minorities, and not for minorities as such. One of the main arguments against guaranteeing minority rights is the fear that this might lead to minority secession and the loss of national territory. After all, international organizations and their human rights charters are created by established states with their own interests to protect.

Whether the silence of international organizations on the issue of minority rights prevents or contributes to ethnic conflicts is a matter of debate. But what is clear is that such clashes have been a long-standing feature of European politics. Examples we examined in Chapters 3 and 4 include the Bretons and Corsicans in France, the Basques and Catalans in Spain, the Turkish minority in Cyprus, the Kurds in Turkey, the Catholics in Northern Ireland, Surinamese and Moluccans in the Netherlands, and the Turks in Germany.

Notwithstanding the widespread tensions caused by such ethnic mingling in Western Europe, however, the level of conflict has, with the exception of Northern Ireland, either diminished or been partially resolved (Chapter 13). In contrast, the scale and nature of ethnic conflict in Central and Eastern Europe has on occasion reached frightening proportions since the collapse of communism in 1989. Can Central and Eastern Europe learn from and/or adopt policies similar to those employed in Western Europe for resolving ethnic conflicts? What lessons can be drawn from conflict in the former Yugoslavia, and how can similar occurrences be prevented? What role can, or should, international organizations play in the resolution and prevention of ethnic, linguistic or religious conflicts? These are important questions in their own right, and there is the additional one raised in Chapter 4: can similar approaches to minorities be used in both Western and Eastern Europe?

This chapter will deal with the problems which minorities and migrants pose for general European stability. It will go on to consider measures which could help alleviate minority problems within states. However, before doing this, we provide a brief review of what constitutes a minority, and of the main mechanisms which have been proposed for the solution of minority problems.

■ Problems of definition and causation

Despite numerous studies, there is no clear definition of a minority. One of the more widely accepted attempts is that of Capotori who defines a minority as:

[a] group numerically inferior to the rest of the population of a state, in a non-dominant position, whose members – being nationals of the state – possess ethnic, religious or linguistic characteristics differing from those of the rest of the population and show, if only implicitly, a sense of solidarity, directed towards preserving their culture, traditions, religion or language   *(Capotori, 1979).*

While this definition distinguishes between ethnic (according to race, culture and origin), religious, and linguistic minorities, it leaves a number of issues unresolved. One is size. Should a group of a mere one hundred be designated a minority, or perhaps the minimum is a thousand, or ten thousand, or a hundred thousand? Nor does minority status necessarily imply smaller numerical size. In Belgium, the Flemings (60 per cent), are the perceived minority, compared with the Walloons (40 per cent). The same is true of the Albanians of Kosovo, in the South of Serbia, who make up 80 per cent of the local population, but are nevertheless considered the 'minority' by the Serbs. The Human Rights Convention of the Council of Europe avoids discussion of numbers and proportions, and simply refers to 'national minorities'.

A further complication is raised by migrants. Analytically, a distinction can be made between minorities and migrants. Minorities are people within a state who are distinct in terms of ethnic, religious or linguistic criteria. Migrants are people who, by choice or permission, live in another country for a specified period, primarily to seek better standards of living. In practice, however, there is a considerable overlap between the two categories with migrants, together with refugees and political asylum seekers, frequently being identified as minorities, as is done by the UN Convention on Refugees of 1951.

More work is needed to operationalize the concept of minorities. Some clarification can be drawn from the study of their demands and from state reactions to these. For example, it is important to determine whether groups want political independence within their own nation-state, or whether they want to preserve their distinct cultural identity within an existing State.

There has been considerable discussion about why demands for greater autonomy are made. To what extent are economic factors responsible, or socio-psychological ones? The main economic factor is likely to be 'perceived economic deprivation' compared with majority groups. Socio-psychological factors can relate to ethnocentrism, which involves the rejection and subordination of minorities who are considered to be culturally different from and inferior to the majority. 'Contrary to much of conventional wisdom, individual economic situations or expectations about the future are less strongly related to nationalism than external threat, ideology, political or socio-psychological factors' (M. McIntosh, L. McIver and P. Abele, 'The Dynamics of Nationalism', unpublished paper, PSA, 1993). This concurs with many studies on voting behaviour which identify religion as the most salient socio-political cleavage. This has important implications for economic development in Eastern Europe, where the effects of economic reconstruction programmes and foreign investment may be hampered by ethnocentric feelings.

■ Political mechanisms for resolving ethnic conflict

A number of different political institutions may be used to control or reduce political tensions between majorities and minorities. These include:

1. federal and regional government
2. consociational democracy
3. constitutional protection, and
4. intervention by international organizations.

We have already discussed federal and regional government extensively in Chapter 13. We review the other alternatives below:

Consociational democracy

Consociational democracy in mixed (or plural) societies allows different groups to create and run their own institutions, including some government and public service agencies. This allows different social groups to administer themselves, and to share power by using 'grand coalitions' to make compromise decisions. The Netherlands is one example of consociational democracy which works exceedingly well. But the model seems to apply less well to places such as Northern Ireland, or Bosnia.

Constitutional provisions

A number of constitutional provisions can be used to safeguard or promote minority interests. In some countries, such as Belgium, the constitution requires a special majority for the passage of certain types of laws. In others, it provides an 'alarm bell' procedure to alert minorities which, under certain circumstances, may then suspend the adoption of a bill. Another form of constitutional protection allows minorities to maximize their participation in public life. In Austria for example, the *proporz* system reserves set proportions of public service occupations for different religious groups.

In a number of states independent advisory bodies, composed of elected representatives of national minorities, provide advice to the legislature or the executive. The Sami (Lapp) parliaments in Norway, Finland and Sweden serve such a purpose (see Table 13.2). Other examples include the Contact Committee for the German minority in Denmark, the Foundation for the Sorbian People in Germany, and the Austrian Ethnic Advisory Councils. Such bodies could serve as a model for non-territorial representation of national minorities, involving both concentrated and dispersed minorities. The Roma gypsies, dispersed across all European countries, would benefit from a co-ordinated approach that transcends individual states.

Certain states promote the representation of national minorities in the legislature by lowering the number of votes needed for the election of minority representatives – the Danish minority in Germany, and national and ethnic minorities in Hungary. Other countries, such as Romania, reserve a minimum number of seats for the national minority. But there is also a fear that these arrangements might foster 'ethnic' parties or fail to give minorities a sufficient number of seats to affect decision-making in the legislature. Conversely, would state-wide parties incorporating minority interests give them any more influence, or would they just contribute to

> **BRIEFING 17.2**
>
> ### The Roma: residents or immigrants?
>
> Gypsies (Roma) are the descendants of groups from North India who migrated west-wards to almost all the countries of Europe in the Middle Ages. They number about 5 million or 1 per cent of the population of Europe outside the ex-Soviet Union. Their largest concentrations of population are shown in Table 13.1. In terms of Chapter 4 they are a 'diaspora' or dispersed minority even in countries where they are numerous.
>
> This is partly due to their semi-nomadic lifestyle. Roma have been astonishingly resistant to assimilation into host populations and at the same time very adaptable in fitting themselves into niches in the society as horse or car dealers, scrap merchants, drug dealers, petty criminals and so on. As the countryside becomes depopulated in Central and Eastern Europe they move into deserted villages. Tensions with the rest of the population are exacerbated by this lifestyle. The Nazi regime classed them with Jews and exterminated perhaps a million during the war. They are often attacked or dis-criminated against throughout Europe. The Roma form a particular problem: are they a minority group or are they migrants?. Can democracies accommodate such a distinctive minority in their midst?

their marginalization? These are empirical questions which have so far defied clear answers.

In contrast to the arrangements which have developed in most of Western Europe, confrontations in Central and Eastern Europe have sometimes taken a violent form involving secession. The Baltic Republics (from the Soviet Union) and Slovenia and Croatia (from Yugoslavia) are examples. Federal approaches have not always worked – in Czechoslovakia, for example – and in many parts of Eastern Europe ethnic conflict is notoriously difficult to resolve. However, there are some encouraging signs. For example, the Ukraine has so far managed to hold together, in spite of different ethnic, religious, and language groups. The Russian autonomous Republics, such as those of the Upper Volga are a promising alternative in spite of the breakdown of compromise in Chechnya. The 'velvet divorce' between the Czech and Slovak Republics is another example of peaceful separation, but whether it will serve as an example for other parts of Central and Eastern Europe remains to be seen.

Minorities versus majorities

In post-1989 Europe, three important problems have emerged. The first relates to tensions between minorities and majorities in Central to Eastern Europe and the issue of self-determination. The second relates to migration from Eastern and Western Europe. The third involves the role of international organizations, such as the EU, the Council of Europe, or the OSCE, in relation to migration and the peace-ful resolution of ethnic conflicts. These three questions are analysed below, starting with the issue of minorities.

What makes the situation in Central and Eastern Europe special is the complex-ity and intensity of ethnic and religious conflicts. In particular the Balkan peninsula, for long a political flash point, is one of the most ethnically, linguistically and religiously complex areas of the world. Ethnic unrest there was one of the main causes of the First World War. There are also deep religious cleavages in Eastern Europe, especially in the Balkans – Catholicism in Slovenia and Croatia, Orthodox in Serbia and Macedonia, and Islam in Bosnia and Albania. In Bosnia the three religions met head on, and tensions were exacerbated by the territorial claims of Serbia and Croatia, and by fears of 'militant Islamic nationalism'.

Communist domination suppressed much of this conflict. But with the end of authoritarian rule in 1989, ethnic feeling once again rose to the surface. Re-establishing national sovereignty has been rather easy, but the restructuring of minority/majority relations has not. However, the events of 1989 offered minorities and majorities an opportunity to renegotiate and to begin (again) the long and difficult process of redefining their national identity. As a result, minorities throughout much of Eastern Europe, following those in the West, have been lobbying for the right to their own cultural and social organizations, political representation and schooling in their mother tongue.

The strength of their demands has often been influenced by so-called 'co-nationals' rights'. These occur where the minorities of one country are 'co-nationals' of the majority in a neighbouring country. Albanians and Hungarians in Serbia, Hungarians in Romania, Russians in Moldova, Poles in Lithuania, Hungarians in Slovakia, Turks in Bulgaria, and Russians in Belarus and the Ukraine live within a relatively short distance of their 'mother country' and share linguistic and cultural ties with it.

But even where there is no co-national problem, ethnic conflicts are often deep and bitter. Partisans of both majorities and minorities are prepared to take drastic steps on behalf of their respective cause. In recent years, people have been slaughtered in Azerbaijan, Bosnia, Georgia, Chechnya and former Yugoslavia. In contrast, west European cross-border ethnic issues have been satisfactorily resolved in the case of the Danish minority in northern Germany, the Tyroleans in Italy, the Germans in Belgium and the Swedish-speaking minority in Finland. The most notorious exception is Northern Ireland.

Ultimately, ethnic conflict is bitter and violent because it involves the territorial unity and integrity of states. Granting the cultural and political rights demanded by minority groups is often perceived as a threat to well-being and security. In Greece, the 'majority' claim that cultural autonomy for a Slav or Muslim minority will lead to territorial secession and eventual re-incorporation into the mother country. In sum, national majorities argue that giving minorities special rights simply strengthens their ties to the foreign countries, and thereby contributes to security threats. This perception, real or imagined, explains why the majority may resort to aggressive nationalism.

That nationalist groups continue to flourish and that the number of nation-states continues to grow, in Europe, as elsewhere in the world, may seem paradoxical. As the world becomes more interdependent and supranational organizations, like the European Union, grow in power, minority and nationalist claims may appear out of place. Yet, internationalization creates global 'demonstration effects', in which the example of one successful case of ethnic nationalism stimulates others, reinforced by growing perceptions of political and economic inequality.

Modern nationalism may not only 'bubble up' from the population, but emerge from economic factors and political elites. These certainly contributed to the break-up of Czechoslovakia and Yugoslavia, and to minority problems in Romania and

Table 17.1 Immigrant
populations in the major
host countries of Europe

Country	Immigrant Group	Size ('000s)	Percent of total population
Estonia	Russians	500	30.0
Latvia	Russian	830	34.0
	Other Ex-Soviet	300	10.0
Lithuania	Russians	400	9.0
Germany	'Ethnic Germans'*	1800	2.1
	Turks–Kurds	1850	2.3
	Croatians	800	1.0
	Italians	400	0.5
Switzerland	Italians	350	5.5
	Croatians, Serbs	200	3.0
	Spanish, Portuguese	200	3.0
	Turks	70	1.0
Netherlands	Caribbean-Surinam	153	1.0
	Indonesian	50	0.3
	Turks	210	1.4
	Arabs	170	1.0
Belgium	Italians	240	2.4
	Arabs	140	1.4
	French	100	1.0
France	Caribbean	1500	2.0
	Arab	2800	4.5
	Spanish	550	1.0
	Italian	550	1.0
Spain	Arabs	300	0.8
Italy	Arab	1500	2.7
	Albanian	90	0.2
Great Britain	Caribbean	580	1.0
	Indian-Pakistani	1640	3.0
	Irish	600	1.0

Note: * Formerly residents in Eastern Europe and Russia.
Sources: Harry Drost, *What's What and Who's Who in Europe* (London, Cassel, 1994); *Kessing's Contemporary Archives* (London, Longman, 1990–96).

Bulgaria. Nationalism among Czechs and Slovaks had at least as much to do with economic protection as ethnic feelings. The conflict in Yugoslavia was strongly influenced by the personal aspirations of a few political leaders. As a result, nationalism is sometimes symbolic of economic concerns as much as a desire for independence.

■ The impact of migration

Legal immigration into Western Europe has been low but steady since the oil crisis of the 1970s, when most countries restricted immigration from outside the European Union. However, it increased slightly in the 1980s. In absolute terms, the foreign population increased most in Germany (by 1 per cent, to reach 8.2 per cent of the total population) while actually declining in France (from 6.8 per cent in 1980 to 6.4 per cent in 1990). However, relatively few immigrants became naturalized citizens in Germany. More did so in France.

Legal immigration increased threefold in Italy during the 1980s, but it is still comparatively low and the total figure remains under 800,000. Illegal immigration may well be higher. Certainly, for the first time in its modern history, Italy has become a country of net immigration rather than of net emigration. The same is true of other southern European countries. The great majority of immigrants, however, are found in the Northern European countries of Germany and France, followed by the UK, Switzerland and Belgium, as Table 17.1 shows. However, this depends in part on whether one regards Russians in the Baltic States as settled residents or immigrants, and on the extent to which the semi-migratory Roma (see Table 13.1) are classed as residents.

The figures in Table 17.1 are generally for legal immigrants. Those for illegal immigrants in Europe are, for obvious reasons, more difficult to establish. The International Labour Organization estimated that in 1991 there were 2,600,000 illegal residents representing some 14 per cent of the total foreign population. The countries most affected seem to be Germany, with 650,000, and Italy with an estimated 600,000 (which may, however, be substantially higher).

The number of asylum seekers is lower but not insignificant. The collapse of the communist regimes and the war in Yugoslavia produced a rapid increase in every country of Western Europe, particularly in Germany and Sweden. In October 1992 the United Nations High Commission for Refugees (UNHCR) reported that 220,000 ex-Yugoslavs had asked for political asylum in Germany, 70,000 in Switzerland, 60,000 in Sweden and 57,500 in Austria. A total of 550,000 had left former Yugoslavia. A further 2 million were displaced within the former Yugoslavia. The number of asylum seekers is now falling because legal and administrative changes have made it more difficult for them to enter some countries in Western Europe.

The removal of barriers between Eastern and Western Europe has made the westward movement of people easier. Germany has become a favoured destination, mainly because of its geographical position and high standard of living. Hence where income disparities are large and movement becomes a possibility, incentives to move are strong, and will grow if unemployment rises in the East. Until the income gap is reduced, pressure to migrate will remain high. This presents Western Europe with a potentially serious and growing political problem.

Immigration and the free movement of people raise fundamental issues about individual rights and European integration. Some observers see free movement as a basic element of human dignity. To them the concept of a 'common European space' is meaningless without substantial freedom of movement. They argue that a new Berlin Wall to keep people out of Western Europe would be as offensive as the old one that kept people inside Eastern Europe. They argue that the issue is not *whether* people should cross from the East to the West, but *how* they are to do so.

This raises the question of how many immigrants Western Europe can absorb without serious social and political disruption. Between 1950 and 1970 almost 3 per cent of the population of Southern Europe shifted into Western and Northern Europe (5 million people). Are these regions capable of accepting another 3 per cent or more from the East? This would mean another 10 million people, in addition to 3 million Germans who live in Central and Eastern Europe but have a constitutional right to reside in Germany.

An influx of immigrants on this scale raises major economic and social issues about jobs, housing and services, to say nothing of the political reaction it might provoke from anti-immigrant political groups. This is particularly the case in Germany which has admitted large numbers of migrants, refugees and political exiles, and is also faced with the economic and social problems of absorbing East Germany. Concerns have also been raised in other Western European countries about political tolerance, as well as the economic advantages of migration, and the issue of citizenship.

The problem is not one for individual countries, but must be tackled on a

BRIEFING 17.3

The Schengen Accords

The Schengen Accords of 1985, with a supplementary agreement in 1990, were signed by nine of the twelve EU member states who agreed to remove border controls between themselves. They also agreed to greater co-operation on immigration control and cross-border police matters. The nine signatories were Belgium, France, Greece, Germany, Italy, Luxembourg, the Netherlands, Portugal and Spain. The Accords were thought to be a key part of the single-market programme. They were supposed to be implemented in 1991, but political and technical problems delayed the start. Denmark, Ireland and the UK did not sign the Accords.

European basis by the EU. In some ways the need for international action makes the problem more difficult. For example, because of internal market arrangements (and the Schengen agreement), migration or legal entry to Germany is migration into the EU. Hence, German immigration legislation and the politicization of immigration in Germany have effects on other member states of the EU.

Host populations often react against immigrants. The feeling that there are too many is strong even among countries with very few. As a consequence, many West European countries, such as Germany, France and Britain, have tightened up entry requirements. They have also introduced repatriation programmes. Germany has also restricted immigration from Poland and the Czech and Slovak Republics, by means of 'good neighbour treaties'.

If it is difficult to cure the ills of huge population migration, what are the alternatives to it? Two means can be envisaged to increase prosperity without relocation in wealthier countries. These involve increased trade and capital flows: trade flows from East to West, and capital flows in the other direction. However, it may be doubted whether free trade agreements between the EU and the Central and Eastern European states will eliminate the income gap, or even reduce it much in the short run. In the long run, however, it is likely that economic reforms and capital investment will stimulate the economies and the exports of Central and Eastern Europe.

On the other hand, migration is far from being a negative development even from a narrowly Western European point of view. Due to demographic changes, the labour force will soon be shrinking. For example, Germans can now retire at sixty, and the sixty-and-over age group represents 21 per cent of Germany's population. It will make up 30 per cent by the year 2020. With fewer workers to pay for more pensions, Germany has increased its retirement age to sixty-five, effective in 2012. Thus, it would appear that Germany needs more young Turks, not fewer. There might also be incentives for the West to employ well-trained and educated workers from the East (although this, of course, drains the more disadvantaged region of its skilled workers).

Since economic development in the regions is interconnected, how can we best promote stable political relations and economic growth across Europe? This is not a question that can be tackled by individual countries. It inevitably involves the contribution made by international organizations, like the Council of Europe, the EU, the CSCE (Conference on Security and Co-operation in Europe) and NATO.

The role of international organizations

Current efforts to link Eastern and Western Europe through international organizations (such as the EU, the Council of Europe, NATO) may give Eastern Europeans a
greater sense of security. Conversely, the isolation of these countries might encourage nationalism, ethnic problems and greater flows of emigration. Much may
depend, therefore, on the capacity of international organizations to create the political frameworks within which the large and urgent problems of ethnic conflict and
migration might be solved, or at least reduced to manageable proportions.

The Council of Europe tries to protect minority rights by setting political standards and by promoting the best cultural and educational standards for governments.
Above all, signatories must undertake to ratify the human rights convention, including its provisions for individual petition and the compulsory jurisdiction of the
European Court of Human Rights. These conditions led the Council to refer applications for membership from Latvia, Lithuania and Estonia which had to have their
constitutional provisions for minority groups examined before membership was
granted. Slovakia was accepted in June 1992 only after promising to repeal laws that
discriminated against ethnic Hungarians. In 1970 Greece, then under military rule,
was effectively forced to resign from the Council, after being found guilty of tortur-
ing political prisoners. It was readmitted after the restoration of democracy in 1974.

Yet the European Convention on Human Rights of the Council of Europe contains no provisions for minority rights. In view of the rapid changes in Central and
Eastern Europe, pressures may mount to correct this omission. At the moment
minority groups are recognized as having 'locus standi' to bring cases against practices which breach the European Convention on Human Rights.

In addition, the European Commission for Democracy, a consultative body of the
Council of Europe, produced a proposal for a European Convention for the
Protection of Minorities in 1991. This was intended for adoption not by the Council
of Europe, but by the CSCE. The CSCE has a long history of involvement in the protection of minority rights, dating back to Principle VII of the Helsinki Final Act of
1975. Since 1990 it has made three particularly important innovations with regard
to minorities.

The first was agreed at the CSCE conference in Copenhagen in 1990 which
adopted a wide-ranging catalogue of responsibilities. For the first time these contained a reference to 'group rights', among them the responsibility to protect the
ethnic, cultural, linguistic and religious identity of minorities.

The second innovation was to assume responsibility for dealing with crises within
states. In 1991, immediately after the abortive Moscow coup, the CSCE declared that
commitments undertaken in regard to human rights 'are matters of direct and legitimate concern to all participating states and do not belong exclusively to the national
affairs of the states concerned'.

The third innovation was the appointment of a High Commissioner for National
Minorities in December 1992 with the task of defusing tensions by promoting dialogue, confidence and co-operation between concerned parties. His main power is
to issue formal notice of 'early warnings'. The High Commissioner can deal only
with new conflicts, not with conflicts which have existed for a long time or which
involve violence, such as the conflict in Northern Ireland or that involving the Kurds
in Turkey. The High Commissioner has been involved in the situation of Russian

minorities in the Baltic and of the Hungarian minority in Slovakia. However, the CSCE has few effective instruments for settling disputes or preventing crises. It has no military apparatus of its own, and verdicts of the court of arbitration, established in 1992, are not binding.

Organizations, like the UN, the Council of Europe and the CSCE, either lack power or resources. In contrast, the EU is more cohesive, has legally binding power, a wider range of policy instruments, considerably more resources, and greater attraction for new members.

One of the original aims of the EU was to be a 'peace community' for the elimination of war, and a 'value community', for democratic and human rights. Although the EU has helped to diffuse aggressive nationalism among its member states, nationalism and the defence of national interests has remained a significant factor in EU affairs. Although there is widespread support for the idea of European integration and co-operation among the populations of EU states, national loyalties and interests remain paramount. Economic benefits are not sufficient on their own to create sentiments of trust, identity, or community in Europe, and there is a long way to go before deep loyalty to Europe, as opposed to nation states, can emerge.

So much for the internal concerns of the EU. How has it responded to developments in Central and Eastern Europe? Two aspects can be identified: the proposal for a stability pact and the decision to consider members from Central Europe. The proposal for a European Stability Pact, launched in 1993, has a particular relevance to the problems of minorities. It stems from the realization that political stability is an essential precondition for economic and social progress in the East. Thus the EU is to offer inducements for these states to work together with the aim of guaranteeing both national frontiers and the rights of minorities, so that tragedies like that of the war in Bosnia (1992–5) do not recur. Beyond that countries wishing to join the EU must establish their democratic credentials and not bring unresolved conflicts with them into the Union.

As well as the European Stability Pact itself, there will be a series of discussions between neighbouring states, and bilateral agreements between particular states. The inaugural conference in Paris in May 1994 was attended by the foreign ministers of some forty European countries, and by representatives of European organizations. However, it did not deal with conflict in the former Yugoslavia and the Caucasus, and countries in these areas were not invited to the conference, with the exception of Slovenia. Albania was invited only as an observer. Two round tables were proposed. One was to explore the treatment of the Russian minorities in the Baltic states, the other was concerned with the Hungarian minorities in Slovakia and Romania. Poland, with only tiny ethnic minorities left, has already concluded bilateral treaties with all seven neighbouring states.

However, the reference to border disputes and to bilateral solutions in the Stability Pact caused consternation among Central and Eastern European states. They believe that the EU is imposing standards on them it does not apply to itself. They also note that while neighbouring states can sometimes play a constructive role in managing minority issues – as Austria has in the Italian South Tyrol, and Ireland is trying to do in Ulster – it is dangerous to give such states a general licence to interfere in their neighbours' affairs. This is especially true in regard to Russia.

The debate continues. Meanwhile the EU decided in 1992 to consider Central European membership. Poland, Hungary and the Czech Republic have subsequently applied. The EU has called on prospective associates to 'assume the obligations of membership by satisfying the economic and political conditions required'. Precise deadlines and criteria were not specified, however.

This leaves the question whether the EU is right to demand that new members should have solved their problems before joining. One of its great achievements, the EU claims, is to create the conditions in which war cannot occur between members, and in which old historical enmities are buried. In other words, the EU claims to be able to resolve the international problems that are beyond the capabilities of independent states. It is perhaps unfair, therefore, to ask individual states to solve their problems before they can join the EU.

Conclusions

Minorities and migration are of great importance for the stability of individual European states and of Europe as a whole. Increasing flows of migrants and refugees, together with the new freedom of movement, pose enormous challenges. Two questions appear to be crucial. First, how is the identity of national minorities to be protected without significantly undermining state cohesion? Secondly, how are we to square the economic needs of migrants, and the political rights of asylum seekers and refugees, with the economic and social problems they often bring, not least the eruption of racist and xenophobic politics? In a nutshell, the task is to devise effective, preventive and confidence-building measures in situations of intolerance, hate and violence towards national minorities or immigrants. It is worth bearing in mind that ethnic, religious, or linguistic homogeneity is not necessary for peace and stability: Switzerland is a good example.

There does not appear to be a single model for striking the delicate balance between majority rule and minority rights. Each minority represents a different case, and each case requires different ways of implementing common principles. What is more, special arrangements have to be worked out at different levels of a society (local, regional and national) according to different patterns and government institutions.

There are significant differences between Western and Eastern Europe in this respect. West Europe has long-established democracies, few serious threats to national integrity, and institutions built on much experience in managing ethnic, cultural, linguistic, and religious diversity. In contrast, CEE states have to contain these in the midst of economic hardship, and in face of serious threats to their integrity. They face the problems of a simultaneous revolution on three fronts: economic restructuring, democratization, and nation-building. This requires imaginative, diverse and adaptable solutions. The success of Russia in accommodating many of its minorities, so far, indicates that solutions can be found even as the Chechen War shows what happens when they can not.

The machinery necessary to resolve the tensions surrounding minorities and migration must be built at the national and international levels. Nationally, differentiated regionalism federal systems and consociational arrangements have been found effective. International organizations can promote economic and democratic development, control immigration flows, and create peace-making and peacekeeping arrangements. A combination of national and international mechanisms can enhance the chances of accommodating minorities and migration and hence promote the prospects for peace and stability in Europe as a whole.

■ Further reading

F. Capotori, *The Rights of Persons Belonging to . . . Minorities* (Baden-Baden, Nomas, 1979).

Stephen Castles and Mark J. Miller, *The Age of Migration: International Population Movements in the Modern World* (London, Macmillan, 1993).

Harry Drost, *Europe* (London, Cassell, 1995).

Hugh Poulton, *The Balkans: Minorities and States in Conflict* (London, Minority Rights Publications, 1993).

G. Schöpflin, *Politics in Eastern Europe* (Oxford, Blackwell, 1993).

Chapter 18

Strategic choices for Europe

Divergent diagnoses

If any further illustration were needed to reinforce the point that European problems transcend the country level, it can be found in the proliferation of international agencies to deal with matters like minorities and migrants. If states can no longer exclusively define the status and rights of groups on their own territory, then indeed power is shifting to the European and international level.

This has long been true of defence, of course. No European state acting on its own can guarantee its citizens' security against external threats. This has to be guaranteed by collective European arrangements and by some organizations, such as NATO, which transcend Europe and operate at a global level. Even so, security is hardly the exclusive concern of any one supranational organization or alliance. NATO may be the main military organization but there is also the Western European Union, on the one hand, and the continual consultations with Russia, on the other. The United Nations also has a role through its sponsorship of peacekeeping operations. Both NATO and the UN of course involve the United States as a key player.

Exclusively European initiatives are more evident in the field of trade and economics, and in cultural and legal agreements. Chapter 1 and Chapter 17 alluded to the importance of these in building up similar institutions and attitudes within the European states, which on a 'liberal' diagnosis of international relations will then contribute to co-operation between States. Liberal democracies are unlikely to go to war with each other. So the solution to guaranteeing European peace is to encourage party competition, free elections, interest groups, and all the other elements of democracy within European States.

At present, it seems, the institutions of pluralist democracy are consolidating themselves in Central and Eastern Europe. These include media (Chapter 6), interest groups (Chapter 7), social movements (Chapter 8), political parties (Chapter 9), parliaments (Chapters 10 and 11) and courts and legal systems (Chapter 14). All these institutions are supported by popular sentiments which are positive towards democracy (Chapter 5). Ultimately, democratic development may be complemented by joining the European Union (Chapter 2) which will foster both economic prosperity and political co-operation among an expanded membership.

As we pointed out in Chapter 1, however, this scenario may be too optimistic. The economies of many of the new democracies are fragile (Chapter 16) and their populations often have no welfare support (Chapter 15). Economic collapse might produce massive movements of population and increase ethnic and nationalist tensions (Chapters 4 and 17). Some states seem unlikely to survive a severe economic crisis of the type which destroyed democracy in so many countries in the 1920s and 1930s. According to the 'realist' school of thought one must construct international arrangements which will survive internal changes of regime because they are built on military alliances. These will secure a balance of power and make international aggression unlikely to succeed, regardless of internal changes within states.

A 'realist' approach thus stresses different aspects of the international situation from those picked out by liberal theorists. A considerable part of the European dilemma over security is that there is little agreement over what the problems are, let alone how to respond to them.

In this chapter we analyse European debates about security. As so much depends on the assumptions they make about international relations (and indeed about human nature) it is difficult to say whether liberals or realists are correct. What we can do, however, is describe their conflicting diagnoses and the way in which they enter, in varying mixes, into contemporary and future responses to the European security situation. Security is the precondition for convergence and democracy. So it is natural to end a book on the New Europe with an account of the various security options which its states can take up over the next decade.

■ Conceptualizing security

The nature of threat

Security is such a commonly cited goal of political leaders and citizens the world over that it might be thought to unite peoples and countries. Paradoxically, however, there is substantial conflict over how it might best be achieved. The purpose of this section is to outline some of the main problems connected with it, to highlight its complexity, and to explain why it is contested.

Fortunately, there is widespread consensus about its most basic definition: security is conventionally taken to be freedom from threat. However, this simply raises two further questions: what is a threat; and what is the appropriate response to it? Specifying the component parts of answers to these questions is, in fact, to construct a security agenda. But, of course, this is not at all easy.

These are three principal features of a threat: its object, its form and its source. We will deal with each of these in turn. First, the object of a threat must be something which is valued. As the value attached to it increases, so also does the danger of the threat. Individuals and groups give first priority to many different values and goals. This explains why we use the term security in a wide variety of settings, such as job security or environmental security or social security. Traditionally, within international relations, security has been taken to be freedom from the threat of war and death. Not surprisingly, war has proved to be an important focus of attention. Nevertheless, individuals do not attach the same value to either war or death. If they believe the threat of war is remote, then other goals, such as welfare security, will figure more prominently in the hierarchy of values.

The second principal aspect of a threat is its form. Insecurity is present only when a threat is perceived. Thus, ignorance may prevent any such perception. A commonly cited example is that of a stranger feeling quite secure while walking, in ignorance, through what locals take as a 'no go' area of a city. But even those who are not ignorant may miscalculate the nature of the situation. For example, a country might engage in a military exercise for practice. This might, however, be taken by a neighbour as preparations for an attack. The result might be accidental or unintentional war. Similarly, we know that perceptions differ substantially between groups and individuals. To members of the IRA, British troops in Northern Ireland are occupying forces; to the British government the troops are 'peacekeeping forces'.

There are also difficulties in assessing the form of a threat so far as it involves calculations about the future. Threat assessment is in effect an estimate or 'guestimate' about the *potential* damage in the future. Usually estimates are based on current and past behaviour. But analysts can disagree about such estimates, if only because current behaviour can be a poor guide to future developments.

The form of the threat also involves the manner in which it may be delivered. Traditionally, analysts of international relations have focused on the military. As weapons have proliferated and diversified, the manner in which military strikes can be made has become substantially more varied. The military is not the only form of threat, however. Threats can also be effected through economic boycotts or sanctions, which may be underwritten by military capabilities.

The third principal feature of a threat is its source. Traditionally, military force has been the main means of delivering a threat. But as often as not it has been a symptom rather than a cause of tension. From 1945–89 the military forces of the Soviet Union clearly constituted a threat to the West. But there was much disagreement about the source of the Soviet threat. For some it lay in the alleged expansionist ambitions of the Soviet government. For others it was caused by the incompatibility of the capitalist and communist systems. For still others it was caused by the massive losses of the Soviet Union during the Second World War, which caused the communists to arm themselves against any possibility of future invasion from the West.

The nature of the response

The construction of a security agenda necessitates not only the identification of the object, the form, and the source of the threat but also the identification of an appropriate response. Once again this is a difficult task with three component parts: whether to deal with symptoms or causes; the appropriate response; and identifying which community's needs should be responded to.

First, there is a decision to be taken on whether the symptom or the cause of the threat should be addressed. To take a non-military example, burglary might be combated by alarm systems, armed householders, the police force, or by fines and prison sentences. All deal with symptoms, but all have different implications. Equally, the response could be directed at the causes of burglary. Once again there are many options, including rehousing, welfare, the reduction of unemployment or social inequalities, treatment of drug addiction problems, and so on. In the context of military security, there are also many different options. Responses to symptoms can vary from attempts to attain military superiority, to alliance formation, to the negotiation of matching force levels. Equally if the response is directed at causes rather than symptoms, the choices again are multiple. Tension could be eradicated by negotiating the removal or conversion of the point at issue, through territorial concessions for example, or through the development of trade or cultural links.

A second consideration is that the response must be appropriate for the threat. If people identify different threats they are likely to respond quite differently. Besides, the response can exacerbate the threat. For example, if burglars know householders have guns they too may arm themselves, thereby transforming unarmed into armed robbery. In the military area this problem is so well known that it has its own special name – 'security dilemma'. The security dilemma exists because the military forces of A, devised to enhance its security, may be seen by B as a threat to B's security. If B then increases *its* military capabilities to improve security, this may well be perceived by A as decreasing its security – and so on, causing an arms race.

The third major problem in deciding on the response to a threat concerns the identification of the community on whose behalf the response is made. This is traditionally seen in terms of national security, which means removing a foreign threat for all citizens. Two main difficulties arise in this context: the national and the international. If a country is reasonably united as a nation, its military will not present domestic problems, being concerned only with external threats. But if the country contains regional separatist or secessionist movements, the military is in danger of having to be used to combat internal 'subversion' and thus becoming embroiled in domestic affairs. At the international level, the act of forming alliances automatically defines 'our' security community. This has the effect of defining countries outside this as hostile – another version of the 'security dilemma' defined above. The creation of alliances will juxtapose one security community against other security communities. In other words, defining members of the community equally defines non-members, who from being neutral may thus become 'enemies'.

In this context, collective defence alliances are commonly established which transform national security communities into international ones, and in doing so reduce the number of national security communities. In other words, collective defence agreements resolve the security dilemma for individual states. But they simply recreate it at the international level.

To summarize, there is widespread agreement on the idea of security as the absence of threat, and on the division of a security agenda into threat and response. The problems begin when attempts are made to elaborate the content of the security agenda. It is possible to identify three elements of threat and three different elements of appropriate response, and to combine these in different ways. So it can readily be seen why there are many different security agendas in Europe. In short, there is general consensus about the goal of security. But attempts to operationalize in the hard world of political reality invariably result in disagreement.

■ Conflicting agendas

The contested nature of security explains why competing ideologies of 'liberalism' and 'realism' can be identified in the debate over the future of Europe. These ideologies have two things in common. They agree on the goal of security, and about the need to create structural arrangements for the political, economic and social conditions necessary to achieve that goal. But they disagree as soon as they attempt to give it substantive content and specify the structural arrangements required. They identify different security threats and different security responses. This illustrates the multi-faceted nature of the European dilemma. Simply focusing on the deployment of military capabilities provides a very impoverished understanding of the problems associated with security.

For the liberal, the fundamental goal is the pursuit of individual freedom within a market economy and a democratic polity. Domestically, security is achieved by consensus about the goals of society and by interdependence among citizens. Those who break the rules of society are dealt with by the police and the courts. International security is sustained in exactly the same way. Thus in a perfect international system of the liberal type, national militaries would become largely redundant and any transgressions of the international code would be dealt with by international courts and a collective security system.

For realists the fundamental goal is the promotion and protection of state sovereignty. The international system consists of a hierarchy of states, distinguished in terms of their power capabilities (chiefly military ones). Since states compete to protect or enhance their positions in the international hierarchy, there is a general condition of international tension. Though the international system contains a substantial degree of conflict, this conflict can be managed, and security achieved, through norms of reciprocity, the balance of power, alliances and spheres of influence. In marked contrast to the liberal design, it is absolutely essential to maintain national forces and military capabilities.

We can readily see how these very differing conceptions of the international situation can lead to very different diagnoses of, and programmes for, European security. Liberals will tend to see democracy, international agreements, and the growth of trade as the major way to enhance peace and stability. The EU could be a major contributor to these. Realists aim at primarily military solutions, stressing concepts like a balance of power, and the need to prevent the power vacuums through the collapse of existing states when there is no obvious successor. Rather than seeing an expansion of the EU as a way of coping with existing tensions, realists are concerned by the possibility that expansion of the EU will dilute its capabilities, thus making it less effective as a counterweight to Russia.

We have already elaborated on the realist and liberal positions when we discussed international relations in Chapter 1. They also enter into 'left' and 'right' divisions between political parties as we saw in Chapter 9. What we should stress here is that these debates will continue into the future. They cannot be resolved by an appeal to past experience, since history is always subject to interpretation from a realist or an idealist-liberal point of view. What does seem to be generally agreed is that Russia will remain overwhelmingly important in future developments. The dominant European power in terms of population, territory and military might, Russia lags behind economically. This combination is potentially explosive, particularly if a world economic downturn inflicts yet more strains on the long-suffering Russian population. The result may destablize not just Russia but also, if mass migration is an outcome, the rest of Europe as well. Alternatively, a resurgent Russian nationalism might encourage military action.

To these eventualities European decision-makers are likely to present different responses – precisely because they are divided between the liberal and realist positions. The longer economic growth continues, and the longer democratic development continues in the East, the more influential liberal diagnoses and prescriptions are likely to become. Conversely an increase in tensions, and in particular any perceived departure in Russia from the path of market reform and democracy, will restore credibility to the realists. In practice the West is likely to rely on both (liberal) inducements and (realist) deterrents; maintaining its alliances and military capabilities at a high level, while seeking military and economic agreements designed to reduce tension.

There will always be arguments based on different views of the world. But actions based upon different arguments may produce a fruitful mix in the end. We must hope that they do. Without a stable settlement with and within Russia, all the political and economic progress of the new Europe during the last decade will be lost, and the legitimate aspirations of its peoples for order, peace and security will once again be disappointed.

◼ Further reading

Barry Buzan, *People States and Fear: An Agenda for International Security* (Brighton, Harvester/Wheatsheaf, 1991).

Palme Commission, *Common Security: A Programme for Disarmament* (London, Pan Books, 1982).

R. D. McKinley and R. Little, *Global Problems and World Order* (London, Pinter, 1986).

P. Shearman (ed.), *Russian Foreign Policy* (Boulder, CO., Westview, 1993).

C. Thomas, *In Search of Security* (Brighton, Wheatsheaf, 1987).

Author Index

Subject Index